D0849626

The Guide for the Perplexed

Unabridged Edition

MOSES MAIMONIDES

MICHAEL FRIEDLÄNDER, TRANSLATOR

COSIMOCLASSICS

NEW YORK

The Guide for the Perplexed: Unabridged Edition
Cover © 2007 Cosimo, Inc.

For information, address:

Cosimo, P.O. Box 416
Old Chelsea Station
New York, NY 10113-0416

or visit our website at:
www.cosimobooks.com

The Guide for the Perplexed: Unabridged Edition was originally published in 1904.

Cover design by www.kerndesign.net

ISBN: 978-1-60206-500-0

The object of this treatise is to enlighten a religious man who
has been trained to believe in the truth of our holy Law,
who conscientiously fulfils his moral and religious duties,
and at the same time has been successful in his philosophical
studies. Human reason has attracted him to abide within
its sphere; and he finds it difficult to accept as correct
the teaching based on the literal interpretation
of the Law, and especially that which he himself
or others derived from those homonymous,
metaphorical, or hybrid expressions. Hence
he is lost in perplexity and anxiety.

—from the "Prefatory Remarks"

PREFACE

The first Edition of the English Translation of Maimonides' *Dalalāt al-Hairin* being exhausted without having fully supplied the demand, I prepared a second, revised edition of the Translation. In the new edition the three volumes of the first edition have been reduced to one volume by the elimination of the notes; besides Hebrew words and phrases have been eliminated or transliterated. By these changes the translator sought to produce a cheap edition in order to bring the work of Maimonides within the reach of all students of Theology and Jewish Literature.

M. FRIEDLÄNDER.

JEWS' COLLEGE, *July* 1904.

PREFACE TO VOLUME ONE OF THE FIRST EDITION

In compliance with a desire repeatedly expressed by the Committee of the Hebrew Literature Society, I have undertaken to translate Maimonides' *Dalalāt al-Ḥairin*, better known by the Hebrew title *Moreh Nebuchim*, and I offer the first instalment of my labours in the present volume. This contains—(1) A short Life of Maimonides, in which special attention is given to his alleged apostasy. (2) An analysis of the whole of the Moreh Nebuchim. (3) A translation of the First Part of this work from the Arabic, with explanatory and critical notes.

Parts of the Translation have been contributed by Mr. Joseph Abrahams, B.A., Ph.D., and Rev. H. Gollancz—the Introduction by the former, and the first twenty-five chapters by the latter.

In conclusion I beg to tender my thanks to Rev. A. Loewy, Editor of the Publications of the Hebrew Literature Society, for his careful revision of my manuscript and proofs, and to Mr. A. Neubauer, M.A., for his kindness in supplying me with such information as I required.

M. FRIEDLÄNDER.

Jews' College, *June* 1881.

CONTENTS

CONTENTS

CHAPTER		PAGE
XLIII	On *kanaf*	57
XLIV	On *'ayin*	58
XLV	On *shama*	58
XLVI, XLVII	On the Attribution of Senses and Sensations to God	59, 63
XLVIII	The Targum of *shama* and raah	64
XLIX	Figurative Expressions applied to Angels	65
L	On Faith	67
LI–LX	On Attributes	68–89
LI	On the Necessity of Proving the Inadmissibility of Attributes in reference to God	68
LII	Classification of Attributes	69
LIII	The Arguments of the Attributists	72
LIV	On Exod. xxxiii. 13 ; xxxiv. 7.	75
LV	On Attributes implying Corporeality, Emotion, Non-existence and Comparison	78
LVI	On Attributes denoting Existence, Life, Power, Wisdom and Will	79
LVII	On the Identity of the Essence of God and His Attributes	80
LVIII	On the Negative Sense of the True Attributes of God	81
LIX	On the Character of the Knowledge of God Consisting of Negations	83
LX	On the Difference between Positive and Negative Attributes	87
LXI	On the Names of God	89
LXII	On the Divine Names composed of Four, Twelve and Forty-two Letters	91
LXIII	On *Ehyeh, Yah* and *Shaddai*	93
LXIV	On "The Name of the Lord," and "The Glory of God"	95
LXV	On the phrase "God spake"	96
LXVI	On Exod. xxxii. 16	98
LXVII	On *shabat* and *nab*	99
LXVIII	On the Terms : The Intellectus, the Intelligens and the Intelligibile	100
LXIX	On the Primal Cause	102
LXX	On the attribute *rokeb ba'arabot*	105
LXXI	The Origin of the *Kalām*	107
LXXII	A Parallel between the Universe and Man.	113
LXXIII	Twelve Propositions of the *Kalām*	120
LXXIV	Proofs of the *Kalām* for *the creatio ex nibilo*	133
LXXV	Proofs of the *Kalām* for the Unity of God	138
LXXVI	Proofs of the *Kalām* for the Incorporeality of God	141

PART II.

The Author's Introduction. The Twenty-Six Propositions employed by the Philosophers to prove the Existence of God — 145

CHAPTER.		
I	Philosophical proofs for the Existence, Incorporeality, and Unity of the First Cause	149
II	On the Existence of Intelligences or purely Spiritual Beings	154
III	The Author adopts the Theory of Aristotle as least open to Objections	156
IV	The Spheres and the Causes of their Motion	156
V	Agreement of the Aristotelian Theory with the Teaching of Scripture	159
VI	What is meant by the Scriptural Term "Angels"	160
VII	The Homonymity of the term "Angel"	162
VIII	On the Music of the Spheres	163
IX	On the Number of the Heavenly Spheres	163
X	The Influence of the Spheres upon the Earth manifests itself in four different ways	164
XI	The Theory of Eccentricity Preferable to that of Epicycles	166
XII	On the Nature of the Divine Influence and that of the Spheres	168
XIII	Three Different Theories about the Beginning of the Universe	171

CONTENTS

PART III.

CONTENTS

CONTENTS

xiii

THE LIFE OF MOSES MAIMONIDES

" Before the sun of Eli had set the sun of Samuel had risen." Before the voice of the prophets had ceased to guide the people, the Interpreters of the Law, the Doctors of the Talmud, had commenced their labours, and before the Academies of Sura and of Pumbadita were closed, centres of Jewish thought and learning were already flourishing in the far West. The circumstances which led to the transference of the head-quarters of Jewish learning from the East to the West in the tenth century are thus narrated in the *Sefer ha-kabbalah* of Rabbi Abraham ben David :

" After the death of Hezekiah, the head of the Academy and Prince of the Exile, the academies were closed and no new Geonim were appointed. But long before that time Heaven had willed that there should be a discontinuance of the pecuniary gifts which used to be sent from Palestine, North Africa and Europe. Heaven had also decreed that a ship sailing from Bari should be captured by Ibn Romahis, commander of the naval forces of Abd-er-rahman al-nasr. Four distinguished Rabbis were thus made prisoners—Rabbi Hushiel, father of Rabbi Hananel, Rabbi Moses, father of Rabbi Hanok, Rabbi Shemarjahu, son of Rabbi Elhanan, and a fourth whose name has not been recorded. They were engaged in a mission to collect subsidies in aid of the Academy in Sura. The captor sold them as slaves ; Rabbi Hushiel was carried to Kairuan, R. Shemarjahu was left in Alexandria, and R. Moses was brought to Cordova. These slaves were ransomed by their brethren and were soon placed in important positions. When Rabbi Moses was brought to Cordova, it was supposed that he was uneducated. In that city there was a synagogue known at that time by the name of *Keneset ha-midrash*, and Rabbi Nathan, renowned for his great piety, was the head of the congregation. The members of the community used to hold meetings at which the Talmud was read and discussed. One day when Rabbi Nathan was expounding the Talmud and was unable to give a satisfactory explanation of the passage under discussion, Rabbi Moses promptly removed the difficulty and at the same time answered several questions whch were submitted to him. Thereupon R. Nathan thus addressed the assembly :—'I am no longer your leader ; that stranger in sackcloth shall henceforth be my teacher, and you shall appoint him to be your chief.' The admiral, on hearing of the high attainments of his prisoner, desired to revoke the sale, but the king would not permit this retraction, being pleased to learn that his Jewish subjects were no longer dependent for their religious instruction on the schools in the East."

Henceforth the schools in the West asserted their independence, and even surpassed the parent institutions. The Caliphs, mostly opulent, gave every encouragement to philosophy and poetry ; and, being generally liberal in sentiment, they entertained kindly feelings towards their Jewish subjects.

These were allowed to compete for the acquisition of wealth and honour on equal terms with their Mohammedan fellow-citizens. Philosophy and poetry were consequently cultivated by the Jews with the same zest as by the Arabs. Ibn Gabirol, Ibn Ḥasdai, Judah ha-levi, Ḥananel, Alfasi, the Ibn Ezras, and others who flourished in that period were the ornament of their age, and the pride of the Jews at all times. The same favourable condition was maintained during the reign of the Omeyades ; but when the Moravides and the Almohades came into power, the horizon darkened once more, and misfortunes threatened to destroy the fruit of several centuries. Amidst this gloom there appeared a brilliant luminary which sent forth rays of light and comfort : this was Moses Maimonides.

Moses, the son of Maimon, was born at Cordova, on the 14th of Nisan, 4895 (March 30, 1135). Although the date of his birth has been recorded with the utmost accuracy, no trustworthy notice has been preserved concerning the early period of his life. But his entire career is a proof that he did not pass his youth in idleness ; his education must have been in harmony with the hope of his parents, that one day he would, like his father and forefathers, hold the honourable office of *Dayyan* or *Rabbi*, and distinguish himself in theological learning. It is probable that the Bible and the Talmud formed the chief subjects of his study ; but he unquestionably made the best use of the opportunities which Mohammedan Spain, and especially Cordova, afforded him for the acquisition of general knowledge. It is not mentioned in any of his writings who were his teachers ; his father, as it seems, was his principal guide and instructor in many branches of knowledge. David Conforte, in his historical work, *Ḳore ha-dorot*, states that Maimonides was the pupil of two eminent men, namely, Rabbi Joseph Ibn Migash and Ibn Roshd (Averroes) ; that by the former he was instructed in the Talmud, and by the latter in philosophy. This statement seems to be erroneous, as Maimonides was only a child at the time when Rabbi Joseph died, and already far advanced in years when he became acquainted with the writings of Ibn Roshd. The origin of this mistake, as regards Rabbi Joseph, can easily be traced. Maimonides in his *Mishneh Tora*, employs, in reference to R. Isaac Alfasi and R. Joseph, the expression " my teachers " (*rabbotai*), and this expression, by which he merely describes his indebtedness to their writings, has been taken in its literal meaning.

Whoever his teachers may have been, it is evident that he was well prepared by them for his future mission. At the age of twenty-three he entered upon his literary career with a treatise on the Jewish Calendar. It is unknown where this work was composed, whether in Spain or in Africa. The author merely states that he wrote it at the request of a friend, whom he, however, leaves unnamed. The subject was generally considered to be very abstruse, and to involve a thorough knowledge of mathematics. Maimonides must, therefore, even at this early period, have been regarded as a profound scholar by those who knew him. The treatise is of an elementary character.—It was probably about the same time that he wrote, in Arabic, an explanation of Logical terms, *Millot higgayon*, which Moses Ibn Tibbon translated into Hebrew.

The earlier period of his life does not seem to have been marked by any incident worth noticing. It may, however, be easily conceived that the later period of his life, which was replete with interesting incidents, engaged the exclusive attention of his biographers. So much is certain, that his youth was beset with trouble and anxiety ; the peaceful development of science and philosophy was disturbed by wars raging between Mohammedans and Christians, and also between the several Mohammedan sects. The Moravides, who had succeeded the Omeyades, were opposed to liberality and toleration ; but they were surpassed in cruelty and fanaticism by their successors. Cordova was taken by the Almohades in the year 1148, when Maimonides was about thirteen years old. The victories of the Almohades, first under the leadership of the Mahadi Ibn Tamurt, and then under Abd-al-mumen, were, according to all testimonies, attended by acts of excessive intolerance. Abd-al-mumen would not suffer in his dominions any other faith but the one which he himself confessed. Jews and Christians had the choice between Islam and emigration or a martyr's death. The *Sefer ha-kabbalah* contains the following description of one of the persecutions which then occurred :

" After the death of R. Joseph ha-levi the study of the Torah was interrupted, although he left a son and a nephew, both of whom had under his tuition become profound scholars. ' The righteous man (R. Joseph) was taken away on account of the approaching evils.' After the death of R. Joseph there came for the Jews a time of oppression and distress. They quitted their homes, ' Such as were for death, to death, and such as were for the sword, to the sword ; and such as were for the famine, to the famine, and such as were for the captivity, to the captivity ' ; and—it might be added to the words of Jeremiah (xv. 2)—' such as were for apostasy, to apostasy.' All this happened through the sword of Ibn Tamurt, who, in 4902 (1142), determined to blot out the name of Israel, and actually left no trace of the Jews in any part of his empire."

Ibn Verga in his work on Jewish martyrdom, in *Shebet Jehudah*, gives the following account of events then happening :—" In the year 4902 the armies of Ibn Tamurt made their appearance. A proclamation was issued that any one who refused to adopt Islam would be put to death, and his property would be confiscated. Thereupon the Jews assembled at the gate of the royal palace and implored the king for mercy. He answered—' It is because I have compassion on you, that I command you to become Muslemim ; for I desire to save you from eternal punishment.' The Jews replied —' Our salvation depends on our observance of the Divine Law ; you are the master of our bodies and of our property, but our souls will be judged by the King who gave them to us, and to whom they will return ; whatever be our future fate, you, O king, will not be held responsible for it.' ' I do not desire to argue with you,' said the king ; ' for I know you will argue according to your own religion. It is my absolute will that you either adopt my religion or be put to death.' The Jews then proposed to emigrate, but the king would not allow his subjects to serve another king. In vain did the Jews implore the nobles to intercede in their behalf ; the king remained inexorable. Thus many congregations forsook their religion ; but within a month the king came to a sudden death ; the son, believing that his father had met with an untimely end as a punishment for his cruelty to the Jews, assured the involuntary converts that it would be indifferent to him what religion they professed. Hence many Jews returned at once to the religion of their fathers, while others hesitated for some time, from fear that the king meant to entrap the apparent converts."

From such records it appears that during these calamities some of the Jews fled to foreign countries, some died as martyrs, and many others submitted for a time to outward conversion. Which course was followed by the family of Maimon ? Did they sacrifice personal comfort and safety to their religious conviction, or did they, on the contrary, for the sake of mere worldly considerations dissemble their faith and pretend that they completely submitted to the dictates of the tyrant ? An answer to this question presents itself in the following note which Maimonides has appended to his commentary on the Mishnah : " I have now finished this work in accordance with my promise, and I fervently beseech the Almighty to save us from error. If there be one who shall discover an inaccuracy in this Commentary or shall have a better explanation to offer, let my attention be directed unto it ; and let me be exonerated by the fact that I have worked with far greater application than any one who writes for the sake of pay and profit, and that I have worked under the most trying circumstances. For Heaven had ordained that we be exiled, and we were therefore driven about from place to place ; I was thus compelled to work at the Commentary while travelling by land, or crossing the sea. It might have sufficed to mention that during that time I, in addition, was engaged in other studies, but I preferred to give the above explanation in order to encourage those who wish to criticise or annotate the Commentary, and at the same time to account for the slow progress of this work. I, Moses, the son of Maimon, commenced it when I was twenty-three years old, and finished it in Egypt, at the age of thirty[-three] years, in the year 1479 Sel. (1168)."

The *Sefer Haredim* of R. Eleazar Askari of Safed contains the following statement of Maimonides :—" On Sabbath evening, the 4th of Iyyar, 4925 (1165), I went on board ; on the following Sabbath the waves threatened to destroy our lives. . . . On the 3rd of Sivan, I arrived safely at Acco, *and was thus rescued from apostasy.* . . . On Tuesday, the 4th of Marḥeshvan, 4926, I left Acco, arrived at Jerusalem after a journey beset with difficulties and with dangers, and prayed on the spot of the great and holy house on the 4th, 5th, and 6th of Marḥeshvan. On Sunday, the 9th of that month, I left Jerusalem and visited the cave of Machpelah, in Hebron."

From these two statements it may be inferred that in times of persecution Maimonides and his family did not seek to protect their lives and property by dissimulation. They submitted to the troubles of exile in order that they might remain faithful to their religion. Carmoly, Geiger, Munk, and others are of opinion that the treatise of Maimonides on involuntary apostasy, as well as the accounts of some Mohammedan authors, contain strong evidence to show that there was a time when the family of Maimon publicly professed their belief in Mohammed. A critical examination of these documents compels us to reject their evidence as inadmissible.—After a long period of trouble and anxiety, the family of Maimon arrived at Fostat, in Egypt, and settled there. David, the brother of Moses Maimonides, carried on a trade in precious stones, while Moses occupied himself with his studies and interested himself in the communal affairs of the Jews.

It appears that for some time Moses was supported by his brother, and when this brother died, he earned a living by practising as a physician ; but he never sought or derived any benefit from his services to his community, or from his correspondence or from the works he wrote for the instruction of his brethren ; the satisfaction of being of service to his fellow-creatures was for him a sufficient reward.

The first public act in which Maimonides appears to have taken a leading part was a decree promulgated by the Rabbinical authorities in Cairo in the year 1167. The decree begins as follows :—" In times gone by, when storms and tempests threatened us, we used to wander about from place to place ; but by the mercy of the Almighty we have now been enabled to find here a resting-place. On our arrival, we noticed to our great dismay that the learned were disunited ; that none of them turned his attention to the needs of the congregation. We therefore felt it our duty to undertake the task of guiding the holy flock, of inquiring into the condition of the community, of " reconciling the hearts of the fathers to their children," and of correcting their corrupt ways. The injuries are great, but we may succeed in effecting a cure, and—in accordance with the words of the prophet—' I will seek the lost one, and that which has been cast out I will bring back, and the broken one I will cure ' (Micah iv. 6). When we therefore resolved to take the management of the communal affairs into our hands, we discovered the existence of a serious evil in the midst of the community," etc.

It was probably about that time that Maimon died. Letters of condolence were sent to his son Moses from all sides, both from Mohammedan and from Christian countries ; in some instances the letters were several months on their way before they reached their destination.

The interest which Maimonides now took in communal affairs did not prevent him from completing the great and arduous work, the Commentary on the Mishnah, which he had begun in Spain and continued during his wanderings in Africa. In this Commentary he proposed to give the quintessence of the Gemara, to expound the meaning of each dictum in the Mishnah, and to state which of the several opinions had received the sanction of the Talmudical authorities. His object in writing this work was to enable those who are not disposed to study the Gemara, to understand the Mishnah, and to facilitate the study of the Gemara for those who are willing to engage in it. The commentator generally adheres to the explanations given in the Gemara, and it is only in cases where the *halakah*, or practical law, is not affected, that he ventures to dissent. He acknowledges the benefit he derived from such works of his predecessors as the Halakot of Alfasi, and the writings of the Geonim, but afterwards he asserted that errors which were discovered in his works arose from his implicit reliance on those authorities. His originality is conspicuous in the Introduction and in the treatment of general principles, which in some instances precedes the exposition of an entire section or chapter, in others that of a single rule. The commentator is generally concise, except when occasion is afforded to treat of ethical and theological principles, or of a scientific subject, such as weights and measures, or mathematical and astronomical problems. Although exhortations to virtue and warnings against vice are found in all parts of his work, they are especially abundant in the Commentary on *Abot*, which is prefaced by a separate psychological treatise, called *The Eight Chapters*. The dictum " He who speaketh much commits a sin," elicited a lesson on the economy of speech ; the explanation of *'olam ha-ba* in the treatise Sanhedrin (xi. 1) led him to discuss the principles of faith, and to lay down the thirteen articles of the Jewish creed. The Commentary was written in Arabic, and was subsequently translated into Hebrew and into other languages. The estimation in which the Commentary was held may be inferred from the following fact : When the Jews in Italy became acquainted with its method and spirit, through a Hebrew translation of one of its parts, they sent to Spain in search of a complete Hebrew version of the Commentary. R. Simḥah, who had been entrusted with the mission, found no copy extant, but he succeeded, through the influence of Rabbi Shelomoh ben Aderet, in causing a Hebrew translation of this important work to be prepared.—In the Introduction, the author states that he has written a Commentary on the Babylonian Talmud treatise Ḥullin and on nearly three entire sections, viz., *Moĕd*, *Nashim*, and *Nezikin*. Of all these Commentaries only the one on *Rosh ha-shanah* is known.

In the year 1172 Maimonides wrote the *Iggeret Teman*, or *Petaḥ-tiḵvah* (" Letter to the Jews in Yemen," or " Opening of hope ") in response to a letter addressed to him by Rabbi Jacob al-Fayumi on the critical condition of the Jews in Yemen. Some of these Jews had been forced into apostasy ; others were made to believe that certain passages in the Bible alluded to the mission of Mohammed ; others again had been misled by an impostor who pretended to be the Messiah. The character and style of Maimonides' reply appear to have been adapted to the intellectual condition of the Jews in Yemen, for whom it was written. These probably read the Bible with Midrashic commentaries, and preferred the easy and attractive *Agadah* to the more earnest study of the *Halakah*. It is therefore not surprising that the letter contains remarks and interpretations which cannot be reconciled with the philosophical and logical method by which all the other works of Maimonides are distinguished. After a few complimentary words, in which the author modestly disputes the justice of the praises lavished upon him, he attempts to prove that the present sufferings of the Jews, together with the numerous instances of apostasy, were foretold by the prophets, especially by Daniel, and must not perplex the faithful. It must be borne in mind, he continues, that the attempts made in past times to do away with the Jewish religion, had invariably failed ; the same would be the fate of the present attempts ; for " religious persecutions are of but short duration." The arguments which profess to demonstrate that in certain Biblical passages allusion is made to Mohammed, are based on interpretations which are totally opposed to common sense. He urges that the Jews, faithfully adhering to their religion, should impress their children with the greatness of the Revelation on Mount Sinai, and of the miracles wrought through Moses ; they also should remain firm in the belief that God will send the Messiah to deliver their nation, but they must abandon futile calculations of the Messianic period, and beware of impostors. Although there be signs which indicate the approach of the promised deliverance, and the times seem to be the period of the last and most cruel persecution mentioned in the visions of Daniel (xi. and xii.), the person in Yemen who pretends to be the Messiah is an impostor, and if care be not taken, he is sure to do mischief. Similar impostors in Cordova, France, and Africa, have deceived the multitude and brought great troubles upon the Jews.—Yet, inconsistently with this sound advice the author gives a positive date of the Messianic time, on the basis of an old tradition; the inconsistency is so obvious that it is impossible to attribute this passage to Maimonides himself. It is probably spurious, and has, perhaps, been added by the translator. With the exception of the rhymed introduction, the letter was written in Arabic, " in order that all should be able to read and understand it "; for that purpose the author desires that copies should be made of it, and circulated among the Jews. Rabbi Naḥum, of the Maghreb, translated the letter into Hebrew.

The success in the first great undertaking of explaining the Mishnah encouraged Maimonides to propose to himself another task of a still more ambitious character. In the Commentary on the Mishnah, it was his object that those who were unable to read the Gemara should be made acquainted with the results obtained by the Amoraim in the course of their discussions on the Mishnah. But the Mishnah, with the Commentary, was not such a code of laws as might easily be consulted in cases of emergency ; only the initiated would be able to find the section, the chapter, and the paragraph in which the desired information could be found. The *halakah* had, besides, been further developed since the time when the Talmud was compiled. The changed state of things had suggested new questions ; these were discussed and settled by the Geonim, whose decisions, being contained in special letters or treatises, were not generally accessible. Maimonides therefore undertook to compile a complete code, which would contain, in the language and style of the Mishnah, and without discussion, the whole of the Written and the Oral Law, all the precepts recorded in the Talmud, Sifra, Sifre and Tosefta, and the decisions of the Geonim. According to the plan of the author, this work was to present a solution of every question touching the religious, moral, or social duties of the Jews. It was not in any way his object to discourage the study of the Talmud and the Midrash ; he only sought to diffuse a knowledge of the Law amongst those who, through incapacity or other circumstances, were precluded from that study. In order to ensure the completeness of the code, the author drew up a list of the six hundred and thirteen precepts of the Pentateuch, divided them into fourteen groups, these again he subdivided, and thus showed how many positive and negative precepts were contained in each section of the Mishneh torah. The principles by which he was guided in this arrangement were laid down in a separate treatise, called *Sefer ha-mizvot*. Works of a similar kind, written by his predecessors, as the *Halakot gedolot* of R. Shimon Kahira, and the several *Azharot* were, according to Maimonides, full of errors, because their authors had not adopted any proper method. But an examination of the rules laid down by Maimonides and of their application leads to the conclusion that his results were not less arbitrary ; as has, in fact, been shown by the criticisms of Naḥmanides. The *Sefer ha-mizvot* was written in Arabic, and thrice translated into Hebrew, namely, by Rabbi Abraham ben Ḥisdai, Rabbi Shelomoh ben Joseph ben Job, and Rabbi Moses Ibn Tibbon. Maimonides himself desired to translate the book into Hebrew, but to his disappointment he found no time.

This *Sefer ha-miẓvot* was executed as a preparation for his principal work, the *Mishneh Torah*, or *Yad ha-ḥazakah*, which consists of an Introduction and fourteen Books. In the Introduction the author first describes the chain of tradition from Moses to the close of the Talmud, and then he explains his method in compiling the work. He distinguishes between the dicta found in the Talmud, Sifre, Sifra, or Tosefta, on the one hand, and the dicta of the Geonim on the other ; the former were binding on all Jews, the latter only as far as their necessity and their utility or the authority of their propounders was recognized. Having once for all stated the sources from which he compiled his work, he did not deem it necessary to name in each case the authority for his opinion or the particular passage from which he derived his dictum. Any addition of references to each paragraph he probably considered useless to the uninformed and superfluous to the learned. At a later time he discovered his error, he being himself unable to find again the sources of some of his decisions. Rabbi Joseph Caro, in his commentary on the *Mishneh Torah*, termed *Keseph Mishneh*, remedied this deficiency. The Introduction is followed by the enumeration of the six hundred and thirteen precepts and a description of the plan of the work, its division into fourteen books, and the division of the latter into sections, chapters, and paragraphs.

According to the author, the *Mishneh Torah* is a mere compendium of the Talmud ; but he found sufficient opportunities to display his real genius, his philosophical mind, and his ethical doctrines. For in stating what the traditional Law enjoined he had to exercise his own judgment, and to decide whether a certain dictum was meant to be taken literally or figuratively ; whether it was the final decision of a majority or the rejected opinion of a minority ; whether it was part of the Oral Law or a precept founded on the scientific views of a particular author ; and whether it was of universal application or was only intended for a special period or a special locality. The first Book, *Sefer ha-madda'*, is the embodiment of his own ethical and theological theories, although he frequently refers to the Sayings of our Sages, and employs the phraseology of the Talmud. Similarly, the section on the Jewish Calendar, *Hilkot ha-'ibur*, may be considered as his original work. In each group of the *halakot*, its source, a certain passage of the Pentateuch, is first quoted, with its traditional interpretation, and then the detailed rules follow in systematic order. The *Mishneh Torah* was written by the author in pure Hebrew ; when subsequently a friend asked him to translate it into Arabic, he said he would prefer to have his Arabic writings translated into Hebrew instead of the reverse. The style is an imitation of the Mishnah ; he did not choose, the author says, the philosophical style, because that would be unintelligible to the common reader ; nor did he select the prophetic style, because that would not harmonize with the subject.

Ten years of hard work by day and by night were spent in the compilation of this code, which had originally been undertaken for " his own benefit, to save him in his advanced age the trouble and the necessity of consulting the Talmud on every occasion." Maimonides knew very well that his work would meet with the opposition of those whose ignorance it would expose, also of those who were incapable of comprehending it, and of those who were inclined to condemn every deviation from their own preconceived notions.

But he had the satisfaction to learn that it was well received in most of the congregations of Israel, and that there was a general desire to possess and study it. This success confirmed him in his hope that at a later time, when all cause for jealousy would have disappeared, the *Mishneh Torah* would be received by all Jews as an authoritative code. This hope has not been realized. The genius, earnestness, and zeal of Maimonides are generally recognized; but there is no absolute acceptance of his dicta. The more he insisted on his infallibility, the more did the Rabbinical authorities examine his words and point out errors wherever they believed that they could discover any. It was not always from base motives, as contended by Maimonides and his followers, that his opinions were criticised and rejected. The language used by Rabbi Abraham ben David in his notes (*hasagot*) on the *Mishneh Torah* appears harsh and disrespectful, if read together with the text of the criticised passage, but it seems tame and mild if compared with expressions used now and then by Maimonides about men who happened to hold opinions differing from his own.

Maimonides received many complimentary letters, congratulating him upon his success; but likewise letters with criticisms and questions respecting individual *halakot*. In most cases he had no difficulty in defending his position. From the replies it must, however, be inferred that Maimonides made some corrections and additions, which were subsequently embodied in his work. The letters addressed to him on the *Mishneh Torah* and on other subjects were so numerous that he frequently complained of the time he had to spend in their perusal, and of the annoyance they caused him; but " he bore all this patiently, as he had learned in his youth to bear the yoke." He was not surprised that many misunderstood his words, for even the simple words of the Pentateuch, " the Lord is one," had met with the same fate. Some inferred from the fact that he treated fully of *'Olam ha-ba*, " the future state of the soul," and neglected to expatiate on the resurrection of the dead, that he altogether rejected that principle of faith. They therefore asked Rabbi Samuel ha-levi of Bagdad to state his opinion; the Rabbi accordingly discussed the subject; but, according to Maimonides, he attempted to solve the problem in a very unsatisfactory manner. The latter thereupon likewise wrote a treatise " On the Resurrection of the Dead," in which he protested his adherence to this article of faith. He repeated the opinion he had stated in the Commentary on the Mishnah and in the *Mishneh Torah*, but " in more words; the same idea being reiterated in various forms, as the treatise was only intended for women and for the common multitude."

These theological studies engrossed his attention to a great extent, but it did not occupy him exclusively. In a letter addressed to R. Jonathan, of Lunel, he says: "Although from my birth the Torah was betrothed to me, and continues to be loved by me as the wife of my youth, in whose love I find a constant delight, strange women whom I at first took into my house as her handmaids have become her rivals and absorb a portion of my time." He devoted himself especially to the study of medicine, in which he distinguished himself to such a degree, according to Alkifti, that " the King of the Franks in Ascalon wanted to appoint him as his physician." Maimonides declined the honour. Alfadhel, the Vizier of Saladin king of Egypt, admired the genius of Maimonides, and bestowed upon him many distinctions. The name of Maimonides was entered on the roll of physicians, he received a pension, and was introduced to the court of Saladin. The method adopted in his professional practice he describes in a letter to his pupil, Ibn Aknin, as follows : " You know how difficult this profession is for a conscientious and exact person who only states what he can support by argument or authority." This method is more fully described in a treatise on hygiene, composed for Alfadhel, son of Saladin, who was suffering from a severe illness and had applied to Maimonides for advice. In a letter to Rabbi Samuel Ibn Tibbon he alludes to the amount of time spent in his medical practice, and says : " I reside in Egypt (or Fostat) ; the king resides in Cairo, which lies about two Sabbath-day journeys from the first-named place. My duties to the king are very heavy. I am obliged to visit him every day, early in the morning ; and when he or any of his children or the inmates of his harem are indisposed, I dare not quit Cairo, but must stay during the greater part of the day in the palace. It also frequently happens that one or two of the royal officers fall sick, and then I have to attend them. As a rule, I go to Cairo very early in the day, and even if nothing unusual happens I do not return before the afternoon, when I am almost dying with hunger ; but I find the antechambers filled with Jews and Gentiles, with nobles and common people, awaiting my return," etc.

Notwithstanding these heavy professional duties of court physician, Maimonides continued his theological studies. After having compiled a religious guide—*Mishneh Torah*—based on Revelation and Tradition, he found it necessary to prove that the principles there set forth were confirmed by philosophy. This task he accomplished in his *Dalalāt al-ḥaïrin*, " The Guide for the Perplexed," of which an analysis will be given below. It was composed in Arabic, and written in Hebrew characters. Subsequently it was translated into Hebrew by Rabbi Samuel Ibn Tibbon, in the lifetime of Maimonides, who was consulted by the translator on all difficult passages. The congregation in Lunel, ignorant of Ibn Tibbon's undertaking, or desirous to possess the most correct translation of the Guide, addressed a very flattering letter to Maimonides, requesting him to translate the work into Hebrew. Maimonides replied that he could not do so, as he had not sufficient leisure for even more pressing work, and that a translation was being prepared by the ablest and fittest man, Rabbi Samuel Ibn Tibbon. A second translation was made later on by Jehudah Alḥarizi. The Guide delighted many, but it also met with much adverse criticism on account of the peculiar views held by Maimonides concerning angels, prophecy, and miracles, especially on account of his assertion that if the Aristotelian proof for the Eternity of the Universe had satisfied him, he would have found no difficulty in reconciling the Biblical account of the Creation with that doctrine. The controversy on the Guide continued long after the death of Maimonides to divide the community, and it is difficult to say how far the author's hope to effect a reconciliation between reason and revelation was realized. His disciple, Joseph Ibn Aknin, to whom the work was dedicated, and who was expected to derive from it the greatest benefit, appears to have been disappointed. His inability to reconcile the two antagonistsic elements of faith and science, he describes allegorically in the form of a letter addressed to Maimonides, in which the following passage occurs : " Speak, for I desire that you be justified; if you can, answer me. Some time ago your beloved daughter, the beautiful and charming Kimah, obtained grace and favour in my sight, and I betrothed her unto me in faithfulness, and married her in accordance with the Law, in the presence of two trustworthy witnesses, viz., our master, Abd-allah and Ibn Roshd. But she soon became faithless to me; she could not have found fault with me, yet she left me and departed from my tent. She does no longer let me behold her pleasant countenance or hear her melodious voice. You have not rebuked or punished her, and perhaps you are the cause of this misconduct. Now, ' send the wife back to the man, for he is '—or might become—' a prophet; he will pray for you that you may live,' and also for her that she may be firm and steadfast. If, however, you do not send her back, the Lord will punish you. Therefore seek peace and pursue it; listen to what our Sages said : ' Blessed be he who restores to the owner his lost property '; for this blessing applies in a higher degree to him who restores to a man his virtuous wife, the crown of her husband." Maimonides replied in the same strain, and reproached his " son-in-law " that he falsely accused his wife of faithlessness after he had neglected her; but he restored him his wife with the advice to be more cautious in future. In another letter Maimonides exhorts Ibn Aknin to study his works, adding, " apply yourself to the study of the Law of Moses; do not neglect it, but, on the contrary, devote to it the best and the most of your time, and if you tell me that you do so, I am satisfied that you are on the right way to eternal bliss."

Of the letters written after the completion of the "Guide," the one addressed to the wise men of Marseilles (1194) is especially noteworthy. Maimonides was asked to give his opinion on astrology. He regretted in his reply that they were not yet in the possession of his *Mishneh Torah*; they would have found in it the answer to their question. According to his opinion, man should only believe what he can grasp with his intellectual faculties, or perceive by his senses, or what he can accept on trustworthy authority. Beyond this nothing should be believed. Astrological statements, not being founded on any of these three sources of knowledge, must be rejected. He had himself studied astrology, and was convinced that it was no science at all. If some dicta be found in the Talmud which appear to represent astrology as a true source of knowledge, these may either be referred to the rejected opinion of a small minority, or may have an allegorical meaning, but they are by no means forcible enough to set aside principles based on logical proof.

The debility of which Maimonides so frequently complained in his correspondence, gradually increased, and he died, in his seventieth year, on the 20th Tebeth, 4965 (1204). His death was the cause of great mourning to all Jews. In Fostat a mourning of three days was kept; in Jerusalem a fast was appointed; a portion of the *tochaḥah* (Lev. xxvi. or Deut. xxix.) was read, and also the history of the capture of the Ark by the Philistines (1 Sam. iv.). His remains were brought to Tiberias. The general regard in which Maimonides was held, both by his contemporaries and by succeeding generations, has been expressed in the popular saying : " From Moses to Moses there was none like Moses."

THE MOREH NEBUCHIM LITERATURE

I. *The Arabic Text.*—The *editio princeps*, the only edition of the original text of the Guide (in Arabic, *Dĕlil*, or *Dalalat al-ḥaïrin*), was undertaken and executed by the late S. Munk. Its title is : *Le Guide des Égarés, traité de Théologie et de Philosophie par Moïse ben Maimon, publié pour la première fois dans l'original Arabe, et accompagné d'une traduction Française et de notes critiques, littéraires et explicatives, par S. Munk* (Paris, 1850–1866). The plan was published, 1833, in *Reflexions sur le culte des anciens Hébreux* (La Bible, par S. Cahen, vol. iv.), with a specimen of two chapters of the Third Part. The text adopted has been selected from the several MSS. at his disposal with great care and judgment. Two Leyden MSS. (cod. 18 and 221), various MSS. of the *Bibliothèque Nationale* (No. 760, very old ; 761 and 758, written by R. Saadia Ibn Danan), and some MSS. of the Bodleian Library were consulted. In the notes which accompany the French translation, the various readings of the different MSS. are fully discussed. At the end of the third volume a list is added of " Variantes des Manuscrits Arabes et des deux Versions Hébraïques."

The library of the British Museum possesses two copies of the Arabic text ; the one Or. 1423 is complete, beautifully written, with explanatory notes in the margin and between the lines. The name of the copyist is not mentioned, nor the date when it has been written. The volume has in the beginning an incomplete index to the Scriptural passages referred to in the *Guide*, and at the end fragments of Psalm cxli. in Arabic and of astronomical tables.

The second copy of the *Dalalat al-ḥaïrin* is contained in the MS. Or. 2423, written in large Yemen Rabbinic characters. It is very fragmentary. The first fragment begins with the last paragraph of the introduction ; there are a few marginal notes in Hebrew.

In the Bodleian Library there are the following copies of the *Dalalat al-ḥaïrin* according to the Catal. of Hebr. MSS. by Dr. A. Neubauer :—

No. 1236. The text is preceded by Jehudah al-Charizi's index of the contents of the chapters, and by an index of Biblical quotations. In the margin there are notes, containing omissions, by different hands, two in Arabic characters. The volume was written 1473.

No. 1237. The Arabic text, with a few marginal notes containing various readings ; the text is preceded by three Hebrew poems, beginning, *De'i bolek, Bi-sedeb tebunot* ; and *Binu be-dat Mosheb*. Fol. 212 contains a fragment of the book (III., xxix.).

No. 1238. Text with a few marginal notes.

No. 1239. The end of the work is wanting in this copy. The second part has forty-nine chapters, as the introduction to Part II. is counted as chapter i.; Part III. has fifty-six chapters, the introduction being counted as chapter i., and chapter xxiv. being divided into two chapters. The index of passages from the Pentateuch follows the ordinary mode of counting the chapters of the *Guide*.

No. 1240. Arabic text transcribed in Arabic characters by Saadiah b. Levi Azankoṭ for Prof. Golius in 1645.

No. 1241. First part of the *Dalalat al-ḥaïrin*, written by Saadiah b. Mordecai b. Mosheh in the year 1431.

No. 1242 contains the same Part, but incomplete.

Nos. 1243, 1244, 1245, and 1246 contain Part II. of the Arabic text, incomplete in Nos. 1245 and 1246.

Nos. 1247, 1248, and 1249 have Part III.; it is incomplete in Nos. 1248 and 1249. No. 1249 was written 1291, and begins with III., viii.

A fragment of the Arabic text, the end of Part III., is contained in No. 407, 2.

No. 2508 includes a fragment of the original (I. ii.-xxxii.), with a Hebrew interlineary translation of some words and a few marginal notes. It is written in Yemen square characters, and is marked as "holy property of the Synagogue of Alsiani."

A fragment (I. i.) of a different recension from the printed is contained in 2422, 16. On the margin the Commentaries of Shem-ṭob and Ephodi are added in Arabic.

A copy of the *Dalalat* is also contained in the Berlin Royal Library MS. Or. Qu., 579 (105 Cat. Steinschneider); it is defective in the beginning and at the end.

The Cairo Genizah at Cambridge contains two fragments : (*a*) I. lxiv. and beginning of lxv; (*b*) II. end of xxxii. and xxxiii. According to Dr. H. Hirschfeld, *Jewish Quarterly Review* (vol. xv. p. 677, they are in the handwriting of Maimonides.

The valuable collection of MSS. in the possession of Dr. M. Gaster includes a fragment of the *Dalalat-al-ḥaïrin* (Codex 605). II. xiii–xv., beginning and end defective.

II. *Translations. a. Hebrew.*—As soon as European Jews heard of the existence of this work, they procured its translation into Hebrew. Two scholars, independently of each other, undertook the task : Samuel Ibn Tibbon and Jehudah al-Ḥarizi. There is, besides, in the *Moreh ha-ṃoreh* of Shemṭob Palquera an original translation of some portions of the *Moreh*. In the *Sifte yeshenim* (No. 112) a rhymed translation of the *Dalalat* by Rabbi Mattityahu Kartin is mentioned. Ibn Tibbon's version is very accurate ; he sacrificed elegance of style to the desire of conscientiously reproducing the author's work, and did not even neglect a particle, however unimportant it may appear. Ibn Tibbon went in his anxiety to retain peculiarities of the original so far as to imitate its ambiguities, e.g., *meẓiut* (I. lviii.) is treated as a masculine noun, only in order to leave it doubtful whether a pronoun which follows agrees with *meẓiut*, " existence," or with *nimẓa*, " existing being," both occurring in the same sentence (Br. Mus. MS. Harl. 7586, marg. note by Ibn Tibbon). When he met with passages that offered any difficulty he consulted Maimonides. Ḥarizi, on the other hand, was less conscientious about words and particles, but wrote in a superior style. *Vox populi*, how-ever, decided in favour of the version of Ibn Tibbon, the rival of which be-came almost forgotten. Also Abraham, the son of Moses Maimonides, in *Milḥamoth ha-shem*, describes Ḥarizi's version as being inaccurate. Most of the modern translations were made from Ibn Tibbon's version. There are, therefore, MSS. of this version almost in every library containing collec-tions of Hebrew books and MSS. It has the title *Moreh-nebuchim*. The British Museum has the following eight copies of Ibn Tibbon's version :—

Harl. 7586 *A.* This codex was written in the year 1284, for Rabbi Shabbatai ben Rabbi Mattityahu. In the year 1340 it came into the possession of Jacob b. Shelomoh ; his son Menaḥem sold it in the year 1378 to R. Mattityahu, son of R. Shabbatai, for fifty gold florins. It was again sold in the year 1461 by Yehiel ben Joab. There is this peculiarity in the writing, that long words at the end of a line are divided, and written half on the one line, half on the next; in words which are vocalized, *patah* is frequently found for *kamez*. There are numerous various readings in the margin. The text is preceded by a poem, written by Joseph Ibn Aknin, pupil of Maimonides, in praise of his master, and beginning *Adon yizro.* This poem is attributed to R. Yehudah ha-Levi (Luzzatto, in his Divan, *Betulat-bat-Yehudah*, p. 104). At the end the copyist adds an epigram, the translation of which is as follows :—

" The Moreh is finished—Praise to Him who formed and created everything—written for the instruction and benefit of the few whom the Lord calleth. Those who oppose the Moreh ought to be put to death ; but those who study and understand it deserve that Divine Glory rest upon them, and inspire them with a spirit from above."

Harl. 7586 *B.* This codex, much damaged in the beginning and at the end, contains the version of Ibn Tibbon, with marginal notes, consisting of words omitted in the text, and other corrections. The version is followed by the poems *Karob meod*, etc., and *De'i bolek*, etc.

Harl. 5507 contains the Hebrew version of Ibn Tibbon, with the translator's preface and marginal notes, consisting of various readings and omissions from the text. The work of Maimonides is followed by Ibn Tibbon's Vocabulary (*millot-zarot*), *Mesharet-mosheh*, '*Arugot ha-mezimmah, Millot biggayon, Ruah-hen,* Alfarabi's *Hathalot,* a Hebrew-Italian vocabulary of logical terms, and an explanation of *koteb.* The passage in Part I., chap. lxxi., which refers to Christianity, has been erased.

Harl. 5525 was the property of Shimshon Kohen Modon. The MS. begins with Harizi's *Kavvanat ha-perakim ;* then follows the text, with a few marginal notes of a later hand, mostly adverse criticisms and references to 'Arama's '*Akedah* and the Biblical commentaries of Abarbanel. There is also a note in Latin. The text is followed by Ibn Tibbon's Vocabulary (*Millot-zarot*) and *Masoret ha-pesukim* (Index to the Biblical quotations in the Moreh). In a poem, beginning *Moreh asher mennu derakav gabehu,* the Moreh is compared to a musical instrument, which delights when played by one that understands music, but is spoiled when touched by an ignorant person.

Add. 27068 (Almanzi coll.). At the end the following remark is added : I, Samuel Ibn Tibbon, finished the translation of this work in the month of Tebet 4965 (1205). The text is preceded by the well-known epigrams, *De'i bolek* and *Moreh-nebuchim sa shelomi ;* the last page contains the epigram *Karob meod.* There are some notes in the margin, mostly referring to various readings.

Add. 14763. This codex, written 1273 at Viterbo, contains the preface of Harizi to his translation of the Moreh and his index of contents, Ibn Tibbon's version with a few marginal notes of different hands, including some remarks of the translator, and the contents of the chapters. The codex contains besides the following treatises : Commentary of Maimonides on Abot ; Comm. of Maim. on Mishnah Sanhedrin x. 1 ; Letter of Maimonides on the Resurrection of the Dead ; Vocabulary of difficult words by Samuel Ibn Tibbon ; Maimonides' Letter to the wise men of Marseilles ; his Letter to Rabbi Jonathan ; *Keter-malkut, Mesharet-mosheh, Ruah-hen, Otot ha-shamayim,* translated from the Arabic by Samuel Ibn Tibbon ; *Hathalot ha-nimzaot,* of Alfarabi ; *Sefer ha-happuah, Mishle hamishim ha-talmidim ;* on the seven zones of the earth ; a fragment of a chronicle from the exile of Babylon down to the fourth year of the Emperor Nicepheros of Constantinople, and a poem, which begins *asher yishal,* and has the following sense:—" If one asks the old and experienced for advice, you may expect his success in all he undertakes ; but if one consults the young, remember the fate of Rehoboam, son of Solomon."

Add. 14764. In addition to the Hebrew version of Ibn Tibbon (from end of I. xxvii.) with a few marginal notes and index, the codex contains at the end of Part I. an Index of references made by the author to explanations given in preceding or succeeding chapters. At the end of the text the statement is added, that the translation was finished in the month of Tebet 968 (1208). The Moreh is followed by *Ruah-hen,* and Ibn Tibbon's Vocabulary of *millot-zarot* (incomplete), and is preceded by four poems in praise of the Moreh, beginning *Shim'u nebone leb, Moreh nebuchim sa shelomi, De'i bolek* and *Nofet mahkim.*

Bibl. Reg. 16 A, xi. This codex, written in Prov. curs. characters in the year 1308, has in front a fragment of III. i., then follows the poem of Meshullam, beginning *Yebgu mezimmotai* (Grätz *Leket-shoshannim,* p. 151), and other poems.

The following MS. copies of Ibn Tibbon's version are included in the Oxford Bodleian Library; the numbers refer to Dr. Neubauer's catalogue of the MSS. :—

1250. An index of the passages from the Bible referred to in the work, and an index of the contents precede the version. The marginal notes contain chiefly omissions.

1251. This codex was written in 1675. The marginal notes contain omissions and explanations.

1252. The marginal notes contain the translator's remarks on I. lxxiv. 4, and III. xlvii. The version is followed by Ibn Tibbon's vocabulary, and his additional remarks on the reasons for the commandments. The MS. was bought by Samuel ben Moses from a Christian after the pillage of Padua, where it had belonged to a Synagogue of foreigners (*lo'azim*) ; he gave it to a Synagogue of the same character at Mantua.

1253. The marginal notes include that of the translator on III. xlvii.

1254, 1. Text with marginal notes containing omissions.

1255. The marginal notes include those of the translator on I. xlvi. and lxxiv. 5.

1256. The marginal notes contain various readings, notes relating to Ḥarizi's translation and the Arabic text ; on fol. 80 there is a note in Latin. There are in this codex six epigrams concerning the Moreh.

1257. Text incomplete ; with marginal notes.

Fragments of the Version are contained in the following codices : 2047, 3, p. 65 ; 2283, 8 ; 2309, 2, and 2336.

Among the MS. copies of the Moreh in the Bibl. Nat. in Paris, there is one that has been the property of R. Eliah Mizraḥi, and another that had been in the hands of Azariah de Rossi (No. 685 and No. 691) ; the Günzburg Library (Paris) possesses a copy (No. 771), that was written 1452 by Samuel son of Isaac for Rabbi Moses de Leon, and Eliah del Medigo's copy of the Moreh is in the possession of Dr. Ginsburg (London) ; it contains six poems, beginning *Moreh nebuchim sa ; Emet moreh emet ; Bi-leshon esh ; Mahba'aru ; Kamu more shav.*

The *editio princeps* of this version has no statement as to where and when it was printed, and is without pagination. According to Fürst (Bibliogr.) it is printed before 1480. The copy in the British Museum has some MS. notes. Subsequent editions contain besides the Hebrew text the Commentaries of Shem-ṭob and Efodi, and the index of contents by Ḥarizi (Venice, 1551, fol.) ; also the Comm. of Crescas and Vocabulary of Ibn Tibbon (Sabionetta, 1553, fol. ; Jessnitz, 1742, fol. etc.) ; the Commentaries of Narboni and S. Maimon (Berlin, 1791) ; the commentaries of Efodi, Shem-ṭob, Crescas and Abarbanel (Warsaw, 1872, 4to) ; German translation and Hebrew Commentary (*Biur*) Part I. (Krotoschin, 1839, 8vo) ; German translation and notes, Part II. (Wien. 1864), Part III. (Frankfort-a-M., 1838).

The Hebrew version of Ibn Tibbon (Part I. to ch. lxxii.) has been translated into Mishnaic Hebrew by M. Levin (Zolkiew, 1829, 4to).

There is only one MS. known of Ḥarizi's version, viz., No. 682 of the Bibliothèque Nationale at Paris. It has been edited by L. Schlosberg, with notes. London, 1851 (Part I.), 1876 (II.), and 1879 (III.). The notes on Part I. were supplied by S. Scheyer.

The first Latin translation of the Moreh has been discovered by Dr. J. Perles among the Latin MSS. of the Munic Library, Catal. Cod. latinorum bibl. regiae Monacensis, tom. 1, pars iii. pag. 208 (Kaish. 36 b), 1700 (7936 b). This version is almost identical with that edited by Augustinus Justinianus,

Paris, 1520, and is based on Harizi's Hebrew version of the Moreh. The name of the translator is not mentioned. In the Commentary of Moses, son of Solomon, of Salerno, on the Moreh, a Latin translation is quoted, and the quotations agree with this version. It is called by this commentator *ha 'atakat ha-noẓrit* (" the Christian translation "), and its author, *ha-ma 'atik ha-noẓer* (lit. " the Christian translator "). Dr. Perles is, however, of opinion that these terms do not necessarily imply that a Christian has made this translation, as the word *noẓer* may have been used here for " Latin." He thinks that it is the result of the combined efforts of Jewish and Christian scholars connected with the court of the German Emperor Frederic II., especially as in the thirteenth century several Jewish scholars distinguished themselves by translating Oriental works into Latin. See Grätz Monatschrift, 1875, Jan.–June, " Die in einer Münchener Handschrift aufgefundene erste lateinische Uebersetzung," etc., von Dr. J. Perles. The title has been variously rendered into Latin : Director neutrorum, directorium dubitantium, director neutrorum, nutantium or dubitantium ; doctor perplexorum.

Gedaliah ibn Yahyah, in *Shalshelet ha-ḳabbalah*, mentions a Latin translation of the Moreh by Jacob Monteno ; but nothing is known of it, unless it be the anonymous translation of the Munich MS., mentioned above. Augustinus Justinianus edited this version (Paris, 1520), with slight alterations and a great number of mistakes. Joseph Scaliger's opinion of this version is expressed in a letter to Casaubonus, as follows : Qui latine vertit, Hebraica, non Arabica, convertit, et quidem sæpe hallucinatur, neque mentem Authoris assequitur. Magna seges mendorum est in Latino. Præter illa quæ ab inertia Interpretis peccata sunt accessit et inertia Librariorum aut Typographorum, e.g., prophetiæ pro philosophiæ ; altitudo pro aptitudo ; bonitatem pro brevitatem. (Buxtorf, Doctor Perplexorum, Præf.)

Johannes Buxtorfius, Fil., translated the Hebrew version of Ibn Tibbon into Latin (Basileæ, 1629, 4to). In the Præfatio ad Lectorem, the translator discusses the life and the works of Maimonides, and dwells especially on the merits and the fate of the *Moreh-nebuchim*. The preface is followed by a Hebrew poem of Rabbi Raphael Joseph of Trèves, in praise of an edition of the Moreh containing the Commentaries of Efodi, Shem-tob, and Crescas.

Italian was the first living language into which the Moreh has been translated. This translation was made by Yedidyah ben Moses (Amadeo de Moïse di Recanati), and dedicated by him to " divotissimo e divinissimo Signor mio il Signor Immanuel da Fano " (i.e., the Kabbalist Menaḥem Azarriah). The translator dictated it to his brother Eliah, who wrote it in Hebrew characters ; it was finished the 8th of February, 1583. The MS. copy is contained in the Royal Library at Berlin, MS. Or. Qu. 487 (M. Steinschneider Catal., etc.)—The Moreh has been translated into Italian a second time, and annotated by D. J. Maroni: Guida degli Smarriti, Firenze, 1870, fol.

The Moreh has been translated into German by R. Fürstenthal (Part I,, Krotoschin, 1839), M. Stern (Part II., Wien, 1864), and S. Scheyer (Part III.. Frankfort-a.-M., 1838). The translation is based on Ibn Tibbon's Hebrew version. The chapters on the Divine Attributes have been translated into

xxxii GUIDE FOR THE PERPLEXED

German, and fully discussed, by Dr. Kaufmann in his *Geschichte der Attri-butcnlehre* (Gotha, 1877). An excellent French translation, based on the Arabic original, has been supplied by the regenerator of the *Guide*, S. Munk. It was published together with the Arabic text (Paris, 1850–1866).

The Moreh has also been translated into the Hungarian language by Dr. Klein. The translation is accompanied by notes (Budapest, 1878–80).

The portion containing the reasons of the Commandments (Part III. ch. xxvi.–xlix.) has been translated into English by James Townley (London, 1827). The translation is preceded by an account on the life and works of Maimonides, and dissertations on various subjects; among others, Talmudical and Rabbinical writings, the Originality of the Institutions of Moses, and Judicial astrology.

III. *Commentaries.*—It is but natural that in a philosophical work like the Moreh, the reader will meet with passages that at first thought seem unintelligible, and require further explanation, and this want has been supplied by the numerous commentators that devoted their attention to the study of the Moreh. Joseph Solomon del Medigo (1591) saw eighteen Commentaries. The four principal ones he characterizes thus (in imitation of the Hagadah for Passover): Moses Narboni is *rasha'*, has no piety, and reveals all the secrets of the Moreh. Shem-ṭob is *ḥakam*, " wise," expounds and criticises; Crescas is *tam*, " simple," explains the book in the style of the Rabbis; Epodi is *she-eno yode'a lishol*, " does not understand to ask," he simply explains in short notes without criticism (*Miktab-aḥuz*; ed. A. Geiger, Berlin, 1840, p. 18). The earliest annotations were made by the author himself on those passages, which the first translator of the Moreh was unable to comprehend. They are contained in a letter addressed to Samuel Ibn Tibbon, beginning, *lefi siklo yehullal ish* (Bodl Library, No. 2218, s.; comp. *The Guide*, etc., I. 21, 343; II. 8, 99). Ibn Tibbon, the translator, likewise added a few notes, which are found in the margin of MSS. of the Hebrew version of the Moreh (on I. xlv. lxxiv.; II. xxiv.; and III. xlvii.—MSS. Bodl. 1252, 1; 1253, 1255, 1257; Brit. Mus. Add. 14,763 and 27,068).

Both translators wrote explanations of the philosophical terms employed in the versions. Ḥarizi wrote his vocabulary first, and Ibn Tibbon, in the introductory remarks, to *Perush millot zarot* (" Explanation of difficult words "), describes his rival's vocabulary as full of blunders. Ibn Tibbon's *Perush* is found almost in every copy of his version, both MS. and print; so also Ḥarizi's index of the contents of the chapters of the Moreh (*Kavvanat ha-peraḳim*).

The following is an alphabetical list of Commentaries on the Moreh :—

Abarbanel (Don Isaak) wrote a Commentary on I. i.–lv.; II. xxxi.–xlv., and a separate book *Shamayim-ḥadashim*, " New Heavens," on II. xix., in which he fully discusses the question concerning *Creatio ex nihilo*. The opinion of Maimonides is not always accepted. Thus twenty-seven objections are raised against his interpretation of the first chapter of Ezekiel. These objections he wrote at Molin, in the house of R. Abraham Treves Ẓarfati. The Commentary is followed by a short essay (*maamar*) on the plan of the Moreh. The method adopted by Abarbanel in all his Commentaries, is also employed in this essay. A series of questions is put forth on the subject, and then the author sets about to answer them. M. J. Landau edited the Commentary without text, with a Preface, and with explanatory notes, called *Moreh li-ẓeîdakah* (Prag. 1831; MS. Bodl. 2385). In addition tc these the same author wrote *Teshubot* "Answers" to several questions asked by Rabbi Shaul ha-Cohen on topics discussed in the Moreh (Venice, 1754).

Abraham Abulafia wrote "Sodot ha-moreh," or *Sitre-torah*, a kabbalistic Commentary on the Moreh. He gives the expression, גן עדן (Paradise), for the number (177) of the chapters of the Moreh. MS. Nat. Bibl. 226, 3. Leipsic Libr. 232, 4. MS. Bodl. 2360, 5, contains a portion of Part III.

Buchner A. Ha-moreh li-zedakah (Warsaw, 1838). Commentary on "The Reasons of the Laws," Moreh III. xxix.–xlix. The Commentary is preceded by an account of the life of Maimonides.

Comtino, Mordecai b. Eliezer, wrote a short commentary on the Moreh (Dr. Ginsburg's collection of MSS. No. 10). Narboni, who "spread light on dark passages in the Guide," is frequently quoted. Reference is also made to his own commentary on Ibn Ezra's *Yesod-mora*.

Crescas (Asher b. Abraham), expresses in the Preface to his Commentary the conviction that he could not always comprehend the right sense of the words of Maimonides, for "there is no searching to his understanding." He nevertheless thinks that his explanations will help "the young" to study the Moreh with profit. A long poem in praise of Maimonides and his work precedes the Preface. His notes are short and clear, and in spite of his great respect of Maimonides, he now and then criticises and corrects him.

David Yahya is named by Joseph Del Medigo (*Miktab-ahuz* ed. A. Geiger, Berlin, 1840 ; p. 18, and note 76), as having written a Commentary on the Moreh.

David ben Yehudah Leon Rabbino wrote *'En ha-kore*, MS. Bodl. 1263. He quotes in his Commentary among others 'Arama's *'Akedat yizhak*. The Preface is written by Immanuel ben Raphael Ibn Meir, after the death of the author.

Efodi is the name of the Commentary written by Isaac ben Moses, who during the persecution of 1391 had passed as Christian under the name of Profiat Duran. He returned to Judaism, and wrote against Christianity the famous satire "Al tehee kaaboteka" ("Be not like your Fathers"), which misled Christians to cite it as written in favour of Christianity. It is addressed to the apostate En Bonet Bon Giorno. The same author also wrote a grammatical work, *Ma'aseh-efod*. The name *Efod* (אפד), is explained as composed of the initials *Amar Profiat Duran*. His Commentary consists of short notes, explanatory of t' .ext. The beginning of this Commentary is contained in an Arabic translation in Ms. Bodl. 2422, 16.

Ephraim Al-Naqavah in *Sha'ar Kebod ha-shem* (MS. Bodl. 939, 2 and 1258, 2), answers some questions addressed to him concerning the Moreh. He quotes Hisdai's *Or adonai*.

Fürstenthal, R., translator and commentator of the Mahzor, added a Biur, short explanatory notes, to his German translation of Part I. of the Moreh (Krotoschin, 1839).

Gershon, Moreh-derek, Commentary on Part I. of the Moreh (MS. Bodl. 1265).

Hillel b. Samuel b. Elazar of Verona explained the Introduction to Part II. (the 25 Propos.). S. H. Halberstam edited this Commentary together with *Tagmule ha-nefesh* of the same author, for the Society *Mekize-nirdamim* (Lyck, 1874).

Joseph ben Aba-mari b. Joseph, of Caspi (Argentière), wrote three Commentaries on the Moreh. The first is contained in a Munich MS. (No. 263) ; and seems to have been recast by the author, and divided into two separate Commentaries : *'Ammude Kesef*, and *Maskiyot Kesef*. The former was to contain plain and ordinary explanation, whilst profound and mysterious matter was reserved for the second (Steinschn. Cat.). In II., chap. xlviii., Caspi finds fault with Maimonides that he does not place the book of Job among the highest class of inspired writings, "its author being undoubtedly Moses." These Commentaries have been edited by T. Werblumer (Frankfort-a.-M., 1848). R. Kirchheim added a Hebrew introduction discussing the character of these commentaries, and describing the manuscripts from which these were copied ; a Biography of the author is added in German.

Joseph Giqatilia wrote notes on the Moreh, printed with "Questions of Shaul ha-kohen" (Venice, 1574. MS. Bodl. 1911, 3).

Joseph b. Isaac ha-Levi's Gib'at ha-Moreh is a short Commentary on portions of the Moreh, with notes by R. Yom-tob Heller, the author of *Tosafot Yom-tob* (Prag., 1612).

Isaac Satanov wrote a commentary on Parts II. and III. of the *Moreh* (see Maimon Solomon p. xxi.).

Isaac ben Shem-tob ibn Shem-tob wrote a lengthy Commentary on the Moreh, Part I. (MS. Brit. Mus. Or. 1388). The object of the Commentary is to show that there is no contradiction between Maimonides and the Divine Law. He praises Maimonides as a true believer in *Creatio ex nibilo*, whilst Ibn Ezra and Gersonides assumed a *prima materia* (*Yozer, kadosh*). Nachmanides is called *ha-hasid ha-gadol*, but is nevertheless blamed, together with Narboni and Zerahyah ha-Levi, for criticising Maimonides, instead of trying to explain startling utterances even in "a forced way" (*bederek rahok*); and Narboni, "in spite of his wisdom, frequently misunderstood the Moreh." At the end of each chapter a *résumé* (*derush*) of the contents of the chapter is given, and the lesson to be derived from it. The MS. is incomplete, chaps. xlvi.–xlviii. are missing.

Kauffmann, D., in his *Geschichte der Atributenlehre*, translated Part I. chap. l.–lxiii. into German, and added critical and explanatory notes.

Kalonymos wrote a kind of introduction to the *Moreh* (*Mesharet Mosheh*), in which he especially discusses the theory of Maimonides on Providence.

Leibnitz made extracts from Buxtorf's Latin version of the *Moreh*, and added his own remarks. *Observationes ad R. Mosen Maimoniden* (Foucher de Careil, C.A., *La Philosophie Juive*, 1861).

Levin, M., wrote *Allon-moreh* as a kind of introduction to his retranslation of Tibbon's Hebrew version into the language of the Mishnah.

Maimon, Solomon, is the author of *Gib'at ha-moreh*, a lengthy commentary on Book I. (Berlin, 1791). The author is fond of expatiating on topics of modern philosophy. In the introduction he gives a short history of philosophy. The commentary on Books II. and III. was written by Isaac Satanov.

Meir ben Jonah ha-mekunneh Ben-shneor wrote a commentary on the *Moreh* in Fez 1560 (MS. Bodl. 1262).

Menahem Kara expounded the twenty-five propositions enumerated in the Introduction to Part II. of the Moreh (MS. Bodl. 1649, 13).

Mordecai Yaffe, in his *Or Yekarot*, or *Pinnat Yikrat*, one of his ten *Lebushim*, comments upon the theories contained in the *Moreh*.

Moses, son of Abraham Provençal, explains the passage in Part I. chap. lxxiii. Prop. 3, in which Maimonides refers to the difference between commensurable and incommensurable lines (MS. Bodl. 2033, 8).

Moses, son of Jehudah Nagari, made an index of the subjects treated in the *Moreh*, indicating in each case the chapters in which allusion is made to the subject. He did so, "in obedience to the advice of Maimonides, to consider the chapters in connected order" (Part I. p. 20). It has been printed together with the questions of Shaul ha-kohen (Venice, 1574).

Moses son of Solomon of Salerno, is one of the earliest expounders of the *Moreh*. He wrote his commentary on Parts I. and II., perhaps together with a Christian scholar. He quotes the opinion of "the Christian scholar with whom he worked together." Thus he names Petrus de Bernia and Nicolo di Giovenazzo. R. Jacob Anatoli, author of the *Malmed ha-talmidim*, is quoted as offering an explanation for the passage from *Pirke di-rabbi Eliezer*, which Maimonides (II. chap. xxvi.) considers as strange and inexplicable (Part I., written 1439; MS. of *Bet ha-midrash*, London; Parts I.–II.,MS. Bodl. 1261, written, 1547; MS. Petersburg, No. 82; Munich MS. 60 and 370).

Moses ha-katan, son of Jehudah, son of Moses, wrote *To'aliyot pirke ha-maamar* (" Lessons taught in the chapters of this work "). It is an index to the *Moreh* (MS. Bodl. 1267).

Moses Leiden explained the 25 Prop. of the Introduction to Part II. (MS. Günzburg, Paris).

Moses Narboni wrote a short commentary at Soria, 1362. He freely criticizes Maimonides, and uses expressions like the following :—" He went too far, may God pardon him" (II. viii.). Is. Euchel ed. Part I. (Berlin, 1791); J. Goldenthal, I. to III. (Wien, 1852). The Bodl. Libr. possesses several MS. copies of this commentary (Nos. 1260, 1264, 2, and 1266).

Munk, S., added to his French translation of the Moreh numerous critical and explanatory notes.

S. Sachs (Ha-tehiyah, Berlin, 1850, p. 8) explains various passages of the Moreh, with a view of discovering the names of those who are attacked by Maimonides without being named.

Scheyer, S., added critical and explanatory notes to his German translation of the Moreh, Part 3, and to the Hebrew version of Ḥarizi, Part 1. He also wrote *Das Psychologische System des Maimonides*, an Introduction to the Moreh (Frankf.-a-M., 1845).

Shem ṭob Ibn Palquera's Moreh ha-moreh consists of 3 parts : (1) a philosophical explanation of the Moreh, (2) a description of the contents of the chapters of the Moreh, Part I, i.–lvii. (Presburg, 1827) ; (3) Corrections of Ibn Tibbon's version. He wrote the book for himself, that in old age he might have a means of refreshing his memory. The study of science and philosophy is to be recommended, but only to those who have had a good training in "the fear of sin." Ibn Roshd (Averroes) is frequently quoted, and referred to as *he-ḥakam ha-nizkar* (the philosopher mentioned above).

Shem-ṭob ben Joseph ben Shem-ṭob had the commentary of *Efodi* before him, which he seems to have quoted frequently *verbatim* without naming him. In the preface he dwells on the merits of the Moreh as the just mediator between religion and philosophy. The commentary of Shem-tobh is profuse, and includes almost a paraphrase of the text. He apologises in conclusion for having written many superfluous notes and added explanation where no explanation was required ; his excuse is that he did not only intend to write a commentary (*biur*) but also a work complete in itself (*ḥibbur*). He often calls the reader's attention to things which are plain and clear.

Shem-ṭob Ibn Shem-ṭob, in *Sefer ha-emunot* (Ferrara, 1556), criticises some of the various theories discussed in the Moreh, and rejects them as heretic. His objections were examined by Moses Al-ashkar, and answered in *Hasagot 'al mah she-katab Rabbi Shem-ṭob neged ha-Rambam* (Ferrara, 1556).

Solomon b. Jehudah ha-nasi wrote in Germany *Sitre-torah*, a kabbalistic commentary on the Moreh, and dedicated it to his pupil Jacob b. Samuel (MS. Bet-ha-midrash, London).

Tabrizi. The twenty-five Propositions forming the introduction to Part 2, have been fully explained by Mohammed Abu-becr ben Mohammed al-tabrizi. His Arabic explanations have been translated by Isaac b. Nathan of Majorca into Hebrew (Ferrara, 1556). At the end the following eulogy is added :—The author of these Propositions is the chief whose sceptre is "wisdom" and whose throne is "understanding," the Israelite prince, that has benefited his nation and all those who love God, etc. : Moses b. Maimon b. Ebed-elohim, the Israelite. . . . May God lead us to the truth. Amen !

Tishbi. In MS. Bodl. 2279, 1, there are some marginal notes on Part III. which are signed Tishbi (Neub. Cat.).

Yaḥya Ibn Suleiman wrote in Arabic a Commentary on the *Guide of the Perplexed.* A fragment is contained in the Berlin MS. Or. Qu., 554, 2 (Steinschneider, Cat. No. 92).

Zeraḥyah b. Isaac ha-Levi. Commentary on the Moreh, I., i.–lxxi., and some other portions of the work. (See Maskir, 1861, p. 125).

MS. Bodl. 2360, 8, contains a letter of Jehudah b. Shelomoh on some passages of the Moreh, and Zeraḥyah's reply.

Anonymous Commentaries.—The MS. Brit. Mus. 1423 contains marginal and interlineary notes in Arabic. No author or date is given, nor is any other commentary referred to in the notes. The explanations given are mostly preceded by a question, and introduced by the phrase, " the answer is," in the same style as is employed in the Hebrew-Arabic Midrash, MS. Brit. Mus. Or. 2213. The Midrashic character is prominent in the notes. Thus the verse " Open, ye gates, that the righteous nation which keepeth the truth may enter in," is explained as meaning : Open, ye gates of wisdom, that human understanding that perceiveth truth may enter. The notes are numerous, especially in the first part, explaining almost every word ; e.g., on " Rabbi " : Why does Maimonides employ this title before the name of his pupil ? The answer is : either the word is not to be taken literally (" master "), but as a mere compliment, or it has been added by later copyists. Of a similar style seem to be the Arabic notes in the Berlin MS. Or. Oct. 258, 2, 8, 10. (Cat. Steinschneider, No. 108.)—Anonymous marginal notes are met with almost in every MS. of the Moreh ; e.g., Brit. Mus. Harl. 5525 ; Add. 14,763, 14,764 ; Bodl. 1264, 1 ; 2282, 10 ; 2423, 3 ; Munich MS., 239, 6.

The explanation of passages from the Pentateuch contained in the Moreh have been collected by D. Ottensosser, and given as an appendix (*Moreh-derek*) to *Derek-selulah* (Pent. with Comm. etc., Furth, 1824).

IV. *Controversies.*—The seemingly new ideas put forth by Maimonides in the Moreh and in the first section of his Mishneh-torah (*Sefer ha-madda'*) soon produced a lively controversy as regards the merits of Maimonides' theories. It was most perplexing to pious Talmudists to learn how Maimonides explained the anthropomorphisms employed in the Bible, the Midrashim and the Talmud, what he thought about the future state of our soul, and that he considered the study of philosophy as the highest degree of Divine worship, surpassing even the study of the Law and the practice of its precepts. The objections and attacks of Daniel of Damascus were easily silenced by a *ḥerem* (excommunication) pronounced against him by the *Rosh ha-golah* Rabbi David. Stronger was the opposition that had its centre in Montpellier. Rabbi Solomon ben Abraham noticed with regret in his own community the fruit of the theories of Maimonides in the neglect of the study of the Law and of the practice of the Divine precepts. It happened to Moses Maimonides what in modern times happened to Moses Mendelssohn. Many so-called disciples and followers of the great master misunderstood or misinterpreted his teaching in support of their dereliction of Jewish law and Jewish practice, and thus brought disrepute on him in the eyes of their opponents. Thus it came that Rabbi Solomon and his disciples turned their wrath against the writings of Maimonides instead of combating the arguments of the pseudo-Maimonists. The latter even accused Solomon of having denounced the Moreh and the *Sefer ha-madda'* to the Dominicans, who condemned these writings to the flames ; when subsequently copies of the Talmud were burnt, and some of the followers of the Rabbi of Montpellier were subjected to cruel tortures, the Maimonists saw in this event a just punishment for offending Maimonides. (Letters of Hillel of Verona, *Ḥemdah Genuzah*, ed. H. Edelmann, p. 18 *sqq.*).

Meir b. Todros ha-levi Abulafia wrote already during the lifetime of Maimonides to the wise men in Lunel about the heretic doctrines he discovered in the works of Maimonides. Ahron b. Meshullam and Shesheth Benvenisti defended Maimonides. About 1232 a correspondence opened between the Maimonists and the Anti-maimonists (Grätz, Gesch. d. J. vii. note I). The Grammarian David Kimḥi wrote in defence of Maimonides three letters to Jehudah Alfachar, who answered each of them in the sense of Rabbi Solomon of Montpellier. Abraham b. Ḥisdai and Samuel b. Abraham Saportas on the side of the Maimonists, took part in the controversy. Meshullam b. Kalonymos b. Todros of Narbonne begged Alfachar to treat Kimḥi with more consideration, whereupon Alfachar resolved to withdraw from the controversy. Naḥmanides, though more on the side of Rabbi Solomon, wrote two letters of a conciliatory character, advising moderation on both sides. Representatives of the congregations of Saragossa, Huesca, Monzon, Kalatajud, and Lerida signed declarations against R. Solomon. A herem was proclaimed from Lunel and Narbonne against the Anti-Maimonists. The son of Maimonides, Abraham, wrote a pamphlet *Milḥamot adonai*, in defence of the writings of his father. The controversy raised about fifty years later by Abba Mari Don Astruc and R. Solomon ben-Aderet of Barcelona, concerned the Moreh less directly. The question was of a more general character : Is the study of philosophy dangerous to the religious belief of young students ? The letters written in this controversy are contained in *Minḥat-ḳenaot* by Abba Mari Don Astruc (Presburg, 1838), and Kitab alrasail of Meir Abulafia ed. J. Brill (Paris, 1871). Yedaya Bedrasi took part in this controversy, and wrote *Ketab hitnaẓlut* in defence of the study of philosophy (Teshubot Rashba, Hanau, 1610, p. 111 b.). The whole controversy ended in the victory of the Moreh and the other writings of Maimonides. Stray remarks are found in various works, some in praise and some in condemnation of Maimonides. A few instances may suffice. Rabbi Jacob Emden in his *Mitpaḥat-sefarim* (Lemberg, 1870, p. 56) believes that parts of the Moreh are spurious ; he even doubts whether any portion of it is the work of " Maimonides, the author of the Mishneh-torah, who was not capable of writing such heretic doctrines." S. D. Luzzato regards Maimonides with great reverence, but this does not prevent him from severely criticising his philosophical theories (Letters to S. Rappoport, No. 79, 83, 266, *Iggeroth Shedal* ed. E. Graber, Przemys'l, 1882), and from expressing his conviction that the saying " From Moses to Moses none rose like Moses," was as untrue as that suggested by Rappoport, " From Abraham to Abraham (Ibn-Ezra) none rose like Abraham." Rabbi Hirsch Chayyuth in *Darke-Mosheh* (Zolkiew, 1840) examines the attacks made upon the writings of Maimonides, and tries to refute them, and to show that they can be reconciled with the teaching of the Talmud.

The Bodl. MS. 2240, 3a, contains a document signed by Josselman and other Rabbis, declaring that they accept the teaching of Maimonides as correct, with the exception of his theory about angels and sacrifices.

Numerous poems were written, both in admiration and in condemnation of the Moreh. Most of them precede or follow the Moreh in the printed editions and in the various MS. copies of the work. A few have been edited in *Dibre-ḥakamim*, pp. 75 and 86 ; in the Literaturblatt d. Or. I. 379, II. 26–27, IV. 748, and *Leket-shoshannim* by Dr. Grätz. In the *Sammelband* of the Mekize Nirdamim (1885) a collection of 69 of these poems is contained, edited and explained by Prof. Dr. A. Berliner. In imitation of the Moreh and with a view of displacing Maimonides' work, the Karaite Ahron II. b. Eliah wrote a philosophical treatise, *Eẓ-ḥayyim* (Ed. F. Delitzsch. Leipzig, 1841).

Of the works that discuss the whole or part of the philosophical system of the Moreh the following are noteworthy :—

Bacher, W. Die Bibilexegese Moses Maimûni's, in the Jahresbericht der Landes Rabbinerschule zu Buda-Pest. 1896.

Eisler, M. Vorlesungen über die jüdischen Philosophen des Mittelalters. Abtheil. II., Moses Maimonides (Wien, 1870).

Geiger, A. Das Judenthum u. seine Geschichte (Breslau, 1865), Zehnte Vorlesung : Aben Ezra u. Maimonides.

Grätz, H. Geschichte d. Juden, VI. p. 363 *sqq*.

Joel, M. Religionsphilosophie des Moses b. Maimon (Breslau, 1859).

Joel, M. Albertus Magnus u. sein Vorhältniss zu Maimonides (Breslau, 1863).

Kaufmann, D.   Geschichte der Attributenlehre, VII.   Gotha, 1874.

Philippsohn, L.   Die Philosophie des Maimonides.   Predigt und Schul-Magazin, I. xviii.   (Magdeburg, 1834.)

Rosin, D.   Die Ethik d. Maimonides (Breslau, 1876).

Rubin, S.   Spinoza u. Maimonides, ein Psychologisch-Philosophisches Antitheton (Wien, 1868).

Scheyer, S.   Das psychologische System des Maimonides.   Frankfort-a.-M., 1845.

Weiss, T. H.   *Beth-Talmud*, I. x. p. 289.

David Yellin and Israel Abrahams, Maimonides.

ANALYSIS OF THE GUIDE FOR THE PERPLEXED

IT is the object of this work " to afford a guide for the perplexed," i.e. " to thinkers whose studies have brought them into collision with religion " (p. 9), "who have studied philosophy and have acquired sound knowledge, and who, while firm in religious matters, are perplexed and bewildered on account of the ambiguous and figurative expressions employed in the holy writings " (p. 5). Joseph, the son of Jehudah Ibn Aknin, a disciple of Maimonides, is addressed by his teacher as an example of this kind of students. It was " for him and for those like him " that the treatise was composed, and to him this work is inscribed in the dedicatory letter with which the Introduction begins. Maimonides, having discovered that his disciple was sufficiently advanced for an exposition of the esoteric ideas in the books of the Prophets, commenced to give him such expositions " by way of hints." His disciple then begged him to give him further explanations, to treat of metaphysical themes, and to expound the system and the method of the Kalām, or Mohammedan Theology.[1] In compliance with this request, Maimonides composed the Guide of the Perplexed. The reader has, therefore, to expect that the subjects mentioned in the disciple's request indicate the design and arrangement of the present work, and that the Guide consists of the following parts :—1. An exposition of the esoteric ideas (sodot) in the books of the Prophets. 2. A treatment of certain metaphysical problems. 3. An examination of the system and method of the Kalām. This, in fact, is a correct account of the contents of the book ; but in the second part of the Introduction, in which the theme of this work is defined, the author mentions only the first-named subject. He observes : " My primary object is to explain certain terms occurring in the prophetic book. Of these some are homonymous, some figurative, and some hybrid terms." " This work has also a second object. It is designed to explain certain obscure figures which occur in the Prophets, and are not distinctly characterised as being figures " (p. 2). Yet from this observation it must not be inferred that Maimonides abandoned his original purpose ; for he examines the Kalām in the last chapters of the First Part (ch. lxx.-lxxvi.), and treats of certain metaphysical themes in the beginning of the Second Part (Introd. and ch. i.-xxv.). But in the passage quoted above he confines himself to a delineation of the *main* object of this treatise, and advisedly leaves unmentioned the other two subjects, which, however important they may be, are here of subordinate interest. Nor did he consider it necessary to expatiate on these subjects ; he only wrote for the student, for whom a mere reference to works on philosophy and science was sufficient. We therefore meet now and then with such phrases as the following : " This is fully discussed in works on metaphysics." By references of this kind the author may have intended to create a taste for the study of philosophical works. But our observation only holds good with regard to the Aristotelian philosophy.

[1] See *infra*, page 4, note 1.

The writings of the Mutakallemim are never commended by him ; he states their opinions, and tells his disciple that he would *not* find any additional argument, even if he were to read all their voluminous works (p. 133). Maimonides was a zealous disciple of Aristotle, although the theory of the Kalām might seem to have been more congenial to Jewish thought and belief.   The Kalām upheld the theory of God's Existence, Incorporeality, and Unity, together with the *creatio ex nihilo*.   Maimonides nevertheless opposed the Kalām, and, anticipating the question, why preference should be given to the system of Aristotle, which included the theory of the Eternity of the Universe, a theory contrary to the fundamental teaching of the Scriptures, he exposed the weakness of the Kalām and its fallacies.

The exposition of Scriptural texts is divided by the author into two parts ; the first part treats of homonymous, figurative, and hybrid terms,[1] employed in reference to God ; the second part relates to Biblical figures and allegories. These two parts do not closely follow each other ; they are separated by the examination of the Kalām, and the discussion of metaphysical problems.   It seems that the author adopted this arrangement for the following reason : first of all, he intended to establish the fact that the Biblical anthropomorphisms do not imply corporeality, and that the Divine Being of whom the Bible speaks could therefore be regarded as identical with the Primal Cause of the philosophers.   Having established this principle, he discusses from a purely metaphysical point of view the properties of the Primal Cause and its relation to the universe.   A solid foundation is thus established for the esoteric exposition of Scriptural passages.   Before discussing metaphysical problems, which he treats in accordance with Aristotelian philosophy, he disposes of the Kalām, and demonstrates that its arguments are illogical and illusory.

The " Guide for the Perplexed " contains, therefore, an Introduction and the following four parts :—1. On homonymous, figurative, and hybrid terms.   2. On the Supreme Being and His relation to the universe, according to the Kalām. 3. On the Primal Cause and its relation to the universe, according to the philosophers.   4. Esoteric exposition of some portions of the Bible (*sodot*) : *a*, Maaseh bereshith, or the history of the Creation (Genesis, ch. i.-iv.) ; *b*, on Prophecy ; *c*, Maaseh mercabbah, or the description of the divine chariot (Ezekiel, ch. i.).

According to this plan, the work ends with the seventh chapter of the Third Part.   The chapters which follow may be considered as an appendix ; they treat of the following theological themes : the Existence of Evil, Omniscience and Providence, Temptations, Design in Nature, in the Law, and in the Biblical Narratives, and finally the true Worship of God.

In the Introduction to the " Guide," Maimonides (1) describes the object of the work and the method he has followed ; (2) treats of similes ; (3) gives " directions for the study of the work " ; and (4) discusses the usual causes of inconsistencies in authors.

1 (pp. 2–3). Inquiring into the root of the evil which the Guide was intended to remove, viz., the conflict between science and religion, the author perceived that in most cases it originated in a misinterpretation of the anthropomorphisms in Holy Writ.   The main difficulty is found in the ambiguity of the words employed by the prophets when speaking of the Divine Being ; the question arises whether they are applied to the Deity and to other things in one and the same sense or equivocally ; in the latter case the author distinguishes between homonyms pure and simple, figures, and hybrid terms.   In order to show that the Biblical anthropomorphisms do not imply the corporeality of the Deity, he seeks in each instance to demonstrate that the expression under exam-

---

[1] See *infra*, page 5, note 4.

ination is a perfect homonym denoting things which are totally distinct from each other, and whenever such a demonstration is impossible, he assumes that the expression is a hybrid term, that is, being employed in one instance figuratively and in another homonymously. His explanation of "form" (*zelem*) may serve as an illustration. According to his opinion, it *invariably* denotes "form" in the philosophical acceptation of the term, viz., the complex of the essential properties of a thing. But to obviate objections he proposes an alternative view, to take *zelem* as a hybrid term that may be explained as a class noun denoting *only* things of the same class, or as a homonym employed for totally different things, viz., "form" in the philosophical sense, and "form" in the ordinary meaning of the word. Maimonides seems to have refrained from explaining anthropomorphisms as figurative expressions, lest by such interpretation he might implicitly admit the existence of a certain relation and comparison between the Creator and His creatures.

Jewish philosophers before Maimonides enunciated and demonstrated the Unity and the Incorporeality of the Divine Being, and interpreted Scriptural metaphors on the principle that "the Law speaks in the language of man" ; but our author adopted a new and altogether original method. The Commentators, when treating of anthropomorphisms, generally contented themselves with the statement that the term under consideration must not be taken in its literal sense, or they paraphrased the passage in expressions which implied a lesser degree of corporeality. The Talmud, the Midrashim, and the Targumim abound in paraphrases of this kind. Saadiah in "*Emunot ve-de'ot*," Bahya in his "*Hobot ha-lebabot*," and Jehudah ha-levi in the "*Cusari*," insist on the necessity and the appropriateness of such interpretations. Saadiah enumerates ten terms which primarily denote organs of the human body, and are figuratively applied to God. To establish this point of view he cites numerous instances in which the terms in question are used in a figurative sense without being applied to God. Saadiah further shows that the Divine attributes are either qualifications of such of God's actions as are perceived by man, or they imply a negation. The correctness of this method was held to be so obvious that some authors found it necessary to apologize to the reader for introducing such well-known topics. From R. Abraham ben David's strictures on the Yad hahazakah it is, however, evident that in the days of Maimonides persons were not wanting who defended the literal interpretation of certain anthropomorphisms. Maimonides, therefore, did not content himself with the vague and general rule, "The Law speaks in the language of man," but sought carefully to define the meaning of each term when applied to God, and to identify it with some transcendental and metaphysical term. In pursuing this course he is sometimes forced to venture upon an interpretation which is much too far-fetched to commend itself even to the supposed philosophical reader. In such instances he generally adds a simple and plain explanation, and leaves it to the option of the reader to choose the one which appears to him preferable. The enumeration of the different meanings of a word is often, from a philological point of view, incomplete ; he introduces only such significations as serve his object. When treating of an imperfect homonym, the several significations of which are derived from one primary signification, he apparently follows a certain system which he does not employ in the interpretation of perfect homonyms. The homonymity of the term is not proved ; the author confines himself to the remark, "It is employed homonymously," even when the various meanings of a word might easily be traced to a common source.

2 (pag. 4–8). In addition to the explanation of homonyms Maimonides undertakes to interpret similes and allegories. At first it had been his intention to write two distinct works—*Sefer ha-nebuah*, "A Book on Prophecy," and *Sefer ha-shevaah*, "A Book of Reconciliation." In the former work he had intended

to explain difficult passages of the Bible, and in the latter to expound such passages in the Midrash and the Talmud as seemed to be in conflict with common sense. With respect to the "Book of Reconciliation," he abandoned his plan, because he apprehended that neither the learned nor the unlearned would profit by it : the one would find it superfluous, the other tedious. The subject of the "Book on Prophecy" is treated in the present work, and also strange passages that occasionally occur in the Talmud and the Midrash are explained.

The treatment of the simile must vary according as the simile is compound or simple. In the first case, each part represents a separate idea and demands a separate interpretation ; in the other case, only one idea is represented, and it is not necessary to assign to each part a separate metaphorical meaning. This division the author illustrates by citing the dream of Jacob (Gen. xxviii. 12 *sqq.*), and the description of the adulteress (Prov. vii. 6 *sqq.*). He gives no rule by which it might be ascertained to which of the two categories a simile belongs, and, like other Commentators, he seems to treat as essential those details of a simile for which he can offer an adequate interpretation. As a general principle, he warns against the confusion and the errors which arise when an attempt is made to expound every single detail of a simile. His own explanations are not intended to be exhaustive ; on the contrary, they are to consist of brief allusions to the idea represented by the simile, of mere suggestions, which the reader is expected to develop and to complete. The author thus aspires to follow in the wake of the Creator, whose works can only be understood after a long and persevering study. Yet it is possible that he derived his preference for a reserved and mysterious style from the example of ancient philosophers, who discussed metaphysical problems in figurative and enigmatic language. Like Ibn Ezra, who frequently concludes his exposition of a Biblical passage with the phrase, "Here a profound idea (*sod*) is hidden," Maimonides somewhat mysteriously remarks at the end of different chapters, "Note this," "Consider it well." In such phrases some Commentators fancied that they found references to metaphysical theories which the author was not willing fully to discuss. Whether this was the case or not, in having recourse to that method he was not, as some have suggested, actuated by fear of being charged with heresy. He expresses his opinion on the principal theological questions without reserve, and does not dread the searching inquiries of opponents ; for he boldly announces that their displeasure would not deter him from teaching the truth and guiding those who are able and willing to follow him, however few these might be. When, however, we examine the work itself, we are at a loss to discover to which parts the professed enigmatic method was applied. His theories concerning the Deity, the Divine attributes, angels, *creatio ex nihilo*, prophecy, and other subjects, are treated as fully as might be expected. It is true that a cloud of mysterious phrases enshrouds the interpretation of *Ma'aseh bereshit* (Gen. i.–iii.) and *Ma'aseh mercabah* (Ez. i.). But the significant words occurring in these portions are explained in the First Part of this work, and a full exposition is found in the Second and Third Parts. Nevertheless the statement that the exposition was never intended to be explicit occurs over and over again. The treatment of the first three chapters of Genesis concludes thus : "These remarks, together with what we have already observed on the subject, and what we may have to add, must suffice both for the object and for the reader we have in view " (II. xxx.). In like manner, he declares, after the explanation of the first chapter of Ezekiel : "I have given you here as many suggestions as may be of service to you, if you will give them a further development. . . . Do not expect to hear from me anything more on this subject, for I have, though with some hesitation, gone as far in my explanation as I possibly could go " (III. vii.).

3 (pag. 8–9). In the next paragraph, headed, "Directions for the Study of

this Work," he implores the reader not to be hasty with his criticism, and to bear in mind that every sentence, indeed every word, had been fully considered before it was written down. Yet it might easily happen that the reader could not reconcile his own view with that of the author, and in such a case he is asked to ignore the disapproved chapter or section altogether. Such disapproval Maimonides attributes to a mere misconception on the part of the reader, a fate which awaits every work composed in a mystical style. In adopting this peculiar style, he intended to reduce to a minimum the violation of the rule laid down in the Mishnah (Ḥagigah ii. 1), that metaphysics should not be taught publicly. The violation of this rule he justifies by citing the following two Mishnaic maxims : " It is time to do something in honour of the Lord " (Berakot ix. 5), and " Let all thy acts be guided by pure intentions " (Abot ii. 17). Maimonides increased the mysteriousness of the treatise, by expressing his wish that the reader should abstain from expounding the work, lest he might spread in the name of the author opinions which the latter never held. But it does not occur to him that the views he enunciates might in themselves be erroneous. He is positive that his own theory is unexceptionally correct, that his esoteric interpretations of Scriptural texts are sound, and that those who differed from him—viz., the Mutakallemim on the one hand, and the unphilosophical Rabbis on the other— are indefensibly wrong. In this respect other Jewish philosophers—e.g. Saadiah and Baḥya—were far less positive ; they were conscious of their own fallibility, and invited the reader to make such corrections as might appear needful. Owing to this strong self-reliance of Maimonides, it is not to be expected that opponents would receive a fair and impartial judgment at his hands.

4 (pag. 9–11). The same self-reliance is noticeable in the next and concluding paragraph of the Introduction. Here he treats of the contradictions which are to be found in literary works, and he divides them with regard to their origin into seven classes. The first four classes comprise the apparent contradictions, which can be traced back to the employment of elliptical speech ; the other three classes comprise the real contradictions, and are due to carelessness and oversight, or they are intended to serve some special purpose. The Scriptures, the Talmud, and the Midrash abound in instances of apparent contradictions ; later works contain real contradictions, which escaped the notice of the writers. In the present treatise, however, there occur only such contradictions as are the result of intention and design.

PART I.

The homonymous expressions which are discussed in the First Part include— (1) nouns and verbs used in reference to God, ch. i. to ch. xlix. ; (2) attributes of the Deity, ch. l. to lx. ; (3) expressions commonly regarded as names of God, ch. lxi. to lxx. In the first section the following groups can be distinguished— (a) expressions which denote form and figure, ch. i. to ch. vi. ; (b) space or relations of space, ch. viii. to ch. xxv. ; (c) parts of the animal body and their functions, ch. xxviii. to ch. xlix. Each of these groups includes chapters not connected with the main subject, but which serve as a help for the better understanding of previous or succeeding interpretations. Every word selected for discussion bears upon some Scriptural text which, according to the opinion of the author, has been misinterpreted. But such phrases as "the mouth of the Lord," and "the hand of the Lord," are not introduced, because their figurative meaning is too obvious to be misunderstood.

The lengthy digressions which are here and there interposed appear like outbursts of feeling and passion which the author could not repress. Yet they are " words fitly spoken in the right place " ; for they gradually unfold the author's theory, and acquaint the reader with those general principles on which he founds the interpretations in the succeeding chapters. Moral reflections are of frequent occurrence, and demonstrate the intimate connexion between a virtuous life and the attainment of higher knowledge, in accordance with the maxim current long before Maimonides, and expressed in the Biblical words, "The fear of the Lord is the beginning of wisdom" (Ps. cxi. 10). No opportunity is lost to inculcate this lesson, be it in a passing remark or in an elaborate essay.

The discussion of the term "*zelem*" (ch. i.) afforded the first occasion for reflections of this kind. Man, "the image of God," is defined as a living and rational being, as though the moral faculties of man were not an essential element of his existence, and his power to discern between good and evil were the result of the first sin. According to Maimonides, the moral faculty would, in fact, not have been required, if man had remained a purely rational being. It is only through the senses that "the knowledge of good and evil" has become indispensable. The narrative of Adam's fall is, according to Maimonides, an allegory representing the relation which exists between sensation, moral faculty, and intellect. In this early part (ch. ii.), however, the author does not yet mention this theory ; on the contrary, every allusion to it is for the present studiously avoided, its full exposition being reserved for the Second Part.

The treatment of *ḥazah* "he beheld" (ch. vi.), is followed by the advice that the student should not approach metaphysics otherwise than after a sound and thorough preparation, because a rash attempt to solve abstruse problems brings nothing but injury upon the inexperienced investigator. The author points to the "nobles of the children of Israel" (Exod. xxiv. 11), who, according to his interpretation, fell into this error, and received their deserved punishment. He gives additional force to these exhortations by citing a dictum of Aristotle to the same effect. In a like way he refers to the allegorical use of certain terms by Plato (ch. xvii.) in support of his interpretation of "*zur*" (*lit.*, "rock") as denoting "Primal Cause."

The theory that nothing but a sound moral and intellectual training would entitle a student to engage in metaphysical speculations is again discussed in the digression which precedes the third group of homonyms (xxxi.–xxxvi.). Man's intellectual faculties, he argues, have this in common with his physical forces, that their sphere of action is limited, and they become inefficient whenever they are overstrained. This happens when a student approaches metaphysics without due preparation. Maimonides goes on to argue that the non-success of metaphysical studies is attributable to the following causes : the transcendental character of this discipline, the imperfect state of the student's knowledge, the persistent efforts which have to be made even in the preliminary studies, and finally the waste of energy and time owing to the physical demands of man. For these reasons the majority of persons are debarred from pursuing the study of metaphysics. Nevertheless, there are certain metaphysical truths which have to be communicated to all men, e.g., that God is One, and that He is incorporeal ; for to assume that God is corporeal, or that He has any properties, or to ascribe to Him any attributes, is a sin bordering on idolatry.

Another digression occurs as an appendix to the second group of homonyms (ch. xxvi.–xxvii.). Maimonides found that only a limited number of terms are applied to God in a figurative sense ; and again, that in the "Targum" of Onkelos some of the figures are paraphrased, while other figures received a literal rendering. He therefore seeks to discover the principle which was applied both in the Sacred Text and in the translation, and he found it in the Talmudical dictum, "The Law speaketh the language of man." For this reason all figures are eschewed which, in their literal sense, would appear to the multitude as implying debasement or a blemish. Onkelos, who rigorously guards himself against using any term that might suggest corporification, gives a literal rendering of figurative terms when there is no cause for entertaining such an apprehension. Maimonides illustrates this rule by the mode in which Onkelos renders "*yarad*" (" he went down,"), when used in reference to God. It is generally paraphrased, but in one exceptional instance, occurring in Jacob's "visions of the night " (Gen. xlvi. 4), it is translated literally ; in this instance the literal rendering does not lead to corporification ; because visions and dreams were generally regarded as mental operations, devoid of objective reality. Simple and clear as this explanation may be, we do not consider that it really explains the method of Onkelos. On the contrary, the translator paraphrased anthropomorphic terms, even when he found them in passages relating to dreams or visions ; and indeed it is doubtful whether Maimonides could produce a single instance in favour of his view. He was equally unsuccessful in his explanation of "*ḥazah*" "he saw" (ch. xlviii.). He says that when the object of the vision was derogatory, it was not brought into direct relation with the Deity ; in such instances the verb is paraphrased, while in other instances the rendering is literal. Although Maimonides grants that the force of this observation is weakened by three exceptions, he does not doubt its correctness.

The next Section (ch. l. to ch. lix.) " On the Divine Attributes " begins with the explanation that "faith" consists in thought, not in mere utterance ; in conviction, not in mere profession. This explanation forms the basis for the subsequent discussion. The several arguments advanced by Maimonides against the employment of attributes are intended to show that those who assume the real existence of Divine attributes may possibly utter with their lips the creed of the Unity and the Incorporeality of God, but they cannot truly believe it. A demonstration of this fact would be needless, if the Attributists had not put forth their false theses and defended them with the utmost tenacity, though with the most absurd arguments.

After this explanation the author proceeds to discuss the impropriety of assigning attributes to God. The Attributists admit that God is the Primal Cause, One, incorporeal, free from emotion and privation, and that He is not comparable to any of His creatures. Maimonides therefore contends that any attributes which, either directly or indirectly, are in contradiction to this creed, should not be applied to God. By this rule he rejects four classes of attributes : viz., those which include a definition, a partial definition, a quality, or a relation.

The definition of a thing includes its efficient cause ; and since God is the Primal Cause, He cannot be defined, or described by a partial definition. A quality, whether psychical, physical, emotional, or quantitative, is always regarded as something distinct from its substratum ; a thing which possesses any quality, consists, therefore, of that quality and a substratum, and should not be called *one*. All relations of time and space imply corporeality ; all relations between two objects are, to a certain degree, a comparison between these two objects. To employ any of these attributes in reference to God would be as much as to declare that God is not the Primal Cause, that He is not One, that He is corporeal, or that He is comparable to His creatures.

There is only one class of attributes to which Maimonides makes no objection, viz. such as describe actions, and to this class belong all the Divine attributes which occur in the Scriptures. The " Thirteen Attributes " (*shelosh esreh middot*, Exod. xxxiv. 6, 7) serve as an illustration. They were communicated to Moses when he, as the chief of the Israelites, wished to know the way in which God governs the universe, in order that he himself in ruling the nation might follow it, and thereby promote their real well-being.

On the whole, the opponents of Maimonides admit the correctness of this theory. Only a small number of attributes are the subject of dispute. The

Scriptures unquestionably ascribe to God Existence, Life, Power, Wisdom, Unity, Eternity, and Will. The Attributists regard these as properties distinct from, but co-existing with, the Essence of God. With great acumen, and with equally great acerbity, Maimonides shows that their theory is irreconcilable with their belief in the Unity and the Incorporeality of God. He points out three different ways of interpreting these attributes :— 1. They may be regarded as descriptive of the works of God, and as declaring that these possess such properties as, in works of man, would appear to be the result of the will, the power, and the wisdom of a living being. 2. The term "existing," "one," "wise," etc., are applied to God and to His creatures homonymously ; as attributes of God they coincide with His Essence ; as attributes of anything beside God they are distinct from the essence of the thing. 3. These terms do not describe a positive quality, but express a negation of its opposite. This third interpretation appears to have been preferred by the author ; he discusses it more fully than the two others. He observes that the knowledge of the incomprehensible Being is solely of a negative character, and he shows by simple and appropriate examples that an approximate knowledge of a thing can be attained by mere negations, that such knowledge increases with the number of these negations, and that an error in positive assertions is more injurious than an error in negative assertions. In describing the evils which arise from the application of positive attributes to God, he unsparingly censures the hymnologists, because he found them profuse in attributing positive epithets to the Deity. On the basis of his own theory he could easily have interpreted these epithets in the same way as he explains the Scriptural attributes of God. His severity may, however, be accounted for by the fact that the frequent recurrence of positive attributes in the literary composition of the Jews was the cause that the Mohammedans charged the Jews with entertaining false notions of the Deity.

The inquiry into the attributes is followed by a treatment of the names of God. It seems to have been beyond the design of the author to elucidate the etymology of each name, or to establish methodically its signification ; for he does not support his explanations by any proof. His sole aim is to show that the Scriptural names of God in their true meaning strictly harmonize with the philosophical conception of the Primal Cause. There are two things which have to be distinguished in the treatment of the Primal Cause : the Primal Cause *per se*, and its relation to the Universe. The first is expressed by the tetragrammaton and its cognates, the second by the several attributes, especially by *rokeb ba'arabot*, " He who rideth on the 'arabot " (Ps. lxviii. 4)

The tetragrammaton exclusively expresses the essence of God, and therefore it is employed as a *nomen proprium*. In the mystery of this name, and others mentioned in the Talmud, as consisting of twelve and of forty-two letters, Maimonides finds no other secret than the solution of some metaphysical problems. The subject of these problems is not actually known, but the author supposes that it referred to the " absolute existence of the Deity." He discovers the same idea in *ehyeh* (Exod. iii. 14), in accordance with the explanation added in the Sacred Text : *asher ehyeh*, "that is, I am." In the course of this discussion he exposes the folly or sinfulness of those who pretend to work miracles by the aid of these and similar names.

With a view of preparing the way for his peculiar interpretation of *rokeb ba'arabot*, he explains a variety of Scriptural passages, and treats of several philosophical terms relative to the Supreme Being. Such expressions as " the word of God," " the work of God," " the work of His fingers," " He made," " He spake," must be taken in a figurative sense ; they merely represent God as the cause that some work has been produced, and that some person has acquired a certain knowledge. The passage, "And He rested on the seventh day" (Exod. xx. 11) is interpreted as follows : On the seventh Day the forces and laws were complete, which during the previous six days were in the state of being established for the preservation of the Universe. They were not to be increased or modified.

It seems that Maimonides introduced this figurative explanation with a view of showing that the Scriptural "God" does not differ from the "Primal Cause" or "Ever-active Intellect" of the philosophers. On the other hand, the latter do not reject the Unity of God, although they assume that the Primal Cause comprises the *causa efficiens*, the *agens*, and the *causa finalis* (or, the cause, the means, and the end) ; and that the Ever-active Intellect comprises the *intelligens*, the *intellectus*, and the *intellectum* (or, the thinking subject, the act of thought, and the object thought of) ; because in this case these apparently different elements are, in fact, identical. The Biblical term corresponding to "Primal Cause" is *rokeb ba'arabot*, "riding on '*arabot*." Maimonides is at pains to prove that '*arabot* denotes "the highest sphere," which causes the motion of all other spheres, and which thus brings about the natural course of production and destruction. By "the highest sphere" he does not understand a material sphere, but the immaterial world of intelligences and angels, "the seat of justice and judgment, stores of life, peace, and blessings, the seat of the souls of the righteous," etc. *Rokeb ba'arabot*, therefore, means : He presides over the immaterial beings, He is the source of their powers, by which they move the spheres and regulate the course of nature. This theory is more fully developed in the Second Part.

The next section (chap. lxxi.–lxxvi.) treats of the Kalām. According to the author, the method of the Kalām is copied from the Christian Fathers, who applied it in the defence of their religious doctrines. The latter examined in their writings the views of the philosophers, ostensibly in search of truth, in reality, however, with the object of supporting their own dogmas. Subsequently Mohammedan theologians found in these works arguments which seemed to confirm the truth of their own religion ; they blindly adopted these arguments, and made no inquiry whence these had been derived. Maimonides rejects *à priori* the theories of the Mutakallemim, because they explain the phenomena in the universe in conformity with preconceived notions, instead of following the scientific method of the philosophers. Among the Jews, especially in the East and in Africa, there were also some who adopted the method of the Kalām ; in doing so they followed the Mu'tazilah (dissenting Mohammedans), not because they found it more correct than the Kalām of the Ashariyah (orthodox Mohammedans), but because at the time when the Jews became acquainted with the Kalām it was only cultivated by the Mu'tazilah. The Jews in Spain, however, remained faithful to the Aristotelian philosophy.

The four principal dogmas upheld by the dominant religions were the *creatio ex nihilo*, the Existence of God, His Incorporeality, and His Unity. By the philosophers the *creatio ex nihilo* was rejected, but the Mutakallemim defended it, and founded upon it their proofs for the other three dogmas. Maimonides adopts the philosophical proofs for the Existence, Incorporeality, and Unity of God, because they must be admitted even by those who deny the *creatio ex nihilo*, the proofs being independent of this dogma. In order to show that the Mutakallemim are mistaken in ignoring the organization of the existing order of things, the author gives a minute description of the analogy between the Universe, or Kosmos, and man, the mikrokosmos (ch. lxxii.). This analogy is merely asserted, and the reader is advised either to find the proof by his own studies, or to accept the fact on the authority of the learned. The *Kalām* does not admit the existence of law, organization, and unity in the universe. Its adherents have, accordingly, no trustworthy criterion to determine whether a thing is possible or impossible. Everything that is conceivable by imagination is by them held as possible. The several parts of the universe are in no relation to each other ; they all consist of equal elements ; they are not composed of substance and properties, but of atoms and accidents : the law of causality is ignored ; man's actions are not the result of will and design, but are mere accidents. Maimonides in enumerating and discussing the twelve fundamental propositions of the *Kalām* (ch. lxiii.), which embody these theories, had apparently no intention to give a complete and impartial account of the *Kalām* ; he solely aimed at exposing the weakness of a system which he regarded as founded not on a sound basis of positive facts, but on mere fiction ; not on the evidences of the senses and of reason, but on the illusions of imagination.

After having shown that the twelve fundamental propositions of the *Kalām* are utterly untenable, Maimonides finds no difficulty in demonstrating the insufficiency of the proofs advanced by the Mutakallemim in support of the above-named dogmas. Seven arguments are cited which the Mutakallemim employ in support of the *creatio ex nihilo*.[1] The first argument is based on the atomic theory, viz., that the universe consists of equal atoms without inherent properties : all variety and change observed in nature must therefore be attributed to an external force. Three arguments are supplied by the proposition that finite things of an infinite number cannot exist (Propos. xi.). Three other arguments derive their support from the following proposition (x.) : Everything that can be imagined can have an actual existence. The present order of things is only one out of the many forms which are possible, and exist through the *fiat* of a determining power.

The Unity of God is demonstrated by the Mutakallemim as follows : Two Gods would have been unable to produce the world ; one would have impeded the work of the other. Maimonides points out that this might have been avoided by a suitable division of labour. Another argument is as follows : The two Beings would have one element in common, and would differ in another ; each would thus consist of two elements, and would not be God. Maimonides might have suggested that the argument moves in a circle, the unity of God being proved by assuming His unity. The following argument is altogether unintelligible : Both Gods are moved to action by will ; the will, being without a substratum, could not act simultaneously in two separate beings. The fallacy of the following argument is clear : The existence of *one* God is proved ; the existence of a second God is not proved, it would be possible ; and as possibility is inapplicable to God, there does not exist a second God. The possibility of ascertaining the existence of God is here confounded with potentiality of existence. Again, if *one* God suffices, the second God is superfluous ; if *one* God is not sufficient, he is not perfect, and cannot be a deity. Maimonides objects that it would not be an imperfection in either deity to act exclusively within their respective provinces. As in the criticism of the first argument, Maimonides

---

[1] Saadiah proves the existence of the Creator in the following way :—1. The Universe is limited, and therefore cannot possess an unlimited force. 2. All things are compounds ; the composition must be owing to some external cause. 3. Changes observed in all beings are effected by some external cause. 4. If time were infinite, it would be impossible to conceive the progress of time from the present moment to the future, or from the past to the present moment. (Emunot vede'ot, ch. i.).—Bahya founds his arguments on three propositions :—1. A thing cannot be its own maker. 2. The series of successive causes is finite. 3. Compounds owe their existence to an external force. His arguments are :—1. The Universe, even the elements, are compounds consisting of substance and form. 2. In the Universe plan and unity is discernible. (Hobot halebabot, ch. i.)

seems here to forget that the existence of separate provinces would require a superior determining Power, and the two Beings would not properly be called Gods.

The weakest of all arguments are, according to Maimonides, those by which the Mutakallemim sought to support the doctrine of God's Incorporeality. If God were corporeal, He would consist of atoms, and would not be *one* ; or He would be comparable to other beings : but a comparison implies the existence of similar and of dissimilar elements, and God would thus not be *one*. A corporeal God would be finite, and an external power would be required to define those limits.

PART II.

The Second Part includes the following sections :—1. Introduction ; 2. Philosophical Proof of the Existence of One Incorporeal Primal Cause (ch. i.) ; 3. On the Spheres and the Intelligences (ii.-xii.) ; 4. On the theory of the Eternity of the Universe (xiii.-xxix.) ; 5. Exposition of Gen. i.-iv. (xxx., xxxi.) ; 6. On Prophecy (xxxii.-xlviii.).

The enumeration of twenty-six propositions, by the aid of which the philosophers prove the Existence, the Unity, and the Incorporeality of the Primal Cause, forms the introduction to the Second Part of this work. The propositions treat of the properties of the finite and the infinite (i.-iii., x.-xii., xvi.), of change and motion (iv.-ix., xiii.-xviii.), and of the possible and the absolute or necessary (xx.-xxv.) ; they are simply enumerated, but are not demonstrated. Whatever the value of these Propositions may be, they were inadequate for their purpose, and the author is compelled to introduce auxiliary propositions to prove the existence of an infinite, incorporeal, and uncompounded Primal Cause. (Arguments I. and III.)

The first and the fourth arguments may be termed cosmological proofs. They are based on the hypothesis that the series of causes for every change is finite, and terminates in the Primal Cause. There is no essential difference in the two arguments : in the first are discussed the causes of the motion of a moving object ; the fourth treats of the causes which bring about the transition of a thing from potentiality to reality. To prove that neither the spheres nor a force residing in them constitute the Primal Cause, the philosophers employed two propositions, of which the one asserts that the revolutions of the spheres are infinite, and the other denies the possibility that an infinite force should reside in a finite object. The distinction between the finite in space and the finite in time appears to have been ignored ; for it is not shown why a force infinite in time could not reside in a body finite in space. Moreover, those who, like Maimonides, reject the eternity of the universe, necessarily reject this proof, while those who hold that the universe is eternal do not admit that the spheres have ever been only potential, and passed from potentiality to actuality. The second argument is supported by the following supplementary proposition : If two elements coexist in a state of combination, and one of these elements is to be found at the same time separate, in a free state, it is certain that the second element is likewise to be found by itself. Now, since things exist which combine in themselves motive power and mass moved by that power, and since mass is found by itself, motive power must also be found by itself independent of mass.

The third argument has a logical character : The universe is either eternal or temporal, or partly eternal and partly temporal. It cannot be eternal in all its parts, as many parts undergo destruction ; it is not altogether temporal, because, if so, the universe could not be reproduced after being destroyed. The continued existence of the universe leads, therefore, to the conclusion that there is an immortal force, the Primal Cause, besides the transient world.

These arguments have this in common, that while proving the existence of a Primal Cause, they at the same time demonstrate the Unity, the Incorporeality, and the Eternity of that Cause. Special proofs are nevertheless superadded for each of these postulates, and on the whole they differ very little from those advanced by the Mohammedan Theologians.

This philosophical theory of the Primal Cause was adapted by Jewish scholars to the Biblical theory of the Creator. The universe is a living, organized being, of which the earth is the centre. Any changes on this earth are due to the revolutions of the spheres ; the lowest or innermost sphere, viz., the one nearest to the centre, is the sphere of the moon ; the outermost or uppermost is " the all-encompassing sphere." Numerous spheres are interposed ; but Maimonides divides all the spheres into four groups, corresponding to the moon, the sun, the planets, and the fixed stars. This division is claimed by the author as his own discovery ; he believes that it stands in relation to the four causes of their motions, the four elements of the sublunary world, and the four classes of beings, viz., the mineral, the vegetable, the animal, and the rational. The spheres have souls, and are endowed with intellect ; their souls enable them to move freely, and the impulse to the motion is given by the intellect in conceiving the idea of the Absolute Intellect. Each sphere has an intellect peculiar to itself ; the intellect attached to the sphere of the moon is called " the active intellect " (*Sekel ha-po'ēl*). In support of this theory numerous passages are cited both from Holy Writ and from post-Biblical Jewish literature. The angels (*elohim, malakim*) mentioned in the Bible are assumed to be identical with the intellects of the spheres ; they are free agents, and their volition invariably tends to that which is good and noble ; they emanate from the Primal Cause, and form a descending series of beings, ending with the active intellect. The transmission of power from one element to the other is called "emanation" (*shefa'*). This transmission is performed without the utterance of a sound ; if any voice is supposed to be heard, it is only an illusion, originating in the human imagination, which is the source of all evils (ch. xii.).

In accordance with this doctrine, Maimonides explains that the three men who appeared to Abraham, the angels whom Jacob saw ascend and descend the ladder, and all other angels seen by man, are nothing but the intellects of the spheres, four in number, which emanate from the Primal Cause (ch. x). In his description of the spheres he, as usual, follows Aristotle. The spheres do not contain any of the four elements of the sublunary world, but consist of a quintessence, an entirely different element. Whilst things on this earth are transient, the beings which inhabit the spheres above are eternal. According to Aristotle, these spheres, as well as their intellects, coexist with the Primal Cause. Maimonides, faithful to the teaching of the Scriptures, here departs from his master, and holds that the spheres and the intellects had a beginning, and were brought into existence by the will of the Creator. He does not attempt to give a positive proof of his doctrine ; all he contends is that the theory of the *creatio ex nihilo* is, from a philosophical point of view, not inferior to the doctrine which asserts the eternity of the universe, and that he can refute all objections advanced against his theory (ch. xiii.–xxviii.).

He next enumerates and criticises the various theories respecting the origin of the Universe, viz. : A. God created the Universe out of nothing. B. God formed the Universe from an eternal substance. C. The Universe originating in the eternal Primal Cause is co-eternal.—It is not held necessary by the author to discuss the view of those who do not assume a Primal Cause, since the existence of such a cause has already been proved (ch. xiii.).

The objections raised to a *creatio ex nihilo* by its opponents are founded partly on the properties of Nature, and partly on those of the Primal Cause. They infer from the properties of Nature the following arguments : (1) The first moving force is eternal ; for if it had a beginning, another motion must have produced it, and then it would not be the First moving force. (2) If the *formless* matter be not eternal, it must have been produced out of another substance ; it would then have a certain form by which it might be distinguished from the primary substance, and then it would not be *formless*. (3) The circular motion of the spheres does not involve the necessity of termination ; and anything that is without an end, must be without a beginning. (4) Anything brought to existence existed previously *in potentia ;* something must therefore have pre-existed of which potential existence could be predicated. Some support for the theory of the eternity of the heavens has been derived from the general belief in the eternity of the heavens.— The properties of the Primal Cause furnished the following arguments :—If it were assumed that the Universe was created from nothing, it would imply that the First Cause had changed from the condition of a potential Creator to that of an actual Creator, or that His will had undergone a change, or that He must be imperfect, because He produced a perishable work, or that He had been inactive during a certain period. All these contingencies would be contrary to a true conception of the First Cause (ch. xiv.).

Maimonides is of opinion that the arguments based on the properties of things in Nature are inadmissible, because the laws by which the Universe is regulated need not have been in force before the Universe was in existence. This refutation is styled by our author "a strong wall built round the Law, able to resist all attacks " (ch. xvii.). In a similar manner the author proceeds against the objections founded on the properties of the First Cause. Purely intellectual beings, he says, are not subject to the same laws as material bodies ; that which necessitates a change in the latter or in the will of man need not produce a change in immaterial beings. As to the belief that the heavens are inhabited by angels and deities, it has not its origin in the real existence of these supernatural beings ; it was suggested to man by meditation on the apparent grandeur of heavenly phenomena (ch. xviii.).

Maimonides next proceeds to explain how, independently of the authority of Scripture, he has been led to adopt the belief in the *creatio ex nihilo*. Admitting that the great variety of the things in the sublunary world can be traced to those immutable laws which regulate the influence of the spheres on the beings below— the variety in the spheres can only be explained as the result of God's free will. According to Aristotle—the principal authority for the eternity of the Universe— it is impossible that a simple being should, according to the laws of nature, be the cause of various and compound beings. Another reason for the rejection of the Eternity of the Universe may be found in the fact that the astronomer Ptolemy has proved the incorrectness of the view which Aristotle had of celestial spheres, although the system of that astronomer is likewise far from being perfect and final (ch. xxiv.). It is impossible to obtain a correct notion of the properties of the heavenly spheres ; "the heaven, even the heavens, are the Lord's, but the earth hath He given to the children of man " (Ps. cxv. 16). The author, observing that the arguments against the *creatio ex nihilo* are untenable, adheres to his theory, which was taught by such prophets as Abraham and Moses. Although each Scriptural quotation could, by a figurative interpretation, be made to agree with the opposite theory, Maimonides declines to ignore the literal sense of a term, unless it be in opposition to well-established truths, as is the case with anthropomorphic expressions ; for the latter, if taken literally, would be contrary to the demonstrated truth of God's incorporeality (ch. xxv.). He is therefore surprised that the author of Pirke-di Rabbi Eliezer ventured to assume the eternity of matter, and he thinks it possible that Rabbi Eliezer carried the license of figurative speech too far. (Ch. xxvi.).

The theory of the *creatio ex nihilo* does not involve the belief that the Universe will at a future time be destroyed ; the Bible distinctly teaches the creation, but not the destruction of the world except in passages which are undoubtedly conceived in a metaphorical sense. On the contrary, respecting certain parts of the Universe it is clearly stated " He established them for ever." (Ps. cxlviii. 5.) The destruction of the Universe would be, as the creation has been, a direct act of the Divine will, and not the result of those immutable laws which govern the Universe. The Divine will would in that case set aside those laws, both in the initial and the final stages of the Universe. Within this interval, however, the laws remain undisturbed (ch. xxvii.). Apparent exceptions, the miracles, originate in these laws, although man is unable to perceive the causal relation. The Biblical account of the creation concludes with the statement that God rested on the seventh day, that is to say, He declared that the work was complete ; no new act of creation was to take place, and no new law was to be introduced. It is true that the second and the third chapters of Genesis appear to describe a new creation, that of Eve, and a new law, viz., that of man's mortality, but these chapters are explained as containing an allegorical representation of man's psychical and intellectual faculties, or a supplemental detail of the contents of the first chapter. Maimonides seems to prefer the allegorical explanation which, as it seems, he had in view without expressly stating it, in his treatment of Adam's sin and punishment. (Part I. ch. ii.) It is certainly inconsistent on the one hand to admit that at the pleasure of the Almighty the laws of nature may become inoperative, and that the whole Universe may become annihilated, and on the other hand to deny, that during the existence of the Universe, any of the natural laws ever have been or ever will be suspended. It seems that Maimonides could not conceive the idea that the work of the All-wise should be, as the Mutakallemim taught—without plan and system, or that the laws once laid down should not be sufficient for all emergencies.

The account of the Creation given in the book of Genesis is explained by the author according to the following two rules : First its language is allegorical ; and, Secondly, the terms employed are homonyms. The words *erez, mayim, ruah,* and *hoshek* in the second verse (ch. i.), are homonyms and denote the four elements : earth, water, air, and fire ; in other instances *erez* is the terrestrial globe, *mayim* is water or vapour, *ruah* denotes wind, and *hoshek* darkness: According to Maimonides, a summary of the first chapter may be given thus ; God created the Universe by producing first the *reshit* the "beginning" Gen. i. 1), or *hathalah,* i.e., the intellects which give to the spheres both existence and motion, and thus become the source of the existence of the entire Universe. At first this Universe consisted of a chaos of elements, but its form was successively developed by the influence of the spheres, and more directly by the action of light and darkness, the properties of which were fixed on the first day of the Creation. In the subsequent five days minerals, plants, animals, and the intellectual beings came into existence. The seventh day, on which the Universe was for the first time ruled by the same natural laws which still continue in operation, was distinguished as a day blessed and sanctified by the Creator, who designed it to proclaim the *creatio ex nihilo* (Exod. xx. 11). The Israelites were moreover commanded to keep this Sabbath in commemoration of their departure from Egypt (Deut. v. 15), because during the period of the Egyptian bondage, they had not been permitted to rest on that day. In the history of the first sin of man, Adam, Eve, and the serpent represent the intellect, the body, and the imagination. In order to complete the imagery, *Samael* or *Satan,* mentioned in the Midrash in connexion with this account, is added as representing man's appetitive faculties. Imagination, the source of error, is directly aided by the appetitive faculty, and the two are intimately connected with the body, to which man generally gives paramount attention, and for the sake of which he indulges in sins ; in the end, however, they subdue the intellect and weaken its power. Instead of obtaining pure and real knowledge, man forms false conceptions; in consequence, the body is subject to suffering, whilst the imagination, instead of being guided by the intellect and attaining a higher development becomes debased and depraved. In the three sons of Adam, Kain, Abel, and Seth, Maimonides finds an allusion to the three elements in man : the vegetable, the animal, and the intellectual. First, the animal element (Abel) becomes extinct ; then the vegetable elements (Kain) are dissolved ; only the third element, the intellect (Seth), survives, and forms the basis of mankind (ch. xxx., xxxi.).

Maimonides having so far stated his opinion in explicit terms, it is difficult to understand what he had in view by the avowal that he could not disclose everything. It is unquestionably no easy matter to adapt each verse in the first chapters of Genesis to the foregoing allegory ; but such an adaptation is, according to the author's own view (Part I., Introd., p. 19), not only unnecessary, but actually objectionable.

In the next section (xxxii.-xlviii.) Maimonides treats of Prophecy. He mentions the following three opinions :—1. Any person, irrespective of his physical or moral qualifications, may be summoned by the Almighty to the mission of a prophet. 2. Prophecy is the highest degree of mental development, and can only be attained by training and study. 3. The gift of prophecy depends on physical, moral, and mental training, combined with inspiration. The author adopts the last-mentioned opinion. He defines prophecy as an emanation (*shefa'*), which through the will of the Almighty descends from the Active Intellect to the intellect and the imagination of thoroughly qualified persons. The prophet is thus distinguished both from wise men whose intellect alone received the necessary impulse from the Active Intellect, and from diviners or dreamers, whose imagination alone has been influenced by the Active Intellect. Although it is assumed that the attainment of this prophetic faculty depends on God's will, this dependence is nothing else but the relation which all things bear to the Primal Cause ; for the Active Intellect acts in conformity with the laws established by the will of God ; it gives an impulse to the intellect of man, and, bringing to light those mental powers which lay dormant, it merely turns potential faculty into real action. These faculties can be perfected to such a degree as to enable man to apprehend the highest truths intuitively, without passing through all the stages of research required by ordinary persons. The same fact is noticed with respect to imagination ; man sometimes forms faithful images of objects and events which cannot be traced to the ordinary channel of information, viz., impressions made on the senses. Since prophecy is the result of a natural process, it may appear surprising that, of the numerous men excelling in wisdom, so few became prophets. Maimonides accounts for this fact by assuming that the moral faculties of such men had not been duly trained. None of them had, in the author's opinion, gone through the moral discipline indispensable for the vocation of a prophet. Besides this, everything which obstructs mental improvement, misdirects the imagination or impairs the physical strength, and precludes man from attaining to the rank of prophet. Hence no prophecy was vouchsafed to Jacob during the period of his anxieties on account of his separation from Joseph. Nor did Moses receive a Divine message during the years which the Israelites, under Divine punishment, spent in the desert. On the other hand, music and song awakened the prophetic power (comp. 2 Kings iii. 15), and

"The spirit of prophecy alights only on him who is wise, strong, and rich" (Babyl. Talm. Shabbat, 92a). Although the preparation for a prophetic mission, the pursuit of earnest and persevering study, as also the execution of the Divine dictates, required physical strength, yet in the moment when the prophecy was received the functions of the bodily organs were suspended. The intellect then acquired true knowledge, which presented itself to the prophet's imagination in forms peculiar to that faculty. Pure ideals are almost incomprehensible ; man must translate them into language which he is accustomed to use, and he must adapt them to his own mode of thinking. In receiving prophecies and communicating them to others the exercise of the prophet's imagination was therefore as essential as that of his intellect, and Maimonides seems to apply to this imagination the term "angel," which is so frequently mentioned in the Bible as the medium of communication between the Supreme Being and the prophet.

Only Moses held his bodily functions under such control that even without their temporary suspension he was able to receive prophetic inspiration ; the interposition of the imagination was in his case not needed : "God spoke to him mouth to mouth" (Num. xii. 8). Moses differed so completely from other prophets that the term "prophet" could only have been applied to him and other men by way of homonymy.

The impulses descending from the Active Intellect to man's intellect and to his imagination produce various effects, according to his physical, moral, and intellectual condition. Some men are thus endowed with extraordinary courage and with an ambition to perform great deeds, or they feel themselves impelled to appeal mightily to their fellowmen by means of exalted and pure language. Such men are filled with "the spirit of the Lord," or, "with the spirit of holiness." To this distinguished class belonged Jephthah, Samson, David, Solomon, and the authors of the Hagiographa. Though above the standard of ordinary men, they were not included in the rank of prophets. Maimonides divides the prophets into two groups, viz., those who receive inspiration in a dream and those who receive it in a vision. The first group includes the following five classes :—1. Those who see symbolic figures ; 2. Those who hear a voice addressing them without perceiving the speaker ; 3. Those who see a man and hear him addressing them ; 4. Those who see an angel addressing them ; 5. Those who see God and hear His voice. The other group is divided in a similar manner, but contains only the first four classes, for Maimonides considered it impossible that a prophet should see God in a vision. This classification is based on the various expressions employed in the Scriptures to describe the several prophecies.

When the Israelites received the Law at Mount Sinai, they distinctly heard the first two commandments, which include the doctrines of the Existence and the Unity of God ; of the other eight commandments, which enunciate moral, not metaphysical truths, they heard the mere "sound of words" ; and it was through the mouth of Moses that the Divine instruction was revealed to them. Maimonides defends this opinion by quotations from the Talmud and the Midrashim.

The theory that imagination was an essential element in prophecy is supported by the fact that figurative speech predominates in the prophetical writings, which abound in figures, hyperbolical expressions and allegories. The symbolical acts which are described in connexion with the visions of the prophets, such as the translation of Ezekiel from Babylon to Jerusalem (Ez. viii. 3), Isaiah's walking about naked and barefoot (Isa. xx. 2), Jacob's wrestling with the angel (Gen. xxxii. 27 *sqq.*), and the speaking of Balaam's ass (Num. xxii. 28), had no positive reality. The prophets, employing an elliptical style, frequently omitted to state that a certain event related by them was part of a vision or a dream. In consequence of such elliptical speech events are described in the Bible as coming directly from God, although they simply are the effect of the ordinary laws of nature, and as such depend on the will of God. Such passages cannot be misunderstood when it is borne in mind that every event and every natural phenomenon can for its origin be traced to the Primal Cause. In this sense the prophets employ such phrases as the following : "And I will command the clouds that they rain no rain upon it" (Isa. v. 6) ; "I have also called my mighty men " (*ibid.* xi. 3).

PART III.

This part contains the following six sections :—1. Exposition of the *ma'aseh mercabah* (Ez. i.), ch. i. vii. ; 2. On the nature and the origin of evil, ch. viii. xii. ; 3. On the object of the creation, ch. xiii.,-xv. ; 4. On Providence and Omniscience, ch. xvi.-xxv. ; 5. On the object of the Divine precepts (*ta'ame ha-mizvot*) and the historical portions of the Bible, ch. xxv.-xl. ; 6. A guide to the proper worship of God.

With great caution Maimonides approaches the explanation of the *ma'aseh mercabah*, the chariot which Ezekiel beheld in a vision (Ez. i.). The mysteries included in the description of the Divine chariot had been orally transmitted from generation to generation, but in consequence of the dispersion of the Jews the chain of tradition was broken, and the knowledge of these mysteries had vanished. Whatever he knew of those mysteries he owed exclusively to his own intellectual faculties ; he therefore could not reconcile himself to the idea that his knowledge should die with him. He committed his exposition of the *ma'aseh mercabah* and the *ma'aseh bereshit* to writing, but did not divest it of its original mysterious character ; so that the explanation was fully intelligible to the initiated—that is to say, to the philosopher —but to the ordinary reader it was a mere paraphrase of the Biblical text.— (Introduction.)

The first seven chapters are devoted to the exposition of the Divine chariot. According to Maimonides three distinct parts are to be noticed, each of which begins with the phrase, "And I saw." These parts correspond to the three parts of the Universe, the sublunary world, the spheres and the intelligences. First of all the prophet is made to behold the material world which consists of the earth and the spheres, and of these the spheres, as the more important, are noticed first. In the Second Part, in which the nature of the spheres is discussed, the author dwells with pride on his discovery that they can be divided into four groups. This discovery he now employs to show that the four "hayyot" (animals) represent the four divisions of the spheres. He points out that the terms which the prophet uses in the description of the *hayyot* are identical with terms applied to the properties of the spheres. For the four *hayyot* or "angels," or *cherubim*, (1) have human form ; (2) have human faces ; (3) possess characteristics of other animals ; (4) have human hands ; (5) their feet are straight and round (cylindrical) ; (6) their bodies are closely joined to each other ; (7) only their faces and their wings are separate ; (8) their substance is transparent and refulgent ; (9) they move uniformly ; (10) each moves in its own direction ; (11) they run ; (12) swift as lightning they return towards their starting point ; and (13) they move in consequence of an extraneous impulse (*ruah*). In a similar manner the spheres are described :—(1) they possess the characteristics of man, viz., life and intellect ; (2) they consist like man of body and soul ; (3) they are strong, mighty and swift, like the ox, the lion, and the eagle ; (4) they perform all manner of work as though they had hands ; (5) they are round, and are not divided into parts ; (6) no vacuum intervenes between one sphere and the other ; (7) they may be considered as one being, but in respect to the intellects, which are the causes of their existence and motion, they appear as four different beings ; (8) they are transparent and refulgent ; (9) each sphere moves uniformly, (10) and according to its special laws ; (11) they revolve with great velocity ; (12) each point returns again to its previous position ; (13) they are self-moving, yet the impulse emanates from an external power.

In the second part of the vision the prophet saw the *ofannim*. These represent the four elements of the sublunary world. For the *ofannim* (1) are connected with the *hayyot* and with the earth ; (2) they have four faces, and are four separate beings, but interpenetrate each other " as though it were a wheel in the midst of a wheel " (Ez. i. 16) ; (3) they are covered with eyes ; (4) they are not self-moving ; (5) they are set in motion by the *hayyot;* (6) their motion is not circular but rectilinear. The same may almost be said of the four elements :— (1) they are in close contact with the spheres, being encompassed by the sphere of the moon ; earth occupies the centre, water surrounds earth, air has its position between water and fire ; (2) this order is not invariably maintained ; the respective portions change and they become intermixed and combined with each other ; (3) though they are only four elements they form an infinite number of things ; (4) not being animated they do not move of their own accord ; (5) they are set in motion by the action of the spheres ; (6) when a portion is displaced it returns in a straight line to its original position.

In the third vision Ezekiel saw a human form above the *hayyot*. The figure was divided in the middle ; in the upper portion the prophet only noticed that it was *hashmal*, (mysterious) ; from the loins downwards there was " the vision of the likeness of the Divine Glory," and " the likeness of the throne." The world of Intelligences was represented by the figure ; these can only be perceived in as far as they influence the spheres, but their relation to the Creator is beyond human comprehension. The Creator himself is not represented in this vision.

The key to the whole vision Maimonides finds in the introductory words, "And the heavens were opened," and in the minute description of the place and the time of the revelation. When pondering on the grandeur of the spheres and their influences, which vary according to time and place, man begins to think of the existence of the Creator. At the conclusion of this exposition Maimonides declares that he will, in the subsequent chapters, refrain from giving further explanation of the *ma'aseh mercabah*. The foregoing summary, however, shows that the opinion of the author on this subject is fully stated, and it is indeed difficult to conceive what additional disclosures he could still have made.

The task which the author has proposed to himself in the Preface he now regarded as accomplished. He has discussed the method of the Kalām, the system of the philosophers, and his own theory concerning the relation between the Primal Cause and the Universe : he has explained the Biblical account of the creation, the nature of prophecy, and the mysteries in Ezekiel's vision. In the remaining portion of the work the author attempts to solve certain theological problems, as though he wished to obviate the following objections, which might be raised to his theory that there is a design throughout the creation, and that the entire Universe is subject to the law of causation :—What is the purpose of the evils which attend human life ? For what purpose was the world created ? In how far does Providence interfere with the natural course of events ? Does God know and foresee man's actions ? To what end was the Divine Law revealed ? These problems are treated seriatim.

All evils, Maimonides holds, originate in the material element of man's existence. Those who are able to emancipate themselves from the tyranny of the body, and unconditionally to submit to the dictates of reason, are protected from many evils. Man should disregard the cravings of the body, avoid them as topics of conversation, and keep his thoughts far away from them ; convivial and erotic songs debase man's noblest gifts—thought and speech. Matter is the partition separating man from the pure Intellects ; it is "the thickness of the cloud" which true knowledge has to traverse before it reaches man. In reality, evil is the mere negative of good : "God saw *all* that He had made, and behold it was very good " (Gen. i. 31). Evil does not exist at all. When evils are mentioned in the Scriptures as the work of God, the Scriptural expressions must not be taken in their literal sense.

There are three kinds of evils :—1. Evils necessitated by those laws of production and destruction by which the species are perpetuated. 2. Evils which men inflict on each other ; they are comparatively few, especially among civilized men. 3. Evils which man brings upon himself, and which comprise the majority of existing evils. The consideration of these three classes of evils leads to the conclusion that "the Lord is good to all, and his tender mercies are over all his works " (Ps. cxlv. 9).

The question, What is the object of the creation ? must be left unanswered. The creation is the result of the will of God. Also those who believe that the Universe is eternal must admit that they are unable to discover the purpose of the Universe. It would, however, not be illogical to assume that the spheres have been created for the sake of man, notwithstanding the great dimensions of the former and the smallness of the latter. Still it must be conceded that, even if mankind were the main and central object of creation, there is no absolute interdependence between them ; for it is a matter of course that, under altered conditions, man could exist without the spheres. All teleological theories must therefore be confined within the limits of the Universe as it now exists. They are only admissible in the relation in which the several parts of the Universe stand to each other ; but the purpose of the Universe as a whole cannot be accounted for. It is simply an emanation from the will of God.

Regarding the belief in Providence, Maimonides enumerates the following five opinions :—1. There is no Providence ; *everything* is subject to chance ; 2. Only a part of the Universe is governed by Providence, viz., the spheres, the species, and such individual beings as possess the power of perpetuating their existence (e.g., the stars) ; the rest—that is, the sublunary world—is left to mere chance. 3. Everthing is predetermined ; according to this theory, revealed Law is inconceivable. 4. Providence assigns its blessings to *all* creatures, according to their merits ; accordingly, all beings, even the lowest animals, if innocently injured or killed, receive compensation in a future life. 5. According to the Jewish belief, all living beings are endowed with free-will ; God is just, and the destiny of man depends on his merits. Maimonides denies the existence of trials inflicted by Divine love, i.e. afflictions which befall man, not as punishments of sin, but as means to procure for him a reward in times to come. Maimonides also rejects the notion that God ordains special temptation. The Biblical account, according to which God tempts men, "to know what is in their hearts," must not be taken in its literal sense ; it merely states that God made the virtues of certain people known to their fellowmen in order that their good example should be followed. Of all creatures man alone enjoys the especial care of Providence : because the acts of Providence are identical with certain influences (*shefa'*) which the Active Intellect brings to bear upon the human intellect; their effect upon man varies according to his physical, moral, and intellectual condition ; irrational beings, however, cannot be affected by these influences. If we cannot in each individual case see how these principles are applied, it must be borne in mind that God's wisdom is far above that of man. The author seems to have felt that his theory has its weak points, for he introduces it as follows :—" My theory is not established by demonstrative proof ; it is based on the authority of the Bible, and it is less subject to refutation than any of the theories previously mentioned."

Providence implies Omniscience, and men who deny this, *eo ipso*, have no belief in Providence. Some are unable to reconcile the fate of man with Divine Justice, and are therefore of opinion that God takes no notice whatever of the events which occur on earth. Others believe that God, being an absolute Unity, cannot possess a knowledge of a multitude of things, or of things that do not yet exist, or the number of which is infinite. These objections, which are based on the nature of man's perception, are illogical ; for God's knowledge cannot be compared to that of man ; it is identical with His essence. Even the Attributists, who assume that God's knowledge is different from His essence, hold that it is distinguished from man's knowledge in the following five points :— 1. It is *one*, although it embraces a plurality. 2. It includes even such things as do not yet exist. 3. It includes things which are infinite in number. 4. It does not change when new objects of perception present themselves. 5. It does not determine the course of events.—However difficult this theory may appear to human comprehension, it is in accordance with the words of Isaiah (lv. 8) : "Your thoughts are not My thoughts, and your ways are not My ways." According to Maimonides, the difficulty is to be explained by the fact that God is the Creator of all things, and His knowledge of the things is not dependent on their existence ; while the knowledge of man is solely dependent on the objects which come under his cognition.

According to Maimonides, the book of Job illustrates the several views which have been mentioned above. Satan, that is, the material element in human existence, is described as the cause of Job's sufferings. Job at first believed that man's happiness depends on riches, health, and children ; being deprived of these sources of happiness, he conceived the notion that Providence is indifferent to the fate of mortal beings. After a careful study of natural phenomena, he rejected this opinion. Eliphaz held that *all* misfortunes of man serve as punishments of past sins. Bildad, the second friend of Job, admitted the existence of those afflictions which Divine love decrees in order that the patient sufferer may be fitted to receive a bountiful reward. Zophar, the third friend of Job, declared that the ways of God are beyond human comprehension ; there is but one explanation assignable to all Divine acts, namely : Such is His Will. Elihu gives a fuller development to this idea ; he says that such evils as befell Job may be remedied once or twice, but the course of nature is not altogether reversed. It is true that by prophecy a clearer insight into the ways of God can be obtained, but there are only few who arrive at that exalted intellectual degree, whilst the majority of men must content themselves with acquiring a knowledge of God through the study of nature. Such a study leads man to the conviction that his understanding cannot fathom the secrets of nature and the wisdom of Divine Providence.

The concluding section of the Third Part treats of the purpose of the Divine precepts. In the Pentateuch they are described as the means of acquiring wisdom, enduring happiness, and also bodily comfort (ch. xxxi.). Generally a distinction is made between "*ḥuḳḳim*" ("statutes") and *mishpaṭim* ("judgments"). The object of the latter is, on the whole, known, but the *ḥuḳḳim* are considered as tests of man's obedience ; no reason is given why they have been enacted. Maimonides rejects this distinction ; he states that all precepts are the result of wisdom and design, that all contribute to the welfare of mankind, although with regard to the *ḥuḳḳim* this is less obvious. The author draws another line of distinction between the general principles and the details of rules.   For the selection and the introduction of the latter there is but one reason, viz. : " Such is the will of God."

The laws are intended to promote man's perfection ; they improve both his mental and his physical condition ; the former in so far as they lead him to the acquisition of true knowledge, the latter through the training of his moral and social faculties.   Each law thus imparts knowledge, improves the moral con- dition of man, or conduces to the well-being of society.   Many revealed laws help to enlighten man, and to correct false opinions.   This object is not always clearly announced.   God in His wisdom sometimes withheld from the knowledge of man the purpose of commandments and actions.   There are other precepts which tend to restrain man's passions and desires.   If the same end is occasionally attainable by other means, it must be remembered that the Divine laws are adapted to the ordinary mental and emotional state of man, and not to exceptional circumstances.   In this work, as in the *Yad ha-ḥazaḳah*, Maimonides divides the laws of the Pentateuch into fourteen groups, and in each group he discusses the principal and the special object of the laws included in it.

In addition to the legislative contents, the Bible includes historical informa- tion ; and Maimonides, in briefly reviewing the Biblical narratives, shows that these are likewise intended to improve man's physical, moral, and intellectual condition.   "It is not a vain thing for you" (Deut. xxxii. 47), and when it proves vain to anyone, it is his own fault.

In the final chapters the author describes the several degrees of human per- fection, from the sinners who have turned from the right path to the best of men, who in all their thoughts and acts cling to the Most Perfect Being, who aspire after the greatest possible knowledge of God, and strive to serve their Maker in the practice of "loving-kindness, righteousness, and justice."   This degree of human perfection can only be attained by those who never forget the presence of the Almighty, and remain firm in their fear and love of God. These servants of the Most High inherit the choicest of human blessings ; they are endowed with wisdom : they are godlike beings.

INTRODUCTION

[Letter of the Author to his Pupil, R. Joseph Ibn Aknin.]

In the name of GOD, Lord of the Universe.

To R. Joseph (may God protect him !), son of R. Jehudah (may his repose
be in Paradise !) :—

" My dear pupil, ever since you resolved to come to me, from a distant
country, and to study under my direction, I thought highly of your thirst
for knowledge, and your fondness for speculative pursuits, which found expression in your poems. I refer to the time when I received your writings
in prose and verse from Alexandria. I was then not yet able to test your
powers of apprehension, and I thought that your desire might possibly exceed
your capacity. But when you had gone with me through a course of astronomy, after having completed the [other] elementary studies which are
indispensable for the understanding of that science, I was still more gratified
by the acuteness and the quickness of your apprehension. Observing your
great fondness for mathematics, I let you study them more deeply, for I felt
sure of your ultimate success. Afterwards, when I took you through a course
of logic, I found that my great expectations of you were confirmed, and I
considered you fit to receive from me an exposition of the esoteric ideas contained in the prophetic books, that you might understand them as they are
understood by men of culture. When I commenced by way of hints, I
noticed that you desired additional explanation, urging me to expound some
metaphysical problems ; to teach you the system of the Mutakallemim ; to
tell you whether their arguments were based on logical proof ; and if not,
what their method was. I perceived that you had acquired some knowledge
in those matters from others, and that you were perplexed and bewildered ;
yet you sought to find out a solution to your difficulty. I urged you to desist
from this pursuit, and enjoined you to continue your studies systematically ;
for my object was that the truth should present itself in connected order,
and that you should not hit upon it by mere chance. Whilst you studied
with me I never refused to explain difficult verses in the Bible or passages in
rabbinical literature which we happened to meet. When, by the will of
God, we parted, and you went your way, our discussions aroused in me a
resolution which had long been dormant. Your absence has prompted me
to compose this treatise for you and for those who are like you, however few
they may be. I have divided it into chapters, each of which shall be sent to
you as soon as it is completed. Farewell ! "

[Prefatory Remarks.]

" Cause me to know the way wherein I should walk, for I lift up my soul unto Thee."
(Psalm cxliii. 8.)

" Unto you, O men, I call, and my voice is to the sons of men." (Prov. viii. 4.)

" Bow down thine ear and hear the words of the wise, and apply thine heart unto my
knowledge." (Prov. xxii. 17.)

My primary object in this work is to explain certain words occurring in the prophetic books. Of these some are homonyms, and of their several meanings the ignorant choose the wrong ones ; other terms which are employed in a figurative sense are erroneously taken by such persons in their primary signification. There are also hybrid terms, denoting things which are of the same class from one point of view and of a different class from another. It is not here intended to explain all these expressions to the unlettered or to mere tyros, a previous knowledge of Logic and Natural Philosophy being indispensable, or to those who confine their attention to the study of our holy Law, I mean the study of the canonical law alone ; for the true knowledge of the Torah is the special aim of this and similar works.

The object of this treatise is to enlighten a religious man who has been trained to believe in the truth of our holy Law, who conscientiously fulfils his moral and religious duties, and at the same time has been successful in his philosophical studies. Human reason has attracted him to abide within its sphere ; and he finds it difficult to accept as correct the teaching based on the literal interpretation of the Law, and especially that which he himself or others derived from those homonymous, metaphorical, or hybrid expressions. Hence he is lost in perplexity and anxiety. If he be guided solely by reason, and renounce his previous views which are based on those expressions, he would consider that he had rejected the fundamental principles of the Law ; and even if he retains the opinions which were derived from those expressions, and if, instead of following his reason, he abandon its guidance altogether, it would still appear that his religious convictions had suffered loss and injury. For he would then be left with those errors which give rise to fear and anxiety, constant grief and great perplexity.

This work has also a second object in view. It seeks to explain certain obscure figures which occur in the Prophets, and are not distinctly characterized as being figures. Ignorant and superficial readers take them in a literal, not in a figurative sense. Even well informed persons are bewildered if they understand these passages in their literal signification, but they are entirely relieved of their perplexity when we explain the figure, or merely suggest that the terms are figurative. For this reason I have called this book *Guide for the Perplexed.*

I do not presume to think that this treatise settles every doubt in the minds of those who understand it, but I maintain that it settles the greater part of their difficulties. No intelligent man will require and expect that on introducing any subject I shall completely exhaust it ; or that on commencing the exposition of a figure I shall fully explain all its parts. Such a course could not be followed by a teacher in a *viva voce* exposition, much less by an author in writing a book, without becoming a target for every foolish conceited person to discharge the arrows of folly at him. Some general principles bearing upon this point have been fully discussed in our works on the Talmud, and we have there called the attention of the reader to many themes of this kind. We also stated (*Mishneh torah*, I. ii. 12, and iv. 10) that the expression *Ma'ase Bereshit* (Account of the Creation) signified " Natural Science," and *Ma'aseh Mercabah* (" Description of the Chariot ") Metaphysics, and we explained the force of the Rabbinical dictum, " The *Ma'aseh Mercabah* must not be fully expounded even in the presence of a single student, unless he be wise and able to reason for himself, and even then you should merely acquaint him with the heads of the different sections of the subject. (Babyl. Talm. *Hagigah*, fol. 11 b). You must, therefore, not expect from me more than such heads. And even these have not been methodically and systematically arranged in this work, but have been, on the contrary, scattered, and are interspersed with other topics which we shall have occasion to explain. My object in adopting this arrangement is that the truths should be at one time apparent, and at another time concealed. Thus we shall not be in opposition to the Divine Will (from which it is wrong to deviate) which has withheld from the multitude the truths required for the knowledge of God, according to the words, " The secret of the Lord is with them that fear Him " (Ps. xxv. 14).

Know that also in Natural Science there are topics which are not to be fully explained. Our Sages laid down the rule, " The *Ma'aseh Bereshith* must not be expounded in the presence of two." If an author were to explain these principles in writing, it would be equal to expounding them unto thousands of men. For this reason the prophets treat these subjects in figures, and our Sages, imitating the method of Scripture, speak of them in metaphors and allegories ; because there is a close affinity between these subjects and metaphysics, and indeed they form part of its mysteries. Do not imagine that these most difficult problems can be thoroughly understood by any one of us. This is not the case. At times the truth shines so brilliantly that we perceive it as clear as day. Our nature and habit then draw a veil over our perception, and we return to a darkness almost as dense as before. We are like those who, though beholding frequent flashes of lightning, still find themselves in the thickest darkness of the night. On some the lightning flashes in rapid succession, and they seem to be in continuous light, and their night is as clear as the day. This was the degree of prophetic excellence attained by (Moses) the greatest of prophets, to whom God said, " But as for thee, stand thou here by Me " (Deut. v. 31), and of whom it is written " the skin of his face shone," etc. (Exod. xxxiv. 29). [Some perceive the prophetic flash at long intervals ; this is the degree of most prophets.] By others only once during the whole night is a flash of lightning perceived. This is the case with those of whom we are informed, " They prophesied, and did not prophesy again " (Num. xi. 25). There are some to whom the flashes of lightning appear with varying intervals; others are in the condition of men, whose darkness is illumined not by lightning, but by some kind of crystal or similar stone, or other substances that possess the property of shining during the night ; and to them even this small amount of light is not continuous, but now it shines and now it vanishes, as if it were " the flame of the rotating sword."

The degrees in the perfection of men vary according to these distinctions. Concerning those who never beheld the light even for one day, but walk in continual darkness, it is written, " They know not, neither will they understand ; they walk on in darkness " (Ps. lxxxii. 5). Truth, in spite of all its powerful manifestations, is completely withheld from them, and the following words of Scripture may be applied to them, " And now men see not the light which is bright in the skies " (Job xxxvii. 21). They are the multitude of ordinary men ; there is no need to notice them in this treatise.

You must know that if a person, who has attained a certain degree of perfection, wishes to impart to others, either orally or in writing, any portion of the knowledge which he has acquired of these subjects, he is utterly unable to be as systematic and explicit as he could be in a science of which the method is well known. The same difficulties which he encountered when investigating the subject for himself will attend him when endeavouring to instruct others ; viz., at one time the explanation will appear lucid, at another time, obscure ; this property of the subject appears to remain the same both to the advanced scholar and to the beginner. For this reason, great theological scholars gave instruction in all such matters only by means of metaphors and allegories. They frequently employed them in forms varying more or less essentially. In most cases they placed the lesson to be illustrated at the beginning, or in the middle, or at the end of the simile. When they could find no simile which from beginning to end corresponded to the idea which was to be illustrated, they divided the subject of the lesson, although in itself one whole, into different parts, and expressed each by a separate figure. Still more obscure are those instances in which one simile is employed to illustrate many subjects, the beginning of the simile representing one thing, the end another. Sometimes the whole metaphor may refer to two cognate subjects in the same branch of knowledge.

If we were to teach in these disciplines, without the use of parables and figures, we should be compelled to resort to expressions both profound and transcendental, and by no means more intelligible than metaphors and similes ; as though the wise and learned were drawn into this course by the Divine Will, in the same way as they are compelled to follow the laws of nature in matters relating to the body. You are no doubt aware that the Almighty, desiring to lead us to perfection and to improve our state of society, has revealed to us laws which are to regulate our actions. These laws, however, presuppose an advanced state of intellectual culture. We must first form a conception of the Existence of the Creator according to our capabilities ; that is, we must have a knowledge of Metaphysics. But this discipline can only be approached after the study of Physics ; for the science of Physics borders on Metaphysics, and must even precede it in the course of our studies, as is clear to all who are familiar with these questions. Therefore the Almighty commenced Holy Writ with the description of the Creation, that is, with Physical Science ; the subject being on the one hand most weighty and important, and on the other hand our means of fully comprehending those great problems being limited. He described those profound truths, which His Divine Wisdom found it necessary to communicate to us, in allegorical, figurative, and metaphorical language. Our Sages have said (Yemen Midrash on Gen. i. 1), " It is impossible to give a full account of the Creation to man. Therefore Scripture simply tells us, In the beginning God created the heavens and the earth " (Gen. i. 1). Thus they have suggested that this subject is a deep mystery, and in the words of Solomon, " Far off and exceedingly deep, who can find it out ? " (Eccles. vii. 24). It has been treated in metaphors in order that the uneducated may comprehend it according to the measure of their faculties and the feebleness of their apprehension, while educated persons may take it in a different sense. In our commentary on the Mishnah we stated our intention to explain difficult problems in the Book on Prophecy and in the Book of Harmony. In the latter we intended to examine all the passages in the Midrash which, if taken literally, appear to be inconsistent with truth and common sense, and must therefore be taken figuratively. Many years have elapsed since I first commenced those works. I had proceeded but a short way when I became dissatisfied with my original plan. For I observed that by expounding these passages by means of allegorical and mystical terms, we do not explain anything, but merely substitute one thing for another of the same nature, whilst in explaining them fully our efforts would displease most people ; and my sole object in planning to write those books was to make the contents of Midrashim and the exoteric lessons of the prophecies intelligible to everybody. We have further noticed that when an ill-informed Theologian reads these Midrashim, he will find no difficulty ; for possessing no knowledge of the properties of things, he will not reject statements which involve impossibilities. When, however, a person who is both religious and well educated reads them, he cannot escape the following dilemma : either he takes them literally, and questions the abilities of the author and the soundness of his mind—doing thereby nothing which is opposed to the principles of our faith,—or he will acquiesce in assuming that the passages in question have some secret meaning, and he will continue to hold the author in high estimation whether he understood the allegory or not. As regards prophecy in its various degrees and the different metaphors used in the prophetic books, we shall give in the present work an explanation, according to a different method. Guided by these considerations I have refrained from writing those two books as I had previously intended. In my larger work, the *Mishnah Torah*, I have contented myself with briefly stating the principles of our faith and its fundamental truths, together with such hints as approach a clear exposition. In this work, however, I address those who have studied philosophy and have acquired sound knowledge, and who while firm in religious matters are perplexed and bewildered on account of the ambiguous and figurative expressions employed in the holy writings. Some chapters may be found in this work which contain no reference whatever to homonyms. Such chapters will serve as an introduction to others ; they will contain some reference to the signification of a homonym which I do not wish to mention in that place, or explain some figure ; point out that a certain expression is a figure ; treat of difficult passages generally misunderstood in consequence of the homonymy they include, or because the simile they contain is taken in place of that which it represents, and *vice versâ*.

Having spoken of similes, I proceed to make the following remark :—The key to the understanding and to the full comprehension of all that the Prophets have said is found in the knowledge of the figures, their general ideas, and the meaning of each word they contain. You know the verse :—

" I have also spoken in similes by the Prophets " (Hosea xii. 10) ; and also the verse, " Put forth a riddle and speak a parable " (Ezek. xvii. 2). And because the Prophets continually employ figures, Ezekiel said, " Does He not speak parables ? " (xxi. 5). Again, Solomon begins his book of Proverbs with the words, " To understand a proverb and figurative speech, the words of the wise and their dark sayings " (Prov. i. 6) ; and we read in Midrash, *Shir ha-shirim Rabba*, i. 1) ; " To what were the words of the Law to be compared before the time of Solomon ? To a well the waters of which are at a great depth, and though cool and fresh, yet no man could drink of them. A clever man joined cord with cord, and rope with rope, and drew up and drank. So Solomon went from figure to figure, and from subject to subject, till he obtained the true sense of the Law." So far go the words of our Sages. I do not believe that any intelligent man thinks that " the words of the Law " mentioned here as requiring the application of figures in order to be understood, can refer to the rules for building tabernacles, for preparing the lulab, or for the four kinds of trustees. What is really meant is the apprehension of profound and difficult subjects, concerning which our Sages said, " If a man loses in his house a sela, or a pearl, he can find it by lighting a taper worth only one issar. Thus the parables in themselves are of no great value, but through them the words of the holy Law are rendered intelligible." These likewise are the words of our Sages ; consider well their statement, that the deeper sense of the words of the holy Law are pearls, and the literal acceptation of a figure is of no value in itself. They compare the hidden meaning included in the literal sense of the simile to a pearl lost in a dark room, which is full of furniture. It is certain that the pearl is in the room, but the man can neither see it nor know where it lies. It is just as if the pearl were no longer in his possession, for, as has been stated, it affords him no benefit whatever until he kindles a light. The same is the case with the comprehension of that which the simile represents. The wise king said, " A word fitly spoken is like apples of gold in vessels of silver " (Prov. xxv. 11). Hear the explanation of what he said :—The word *maskiyoth*, the Hebrew equivalent for " vessels," denotes " filigree network "—i.e., things in which there are very small apertures, such as are frequently wrought by silversmiths. They are called in Hebrew *maskiyyoth* (lit. " transpicuous," from the verb *sakah*, " he saw," a root which occurs also in the Targum of Onkelos, Gen. xxvi. 8), because the eye penetrates through them. Thus Solomon meant to say, " Just as apples of gold in silver filigree with small apertures, so is a word fitly spoken."

See how beautifully the conditions of a good simile are described in this figure ! It shows that in every word which has a double sense, a literal one and a figurative one, the plain meaning must be as valuable as silver, and the hidden meaning still more precious ; so that the figurative meaning bears the same relation to the literal one as gold to silver. It is further necessary that the plain sense of the phrase shall give to those who consider it some notion of that which the figure represents. Just as a golden apple overlaid with a network of silver, when seen at a distance, or looked at superficially, is mistaken for a silver apple, but when a keen-sighted person looks at the object well, he will find what is within, and see that the apple is gold. The same is the case with the figures employed by prophets. Taken literally, such expressions contain wisdom useful for many purposes, among others, for the amelioration of the condition of society ; e.g., the Proverbs (of Solomon), and similar sayings in their literal sense. Their hidden meaning, however, is profound wisdom, conducive to the recognition of real truth.

Know that the figures employed by prophets are of two kinds : first, where every word which occurs in the simile represents a certain idea ; and secondly, where the simile, as a whole, represents a general idea, but has a great many points which have no reference whatever to that idea ; they are simply required to give to the simile its proper form and order, or better to conceal the idea ; the simile is therefore continued as far as necessary, according to its literal sense. Consider this well.

An example of the first class of prophetic figures is to be found in Genesis : —" And, behold, a ladder set up on the earth, and the top of it reached to heaven ; and, behold, the angels of God ascending and descending on it " (Gen. xxviii. 12). The word " ladder " refers to one idea ; " set up on the earth " to another ; " and the top of it reached to heaven " to a third ; " angels of God " to a fourth ; " ascending " to a fifth ; " descending " to a sixth ; " the Lord stood above it " (ver. 13) to a seventh. Every word in this figure introduces a fresh element into the idea represented by the figure.

An example of the second class of prophetic figures is found in Proverbs (vii. 6–26) :—" For at the window of my house I looked through my casement, and beheld among the simple ones ; I discerned among the youths a young man void of understanding, passing through the street near her corner : and he went the way to her house, in the twilight, in the evening, in the black and dark night : and, behold, there met him a woman with the attire of a harlot, and subtil of heart. (She is loud and stubborn ; her feet abide not in her house : now she is without, now in the streets, and lieth in wait in every corner.) So she caught him, and kissed him, and with an impudent face said unto him, I have peace offerings with me ; this day have I paid my vows. Therefore came I forth to meet thee, diligently to seek thy face, and I have found thee. I have decked my bed with coverings of tapestry, with striped cloths of the yarn of Egypt. I have perfumed my bed with myrrh, aloes, and cinnamon. Come, let us take our fill of love until the morning : let us solace ourselves with loves. For the goodman is not at home, he is gone a long journey : he hath taken a bag of money with him, and will come home at the day appointed. With her much fair speech she caused him to yield, with the flattering of her lips she forced him. He goeth after her straightway, as an ox goeth to the slaughter, or as fetters to the correction of a fool : till a dart strike through his liver ; as a bird hasteth to the snare, and knoweth not that it is for his life. Hearken unto me now therefore, O ye children, and attend to the words of my mouth. Let not thine heart decline to her ways, go not astray in her paths. For she hath cast down many wounded : yea, many strong men have been slain by her."

The general principle expounded in all these verses is to abstain from excessive indulgence in bodily pleasures. The author compares the body, which is the source of all sensual pleasures, to a married woman who at the same time is a harlot. And this figure he has taken as the basis of his entire book. We shall hereafter show the wisdom of Solomon in comparing sensual pleasures to an adulterous harlot. We shall explain how aptly he concludes that work with the praises of a faithful wife who devotes herself to the welfare of her husband and of her household. All obstacles which prevent man from attaining his highest aim in life, all the deficiencies in the character of man, all his evil propensities, are to be traced to the body alone. This will be explained later on. The predominant idea running throughout the figure is, that man shall not be entirely guided by his animal, or material nature ; for the material substance of man is identical with that of the brute creation.

An adequate explanation of the figure having been given, and its meaning having been shown, do not imagine that you will find in its application a corresponding element for each part of the figure ; you must not ask what is meant by " I have peace offerings with me " (ver. 14) ; by " I have decked my bed with coverings of tapestry " (ver. 16) ; or what is added to the force of the figure by the observation " for the goodman is not at home " (ver. 19), and so on to the end of the chapter. For all this is merely to complete the illustration of the metaphor in its literal meaning. The circumstances described here are such as are common to adulterers. Such conversations take place between all adulterous persons. You must well understand what I have said, for it is a principle of the utmost importance with respect to those things which I intend to expound. If you observe in one of the chapters that I explained the meaning of a certain figure, and pointed out to you its general scope, do not trouble yourself further in order to find an interpretation of each separate portion, for that would lead you to one of the two following erroneous courses ; either you will miss the sense included in the metaphor, or you will be induced to explain certain things which require no explanation, and which are not introduced for that purpose. Through this unnecessary trouble you may fall into the great error which besets most modern sects in their foolish writings and discussions ; they all endeavour to find some hidden meaning in expressions which were never uttered by the author in that sense. Your object should be to discover in most of the figures the general idea which the author wishes to express. In some instances it will be sufficient if you understand from my remarks that a certain expression contains a figure, although I may offer no further comment. For when you know that it is not to be taken literally, you will understand at once to what subject it refers. My statement that it is a figurative expression will, as it were, remove the screen from between the object and the observer.

Directions for the Study of this Work.

If you desire to grasp all that is contained in this book so that nothing shall escape your notice, consider the chapters in connected order. In studying each chapter, do not content yourself with comprehending its principal subject, but attend to every term mentioned therein, although it may seem to have no connection with the principal subject. For what I have written in this work was not the suggestion of the moment ; it is the result of deep study and great application. Care has been taken that nothing that appeared doubtful should be left unexplained. Nothing of what is mentioned is out of place, every remark will be found to illustrate the subject-matter of the respective chapter. Do not read superficially, lest you do me an injury, and derive no benefit for yourself. You must study thoroughly and read continually ; for you will then find the solution of those important problems of religion, which are a source of anxiety to all intelligent men. I adjure any reader of my book, in the name of the Most High, not to add any explanation even to a single word ; nor to explain to another any portion of it except such passages as have been fully treated of by previous theological authorities ; he must not teach others anything that he has learnt from my work alone, and that has not been hitherto discussed by any of our authorities. The reader must, moreover, beware of raising objections to any of my statements, because it is very probable that he may understand my words to mean the exact opposite to what I intended to say. He will injure me, while I endeavoured to benefit him. " He will requite me evil for good." Let the reader make a careful study of this work ; and if his doubt be removed on even one point, let him praise his Maker and rest contented with the knowledge he has acquired. But if he derive from it no benefit whatever, he may consider the book as if it had never been written. Should he notice any opinions with which he does not agree, let him endeavour to find a suitable explanation, even if it seem far-fetched, in order that he may judge me charitably. Such a duty we owe to every one. We owe it especially to our scholars and theologians, who endeavour to teach us what is the truth according to the best of their ability. I feel assured that those of my readers who have not studied philosophy, will still derive profit from many a chapter. But the thinker whose studies have brought him into collision with religion, will, as I have already mentioned, derive much benefit from every chapter. How greatly will he rejoice ! How agreeably will my words strike his ears ! Those, however, whose minds are confused with false notions and perverse methods, who regard their misleading studies as sciences, and imagine themselves philosophers, though they have no knowledge that could truly be termed science, will object to many chapters, and will find in them many insuperable difficulties, because they do not understand their meaning, and because I expose therein the absurdity of their perverse notions, which constitute their riches and peculiar treasure, " stored up for their ruin." God knows that I hesitated very much before writing on the subjects contained in this work, since they are profound mysteries ; they are topics which, since the time of our captivity have not been treated by any of our scholars as far as we possess their writings ; how then shall I now make a beginning and discuss them ? But I rely on two precedents : first, to similar cases our Sages applied the verse, " It is time to do something in honour of the Lord : for they have made void thy law " (Ps. cxix. 126). Secondly, they have said, " Let all thy acts be guided by pure intentions." On these two principles I relied while composing some parts of this work. Lastly, when I have a difficult subject before me—when I find the road narrow, and can see no other way of teaching a well established truth except by pleasing one intelligent man and displeasing ten thousand fools—I prefer to address myself to the one man, and to take no notice whatever of the condemnation of the multitude ; I prefer to extricate that intelligent man from his embarrassment and show him the cause of his perplexity, so that he may attain perfection and be at peace.

Introductory Remarks.

[ON METHOD.]

THERE are seven causes of inconsistencies and contradictions to be met with in a literary work. The first cause arises from the fact that the author collects the opinions of various men, each differing from the other, but neglects to mention the name of the author of any particular opinion. In such a work contradictions or inconsistencies must occur, since any two statements may belong to two different authors. Second cause : The author holds at first one opinion which he subsequently rejects ; in his work, however, both his original and altered views are retained. Third cause: The passages in question are not all to be taken literally ; some only are to be understood in their literal sense, while in others figurative language is employed, which includes another meaning besides the literal one : or, in the apparently inconsistent passages, figurative language is employed which, if taken literally, would seem to be contradictories or contraries. Fourth cause : The premises are not identical in both statements, but for certain reasons they are not fully stated in these passages ; or two propositions with different subjects which are expressed by the same term without having the difference in meaning pointed out, occur in two passages. The contradiction is therefore only apparent, but there is no contradiction in reality. The fifth cause is traceable to the use of a certain method adopted in teaching and expounding profound problems. Namely, a difficult and obscure theorem must sometimes be mentioned and assumed as known, for the illustration of some elementary and intelligible subject which must be taught beforehand, the commencement being always made with the easier thing. The teacher must therefore facilitate, in any manner which he can devise, the explanation of those theorems, which have to be assumed as known, and he must content himself with giving a general though somewhat inaccurate notion on the subject. It is, for the present, explained according to the capacity of the students, that they may comprehend it as far as they are required to understand the subject. Later on, the same subject is thoroughly treated and fully developed in its right place. Sixth cause : The contradiction is not apparent, and only becomes evident through a series of premises. The larger the number of premises necessary to prove the contradiction between the two conclusions, the greater is the chance that it will escape detection, and that the author will not perceive his own inconsistency. Only when from each conclusion, by means of suitable premises, an inference is made, and from the enunciation thus inferred, by means of proper arguments, other conclusions are formed, and after that process has been repeated many times, then it becomes clear that the original conclusions are contradictories or contraries. Even able writers are liable to overlook such inconsistencies. If, however, the contradiction between the original statements can at once be discovered, and the author, while writing the second, does not think of the first, he evinces a greater deficiency, and his words deserve no notice whatever. Seventh cause: It is sometimes necessary to introduce such metaphysical matter as may partly be disclosed, but must partly be concealed ; while, therefore, on one occasion the object which the author has in view may demand that the metaphysical problem be treated as solved in one way, it may be convenient on another occasion to treat it as solved in the opposite way. The author must endeavour, by concealing the fact as much as possible, to prevent the uneducated reader from perceiving the contradiction.

Inconsistencies occurring in the Mishnah and Boraitot are traceable to the first cause. You meet frequently in the Gemara with passages like the following :—" Does not the beginning of the passage contradict the end ? No ; the beginning is the dictum of a certain Rabbi ; the end that of another " ; or " Rabbi (Jehudah ha-Nasi) approved of the opinion of a certain rabbi in one case and gave it therefore anonymously, and having accepted that of another rabbi in the other case he introduced that view without naming the authority " ; or " Who is the author of this anonymous dictum ? Rabbi A." " Who is the author of that paragraph in the Mishnah ? Rabbi B." Instances of this kind are innumerable.

Apparent contradictions or differences occurring in the Gemara may be traced to the first cause and to the second, as e.g., " In this particular case he agrees with this rabbi " ; or " He agrees with him in one point, but differs from him in another " ; or " These two dicta are the opinions of two Amoraim, who differ as regards the statement made by a certain rabbi." These are examples of contradictions traceable to the first cause. The following are instances which may be traced to the second cause. " Rabba altered his opinion on that point " ; it then becomes necessary to consider which of the two opinions came second. Again, " In the first recension of the Talmud by Rabbi Ashi, he made one assertion, and in the second a different one."

The inconsistencies and contradictions met with in some passages of the prophetic books, if taken literally, are all traceable to the third or fourth cause, and it is exclusively in reference to this subject that I wrote the present Introduction. You know that the following expression frequently occurs, " One verse says this, another that," showing the contradiction, and explaining that either some premise is wanting or the subject is altered. Comp. " Solomon, it is not sufficient that thy words contradict thy father ; they are themselves inconsistent, etc." Many similar instances occur in the writings of our Sages. The passages in the prophetical books which our Sages have explained, mostly refer to religious or moral precepts. Our desire, however, is to discuss such passages as contain apparent contradictions in regard to the principles of our faith. I shall explain some of them in various chapters of the present work ; for this subject also belongs to the secrets of the Torah.

Contradictions traceable to the seventh cause occurring in the prophetical works require special investigation ; and no one should express his opinion on that matter by reasoning and arguing without weighing the matter well in his mind.

Inconsistencies in the writings of true philosophers are traceable to the fifth cause. Contradictions occurring in the writings of most authors and commentators, such as are not included in the above-mentioned works, are due to the sixth cause. Many examples of this class of contradictions are found in the Midrash and the Agada ; hence the saying, " We must not raise questions concerning the contradictions met with in the Agada." You may also notice in them contradictions due to the seventh cause. Any inconsistency discovered in the present work will be found to arise in consequence of the fifth cause or the seventh. Notice this, consider its truth, and remember it well, lest you misunderstand some of the chapters in this book.

Having concluded these introductory remarks I proceed to examine those expressions, to the true meaning of which, as apparent from the context, it is necessary to direct your attention. This book will then be a key admitting to places the gates of which would otherwise be closed. When the gates are opened and men enter, their souls will enjoy repose, their eyes will be gratified, and even their bodies, after all toil and labour, will be refreshed.

PART I

" Open ye the gates, that the righteous nation which keepeth the truth may enter in."—(Isa. xxvi. 2.)

CHAPTER I

SOME have been of opinion that by the Hebrew *ẓelem*, the shape and figure of a thing is to be understood, and this explanation led men to believe in the corporeality [of the Divine Being] : for they thought that the words " Let us make man in our *ẓelem* " (Gen.i. 26), implied that God had the form of a human being, i.e., that He had figure and shape, and that, consequently, He was corporeal. They adhered faithfully to this view, and thought that if they were to relinquish it they would *eo ipso* reject the truth of the Bible : and further, if they did not conceive God as having a body possessed of face and limbs, similar to their own in appearance, they would have to deny even the existence of God. The sole difference which they admitted, was that He excelled in greatness and splendour, and that His substance was not flesh and blood. Thus far went their conception of the greatness and glory of God. The incorporeality of the Divine Being, and His unity, in the true sense of the word—for there is no real unity without incorporeality—will be fully proved in the course of the present treatise. (Part II., ch. i.) In this chapter it is our sole intention to explain the meaning of the words *ẓelem* and *demut*. I hold that the Hebrew equivalent of " form " in the ordinary acceptation of the word, viz., the figure and shape of a thing, is *toär*. Thus we find " [And Joseph was] beautiful in *toär* ('form'), and beautiful in appearance" (Gen. xxxix. 6) : " What form (*toär*) is he of ? " (1 Sam. xxviii. 14) : " As the form (*toär*) of the children of a king " (Judges viii. 18). It is also applied to form produced by human labour, as " He marketh its form (*toär*) with a line," " and he marketh its form (*toar*) with the compass " (Isa. xliv. 13). This term is not at all applicable to God. The term *ẓelem*, on the other hand, signifies the specific form, viz., that which constitutes the essence of a thing, whereby the thing is what it is ; the reality of a thing in so far as it is that particular being. In man the " form " is that constituent which gives him human perception : and on account of this intellectual perception the term *ẓelem* is employed in the sentences " In the *ẓelem* of God he created him " (Gen. i. 27). It is therefore rightly said, " Thou despisest their *ẓelem* " (Ps. lxiii. 20) ; the " contempt " can only concern the soul— the specific form of man, not the properties and shape of his body. I am also of opinion that the reason why this term is used for " idols " may be found in the circumstance that they are worshipped on account of some idea represented by them, not on account of their figure and shape. For the same reason the term is used in the expression, " the forms (*ẓalme*) of your emerods " (1 Sam. vi. 5), for the chief object was the removal of the injury caused by the emerods, not a change of their shape. As, however, it must be admitted that the term *zelem* is employed in these two cases, viz. " the images of the emerods " and " the idols " on account of the external shape, the term *zelem* is either a homonym or a hybrid term, and would denote both the specific form and the outward shape, and similar properties relating to the dimensions and the shape of material bodies ; and in the phrase " Let us make man in our *zelem* " (Gen. i. 26), the term signifies " the specific form " of man, viz., his intellectual perception, and does not refer to his " figure " or " shape." Thus we have shown the difference between *zelem* and *toär*, and explained the meaning of *zelem*.

Demut is derived from the verb *damah*, " he is like." This term likewise denotes agreement with regard to some abstract relation : comp. " I am like a pelican of the wilderness " (Ps. cii. 7) ; the author does not compare himself to the pelican in point of wings and feathers, but in point of sadness. " Nor any tree in the garden of God was like unto him in beauty" (Ezek. xxxi. 8) ; the comparison refers to the idea of beauty. " Their poison is like the poison of a serpent " (Ps. lviii. 5) ; " He is like unto a lion " (Ps. xvii. 12) ; the resemblance indicated in these passages does not refer to the figure and shape, but to some abstract idea. In the same manner is used " the likeness of the throne " (Ezek. i. 26); the comparison is made with regard to greatness and glory, not, as many believe, with regard to its square form, its breadth, or the length of its legs : this explanation applies also to the phrase " the likeness of the *hayyot* (" living creatures," Ezek. i. 13).

As man's distinction consists in a property which no other creature on earth possesses, viz., intellectual perception, in the exercise of which he does not employ his senses, nor move his hand or his foot, this perception has been compared—though only apparently, not in truth—to the Divine perception, which requires no corporeal organ. On this account, i.e., on account of the Divine intellect with which man has been endowed, he is said to have been made in the form and likeness of the Almighty, but far from it be the notion that the Supreme Being is corporeal, having a material form.

CHAPTER II

SOME years ago a learned man asked me a question of great importance ; the problem and the solution which we gave in our reply deserve the closest attention. Before, however, entering upon this problem and its solution I must premise that every Hebrew knows that the term *Elohim* is a homonym, and denotes God, angels, judges, and the rulers of countries, and that Onkelos the proselyte explained it in the true and correct manner by taking *Elohim* in the sentence, " and ye shall be like *Elohim* " (Gen. iii. 5) in the last-mentioned meaning, and rendering the sentence " and ye shall be like princes." Having pointed out the homonymity of the term " *Elohim* " we return to the question under consideration. " It would at first sight," said the objector, " appear from Scripture that man was originally intended to be perfectly equal to the rest of the animal creation, which is not endowed with intellect, reason, or power of distinguishing between good and evil : but that Adam's disobedience to the command of God procured him that great per-

fection which is the peculiarity of man, viz., the power of distinguishing between good and evil—the noblest of all the faculties of our nature, the essential characteristic of the human race. It thus appears strange that the
punishment for rebelliousness should be the means of elevating man to a
pinnacle of perfection to which he had not attained previously. This is
equivalent to saying that a certain man was rebellious and extremely wicked,
wherefore his nature was changed for the better, and he was made to shine
as a star in the heavens." Such was the purport and subject of the question,
though not in the exact words of the inquirer. Now mark our reply, which
was as follows :—" You appear to have studied the matter superficially, and
nevertheless you imagine that you can understand a book which has been the
guide of past and present generations, when you for a moment withdraw from
your lusts and appetites, and glance over its contents as if you were reading
a historical work or some poetical composition. Collect your thoughts and
examine the matter carefully, for it is not to be understood as you at first
sight think, but as you will find after due deliberation ; namely, the intellect
which was granted to man as the highest endowment, was bestowed on him
before his disobedience. With reference to this gift the Bible states that
" man was created in the form and likeness of God." On account of this gift
of intellect man was addressed by God, and received His commandments, as
it is said : " And the Lord God commanded Adam " (Gen. ii. 16)—for no
commandments are given to the brute creation or to those who are devoid of
understanding. Through the intellect man distinguishes between the true
and the false. This faculty Adam possessed perfectly and completely. The
right and the wrong are terms employed in the science of apparent truths
(morals), not in that of necessary truths, as, e.g , it is not correct to say, in
reference to the proposition " the heavens are spherical," it is " good " or to
declare the assertion that " the earth is flat " to be " bad " ; but we say of
the one it is true, of the other it is false. Similarly our language expresses
the idea of true and false by the terms *emet* and *sheker*, of the morally right
and the morally wrong, by *tob* and *ra'*. Thus it is the function of the intellect to discriminate between the true and the false—a distinction which is
applicable to all objects of intellectual perception. When Adam was yet in
a state of innocence, and was guided solely by reflection and reason—on
account of which it is said : " Thou hast made him (man) little lower than
the angels " (Ps. viii. 6)—he was not at all able to follow or to understand
the principles of apparent truths ; the most manifest impropriety, viz., to
appear in a state of nudity, was nothing unbecoming according to his idea: he
could not comprehend why it should be so. After man's disobedience, however, when he began to give way to desires which had their source in his
imagination and to the gratification of his bodily appetites, as it is said," And
the wife saw that the tree was good for food and delightful to the eyes "
(Gen. iii. 6), he was punished by the loss of part of that intellectual faculty
which he had previously possessed. He therefore transgressed a command
with which he had been charged on the score of his reason ; and having obtained a knowledge of the apparent truths, he was wholly absorbed in the
study of what is proper and what improper. Then he fully understood the
magnitude of the loss he had sustained, what he had forfeited, and in what
situation he was thereby placed. Hence we read, " And ye shall be like

elohim, knowing good and evil," and not "knowing" or "discerning the true and the false": while in necessary truths we can only apply the words "true and false," not "good and evil." Further observe the passage, "And the eyes of both were opened, and they knew they were naked" (Gen. iii. 7): it is not said, "And the eyes of both were opened, and they *saw*"; for what the man had seen previously and what he saw after this circumstance was precisely the same; there had been no blindness which was now removed, but he received a new faculty whereby he found things wrong which previously he had not regarded as wrong. Besides, you must know that the Hebrew word *pakaḥ* used in this passage is exclusively employed in the figurative sense of receiving new sources of knowledge, not in that of regaining the sense of sight. Comp., "God opened her eyes" (Gen. xxi. 19). "Then shall the eyes of the blind be opened" (Isaiah xxxviii. 8). "Open ears, he heareth not" (ibid. xlii. 20), similar in sense to the verse, "Which have eyes to see, and see not" (Ezek. xii. 2). When, however, Scripture says of Adam, "He changed his face (*panav*) and thou sentest him forth" (Job xiv. 20), it must be understood in the following way: On account of the change of his original aim he was sent away. For *panim,* the Hebrew equivalent of face, is derived from the verb *panah,* "he turned," and signifies also "aim," because man generally turns his face towards the thing he desires. In accordance with this interpretation, our text suggests that Adam, as he altered his intention and directed his thoughts to the acquisition of what he was forbidden, he was banished from Paradise: this was his punishment; it was measure for measure. At first he had the privilege of tasting pleasure and happiness, and of enjoying repose and security; but as his appetites grew stronger, and he followed his desires and impulses, (as we have already stated above), and partook of the food he was forbidden to taste, he was deprived of everything, was doomed to subsist on the meanest kind of food, such as he never tasted before, and this even only after exertion and labour, as it is said, "Thorns and thistles shall grow up for thee" (Gen. iii. 18), "By the sweat of thy brow," etc., and in explanation of this text continues, "And the Lord God drove him from the Garden of Eden, to till the ground whence he was taken." He was now with respect to food and many other requirements brought to the level of the lower animals; comp., "Thou shalt eat the grass of the field" (Gen. iii. 18). Reflecting on his condition, the Psalmist says, "Adam unable to dwell in dignity, was brought to the level of the dumb beast" (Ps. xlix. 13).

"May the Almighty be praised, whose design and wisdom cannot be fathomed."

CHAPTER III

It might be thought that the Hebrew words *temunah* and *tabnit* have one and the same meaning, but this is not the case. *Tabnit,* derived from the verb *banah* (he built), signifies the build and construction of a thing—that is to say, its figure, whether square, round, triangular, or of any other shape. Comp. "the pattern (*tabnit*) of the Tabernacle and the pattern (*tabnit*) of all its vessels" (Exod. xxv. 9); "according to the pattern (*tabnit*) which thou wast shown upon the mount" (Exod. xxv. 40); "the form of any bird" (Deut. iv. 17); "the form (*tabnit*) of a hand" (Ezek. viii. 3); "the pattern (*tabnit*) of the porch " (1 Chron. xxviii. 11). In all these quotations it is the shape which is referred to. Therefore the Hebrew language never employs the word *tabnit* in speaking of the qualities of God Almighty.

The term *temunah*, on the other hand, is used in the Bible in three different senses. It signifies, first, the outlines of things which are perceived by our bodily senses, i.e., their shape and form ; as, e.g., " And ye make an image the form (*temunat*) of some likeness " (Deut. iv. 16) ; " for ye saw no likeness " (*temunah*) (Deut. iv. 15). Secondly, the forms of our imagination, i.e., the impressions retained in imagination when the objects have ceased to affect our senses. In this sense it is used in the passage which begins " In thoughts from the visions of the night " (Job iv. 13), and which concludes " it remained but I could not recognize its sight, only an image—*temunah*— was before my eyes," i.e., an image which presented itself to my sight during sleep. Thirdly, the true form of an object, which is perceived only by the intellect : and it is in this third signification that the term is applied to God. The words " And the similitude of the Lord shall he behold " (Num. xii. 8) therefore mean " he shall comprehend the true essence of the Lord."

CHAPTER IV

THE three verbs *raah*, *hibbit*, and *ḥazah*, which denote " he perceived with the eye," are also used figuratively in the sense of intellectual perception. As regards the first of these verbs this is well known, e.g., " And he looked (*va-yar*) and behold a well in the field " (Gen. xxix. 2) : here it signifies ocular perception ; " yea, my heart has seen (*raah*) much of wisdom and of knowledge " (Eccles. i. 16) ; in this passage it refers to the intellectual perception.

In this figurative sense the verb is to be understood, when applied to God ; e.g., " I saw (*raïti*) the Lord " (1 Kings xxii. 19) ; " And the Lord appeared (*va-yera*) unto him " (Gen. xviii. 1) ; " And God saw (*va-yar*) that it was good " (Gen. i. 10) ; " I beseech thee, show me (*hareni*) thy glory " (Exod. xxxiii. 18) ; " And they saw (*va-yiru*) the God of Israel " (Exod. xxiv. 10). All these instances refer to intellectual perception, and by no means to perception with the eye as in its literal meaning : for, on the one hand, the eye can only perceive a corporeal object, and in connection with it certain accidents, as colour, shape, etc. ; and, on the other hand, God does not perceive by means of a corporeal organ, as will be explained.

In the same manner the Hebrew *hibbit* signifies "he viewed" with the eye ; comp. " Look (*tabbit*) not behind thee " (Gen. xix. 17) ; " But his wife looked (*va-tabbet*) back from him " (Gen. xix. 26) ; " And if one look (*ve-nibbat*) unto the land " (Isa. v. 30) ; and figuratively, " to view and observe " with the intellect, " to contemplate " a thing till it be understood. In this sense the verb is used in passages like the following : " He hath not beheld (*hibbit*) iniquity in Jacob " (Num. xxiii. 21) ; for " iniquity " cannot be seen with the eye. The words, " And they looked (*ve-hibbitu*) after Moses " (Exod. xxxiii. 8)—in addition to the literal understanding of the phrase— were explained by our Sages in a figurative sense. According to them, these words mean that the Israelites examined and criticised the actions and sayings of Moses. Compare also " Contemplate (*habbet*), I pray thee, the heaven "

(Gen. xv. 5) ; for this took place in a prophetic vision. This verb, when applied to God, is employed in this figurative sense ; e.g., " to look (*me-habbit*) upon God " (Exod. iii. 6) ; " And the similitude of the Lord shall he behold " (*yabbit*) (Num. xii. 8) ; " And thou canst not look (*habbet*) on iniquity " (Hab. i. 13).

The same explanation applies to *ḥazah*. It denotes to view with the eye, as : " And let our eye look (*ve-taḥaz*) upon Zion " (Mic. iv. 11) ; and also figuratively, to perceive mentally : " which he saw (*ḥazah*) concerning Judah and Jerusalem " (Isa. i. 1) ; " The word of the Lord came unto Abraham in a vision " (*maḥazeh*) (Gen. xv. 1) : in this sense *ḥazah* is used in the phrase, " Also they saw (*va-yeḥezu*) God " (Exod. xxiv. 11). Note this well.

CHAPTER V

When the chief of philosophers [Aristotle] was about to inquire into some very profound subjects, and to establish his theory by proofs, he commenced his treatise with an apology, and requested the reader to attribute the author's inquiries not to presumption, vanity, egotism, or arrogance, as though he were interfering with things of which he had no knowledge, but rather to his zeal and his desire to discover and establish true doctrines, as far as lay in human power. We take the same position, and think that a man, when he commences to speculate, ought not to embark at once on a subject so vast and important ; he should previously adapt himself to the study of the several branches of science and knowledge, should most thoroughly refine his moral character and subdue his passions and desires, the offspring of his imagination ; when, in addition, he has obtained a knowledge of the true fundamental propositions, a comprehension of the several methods of inference and proof, and the capacity of guarding against fallacies, then he may approach the investigation of this subject. He must, however, not decide any question by the first idea that suggests itself to his mind, or at once direct his thoughts and force them to obtain a knowledge of the Creator, but he must wait modestly and patiently, and advance step by step.

In this sense we must understand the words " And Moses hid his face, for he was afraid to look upon God " (Exod. iii. 6), though retaining also the literal meaning of the passage, that Moses was afraid to gaze at the light which appeared to his eye ; but it must on no account be assumed that the Being which is exalted far above every imperfection can be perceived by the eye. This act of Moses was highly commended by God, who bestowed on him a well deserved portion of His goodness, as it is said : " And the similitude of the Lord shall he behold " (Num. xii. 8). This, say our Sages, was the reward for having previously hidden his face, lest he should gaze at the Eternal. (*Talm. B. Berakot F a.*)

But " the nobles of the Children of Israel " were impetuous, and allowed their thoughts to go unrestrained : what they perceived was but imperfect. Therefore it is said of them, " And they saw the God of Israel, and there was under his feet," etc. (Exod. xxiv. 10) ; and not merely, " and they saw the God of Israel " ; the purpose of the whole passage is to criticize their act of seeing and not to describe it. They are blamed for the nature of their perception, which was to a certain extent corporeal—a result which necessarily followed, from the fact that they ventured too far before being perfectly prepared. They deserved to perish, but at the intercession of Moses this fate was averted by God for the time. They were afterwards burnt at Taberah, except Nadab and Abihu, who were burnt in the Tabernacle of the congregation, according to what is stated by authentic tradition. (*Midr. Rabba ad locum.*)

If such was the case with them, how much more is it incumbent on us who are inferior, and on those who are below us, to persevere in perfecting our knowledge of the elements, and in rightly understanding the preliminaries which purify the mind from the defilement of error ; then we may enter the holy and divine camp in order to gaze : as the Bible says, " And let the priests also, which come near to the Lord, sanctify themselves, lest the Lord break forth upon them " (Exod. xix. 22). Solomon, also, has cautioned all who endeavour to attain this high degree of knowledge in the following figurative terms, " Keep thy foot when thou goest to the house of God " (Eccles. iv. 17).

I will now return to complete what I commenced to explain. The nobles of the Children of Israel, besides erring in their perception, were, through this cause, also misled in their actions ; for in consequence of their confused perception, they gave way to bodily cravings. This is meant by the words, " Also they saw God and did eat and drink " (Exod. xxiv. 11). The principal part of that passage, viz., " And there was under his feet as it were a paved work of a sapphire stone " (Exod. xxiv. 10), will be further explained in the course of the present treatise (ch. xxviii.). All we here intend to say is, that wherever in a similar connection any one of the three verbs mentioned above occurs, it has reference to intellectual perception, not to the sensation of sight by the eye ; for God is not a being to be perceived by the eye.

It will do no harm, however, if those who are unable to comprehend what we here endeavour to explain should refer all the words in question to sensuous perception, to seeing lights created [for the purpose], angels, or similar beings.

CHAPTER VI

THE two Hebrew nouns *ish* and *ishshah* were originally employed to designate the " male and female " of human beings, but were afterwards applied to the " male and female " of the other species of the animal creation. For instance, we read, " Of every clean beast thou shalt take to thee by sevens," *ish ve-ishto* (Gen. vii. 2), in the same sense as *ish ve-ishshah*, " male and female." The term *zakar u-nekebah* was afterwards applied to anything designed and prepared for union with another object Thus we read, " The five curtains shall be coupled together, one (*ishshah*) to the other " (*ahotah*) (Exod. xxvi. 3).

It will easily be seen that the Hebrew equivalents for " brother and sister " are likewise treated as homonyms, and used, in a figurative sense, like *ish* and *ishshah*.

CHAPTER VII

IT is well known that the verb *yalad* means " to bear," " they have born (*ve-yaledu*) him children " (Deut. xxi. 15). The word was next used in a figurative sense with reference to various objects in nature, meaning, " to create," e.g. " before the mountains were created " (*yulladu*) (Ps. xc. 2) ; also, " to produce," in reference to that which the earth causes to come forth as if by birth, e.g., " He will cause her to bear (*holidah*) and bring forth " (Isa. lv. 10). The verb further denotes, " to bring forth," said of changes in the process of time, as though they were things which were born, e.g., " for thou knowest not what a day may bring forth " (*yeled*) (Prov. xxvii. 1). Another figurative use of the word is its application to the formation of thoughts and ideas, or of opinions resulting from them ; comp. " and brought forth (*ve-yalad*) falsehood " (Ps. vii. 14) ; also, " and they please themselves in the children (*yalde*) of strangers " (Isa. ii. 6), i.e., " they delight in the opinions of strangers." Jonathan the son of Uzziel paraphrases this passage, " they walk in the customs of other nations."

A man who has instructed another in any subject, and has improved his knowledge, may in like manner be regarded as the parent of the person taught, because he is the author of that knowledge ; and thus the pupils of the prophets are called " sons of the prophets," as I shall explain when treating of the homonymity of *ben* (son). In this figurative sense, the verb *yalad* (to bear) is employed when it is said of Adam, " And Adam lived an hundred and thirty years, and begat (*va-yoled*) a son in his own likeness, in his form " (Gen. v. 3). As regards the words, " the form of Adam, and his likeness," we have already stated (ch. i.) their meaning. Those sons of Adam who were born before that time were not human in the true sense of the word, they had not " the form of man." With reference to Seth who had been instructed, enlightened and brought to human perfection, it could rightly be said, " he (Adam) begat *a son* in his likeness, in his form." It is acknowledged that a man who does not possess this " form " (the nature of which has just been explained) is not human, but a mere animal in human shape and form. Yet such a creature has the power of causing harm and injury : a power which does not belong to other creatures. For those gifts of intelligence and judgment with which he has been endowed for the purpose of acquiring perfection, but which he has failed to apply to their proper aim, are used by him for wicked and mischievous ends ; he begets evil things, as though he merely resembled man, or simulated his outward appearance. Such was the condition of those sons of Adam who preceded Seth. In reference to this subject the Midrash says : " During the 130 years when Adam was under rebuke he begat spirits, i.e., demons ; when, however, he was again restored to divine favour " he begat in his likeness, in his form." This is the sense of the passage, " Adam lived one hundred and thirty years, and he begat in his likeness, in his form " (Gen. v. 3).

CHAPTER VIII

ORIGINALLY the Hebrew term *makom* (place) applied both to a particular spot and to space in general ; subsequently it received a wider signification and denoted " position," or " degree," as regards the perfection of man in certain things. We say, e.g., this man occupies a certain place in such and such a subject. In this sense this term, as is well known, is frequently used by authors, e.g., " He fills his ancestors' place (*makom*) in point of wisdom and piety " ; " the dispute still remains in its place " (*makom*), i.e., *in statu quo* [*ante*]. In the verse, " Blessed be the glory of the Lord from His place " (*mekomo*) (Ezek. iii. 12), *makom* has this figurative meaning, and the verse may be paraphrased " Blessed be the Lord according to the exalted nature of His existence," and wherever *makom* is applied to God, it expresses the same idea, namely, the distinguished position of His existence, to which nothing is equal or comparable, as will be shown below (chap. lvi.).

It should be observed that when we treat in this work of any homonym, we do not desire you to confine yourself to that which is stated in that particular chapter ; but we open for you a portal and direct your attention to those significations of the word which are suited to our purpose, though they may not be complete from a philological point of view. You should examine the prophetical books and other works composed by men of science, notice the meaning of every word which occurs in them, and take homonyms in that sense which is in harmony with the context. What I say in a particular passage is a key for the comprehension of all similar passages. For example, we have explained here *makom* in the sentence " Blessed be the glory of the Lord from His place " (*mekomo*) ; but you must understand that the word *makom* has the same signification in the passage " Behold, a place (*makom*) is with me " (Exod. xxxiii. 26), viz., a certain degree of contemplation and intellectual intuition (not of ocular inspection), in addition to its literal meaning " a place," viz., the mountain which was pointed out to Moses for seclusion and for the attainment of perfection.

CHAPTER IX

THE original meaning of the word *kisse*, " throne," requires no comment. Since men of greatness and authority, as, e.g., kings, use the throne as a seat, and " the throne " thus indicates the rank, dignity, and position of the person for whom it is made, the Sanctuary has been styled " the throne," inasmuch as it likewise indicates the superiority of Him who manifests Himself, and causes His light and glory to dwell therein. Comp. " A glorious throne on high from the beginning is the place of our sanctuary " (Jer. xvii.12). For the same reason the heavens are called " throne," for to the mind of him who observes them with intelligence they suggest the Omnipotence of the Being which has called them into existence, regulates their motions, and governs the sublunary world by their beneficial influence : as we read, " Thus saith the Lord, The heavens are my throne and the earth my footstool " (Isa. lxvi. 1) ; i.e., they testify to my Existence, my Essence, and my Omnipotence, as the throne testifies to the greatness of him who is worthy to occupy it.

This is the idea which true believers should entertain ; not, however, that the Omnipotent, Supreme God is supported by any material object ; for God is incorporeal, as we shall prove further on ; how, then, can He be said to occupy any space, or rest on a body ? The fact which I wish to point out is this : every place distinguished by the Almighty, and chosen to receive His light and splendour, as, for instance, the Sanctuary or the Heavens, is termed " throne " ; and, taken in a wider sense, as in the passage " For my hand is upon the throne of God " (Exod. xvii. 16), " the throne " denotes here the Essence and Greatness of God. These, however (the Essence and Greatness of God) need not be considered as something separate from the God Himself or as part of the Creation, so that God would appear to have existed both without the throne, and with the throne; such a belief would be undoubtedly heretical. It is distinctly stated, "Thou, O Lord, remainest for ever; Thy throne from generation to generation" (Lam. v. 19). By "Thy throne" we must, therefore, understand something inseparable from God. On that account, both here and in all similar passages, the word "throne" denotes God's Greatness and Essence, which are inseparable from His Being.

Our opinion will be further elucidated in the course of this Treatise.

CHAPTER X

WE have already remarked that when we treat in this work of homonyms, we have not the intention to exhaust the meanings of a word (for this is not a philological treatise); we shall mention no other significations but those which bear on our subject. We shall thus proceed in our treatment of the terms 'alah and yarad.

These two words, 'alah, "he went up," and yarad, "he went down," are Hebrew terms used in the sense of ascending and descending. When a body moves from a higher to a lower place, the verb yarad, "to go down," is used; when it moves from a lower to a higher place, 'alah, "to go up," is applied. These two verbs were afterwards employed with regard to greatness and power. When a man falls from his high position, we say "he has come down," and when he rises in station "he has gone up." Thus the Almighty says, "The stranger that is within thee shall get up above thee very high, and thou shalt come down very low" (Deut. xxviii. 43). Again, "The Lord thy God will set thee on high ('elyon) above all nations of the earth" (Deut. xxviii. 1): "And the Lord magnified Solomon exceedingly" (lema'alah) (1 Chron. xxix. 25). The Sages often employ these expressions, as: "In holy matters men must ascend (ma'alin) and not descend (moridin)." The two words are also applied to intellectual processes, namely, when we reflect on something beneath ourselves we are said to go down, and when our attention is raised to a subject above us we are said to rise.

Now, we occupy a lowly position, both in space and rank in comparison with the heavenly sphere, and the Almighty is Most High not in space, but with respect to absolute existence, greatness and power. When it pleased the Almighty to grant to a human being a certain degree of wisdom or prophetic inspiration, the divine communication thus made to the prophet and the entrance of the Divine Presence into a certain place is termed (yeridah), "descending," while the termination of the prophetic communication or the departure of the divine glory from a place is called 'aliyah, "ascending."

The expressions "to go up" and "to go down," when used in reference to God, must be interpreted in this sense. Again, when, in accordance with the divine will, some misfortune befalls a nation or a region of the earth, and when the biblical account of that misfortune is preceded by the statement that the Almighty visited the actions of the people, and that He punished

them accordingly, then the prophetic author employs the term " to descend " :
for man is so low and insignificant that his actions would not be visited and
would not bring punishment on him, were it not for the divine will : as is
clearly stated in the Bible, with regard to this idea, " What is man that thou
shouldst remember him, and the son of man that thou shouldst visit him "
(Ps. viii. 5).

The design of the Deity to punish man is, therefore, introduced by the
verb " to descend "; comp. " Go to, let us go down and there confound
their language " (Gen. xi. 7); " And the Lord came down to see " (Gen. xi.
5); " I will go down now and see " (Gen. xviii. 21). All these instances
convey the idea that man here below is going to be punished.

More numerous, however, are the instances of the first case, viz., in which
these verbs are used in connection with the revelation of the word and of the
glory of God, e.g., " And I will come down and talk with thee there " (Num.
xi. 17); " And the Lord came down upon Mount Sinai " (Exod. xix. 20);
" The Lord will come down in the sight of all the people " (Exod. xix. 11);
" And God went up from him " (Gen. xxxv. 13); " And God went up from
Abraham " (Gen. xvii. 22). When, on the other hand, it says, " And Moses
went up unto God " (Exod. xix. 3), it must be taken in the third signification
of these verbs, in addition to its literal meaning that Moses also ascended to
the top of the mount, upon which a certain material light (the manifestation
of God's glory) was visible ; but we must not imagine that the Supreme
Being occupies a place to which we can ascend, or from which we can descend.
He is far from what the ignorant imagine.

CHAPTER XI

THE primary meaning of the Hebrew *yashab* is " he was seated," as " Now
Eli the priest sat (*yashab*) upon a seat " (1 Sam. i. 9) ; but, since a person can
best remain motionless and at rest when sitting, the term was applied to
everything that is permanent and unchanging ; thus, in the promise that
Jerusalem should remain constantly and permanently in an exalted condition,
it is stated, " She will rise and sit in her place " (Zech. xiv. 10) ; further,
" He maketh the woman who was childless to sit as a joyful mother of children " (Ps. cxiii. 9) ; i.e., He makes her happy condition to be permanent
and enduring.

When applied to God, the verb is to be taken in that latter sense :
" Thou O Lord, remainest (*tesheb*) for ever " (Lam. v. 19) ; " O thou
who sittest (*ha-yoshebi*) in the heavens " (Ps. cxxiii. 1) ; " He who sitteth
in the heavens " (ii. 4), i.e., He who is everlasting, constant, and in no
way subject to change ; immutable in His Essence, and as He consists of
nought but His Essence, He is mutable in no way whatever ; not mutable
in His relation to other things ; for there is no relation whatever existing
between Him and any other being, as will be explained below, and therefore
no change as regards such relations can take place in Him. Hence He is
immutable in every respect, as He expressly declares, " I, the Lord, do not
change " (Mal. iii. 6) ; i.e., in Me there is not any change whatever. This
idea is expressed by the term *yashab* when referring to God.

The verb, when employed of God, is frequently complemented by " the Heavens," inasmuch as the heavens are without change or mutation, that is to say, they do not individually change, as the individual beings on earth, by transition from existence into non-existence.

The verb is also employed in descriptions of God's relation (the term " relation " is here used as a homonym) to existing *species* of evanescent things ; for those species are as constant, well organized, and unvarying as the individuals of the heavenly hosts. Thus we find, " Who sitteth over the circle of the earth " (Isa. xl. 22), Who remains constantly and unremittingly over the sphere of the earth; that is to say, over the things that come into existence within that sphere.

Again, " The Lord sitteth upon the flood " (Ps. xxix. 10), i.e., despite the change and variation of earthly objects, no change takes place with respect to God's relation (to the earth) : His relation to each of the things which come into existence and perish again is stable and constant, for it concerns only the existing species and not the individuals. It should therefore be borne in mind, that whenever the term " sitting " is applied to God, it is used in this sense.

CHAPTER XII

THE term *kam* (he rose) is a homonym. In one of its significations it is the opposite of " to sit," as " He did not rise (*kam*) nor move for him " (Esth. v. 9). It further denotes the confirmation and verification of a thing, e.g. : " The Lord will verify (*yakem*) His promise " (1 Sam. i. 23) ; " The field of Ephron was made sure (*va-yakom*) as the property of Abraham " (Gen. xxiii. 17). " The house that is in the walled city shall be established (*ve-kam*) " (Lev. xxv. 30) ; " And the kingdom of Israel shall be firmly established (*ve-kamah*) in thy hand " (1 Sam. xxiv. 20). It is always in this sense that the verb is employed with reference to the Almighty ; as " Now shall I rise (*akum*), saith the Lord " (Ps. xii. 7), which is the same as saying, " Now shall I verify my word and my dispensation for good or evil." " Thou shalt arise (*takum*) and have mercy upon Zion " (Ps. cii. 13), which means : Thou wilt establish what thou hast promised, viz., that thou wouldst pity Zion.

Generally a person who resolves to set about a matter, accompanies his resolve by rising, hence the verb is employed to express " to resolve " to do a certain thing ; as, " That my son hath stirred up my servant against me " (1 Sam. xxii. 8). The word is figuratively used to signify the execution of a divine decree against a people sentenced to extermination, as " And I will rise against the house of Jeroboam " (Amos vii. 9) ; " but he will arise against the house of the evildoers " (Isa. xxxi. 2). Possibly in Psalm xii. 7 the verb has this latter sense, as also in Psalm cii. 13, namely : Thou wilt rise up against her enemies.

There are many passages to be interpreted in this manner, but in no way should it be understood that He rises or sits—far be such a notion ! Our Sages expressed this idea in the formula, " In the world above there is neither sitting nor standing (*'amidah*) " ; for the two verbs *'amad* and *kam* are synonyms [and what is said about the former is also applicable to the latter].

CHAPTER XIII

THE term *'amad* (he stood) is a homonym signifying in the first instance " to stand upright," as " When he stood (*be-'omdo*) before Pharaoh " (Gen. xli. 46) ; " Though Moses and Samuel stood (*ya'amod*) " (Jer. xv. 1) ; " He stood by them " (Gen. xviii. 8). It further denotes " cessation and interruption," as " but they stood still (*'amedu*) and answered no more " (Job xxxii. 16) ; " and she ceased (*va-ta'amod*) to bear " (Gen. xxix. 35). Next it signifies " to be enduring and lasting," as, " that they may continue (*yo-'amedu*) many days " (Jer. xxxii. 14) ; " Then shalt thou be able to endure (*'amod*) " (Exod. xviii. 23) ; " His taste remained (*'amad*) in him " (Jer. xlviii. 11), i.e., it has continued and remained in existence without any change ; " His righteousness standeth for ever " (Ps. cxi. 3), i.e., it is permanent and everlasting. The verb applied to God must be understood in this latter sense, as in Zechariah xiv. 4, " And his feet shall stand (*ve-'amedu*) in that day upon the Mount of Olives " (Zech. xiv. 4), " His causes, i.e., the events of which He is the cause, will remain efficient," etc. This will be further elucidated when we speak of the meaning of *regel* (foot). (*Vide infra*, chap. xxviii.) In the same sense is this verb employed in Deuteronomy v. 28, " But as for thee, stand thou here by me," and Deuteronomy v. 5, " I stood between the Lord and you."

CHAPTER XIV

THE homonymous term *adam* is in the first place the name of the first man, being, as Scripture indicates, derived from *adamah*, "earth." Next, it means " mankind," as " My spirit shall not strive with man (*adam*) " (Gen. vi. 3). Again " Who knoweth the spirit of the children of man (*adam*) " (Eccles. iii. 21) ; " so that a man (*adam*) has no pre-eminence above a beast " (Eccles. iii. 19). Adam signifies also " the multitude," " the lower classes " as opposed to those distinguished from the rest, as " Both low (*bene adam*) and high (*bene ish*) " (Ps. xlix. 3).

It is in this third signification that it occurs in the verses, " The sons of the higher order (*Elohim*) saw the daughters of the lower order (*adam*) " (Gen. vi. 2) ; and " Forsooth ! as the humble man (*adam*) you shall die " (Ps. lxxxii. 7).

CHAPTER XV

ALTHOUGH the two roots *nazab* and *yazab* are distinct, yet their meaning is, as you know, identical in all their various forms.

The verb has several meanings : in some instances it signifies " to stand " or " to place oneself," as " And his sister stood (*va-tetazzab*) afar off " (Exod. ii. 4) ; " The kings of the earth set themselves " (*yityazzebu*) (Ps. ii. 2) ; " They came out and stood " (*nizzabim*) (Num. xvi. 27). In other instances it denotes continuance and permanence, as, " Thy word is established (*nizzab*) in Heaven " (Ps. cxix. 89), i.e., it remains for ever.

Whenever this term is applied to God it must be understood in the latter sense, as, " And, behold, the Lord stood (*nizzab*) upon it " (Gen. xxviii. 13), i.e., appeared as eternal and everlasting " upon it," namely, upon the ladder, the upper end of which reached to heaven, while the lower end touched the earth. This ladder all may climb up who wish to do so, and they must ultimately attain to a knowledge of Him who is above the summit of the ladder, because He remains upon it permanently. It must be well understood that the term " upon it " is employed by me in harmony with this metaphor. " Angels of God " who were going up represent the prophets. That the term " angel " was applied to prophets may clearly be seen in the following passages : " He sent an angel " (Num. xx. 16) ; " And an angel of the Lord came up from Gilgal to Bochim" (Judges ii. 1). How suggestive, too, is the expression " ascending and descending on it " ! The ascent is mentioned before the descent, inasmuch as the " ascending " and arriving at a certain height of the ladder precedes the " descending," i.e., the application of the knowledge acquired in the ascent for the training and instruction of mankind. This application is termed " descent," in accordance with our explanation of the term *yarad* (chapter x.).

To return to our subject. The phrase " stood upon it " indicates the permanence and constancy of God, and does not imply the idea of physical position. This is also the sense of the phrase " Thou shalt stand upon the rock " (Exod. xxxiii. 21). It is therefore clear that *nizzab* and *'amad* are identical in this figurative signification. Comp. " Behold, I will stand (*'omed*) before thee there upon the rock in Horeb " (Exod. xvii. 6).

CHAPTER XVI

THE word *zur* (rock) is a homonym. First, it denotes " rock," as " And thou shalt smite the rock " (*zur*) (Exod. xvii. 6). Then, " hard stone," like the flint, e.g., " Knives of stone " (*zurim*) (Josh. v. 2). It is next employed to signify the quarry from which the stones are hewn ; comp. " Look unto the rock (*zur*) whence ye are hewn " (Isa. li. 1). From this latter meaning of the term another figurative notion was subsequently derived, viz., " the root and origin " of all things. It is on this account that after the words " Look to the rock whence ye are hewn," the Prophet continues, " Look unto Abraham your father," from which we evidently may infer that the words " Abraham your father " serve to explain " the rock whence ye are hewn " ; and that the Prophet meant to say, " Walk in his ways, put faith in his instruction, and conduct yourselves according to the rule of his life ! for the properties contained in the quarry should be found again in those things which are formed and hewn out of it."

It is in the latter sense that the Almighty is called " rock," He being the origin and the *causa efficiens* of all things besides Himself. Thus we read, " He is the Rock, His work is perfect " (Deut. xxxii. 4) ; " Of the Rock that begat thee thou art unmindful " (Deut. xxxii. 18) ; " Their Rock had sold them " (xxxi. 30) ; " There is no rock like our God " (1 Sam. ii. 2) : " The Rock of Eternity " (Isa. xxvi. 4). Again, " And thou shalt stand upon the Rock " (Exod. xxxiii. 21), i.e., Be firm and steadfast in the conviction that God is the source of all things, for this will lead you towards the knowledge of the Divine Being. We have shown (chap. viii.) that the words " Behold, a place is with me " (Exod. xxxiii. 21) contain the same idea.

CHAPTER XVII

Do not imagine that only Metaphysics should be taught with reserve to the common people and to the uninitiated ; for the same is also the case with the greater part of Natural Science. In this sense we have repeatedly made use of the expression of the Sages, " Do not expound the chapter on the Creation in the presence of two " [*vide* Introd. page 2]. This principle was not peculiar to our Sages ; ancient philosophers and scholars of other nations were likewise wont to treat of the *principia rerum* obscurely, and to use figurative language in discussing such subjects. Thus Plato and his predecessors called Substance the female, and Form the male. (You are aware that the *principia* of all existing transient things are three, viz., Substance, Form, and Absence of a particular form ; the last-named principle is always inherent in the substance, for otherwise the substance would be incapable of receiving a new form ; and it is from this point of view that absence [of a particular form] is included among the *principia*. As soon, then, as a substance has received a certain form, the privation of that form, namely, of that which has just been received, has ceased, and is replaced by the privation of another form, and so on with all possible forms, as is explained in treatises on natural philosophy.) —Now, if those philosophers who have nothing to fear from a lucid explanation of these metaphysical subjects still were in the habit of discussing them in figures and metaphors, how much more should we, having the interest of religion at heart, refrain from elucidating to the mass any subject that is beyond their comprehension, or that might be taken in a sense directly opposite to the one intended. This also deserves attention.

CHAPTER XVIII

THE three words *karab*, " to come near," *naga'*, " to touch," and *nagash*, "to approach," sometimes signify " contact " or " nearness in space," sometimes the approach of man's knowledge to an object, as if it resembled the physical approach of one body to another. As to the use of *karab* in the first meaning, viz., to draw near a certain spot, comp. " As he drew near (*karab*) the camp " (Exod. xxxii. 19) ; " And Pharaoh drew near (*hikrib*) (Exod. xiv. 10). *Naga'*, in the first sense, viz., expressing the contact of two bodies, occurs in " And she cast it (*va-tagga'*) at his feet " (Exod. iv. 25) ; " He caused it to touch (*va-yagga'*) my mouth " (Isa. vi. 7). And *nagash* in the first sense, viz., to approach or move towards another person, is found, e.g., in " And Judah drew near (*va-yiggash*) unto him " (Gen. xliv. 1).

The second meaning of these three words is " approach by means of knowledge," or " contact by comprehension," not in reference to space. As to *naga'* in this second sense, comp. " for her judgment reacheth (*naga'*) unto heaven " (Jer. li. 9). An instance of *karab* being used in this meaning is contained in the following passage, " And the cause that is too hard for you, bring (*takribun*) it unto me " (Deut. i. 17) ; this is equivalent to saying, " Ye shall make it known unto me." The verb *karab* (in the Hiphil) is thus employed in the sense of giving information concerning a thing. The verb *nagash* is used figuratively in the phrase, " And Abraham drew near (*va-yiggash*), and said " (Gen. xviii. 23) ; this took place in a prophetic vision and in a trance, as will be explained (Part I. chap. xxi., and Part II. chap. xli.; also in " Forasmuch as this people draw near (*niggash*) me with their mouths and with their lips " (Isa. xxix. 13). Wherever a word denoting approach or contact is employed in the prophetic writings to describe a certain relation between the Almighty and any created being, it has to be understood in this latter sense [viz., to approach mentally]. For, as will be proved in this treatise (II. chap. iv.), the Supreme is incorporeal, and consequently He does not approach or draw near a thing, nor can aught approach or touch Him ; for when a being is without corporeality, it cannot occupy space, and all idea of approach, contact, distance, conjunction, separation, touch, or proximity is inapplicable to such a being.

There can be no doubt respecting the verses " The Lord is nigh (*karob*) unto all them that call upon him " (Ps. cxlv. 18) ; " They take delight in approaching (*kirbat*) to God " (Isa. lviii. 2) ; " The nearness (*kirbat*) of God is pleasant to me " (Ps. lxxiii. 28) ; all such phrases intimate a spiritual approach, i.e., the attainment of some knowledge, not, however, approach in space. Thus also " who hath God so nigh (*kerobim*) unto him " (Deut. iv. 7) ; " Draw thou near (*kerab*) and hear " (Deut. v. 27) ; " And Moses alone shall draw near (*ve-niggash*) the Lord ; but they shall not come nigh (*yiggashu*) " (Exod. xxiv. 2).

If, however, you wish to take the words " And Moses shall draw near " to mean that he shall draw near a certain place in the mountain, whereon the Divine Light shone, or, in the words of the Bible, " where the glory of the Lord abode," you may do so, provided you do not lose sight of the truth that there is no difference whether a person stand at the centre of the earth or at the highest point of the ninth sphere, if this were possible ; he is no further away from God in the one case, or nearer to Him in the other ; those only approach Him who obtain a knowledge of Him ; while those who remain ignorant of Him recede from Him. In this approach towards, or recession from God there are numerous grades one above the other, and I shall further elucidate, in one of the subsequent chapters of the Treatise (I. chap. lx., and II. chap. xxxvi.) what constitutes the difference in our perception of God.

In the passage, " Touch (*ga'*) the mountains, and they shall smoke " (Ps. cxliv. 5), the verb " touch " is used in a figurative sense, viz., " Let thy word touch them." So also the words, " Touch thou him himself " (Job ii. 5), have the same meaning as " Bring thy infliction upon him." In a similar manner must this verb, in whatever form it may be employed, be interpreted in each place, according to the context ; for in some cases it denotes contact of two material objects, in others knowledge and comprehension of a thing, as if he who now comprehends anything which he had not comprehended previously had thereby approached a subject which had been distant from him. This point is of considerable importance.

CHAPTER XIX

THE term *male* is a homonym which denotes that one substance enters another, and fills it, as " And she filled (*va-temalle*) her pitcher " (Gen. xxiv. 16) ; " An omer-full (*melo*) for each " (Exod. xvi. 32), and many other instances. Next, it signifies the expiration or completion of a fixed period

of time, as " And when her days to be delivered were fulfilled (*va-yimleü*) "
(Gen. xxv. 24) ; " And forty days were completed (*va-yimleü*) for him "
(Gen. l. 3). It further denotes attainment of the highest degree of excellency, as " Full (*male*) with the blessing of the Lord " (Deut. xxxiii. 23) ;
" Them hath he filled (*mille*) with wisdom of heart " (Exod. xxxv. 35) ; " He
was filled (*va-yimmale*) with wisdom, and understanding, and cunning "
(1 Kings vii. 14). In this sense it is said " The whole earth is full (*melo*) of
his glory " (Isa. vi. 4), " All the earth gives evidence of his perfection,"
i.e. leads to a knowledge of it. Thus also " The glory of the Lord filled
(*male*) the tabernacle " (Exod. xl. 34) ; and, in fact, every application of the
word to God must be interpreted in this manner ; and not that He has a
body occupying space. If, on the other hand, you prefer to think that in
this passage by " the glory of the Lord," a certain light created for the purpose is to be understood, that such light is always termed " glory," and that
such light " filled the tabernacle," we have no objection.

CHAPTER XX

THE word *ram* (high) is a homonym, denoting elevation in space, and elevation
in dignity, i.e., greatness, honour, and power. It has the first meaning in
" And the ark was lifted up (*va-tarom*) above the earth " (Gen. vii. 17) ; and
the latter meaning in " I have exalted (*harimoti*) one chosen out of the
people " (Ps. lxxxix. 20 ; " Forasmuch as I have exalted (*harimoti*) thee from
amongst the dust " (1 Kings xvi. 2) ; " Forasmuch as I exalted (*harimoti*)
thee from among the people " (1 Kings xiv. 7).

Whenever this term is employed in reference to God, it must be taken in
the second sense : " Be thou exalted (*rumah*), O God, above the heavens "
(Ps. lvii. 12). In the same manner does the root *nasa* (to lift up) denote both
elevation in space and elevation in rank and dignity. In the former sense it occurs
in " And they lifted up (*va-yisseü*) their corn upon their asses " (Gen. xlii.
26) ; and there are many instances like this in which this verb has the meaning " to carry," " to move " from place to place ; for this implies elevation
in space. In the second sense we have " And his kingdom shall be exalted "
(*ve-tinnase*) (Num. xxiv. 7) ; " And he bare them, and carried them "
(*va-yenasseëm*) (Isa. lxiii. 9) ; " Wherefore do ye exalt yourselves " (*titnasseü*)
(Num. xvi. 3).

Every form of this verb when applied to God has this latter sense—e.g.,
" Lift up thyself (*hinnase*), thou judge of the earth " (Ps. xciv. 2) ; " Thus
saith the High (*ram*) and Exalted (*nissa*) One " (Isa. lvii. 15)—denoting elevation in rank, quality, and power, and not elevation in space.

You may be surprised that I employ the expression, " elevation in rank,
quality, and power," and you may say, " How can you assert that several
distinct expressions denote the same thing ? " It will be explained later on
(chap. l. *seqq.*) that those who possess a true knowledge of God do not consider that He possesses many attributes, but believe that these various attributes which describe His Might, Greatness, Power, Perfection, Goodness,
etc., are identical, denoting His Essence, and not anything extraneous to His
Essence. I shall devote special chapters to the Names and Attributes of

God ; our intention here is solely to show that " high and exalted " in the passage quoted denote elevation in rank, not in space.

CHAPTER XXI

In its primary signification the Hebrew *abar,* " to pass," refers to the motion of a body in space, and is chiefly applied to living creatures moving at some distance in a straight line, e.g., " And He passed over (*abar*) before them " (Gen. xxxiii. 3) ; " Pass (*abor*) before the people " (Exod. xvii. 5). Instances of this kind are numerous. The verb was next applied to the passage of sound through air, as " And they caused a sound to pass (*va-ya'abiru*) through-out the camp " (Exod. xxxvi. 6) ; " That I hear the Lord's people spreading the report " (*ma'abirim*) (1 Sam. ii. 24).

Figuratively it denoted the appearance of the Light and the Divine Presence (Shechinah) which the prophets perceived in their prophetic visions, as it is said," And behold a smoking furnace, and a burning lamp that passed (*abar*) between those pieces " (Gen. xv. 17). This took place in a prophetic vision, for the narrative commences, " And a deep sleep fell upon Abram." The verb has this latter meaning in Exodus xii. 12, " And I shall pass (*ve-'abarti*) through the land of Egypt " (denoting " I shall reveal myself," etc.), and in all similar phrases.

The verb is next employed to express that a person has gone too far, and transgressed the usual limit, in the performance of some act, as " And as a man who is drinking wine has passed (*abarv*) the proper limit " (Jer. xxiii. 9).

It is also used figuratively to denote : to abandon one aim, and turn to a different aim and object, e.g., " He shot an arrow, causing it to miss the aim (*leha'abiro*) " (1 Sam. xx. 36). This is the sense, it appears to me, of this verb in " And the Lord passed by (*va-ya'abor*) before his face " (Exod. xxxiv. 6). I take " his face " to mean " the face of God " ; our Teachers likewise interpreted " his face " as being identical with " the face of God." And, although this is found in the midst of Agadic interpretations which would be out of place in this our work, yet it is some support of our view, that the pronoun " his " is employed in this passage as a substitute for " God's "—and the whole passage could in my opinion be explained as follows : Moses sought to attain to a certain perception which is called " the perception of the Divine face," a term occurring in the phrase " My face cannot be seen " ; but God vouchsafed to him a perception of a lower degree, viz., the one called, " the seeing of the back," in the words, " And thou shalt see my back " (Exod. xxxiii. 23). We have mentioned this subject in our work *Mishneh Torah.* Accordingly, it is stated in the above-mentioned passage that the Lord withheld from Moses that perception which is termed " the seeing of the Divine face," and sub-stituted for it another gift, viz., the knowledge of the acts attributed to God, which, as I shall explain (chap. liv.) are considered to be different and separate attributes of the Supreme. In asserting that God withheld from Moses (the higher knowledge) I mean to say that this knowledge was un-attainable, that by its nature it was inaccessible to Moses ; for man, whilst able to gain perfection by applying his reasoning faculties to the attainment of what is within the reach of his intellect, either weakens his reason or loses

it altogether as soon as he ventures to seek a higher degree of knowledge—
as I shall elucidate in one of the chapters of this work—unless he be granted
a special aid from heaven, as is described in the words, " And I will cover
thee with my hand until I pass by " (Exod. xxxiii. 23).

Onkelos, in translating this verse, adopts the same method which he applies
to the explanation of similar passages, viz., every expression implying corporeality or corporal properties, when referring to God, he explains by
assuming an ellipsis of a *nomen regens* before " God," thus connecting the
expression (of corporeality) with another word which is supplied, and which
governs the genitive " God " ; e.g., " And behold the Lord stood upon it "
(Gen. xxviii. 13), he explains, " The glory of the Lord stood arrayed above
it." Again, " The Lord watch between me and thee " (Gen. xxxi. 49), he
paraphrases," The word of the Lord shall watch." This is his ordinary method
in explaining Scripture. He applies it also to Exod. xxxiv. 6, which he paraphrases, " The Lord caused his Presence to pass before his face and called."
According to this rendering the thing which passed was unquestionably
some physical object, the pronoun " his " refers to Moses, and the phrase
ʻ*al panav* is identical with *lefanav*, " before him." Comp. " So went the
present over before him " (ʻ*al panav*) (Gen. xxxii. 22). This is likewise an
appropriate and satisfactory explanation ; and I can adduce still further
support for the opinion of Onkelos from the words " while my glory passeth
by " (*ba-ʻabor*) (Exod. xxxiii. 22), which expressly state that the passing object
was something ascribed to God, not God Himself ; and of this Divine glory
it is also said, " until I pass by," and " And the Lord passed by before him."

Should it, however, be considered necessary to assume here an ellipsis,
according to the method of Onkelos, who supplies in some instances the term
" the Glory," in others " the Word," and in others " the Divine Presence,"
as the context may require in each particular case, we may also supply here
the word " voice," and explain the passage, " And a voice from the Lord
passed before him and called." We have already shown that the verb ʻ*abar*,
" he passed," can be applied to the voice, as in " And they caused a voice to
pass through the camp " (Exod. xxxvi. 6). According to this explanation,
it was the voice which called. No objection can be raised to applying the
verb *kara* (he called) to *kol* (voice), for a similar phrase occurs in the Bible
in reference to God's commands to Moses, " He heard the voice speaking
unto him " ; and, in the same manner as it can be said " the voice spoke,"
we may also say " the voice called " ; indeed, we can even support this application of the verbs " to say," and " to call," to " the voice," by parallel
passages, as " A voice saith ' Cry,' and it says ' What shall I cry ? ' " (Isa. xl. 6).
According to this view, the meaning of the passage under discussion would
be : " A voice of God passed before him and called, ' Eternal, Eternal, All-
powerful, All-merciful, and All-gracious ! ' " (The word Eternal is repeated ;
it is in the vocative, for the Eternal is the one who is called. Comp. Moses,
Moses ! Abraham, Abraham !) This, again, is a very appropriate explanation of the text.

You will surely not find it strange that this subject, so profound and difficult, should bear various interpretations ; for it will not impair the force of
the argument with which we are here concerned. Either explanation may
be adopted ; you may take that grand scene altogether as a prophetic vision,

and the whole occurrence as a mental operation, and consider that what Moses sought, what was withheld from him, and what he attained, were things perceived by the intellect without the use of the senses (as we have explained above) : or you may assume that in addition there was a certain ocular perception of a material object, the sight of which would assist intellectual perception.   The latter is the view of Onkelos, unless he assumes that in this instance the ocular perception was likewise a prophetic vision, as was the case with " a smoking furnace and a burning lamp that passed between those pieces " (Gen. xv. 17), mentioned in the history of Abraham.   You may also assume that in addition there was a perception of sound, and that there was a voice which passed before him, and was undoubtedly something material.   You may choose either of these opinions, for our sole intention and purpose is to guard you against the belief that the phrase " and the Lord passed," is analogous to " pass before the people " (Exod. xvii. 5), for God, being incorporeal, cannot be said to move, and consequently the verb " to pass " cannot with propriety be applied to Him in its primary signification.

CHAPTER XXII

In Hebrew, the verb *bo* signifies " to come " as applied to a living being, i.e., its arrival at a certain place, or approach to a certain person, as " Thy brother came (*ba*) with subtilty " (Gen. xxvii. 35).   It next denotes (with regard to a living being) " to enter " a certain place, e.g., " And when Joseph came (*va-yabo*) into the house " (Gen. xliii. 26) ; " When ye come (*ta-boü*) into the land " (Exod. xii. 25).   The term was also employed metaphorically in the sense of " to come " applied to a certain event, that is, to something incorporeal, as " When thy sayings come to pass (*yabo*) " (Judg. xiii. 17) ; " Of that which will come (*yaboü*) over thee " (Isa. xlvii. 13).   Nay, it is even applied to privatives, e.g., " Yet evil came (*va-yabo*) " '(Job iii. 26) ; " And darkness came (*va-yabo*) "   Now, since the word has been applied to incorporeal things, it has also been used in reference to God—to the fulfilment of His word, or to the manifestation of His Presence (the Shechinah).   In this figurative sense it is said, " Lo, I come (*ba*) unto thee in a thick cloud " (Exod. xix. 9) ; " For the Lord the God of Israel cometh (*ba*) through it " (Ezek. xliv. 2).   In these and all similar passages, the coming of the Shechinah is meant, but the words, " And the Lord my God shall come (*u-ba*) " (Zech. xiv. 5) are identical with " His word will come," that is to say, the promises which He made through the Prophets will be fulfilled ; therefore Scripture adds " all the holy ones that are with thee," that is to say, " The word of the Lord my God will be performed, which has been spoken by all the holy ones who are with thee, who address the Israelites."

CHAPTER XXIII

Yaza (" he came out ") is the opposite of *ba* (" he came in ").   The term *yaza* is applied to the motion of a body from a place in which it had previously rested, to another place (whether the body be a living being or not), e.g., " And when they were gone out (*yazeü*) of the city " (Gen. xliv. 4) ; " If fire break out (*teze*) " (Exod. xxii. 5).   It was then figuratively employed to denote the appearance of something incorporeal, as, " The word went out (*yaẓa*) of the king's mouth " (Esth. vii. 8) ; " When this deed of the queen shall come abroad (*yeẓe*) unto all women " (Esth. i. 17), that is to say, " the report will spread." Again, " For out of Zion shall go forth (*teẓe*) the Law " (Isa. ii. 3) ; further, " The sun had risen (*yaẓa*) upon the earth " (Gen. xix. 23), i.e., its light became visible.

In this figurative sense we must take every expression of coming out when applied to the Almighty, e.g., " Behold, the Lord cometh out (*yoẓe*) of his place " (Isa. xxvi. 21), i.e., " The word of God, which until now has been in secret, cometh out, and will become manifest," i.e., something will come into being which had not existed before ; for everything new emanating from God is ascribed to His word. Comp. " By the word of the Lord were the heavens made, and all the host of them by the breath of his mouth " (Ps. xxxiii. 6). This is a simile taken from the conduct of kings, who employ the word as the means of carrying their will into effect. God, however, requires no instrument wherewith to operate in order to perform anything ; the effect is produced solely by His will alone. He does not employ any kind of speech, as will be explained further on (chap. lv.).

The verb " to come out " is thus employed to designate the manifestation of a certain work of God, as we noticed in our interpretation of the phrase, " Behold, the Lord cometh out of his place." In a similar manner the term *shub*, " to return," has been figuratively employed to denote the discontinuance of a certain act according to the will of God, as in " I will go and return to my place " (Hosea v. 15) ; that is to say, the Divine presence (Shechinah) which had been in our midst departed from us, the consequence of which has been the absence of Divine protection from amongst us. Thus the Prophet foretelling misfortune says, " And I will hide my face from them, and they shall be devoured " (Deut. xxxi. 17) ; for, when man is deprived of Divine protection he is exposed to all dangers, and becomes the butt of all fortuitous circumstances ; his fortune and misfortune then depend on chance. Alas ! how terrible a threat !—This is the idea contained in the words, " I will go and return to my place " (Hos. v. 15).

CHAPTER XXIV

THE term *halak* is likewise one of the words which denote movements performed by living beings, as in " And Jacob went (*halak*) on his way " (Gen. xxxii. 1), and in many other instances. The verb " to go " was next employed in describing movements of objects less solid than the bodies of living beings, comp. " And the waters were going on (*halok*) decreasing " (Gen. viii. 5) ; " And the fire went along (*va-tihalak*) upon the ground " (Exod. ix. 23). Then it was employed to express the spreading and manifestation of something incorporeal, comp. " The voice thereof shall go like a serpent " (Jer. xlvi. 22) ; again, " The voice of the Lord God walking in the garden " (Gen. iii. 8). It is " the voice " that is qualified by " walking."

Whenever the word " to go " is used in reference to God, it must be taken in this figurative sense, i.e., it applies to incorporeal things, and signifies either the manifestation of something incorporeal, or the withdrawal of the Divine protection, an act corresponding in lifeless beings to the removal of a thing, in living beings to the departure of a living being, " walking." The withdrawal of God's protection is called in the Bible " the hiding of God's countenance, as in Deuteronomy xxxi. 18, " As for me, I will hide my countenance." On the same ground it has been designated " going away," or moving away from a thing, comp. " I will depart and return to my place " (Hos. v. 15). But in the passage, " And the anger of the Lord was kindled against them, and he went " (Num. xii. 9), the two meanings of the verb are combined. viz., the withdrawal of the Divine protection, expressed by " and he went," and the revelation, manifestation, and appearance of something namely, of the anger which went forth and reached them, in consequence of which Miriam became " leprous, white as snow." The expression " to walk " was further applied to conduct, which concerns only the inner life, and which requires no bodily motion, as in the following passages, " And thou shalt walk in his ways " (Deut. xxviii. 9) ; " Ye shall walk after the Lord your God " (Deut. xiii. 5) ; " Come ye, and let us walk in the light of the Lord." (Isa. ii. 5).

CHAPTER XXV

THE Hebrew *shakan*, as is well known, signifies " to dwell," as, " And he was dwelling (*shoken*) in the plains of Mamre " (Gen. xiv. 13) ; " And it came to pass, when Israel dwelt (*bishekon*) " (Gen. xxxv. 22). This is the most common meaning of the word. But " dwelling in a place " consists in the continued stay in a place, general or special ; when a living being dwells long in a place, we say that it stays in that place, although it unquestionably moves about in it, comp. " And he was staying in the plains of Mamre " (Gen. xiv. 13), and, " And it came to pass, when Israel stayed " (Gen. xxxv. 22).

The term was next applied metaphorically to inanimate objects, i.e., to everything which has settled and remains fixed on one object, although the object on which the thing remains is not a place, and the thing itself is not a living being ; for instance, " Let a cloud dwell upon it [the day] " (Job iii. 5) ; there is no doubt that the cloud is not a living being, and that the day is not a corporeal thing, but a division of time.

In this sense the term is employed in reference to God, that is to say, to denote the continuance of His Divine Presence (Shechinah) or of His Providence in some place where the Divine Presence manifested itself constantly, or in some object which was constantly protected by Providence. Comp. " And the glory of the Lord abode " (Exod. xxiv. 16) ; " And I will dwell among the children of Israel " (Exod. xxix. 45) ; " And for the goodwill of him that dwelt in the bush " (Deut. xxxiii. 16). Whenever the term is applied to the Almighty, it must be taken consistently with the context in the sense either as referring to the Presence of His Shechinah (i.e., of His light that was created for the purpose) in a certain place, or of the continuance of His Providence protecting a certain object.

CHAPTER XXVI

YOU, no doubt, know the Talmudical saying, which includes in itself all the various kinds of interpretation connected with our subject. It runs thus :

" The Torah speaks according to the language of man," that is to say, expressions, which can easily be comprehended and understood by all, are applied to the Creator. Hence the description of God by attributes implying corporeality, in order to express His existence ; because the multitude of people do not easily conceive existence unless in connection with a body, and that which is not a body nor connected with a body has for them no existence. Whatever we regard as a state of perfection, is likewise attributed to God, as expressing that He is perfect in every respect, and that no imperfection or deficiency whatever is found in Him. But there is not attributed to God anything which the multitude consider a defect or want ; thus He is never represented as eating, drinking, sleeping, being ill, using violence, and the like. Whatever, on the other hand, is commonly regarded as a state of perfection is attributed to Him, although it is only a state of perfection in relation to ourselves ; for in relation to God, what we consider to be a state of perfection, is in truth the highest degree of imperfection. If, however, men were to think that those human perfections were absent in God, they would consider Him as imperfect.

You are aware that locomotion is one of the distinguishing characteristics of living beings, and is indispensable for them in their progress towards perfection. As they require food and drink to supply animal waste, so they require locomotion, in order to approach that which is good for them and in harmony with their nature, and to escape from what is injurious and contrary to their nature. It makes, in fact, no difference whether we ascribe to God eating and drinking or locomotion ; but according to human modes of expression, that is to say, according to common notions, eating and drinking would be an imperfection in God, while motion would not, in spite of the fact that the necessity of locomotion is the result of some want. Furthermore, it has been clearly proved, that everything which moves is corporeal and divisible ; it will be shown below that God is incorporeal and that He can have no locomotion ; nor can rest be ascribed to Him ; for rest can only be applied to that which also moves. All expressions, however, which imply the various modes of movement in living beings, are employed with regard to God in the manner we have described and in the same way as life is ascribed to Him ; although motion is an accident pertaining to living beings, and there is no doubt that, without corporeality, expressions like the following could not be imagined : " to descend, to ascend, to walk, to place, to stand, to surround, to sit, to dwell, to depart, to enter, to pass, etc.

It would have been superfluous thus to dilate on this subject, were it not for the mass of the people, who are accustomed to such ideas. It has been necessary to expatiate on the subject, as we have attempted, for the benefit of those who are anxious to acquire perfection, to remove from them such notions as have grown up with them from the days of youth.

CHAPTER XXVII

ONKELOS the Proselyte, who was thoroughly acquainted with the Hebrew and Chaldaic languages, made it his task to oppose the belief in God's corporeality. Accordingly, any expression employed in the Pentateuch in reference to God, and in any way implying corporeality, he paraphrases in consonance with the context. All expressions denoting any mode of motion, are explained by Him to mean the appearance or manifestation of a certain light that had been created [for the occasion], i.e., the Shekhinah (Divine Presence), or Providence. Thus he paraphrases " the Lord will come down " (Exod. xix. 11), " The Lord will manifest Himself "; "And God came down " (xvi. 20), " And God manifested Himself " ; and does not say "And God came down " ; " I will go down now and see " (Gen. xviii. 21), he paraphrases, " I will manifest myself now and see." This is his rendering [of the verb *yarad*, " he went down," when used in reference to God] throughout his version, with the exception of the following passage, " I will go down (*ered*) with thee into Egypt " (Gen. xlvi. 4), which he renders literally. A remarkable proof of this great man's talents, the excellence of his version, and the correctness of his interpretation ! By this version he discloses to us an important principle as regards prophecy.

This narrative begins : " And God spake unto Israel in the visions of the night, and said, Jacob, Jacob, etc. And He said, I am God, etc., I will go down with thee into Egypt " (Gen. xlvi. 2, 3). Seeing that the whole narrative is introduced as a vision of the night, Onkelos did not hesitate to translate literally the words addressed to Jacob in the nocturnal vision, and thus gave a faithful account of the occurrence. For the passage in question contains a statement of what Jacob was told, not what actually took place, as is the case in the words, " And the Lord came down upon Mount Sinai " (Exod. xix. 20). Here we have an account of what actually occurred in the physical world ; the verb *yarad* is therefore paraphrased " He manifested Himself," and entirely detached from the idea of motion. Accounts of what happened in the imagination of man, I mean of what he was told, are not altered. A most remarkable distinction !

Hence you may infer that there is a great difference between a communication, designated as having been made in a dream, or a vision of the night, and a vision or a manifestation simply introduced with phrases like " And the word of the Lord came unto me, saying " ; " And the Lord spake unto me, saying."

According to my opinion, it is also possible that Onkelos understood *Elohim* in the above passage to signify " angel," and that for this reason he did not hesitate to translate literally, " I will go down with thee to Egypt." Do not think it strange that Onkelos should have believed the *Elohim*, who said to Jacob, " I am God, the God of thy father " (*ib.* 3), to be an angel, for this sentence can, in the same form, also have been spoken by an angel. Thus Jacob says, " And the angel of God spake unto me in a dream, saying, Jacob. And I said, Here am I, " etc. (Gen. xxxi. 11) ; and concludes the report of the angel's words to him in the following way, " I am the God of Bethel, where thou anointedst the pillar, and where thou vowedst a vow *unto me* " (*ib.* 13), although there is no doubt that Jacob vowed to God, not to the angel. It is the usual practice of prophets to relate words addressed to them by an angel in the name of God, as though God Himself had spoken to them. Such passages are all to be explained by supplying the *nomen regens*, and by considering them as identical with " I am the messenger of the God of thy father," " I am the messenger of God who appeared to thee in Bethel," and the like. Prophecy with its various degrees, and the nature of angels, will be fully discussed in the sequel, in accordance with the object of this treatise (II. chap. xiv.).

CHAPTER XXVIII

THE term *regel* is homonymous, signifying, in the first place, the foot of a living being; comp. " Foot for foot " (Exod. xxi. 24). Next it denotes an object which follows another ; comp. " And all the people that follow thee " (lit. that are at thy feet) (*ib*. xi. 18). Another signification of the word is " cause " ; comp. " And the Lord hath blessed thee, I being the cause " (*leragli*) (Gen. xxx. 30), i.e., for my sake ; for that which exists for the sake of another thing has the latter for its final cause. Examples of the term used in this sense are numerous. It has that meaning in Genesis xxxiii. 14, " Because (*leregel*) of the cattle that goeth before me, and because (*leregel*) of the children."

Consequently, the Hebrew text, of which the literal rendering is : " And his feet shall stand in that day upon the Mount of Olives " (Zech. xiv. 4) can be explained in the following way : " And the things caused by him (*raglav*) on that day upon the Mount of Olives, that is to say, the wonders which will then be seen, and of which God will be the Cause or the Maker, will remain permanently." To this explanation does Jonathan son of Uziel incline in paraphrasing the passage, " And he will appear in his might on that day upon the Mount of Olives. He generally expresses terms denoting those parts of the body by which contact and motion are effected, by " his might " [when referring to God], because all such expressions denote acts done by His Will.

In the passage (Exod. xxiv. 10, lit., " And there was under his feet, like the action of the whiteness of a sapphire stone "), Onkelos, as you know, in his version, considers the word (*raglav*) " his feet " as a figurative expression and a substitute for " throne " ; the words " under his feet " he therefore paraphrases, " And under the throne of his glory." Consider this well, and you will observe with wonder how Onkelos keeps free from the idea of the corporeality of God, and from everything that leads thereto, even in the remotest degree. For he does not say, " and under His throne " ; the direct relation of the throne to God, implied in the literal sense of the phrase " His throne," would necessarily suggest the idea that God is supported by a material object, and thus lead directly to the corporeality of God ; he therefore refers the throne to His glory, i.e., to the Shekhinah, which is a light created for the purpose.

Similarly he paraphrases the words, " For my hand I lift up to the throne of God " (Exod. xvii. 16), " An oath has been uttered by God, whose Shekhinah is upon the throne of his glory." This principle found also expression in the popular phrase, " the Throne of the Glory."

We have already gone too far away from the subject of this chapter, and touched upon things which will be discussed in other chapters ; we will now return to our present theme. You are acquainted with the version of Onkelos [of the passage quoted]. He contents himself with excluding from his version all expressions of corporeality in reference to God, and does not show us what they (the nobles of the children of Israel Exod. xxiv. 10) perceived, or what is meant by that figure.   In all similar instances Onkelos also abstains from entering into such questions, and only endeavours to exclude every expression implying corporeality; for the incorporeality of God is a demonstrative truth and an indispensable element in our faith; he could decidedly state all that was necessary in that respect.   The interpretation of a simile is a doubtful thing; it may possibly have that meaning, but it may also refer to something else.   It contains besides very profound matter, the understanding of which is not a fundamental element in our faith, and the comprehension of which is not easy for the common people.   Onkelos, therefore, did not enter at all into this subject.

We, however, remaining faithful to our task in this treatise, find ourselves compelled to give our explanation.   According to our opinion " under his feet " (*raglav*) denotes " under that of which He is the cause," " that which exists through Him," as we have already stated.   They (the nobles of the children of Israel) therefore comprehended the real nature of the *materia prima*, which emanated from Him, and of whose existence He is the only cause.   Consider well the phrase, " like the action of the whiteness of the sapphire stone."   If the colour were the point of comparison, the words, " as the whiteness of the sapphire stone " would have sufficed; but the addition of " like the action " was necessary, because matter, as such, is, as you are well aware, always receptive and passive, active only by some accident.   On the other hand, form, as such, is always active, and only passive by some accident, as is explained in works on Physics.   This explains the addition of " *like* the action " in reference to the *materia prima*.   The expression " the whiteness of the sapphire " refers to the transparency, not to the white *colour*; for " the whiteness " of the sapphire is not a white *colour*, but the property of being transparent.   Things, however, which are transparent, have no colour of their own, as is proved in works on Physics; for if they had a colour they would not permit all the colours to pass through them nor would they receive colours; it is only when the transparent object is totally colourless, that it is able to receive successively all the colours.   In this respect it (the whiteness of the sapphire) is like the *materia prima*, which as such is entirely formless, and thus receives all the forms one after the other.   What they (the nobles of the children of Israel) perceived was therefore the *materia prima*, whose relation to God is distinctly mentioned, because it is the source of those of his creatures which are subject to genesis and destruction, and has been created by him.   This subject also will be treated later on more fully.

Observe that you must have recourse to an explanation of this kind, even when adopting the rendering of Onkelos, " And under the throne of His glory "; for in fact the *materia prima* is also under the heavens, which are called " throne of God," as we have remarked above.   I should not have thought of this unusual interpretation, or hit on this argument were it not for an utterance of R. Eliezer ben Hyrcanus, which will be discussed in one of the parts of this treatise (II. chap. xxvi.).   The primary object of every intelligent person must be to deny the corporeality of God, and to believe that all those perceptions (described in the above passage) were of a spiritual not of a material character.   Note this and consider it well.

CHAPTER XXIX

THE term *'ezeb* is homonymous, denoting, in the first place, pain and trembling; comp. "In sorrow (*be-'ezeb*) thou shalt bring forth children" (Gen. iii. 16). Next it denotes anger; comp. "And his father had not made him angry (*'azabo*) at any time" (1 Kings i. 6); "for he was angry (*ne'ezab*) for the sake of David" (1 Sam. xx. 34). The term signifies also provocation; comp. "They rebelled, and vexed (*'izzebu*) his holy spirit" (Isa. lxiii. 10); "and provoked (*ya'azibahu*) him in the desert" (Ps. lxxviii. 40); "If there be any way of provocation (*'ozeb*) in me" (*ib.* cxxxix. 24); "Every day they rebel (*ye'azzebu*) against my words" (*ib.* lvi. 6).

In Genesis vi. 6 the word has either the second or the third signification. In the first case, the sense of the Hebrew *va-yit'azzeb el libbo* is "God was angry with them on account of the wickedness of their deeds"; as to the words "to his heart" used here, and also in the history of Noah (*ib.* viii. 21) I will here explain what they mean. With regard to man, we use the expression "he said to himself," or "he said in his heart," in reference to a subject which he did not utter or communicate to any other person. Similarly the phrase "And God said in his heart," is used in reference to an act which God decreed without mentioning it to any prophet at the time the event took place according to the will of God. And a figure of this kind is admissible, since "the Torah speaketh in accordance with the language of man" (*supra* c. xxvi.). This is plain and clear. In the Pentateuch no distinct mention is made of a message sent to the wicked generation of the flood, cautioning or threatening them with death; therefore, it is said concerning them, that God was angry with them in His heart; likewise when He decreed that no flood should happen again, He did not tell a prophet to communicate it to others, and for that reason the words "in his heart" are added.

Taking the verb in the third signification, we explain the passage thus: "And man rebelled against God's will concerning him"; for *leb* (heart) also signifies "will," as we shall explain when treating of the homonymity of *leb* (heart).

CHAPTER XXX

IN its primary meaning *akal* (to eat) is used in the sense of taking food by animals; this needs no illustration. It was afterwards observed that eating includes two processes—(1) the loss of the food, i.e., the destruction of its form, which first takes place; (2) the growth of animals, the preservation of their strength and their existence, and the support of all the forces of their body, caused by the food they take.

The consideration of the first process led to the figurative use of the verb in the sense of "consuming," "destroying"; hence it includes all modes of depriving a thing of its form; comp. "And the land of your enemies shall destroy (lit. eat) you" (Lev. xxvi. 38); "A land that destroyeth (lit. eateth) the inhabitants thereof" (Num. xiii. 32); "Ye shall be destroyed (lit. eaten) with the sword" (Isa. i. 6); "Shall the sword destroy (lit. eat)" (2 Sam. ii. 26); "And the fire of the Lord burnt among them, and destroyed (lit. ate) them that were in the uttermost parts of the camp" (Num. xi. 1);

" (God) is a destroying (lit. eating) fire " (Deut. iv. 24), that is, He destroys those who rebel against Him, as the fire destroys everything that comes within its reach. Instances of this kind are very frequent.

With reference to the second effect of the act of eating, the verb " to eat " is figuratively used in the sense of " acquiring wisdom," " learning " ; in short, for all intellectual perceptions. These preserve the human form (intellect) constantly in the most perfect manner, in the same way as food preserves the body in its best condition. Comp. " Come ye, buy and eat " (Isa. lv. 1) ; " Hearken diligently unto me, and eat ye that which is good " (ib. 2) ; " It is not good to eat much honey " (Prov. xxv. 27) ; " My son, eat thou honey, because it is good, and the honeycomb, which is sweet to thy taste ; so shall the knowledge of wisdom be unto thy soul " (ib. xxiv. 13, 14).

This figurative use of the verb " to eat " in the sense of " acquiring wisdom " is frequently met with in the Talmud, e.g., " Come, eat fat meat at Raba's (Baba Bathra 22a) ; comp. "All expressions of ' eating ' and ' drinking ' found in this book (of Proverbs) refer to wisdom," or, according to another reading, " to the Law " (Koh. rabba on Eccl. iii. 13). Wisdom has also been frequently called " water," e.g., " Ho, every one that thirsteth, come ye to the waters " (Isa. lv. 1).

The figurative meaning of these expressions has been so general and common, that it was almost considered as its primitive signification, and led to the employment " of hunger " and " thirst " in the sense of " absence of wisdom and intelligence " ; comp. " I will send a famine in the land, not a famine of bread, nor a thirst for water, but of hearing the words of the Lord " ; " My soul thirsteth for God, for the living God " (Ps. xlii. 3). Instances of this kind occur frequently. The words, " With joy shall ye draw water out of the wells of salvation " (Isa. xii. 3), are paraphrased by Jonathan son of Uzziel thus : " You will joyfully receive new instruction from the chosen of the righteous." Consider how he explains " water " to indicate " the wisdom which will then spread," and " the wells " (ma'ayene) as being identical with " the eyes of the congregation " (Num. xv. 24), in the sense of " the chiefs," or " the wise." By the phrase, " from the chosen of the righteous," he expresses his belief that righteousness is true salvation. You now see how he gives to every word in this verse some signification referring to wisdom and study. This should be well considered.

CHAPTER XXXI

KNOW that for the human mind there are certain objects of perception which are within the scope of its nature and capacity ; on the other hand, there are, amongst things which actually exist, certain objects which the mind can in no way and by no means grasp : the gates of perception are closed against it. Further, there are things of which the mind understands one part, but remains ignorant of the other ; and when man is able to comprehend certain things, it does not follow that he must be able to comprehend everything. This also applies to the senses : they are able to perceive things, but not at every distance ; and all other powers of the body are limited in a similar way. A man can, e.g., carry two kikkar, but he cannot carry ten kikkar. How individuals of the same species surpass each other in these sensations and in other bodily faculties is universally known, but there is a limit to them, and their power cannot extend to every distance or to every degree.

All this is applicable to the intellectual faculties of man. There is a considerable difference between one person and another as regards these faculties, as is well known to philosophers. While one man can discover a certain thing by himself, another is never able to understand it, even if taught by means of all possible expressions and metaphors, and during a long period ; his mind can in no way grasp it, his capacity is insufficient for it. This distinction is not unlimited. A boundary is undoubtedly set to the human mind which it cannot pass. There are things (beyond that boundary) which are acknowledged to be inaccessible to human understanding, and man does not show any desire to comprehend them, being aware that such knowledge is impossible, and that there are no means of overcoming the difficulty ; e.g., we do not know the number of stars in heaven, whether the number is even or odd ; we do not know the number of animals, minerals, or plants, and the like. There are other things, however, which man very much desires to know, and strenuous efforts to examine and to investigate them have been made by thinkers of all classes, and at all times. They differ and disagree, and constantly raise new doubts with regard to them, because their minds are bent on comprehending such things, that is to say, they are moved by desire ; and every one of them believes that he has discovered the way leading to a true knowledge of the thing, although human reason is entirely unable to demonstrate the fact by convincing evidence.—For a proposition which can be proved by evidence is not subject to dispute, denial, or rejection ; none but the ignorant would contradict it, and such contradiction is called " denial of a demonstrated proof." Thus you find men who deny the spherical form of the earth, or the circular form of the line in which the stars move, and the like ; such men are not considered in this treatise. This confusion prevails mostly in metaphysical subjects, less in problems relating to physics, and is entirely absent from the exact sciences. Alexander Aphrodisius said that there are three causes which prevent men from discovering the exact truth : first, arrogance and vainglory ; secondly, the subtlety, depth, and difficulty of any subject which is being examined ; thirdly, ignorance and want of capacity to comprehend what might be comprehended. These causes are enumerated by Alexander. At the present time there is a fourth cause not mentioned by him, because it did not then prevail, namely, habit and training. We naturally like what we have been accustomed to, and are attracted towards it. This may be observed amongst villagers ; though they rarely enjoy the benefit of a douche or bath, and have few enjoyments, and pass a life of privation, they dislike town life and do not desire its pleasures, preferring the inferior things to which they are accustomed, to the better things to which they are strangers ; it would give them no satisfaction to live in palaces, to be clothed in silk, and to indulge in baths, ointments, and perfumes.

The same is the case with those opinions of man to which he has been accustomed from his youth ; he likes them, defends them, and shuns the opposite views. This is likewise one of the causes which prevent men from finding truth, and which make them cling to their habitual opinions. Such is, e.g., the case with the vulgar notions with respect to the corporeality of God, and many other metaphysical questions, as we shall explain. It is the result of long familiarity with passages of the Bible, which they are accustomed to respect and to receive as true, and the literal sense of which implies the corporeality of God and other false notions ; in truth, however, these words were employed as figures and metaphors for reasons to be mentioned below.   Do not imagine that what we have said of the insufficiency of our understanding and of its limited extent is an assertion founded only on the Bible ; for philosophers likewise assert the same, and perfectly understand it, without having regard to any religion or opinion.   It is a fact which is only doubted by those who ignore things fully proved.   This chapter is intended as an introduction to the next.

CHAPTER XXXII

You must consider, when reading this treatise, that mental perception, because connected with matter, is subject to conditions similar to those to which physical perception is subject.   That is to say, if your eye looks around, you can perceive all that is within the range of your vision ; if, however, you overstrain your eye, exerting it too much by attempting to see an object which is too distant for your eye, or to examine writings or engravings too small for your sight, and forcing it to obtain a correct perception of them, you will not only weaken your sight with regard to that special object, but also for those things which you otherwise are able to perceive : your eye will have become too weak to perceive what you were able to see before you exerted yourself and exceeded the limits of your vision.

The same is the case with the speculative faculties of one who devotes himself to the study of any science.   If a person studies too much and exhausts his reflective powers, he will be confused, and will not be able to apprehend even that which had been within the power of his apprehension. For the powers of the body are all alike in this respect.

The mental perceptions are not exempt from a similar condition.   If you admit the doubt, and do not persuade yourself to believe that there is a proof for things which cannot be demonstrated, or to try at once to reject and positively to deny an assertion the opposite of which has never been proved, or attempt to perceive things which are beyond your perception, then you have attained the highest degree of human perfection, then you are like R. Akibha, who " in peace entered [the study of these theological problems], and came out in peace."   If, on the other hand, you attempt to exceed the limit of your intellectual power, or at once to reject things as impossible which have never been proved to be impossible, or which are in fact possible, though their possibility be very remote, then you will be like Elisha Aḥer ; you will not only fail to become perfect, but you will become exceedingly imperfect. Ideas founded on mere imagination will prevail over you, you will incline toward defects, and toward base and degraded habits, on account of the confusion which troubles the mind, and of the dimness of its light, just as weakness of sight causes invalids to see many kinds of unreal images, especially when they have looked for a long time at dazzling or at very minute objects.

Respecting this it has been said, " Hast thou found honey ? eat so much as is sufficient for thee, lest thou be filled therewith, and vomit it " (Prov. xxv. 16).   Our Sages also applied this verse to Elisha Aḥer.

How excellent is this simile! In comparing knowledge to food (as we observed in chap. xxx.), the author of Proverbs mentions the sweetest food, namely, honey, which has the further property of irritating the stomach, and of causing sickness. He thus fully describes the nature of knowledge. Though great, excellent, noble and perfect, it is injurious if not kept within bounds or not guarded properly; it is like honey which gives nourishment and is pleasant, when eaten in moderation, but is totally thrown away when eaten immoderately. Therefore, it is not said " lest thou be filled and loathe it," but " lest thou vomit it." The same idea is expressed in the words, " It is not good to eat much honey " (Prov. xxv. 27); and in the words, " Neither make thyself over-wise; why shouldst thou destroy thyself ? " (Eccles. vii. 16); comp. " Keep thy foot when thou goest to the house of God " (*ibid.* v. 1). The same subject is alluded to in the words of David, " Neither do I exercise myself in great matters, or in things too high for me " (Ps. cxxxi. 2), and in the sayings of our Sages : " Do not inquire into things which are too difficult for thee, do not search what is hidden from thee ; study what you are allowed to study, and do not occupy thyself with mysteries." They meant to say, Let thy mind only attempt things which are within human perception ; for the study of things which lie beyond man's comprehension is extremely injurious, as has been already stated. This lesson is also contained in the Talmudical passage, which begins, " He who considers four things," etc., and concludes, " He who does not regard the honour of his Creator " ; here also is given the advice which we have already mentioned, viz., that man should not rashly engage in speculation with false conceptions, and when he is in doubt about anything, or unable to find a proof for the object of his inquiry, he must not at once abandon, reject and deny it ; he must modestly keep back, and from regard to the honour of his Creator, hesitate [from uttering an opinion] and pause. This has already been explained.

It was not the object of the Prophets and our Sages in these utterances to close the gate of investigation entirely, and to prevent the mind from comprehending what is within its reach, as is imagined by simple and idle people, whom it suits better to put forth their ignorance and incapacity as wisdom and perfection, and to regard the distinction and wisdom of others as irreligion and imperfection, thus taking darkness for light and light for darkness. The whole object of the Prophets and the Sages was to declare that a limit is set to human reason where it must halt. Do not criticise the words used in this chapter and in others in reference to the mind, for we only intended to give some idea of the subject in view, not to describe the essence of the intellect ; for other chapters have been dedicated to this subject.

CHAPTER XXXIII

You must know that it is very injurious to begin with this branch of philosophy, viz., Metaphysics ; or to explain [at first] the sense of the similes occurring in prophecies, and interpret the metaphors which are employed in historical accounts and which abound in the writings of the Prophets. On the contrary, it is necessary to initiate the young and to instruct the less intelligent according to their comprehension ; those who appear to be talented and to have capacity for the higher method of study, i.e., that based on proof and on true logical argument, should be gradually advanced towards perfection, either by tuition or by self-instruction. He, however, who begins with Metaphysics, will not only become confused in matters of religion, but will fall into complete infidelity. I compare such a person to an infant fed with wheaten bread, meat and wine ; it will undoubtedly die, not because such food is naturally unfit for the human body, but because of the weakness of the child, who is unable to digest the food, and cannot derive benefit from it. The same is the case with the true principles of science. They were presented in enigmas, clad in riddles, and taught by all wise men in the most mysterious way that could be devised, not because they contain some secret evil, or are contrary to the fundamental principles of the Law (as fools think who are only philosophers in their own eyes), but because of the incapacity of man to comprehend them at the beginning of his studies : only slight allusions have been made to them to serve for the guidance of those who are capable of understanding them. These sciences were, therefore, called Mysteries (*sodoth*), and Secrets of the Law (*sitre torah*), as we shall explain.

This also is the reason why " the Torah speaks the language of man," as we have explained, for it is the object of the Torah to serve as a guide for the instruction of the young, of women, and of the common people ; and as all of them are incapable to comprehend the true sense of the words, tradition was considered sufficient to convey all truths which were to be established ; and as regards ideals, only such remarks were made as would lead towards a knowledge of their existence, though not to a comprehension of their true essence. When a man attains to perfection, and arrives at a knowledge of the " Secrets of the Law," either through the assistance of a teacher or by self-instruction, being led by the understanding of one part to the study of the other, he will belong to those who faithfully believe in the true principles, either because of conclusive proof, where proof is possible, or by forcible arguments, where argument is admissible ; he will have a true notion of those things which he previously received in similes and metaphors, and he will fully understand their sense. We have frequently mentioned in this treatise the principle of our Sages " not to discuss the *Ma'aseh Mercabah* even in the presence of one pupil, except he be wise and intelligent ; and then only the headings of the chapters are to be given to him." We must, therefore, begin with teaching these subjects according to the capacity of the pupil, and on two conditions, first, that he be wise, i.e., that he should have successfully gone through the preliminary studies, and secondly that he be intelligent, talented, clear-headed, and of quick perception, that is, " have a mind of his own " (*mebin midda'ato*), as our Sages termed it.

I will now proceed to explain the reasons why we should not instruct the multitude in pure metaphysics, or begin with describing to them the true essence of things, or with showing them that a thing must be as it is, and cannot be otherwise. This will form the subject of the next chapter ; and I proceed to say—

CHAPTER XXXIV

There are five reasons why instruction should not begin with Metaphysics, but should at first be restricted to pointing out what is fitted for notice and what may be made manifest to the multitude.

First Reason.—The subject itself is difficult, subtle and profound, " Far off and exceeding deep, who can find it out ? " (Eccles. vii. 24). The following words of Job may be applied to it : " Whence then cometh wisdom ? and where is the place of understanding ? " (Job xxviii. 20). Instruction should not begin with abstruse and difficult subjects. In one of the similes contained in the Bible, wisdom is compared to water, and amongst other interpretations given by our Sages of this simile, occurs the following : He who can swim may bring up pearls from the depth of the sea, he who is unable to swim will be drowned, therefore only such persons as have had proper instruction should expose themselves to the risk.

Second Reason.—The intelligence of man is at first insufficient ; for he is not endowed with perfection at the beginning, but at first possesses perfection only *in potentiâ*, not in fact. Thus it is said, " And man is born a wild ass " (Job xi. 12). If a man possesses a certain faculty *in potentiâ*, it does not follow that it must become in him a reality. He may possibly remain deficient either on account of some obstacle, or from want of training in practices which would turn the possibility into a reality. Thus it is distinctly stated in the Bible, " Not many are wise " (*ib.*, xxxii. 9) ; also our Sages say, " I noticed how few were those who attained to a higher degree of perfection " (B. T. Succah 45*a*). There are many things which obstruct the path to perfection, and which keep man away from it. Where can he find sufficient preparation and leisure to learn all that is necessary in order to develop that perfection which he has *in potentiâ* ?

Third Reason.—The preparatory studies are of long duration, and man, in his natural desire to reach the goal, finds them frequently too wearisome, and does not wish to be troubled by them. Be convinced that, if man were able to reach the end without preparatory studies, such studies would not be preparatory but tiresome and utterly superfluous. Suppose you awaken any person, even the most simple, as if from sleep, and you say to him, Do you not desire to know what the heavens are, what is their number and their form ; what beings are contained in them ; what the angels are ; how the creation of the whole world took place ; what is its purpose, and what is the relation of its various parts to each other ; what is the nature of the soul ; how it enters the body ; whether it has an independent existence, and if so, how it can exist independently of the body ; by what means and to what purpose, and similar problems. He would undoubtedly say " Yes," and show a natural desire for the true knowledge of these things ; but he will wish to satisfy that desire and to attain to that knowledge by listening to a few words from you. Ask him to interrupt his usual pursuits for a week, till he learn all this, he would not do it, and would be satisfied and contented with imaginary and misleading notions ; he would refuse to believe that there is anything which requires preparatory studies and persevering research.

You, however, know how all these subjects are connected together ; for there is nothing else in existence but God and His works, the latter including all existing things besides Him ; we can only obtain a knowledge of Him through His works ; His works give evidence of His existence, and show what must be assumed concerning Him, that is to say, what must be attributed to Him either affirmatively or negatively.   It is thus necessary to examine all things according to their essence, to infer from every species such true and well established propositions as may assist us in the solution of metaphysical problems.   Again, many propositions based on the nature of numbers and the properties of geometrical figures, are useful in examining things which must be negatived in reference to God, and these negations will lead us to further inferences.   You will certainly not doubt the necessity of studying astronomy and physics, if you are desirous of comprehending the relation between the world and Providence as it is in reality, and not according to imagination. There are also many subjects of speculation, which, though not preparing the way for metaphysics, help to train the reasoning power, enabling it to understand the nature of a proof, and to test truth by characteristics essential to it.   They remove the confusion arising in the minds of most thinkers, who confound accidental with essential properties, and likewise the wrong opinions resulting therefrom.   We may add, that although they do not form the basis for metaphysical research, they assist in forming a correct notion of these things, and are certainly useful in many other things connected with that discipline.   Consequently he who wishes to attain to human perfection, must therefore first study Logic, next the various branches of Mathematics in their proper order, then Physics, and lastly Metaphysics.   We find that many who have advanced to a certain point in the study of these disciplines become weary, and stop; that others, who are endowed with sufficient capacity, are interrupted in their studies by death, which surprises them while still engaged with the preliminary course.   Now, if no knowledge whatever had been given to us by means of tradition, and if we had not been brought to the belief in a thing through the medium of similes, we would have been bound to form a perfect notion of things with their essential characteristics, and to believe only what we could prove : a goal which could only be attained by long preparation.   In such a case most people would die, without having known whether there was a God or not, much less that certain things must be asserted about Him, and other things denied as defects. From such a fate not even " one of a city or two of a family " (Jer. iii. 14) would have escaped.

As regards the privileged few, " the remnant whom the Lord calls " (Joel iii. 5), they only attain the perfection at which they aim after due preparatory labour.   The necessity of such a preparation and the need of such a training for the acquisition of real knowledge, has been plainly stated by King Solomon in the following words : " If the iron be blunt, and he do not whet the edge, then must he put to more strength ; and it is profitable to prepare for wisdom " (Eccles. x. 10) ; " Hear counsel, and receive instruction, that thou mayest be wise in thy latter end " (Prov. xix. 20).

There is still another urgent reason why the preliminary disciplines should be studied and understood.   During the study many doubts present themselves, and the difficulties, or the objections raised against certain assertions, are soon understood, just as the demolition of a building is easier than its erection ; while, on the other hand, it is impossible to prove an assertion, or to remove any doubts, without having recourse to several propositions taken from these preliminary studies.   He who approaches metaphysical problems without proper preparation is like a person who journeys towards a certain place, and on the road falls into a deep pit, out of which he cannot rise, and he must perish there; if he had not gone forth, but had remained at home, it would have been better for him.

Solomon has expatiated in the book of Proverbs on sluggards and their indolence, by which he figuratively refers to indolence in the search after wisdom. He thus speaks of a man who desires to know the final results, but does not exert himself to understand the preliminary disciplines which lead to them, doing nothing else but desire. " The desire of the slothful killeth him; for his hands refuse to labour. He coveteth greedily all the day long; but the righteous giveth, and spareth not " (Prov. xxi. 25, 26); that is to say, if the desire killeth the slothful, it is because he neglects to seek the thing which might satisfy his desire, he does nothing but desire, and hopes to obtain a thing without using the means to reach it. It would be better for him were he without that desire. Observe how the end of the simile throws light on its beginning. It concludes with the words " but the righteous giveth, and spareth not "; the antithesis of " righteous " and " slothful " can only be justified on the basis of our interpretation. Solomon thus indicates that only such a man is righteous who gives to everything its due portion; that is to say, who gives to the study of a thing the whole time required for it, and does not devote any part of that time to another purpose. The passage may therefore be paraphrased thus : And the righteous man devotes his ways to wisdom, and does not withhold any of them." Comp. " Give not thy strength unto women " (Prov. xxxi. 3).

The majority of scholars, that is to say, the most famous in science, are afflicted with this failing, viz., that of hurrying at once to the final results, and of speaking about them, without treating of the preliminary disciplines. Led by folly or ambition to disregard those preparatory studies, for the attainment of which they are either incapable or too idle, some scholars endeavour to prove that these are injurious or superfluous. On reflection the truth will become obvious.

The Fourth Reason is taken from the physical constitution of man. It has been proved that moral conduct is a preparation for intellectual progress, and that only a man whose character is pure, calm and steadfast, can attain to intellectual perfection; that is, acquire correct conceptions. Many men are naturally so constituted that all perfection is impossible; e.g., he whose heart is very warm and is himself very powerful, is sure to be passionate, though he tries to counteract that disposition by training; he whose testicles are warm, humid, and vigorous, and the organs connected therewith are surcharged, will not easily refrain from sin, even if he makes great efforts to restrain himself. You also find persons of great levity and rashness, whose excited manners and wild gestures prove that their constitution is in disorder, and their temperament so bad that it cannot be cured. Such persons can never attain to perfection; it is utterly useless to occupy oneself with them on such a subject [as Metaphysics]. For this science is, as you know, different from the science of Medicine and of Geometry, and, from the reason already mentioned, it is not every person who is capable of approaching it. It is impossible for a man to study it successfully without moral preparation; he must acquire the highest degree of uprightness and integrity, " for the froward is an abomination to the Lord, but His secret is

with the righteous " (Prov. iii. 32).   Therefore it was considered inadvisable
to teach it to young men ; nay, it is impossible for them to comprehend it,
on account of the heat of their blood and the flame of youth, which confuses
their minds ; that heat, which causes all the disorder, must first disappear ;
they must have become moderate and settled, humble in their hearts, and
subdued in their temperament ; only then will they be able to arrive at the
highest degree of the perception of God, i.e., the study of Metaphysics, which
is called *Ma'aseh Mercabah* Comp. "The Lord is nigh unto them that
are of a broken heart " (Ps. xxxiv. 18) ; " I dwell in the high and lofty place,
with him also that is of a contrite and humble spirit ; to revive the spirit of
the humble, and to revive the heart of the contrite ones " (Isa. lvii. 15).

   Therefore the rule, " the headings of the sections may be confided to him,"
is further restricted in the Talmud, in the following way : The headings of
the sections must only be handed down to an Ab-bet-din (President of the
Court), whose heart is full of care, i.e., in whom wisdom is united with
humility, meekness, and a great dread of sin. It is further stated there :
" The secrets of the Law can only be communicated to a counsellor, scholar,
and good orator." These qualities can only be acquired if the physical constitution of the student favour their development. You certainly know that
some persons, though exceedingly able, are very weak in giving counsel, while
others are ready with proper counsel and good advice in social and political
matters. A person so endowed is called " counsellor " and may be unable
to comprehend purely abstract notions, even such as are similar to common
sense. He is unacquainted with them, and has no talent whatever for them ;
we apply to him the words : " Wherefore is there a price in the hand of a
fool to get wisdom, seeing he hath no heart to it ? " (Prov. xvii. 16). Others
are intelligent and naturally clear-sighted, able to convey complicated ideas
in concise and well chosen language,—such a person is called " a good
orator," but he has not been engaged in the pursuit of science, or has not
acquired any knowledge of it. Those who have actually acquired a knowledge of the sciences, are called " wise in arts " (or " scholars ") ; the Hebrew term for " wise in arts "—*ḥakam ḥarashim*—has been explained in
the Talmud as implying, that when such a man speaks, all become, as it were,
speechless.

   Now, consider how, in the writings of the Rabbis, the admission of a person
into discourses on metaphysics is made dependent on distinction in social
qualities, and study of philosophy, as well as on the possession of clear-
sightedness, intelligence, eloquence, and ability to communicate things by
slight allusions. If a person satisfies these requirements, the secrets of the
Law are confided to him. In the same place we also read the following passage :—R. Jochanan said to R. Elasar, " Come, I will teach you *Ma'aseh
Mercabah*." The reply was, " I am not yet old," or in other words, I have
not yet become old, I still perceive in myself the hot blood and the rashness
of youth. You learn from this that, in addition to the above-named good
qualities, a certain age is also required. How, then, could any person speak
on these metaphysical themes in the presence of ordinary people, of children,
and of women !

   Fifth Reason.—Man is disturbed in his intellectual occupation by the
necessity of looking after the material wants of the body, especially if the

necessity of providing for wife and children be superadded; much more so if he seeks superfluities in addition to his ordinary wants, for by custom and bad habits these become a powerful motive. Even the perfect man to whom we have referred, if too busy with these necessary things, much more so if busy with unnecessary things, and filled with a great desire for them—must weaken or altogether lose his desire for study, to which he will apply himself with interruption, lassitude, and want of attention. He will not attain to that for which he is fitted by his abilities, or he will acquire imperfect knowledge, a confused mass of true and false ideas. For these reasons it was proper that the study of Metaphysics should have been exclusively cultivated by privileged persons, and not entrusted to the common people. It is not for the beginner, and he should abstain from it, as the little child has to abstain from taking solid food and from carrying heavy weights.

CHAPTER XXXV

Do not think that what we have laid down in the preceding chapters on the importance, obscurity, and difficulty of the subject, and its unsuitableness for communication to ordinary persons, includes the doctrine of God's incorporeality and His exemption from all affections (πάθη). This is not the case. For in the same way as all people must be informed, and even children must be trained in the belief that God is One, and that none besides Him is to be worshipped, so must all be taught by simple authority that God is incorporeal; that there is no similarity in any way whatsoever between Him and His creatures; that His existence is not like the existence of His creatures, His life not like that of any living being, His wisdom not like the wisdom of the wisest of men; and that the difference between Him and His creatures is not merely quantitative, but absolute [as between two individuals of two different classes]; I mean to say that all must understand that our wisdom and His, or our power and His do not differ quantitatively or qualitatively, or in a similar manner; for two things, of which the one is strong and the other weak, are necessarily similar, belong to the same class, and can be included in one definition. The same is the case with all other comparisons; they can only be made between two things belonging to the same class, as has been shown in works on Natural Science. Anything predicated of God is totally different from our attributes; no definition can comprehend both; therefore His existence and that of any other being totally differ from each other, and the term existence is applied to both homonymously, as I shall explain.

This suffices for the guidance of children and of ordinary persons who must believe that there is a Being existing, perfect, incorporeal, not inherent in a body as a force in it—God, who is above all kinds of deficiency, above all affections. But the question concerning the attributes of God, their inadmissibility, and the meaning of those attributes which are ascribed to Him; concerning the Creation, His Providence, in providing for everything; concerning His will, His perception, His knowledge of everything; concerning prophecy and its various degrees; concerning the meaning of His names which imply the idea of unity, though they are more than one; all these things are very difficult problems, the true " Secrets of the Law " the "secrets" mentioned so frequently in the books of the Prophets, and in the words of our Teachers, the subjects of which we should only mention the headings of the chapters, as we have already stated, and only in the presence of a person satisfying the above-named conditions.

That God is incorporeal, that He cannot be compared with His creatures, that He is not subject to external influence ; these are things which must be explained to every one according to his capacity, and they must be taught by way of tradition to children and women, to the stupid and ignorant, as they are taught that God is One, that He is eternal, and that He alone is to be worshipped. Without incorporeality there is no unity, for a corporeal thing is in the first case not simple, but composed of matter and form which are two separate things by definition, and secondly, as it has extension it is also divisible. When persons have received this doctrine, and have been trained in this belief, and are in consequence at a loss to reconcile it with the writings of the Prophets, the meaning of the latter must be made clear and explained to them by pointing out the homonymity and the figurative application of certain terms discussed in this part of the work. Their belief in the unity of God and in the words of the Prophets will then be a true and perfect belief.

Those who are not sufficiently intelligent to comprehend the true interpretation of these passages in the Bible, or to understand that the same term admits of two different interpretations, may simply be told that the scriptural passage is clearly understood by the wise, but that they should content themselves with knowing that God is incorporeal, that He is never subject to external influence, as passivity implies a change, while God is entirely free from all change, that He cannot be compared to anything besides Himself, that no definition includes Him together with any other being, that the words of the Prophets are true, and that difficulties met with may be explained on this principle. This may suffice for that class of persons, and it is not proper to leave them in the belief that God is corporeal, or that He has any of the properties of material objects, just as there is no need to leave them in the belief that God does not exist, that there are more Gods than one, or that any other being may be worshipped.

CHAPTER XXXVI

I SHALL explain to you, when speaking on the attributes of God, in what sense we can say that a particular thing pleases Him, or excites His anger and His wrath, and in reference to certain persons that God was pleased with them, was angry with them, or was in wrath against them. This is not the subject of the present chapter ; I intend to explain in it what I am now going to say. You must know, that in examining the Law and the books of the Prophets, you will not find the expressions " burning anger," " provocation, " or " jealousy " applied to God except in reference to idolatry ; and that none but the idolater called "enemy," " adversary," or "hater of the Lord. " Comp. "And ye serve other gods,. . . and then the Lord's wrath will be kindled against you " (Deut. xi. 16, 17) ; " Lest the anger of the Lord thy God be kindled against thee. " etc. (*ib*. vi. 15) ; " To provoke him to anger through the work of your hands " (*ib*. xxxi. 29) ; " They have moved me to jealousy with that which is not God ; they have provoked me to anger with their vanities " (*ib.* xxxii. 21) ; " For the Lord thy God is a jealous God " (*ib.* vi. 15) ; " Why have they provoked me to anger with their graven images, and with strange vanities ? " (Jer. viii. 19) ; " Because of the provoking of his sons and of his daughters " (Deut. xxxii. 19) ; " For a fire is kindled in mine anger " (*ib.* 22) ; " The Lord will take vengeance on His adversaries, and he reserveth wrath for his enemies " (Nah. i. 2) ; " And repayeth them that hate Him " (Deut. vii. 10) ; " Until He hath driven out His enemies from before Him " (Num. xxxii. 21) ; " Which the Lord thy God hateth " (Deut. xvi. 22) ; " For every abomination to the Lord, which He hateth, have they done unto their gods " (*ib.* xii. 31). Instances like these are innumerable ; and if you examine all the examples met with in the holy writings, you will find that they confirm our view.

The Prophets in their writings laid special stress on this, because it concerns errors in reference to God, i.e., it concerns idolatry. For if any one believes that, e.g., Zaid is standing, while in fact he is sitting, he does not deviate from truth so much as one who believes that fire is under the air, or that water is under the earth, or that the earth is a plane, or things similar to these. The latter does not deviate so much from truth as one who believes that the sun consists of fire, or that the heavens form a hemisphere, and similar things ; in the third instance the deviation from truth is less than the deviation of a man who believes that angels eat and drink, and the like. The latter again deviates less from truth than one who believes that something besides God is to be worshipped ; for ignorance and error concerning a great thing, i.e., a thing which has a high position in the universe, are of greater importance than those which refer to a thing which occupies a lower place ;—by " error " I mean the belief that a thing is different from what it really is ; by " ignorance," the want of knowledge respecting things the knowledge of which can be obtained.

If a person does not know the measure of the cone, or the sphericity of the sun, it is not so important as not to know whether God exists, or whether the world exists without a God ; and if a man assumes that the cone is half (of the cylinder), or that the sun is a circle, it is not so injurious as to believe that God is more than One. You must know that idolaters when worshipping idols do not believe that there is no God besides them ; and no idolater ever did assume that any image made of metal, stone, or wood has created the heavens and the earth, and still governs them. Idolatry is founded on the idea that a particular form represents the agent between God and His creatures. This is plainly said in passages like the following : " Who would not fear thee, O king of nations ? " (Jer. x. 7) ; " And in every place incense is offered unto my name " (Mal. i. 11) ; by " my name " allusion is made to the Being which is called by them [i.e., the idolaters] " the First Cause." We have already explained this in our larger work (*Mishneh Torah*, I. On Idolatry, chap. i.), and none of our co-religionists can doubt it.

The infidels, however, though believing in the existence of the Creator, attack the exclusive prerogative of God, namely, the service and worship which was commanded, in order that the belief of the people in His existence should be firmly established, in the words, " And you shall serve the Lord," etc. (Exod. xxiii. 25). By transferring that prerogative to other beings, they cause the people, who only notice the rites, without comprehending their meaning or the true character of the being which is worshipped, to renounce their belief in the existence of God. They were therefore punished with death ; comp. " Thou shalt save alive nothing that breatheth " (Deut. xx. 16). The object of this commandment, as is distinctly stated, is to extirpate that false opinion, in order that other men should not be corrupted by it any more ; in the words of the Bible " that they teach you not," etc. (*ib.* 18). They are called " enemies," " foes," " adversaries " ; by worshipping idols they are said to provoke God to jealousy, anger, and wrath. How great, then, must be the offence of him who has a wrong opinion of God Himself, and believes Him to be different from what He truly is, i.e., assumes that He does not exist, that He consists of two elements, that He is corporeal, that He is subject to external influence, or ascribes to Him any defect whatever. Such a person is undoubtedly worse than he who worships idols in the belief that they, as agents, can do good or evil.

Therefore bear in mind that by the belief in the corporeality or in anything connected with corporeality, you would provoke God to jealousy and wrath, kindle His fire and anger, become His foe, His enemy, and His adversary in a higher degree than by the worship of idols. If you think that there is an excuse for those who believe in the corporeality of God on the ground of their training, their ignorance or their defective comprehension, you must make the same concession to the worshippers of idols ; their worship is due to ignorance, or to early training, " they continue in the custom of their fathers." (T. B. Ḥullin, 13a) You will perhaps say that the literal interpretation of the Bible causes men to fall into that doubt, but you must know that idolaters were likewise brought to their belief by false imaginations and ideas. There is no excuse whatever for those who, being unable to think for themselves, do not accept [the doctrine of the incorporeality of God] from the true philosophers. I do not consider those men as infidels who are unable to prove the incorporeality, but I hold those to be so who do not believe it, especially when they see that Onkelos and Jonathan avoid [in reference to God] expressions implying corporeality as much as possible. This is all I intended to say in this chapter.

CHAPTER XXXVII

THE Hebrew term *panim* (face) is homonymous ; most of its various meanings have a figurative character. It denotes in the first place the face of a living being ; comp. " And all *faces* are turned into paleness " (Jer. xxx. 6) ; " Wherefore are your *faces* so sad ? " (Gen. xl. 7). In this sense the term occurs frequently.

The next meaning of the word is " anger " ; comp. " And her anger (*paneha*) was gone " (1 Sam. i. 18). Accordingly, the term is frequently used in reference to God in the sense of anger and wrath ; comp. " The anger (*pene*) of the Lord hath divided them " (Lam. iv. 16) ; " The anger (*pene*) of the Lord is against them that do evil " (Ps. xxxiv. 17) ; " Mine anger (*panai*) shall go and I will give thee rest " (Exod. xxxiii. 14) ; " Then will I set mine anger " (*panai*) (Lev. xx. 3) ; there are many other instances.

Another meaning of the word is " the presence and existence of a person " ;

comp. " He died in the presence (*pene*) [i.e., in the lifetime] of all his brethren " (Gen. xxv. 18) ; " And in the presence (*pene*) of all the people I will
be glorified " (Lev. x. 3) ; ." He will surely curse thee in thy very presence "
(*paneka*) (Job i. 11).   In the same sense the word is used in the following
passage, " And the Lord spake unto Moses face to face," i.e., both being
present, without any intervening medium between them.   Comp. " Come,
let us look one another in the face " (2 Kings xiv. 8) ; and also " The Lord
talked with you face to face " (Deut. v. 4) ; instead of which we read more
plainly in another place, " Ye heard the voice of the words, but saw no
similitude ; only ye heard a voice " (*ib.* iv. 12).   The hearing of the voice
without seeing any similitude is termed " face to face."   Similarly do the
words, " And the Lord spake unto Moses face to face " correspond to
" There he heard the voice of one speaking unto him " (Num. vii. 89), in the
description of God's speaking to Moses.   Thus it will be clear to you that
the perception of the Divine voice without the intervention of an angel is
expressed by " face to face."   In the same sense the word *panim* must be
understood in " And my face (*panai*) shall not be seen " (Exod. xxxiii. 23) ;
i.e., my true existence, as it is, cannot be comprehended.

The word *panim* is also used in Hebrew as an adverb of place, in the sense
of " before," or " between the hands."   In this sense it is frequently employed in reference to God ; so also in the passage, " And my face (*panai*)
shall not be seen," according to Onkelos, who renders it, " And those before
me shall not be seen."   He finds here an allusion to the fact, that there are
also higher created beings of such superiority that their true nature cannot
be perceived by man ; viz., the ideals, separate intellects, which in their
relation to God are described as being constantly before Him, or between
His hands, i.e., as enjoying uninterruptedly the closest attention of Divine
Providence.   He, i.e., Onkelos, considers that the things which are described
as completely perceptible are those beings which, as regards existence, are
inferior to the ideals, viz., substance and form ; in reference to which we are
told, " And thou shalt see that which is behind me " (*ibid.*), i.e., beings, from
which, as it were, I turn away, and which I leave behind me.   This figure is
to represent the utter remoteness of such beings from the Deity.   You shall
later on (chap. liv.) hear my explanation of what Moses, our teacher, asked for.

The word is also used as an adverb of time, meaning " before."   Comp.
" In former time (*le-phanim*) in Israel " (Ruth iv. 7) ; " Of old (*le-phanim*)
hast Thou laid the foundation of the earth " (Ps. cii. 25).

Another signification of the word is " attention and regard."   Comp.
" Thou shalt not have regard (*pene*) to the poor " (Lev. xx. 15) ; " And a
person receiving attention (*panim*) " (Isa. iii. 3) ; " Who does not show regard (*panim*)," etc. (Deut. x. 17, etc.).   The word *panim* (face) has a similar
signification in the blessing, " The Lord turn his face to thee " (i.e., The
Lord let his providence accompany thee), " and give thee peace."

CHAPTER XXXVIII

THE Hebrew term *ahor* is a homonym.   It is a noun, signifying " back."
Comp. " Behind (*ahare*) the tabernacle " (Exod. xxvi. 12) ; " The spear came
out behind him (*aharav*) " (2 Sam. ii. 23).

It is next used in reference to time, signifying " after " ; " neither after him (*aḥarav*) arose there any like him " (2 Kings xxiii. 25) ; " After (*aḥar*) these things " (Gen. xv. 1). In this sense the word occurs frequently.

The term includes also the idea of following a thing and of conforming with the moral principles of some other being. Comp. " Ye shall walk after (*aḥare*) the Lord, your God " (Deut. xiii. 5) ; " They shall walk after (*aḥare*) the Lord " (Hos. xi. 10), i.e., follow His will, walk in the way of His actions, and imitate His virtues ; " He walked after (*aḥare*) the commandment " (*ib.* v. 11). In this sense the word occurs in Exodus xxxiii. 20, " And thou shalt see my back " (*aḥorai*) ; thou shalt perceive that which follows me, is similar to me, and is the result of my will, i.e., all things created by me, as will be explained in the course of this treatise.

CHAPTER XXXIX

THE Hebrew *leb* (heart) is a homonymous noun, signifying that organ which is the source of life to all beings possessing a heart. Comp. " And thrust them through the heart of Absalom " (1 Sam. xviii. 14).

This organ being in the middle of the body, the word has been figuratively applied to express " the middle part of a thing." Comp. " unto the midst (*leb*) of heaven " (Deut. iv. 11) ; " the midst (*labbath*) of fire " (Exod. iii. 2).

It further denotes " thought." Comp. " Went not mine heart with thee ? " (2 Kings v. 26), i.e., I was with thee in my thought when a certain event happened. Similarly must be explained, " And that ye seek not after your own heart " (Num. xv. 39), i.e., after your own thoughts ; " Whose heart (i.e., whose thought), turneth away this day " (Deut. xxix. 18).

The word further signifies " counsel." Comp. " All the rest of Israel were of one heart (i.e., had one plan) to make David king " (1 Chron. xii. 38) ; " but fools die for want of heart," i.e., of counsel ; " My heart (i.e., my counsel) shall not turn away from this so long as I live " (Job xxvii. 6) ; for this sentence is preceded by the words, " My righteousness I hold fast, and will not let it go " ; and then follows, " my heart shall never turn away from this."—As regards the expression *yeḥeraf*, I think that it may be compared with the same verb in the form *neḥrefet*, " a handmaid betrothed (*neḥrefet*) to a man " (Lev. xix. 20), where *neḥrefeth* is similar in meaning to the Arabic *munḥarifat*, " turning away," and signifies " turning from the state of slavery to that of marriage."

Leb (heart) denotes also " will " ; comp. " And I shall give you pastors according to my will (*libbi*) " (Jer. iii. 15), " Is thine heart right as my heart is ? " (2 Kings x. 15), i.e., is thy will right as my will is ? In this sense the word has been figuratively applied to God. Comp. " That shall do according to that which is in mine heart and in my soul " (1 Sam. ii. 35), i.e., according to My will ; " And mine eyes and mine heart (i.e., My providence and My will) shall be there perpetually " (1 Kings ix. 3).

The word is also used in the sense of " understanding." Comp. " For vain man will be endowed with a heart " (Job xi. 12), i.e., will be wise ; " A wise man's heart is at his right hand " (Eccles. x. 2), i.e., his understanding is engaged in perfect thoughts, the highest problems. Instances of this kind are numerous. It is in this sense, namely, that of understanding, that the word is used whenever figuratively applied to God; but exceptionally it is also used in the sense of " will." It must, in each passage, be explained in accordance with the context. Also, in the following and similar passages, it signifies " understanding " ; " Consider it in thine heart " (Deut. iv. 39); " And none considereth in his heart " (Isa. xliv. 19). Thus, also, " Yet the Lord hath not given you an heart to perceive," is identical in its meaning with " Unto thee it was shown that thou mightest know " (Deut. iv. 35).

As to the passage, " And thou shalt love the Lord thy God with all thine heart " (*Ib.* vi. 5), I explain " with all thine heart " to mean " with all the powers of thine heart," that is, with all the powers of the body, for they all have their origin in the heart; and the sense of the entire passage is : make the knowledge of God the aim of all thy actions, as we have stated in our Commentary on the Mishnah (Aboth, *Eight Chapters*, v.), and in our Mishneh Torah, yesode hatorah, chap. ii. 2.

CHAPTER XL

Ruaḥ is a homonym, signifying " air," that is, one of the four elements. Comp. " And the air of God moved " (Gen. i. 2).

It denotes also, " wind." Comp. " And the east wind (*ruaḥ*) brought the locusts " (Exod. x. 13); " west wind " (*ruaḥ*) (*ib.* 19). In this sense the word occurs frequently.

Next, it signifies " breath." Comp. " A breath (*ruaḥ*) that passeth away, and does not come again " (Ps. lxxviii. 39); " wherein is the breath (*ruaḥ*) of life " (Gen. vii. 15).

It signifies also that which remains of man after his death, and is not subject to destruction. Comp. " And the spirit (*ruaḥ*) shall return unto God who gave it " (Eccles. xii. 7).

Another signification of this word is " the divine inspiration of the prophets whereby they prophesy "—as we shall explain, when speaking on prophecy, as far as it is opportune to discuss this subject in a treatise like this.— Comp. " And I will take of the spirit (*ruaḥ*) which is upon thee, and will put it upon them " (Num. xi. 17); " And it came to pass, when the spirit (*ruaḥ*) rested upon them " (*ib.* 25); " The spirit (*ruaḥ*) of the Lord spake by me " (2 Sam. xxiii. 2). The term is frequently used in this sense.

The meaning of " intention," " will," is likewise contained in the word *ruaḥ*. Comp. " A fool uttereth all his spirit " (*ruaḥ*) (Prov. xxix. 11), i.e., his intention and will; " And the spirit (*ruaḥ*) of Egypt shall fail in the midst thereof, and I will destroy the counsel thereof " (Isa. xix. 3), i.e., her intentions will be frustrated, and her plans will be obscured; " Who has comprehended the spirit (*ruaḥ*) of the Lord, or who is familiar with his counsel that he may tell us ? " (Isa. xl. 13), i.e., Who knows the order fixed by His will, or perceives the system of His Providence in the existing world, that he may tell us ? as we shall explain in the chapters in which we shall speak on Providence.

Thus the Hebrew *ruaḥ*, when used in reference to God, has generally the fifth signification; sometimes, however, as explained above, the last signification, viz., " will." The meaning of the word in each individual case is therefore to be determined by the context.

CHAPTER XLI

THE Hebrew *nefesh* (soul) is a homonymous noun, signifying the vitality which is common to all living, sentient beings. E.g. " wherein there is a living soul " (*nefesh*) (Gen. i. 30). It denotes also blood," as in " Thou shalt not eat the blood (*nefesh*) with the meat " (Deut. xii. 23). Another signification of the term is " reason," that is, the distinguishing characteristic of man, as in " As the Lord liveth that made us this soul " (Jer. xxxviii. 16). It denotes also the part of man that remains after his death (*nefesh*, soul); comp. " But the soul (*nefesh*) of my lord shall be bound in the bundle of life " (1 Sam. xxv. 29). Lastly, it denotes " will " ; comp. " To bind his princes at his will " (*be-nafsho*) (Ps. cv. 22) ; Thou wilt not deliver me unto the will (*be-nefesh*) of my enemies " (Ps. xli. 3) ; and according to my opinion, it has this meaning also in the following passages, " If it be your will (*nafshe-kem*) that I should bury my dead " (Gen. xxiii. 8) ; " Though Moses and Samuel stood before me, yet my will (*nafshi*) could not be toward this people " (Jer. xv. 1), that is, I had no pleasure in them, I did not wish to preserve them. When *nefesh* is used in reference to God, it has the meaning " will," as we have already explained with reference to the passage, " That shall do according to that which is in my will (*bi-lebabi*) and in mine intention (*be-nafshi*) " (1 Sam. ii. 35). Similarly we explain the phrase, " And his will (*nafsho*) to trouble Israel ceased " (Judg. x. 16). Jonathan, the son of Uzziel [in the Targum of the Prophets], did not translate this passage, because he understood *nafshi* to have the first signification, and finding, therefore, in these words sensation ascribed to God, he omitted them from his translation. If, however, *nefesh* be here taken in the last signification, the sentence can well be explained. For in the passage which precedes, it is stated that Providence abandoned the Israelites, and left them on the brink of death ; then they cried and prayed for help, but in vain. When, however, they had thoroughly repented, when their misery had increased, and their enemy had had power over them, He showed mercy to them, and His will to continue their trouble and misery ceased. Note it well, for it is remarkable. The preposition *ba* in this passage has the force of the preposition *min* (" from " or " of ") ; and *ba'amal* is identical with *me'amal*. Grammarians give many instances of this use of the preposition *ba* : " And that which remaineth of (*ba*) the flesh and of (*ba*) the bread " (Lev. viii. 32) ; " If there remains but few of (*ba*) the years " (*ib.* xxv. 52) ; " Of (*ba*) the strangers and of (*ba*) those born in the land " (Exod. xii. 19).

CHAPTER XLII

Ḥai (" living ") signifies a sentient organism (lit. " growing " and " having sensation "), comp. " Every moving thing that liveth " (Gen. ix. 3) ; it also denotes recovery from a severe illness : " And was recovered (*va-yeḥi*) of his sickness " (Isa. xxxviii. 9) ; " In the camp till they recovered " (*ḥayotam*) (Josh. v. 8) ; " quick, raw (*ḥai*) flesh " (Lev. xiii. 10).

Mavet signifies " death " and " severe illness," as in " His heart died (*va-yamot*) within him, and he became as a stone " (1 Sam. xxv. 37), that is, his illness was severe. For this reason it is stated concerning the son of the woman of Zarephath, " And his sickness was so sore, that there was no breath left in him " (1 Kings xvii. 17). The simple expression *va-yamoth* would have given the idea that he was very ill, near death, like Nabal when he heard what had taken place.

Some of the Andalusian authors say that his breath was suspended, so that no breathing could be perceived at all, as sometimes an invalid is seized with a fainting fit or an attack of asphyxia, and it cannot be discovered whether he is alive or dead ; in this condition the patient may remain a day or two.

The term *ḥai* has also been employed in reference to the acquisition of wisdom. Comp. " So shall they be life (*ḥayyim*) unto thy soul " (Prov. iii. 22) ; " For whoso findeth me findeth life " (*ib.* viii. 35) ; " For they are life (*ḥayyim*) to those that find them " (*ib.* iv. 22). Such instances are numerous. In accordance with this metaphor, true principles are called life, and corrupt principles death. Thus the Almighty says, " See, I have set before thee this day life and good and death and evil " (Deut. xxx. 15), showing that " life " and " good," " death " and " evil," are identical, and then He explains these terms. In the same way I understand His words, " That ye may live " (*ib.* v. 33), in accordance with the traditional interpretation of " That it may be well with thee " [*scil.* in the life to come] (*ib.* xxii. 7). In consequence of the frequent use of this figure in our language our Sages said, " The righteous even in death are called living, while the wicked even in life are called dead." (*Talm. B. Berakhoth*, p. 78). Note this well.

CHAPTER XLIII

THE Hebrew *kanaf* is a homonym ; most of its meanings are metaphorical. Its primary signification is " wing of a flying creature," e.g., " Any winged (*kanaf*) fowl that flieth in the air " (Deut. iv. 17).

The term was next applied figuratively to the wings or corners of garments ; comp. " upon the four corners (*kanfoth*) of thy vesture " (*ib.* xxii. 12).

It was also used to denote the ends of the inhabited part of the earth, and the corners that are most distant from our habitation. Comp. " That it might take hold of the ends (*kanfoth*) of the earth " (Job xxxviii. 13) ; " From the utttermost part (*kenaf*) of the earth have we heard songs " (Isa. xxiv. 16).

Ibn Ganaḥ (in his Book of Hebrew Roots) says that *kenaf* is used in the sense of " concealing," in analogy with the Arabic *kanaftu alshaian*, " I have hidden something," and accordingly explains, Isaiah xxx. 20, " And thy teacher will no longer be hidden or concealed." It is a good explanation, and I think that *kenaf* has the same meaning in Deuteronomy xxiii. 1, " He shall not take away the cover (*kenaf*) of his father " ; also in, " Spread, therefore, thy cover (*kenafeka*) over thine handmaid " (Ruth iii. 9). In this sense, I think, the word is figuratively applied to God and to angels (for angels are not corporeal, according to my opinion, as I shall explain). Ruth ii. 12 must therefore be translated " Under whose protection (*kenafav*) thou art come to trust " ; and wherever the word occurs in reference to angels, it means concealment. You have surely noticed the words of Isaiah (Isa. vi. 2), " With twain he covered his face, and with twain he covered his feet." Their meaning is this : The cause of his (the angel's) existence is hidden and concealed; this is meant by the covering of the face. The things of which he (the angel) is the cause, and which are called " his feet " (as I stated in speaking of the homonym *regel*), are likewise concealed ; for the actions of the intelligences are not seen, and their ways are, except after long study, not understood, on account of two reasons—the one of which is contained in their own properties, the other in ourselves ; that is to say, because our perception is imperfect and the ideals are difficult to be fully comprehended. As regards the phrase " and with twain he flieth," I shall explain in a special chapter (xlix.) why flight has been attributed to angels.

CHAPTER XLIV

The Hebrew *‘ayin* is a homonym, signifying " fountain " ; e.g., " By a fountain (*‘en*) of water " (Gen. xvi. 7). It next denotes " eye " ; comp. (*‘ayin*) " Eye for eye " (Exod. xxi. 24). Another meaning of the word is " providence," as it is said concerning Jeremiah, " Take him and direct thine attention (*eneka*) to him " (Jer. xxxix. 12). In this figurative sense it is to be understood when used in reference to God ; e.g., " And my providence and my pleasure shall be there perpetually " (1 Kings ix. 3), as we have already explained (page 140) ; " The eyes (*‘ene*), i.e., the Providence of the Lord thy God, are always upon it " (Deut. xi. 12) ; " They are the eyes (*‘ene*) of the Lord, which run to and fro through the whole earth " (Zech. iv. 10), i.e., His providence is extended over everything that is on earth, as will be explained in the chapters in which we shall treat of Providence. When, however, the word " eye " is connected with the verb " to see," (*raah or ḥazah*) as in " Open thine eyes, and see " (1 Kings xix. 16) ; " His eyes behold " (Ps. xi. 4), the phrase denotes perception of the mind, not that of the senses ; for every sensation is a passive state, as is well known to you, and God is active, never passive, as will be explained by me.

CHAPTER XLV

Shama‘ is used homonymously. It signifies " to hear," and also " to obey." As regards the first signification, comp. " Neither let it be heard out of thy mouth " (Exod. xxiii. 13) ; " And the fame thereof was heard in Pharaoh's house " (Gen. xlv. 16). Instances of this kind are numerous.

Equally frequent are the instances of this verb being used in the sense of " to obey " : " And they hearkened (*shame‘u*) not unto Moses " (Exod. vi. 9). " If they obey (*yishme‘u*) and serve him (Job xxxvi. 11) ; " Shall we then hearken (*nishma‘*) unto you " (Neh. xiii. 27) ; " Whosoever will not hearken (*yishma‘*) unto thy words " (Josh. i. 18).

The verb also signifies " to know " (" to understand "), comp. " A nation whose tongue, i.e., its language, thou shalt not understand " (*tishma‘*) (Deut. xxviii. 49). The verb *shama‘*, used in reference to God, must be taken in the sense of perceiving, which is part of the third signification, whenever, according to the literal interpretation of the passage, it appears to have the first meaning : comp. " And the Lord heard it " (Num. xi. 1) ; " For that He heareth your murmurings " (Exod. xvi. 7). In all such passages mental perception is meant. When, however, according to the literal interpretation the verb appears to have the second signification, it implies that God re-sponded to the prayer of man and fulfilled his wish, or did not respond and did not fulfil his wish : " I will surely hear his cry " (Exod. xxii. 23) ; " I will hear, for I am gracious " (*ib.* 27) ; " Bow down thine ear, and hear " (2 Kings xix. 16) ; " But the Lord would not hearken to your voice, nor give ear unto you " (Deut. i. 45) ; " Yea, when ye make many prayers, I will not hear " (Isa. i. 15) ; " For I will not hear thee " (Jer. vii. 16). There are many instances in which *shama*ꞌ has this sense.

Remarks will now be presented to you on these metaphors and similes, which will quench your thirst, and explain to you all their meanings without leaving a doubt.

CHAPTER XLVI

WE have already stated, in one of the chapters of this treatise, that there is a great difference between bringing to view the existence of a thing and de-monstrating its true essence. We can lead others to notice the existence of an object by pointing to its accidents, actions, or even most remote relations to other objects : e.g., if you wish to describe the king of a country to one of his subjects who does not know him, you can give a description and an account of his existence in many ways. You will either say to him, the tall man with a fair complexion and grey hair is the king, thus describing him by his acci-dents ; or you will say, the king is the person round whom are seen a great multitude of men on horse and on foot, and soldiers with drawn swords, over whose head banners are waving, and before whom trumpets are sounded ; or it is the person living in the palace in a particular region of a certain country ; or it is the person who ordered the building of that wall, or the construction of that bridge ; or by some other similar acts and things relating to him. His existence can be demonstrated in a still more indirect way, e.g., if you are asked whether this land has a king, you will undoubtedly answer in the affirmative. " What proof have you ? " " The fact that this banker here, a weak and little person, stands before this large mass of gold pieces, and that poor man, tall and strong, who stands before him asking in vain for alms of the weight of a carob-grain, is rebuked and is compelled to go away by the mere force of words ; for had he not feared the king, he would, without hesitation, have killed the banker, or pushed him away and taken as much of the money as he could." Conse-quently, this is a proof that this country has a ruler and his existence is proved by the well-regulated affairs of the country, on account of which the king is respected and the punishments decreed by him are feared. In this whole example nothing is mentioned that indicated his characteristics, and his essential properties, by virtue of which he is king. The same is the case with the information concerning the Creator given to the ordinary classes of men in all prophetical books and in the Law. For it was found necessary to teach all of them that God exists, and that He is in every respect the most perfect Being, that is to say, He exists not only in the sense in which the earth and the heavens exist, but He exists and possesses life, wisdom, power, activity, and all other properties which our belief in His existence must in-clude, as will be shown below. That God exists was therefore shown to ordinary men by means of similes taken from physical bodies ; that He is living, by a simile taken from motion, because ordinary men consider only the body as fully, truly, and undoubtedly existing ; that which is connected with a body but is itself not a body, although believed to exist, has a lower degree of existence on account of its dependence on the body for existence.   That, however, which is neither itself a body, nor a force within a body, is not existent according to man's first notions, and is above all excluded from the range of imagination.   In the same manner motion is considered by the ordinary man as identical with life ; what cannot move voluntarily from place to place has no life, although motion is not part of the definition of life, but an accident connected with it.   The perception by the senses, especially by hearing and seeing, is best known to us ; we have no idea or notion of any other mode of communication between the soul of one person and that of another than by means of speaking, i.e., by the sound produced by lips, tongue, and the other organs of speech.   When, therefore, we are to be informed that God has a *knowledge* of things, and that communication is made by Him to the Prophets who convey it to us, they represent Him to us as seeing and hearing, i.e., as perceiving and knowing those things which can be seen and heard.   They represent Him to us as speaking, i.e., that communications from Him reach the Prophets ; that is to be understood by the term "prophecy," as will be fully explained.   God is described as working, because we do not know any other mode of producing a thing except by direct touch.   He is said to have a soul in the sense that He is living, because all living beings are generally supposed to have a soul ; although the term soul is, as has been shown, a homonym.

Again, since we perform all these actions only by means of corporeal organs, we figuratively ascribe to God the organs of locomotion, as feet, and their soles ; organs of hearing, seeing, and smelling, as ear, eye, and nose ; organs and substance of speech, as mouth, tongue, and sound ; organs for the performance of work, as hand, its fingers, its palm, and the arm.   In short, these organs of the body are figuratively ascribed to God, who is above all imperfection, to express that He performs certain acts ; and these acts are figuratively ascribed to Him to express that He possesses certain perfections different from those acts themselves.   E.g., we say that He has eyes, ears, hands, a mouth, a tongue, to express that He sees, hears, acts, and speaks ; but seeing and hearing are attributed to Him to indicate simply that He perceives.   You thus find in Hebrew instances in which the perception of the one sense is named instead of the other ; thus, " See the word of the Lord " (Jer. ii. 31), in the same meaning as " Hear the word of the Lord," for the sense of the phrase is, " Perceive what He says " ; similarly the phrase, " See the smell of my son " (Gen. xxvii. 27) has the same meaning as " Smell the smell of my son," for it relates to the perception of the smell.   In the same way are used the words, " And all the people saw the thunders and the lightnings " (Exod. xx. 15), although the passage also contains the description of a prophetical vision, as is well known and understood among our people.   Action and speech are likewise figuratively applied to God, to express that a certain influence has emanated from Him, as will be explained (chap. lxv and chap. lxvi.).   The physical organs which are attributed to God in the writings of the Prophets are either organs of locomotion, indicating life; organs of sensation, indicating perception; organs of touch, indicating action; or organs of speech, indicating the divine inspiration of the Prophets, as will be explained.

The object of all these indications is to establish in our minds the notion of the existence of a living being, the Maker of everything, who also possesses a knowledge of the things which He has made. We shall explain, when we come to speak of the inadmissibility of Divine attributes, that all these various attributes convey but one notion, viz., that of the essence of God. The sole object of this chapter is to explain in what sense physical organs are ascribed to the Most Perfect Being, namely, that they are mere indications of the actions generally performed by means of these organs. Such actions being perfections respecting ourselves, are predicated of God, because we wish to express that He is most perfect in every respect, as we remarked above in explaining the Rabbinical phrase, " The language of the Torah is like the language of man." Instances of organs of locomotion being applied to the Creator occur as follows :—" My footstool " (Isa. lxvi. 1); " the place of the soles of my feet " (Ezek. xliii. 7). For examples of organs of touch applied to God, comp. " the hand of the Lord " (Exod. ix. 3); "with the finger of God " (ib. xxxi. 18); " the work of thy fingers " (Ps. viii. 4), " And thou hast laid thine hand upon me " (ib. cxxxix. 5); " The arm of the Lord " (Isa. liii. 1); " Thy right hand, O Lord " (Exod. xv. 6). In instances like the following, organs of speech are attributed to God : " The mouth of the Lord has spoken " (Isa. i. 20); " And He would open His lips against thee " (Job xi. 5); " The voice of the Lord is powerful " (Ps. xxix. 4); " And his tongue as a devouring fire " (Isa. xxx. 27). Organs of sensation are attributed to God in instances like the following : " His eyes behold, His eyelids try " (Ps. xi. 4); " The eyes of the Lord which run to and fro " (Zech. iv. 10); " Bow down thine ear unto me, and hear " (2 Kings xix. 16); " You have kindled a fire in my nostril " (Jer. xvii. 5). Of the inner parts of the human body only the heart is figuratively applied to God, because " heart " is a homonym, and denotes also " intellect "; it is besides the source of animal life. In phrases like " my bowels are troubled for him " (Jer. xxxi. 20); " The sounding of thy bowels " (Isa. lxiii. 15), the term " bowels " is used in the sense of " heart "; for the term " bowels " is used both in a general and in a specific meaning; it denotes specifically " bowels," but more generally it can be used as the name of any inner organ, including " heart." The correctness of this argument can be proved by the phrase " And thy law is within my bowels " (Ps. xl. 9), which is identical with " And thy law is within my heart." For that reason the prophet employed in this verse the phrase " my bowels are troubled " (and " the sounding of thy bowels "); the verb *hamah* is in fact used more frequently in connection with " heart," than with any other organ; comp. " My heart maketh a noise (*homeh*) in me " (Jer. iv. 19). Similarly, the shoulder is never used as a figure in reference to God, because it is known as a mere instrument of transport, and also comes into close contact with the thing which it carries. With far greater reason the organs of nutrition are never attributed to God; they are at once recognized as signs of imperfection. In fact all organs, both the external and the internal, are employed in the various actions of the soul; some, as e.g., all inner organs, are the means of preserving the individual for a certain time; others, as the organs of generation, are the means of preserving the species; others are the means of improving the condition of man and bringing his actions to perfection, as the hands, the feet, and the eyes, all of which tend to render motion, action, and perception more perfect. Animate beings require motion in order to be able to approach that which is conducive to their welfare, and to move away from the opposite; they require the senses in order to be able to discern what is injurious to them and what is beneficial. In addition, man requires various kinds of handiwork, to prepare his food, clothing, and dwelling; and he is compelled by his physical constitution to perform such work, namely, to prepare what is good for him. Some kinds of work also occur among certain animals, as far as such work is required by those animals. I do not believe that any man can doubt the correctness of the assertion that the Creator is not in need of anything for the continuance of His existence, or for the improvement of His condition. Therefore, God has no organs, or, what is the same, He is not corporeal; His actions are accomplished by His Essence, not by any organ, and as undoubtedly physical forces are connected with the organs, He does not possess any such forces, that is to say, He has, besides His Essence, nothing that could be the cause of His action, His knowledge, or His will, for attributes are nothing but forces under a different name. It is not my intention to discuss the question in this chapter. Our Sages laid down a general principle, by which the literal sense of the physical attributes of God mentioned by the prophets is rejected; a principle which evidently shows that our Sages were far from the belief in the corporeality of God, and that they did not think any person capable of misunderstanding it, or entertaining any doubt about it. For that reason they employ in the Talmud and the Midrashim phrases similar to those contained in the prophecies, without any circumlocution; they knew that there could not be any doubt about their metaphorical character, or any danger whatever of their being misunderstood; and that all such expressions would be understood as figurative [language], employed to communicate to the intellect the notion of His existence. Now, it was well known that in figurative language God is compared to a king who commands, cautions, punishes, and rewards, his subjects, and whose servants and attendants publish his orders, so that they might be acted upon, and they also execute whatever he wishes. Thus the Sages adopted that figure, used it frequently, and introduced such speech, consent, and refusal of a king, and other usual acts of kings, as became necessary bʃ that figure. In all these instances they were sure that no doubt or confusion would arise from it. The general principle alluded to above is contained in the following saying of our Sages, mentioned in Bereshith Rabba (c. xxvii.), "Great was the power of the Prophets; they compared the creature to its Creator; comp. 'And over the resemblance of the throne was a resemblance like the appearance of man'" (Ezek. i. 26). They have thus plainly stated that all those images which the Prophets perceived, i.e. in prophetic visions, are images created by God. This is perfectly correct; for every image in our imagination has been created. How pregnant is the expression, "Great is their boldness!" They indicated by it, that they themselves found it very remarkable; for whenever they perceived a word or act difficult to explain, or apparently objectionable, they used that phrase; e.g., a certain Rabbi has performed the act (of "ḥali ah") with a slipper, alone and by night. Another Rabbi, thereupon exclaimed "How great is his boldness to have followed the opinion of the minority." The Chaldee phrase *rab gubreh* in the original of the latter quotation, and the Hebrew *gadol koḥo* in that of the former quotation, have the same meaning, viz., Great is the power of (or the boldness of). Hence, in the preceding quotation, the sense is, How remarkable is the language which the Prophets were obliged to use when they speak of God the Creator in terms signifying properties of beings created by Him. This deserves attention. Our Sages have thus stated in distinct and plain terms that they are far from believing in the corporeality of God; and in the figures and forms seen in a prophetical vision, though belonging to created beings, the Prophets, to use the words of our Sages, "compared the creature to its Creator." If, however, after these explanations, any one wishes out of malice to cavil at them, and to find fault with them, though their method is neither comprehended nor understood by him, the Sages o.b.m. will sustain no injury by it.

CHAPTER XLVII

WE have already stated several times that the prophetic books never attribute to God anything which ordinary men consider a defect, or which they cannot in their imagination combine with the idea of the Almighty, although such terms may not otherwise be different from those which were employed as metaphors in relation to God. Indeed all things which are attributed to God are considered in some way to be perfection, or can at least be imagined [as appertaining to Him].

We must now show why, according to this principle, the senses of hearing, sight and smell, are attributed to God, but not those of taste and touch. He is equally elevated above the use of all the five senses; they are all defective as regards perception, even for those who have no other source of knowledge; because they are passive, receive impressions from without, and are subject to interruptions and sufferings, as much as the other organs of the body. By saying that God sees, we mean to state that He perceives visible things; "He hears" is identical with saying "He perceives audible things"; in the same way we might say, "He tastes and He touches," in the sense of "He perceives objects which man perceives by means of taste and touch." For, as regards perception, the senses are identical; if we deny the existence of one sensation in God, we must deny that of all other sensations, i.e., the perceptions of the five senses; and if we attribute the existence of one sensation to Him, i.e., the perception appertaining to one of the senses, we must attribute all the five sensations. Nevertheless, we find in Holy Writ, "And God saw" (Gen. vi. 5); "And God heard" (Num. xi. 1); "And God smelt" (Gen. viii. 21); but we do not meet with the expressions, "And God tasted," "And God touched." According to our opinion the reason of this is to be found in the idea, which has a firm hold in the minds of all men, that God does not come into contact with a body in the same manner as one body comes into contact with another, since He is not even seen by the eye. While these two senses, namely, taste and touch, only act when in close contact with the object, by sight, hearing, and smell, even distant objects are perceived. These, therefore, were considered by the multitude appropriate expressions [to be figuratively applied to God]. Besides, the object in figuratively applying the sensations to Him, could only have been to express that He perceives our actions; but hearing and sight are sufficient for that, namely, for the perception of what a man does or says. Thus our Sages, among other admonitions, gave the following advice and warning: " Know what is above thee, a seeing eye, and a hearing ear." (Mishnah Abot, ii. 1.)

You, however, know that, strictly speaking, the condition of all the sensations is the same, that the same argument which is employed against the existence of touch and taste in God, may be used against sight, hearing, and smell; for they all are material perceptions and impressions which are subject to change. There is only this difference, that the former, touch and taste, are at once recognized as deficiencies, while the others are considered as perfections. In a similar manner the defect of the imagination is easily seen, less easily that of thinking and reasoning. Imagination (*ra'ayon*) therefore, was never employed as a figure in speaking of God, while thought and reason are figuratively ascribed to Him. Comp. " The thoughts which the Lord thought " (Jer. xlix. 20); " And with his understanding he stretched out the heavens " (*ib.* x. 12). The inner senses were thus treated in the same way as the external; some are figuratively applied to God, some not. All this is according to the language of man; he ascribes to God what he considers a perfection, and does not ascribe to Him what he considers a defect. In truth, however, no real attribute, implying an addition to His essence, can be applied to Him, as will be proved.

CHAPTER XLVIII

WHENEVER in the Pentateuch the term " to hear " is applied to God, Onkelos, the Proselyte, does not translate it literally, but paraphrases it, merely expressing that a certain speech reached Him, i.e., He perceived it, or that He accepted it or did not accept, when it refers to supplication and prayer as its object. The words " God heard " are therefore paraphrased by him regularly either, " It was heard before the Lord," or " He accepted " when employed in reference to supplication and prayer; [e.g.] " I will surely accept," lit. " I will surely hear " (Exod. xxii. 22). This principle is followed by Onkelos in his translation of the Pentateuch without any exception. But as regards the verb " to see," (*raah*), his renderings vary in a remarkable manner, and I was unable to discern his principle or method. In some instances he translates literally, " and God saw "; in others he paraphrases " it was revealed before the Lord." The use of the phrase *va-ḥaza adonai* by Onkelos is sufficient evidence that the term *ḥaza* in Chaldee is homonymous, and that it denotes mental perception as well as the sensation of sight. This being the case, I am surprised that, in some instances avoiding the literal rendering, he substituted for it " And it was revealed before the Lord." When I, however, examined the various readings in the version of Onkelos, which I either saw myself or heard from others during the time of my studies, I found that the term " to see " when connected with wrong, injury, or violence, was paraphrased, " It was manifest before the Lord."

There is no doubt that the term *ḥaza* in Chaldee denotes complete apprehension and reception of the object in the state in which it has been perceived. When Onkelos, therefore, found the verb "to see" connected with the object "wrong," he did not render it literally, but paraphrased it, "It was revealed before the Lord." Now, I noticed that in all instances of the Pentateuch where seeing is ascribed to God, he translated it literally, except those instances which I will mention to you : "For my affliction was revealed before the Lord" (Gen. xxix. 32) ; "For all that Laban doeth unto thee is revealed before me" (*ib.* xxxi. 12) ;—although the first person in the sentence refers to the angel [and not to God], Onkelos does not ascribe to him that perception which implies complete comprehension of the object, because the object is "iniquity"—"The oppression of the children of Israel was known to the Lord" (Exod. ii. 25) ; "The oppression of my people was surely known to me" (*ib.* iii. 7) ; "The affliction is known to me" (*ib.* 9) ; "Their oppression is known to me" (*ib.* iv. 31) ; "This people is known to me" (*ib.* xxxii. 9), i.e., their rebellion is known to me— comp. the Targum of the passage, "And God saw the children of Israel" (*ib.* ii. 25), which is equal to "He saw their affliction and their trouble"— "And it was known to the Lord, and he abhorred them" (Deut. xxxii. 19) ; "It was known to him that their power was gone" (*ib.* 36) ; in this instance the object of the perception is likewise the wrong done to the Israelites, and the increasing power of the enemy. In all these examples Onkelos is consistent, following the maxim expressed in the words, "Thou canst not look on iniquity" (Hab. i. 13) ; wherefore he renders the verb "to see," when referring to oppression or rebellion, It is revealed before him, etc. This appropriate and satisfactory explanation, the correctness of which I do not doubt, is weakened by three passages, in which, according to this view, I expected to find the verb "to see" paraphrased "to be revealed before him," but found instead the literal rendering "to see" in the various copies of the Targum. The following are the three passages : "And God saw that the wickedness of man was great upon the earth" (Gen. vi. 6) ; "And the Lord saw the earth, and behold it was corrupt" (*ib.* vi. 12) ; "and God saw that Leah was hated" (*ib.* xxx. 31). It appears to me that in these passages there is a mistake, which has crept into the copies of the Targum, since we do not possess the Targum in the original manuscript of Onkelos, for in that case we should have assumed that he had a satisfactory explanation of it.

In rendering Genesis xxii. 8, "the lamb is known to the Lord," he either wished to indicate that the Lord was not expected to seek and to bring it, or he considered it inappropriate, in Chaldee to connect the divine perception with one of the lower animals.

However, the various copies of the Targum must be carefully examined with regard to this point, and if you still find those passages the same as I quoted them, I cannot explain what he meant.

CHAPTER XLIX

THE angels are likewise incorporeal ; they are intelligences without matter, but they are nevertheless created beings, and God created them, as will be

explained below. In Bereshith Rabbah (on Gen. iii. 24) we read the following remark of our Sages : " The angel is called ' the flame of the sword which
turned every way ' (Gen. iii. 24), in accordance with the words, ' His ministers a flaming fire ' (Ps. civ. 4) ; the attribute, ' which turned every way ' is
added, because angels are changeable in form ; they appear at one time as
males, at another as females ; now as spirits ; now as angels." By this
remark they clearly stated that angels are incorporeal, and have no permanent bodily form independent of the mind [of him who perceives them],
they exist entirely in prophetic vision, and depend on the action of the
imaginative power, as will be explained when speaking on the true meaning
of prophecy. As to the words " at another time as females," which imply
that the Prophets in prophetical vision perceived angels also in the form of
women, they refer to the vision of Zechariah (v. 9), "And, behold, there
came out two women, and the wind was in their wings." You know very
well how difficult it is for men to form a notion of anything immaterial,
and entirely devoid of corporeality, except after considerable training : it is
especially difficult for those who do not distinguish between objects of the
intellect and objects of the imagination, and depend mostly on the mere
imaginative power. They believe that all imagined things exist or at least
have the possibility of existing ; but that which cannot be imagined does not
exist, and cannot exist. For persons of this class—and the majority of
thinkers belong to it—cannot arrive at the true solution of any question, or
at the explanation of anything doubtful. On account of this difficulty the
prophetic books contain expressions which, taken literally, imply that angels
are corporeal, moving about, endowed with human form, receiving commands of God, obeying His word and performing whatever He wishes,
according to His command. All this only serves to lead to the belief that
angels exist, and are alive and perfect, in the same way as we have explained
in reference to God. If the figurative representation of angels were limited
to this, their true essence would be believed to be the same as the essence of
God, since, in reference to the Creator expressions are likewise employed,
which literally imply that He is corporeal, living, moving and endowed with
human form. In order, therefore, to give to the mind of men the idea that
the existence of angels is lower than the existence of God, certain forms of
lower animals were introduced in the description of angels. It was
thereby shown, that the existence of God is more perfect than that
of angels, as much as man is more perfect than the lower animals.
Nevertheless no organ of the brute creation was attributed to the angels
except wings. Without wings the act of flying appears as impossible as
that of walking without legs ; for these two modes of motion can only be
imagined in connection with these organs. The motion of flying has been
chosen as a symbol to represent that angels possess life, because it is the most
perfect and most sublime movement of the brute creation. Men consider
this motion a perfection to such an extent that they themselves wish to be
able to fly, in order to escape easily what is injurious, and to obtain quickly
what is useful, though it be at a distance. For this reason this motion has
been attributed to the angels.

There is besides another reason. The bird in its flight is sometimes visible,
sometimes withdrawn from our sight ; one moment near to us, and in the

next far off ; and these are exactly the circumstances which we must associate with the idea of angels, as will be explained below. This imaginary perfection, the motion of flight, being the exclusive property of the brute creation, has never been attributed to God. You must not be misled by the passage, "And he rode upon a cherub, and he did fly " (Ps. xviii. 10), for it is the cherub that did fly, and the simile only serves to denote the rapid arrival of that which is referred to in that passage. Comp.: " Behold, the Lord rideth upon a swift cloud, and shall come into Egypt " (Isa. xix. 1) ; that is, the punishment alluded to will come down quickly upon Egypt. Nor should expressions like " the face of an ox," " the face of a lion," " the face of an eagle," " the sole of the foot of a calf," found in the prophecies of Ezekiel (i. 10 and 7) mislead you ; for all these are explained in a different manner, as you will learn later, and besides, the prophet only describes the animals (*ḥay-yot*). The subject will be explained (III. i.), though by mere hints, as far as necessary, for directing your attention to the true interpretation.

The motion of flying, frequently mentioned in the Bible, necessitates, according to our imagination, the existence of wings ; wings are therefore given to the angels as symbols expressive of their existence, not of their true essence. You must also bear in mind that whenever a thing moves very quickly, it is said to fly, as that term implies great velocity of motion. Comp. " As the eagle flieth " (Deut. xxviii. 49). The eagle flies and moves with greater velocity than any other bird, and therefore it is introduced in this simile. Furthermore, the wings are the organs [lit. causes] of flight ; hence the number of the wings of angels in the prophetic vision corresponds to the number of the causes which set a thing in motion, but this does not belong to the theme of this chapter. (Comp. II. iv. and x.)

CHAPTER L

WHEN reading my present treatise, bear in mind that by " faith " we do not understand merely that which is uttered with the lips, but also that which is apprehended by the soul, the conviction that the object [of belief] is exactly as it is apprehended. If, as regards real or supposed truths, you content yourself with giving utterance to them in words, without apprehending them or believing in them, especially if you do not seek real truth, you have a very easy task as, in fact, you will find many ignorant people professing articles of faith without connecting any idea with them.

If, however, you have a desire to rise to a higher state, viz., that of reflection, and truly to hold the conviction that God is One and possesses true unity, without admitting plurality or divisibility in any sense whatever, you must understand that God has no essential attribute in any form or in any sense whatever, and that the rejection of corporeality implies the rejection of essential attributes. Those who believe that God is One, and that He has many attributes, declare the unity with their lips, and assume plurality in their thoughts. This is like the doctrine of the Christians, who say that He is one and He is three, and that the three are one. Of the same character is the doctrine of those who say that God is One, but that He has many attributes ; and that He with His attributes is One, although they deny corporeality and affirm His most absolute freedom from matter ; as if our object were to seek forms of expression, not subjects of belief. For belief is only possible after the apprehension of a thing ; it consists in the conviction that the thing apprehended has its existence beyond the mind [in reality] exactly as it is conceived in the mind. If in addition to this we are convinced that the thing cannot be different in any way from what we believe it to be, and that no reasonable argument can be found for the rejection of the belief or for the admission of any deviation from it, then the belief is true. Renounce desires and habits, follow your reason, and study what I am going to say in the chapters which follow on the rejection of the attributes ; you will then be fully convinced of what we have said ; you will be of those who truly conceive the Unity of God, not of those who utter it with their lips without thought, like men of whom it has been said, " Thou art near in their mouth, and far from their reins " (Jer. xii. 2). It is right that a man should belong to that class of men who have a conception of truth and understand it, though they do not speak of it. Thus the pious are advised and addressed, " Commune with your own heart upon your bed and be still. Selah." (Ps. iv. 5.)

CHAPTER LI

There are many things whose existence is manifest and obvious ; some of these are innate notions or objects of sensation, others are nearly so ; and in fact they would require no proof if man had been left in his primitive state. Such are the existence of motion, of man's free will, of phases of production and destruction, and of the natural properties perceived by the senses, e.g., the heat of fire, the coldness of water, and many other similar things. False notions, however, may be spread either by a person labouring under error, or by one who has some particular end in view, and who establishes theories contrary to the real nature of things, by denying the existence of things perceived by the senses, or by affirming the existence of what does not exist. Philosophers are thus required to establish by proof things which are self-evident, and to disprove the existence of things which only exist in man's imagination. Thus Aristotle gives a proof for the existence of motion, because it had been denied ; he disproves the reality of atoms, because it had been asserted.

To the same class belongs the rejection of essential attributes in reference to God. For it is a self-evident truth that the attribute is not inherent in the object to which it is ascribed, but it is superadded to its essence, and is consequently an *accident* ; if the attribute denoted the essence [τὸ τί ἦν εἶναι] of the object, it would be either mere tautology, as if, e.g., one would say " man is man," or the explanation of a name, as, e.g., " man is a speaking animal " ; for the words " speaking animal " include the true essence of man, and there is no third element besides life and speech in the definition of man ; when he, therefore, is described by the attributes of life and speech, these are nothing but an explanation of the name " man," that is to say, that the thing which is called man, consists of life and speech. It will now be clear that the attribute must be one of two things, either the essence of the object described—in that case it is a mere explanation of a name, and on that account we might admit the attribute in reference to God, but we reject it from another cause as will be shown—or the attribute is something different from the object described, some extraneous superadded element; in that case the attribute would be an accident, and he who merely rejects the appellation " accidents " in reference to the attributes of God, does not thereby alter their character; for everything superadded to the essence of an object joins it without forming part of its essential properties, and that constitutes an accident. Add to this the logical consequence of admitting many attributes, viz., the existence of many eternal beings. There cannot be any belief in the unity of God except by admitting that He is one simple substance, without any composition or plurality of elements; one from whatever side you view it, and by whatever test you examine it; not divisible into two parts in any way and by any cause, nor capable of any form of plurality either objectively or subjectively, as will be proved in this treatise.

Some thinkers have gone so far as to say that the attributes of God are neither His essence nor anything extraneous to His essence. This is like the assertion of some theorists, that the ideals, i.e., the *universalia*, are neither existing nor non-existent, and like the views of others, that the atom does not fill a definite place, but keeps an atom of space occupied; that man has no freedom of action at all, but has acquirement. Such things are only said; they exist only in words, not in thought, much less in reality. But as you know, and as all know who do not delude themselves, these theories are preserved by a multitude of words, by misleading similes sustained by declamation and invective, and by numerous methods borrowed both from dialectics and sophistry. If after uttering them and supporting them by such words, a man were to examine for himself his own belief on this subject, he would see nothing but confusion and stupidity in an endeavour to prove the existence of things which do not exist, or to find a mean between two opposites that have no mean. Or is there a mean between existence and non-existence, or between the identity and non-identity of two things? But, as we said, to such absurdities men were forced by the great licence given to the imagination, and by the fact that every existing material thing is necessarily imagined as a certain substance possessing several attributes; for nothing has ever been found that consists of one simple substance without any attribute. Guided by such imaginations, men thought that God was also composed of many different elements, viz., of His essence and of the attributes superadded to His essence. Following up this comparison, some believed that God was corporeal, and that He possessed attributes; others, abandoning this theory, denied the corporeality, but retained the attributes. The adherence to the literal sense of the text of Holy Writ is the source of all this error, as I shall show in some of the chapters devoted to this theme.

CHAPTER LII

EVERY description of an object by an affirmative attribute, which includes the assertion that an object is of a certain kind, must be made in one of the following five ways :—

First. The object is described by its *definition*, as e.g., man is described as a being that lives and has reason; such a description, containing the true essence of the object, is, as we have already shown, nothing else but the explanation of a name. All agree that this kind of description cannot be given of God ; for there are no previous causes to His existence, by which He could be defined : and on that account it is a well-known principle, received by all the philosophers, who are precise in their statements, that no definition can be given of God.

Secondly. An object is described by *part of its definition*, as when, e.g., man is described as a living being or as a rational being. This kind of description includes the necessary connection [of the two ideas] ; for when we say that every man is rational we mean by it that every being which has the characteristics of man must also have reason. All agree that this kind of description is inappropriate in reference to God ; for if we were to speak of a portion of His essence, we should consider His essence to be a compound. The inappropriateness of this kind of description in reference to God is the same as that of the preceding kind.

Thirdly. An object is described by something different from its true essence, by something that does not complement or establish the essence of the object. The description, therefore, relates to a *quality* ; but quality, in its most general sense, is an accident. If God could be described in this way, He would be the substratum of accidents : a sufficient reason for re-jecting the idea that He possesses quality, since it diverges from the true conception of His essence. It is surprising how those who admit the appli-cation of attributes to God can reject, in reference to Him, comparison and qualification. For when they say " He cannot be qualified," they can only mean that He possesses no quality ; and yet every positive essential attribute of an object either constitutes its essence,—and in that case it is identical with the essence,—or it contains a quality of the object.

There are, as you know, four kinds of quality ; I will give you instances of attributes of each kind, in order to show you that this class of attributes cannot possibly be applied to God. (*a*) A man is described by any of his intellectual or moral qualities, or by any of the dispositions appertaining to him as an animate being, when, e.g., we speak of a person who is a carpenter, or who shrinks from sin, or who is ill. It makes no difference whether we say, a carpenter, or a sage, or a physician ; by all these we represent certain phy-sical dispositions ; nor does it make any difference whether we say " sin-fearing " or " merciful." Every trade, every profession, and every settled habit of man are certain physical dispositions. All this is clear to those who have occupied themselves with the study of Logic. (*b*) A thing is described by some physical quality it possesses, or by the absence of the same, e.g., as being soft or hard. It makes no difference whether we say " soft or hard," or " strong or weak " ; in both cases we speak of physical conditions. (*c*) A man is described by his passive qualities, or by his emotions ; we speak, e.g., of a person who is passionate, irritable, timid, merciful, without implying that these conditions have become permanent. The description of a thing by its colour, taste, heat, cold, dryness, and moisture, belongs also to this class of attributes. (*d*) A thing is described by any of its qualities resulting from quantity as such ; we speak, e.g., of a thing which is long, short, curved, straight, etc.

Consider all these and similar attributes, and you will find that they cannot be employed in reference to God. He is not a magnitude that any quality resulting from quantity as such could be possessed by Him ; He is not affected by external influences, and therefore does not possess any quality resulting from emotion. He is not subject to physical conditions, and therefore does not possess strength or similar qualities ; He is not an animate being, that He should have a certain disposition of the soul, or acquire certain properties, as meekness, modesty, etc., or be in a state to which animate beings as such are subject, as, e.g., in that of health or of illness. Hence it follows that no attribute coming under the head of quality in its widest sense, can be predicated of God. Consequently, these three classes of attributes, describing the essence of a thing, or part of the essence, or a quality of it, are clearly inadmissible in reference to God, for they imply composition, which, as we shall prove, is out of question as regards the Creator. We say, with regard to this latter point, that He is *absolutely* One.

Fourthly. A thing is described by its *relation* to another thing, e.g., to time, to space, or to a different individual ; thus we say, Zaid, the father of A, or the partner of B, or who dwells at a certain place, or who lived at a stated time. This kind of attribute does not necessarily imply plurality or change in the essence of the object described ; for the same Zaid, to whom reference is made, is the partner of Amru, the father of Becr, the master of Khalid, the friend of Zaid, dwells in a certain house, and was born in a certain year. Such relations are not the essence of a thing, nor are they so intimately connected with it as qualities. At first thought, it would seem that they may be employed in reference to God, but after careful and thorough consideration we are convinced of their inadmissibility. It is quite clear that there is no relation between God and time or space. For time is an accident connected with motion, in so far as the latter includes the relation of anteriority and posteriority, and is expressed by number, as is explained in books devoted to this subject ; and since motion is one of the conditions to which only material bodies are subject, and God is immaterial, there can be no relation between Him and time. Similarly there is no relation between Him and space. But what we have to investigate and to examine is this : whether some real relation exists between God and any of the substances created by Him, by which He could be described ? That there is no correlation between Him and any of His creatures can easily be seen ; for the characteristic of two objects correlative to each other is the equality of their reciprocal relation. Now, as God has absolute existence, while all other beings have only possible existence, as we shall show, there consequently cannot be any correlation [between God and His creatures]. That a certain kind of relation does exist between them is by some considered possible, but wrongly. It is impossible to imagine a relation between intellect and sight, although, as we believe, the same kind of existence is common to both ; how, then, could a relation be imagined between any creature and God, who has nothing in common with any other being ; for even the term existence is applied to Him and other things, according to our opinion, only by way of pure homonymity. Consequently there is no relation whatever between Him and any other being. For whenever we speak of a relation between two things, these belong to the same kind ; but when two things belong to different kinds though of the same class, there is no relation between them. We therefore do not say, this red compared with that green, is more, or less, or equally intense, although both belong to the same class—colour ;

when they belong to two different classes, there does not appear to exist any relation between them, not even to a man of ordinary intellect, although the two things belong to the same category ; e.g., between a hundred cubits and the heat of pepper there is no relation, the one being a quality, the other a quantity ; or between wisdom and sweetness, between meekness and bitterness, although all these come under the head of quality in its more general signification. How, then, could there be any relation between God and His creatures, considering the important difference between them in respect to true existence, the greatest of all differences. Besides, if any relation existed between them, God would be subject to the accident of relation ; and although that would not be an accident to the essence of God, it would still be, to some extent, a kind of accident. You would, therefore, be wrong if you applied affirmative attributes in their literal sense to God, though they contained only relations ; these, however, are the most appropriate of all attributes, to be employed, in a less strict sense, in reference to God, because they do not imply that a plurality of eternal things exists, or that any change takes place in the essence of God, when those things change to which God is in relation.

Fifthly. A thing is described by its *actions* ; I do not mean by " its actions " the inherent capacity for a certain work, as is expressed in " carpenter," " painter," or " smith "—for these belong to the class of qualities which have been mentioned above—but I mean the action the latter has performed—we speak, e.g., of Zaid, who made this door, built that wall, wove that garment. This kind of attributes is separate from the essences of the thing described, and, therefore, appropriate to be employed in describing the Creator, especially since we know that these different actions do not imply that different elements must be contained in the substance of the agent, by which the different actions are produced, as will be explained. On the contrary, all the actions of God emanate from His essence, not from any extraneous thing superadded to His essence, as we have shown.

What we have explained in the present chapter is this : that God is one in every respect, containing no plurality or any element superadded to His essence : and that the many attributes of different significations applied in Scripture to God, originate in the multitude of His actions, not in a plurality existing in His essence, and are partly employed with the object of conveying to us some notion of His perfection, in accordance with what we consider perfection, as has been explained by us. The possibility of one simple substance excluding plurality, though accomplishing different actions, will be illustrated by examples in the next chapter.

CHAPTER LIII

THE circumstance which caused men to believe in the existence of divine attributes is similar to that which caused others to believe in the corporeality of God. The latter have not arrived at that belief by speculation, but by following the literal sense of certain passages in the Bible. The same is the case with the attributes ; when in the books of the Prophets and of the Law, God is described by attributes, such passages are taken in their literal sense, and it is then believed that God possesses attributes ; as if He were to be exalted above corporeality, and not above things connected with corporeality, i.e., the accidents, I mean psychical dispositions, all of which are qualities [and connected with corporeality]. Every attribute which the followers of this doctrine assume to be essential to the Creator, you will find to express, although they do not distinctly say so, a quality similar to those which they are accustomed to notice in the bodies of all living beings. We apply to all such passages the principle, " The Torah speaketh in the language of man," and say that the object of all these terms is to describe God as the most perfect being, not as possessing those qualities which are only perfections in relation to created living beings. Many of the attributes express different acts of God, but that difference does not necessitate any difference as regards Him from whom the acts proceed. This fact, viz., that from one agency different effects may result, although that agency has not free will, and much more so if it has free will, I will illustrate by an instance taken from our own sphere. Fire melts certain things and makes others hard, it boils and burns, it bleaches and blackens. If we described the fire as bleaching, blackening, burning, boiling, hardening and melting, we should be correct, and yet he who does not know the nature of fire, would think that it included six different elements, one by which it blackens, another by which it bleaches, a third by which it boils, a fourth by which it consumes, a fifth by which it melts, a sixth by which it hardens things—actions which are opposed to one another, and of which each has its peculiar property. He, however, who knows the nature of fire, will know that by virtue of one quality in action, namely, by heat, it produces all these effects. If this is the case with that which is done by nature, how much more is it the case with regard to beings that act by free will, and still more with regard to God, who is above all description. If we, therefore, perceive in God certain relations of various kinds—for wisdom in us is different from power, and power from will—it does by no means follow that different elements are really contained in Him, that He contains one element by which He knows, another by which He wills, and another by which He exercises power, as is, in fact, the signification of the attributes of God] according to the Attributists. Some of them express it plainly, and enumerate the attributes as elements added to the essence. Others, however, are more reserved with regard to this matter, but indicate their opinion, though they do not express it in distinct and intelligible words. Thus, e.g., some of them say : " God is omnipotent by His essence, wise by His essence, living by His essence, and endowed with a will by His essence." (I will mention to you, as an instance, man's reason, which being one faculty and implying no plurality, enables him to know many arts and sciences ; by the same faculty man is able to sow, to do carpenter's work, to weave, to build, to study, to acquire a knowledge of geometry, and to govern a state. These various acts resulting from one simple faculty, which involves no plurality, are very numerous ; their number, that is, the number of the actions originating in man's reason, is almost infinite. It is therefore intelligible how in reference to God, those different actions can be caused by one simple substance, that does not include any plurality or any additional element. The attributes found in Holy Scripture are either qualifications of His actions, without any reference to His essence, or indicate absolute perfection, but do not imply that the essence of God is a compound of various elements.) For in not admitting the *term* " compound," they do not reject the *idea* of a compound when they admit a substance with attributes.

There still remains one difficulty which led them to that error, and which I am now going to mention. Those who assert the existence of the attributes do not found their opinion on the variety of God's actions ; they say it is true that one substance can be the source of various effects, but His essential attributes cannot be qualifications of His actions, because it is impossible to imagine that the Creator created Himself. They vary with regard to the so-called essential attributes—I mean as regards their number—according to the text of the Scripture which each of them follows. I will enumerate those on which all agree, and the knowledge of which they believe that they have derived from reasoning, not from some words of the Prophets, namely, the following four :—life, power, wisdom, and will. They believe that these are four different things, and such perfections as cannot possibly be absent from the Creator, and that these cannot be qualifications of His actions. This is their opinion. But you must know that wisdom and life in reference to God are not different from each other ; for in every being that is conscious of itself, life and wisdom are the same thing, that is to say, if by wisdom we understand the consciousness of self. Besides, the subject and the object of that consciousness are undoubtedly identical [as regards God] ; for according to our opinion, He is not composed of an element that apprehends, and another that does not apprehend ; He is not like man, who is a combination of a conscious soul and an unconscious body. If, therefore, by " wisdom " we mean the faculty of self-consciousness, wisdom and life are one and the same thing. They, however, do not speak of wisdom in this sense, but of His power to apprehend His creatures. There is also no doubt that power and will do not exist in God in reference to Himself ; for He cannot have power or will as regards Himself ; we cannot imagine such a thing. They take these attributes as different relations between God and His creatures, signifying that He has power in creating things, will in giving to things existence as He desires, and wisdom in knowing what He created. Consequently, these attributes do not refer to the essence of God, but express relations between Him and His creatures.

Therefore we, who truly believe in the Unity of God, declare, that as we do not believe that some element is included in His essence by which He created the heavens, another by which He created the [four] elements, a third by which He created the ideals, in the same way we reject the idea that His essence contains an element by which He has power, another element by which He has will, and a third by which He has a knowledge of His creatures. On the contrary, He is a simple essence, without any additional element whatever ; He created the universe, and knows it, but not by any extraneous force. There is no difference whether these various attributes refer to His actions or to relations between Him and His works ; in fact, these relations, as we have also shown, exist only in the thoughts of men. This is what we must believe concerning the attributes occurring in the books of the Prophets ; some may also be taken as expressive of the perfection of God by way of comparison with what we consider as perfections in us, as we shall explain.

CHAPTER LIV

THE wisest man, our Teacher Moses, asked two things of God, and received a reply respecting both. The one thing he asked was, that God should let him know His true essence ; the other, which in fact he asked first, that God should let him know His attributes. In answer to both these petitions God promised that He would let him know all His attributes, and that these were nothing but His actions. He also told him that His true essence could not be perceived, and pointed out a method by which he could obtain the utmost knowledge of God possible for man to acquire. The knowledge obtained by Moses has not been possesssed by any human being before him or after him. His petition to know the attributes of God is contained in the following words : " Show me now thy way, that I may know thee, that I may find grace in thy sight " (Exod. xxxiii. 13). Consider how many excellent ideas found expression in the words, " Show me thy way, that I may know thee." We learn from them that God is known by His attributes, for Moses believed that he knew Him, when he was shown the way of God. The words " That I may find grace in thy sight," imply that he who knows God finds grace in His eyes. Not only is he acceptable and welcome to God who fasts and prays, but everyone who knows Him. He who has no knowledge of God is the object of His wrath and displeasure. The pleasure and the displeasure of God, the approach to Him and the withdrawal from Him are proportional to the amount of man's knowledge or ignorance concerning the Creator. We have already gone too far away from our subject, let us now return to it.

Moses prayed to God to grant him knowledge of His attributes, and also pardon for His people ; when the latter had been granted, he continued to pray for the knowledge of God's essence in the words, " Show me thy glory " (*ib.* 18), and then received, respecting his first request, " Show me thy way," the following favourable reply, " I will make all my goodness to pass before thee " (*ib.* 19) ; as regards the second request, however, he was told, " Thou canst not see my face " (*ib.* 20). The words " all my goodness " imply that God promised to show him the whole creation, concerning which it has been stated, " And God saw everything that he had made, and, behold, it was very good " (Gen. i. 31) ; when I say " to show him the whole creation," I mean to imply that God promised to make him comprehend the nature of all things, their relation to each other, and the way they are governed by God both in reference to the universe as a whole and to each creature in particular. This knowledge is referred to when we are told of Moses, " he is firmly established in all mine house " (Num. xii. 7) ; that is, " his knowledge of all the creatures in My universe is correct and firmly established " ; for false opinions are not firmly established. Consequently the knowledge of the works of God is the knowledge of His attributes, by which He can be known. The fact that God promised Moses to give him a knowledge of His works, may be inferred from the circumstance that God taught him such attributes as refer exclusively to His works, viz., " merciful and gracious, longsuffering and abundant in goodness," etc., (Exod. xxxiv. 6). It is therefore clear that the ways which Moses wished to know, and which God taught him, are the actions emanating from God. Our Sages call them *middot* (qualities), and speak of the thirteen *middoth* of God (Talm. B. Rosh ha-shanah, p. 17*b*); they used the term also in reference to man; comp. "there are four different *middoth* (characters) among those who go to the house of learning"; "There are four different *middoth* (characters) among those who give charity" (Mishnah *Abot*, v. 13, 14). They do not mean to say that God really possesses *middot* (qualities), but that He performs actions similar to such of our actions as originate in certain qualities, i.e., in certain psychical dispositions; not that God has really such dispositions. Although Moses was shown "all His goodness," i.e., all His works, only the thirteen *middot* are mentioned, because they include those acts of God which refer to the creation and the government of mankind, and to know these acts was the principal object of the prayer of Moses. This is shown by the conclusion of his prayer, "that I may know thee, that I may find grace in thy sight, and consider that this nation is thy people" (Exod. xxxiii. 16), that is to say, the people whom I have to rule by certain acts in the performance of which I must be guided by Thy own acts in governing them. We have thus shown that "the ways" used in the Bible, and "*middot*" used in the Mishnah, are identical, denoting the acts emanating from God in reference to the universe.

Whenever any one of His actions is perceived by us, we ascribe to God that emotion which is the source of the act when performed by ourselves, and call Him by an epithet which is formed from the verb expressing that emotion. We see, e.g., how well He provides for the life of the embryo of living beings; how He endows with certain faculties both the embryo itself and those who have to rear it after its birth, in order that it may be protected from death and destruction, guarded against all harm, and assisted in the performance of all that is required [for its development]. Similar acts, when performed by us, are due to a certain emotion and tenderness called mercy and pity. God is, therefore, said to be merciful; e.g., "Like as a father is merciful to his children, so the Lord is merciful to them that fear Him" (Ps. ciii. 13); "And I will spare them, as a man spareth (*yaḥamol*) his own son that serveth him" (Mal. iii. 17). Such instances do not imply that God is influenced by a feeling of mercy, but that acts similar to those which a father performs for his son, out of pity, mercy and real affection, emanate from God solely for the benefit of His pious men, and are by no means the result of any impression or change—[produced in God].—When we give something to a person who has no claim upon us, we perform an act of grace; e.g., "Grant them graciously unto us" (Judges xxi. 22). [The same term is used in reference to God, e.g.] "which God hath graciously given" (Gen. xxxiii. 5); "Because God hath dealt graciously with me" (*ib.* 11). Instances of this kind are numerous. God creates and guides beings who have no claim upon Him to be created and guided by Him; He is therefore called gracious (*ḥannun*).—His actions towards mankind also include great calamities, which overtake individuals and bring death to them, or affect whole families and even entire regions, spread death, destroy generation after generation, and spare nothing whatsoever. Hence there occur inundations, earthquakes, destructive storms, expeditions of one nation against the other for the sake of destroying it with the sword and blotting out its memory, and many other evils of the same kind. Whenever such evils are caused by us to any person, they originate in great anger, violent jealousy, or a desire for revenge. God is therefore called, because of these acts, " jealous," " revengeful," " wrathful," and "keeping anger" (Nah. i. 2); that is to say, He performs acts similar to those which, when performed by us, originate in certain psychical dispositions, in jealousy, desire for retaliation, revenge, or anger; they are in accordance with the guilt of those who are to be punished, and not the result of any emotion; for He is above all defect ! The same is the case with all divine acts; though resembling those acts which emanate from our passions and psychical dispositions, they are not due to anything superadded to His essence.—The governor of a country, if he is a prophet, should conform to these attributes. Acts [of punishment] must be performed by him moderately and in accordance with justice, not merely as an outlet of his passion. He must not let loose his anger, nor allow his passion to overcome him; for all passions are bad, and they must be guarded against as far as it lies in man's power. At times and towards some persons he must be merciful and gracious, not only from motives of mercy and compassion, but according to their merits; at other times and towards other persons he must evince anger, revenge, and wrath in proportion to their guilt, but not from motives of passion. He must be able to condemn a person to death by fire without anger, passion, or loathing against him, and must exclusively be guided by what he perceives of the guilt of the person, and by a sense of the great benefit which a large number will derive from such a sentence. You have, no doubt, noticed in the Torah how the commandment to annihilate the seven nations, and " to save alive nothing that breatheth " (Deut. xx. 16) is followed immediately by the words, " That they teach you not to do after all their abominations, which they have done unto their gods; so should you sin against the Lord your God " (*ib.* 18); that is to say, you shall not think that this commandment implies an act of cruelty or of retaliation; it is an act demanded by the tendency of man to remove everything that might turn him away from the right path, and to clear away all obstacles in the road to perfection, that is, to the knowledge of God. Nevertheless, acts of mercy, pardon, pity, and grace should more frequently be performed by the governor of a country than acts of punishment; seeing that all the thirteen *middoth* of God are attributes of mercy with only one exception, namely, " visiting the iniquity of the fathers upon the children " (Exod. xxxiv. 7); for the meaning of the preceding attribute (in the original *ve-nakkeh lo yenakkeh*) is " and he will not utterly destroy "; (and not " He will by no means clear the guilty "); comp. "And she will be utterly destroyed (*ve-nikketah*), she shall sit upon the ground " (Isa. iii. 26). When it is said that God is visiting the iniquity of the fathers upon the children, this refers exclusively to the sin of idolatry, and to no other sin. That this is the case may be inferred from what is said in the ten commandments, " upon the third and fourth generation of my enemies " (Exod. xx. 5), none except idolaters being called " enemy "; comp. also " every abomination to the Lord, which he hateth " (Deut. xii. 31). It was, however, considered sufficient to extend the punishment to the fourth generation, because the fourth generation is the utmost a man can see of his posterity; and when, therefore, the idolaters of a place are destroyed, the old man worshipping idols is killed, his son, his grandson, and his great-grandson, that is, the fourth generation.

By the mention of this attribute we are, as it were, told that His command-ments, undoubtedly in harmony with His acts, include the death even of the little children of idolaters because of the sin of their fathers and grand-fathers. This principle we find frequently applied in the Law, as, e.g., we read concerning the city that has been led astray to idolatry, "destroy it utterly, and all that is therein" (Deut. xiii. 15). All this has been ordained in order that every vestige of that which would lead to great injury should be blotted out, as we have explained.

We have gone too far away from the subject of this chapter, but we have shown why it has been considered sufficient to mention only these (thirteen) out of all His acts; namely, because they are required for the good govern-ment of a country; for the chief aim of man should be to make himself, as far as possible, similar to God : that is to say, to make his acts similar to the acts of God, or as our Sages expressed it in explaining the verse, " Ye shall be holy " (Lev. xxi. 2) : " He is gracious, so be you also gracious ; He is merciful, so be you also merciful."

The principal object of this chapter was to show that all attributes ascribed to God are attributes of His acts, and do not imply that God has any quali-ties.

CHAPTER LV

We have already, on several occasions, shown in this treatise that everything that implies corporeality or passiveness, is to be negatived in reference to God, for all passiveness implies change ; and the agent producing that state is undoubtedly different from the object affected by it ; and if God could be affected in any way whatever, another being beside Him would act on Him and cause change in Him. All kinds of non-existence must likewise be negatived in reference to Him ; no perfection whatever can therefore be imagined to be at one time absent from Him, and at another present in Him : for if this were the case, He would [at a certain time] only be potentially perfect. Potentiality always implies non-existence, and when anything has to pass from potentiality into reality, another thing that exists in reality is required to effect that transition. Hence it follows that all perfections must really exist in God, and none of them must in any way be a mere potentiality. Another thing likewise to be denied in reference to God, is similarity to any existing being. This has been generally accepted, and is also mentioned in the books of the Prophets ; e.g., " To whom, then, will you liken me ? " (Isa. xl. 25) ; " To whom, then, will you liken God ? " (*ib.* 18) ; " There is none like unto Thee " (Jer. x. 6). Instances of this kind are frequent. In short, it is necessary to demonstrate by proof that nothing can be predicated of God that implies any of the following four things : corporeality, emotion or change, non-existence,—e.g., that something would be potential at one time and real at another—and similarity with any of His creatures. In this respect our know-ledge of God is aided by the study of Natural Science. For he who is ignorant of the latter cannot understand the defect implied in emotions, the difference between potentiality and reality, the non-existence implied in all potentiality, the inferiority of a thing that exists *in potentiâ* to that which moves in order to cause its transition from potentiality into reality, and the inferiority of that which moves for this purpose compared with its condition when the transition has been effected. He who knows these things, but without their proofs, does not know the details which logically result from these general propositions ; and therefore he cannot prove that God exists, or that the [four] things mentioned above are inadmissible in reference to God.

Having premised these remarks, I shall explain in the next chapter the error of those who believe that God has essential attributes ; those who have some knowledge of Logic and Natural Science will understand it.

CHAPTER LVI

SIMILARITY is based on a certain relation between two things ; if between two things no relation can be found, there can be no similarity between them, and there is no relation between two things that have no similarity to each other ; e.g., we do not say this heat is similar to that colour, or this voice is similar to that sweetness. This is self-evident. Since the existence of a relation between God and man, or between Him and other beings has been denied, similarity must likewise be denied. You must know that two things of the same kind—i.e., whose essential properties are the same, and which are distinguished from each other by greatness and smallness, strength and weakness, etc.—are necessarily similar, though different in this one way ; e.g., a grain of mustard and the sphere of the fixed stars are similar as regards the three dimensions, although the one is exceedingly great, the other exceedingly small, the property of having [three] dimensions is the same in both ; or the heat of wax melted by the sun and the heat of the element of fire, are similar as regards heat ; although the heat is exceedingly great in the one case, and exceedingly small in the other, the existence of that quality (heat) is the same in both. Thus those who believe in the presence of essential attributes in God, viz., Existence, Life, Power, Wisdom, and Will, should know that these attributes, when applied to God, have not the same meaning as when applied to us, and that the difference does not only consist in magnitude, or in the degree of perfection, stability, and durability. It cannot be said, as they practically believe, that His existence is only more stable, His life more permanent, His power greater, His wisdom more perfect, and His will more general than ours, and that the same definition applies to both. This is in no way admissible, for the expression " more than " is used in comparing two things as regards a certain attribute predicated of both of them in exactly the same sense, and consequently implies similarity [between God and His creatures]. When they ascribe to God essential attributes, these so-called essential attributes should not have any similarity to the attributes of other things, and should according to their own opinion not be included in one of the same definition, just as there is no similarity between the essence of God and that of other beings. They do not follow this principle, for they hold that one definition may include them, and that, nevertheless, there is no similarity between them. Those who are familiar with the meaning of similarity will certainly understand that the term existence, when applied to God and to other beings, is perfectly homonymous. In like manner, the terms Wisdom, Power, Will, and Life are applied to God and to other beings by way of perfect homonymity, admitting of no comparison whatever. Nor must you think that these attributes are employed as hybrid terms; for hybrid terms are such as are applied to two things which have a similarity to each other in respect to a certain property which is in both of them an accident, not an essential, constituent element. The attributes of God, however, are not considered as accidental by any intelligent person, while all attributes applied to man are accidents, according to the Mutakallemim. I am therefore at a loss to see how they can find any similarity [between the attributes of God and those of man]; how their definitions can be identical, and their significations the same! This is a decisive proof that there is, in no way or sense, anything common to the attributes predicated of God, and those used in reference to ourselves; they have only the same names, and nothing else is common to them. Such being the case, it is not proper to believe, on account of the use of the same attributes, that there is in God something additional to His essence, in the same way as attributes are joined to our essence. This is most important for those who understand it. Keep it in memory, and study it thoroughly, in order to be well prepared for that which I am going to explain to you.

CHAPTER LVII

ON attributes; remarks more recondite than the preceding. It is known that existence is an accident appertaining to all things, and therefore an element superadded to their essence. This must evidently be the case as regards everything the existence of which is due to some cause; its existence is an element superadded to its essence. But as regards a being whose existence is not due to any cause—God alone is that being, for His existence, as we have said, is absolute—existence and essence are perfectly identical; He is not a substance to which existence is joined as an accident, as an additional element. His existence is always absolute, and has never been a new element or an accident in Him. Consequently God exists without possessing the attribute of existence. Similarly He lives, without possessing the attribute of life; knows, without possessing the attribute of knowledge; is omnipotent without possessing the attribute of omnipotence; is wise, without possessing the attribute of wisdom; all this reduces itself to one and the same entity; there is no plurality in Him, as will be shown. It is further necessary to consider that unity and plurality are accidents supervening to an object according as it consists of many elements or of one. This is fully explained in the book called Metaphysics. In the same way as number is not the substance of the things numbered, so is unity not the substance of the thing which has the attribute of unity, for unity and plurality are accidents belonging to the category of discrete quantity, and supervening to such objects as are capable of receiving them.

To that being, however, which has truly simple, absolute existence, and in which composition is inconceivable, the accident of unity is as inadmissible as the accident of plurality; that is to say, God's unity is not an element superadded, but He is One without possessing the attribute of unity. The investigation of this subject, which is almost too subtle for our understanding, must not be based on current expressions employed in describing it, for these are the great source of error. It would be extremely difficult for us to find, in any language whatsoever, words adequate to this subject, and we can only employ inadequate language. In our endeavour to show that God does not include a plurality, we can only say " He is one," although " one " and " many " are both terms which serve to distinguish quantity. We therefore make the subject clearer, and show to the understanding the way of truth by saying He is one but does not possess the attribute of unity.

The same is the case when we say God is the First (*Kadmon*), to express that He has not been created ; the term " First " is decidedly inaccurate, for it can in its true sense only be applied to a being that is subject to the relation of time ; the latter, however, is an accident to motion which again is connected with a body. Besides the attribute " first " is a relative term, being in regard to time the same as the terms " long " and " short " are in regard to a line. Both expressions, " first " and " created," are equally inadmissible in reference to any being to which the attribute of time is not applicable, just as we do not say " crooked " or " straight " in reference to taste, " salted " or " insipid " in reference to the voice. These subjects are not unknown to those who have accustomed themselves to seek a true understanding of the things, and to establish their properties in accordance with the abstract notions which the mind has formed of them, and who are not misled by the inaccuracy of the words employed. All attributes, such as " the First," " the Last," occurring in the Scriptures in reference to God, are as metaphorical as the expressions " ear " and " eye." They simply signify that God is not subject to any change or innovation whatever ; they do not imply that God can be described by time, or that there is any comparison between Him and any other being as regards time, and that He is called on that account " the first " and " the last." In short, all similar expressions are borrowed from the language commonly used among the people. In the same way we use " One " in reference to God, to express that there is nothing similar to Him, but we do not mean to say that an attribute of unity is added to His essence.

CHAPTER LVIII

THIS chapter is even more recondite than the preceding. Know that the negative attributes of God are the true attributes : they do not include any incorrect notions or any deficiency whatever in reference to God, while positive attributes imply polytheism, and are inadequate, as we have already shown. It is now necessary to explain how negative expressions can in a certain sense be employed as attributes, and how they are distinguished from positive attributes. Then I shall show that we cannot describe the Creator by any means except by negative attributes. An attribute does not exclusively belong to the one object to which it is related ; while qualifying one thing, it can also be employed to qualify other things, and is in that case not peculiar to that one thing. E.g., if you see an object from a distance, and on enquiring what it is, are told that it is a living being, you have certainly learnt an attribute of the object seen, and although that attribute does not exclusively belong to the object perceived, it expresses that the object is not a plant or a mineral. Again, if a man is in a certain house, and you know that something is in the house, but not exactly what, you ask what is in that house, and you are told, not a plant nor a mineral. You have thereby obtained some special knowledge of the thing ; you have learnt that it is a living being, although you do not yet know what kind of a living being it is. The negative attributes have this in common with the positive, that they necessarily circumscribe the object to some extent, although such circumscription consists only in the exclusion of what otherwise would not be excluded. In the following point, however, the negative attributes are distinguished from the positive. The positive attributes, although not peculiar to one thing, describe a portion of what we desire to know, either some part of its essence or some of its accidents ; the negative attributes, on the other hand, do not, as regards the essence of the thing which we desire to know, in any way tell us what it is, except it be indirectly, as has been shown in the instance given by us.

After this introduction, I would observe that,—as has already been shown —God's existence is absolute, that it includes no composition, as will be proved, and that we comprehend only the fact that He exists, not His essence. Consequently it is a false assumption to hold that He has any positive attribute ; for He does not possess existence in addition to His essence ; it therefore cannot be said that the one may be described as an attribute [of the other] ; much less has He [in addition to His existence] a compound essence, consisting of two constituent elements to which the attribute could refer ; still less has He accidents, which could be described by an attribute. Hence it is clear that He has no positive attribute what-ever. The negative attributes, however, are those which are necessary to direct the mind to the truths which we must believe concerning God ; for, on the one hand, they do not imply any plurality, and, on the other, they convey to man the highest possible knowledge of God ; e.g., it has been established by proof that some being must exist besides those things which can be perceived by the senses, or apprehended by the mind ; when we say of this being, that it exists, we mean that its non-existence is impossible. We then perceive that such a being is not, for instance, like the four elements, which are inanimate, and we therefore say that it is living, expressing thereby that it is not dead. We call such a being incorporeal, because we notice that it is unlike the heavens, which are living, but material. Seeing that it is also different from the intellect, which, though incorporeal and living, owes its existence to some cause, we say it is the first, expressing thereby that its existence is not due to any cause. We further notice, that the existence, that is the essence, of this being is not limited to its own existence ; many existences emanate from it, and its influence is not like that of the fire in producing heat, or that of the sun in sending forth light, but consists in constantly giving them stability and order by well-established rule, as we shall show : we say, on that account, it has power, wisdom, and will, i.e., it is not feeble or ignorant, or hasty, and does not abandon its creatures ; when we say that it is not feeble, we mean that its existence is capable of producing the exist-ence of many other things ; by saying that it is not ignorant, we mean " it perceives " or " it lives,"—for everything that perceives is living—by saying " it is not hasty, and does not abandon its creatures," we mean that all these creatures preserve a certain order and arrangement ; they are not left to themselves; they are not produced aimlessly, but whatever condition they receive from that being is given with design and intention. We thus learn that there is no other being like unto God, and we say that He is One, i.e., there are not more Gods than one.

It has thus been shown that every attribute predicated of God either denotes the quality of an action, or—when the attribute is intended to convey some idea of the Divine Being itself, and not of His actions—the negation of the opposite. Even these negative attributes must not be formed and applied to God, except in the way in which, as you know, sometimes an attribute is negatived in reference to a thing, although that attribute can naturally never be applied to it in the same sense, as, e.g., we say, " This wall does not see." Those who read the present work are aware that, notwithstanding all the efforts of the mind, we can obtain no knowledge of the essence of the heavens—a revolving substance which has been measured by us in spans and cubits, and examined even as regards the proportions of the several spheres to each other and respecting most of their motions—although we know that they must consist of matter and form ; but the matter not being the same as sublunary matter, we can only describe the heavens in terms expressing negative properties, but not in terms denoting positive qualities. Thus we say that the heavens are not light, not heavy, not passive and therefore not subject to impressions, and that they do not possess the sensations of taste and smell ; or we use similar negative attributes. All this we do, because we do not know their substance. What, then, can be the result of our efforts, when we try to obtain a knowledge of a Being that is free from substance, that is most simple, whose existence is absolute, and not due to any cause, to whose perfect essence nothing can be superadded, and whose perfection consists, as we have shown, in the absence of all defects. All we understand is the fact that He exists, that He is a Being to whom none of His creatures is similar, who has nothing in common with them, who does not include plurality, who is never too feeble to produce other beings, and whose relation to the universe is that of a steersman to a boat ; and even this is not a real relation, a real simile, but serves only to convey to us the idea that God rules the universe ; that is, that He gives it duration, and preserves its necessary arrangement. This subject will be treated more fully. Praised be He ! In the contemplation of His essence, our comprehension and knowledge prove insufficient ; in the examination of His works, how they necessarily result from His will, our knowledge proves to be ignorance, and in the endeavour to extol Him in words, all our efforts in speech are mere weakness and failure !

CHAPTER LIX

THE following question might perhaps be asked : Since there is no possibility of obtaining a knowledge of the true essence of God, and since it has also been proved that the only thing that man can apprehend of Him is the fact that He exists, and that all positive attributes are inadmissible, as has been shown ; what is the difference among those who have obtained a knowledge of God ? Must not the knowledge obtained by our teacher Moses, and by Solomon, be the same as that obtained by any one of the lowest class of philosophers, since there can be no addition to this knowledge ?   But, on the other hand, it is generally accepted among theologians and also among philosophers, that there can be a great difference between two persons as regards the knowledge of God obtained by them.   Know that this is really the case, that those who have obtained a knowledge of God differ greatly from each other ; for in the same way as by each additional attribute an object is more specified, and is brought nearer to the true apprehension of the observer, so by each additional negative attribute you advance toward the knowledge of God, and you are nearer to it than he who does not negative, in reference to God, those qualities which you are convinced by proof must be negatived.   There may thus be a man who after having earnestly devoted many years to the pursuit of one science, and to the true understanding of its principles, till he is fully convinced of its truths, has obtained as the sole result of this study the conviction that a certain quality must be negatived in reference to God, and the capacity of demonstrating that it is impossible to apply it to Him.   Superficial thinkers will have no proof for this, will doubtfully ask, Is that thing existing in the Creator, or not ?   And those who are deprived of sight will positively ascribe it to God, although it has been clearly shown that He does not possess it.   E.g., while I show that God is incorporeal, another doubts and is not certain whether He is corporeal or incorporeal ; others even positively declare that He is corporeal, and appear before the Lord with that belief.   Now see how great the difference is between these three men ; the first is undoubtedly nearest to the Almighty ; the second is remote, and the third still more distant from Him.   If there be a fourth person who holds himself convinced by proof that emotions are impossible in God, while the first who rejects the corporeality, is not convinced of that impossibility, that fourth person is undoubtedly nearer the knowledge of God than the first, and so on, so that a person who, convinced by proof, negatives a number of things in reference to God, which according to our belief may possibly be in Him or emanate from Him, is undoubtedly a more perfect man than we are, and would surpass us still more if we positively believed these things to be properties of God.   It will now be clear to you, that every time you establish by proof the negation of a thing in reference to God, you become more perfect, while with every additional positive assertion you follow your imagination and recede from the true knowledge of God.   Only by such ways must we approach the knowledge of God, and by such researches and studies as would show us the inapplicability of what is inadmissible as regards the Creator, not by such methods as would prove the necessity of ascribing to Him anything extraneous to His essence, or asserting that He has a certain perfection, when we find it to be a perfection in relation to us.   The perfections are all to some extent acquired properties, and a property which must be acquired does not exist in everything capable of making such acquisition.

You must bear in mind, that by affirming anything of God, you are removed from Him in two respects ; first, whatever you affirm, is only a perfection in relation to us ; secondly, He does not possess anything superadded to this essence ; His essence includes all His perfections, as we have shown. Since it is a well-known fact that even that knowledge of God which is accessible to man cannot be attained except by negations, and that negations do not convey a true idea of the being to which they refer, all people, both of past and present generations, declared that God cannot be the object of human comprehension, that none but Himself comprehends what He is, and that our knowledge consists in knowing that we are unable truly to comprehend Him. All philosophers say, " He has overpowered us by His grace, and is invisible to us through the intensity of His light," like the sun which cannot be perceived by eyes which are too weak to bear its rays. Much more has been said on this topic, but it is useless to repeat it here. The idea is best expressed in the book of Psalms, " Silence is praise to Thee " (lxv. 2). It is a very expressive remark on this subject ; for whatever we utter with the intention of extolling and of praising Him, contains something that cannot be applied to God, and includes derogatory expressions ; it is therefore more becoming to be silent, and to be content with intellectual reflection, as has been recommended by men of the highest culture, in the words " Commune with your own heart upon your bed, and be still " (Ps. iv. 4). You must surely know the following celebrated passage in the Talmud—would that all passages in the Talmud were like that !—although it is known to you, I quote it literally, as I wish to point out to you the ideas contained in it : " A certain person, reading prayers in the presence of Rabbi Haninah, said, ' God, the great, the valiant and the tremendous, the powerful, the strong, and the mighty.'—The rabbi said to him, Have you finished all the praises of your Master ? The three epithets, ' God, the great, the valiant and the tremendous,' we should not have applied to God, had Moses not mentioned them in the Law, and had not the men of the Great Synagogue come forward subsequently and established their use in the prayer ; and you say all this ! Let this be illustrated by a parable. There was once an earthly king, possessing millions of gold coin ; he was praised for owning millions of silver coin ; was this not really dispraise to him ? " Thus far the opinion of the pious rabbi. Consider, first, how repulsive and annoying the accumulation of all these positive attributes was to him ; next, how he showed that, if we had only to follow our reason, we should never have composed these prayers, and we should not have uttered any of them. It has, however, become necessary to address men in words that should leave some idea in their minds, and, in accordance with the saying of our Sages, " The Torah speaks in the language of men," the Creator has been described to us in terms of our own perfections ; but we should not on that account have uttered any other than the three above-mentioned attributes, and we should not have used them as names of God except when meeting with them in reading the Law. Subsequently, the men of the Great Synagogue, who were prophets, introduced these expressions also into the prayer, but we should not on that account use [in our prayers] any other attributes of God. The principal lesson to be derived from this passage is that there are two reasons for our employing those phrases in our prayers : first, they occur in the Pentateuch ; secondly, the Prophets introduced them into the prayer. Were it not for the first reason, we should never have uttered them ; and were it not for the second reason, we should not have copied them from the Pentateuch to recite them in our prayers ; how then could we approve of the use of those numerous attributes ! You also learn from this that we ought not to mention and employ in our prayers all the attributes we find applied to God in the books of the Prophets; for he does not say, " Were it not that Moses, our Teacher, said them, we should not have been able to use them "; but he adds another condition—" and had not the men of the Great Synagogue come forward and established their use in the prayer," because only for that reason are we allowed to use them in our prayers. We cannot approve of what those foolish persons do who are extravagant in praise, fluent and prolix in the prayers they compose, and in the hymns they make in the desire to approach the Creator. They describe God in attributes which would be an offence if applied to a human being; for those persons have no knowledge of these great and important principles, which are not accessible to the ordinary intelligence of man. Treating the Creator as a familiar object, they describe Him and speak of Him in any expressions they think proper; they eloquently continue to praise Him in that manner, and believe that they can thereby influence Him and produce an effect on Him. If they find some phrase suited to their object in the words of the Prophets they are still more inclined to consider that they are free to make use of such texts—which should at least be explained—to employ them in their literal sense, to derive new expressions from them, to form from them numerous variations, and to found whole compositions on them. This license is frequently met with in the compositions of the singers, preachers, and others who imagine themselves to be able to compose a poem. Such authors write things which partly are real heresy, partly contain such folly and absurdity that they naturally cause those who hear them to laugh, but also to feel grieved at the thought that such things can be uttered in reference to God. Were it not that I pitied the authors for their defects, and did not wish to injure them, I should have cited some passages to show you their mistakes; besides, the fault of their compositions is obvious to all intelligent persons. You must consider it, and think thus: If slander and libel is a great sin, how much greater is the sin of those who speak with looseness of tongue in reference to God, and describe Him by attributes which are far below Him; and I declare that they not only commit an ordinary sin, but unconsciously at least incur the guilt of profanity and blasphemy. This applies both to the multitude that listens to such prayers, and to the foolish man that recites them. Men, however, who understand the fault of such compositions, and, nevertheless, recite them, may be classed, according to my opinion, among those to whom the following words are applied: " And the children of Israel used words that were not right against the Lord their God " (2 Kings xvii. 9); and " utter error against the Lord " (Isa. xxxii. 6). If you are of those who regard the honour of their Creator, do not listen in any way to them, much less utter what they say, and still less compose such prayers. knowing how great is the offence of one who hurls aspersions against the Supreme Being. There is no necessity at all for you to use positive attributes of God with the view of magnifying Him in your thoughts, or to go beyond the limits which the men of the Great Synagogue have introduced in the prayers and in the blessings, for this is sufficient for all purposes, and even more than sufficient, as Rabbi Haninah said. Other attributes, such as occur in the books of the Prophets, may be uttered when we meet with them in reading those books; but we must bear in mind what has already been explained, that they are either attributes of God's actions, or expressions implying the negation of the opposite. This likewise should not be divulged to the multitude ; but a reflection of this kind is fitted for the few only who believe that the glorification of God does not consist in *uttering* that which is not to be uttered, but in *reflecting* on that on which man should reflect.

We will now conclude our exposition of the wise words of R. Ḥaninah. He does not employ any such simile as : " A king who possesses millions of gold denarii, and is praised as having hundreds " ; for this would imply that God's perfections, although more perfect than those ascribed to man are still of the same kind ; but this is not the case, as has been proved. The excellence of the simile consists in the words : " who possesses golden denarii, and is praised as having silver denarii " ; this implies that these attributes, though perfections as regards ourselves, are not such as regards God ; in reference to Him they would all be defects, as is distinctly suggested in the remark, " Is this not an offence to Him ? "

I have already told you that all these attributes, whatever perfection they may denote according to your idea, imply defects in reference to God, if applied to Him in the same sense as they are used in reference to ourselves. Solomon has already given us sufficient instruction on this subject by saying, " For God is in heaven, and thou upon earth ; therefore let thy words be few " (Eccles. v. 2).

CHAPTER LX

I WILL give you in this chapter some illustrations, in order that you may better understand the propriety of forming as many negative attributes as possible, and the impropriety of ascribing to God any positive attributes. A person may know for certain that a " ship " is in existence, but he may not know to what object that name is applied, whether to a substance or to an accident ; a second person then learns that the ship is not an accident ; a third, that it is not a mineral ; a fourth, that it is not a plant growing in the earth ; a fifth, that it is not a body whose parts are joined together by nature ; a sixth, that it is not a flat object like boards or doors ; a seventh, that it is not a sphere ; an eighth, that it is not pointed ; a ninth, that it is not round-shaped ; nor equilateral ; a tenth, that it is not solid. It is clear that this tenth person has almost arrived at the correct notion of a " ship " by the foregoing negative attributes, as if he had exactly the same notion as those have who imagine it to be a wooden substance which is hollow, long, and composed of many pieces of wood, that is to say, who know it by positive attributes. Of the other persons in our illustration, each one is more remote from the correct notion of a ship than the next mentioned, so that the first knows nothing about it but the name. In the same manner you will come nearer to the knowledge and comprehension of God by the negative attributes. But you must be careful, in what you negative, to negative by proof, not by mere words, for each time you ascertain by proof that a certain thing, believed to exist in the Creator, must be negatived, you have undoubtedly come one step nearer to the knowledge of God.

It is in this sense that some men come very near to God, and others remain exceedingly remote from Him, not in the sense of those who are deprived of vision, and believe that God occupies a place, which man can physically approach or from which he can recede.   Examine this well, know it, and be content with it.   The way which will bring you nearer to God has been clearly shown to you ; walk in it, if you have the desire.   On the other hand, there is a great danger in applying positive attributes to God.   For it has been shown that every perfection we could imagine, even if existing in God in accordance with the opinion of those who assert the existence of attributes, would in reality not be of the same kind as that imagined by us, but would only be called by the same name, according to our explanation ; it would in fact amount to a negation.   Suppose, e.g., you say He has knowledge, and that knowledge, which admits of no change and of no plurality, embraces many changeable things ;   His knowledge remains unaltered, while new things are constantly formed, and His knowledge of a thing before it exists, while it exists, and when it has ceased to exist, is the same without the least change : you would thereby declare that His knowledge is not like ours ; and similarly that His existence is not like ours.   You thus necessarily arrive at some negation, without obtaining a true conception of an essential attri- bute ; on the contrary, you are led to assume that there is a plurality in God, and to believe that He, though one essence, has several unknown attributes. For if you intend to affirm them, you cannot compare them with those attributes known by us, and·they are consequently not of the same kind. You are, as it were, brought by the belief in the reality of the attributes, to say that God is one subject of which several things are predicated ; though the subject is not like ordinary subjects, and the predicates are not like ordi- nary predicates.   This belief would ultimately lead us to associate other things with God, and not to believe that He is One.   For of every subject certain things can undoubtedly be predicated, and although in reality sub- ject and predicate are combined in one thing, by the actual definition they consist of two elements, the notion contained in the subject not being the same as that contained in the predicate.   In the course of this treatise it will be proved to you that God cannot be a compound, and that He is simple in the strictest sense of the word.

I do not merely declare that he who affirms attributes of God has not suffi- cient knowlenge concerning the Creator, admits some association with God, or conceives Him to be different from what He is ; but I say that he uncon- sciously loses his belief in God.   For he whose knowledge concerning a thing is insufficient, understands one part of it while he is ignorant of the other, as, e.g., a person who knows that man possesses life, but does not know that man possesses understanding ; but in reference to God, in whose real exist- ence there is no plurality, it is impossible that one thing should be known, and another unknown.   Similarly he who associates an object with [the pro- perties of] another object, conceives a true and correct notion of the one object. and applies that notion also to the other ; while those who admit the attributes of God, do not consider them as identical with His essence, but as extraneous elements.   Again, he who conceives an incorrect notion of an object, must necessarily have a correct idea of the object to some ex- tent ; he, however, who says that taste belongs to the category of quantity has not, according to my opinion, an incorrect notion of taste, but is entirely ignorant of its nature, for he does not know to what object the term " taste " is to be applied.—This is a very difficult subject ; consider it well.

According to this explanation you will understand, that those who do not recognize, in reference to God, the negation of things, which others negative by clear proof, are deficient in the knowledge of God, and are remote from comprehending Him. Consequently, the smaller the number of things is which a person can negative in relation to God, the less he knows of Him, as has been explained in the beginning of this chapter; but the man who affirms an attribute of God, knows nothing but the same; for the object to which, in his imagination, he applies that name, does not exist; it is a mere fiction and invention, as if he applied that name to a non-existing being, for there is, in reality, no such object. E.g., some one has heard of the elephant, and knows that it is an animal, and wishes to know its form and nature. A person, who is either misled or misleading, tells him it is an animal with one leg, three wings, lives in the depth of the sea, has a transparent body; its face is wide like that of a man, has the same form and shape, speaks like a man, flies sometimes in the air, and sometimes swims like a fish. I should not say, that he described the elephant incorrectly, or that he has an insufficient knowledge of the elephant, but I would say that the thing thus described is an invention and fiction, and that in reality there exists nothing like it; it is a non-existing being, called by the name of a really existing being, and like the griffin, the centaur, and similar imaginary combinations for which simple and compound names have been borrowed from real things. The present case is analogous; namely, God, praised be His name, exists, and His existence has been proved to be absolute and perfectly simple, as I shall explain. If such a simple, absolutely existing essence were said to have attributes, as has been contended, and were combined with extraneous elements, it would in no way be an existing thing, as has been proved by us; and when we say that that essence, which is called "God," is a substance with many properties by which it can be described, we apply that name to an object which does not at all exist. Consider, therefore, what are the consequences of affirming attributes to God! As to those attributes of God which occur in the Pentateuch, or in the books of the Prophets, we must assume that they are exclusively employed, as has been stated by us, to convey to us some notion of the perfections of the Creator, or to express qualities of actions emanating from Him.

CHAPTER LXI

It is well known that all the names of God occurring in Scripture are derived from His actions, except one, namely, the Tetragrammaton, which consists of the letters *yod, hé, vau* and *hé*. This name is applied exclusively to God, and is on that account called *Shem ha-meforash*, "The nomen proprium." It is the distinct and exclusive designation of the Divine Being; whilst His other names are common nouns, and are derived from actions, to which some of our own are similar, as we have already explained. Even the name *Adonay*, "Lord," which has been substituted for the Tetragrammaton, is derived from the appellative "lord"; comp. "The man who is the lord (*adone*) of the land spake roughly to us" (Gen. xliii. 30). The difference between *Adoni*, "my lord," (with *ḥirek* under the *nun*), or *Adonay* with *kamez*), is similar to the difference between *Sari*, "my prince," and

Saraï, Abraham's wife (*ib.* xvi. 1), the latter form denoting majesty and distinction. An angel is also addressed as "*Adonay*"; e.g., "*Adonay* (My lord), pass not away, I pray thee" (*ib.* xviii. 3). I have restricted my explanation to the term *Adonay*, the substitute for the Tetragrammaton, because it is more commonly applied to God than any of the other names which are in frequent use, like *dayyan*, "judge," *shadday*, "almighty," *zaddik*, "righteous," *hannun*, "gracious," *rahum* "merciful," and *elohim* "chief"; all these terms are unquestionably appellations and derivatives. The derivation of the name, consisting of *yod*, *hé*, *vau*, and *hé*, is not positively known, the word having no additional signification. This sacred name, which, as you know, was not pronounced except in the sanctuary by the appointed priests, when they gave the sacerdotal blessing, and by the high priest on the Day of Atonement, undoubtedly denotes something which is peculiar to God, and is not found in any other being. It is possible that in the Hebrew language, of which we have now but a slight knowledge, the Tetragrammaton, in the way it was pronounced, conveyed the meaning of "absolute existence." In short, the majesty of the name and the great dread of uttering it, are connected with the fact that it denotes God Himself, without including in its meaning any names of the things created by Him. Thus our Sages say: "'My name' (Num. vi. 27) means the name which is peculiar to Me." All other names of God have reference to qualities, and do not signify a simple substance, but a substance with attributes, they being derivatives. On that account it is believed that they imply the presence of a plurality in God, I mean to say, the presence of attributes, that is, of some extraneous element superadded to His essence. Such is the meaning of all derivative names; they imply the presence of some attribute and its substratum, though this be not distinctly named. As, however, it has been proved, that God is not a substratum capable of attributes, we are convinced that those appellatives when employed as names of God, only indicate the relation of certain actions to Him, or they convey to us some notion of His perfection.

Hence R. Haninah would have objected to the expression "the great, the mighty, and the tremendous," had it not been for the two reasons mentioned by him; because such expressions lead men to think that the attributes are essential, i.e., they are perfections actually present in God. The frequent use of names of God derived from actions, led to the belief that He had as many [essential] attributes as there were actions from which the names were derived. The following promise was therefore made, implying that mankind will at a certain future time understand this subject, and be free from the error it involves: "In that day will the Lord be One, and His name One" (Zech. xiv. 9). The meaning of this prophecy is this: He being One, will then be called by one name, which will indicate the essence of God; but it does not mean that His sole name will be a derivative [viz., "One"]. In the *Pirke Rabbi Eliezer* (chap. iii.) occurs the following passage: "Before the universe was created, there was only the Almighty and His name." Observe how clearly the author states that all these appellatives employed as names of God came into existence after the Creation. This is true; for they all refer to actions manifested in the Universe. If, however, you consider His essence as separate and as abstracted from all actions, you will not describe it by an appellative, but by a proper noun, which exclusively indicates that essence. Every other name of God is a derivative, only the Tetragrammaton is a real *nomen proprium*, and must not be considered from any other point of view. You must beware of sharing the error of those who write amulets (*kameot*). Whatever you hear from them, or read in their works, especially in reference to the names which they form by combination, is utterly senseless; they call these combinations *shemot* (names) and believe that their pronunciation demands sanctification and purification, and that by using them they are enabled to work miracles. Rational persons ought not to listen to such men, nor in any way believe their assertions. No other name is called *shem ha-meforash* except this Tetragrammaton, which is written, but is not pronounced according to its letters. The words, "Thus shall ye bless the children of Israel" (Num. vi. 23) are interpreted in Siphri as follows: "'*Thus*,' in the holy language; again '*thus*,' with the *Shem ha-meforash*." The following remark is also found there: "In the sanctuary [the name of God is pronounced] as it is spelt, but elsewhere by its substitutes." In the Talmud, the following passage occurs: "'*Thus*,' i.e., with the *shem ha-meforash*.—You say [that the priests, when blessing the people, had to pronounce] the *shem ha-meforash*; this was perhaps not the case, and they may have used other names instead.—We infer it from the words: 'And they shall put My name' (Num. vi. 27), i.e., My name, which is peculiar to Me." It has thus been shown that the *shem ha-meforash* (the proper name of God) is the Tetragrammaton, and that this is the only name which indicates nothing but His essence, and therefore our Sages in referring to this sacred term said "'*My name*' means the one which is peculiar to Me alone."

In the next chapter I will explain the circumstances which brought men to a belief in the power of *Shemot* (names of God); I will point out the main subject of discussion, and lay open to you its mystery, and then not any doubt will be left in your mind, unless you prefer to be misguided.

CHAPTER LXII

WE were commanded that, in the sacerdotal blessing, the name of the Lord should be pronounced as it is written in the form of the Tetragrammaton, the *shem ha-meforash*. It was not known to every one how the name was to be pronounced, what vowels were to be given to each consonant, and whether some of the letters capable of reduplication should receive a dagesh. Wise men successively transmitted the pronunciation of the name; it occurred only once in seven years that the pronunciation was communicated to a distinguished disciple. I must, however, add that the statement, "The wise men communicated the Tetragrammaton to their children and their disciples once in seven years," does not only refer to the pronunciation but also to its meaning, because of which the Tetragrammaton was made a *nomen proprium* of God, and which includes certain metaphysical principles.

Our Sages knew in addition a name of God which consisted of twelve letters, inferior in sanctity to the Tetragrammaton. I believe that this was not a single noun, but consisted of two or three words, the sum of their letters being twelve, and that these words were used by our Sages as a substitute for the Tetragrammaton, whenever they met with it in the course of their reading the Scriptures, in the same manner as we at present substitute for it *aleph, daleth,* etc. [i.e., *Adonay,* " the Lord "]. There is no doubt that this name also, consisting of twelve letters, was in this sense more distinctive than the name *Adonay* : it was never withheld from any of the students ; whoever wished to learn it, had the opportunity given to him without any reserve : not so the Tetragrammaton ; those who knew it did not communicate it except to a son or a disciple, once in seven years, When, however, unprincipled men had become acquainted with that name which consists of twelve letters and in consequence had become corrupt in faith—as is sometimes the case when persons with imperfect knowledge become aware that a thing is not such as they had imagined—the Sages concealed also that name, and only communicated it to the worthiest among the priests, that they should pronounce it when they blessed the people in the Temple ; for the Tetragrammeton was then no longer uttered in the sanctuary on account of the corruption of the people. There is a tradition, that with the death of Simeon the Just, his brother priests discontinued the pronunciation of the Tetragrammaton in the blessing ; they used, instead, this name of twelve letters. It is further stated, that at first the name of twelve letters was communicated to every man ; but when the number of impious men increased it was only entrusted to the worthiest among the priests, whose voice, in pronouncing it, was drowned amid the singing of their brother priests. Rabbi Tarphon said, " Once I followed my grandfather to the daïs [where the blessing was pronounced] ; I inclined my ear to listen to a priest [who pronounced the name], and noticed that his voice was drowned amid the singing of his brother priests."

There was also a name of forty-two letters known among them. Every intelligent person knows that one word of forty-two letters is impossible. But it was a phrase of several words which had together forty-two letters. There is no doubt that the words had such a meaning as to convey a correct notion of the essence of God, in the way we have stated. This phrase of so many letters is called a name because, like other proper nouns, they represent one single object, and several words have been employed in order to explain more clearly the idea which the name represents ; for an idea can more easily be comprehended if expressed in many words. Mark this and observe now that the instruction in regard to the names of God extended to the signification of each of those names, and did not confine itself to the pronunciation of the single letters which, in themselves, are destitute of an idea. *Shem ha-meforash* applied neither to the name of forty-two letters nor to that of twelve, but only to the Tetragrammaton, the proper name of God, as we have explained. Those two names must have included some metaphysical ideas. It can be proved that one of them conveyed profound knowledge, from the following rule laid down by our Sages : " The name of forty-two letters is exceedingly holy ; it can only be entrusted to him who is modest, in the midway of life, not easily provoked to anger, temperate, gentle, and who speaks kindly to his fellow men. He who understands it, is cautious with it, and keeps it in purity, is loved above and is liked here below ; he is respected by his fellow men ; his learning remaineth with him, and he enjoys both this world and the world to come." So far in the Talmud. How grievously has this passage been misunderstood! Many believe that the forty-two letters are merely to be pronounced mechanically; that by knowledge of these, without any further interpretation, they can attain to these exalted ends, although it is stated that he who desires to obtain a knowledge of that name must be trained in the virtues named before, and go through all the great preparations which are mentioned in that passage. On the contrary, it is evident that all this preparation aims at a knowledge of Metaphysics, and includes ideas which constitute the " secrets of the Law," as we have explained (chap. xxxv.). In works on Metaphysics it has been shown that such knowledge, i.e., the perception of the active intellect, can never be forgotten; and this is meant by the phrase " his learning remaineth with him."

When bad and foolish men were reading such passages, they considered them to be a support of their false pretensions and of their assertion that they could, by means of an arbitrary combination of letters, form a *shem* (" a name ") which would act and operate miraculously when written or spoken in a certain particular way. Such fictions, originally invented by foolish men, were in the course of time committed to writing, and came into the hands of good but weak-minded and ignorant persons who were unable to discriminate between truth and falsehood, and made a secret of these *shemot* (names). When after the death of such persons those writings were discovered among their papers, it was believed that they contained truths; for, " The simple believeth every word " (Prov. xiv. 15).

We have already gone too far away from our interesting subject and recondite inquiry, endeavouring to refute a perverse notion, the absurdity of which every one must perceive who gives a thought to the subject. We have, however, been compelled to mention it, in treating of the divine names, their meanings, and the opinions commonly held concerning them. We shall now return to our theme. Having shown that all names of God, with the exception of the Tetragrammaton (*Shem ha-meforash*), are appellatives, we must now, in a separate chapter, speak on the phrase *Ehyeh asher Ehyeh*, (Exod. iii. 14), because it is connected with the difficult subject under discussion, namely, the inadmissibility of divine attributes.

CHAPTER LXIII

BEFORE approaching the subject of this chapter, we will first consider the words of Moses, " And they shall say unto me, What is His name? what shall I say unto them? " (Exod. iii. 13), How far was this question, anticipated by Moses, appropriate, and how far was he justified in seeking to be prepared with the answer? Moses was correct in declaring, " But, behold, they will not believe me, for they will say, The Lord hath not appeared unto thee " (*ib*. iv. 1); for any man claiming the authority of a prophet must expect to meet with such an objection so long as he has not given a proof of his mission. Again, if the question, as appears at first sight, referred only to the name, as a mere utterance of the lips, the following dilemma would present itself: either the Israelites knew the name, or they had never heard it; if the name was known to them, they would perceive in it no argument in favour of the mission of Moses, his knowledge and their knowledge of the divine name being the same.   If, on the other hand, they had never heard it mentioned, and if the knowledge of it was to prove the mission of Moses, what evidence would they have that this was really the name of God ?   Moreover, after God had made known that name to Moses, and had told him, " Go and gather the elders of Israel, . . . and they shall hearken to thy voice " (*ib.* xvi. 18), he replied, " Behold, they will not believe me nor hearken unto my voice," although God had told him, " And they will hearken to thy voice " ; whereupon God answered, " What is that in thine hand ? " and he said, " A rod " (*ib.* iv. 2).   In order to obviate this dilemma, you must understand what I am about to tell you.   You know how widespread were in those days the opinions of the Sabeans ; all men, except a few individuals, were idolaters, that is to say, they believed in spirits, in man's power to direct the influences of the heavenly bodies, and in the effect of talismans.   Any one who in those days laid claim to authority, based it either, like Abraham, on the fact that, by reasoning and by proof he had been convinced of the existence of a Being who rules the whole Universe, or that some spiritual power was conferred upon him by a star, by an angel, or by a similar agency ; but no one could establish his claim on prophecy, that is to say, on the fact that God had spoken to him, or had entrusted a mission to him ; before the days of Moses no such assertion had ever been made.   You must not be misled by the statements that God spoke to the Patriarchs, or that He had appeared to them.   For you do not find any mention of a prophecy which appealed to others, or which directed them.   Abraham, Isaac, or Jacob, or any other person before them did not tell the people, " God said unto me, you shall do this thing, or you shall not do that thing." or " God has sent me to you." Far from it ! for God spoke to them on nothing but of what especially concerned them, i.e., He communicated to them things relating to their perfection, directed them in what they should do, and foretold them what the condition of their descendants would be ; nothing beyond this.   They guided their fellow-men by means of argument and instruction, as is implied, according to the interpretation generally received amongst us, in the words " and the souls that they had gotten in Haran " (Gen. xii. 5).   When God appeared to our Teacher Moses, and commanded him to address the people and to bring them the message, Moses replied that he might first be asked to prove the existence of God in the Universe, and that only after doing so he would be able to announce to them that God had sent him.   For all men, with few exceptions, were ignorant of the existence of God ; their highest thoughts did not extend beyond the heavenly sphere, its forms or its influences.   They could not yet emancipate themselves from sensation, and had not yet attained to any intellectual perfection.   Then God taught Moses how to teach them, and how to establish amongst them the belief in the existence of Himself, namely, by saying *Ehyeh asher Ehyeh*, a name derived from the verb *hayah* in the sense of " existing," for the verb *hayah* denotes " to be," and in Hebrew no difference is made between the verbs " to be " and " to exist."   The principal point in this phrase is that the same word which denotes " existence," is repeated as an attribute.   The word *asher*, " that," corresponds to the Arabic *illadi* and *illati*, and is an incomplete noun that must be completed by another noun ; it may be considered as the subject of the predicate which follows.   The first noun which is to be described is *ehyeh* ; the second, by which the first is described, is likewise *ehyeh*, the identical word, as if to show that the object which is to be described and the attribute by which it is described are in this case necessarily identical. This is, therefore, the expression of the idea that God exists, but not in the ordinary sense of the term ; or, in other words, He is " the existing Being which is the the existing Being," that is to say, the Being whose existence is absolute. The proof which he was to give consisted in demonstrating that there is a Being of absolute existence, that has never been and never will be without existence. This I will clearly prove (II. Introd. Prop. 20 and chap. i.).

God thus showed Moses the proofs by which His existence would be firmly established among the wise men of His people. Therefore the explanation of the name is followed by the words, " Go, gather the elders of Israel," and by the assurance that the elders would understand what God had shown to him, and would accept it, as is stated in the words, " And they will hearken to thy voice." Then Moses replied as follows : They will accept the doctrine that God exists convinced by these intelligible proofs. But, said Moses, by what means shall I be able to show that this existing God has sent me ? Thereupon God gave him the sign. We have thus shown that the question, " What is His name ? " means " Who is that Being, which according to thy belief has sent thee ? " The sentence, " What is his name " (instead of, Who is He), has here been used as a tribute of praise and homage, as though it had been said, Nobody can be ignorant of Thy essence and of Thy real existence ; if, nevertheless, I ask what is Thy name, I mean, What idea is to be expressed by the name ? (Moses considered it inappropriate to say to God that any person was ignorant of God's existence, and therefore described the Israelites as ignorant of God's name, not as ignorant of Him who was called by that name.)—The name *Jah* likewise implies eternal existence. *Shadday*, however, is derived from *day*, " enough " ; comp. " for the stuff they had was sufficient " (*dayyam*, Exod. xxxvi. 7) ; the *shin* is equal to *asher*, " which," as in *she-kebar*, " which already " (Eccles. ii. 16). The name *Shadday*, therefore, signifies " he who is sufficient " ; that is to say, He does not require any other being for effecting the existence of what He created, or its conservation : His existence is sufficient for that. In a similar manner the name *hasin* implies " strength " ; comp. " he was strong (*hason*) as the oaks " (Amos ii. 9). The same is the case with " rock," which is a homonym, as we have explained (chap. xvi.). It is, therefore, clear that all these names of God are appellatives, or are applied to God by way of homonymy, like *zur* and others, the only exception being the tetragrammaton, the *Shem ha-meforash* (the *nomen proprium* of God), which is not an appellative ; it does not denote any attribute of God, nor does it imply anything except His existence. Absolute existence includes the idea of eternity, i.e., the necessity of existence. Note well the result at which we have arrived in this chapter.

CHAPTER LXIV

KNOW that in some instances by the phrase " the name of the Lord," nothing but the name alone is to be understood ; comp. " Thou shalt not take the name of the Lord thy God in vain" (Exod. xx. 7); "And he that blasphemeth the name of the Lord" (Lev. xxiv. 16). This occurs in numerous other passages. In other instances it means the essence and reality of God Himself, as in the phrase "They shall say to me, What is his name"? Sometimes it stands for "the word of God," so that "the name of God," "the word of God," and "the command of God," are identical phrases; comp. "for my name is in him" (Exod. xxiii. 21), that is, My word or My command is in him; i.e., he is the instrument of My desire and will. I shall explain this fully in treating of the homonymity of the term "angel" (II. chap. vi. and xxxiv.).—The same is the case with "The glory of the Lord." The phrase sometimes signifies "the material light," which God caused to rest on a certain place in order to show the distinction of that place, e.g., "And the glory of the Lord (*kebod adonay*) abode upon Mount Sinai and the cloud covered it" (Exod. xxiv. 16): "And the glory of the Lord filled the tabernacle" (*ib.* xl. 35). Sometimes the essence, the reality of God is meant by that expression, as in the words of Moses, "Show me *thy glory*" (*ib.* xxxiii. 18), to which the reply was given, "For no man shall see *me* and live" (*ib.* xx.). This shows that the glory of the Lord in this instance is the same as He Himself, and that "Thy glory" has been substituted for "Thyself," as a tribute of homage; an explanation which we also gave of the words, "And they shall say unto me, What is his name?" Sometimes the term "glory" denotes the glorification of the Lord by man or by any other being. For the true glorification of the Lord consists in the comprehension of His greatness, and all who comprehend His greatness and perfection, glorify Him according to their capacity, with this difference, that man alone magnifies God in words, expressive of what he has received in his mind, and what he desires to communicate to others. Things not endowed with comprehension, as e.g., minerals, may also be considered as glorifying the Lord, for by their natural properties they testify to the omnipotence and wisdom of their Creator, and cause him who examines them to praise God, by means of speech or without the use of words, if the power of speech be wanting. In Hebrew this licence has been extended still further, and the use of the verb "to speak" has been admitted as applicable in such a case; things which have no comprehension are therefore said to give utterance to praise, e.g., "All my bones shall say, Lord, who is like unto thee?" (Ps. xxxv. 10). Because a consideration of the properties of the bones leads to the discovery of that truth, and it is through them that it became known, they are represented as having uttered the divine praise; and since this [cause of God's praise] is itself called "praise," it has been said "the fulness of the whole earth is his praise" (Isa. vi. 3), in the same sense as "the earth is full of his praise" (Hab. iii. 3). As to *kabod* being employed in the sense of praise, comp. "Give praise (*kabod*) to the Lord your God" (Jer. xiii. 16); also "and in his temple does every one speak of his praise (*kabod*)" (Ps. xxix. 9), etc. Consider well the homonymity of this term, and explain it in each instance in accordance with the context; you will thus escape great embarrassment.

CHAPTER LXV

AFTER you have advanced thus far, and truly comprehended that God exists without having the attribute of existence, and that He is One, without having the attribute of unity, I do not think that I need explain to you the inadmissibility of the attribute of speech in reference to God, especially since our people generally believe that the Law, i.e., the word ascribed to Him, was created. Speech is attributed to Him, in so far as the word which Moses heard, was produced and brought to existence by God in the same manner as He produced all His other works and creations. As we shall have to speak more fully on prophecy, we shall here merely show that speech is attributed to God in the same way as all other actions, which are similar to our own. When we are told that God addressed the Prophets and spoke to them, our minds are merely to receive a notion that there is a Divine knowledge to which the Prophets attain ; we are to be impressed with the idea that the things which the Prophets communicate to us come from the Lord, and are not altogether the products of their own conceptions and ideas. This subject, which we have already mentioned above, will receive further explanation. It is the object of this chapter to show that the words " speaking " and " saying " are synonymous terms denoting (a) " Speech " ; as, e.g., " Moses shall speak (*yedabber*) " (Exod. xix. 19) ; " And Pharaoh said (*va-yomer*) " (*ib.* v. 5) ; (b) " Thought " as formed in the mind without being expressed in words ; e.g., " And I thought (*ve-amarti*) in my heart " (Eccles. ii. 15) ; " And I thought (*vedibbarti*) in my heart " (*ib.*) ; " And thy heart will imagine (*yedabber*) " (Prov. xxiii. 33) ; " Concerning Thee my heart thought (*amar*) " (Ps. xxvii. 8) ; " And Esau thought (*va-yomer*) in his heart " (Gen. xxvii. 41) ; examples of this kind are numerous ; (c) Will ; e.g., " And he said (*va-yomer*) to slay David " (2 Sam. xxi. 16), that is to say, he wished or he intended to slay him ; " Dost thou desire (*omer*) to slay me " (Exod. ii. 14) ; " And the whole congragation intended (*va-yomeru*) to stone them " (Num. xiv. 10). Instances of this kind are likewise numerous.

The two terms, when applied to God, can only have one of the two last-mentioned significations, viz., he wills and he desires, or he thinks, and there is no difference whether the divine thought became known to man by means of an actual voice, or by one of those kinds of inspiration which I shall explain further on (II. chap. xxxviii.). We must not suppose that in speaking God employed voice or sound, or that He has a soul in which the thoughts reside, and that these thoughts are things superadded to His essence ; but we ascribe and attribute to Him thoughts in the same manner as we ascribe to Him any other attributes. The use of these words in the sense of will and desire, is based, as I have explained, on the homonymity of these terms. In addition they are figures borrowed from our common practices, as has been already pointed out. For we cannot, at a first glance, see how anything can be produced by a mere desire ; we think that he who wishes to produce a thing, must perform a certain act, or command some one else to perform it. Therefore the command is figuratively ascribed to God when that takes place which He wishes, and we then say that He commanded that a certain thing should be accomplished. All this has its origin in our comparing the acts of God to our own acts, and also in the use of the term *amar* in the sense of " He desired," as we have already explained. The words " And He said," occurring in the account of the creation, signify " He wished," or " He desired." This has already been stated by other authors, and is well known. A proof for this, namely that the phrase " God said," in the first chapter of Genesis, must be taken in a figurative sense " He willed," and not in its literal meaning, is found in the circumstance that a command can only be given to a being which exists and is capable of receiving the command. Comp. " By the word of the Lord were the heavens made, and all the host of them by the breath of his mouth " (Ps. xxxiii. 6). " His mouth," and " the breath of his mouth," are undoubtedly figurative expressions, and the same is the case with " His word " and " His speech." The meaning of the verse is therefore that they [the heavens and all their host] exist through His will and desire. All our eminent authorities are cognisant of this ; and, I need not explain that in Hebrew *amar* and *dibber* have the same meaning, as is proved by the passage, " For it has heard all the words (*imre*) of the Lord which he spake (*dibber*) unto us " (Josh. xxiv. 27).

CHAPTER LXVI

" And the tables were the work of God " (Exod. xxxii. 16), that is to say, they were the product of nature, not of art ; for all natural things are called " the work of the Lord," e.g., " These see the works of the Lord " (Ps. cvii. 24) ; and the description of the several things in nature, as plants, animals, winds, rain, etc., is followed by the exclamation, " O Lord, how manifold are thy works ! " (Ps. civ. 24). Still more striking is the relation between God and His creatures, as expressed in the phrase, " The cedars of Lebanon, which he hath planted " (*ib.* 16) ; the cedars being the product of nature, and not of art, are described as having been planted by the Lord. Similarly we explain, " And the writing was the writing of God " (Exod. xxxii. 16) ; the relation in which the writing stood to God has already been defined in the words " written with the finger of God " (*ib.* xxxi. 18), and the meaning of this phrase is the same as that of " the work of thy fingers " (Ps. viii. 4). this being said of the heavens ; of the latter it has been stated distinctly that they were made by a word ; comp. " By the word of the Lord were the heavens made " (*ib.* xxxiii. 6). Hence you learn that in the Bible, the creation of a thing is figuratively expressed by terms denoting " word " and " speech " The same thing which according to one passage has been made by the word, is represented in another passage as made by the " finger of God." The phrase " written by the finger of God " is therefore identical with " written by the word of God " ; and if the latter phrase had been used, it would have been equal to " written by the will and desire of God." Onkelos adopted in this place a strange explanation, and rendered the words literally " written by the finger of the Lord " ; he thought that " the finger " was a certain thing ascribed to God ; so that " the finger of the Lord " is to be interpreted in the same way as " the mountain of God " (Exod. iii. 1), " the rod of God " (*ib.* iv. 20), that is, as being an instrument created by Him, which by His will engraved the writing on the tables. I cannot see why Onkelos preferred this explanation. It would have been more reasonable to say " written by the word of the Lord," in imitation of the verse " By the word of the Lord the heavens were made." Or was the creation of the writing on the tables more difficult than the creation of the stars in the spheres ? As the latter were made by the direct will of God, not by means of an instrument, the writing may also have been produced by His direct will, not by means of an instrument. You know what the Mishnah says, " Ten things were created on Friday in the twilight of the evening, and " the writing " is one of the ten things. This shows how generally it was assumed by our forefathers that the writing of the tables was produced in the same manner as the rest of the creation, as we have shown in our Commentary on the Mishnah (*Aboth*, v. 6).

CHAPTER LXVII

SINCE the verb " to say " has been figuratively used to express the will of the Creator, and the phrase " And he said " has repeatedly been employed in the account of all the things created in " the six days of the beginning," the expression " to rest " has likewise been figuratively applied to God in reference to the Sabbath-day, on which there was no creation ; it is therefore said, " And he rested (*va-yishbot*) on the seventh day " (Gen. ii. 2). For " to leave off speaking " is, in Hebrew, likewise expressed by the same verb, as, e.g., " So these three men ceased (*va-yishbetu*) to answer Job " (Job xxxii. 1) ; also by *nuah*, as, in " They spake to Nabal according to all those words in the name of David, and ceased (*va-yanuhu*) " (1 Sam. xxv. 9). In my opinion, (*va-yanuhu*) means " they ceased to speak," and waited for the answer ; for no allusion to exertion whatever having previously been mentioned, the words, " and they rested," in its primary signification, would have been entirely out of place in that narrative, even if the young men who spoke had really used some exertion. The author relates that having delivered that whole speech, which, as you find, consisted of gentle expressions, they were silent, that is to say, they did not add any word or act by which the reply of Nabal could be justified ; it being the object of the entire passage to represent Nabal's conduct as extremely reprehensible. In that sense [viz., " to cease," or " to leave off "] the verb *nuah* is used in the phrase " And he left off (*va-yanah*) on the seventh day."

Our Sages, and some of the Commentators, took, however, *nuah* in its primary sense " to rest," but as a transitive form (hiphil), explaining the phrase thus : " and he gave rest to the world on the seventh day," i.e., no further act of creation took place on that day.

It is possible that the word *va-yanah* is derived either from *yanah*, a verb of the class *pe-yod*, or *nahah*, a verb of the class *lamed-he*, and has this meaning : " he established " or " he governed " the Universe in accordance with the properties it possessed on the seventh day " ; that is to say, while on each of the six days events took place contrary to the natural laws now in operation throughout the Universe, on the seventh day the Universe was merely upheld and left in the condition in which it continues to exist. Our explanation is not impaired by the fact that the form of the word deviates from the rules of verbs of these two classes ; for there are frequent exceptions to the rules of conjugations, and especially of the weak verbs ; and any interpretation which removes such a source of error must not be abandoned because of certain grammatical rules. We know that we are ignorant of the sacred language, and that grammatical rules only apply to the majority of cases.— The same root is also found as a verb 'ayin-*vav* in the sense " to place " and

" to set," as e.g., " and it shall be established and she shall be placed (*ve-hunniḥaḥ*) there upon her own base " (Zech. v. 11), and " she suffered neither the birds of the air to settle (*la-nuaḥ*) on them " (2 Sam. xxi. 10). According to my opinion, the verb has the same signification in Hab. iii. 16, " that I might remain firm (*anuaḥ*) in the day of trouble."

· The word (*va-yinnafash*) is a verb derived from *nefesh*, the homonymity of which we have already explained (chap. xli.), namely, that it has the signification of intention or will; (*va-yinnafash*) accordingly means : " that which he desired was accomplished, and what he wished had come into existence."

CHAPTER LXVIII

You are acquainted with the well-known principle of the philosophers that God is the *intellectus*, the *ens intelligens*, and the *ens intelligibile*. These three things are in God one and the same, and do not in any way constitute a plurality. We have also mentioned it in our larger work, " *Mishneh Torah*," and we have explained there that it is a fundamental principle of our religion, namely, that He is absolutely one, that nothing combines with Him ; that is to say, there is no Eternal thing besides Him. On that account we say *ḥai adonay*, " the Lord liveth " (Ruth iii. 13), and not *ḥe adonay*, " the life of the Lord," for His life is not a thing distinct from His essence, as we have explained in treating of the inadmissibility of the attributes. There is no doubt that he who has not studied any works on mental philosophy, who has not comprehended the nature of the mind, who has no knowledge of its essence, and considers it in no other way than he would consider the nature of whiteness and of blackness, will find this subject extremely difficult, and to him our principle that the *intellectus*, the *intelligens*, and the *intelligibile*, are in God one and the same thing, will appear as unintelligible as if we said that the whiteness, the whitening substance, and the material which is whitened are one and the same thing. And, indeed, many ignorant people refute at once our principle by using such comparisons,. Even amongst those who imagine that they are wise, many find this subject difficult, and are of opinion that it is impossible for the mind to grasp the truth of this proposition, although it is a demonstrated truth, as has been shown by Metaphysicians. I will tell you now what has been proved. Man, before comprehending a thing, comprehends it in potentia (δυνάμει) ; when, however, he comprehends a thing, e.g., the form of a certain tree which is pointed out to him, when he abstracts its form from its substance, and reproduces the abstract form, an act performed by the intellect, he comprehends in reality (ἐνεργείᾳ), and the intellect which he has acquired in actuality, is the abstract form of the tree in man's mind. For in such a case the intellect is not a thing distinct from the thing comprehended. It is therefore clear to you that the thing comprehended is the abstract form of the tree, and at the same time it is the intellect in action ; and that the intellect and the abstract form of the tree are not two different things, for the intellect in action is nothing but the thing comprehended, and that agent by which the form of the tree has been turned into an intellectual and abstract object, namely, that which comprehends, is undoubtedly the intellect in action.

All intellect is identical with its action ; the intellect in action is not a thing different from its action, for the true nature and assence of the intellect is comprehension, and you must not think that the intellect in action is a thing existing by itself, separate from comprehension, and that comprehension is a different thing connected with it ; for the very essence of the intellect is comprehension. In assuming an intellect in action you assume the comprehension of the thing comprehended. This is quite clear to all who have made themselves familiar with the figurative language common to this discipline. You therefore accept it as proved that the intellect consists in its action, which is its true nature and essence. Consequently the very thing by which the form of that tree has been made abstract and intelligible, viz., the intellect, is at the same time the *intelligens*, for the intellect is itself the *agens* which abstracts the form and comprehends it, and that is the action, on account of which it is called the *intelligens ;* but itself and its action are identical ; and that which is called intellect in action consists [in the above-mentioned instance] of nothing else but of the form of the tree. It must now be obvious to you that whenever the intellect is found in action, the intellect and the thing comprehended are one and the same thing ; and also that the function of all intellect, namely, the act of comprehending, is its essence. The intellect, that which comprehends and that which is comprehended, are therefore the same, whenever a real comprehension takes place. But, when we speak of the power of comprehension, we necessarily distinguish two things : the power itself, and the thing which can be comprehended ; e.g., that hylic intellect of Zaid is the power of comprehension, and this tree is, in like manner, a thing which is capable of being comprehended ; these, undoubtedly, are two different things. When, however, the potential is replaced by the actual, and when the form of the tree has really been comprehended, the form comprehended is the intellect, and it is by that same intellect, by the intellect in action, that the tree has been converted into an abstract idea, and has been comprehended. For everything in which a real action takes place exists in reality. On the other hand, the power of comprehension, and the object capable of comprehension are two things ; but that which is only potential cannot be imagined otherwise than in connexion with an object possessing that capacity, as, e.g., man, and thus we have three things : the man who possesses the power, and is capable of comprehending ; that power itself, namely, the power of comprehension, and the object which presents itself as an object of comprehension, and is capable of being comprehended ; to use the foregoing example, the man, the hylic intellect, and the abstract form of the tree, are three different things. They become one and the same thing when the intellect is in action, and you will never find the intellect different from the comprehensible object, unless the power of comprehending and the power of being comprehended be referred to. Now, it has been proved, that God is an intellect which always is in action, and that—as has been stated, and as will be proved hereafter—there is in Him at no time a mere potentiality, that He does not comprehend at one time, and is without comprehension at another time, but He comprehends constantly ; consequently, He and the things comprehended are one and the same thing, that is to say, His essence ; and the act of comprehending because of which it is said that He comprehends, is the intellect itself, which is likewise His essence, God is therefore always the *intellectus*, the *intelligens*, and the *intelligibile*.

We have thus shown that the identity of the intellect, the *intelligens* and the *intelligibile*, is not only a fact as regards the Creator, but as regards all intellect, when in action. There is, however, this difference, that from time to time our intellect passes over from mere potentiality to reality, and that the pure intellect, i.e., the active intellect, finds sometimes obstacles, though not in itself, but accidentally in some external cause. It is not our present intention to explain this subject, but we will merely show that God alone, and none besides Him, is an intellect constantly in action, and there is, neither in Himself nor in anything beside Him, any obstacle whereby His comprehension would be hindered. Therefore He always includes the *intelligens*, the *intellectus*, and the *intelligibile*, and His essence is at the same time the *intelligens*, the *intelligibile*, and the *intellectus*, as is necessarily the case with all intellect in action.

We have reiterated this idea in the present chapter because it is exceedingly abstruse, and I do not apprehend that the reader will confound intellectual comprehension with the representative faculty—with the reproduction of the material image in our imagination, since this work is designed only for those who have studied philosophy, and who know what has already been said on the soul and its faculties.

CHAPTER LXIX

THE philosophers, as you know, call God the First Cause (in Hebrew '*illah* and *sibbah*) : but those who are known by the name of Mutakallemim are very much opposed to the use of that name, and call Him *Agens*, believing that there is a great difference whether we say that God is the Cause or that He is the *Agens*. They argue thus : If we say that God is the Cause, the co-existence of the Cause with that which was produced by that Cause would necessarily be implied ; this again would involve the belief that the Universe was eternal, and that it was inseparable from God. When, however, we say that God is the *Agens*, the co-existence of the *Agens* with its product is not implied ; for the *agens* can exist anterior to its product ; we cannot even imagine how an *agens* can be in action unless it existed before its own production. This is an argument advanced by persons who do not distinguish between the potential and the actual. You, however, should know that in this case there is no difference whether you employ the term " cause " or " *agens* " ; for if you take the term " cause " in the sense of a mere potentiality, it precedes its effect ; but if you mean the cause in action, then the effect must necessarily co-exist with the cause in action. The same is the case with the *agens* ; take it as an *agens* in reality, the work must necessarily co-exist with its *agens*. For the builder, before he builds the house, is not in reality a builder, but has the faculty for building a house—in the same way as the materials for the house before it is being built are merely *in potentiâ*—but when the house has been built, he is the builder in reality, and his product must likewise be in actual existence. Nothing is therefore gained by choosing the term " *agens* " and rejecting the term " cause." My object here is to show that these two terms are equal, and in the same manner as we call God an *Agens*, although the work does not yet exist, only because there is no hindrance or obstacle which might prevent Him from doing it whenever He pleases, we may also call Him the Cause, although the effect may not yet be in existence.

The reason why the philosophers called God the Cause, and did not call Him the *Agens*, is not to be sought in their belief that the universe is eternal, but in other motives, which I will briefly describe to you. It has been shown in the science of Physics that everything, except the Primal Cause, owes its origin to the following four causes :—the substance, the form, the *agens*, the final cause. These are sometimes direct, sometimes indirect causes ; but each by itself is called " a cause." They also believe—and I do not differ from their opinion—that God Himself is the *agens*, the form, and the end ; therefore they call God " the Cause," in order to express that He unites in Himself these three causes, viz., that He is the *agens*, the form, and the final cause of the universe. In the present chapter I only wish to show you in what sense it may be said of God that He is the *agens*, the form, and also the final cause of the universe. You need not trouble yourself now with the question whether the universe has been created by God, or whether, as the philosophers have assumed, it is eternal, co-existing with Him. You will find [in the pages of this treatise] full and instructive information on the subject. Here I wish to show that God is the " cause " of every event that takes place in the world, just as He is the Creator of the whole universe as it now exists. It has already been explained in the science of Physics, that a cause must again be sought for each of the four divisions of causes. When we have found for any existing thing those four causes which are in immediate con-nexion with it, we find for these again causes, and for these again other causes, and so on until we arrive at the first causes. E.g., a certain produc-tion has its *agens*, this *agens* again has its *agens*, and so on and on until at last we arrive at a first *agens*, which is the true *agens* throughout all the inter-vening links. If the letter *aleph* be moved by *bet*, *bet* by *gimel*, *gimel* by *dalet*, and *dalet* by *hé* — and as the series does not extend to infinity, ler us stop at *hé*—there is no doubt that the *hé* moves the letters *aleph*, *bet*, *gimel*, and *dalet*, and we say correctly that the *aleph* is moved by *hé*. In that sense everything occurring in the universe, although directly produced by certain nearer causes, is ascribed to the Creator, as we shall explain. He is the *Agens*, and He is therefore the ultimate cause. We shall also find, after careful examination, that every physical and transient form must be preceded by another such form, by which the substance has been fitted to receive the next form ; the previous form again has been preceded by another, and we arrive at length at that form which is necessary for the existence of all intermediate forms, which are the causes of the present form. That form to which the forms of all existing things are traced is God. You must not imagine that when we say that God is the first form of all forms existing in the Universe, we refer to that first form which Aristotle, in the Book of Metaphysics, describes as being without beginning and without end, for he treats of a form which is a physical, and not a purely intellectual one. When we call God the ultimate form of the universe, we do not use this term in the sense of form connected with substance, namely, as the form of that substance, as though God were the form of a material being. It is not in this sense that we use it, but in the following : Everything existing and endowed with a form, is whatever it is through its form, and when that form is destroyed its whole existence terminates and is obliterated. The same is the case as regards the relation between God and all distant causes of existing beings ; it is through the existence of God that all things exist, and it is He who maintains their existence by that process which is called emanation (in Hebrew *shepha'*), as will be explained in one of the chapters of the present work. If God did not exist, suppose this were possible, the universe would not exist, and there would be an end to the existence of the distant causes, the final effects, and the intermediate causes. Consequently God maintains the same relation to the world as the form has to a thing endowed with a form ; through the form it is what it is, and on it the reality and essence of the thing depends. In this sense we may say that God is the ultimate form, that He is the form of all forms ; that is to say, the existence and continuance of all forms in the last instance depend on Him, the forms are maintained by Him, in the same way as all things endowed with forms retain their existence through their forms. On that account God is called, in the sacred language, *ḥe ha-'olamim*, "the life of the Universe," as will be explained (chap. lxxii.). The same argument holds good in reference to all final causes. If you assign to a thing a certain purpose, you can find for that purpose another purpose. We mention, e.g., a (wooden) chair ; its substance is wood, the joiner is its *agens*, the square its form, and its purpose is that one should sit upon it. You may then ask, For what purpose does one sit upon it ? The answer will be that he who is sitting upon it desires to be high above the ground. If again you ask, For what purpose does he desire to be high above the ground, you will receive the answer that he wishes to appear high in the eyes of those who see him. For what purpose does he wish to appear higher in the eyes of those who see him ? That the people may respect and fear him. What is the good of his being feared ? His commands will be respected. For what purpose are his commands to be respected ? That people shall refrain from injuring each other. What is the object of this precaution ? To maintain order amongst the people. In this way one purpose necessitates the pre-existence of another, except the final purpose, which is the execution of the will of God, according to one of the opinions which have been propounded, as will be explained (III. xiii. and xvii.), and the final answer will be, "It is the will of God." According to the view of others, which will likewise be explained, the final purpose is the execution of the decree of His wisdom, and the final answer will be, "It has been decreed by His wisdom." According to either opinion, the series of the successive purposes terminates, as has been shown, in God's will or wisdom, which, in our opinion, are identical with His essence, and are not any thing separate from Himself or different from His essence. Consequently, God is the final purpose of everything. Again, it is the aim of everything to become, according to its faculties, similar to God in perfection ; this is meant by the expression, "His will, which is identical with His essence," as will be shown below (*ibid.*). In this sense God is called the End of all ends.

I have thus explained to you in what sense God is said to be the *Agens*, the Form, and the End. This is the reason why the philosophers not only call

Him " the Maker " but also the " Cause." Some of the scholars belonging to the Mutakallemim (Mohammedan theologians), went so far in their folly and in their vainglory as to say that the non-existence of the Creator, if that were possible, would not necessarily imply the non-existence of the things created by Him, i.e., the Universe : for a production need not necessarily cease to exist when the producer, after having produced it, has ceased to exist. They would be right, if God were only the maker of the Universe, and if its permanent existence were not dependent on Him. The store-house does not cease to exist at the death of the builder ; for he does not give permanent existence to the building. God, however, is Himself the form of the Universe, as we have already shown, and it is He who causes its continuance and permanency. It is therefore wrong to say that a thing can remain durable and permanent, after the being that makes it durable and permanent has ceased to exist, since that thing can possess no more durability and permanency than it has received from that being. Now you understand the greatness of the error into which they have fallen through their assumption that God is only the *Agens*, and not the End or the Form.

CHAPTER LXX

THE term *rakab*, " to ride," is a synonym. In its primary signification it is applied to man's riding on an animal, in the usual way ; e.g., " Now he was riding (*rokeb*) upon his ass " (Num. xxii. 22). It has then been figu-ratively used to denote " dominion over a thing " ; because the rider governs and rules the animal he rides upon ; e.g., " He made him ride (*yarkibehu*) on the high places of the earth " (Deut. xxxii. 13) ; " and I will cause thee to ride (*ve-hirkabtika*) upon the high places of the earth " (Isa. lviii. 14), that is, you shall have dominion over the highest (people) on earth ; " I will make Ephraim to ride (*arkib*) " (Hos. x. 11), i.e., I shall give him rule and dominion. In this same sense it is said of God, " who rideth (*rokeb*) upon the heaven in thy help " (Deut. xxxiii. 26), that is, who rules the heaven ; and " Him that rideth (*la-rokeb*) upon the 'arabot " (Ps. lxviii. 4), i.e., who rules the 'arabot, the uppermost, all-encompassing sphere. It has also been repeatedly stated by our Sages that there are seven *reki'im* (firma-ments, heavens), and that the uppermost of them, the all-surrounding, is called 'arabot. Do not object to the number seven given by them, al-though there are more *reki'im*, for there are spheres which contain several circles (*gilgallim*), and are counted as one ; this is clear to those who have studied that subject, and I shall also explain it ; here I wish merely to point out that our Sages always assumed that 'arabot is the uppermost sphere. The 'arabot is also referred to in the words, " who rideth upon the heaven in thy help." Thus we read in Talm. B. *Hagigah*, p. 12, " The high and exalted dwelleth on 'arabot, as it is said, ' Extol Him that rideth upon 'arabot ' " (Ps. lxviii. 4). How is it proved that " heaven " and " 'arabot " are identical ? The one passage has " who rideth on 'arabot," the other " who rideth upon the heaven." Hence it is clear that in all these passages reference is made to the same all-surrounding sphere, concerning which you will hereafter (II. xxiv.) receive more information. Consider well that the expression " dwelling over it," is used by them, and not " dwelling in it." The latter expression would have implied that God occupies a place or is a power in the sphere, as was in fact believed by the Sabeans, who held that God was the soul of the sphere. By saying " dwelling over it," they indicated that God was separate from the sphere, and was not a power in it. Know also that the term " riding upon the heavens," has figuratively been applied to God in order to show the following excellent comparison. The rider is better than the animal upon which he rides—the comparative is only used for the sake of convenience, for the rider is not of the same class as the animal upon which he rides—furthermore, the rider moves the animal and leads it as he likes ; it is as it were his instrument, which he uses according to his will ; he is separate from it, apart from it, not connected with it. In like manner the uppermost sphere, by the rotation of which everything moveable is set in motion, is moved by God, who is separate from the sphere, and is not a power in it. In *Bereshit Rabba* we read that in commenting on the Divine words, " The eternal God is a refuge " (lit., a dwelling, Deut. xxxiii. 27), our Sages said, " He is the dwelling of His world, the world is not His dwelling." This explanation is then followed by the remark, " The horse is secondary to the rider, the rider is not subservient to the horse ; this is meant by ' Thou wilt ride upon thy horses ' " (Hab. iii. 8). Consider and learn how they described the relation of God to the sphere, asserting that the latter is His instrument, by means of which He rules the universe. For whenever you find our Sages saying that in a certain heaven are certain things, they do not mean to say that in the heavens there are any extraneous things, but that from a certain heaven the force emanates which is required for the production of certain things, and for their continuing in proper order. The proof for my statement you may find in the following sayings of our Sages—" The '*arabot*, in which there are justice, charity, right, treasures of life and peace, treasures of blessing, of the souls of the righteous, of the souls and the spirits of those to be born, and of the dew by which God will at some future time revive the dead, etc." It is clear that the things enumerated here are not material, and do not occupy a place—for " dew " is not to be taken in its literal sense. —Consider also that here the phrase " in which," meaning " in the '*arabot*," is used, and not " over which," as if to say that all the things existing in the universe derive their existence from powers emanating from the '*arabot*, which God made to be the origin and the place of these powers. They are said to include " the treasures of life " ; a perfectly true and correct assertion ! For all existing life originates in that treasure of life, as will be mentioned below (chap. lxii., and II. chap. x.). Reflect on the fact that the souls of the righteous as well as the souls and the spirits of those to be born are mentioned here ! How sublime is this idea to him who understands it ! for the soul that remains after the death of man, is not the soul that lives in a man when he is born ; the latter is a mere faculty, while that which has a separate existence after death, is a reality ; again, the soul and the spirit of man during his life are two different things ; therefore the souls and the spirits are both named as existing in man ; but separate from the body only one of them exists. We have already explained the homonymity of *ruaḥ* (spirit) in this work, and also at the end of *Sefer ha madda* (*Mishneh torah Hil. teshubah*, viii. 3–4) we treated of the homonymity of these expressions. Consider how these excellent and true ideas, comprehended only by the greatest philosophers, are found scattered in the Midrashim. When a student who disavows truth reads them, he will at first sight deride them, as being contrary to the real state of things. The cause of this is the circumstance, that our Sages spoke of these subjects in metaphors ; they are too difficult for the common understanding of the people, as has been noticed by us several times.

I will now return to the subject which I commenced to explain, in order to bring it to a conclusion. Our Sages commenced to adduce proofs from Scripture for their assertion that the things enumerated above are contained in the 'arabot. As to justice and right they quote " Justice and judgment are the habitation of thy throne " (Ps. lxxxix. 18). In the same way they prove their assertion concerning all things enumerated by them, by showing that they are described as being related to God, as being near Him. Note this. In the *Pirke Rabbi Eliezer* it is said : God created seven rekiʿim (heavens), and out of all of them He selected the 'araboth for His royal throne ; comp. " Exalt him who rideth upon the 'arabot " (Ps. lxviii. 4). These are his (Rabbi Eliezer's) words. Note them likewise.

You must know that in Hebrew the collective noun denoting animals used for riding is " mercabah." Instances of this noun are not rare. " And Joseph made ready his chariot " *(merkabto)* (Gen. xlvi. 29) ; " in the second chariot " *(be-mirkebet)* *(ib.* xli. 43) ; " Pharaoh's chariots " *(markebot)* (Exod. xv. 4). The following passage especially proves that the Hebrew *merkabah* denotes a collection of animals : " And a *merkabah* came up and went out of Egypt for six hundred shekels of silver, and a horse for an hundred and fifty " (1 Kings x. 21). Hence we may learn that *mercabah* denotes here four horses. Therefore I think that when it was stated, according to the literal sense of the words, that four *Hayyot* (beasts) carry the Throne of Glory, our Sages called this " *mercabah* " on account of its similarity with the mercabah consisting of four single animals. So far has the theme of this chapter carried us, and we shall be compelled to make many further remarks on this subject. Here, however, it is our object, and the aim of all we have said, to show that " who rideth upon heaven " (Deut. xxxiii. 26) means " who sets the all-surrounding sphere in motion, and turns it by His power and will." The same sense is contained in the conclusion of that verse : " and in his excellency the spheres," i.e., who in His excellency moves the spheres *(shehakim)*. In reference to the first sphere, the 'arabot, the verb " to ride " is used, in reference to the rest, the noun " excellency," because through the motion of the uppermost sphere in its daily circuit, all the spheres move, participating as parts in the motion of the whole ; and this being that great power that sets everything in motion, it is called " excellency." Let this subject constantly remain in your memory when you study what I am going to say ; for it—i.e., the motion of the uppermost sphere— is the greatest proof for the existence of God, as I shall demonstrate. Note this.

CHAPTER LXXI

KNOW that many branches of science relating to the correct solution of these problems, were once cultivated by our forefathers, but were in the course of time neglected, especially in consequence of the tyranny which barbarous nations exercised over us. Besides, speculative studies were not open to all men, as we have already stated (Introd. p. 2, and I. chap. xxxi.), only the subjects taught in the Scriptures were accessible to all. Even the traditional Law, as you are well aware, was not originally committed to writing, in conformity with the rule to which our nation generally adhered, " Things which I have communicated to you orally, you must not communicate to others in writing." With reference to the Law, this rule was very opportune ; for while it remained in force it averted the evils which happened subsequently, viz., great diversity of opinion, doubts as to the meaning of written words, slips of the pen, dissensions among the people, formation of new sects, and confused notions about practical subjects. The traditional teaching was in fact, according to the words of the Law, entrusted to the Great Tribunal, as we have already stated in our works on the Talmud. (Introd. to *Mishneh Torah* and Introd. to Commen. on the Mishnah).

Care having been taken, for the sake of obviating injurious influences, that the Oral Law should not be recorded in a form accessible to all, it was but natural that no portion of " the secrets of the Law " (i.e., metaphysical problems) would be permitted to be written down or divulged for the use of all men. These secrets, as has been explained, were orally communicated by a few able men to others who were equally distinguished. Hence the principle applied by our teachers, " The secrets of the Law can only be entrusted to him who is a councillor, a cunning artificer, etc." The natural effect of this practice was that our nation lost the knowledge of those important disciplines. Nothing but a few remarks and allusions are to be found in the Talmud and the Midrashim, like a few kernels enveloped in such a quantity of husk, that the reader is generally occupied with the husk, and forgets that it encloses a kernel.

In addition you will find that in the few works composed by the Geonim and the Karaites on the unity of God and on such matter as is connected with this doctrine, they followed the lead of the Mohammedan Mutakallemim, and what they wrote is insignificant in comparison with the kindred works of the Mohammedans. It also happened, that at the time when the Mohammedans adopted this method of the Kalam, there arose among them a certain sect, called Mu'tazilah, i.e., Separatists. In certain things our scholars followed the theory and the method of these Mu'tazilah. Although another sect, the Asha'ariyah, with their own peculiar views, was subsequently established amongst the Mohammedans, you will not find any of these views in the writings of our authors ; not because these authors preferred the opinions of the first-named sect to those of the latter, but because they chanced first to become acquainted with the theory of the Mu'tazilah, which they adopted and treated as demonstrated truth. On the other hand our Andalusian scholars followed the teachings of the philosophers, from whom they accepted those opinions which were not opposed to our own religious principles. You will find that they did not adopt any of the methods of the Mutakallemim ; in many respects they approached the view expressed in the present treatise, as may be noticed in the few works which were recently written by authors of that school. You should also know that whatever the Mohammedans, that is, the Mu'tazilah and the Asha'ariyah, said on those subjects, consists in nothing but theories founded on propositions which are taken from the works of those Greek and Syrian scholars who attempted to oppose the system of the philosophers, and to refute their arguments. The following was the cause of that opposition : At the time when the Christian Church brought the Greeks and Syrians into its fold, and promulgated its well-known dogmas, the opinions of the philosophers were current amongst those nations ; and whilst philosophy flourished, kings became defenders of the Christian faith. The learned Greek and Syrian Christians of the age, seeing that their dogmas were unquestionably exposed to severe attacks from the existing philosophical systems, laid the foundation for this science of Dogmatics ; they commenced by putting forth such propositions as would support their doctrines, and be useful for the refutation of opinions opposed to the funda-mental principles of the Christian religion.

When the Mohammedans caused Arabic translations of the writings of the Philosophers to be made, those criticisms were likewise translated. When the opinions of John the Grammarian, of Ibn Adi, and of kindred authors on those subjects were made accessible to them, they adopted them, and imagined that they had arrived at the solution of important problems. Moreover, they selected from the opinions of the ancient philosophers what-ever seemed serviceable to their purposes, although later critics had proved that those theories were false ; as, e.g., the theories of atoms and of a *vacuum*. They believed that the discussions of those authors were of a general char-acter, and contained propositions useful for the defence of positive religion. At a subsequent period the same theories were more fully developed, and presented an aspect unknown to those Theologians of the Greeks and other nations who were the immediate successors of the Philosophers. At a later time, when the Mohammedans adopted certain peculiar theological theories they were naturally obliged to defend them ; and when their new theories, again became the subject of controversy among them, each party laid down such propositions as suited their special doctrine.

Their arguments undoubtedly involved certain principles which concerned the three communities—Jews, Christians, and Mohammedans, such as the *creatio ex nihilo*, which afforded support to the belief in miracles and to vari-ous other doctrines. There are, however, other subjects of belief which the Christians and Mohammedans have undertaken to defend, such as the doctrine of the Trinity in the theological works of the former, and " the Word " in the works of some Mohammedan sects ; in order to prove the dogmas which they thus desired to establish, they were compelled to resort to certain hypotheses. It is not our object to criticize things which are peculiar to either creed, or books which were written exclusively in the interest of the one community or the other. We merely maintain that the earlier Theologians, both of the Greek Christians and of the Mohammedans, when they laid down their propositions, did not investigate the real pro-perties of things ; first of all they considered what must be the properties of the things which should yield proof for or against a certain creed ; and when this was found they asserted that the thing must be endowed with those properties ; then they employed the same assertion as a proof for the iden-tical arguments which had led to the assertion, and by which they either supported or refuted a certain opinion. This course was followed by able men who originated this method, and adopted it in their writings. They professed to be free from preconceived opinions, and to have been led to a stated result by actual research. Therefore when philosophers of a subsequent date studied the same writings they did not perceive the true character of the arguments ; on the contrary, they found in the ancient works strong proofs and a valuable support for the acceptance or the rejection of certain opinions, and thus thought that, so far as religious principles were concerned, there was no necessity whatever to prove or refute any of their propositions, and that the first Mutakallemim had discussed those subjects with the sole object of defeating certain views of the philosophers, and demonstrating the insufficiency of their proofs. Persons who hold this opinion, do not suspect how much they are mistaken ; for the first Mutakallemim tried to prove a proposition when it was expedient to demonstrate its truth ; and to disprove it, when its rejection was desirable, and when it was contrary to the opinion which they wished to uphold, although the contradiction might only become obvious after the application of a hundred successive propositions. In this manner the earlier Mutakallemim effected a radical cure of the malady ! I tell you, however, as a general rule, that Themistius was right in saying that the properties of things cannot adapt themselves to our opinions, but our opinions must be adapted to the existing properties.

Having studied the works of these Mutakallemim, as far as I had an opportunity, just as I had studied the writings of the philosophers according to the best of my ability, I found that the method of all Mutakallemim was the same in its general characteristics, namely, they assume that the really existing form of things proves nothing at all, because it is merely one of the various phases of the things, the opposite of which is equally admissible to our minds. In many instances these Theologians were guided by their imagination, and thought that they were following the dictates of the intellect. They set forth the propositions which I shall describe to you, and demonstrated by their peculiar mode of arguing that the Universe had a beginning. The theory of the *creatio ex nihilo* being thus established, they asserted, as a logical consequence, that undoubtedly there must be a Maker who created the Universe. Next they showed that this Maker is One, and from the Unity of the Creator they deduced His Incorporeality. This method was adopted by every Mohammedan Mutakallem in the discussion of this subject, and by those of our co-religionists who imitated them and walked in their footsteps Although the Mutakallemim disagree in the methods of their proofs, and employ different propositions in demonstrating the act of creation or in rejecting the eternity of the Universe, they invariably begin with proving the *creatio ex nihilo*, and establish on that proof the existence of God. I have examined this method, and find it most objectionable. It must be rejected, because all the proofs for the creation have weak points, and cannot be considered as convincing except by those who do not know the difference between a proof, a dialectical argument, and a sophism. Those who understand the force of the different methods will clearly see that all the proofs for the creation are questionable, because propositions have been employed which have never been proved. I think that the utmost that can be effected by believers in the truth of Revelation is to expose the shortcomings in the proofs of philosophers who hold that the Universe is eternal, and if forsooth a man has effected this, he has accomplished a great deed ! For it is well known to all clear and correct thinkers who do not wish to deceive themselves, that this question, namely, whether the Universe has been created or is eternal, cannot be answered with mathematical certainty ; here human intellect must pause. We shall have occasion to speak more fully on this subject, but for the present it may suffice to state that the philosophers have for the last three thousand years been continually divided on that subject, as far as we can learn from their works and the record of their opinions.

Such being the nature of this theory, how can we employ it as an axiom and establish on it the existence of the Creator ? In that case the existence of God would be uncertain ; if the universe had a beginning, God does exist ; if it be eternal, God does not exist ; the existence of God would therefore remain either an open question, or we should have to declare that the creation had been proved, and compel others by mere force to accept this doctrine, in order thus to be enabled to declare that we have proved the existence of God. Such a process is utterly inadmissible. The true method, which is based on a logical and indubitable proof, consists, according to my opinion, in demonstrating the existence of God, His unity, and His incorporeality by such philosophical arguments as are founded on the theory of the eternity of the Universe. I do not propose this method as though I believed in the eternity of the Universe, for I do not follow the philosophers on this point, but because by the aid of this method these three principles, viz., the existence of God, His unity and His incorporeality can be fully proved and verified, irrespectively of the question whether the universe has had a beginning or not. After firmly establishing these three principles by an exact proof, we shall treat of the problem of creation and discuss it as fully as possible. You are at liberty to content yourself with the declaration of the Mutakallemim, and to believe that the act of creation has been demonstrated by proof ; nor can there be any harm if you consider it unproven that the universe had a beginning, and accept this theory as supported by the authority of the Prophets. Before you learn our opinion on prophecy, which will be given in the present work, do not ask, how could the belief in prophecy be justified, if it were assumed that the universe was eternal, We will not now expatiate on that subject. You should, however, know that some of the propositions, started and proved by the Radicals, i.e., the Mutakallemim, in order to prove the act of creation, imply an order of things contrary to that which really exists, and involve a complete change in the laws of nature ; this fact will be pointed out to you, for it will be necessary to mention their propositions and their argumentation. My method, as far as I now can explain it in general terms, is as follows. The universe is either eternal or has had a beginning ; if it had a beginning, there must necessarily exist a being which caused the beginning ; this is clear to common sense ; for a thing that has had a beginning, cannot be the cause of its own beginning, another must have caused it. The universe was, therefore, created by God. If on the other hand the universe were eternal, it could in various ways be proved that apart from the things which constitute the universe, there exists a being which is neither body nor a force in a body, and which is one, eternal, not preceded by any cause, and immutable. That being is God. You see that the proofs for the Existence, the Unity and the Incorporeality of God must vary according to the propositions admitted by us. Only in this way can we succeed in obtaining a perfect proof, whether we assume the eternity or the creation of the universe. For this reason you will find in my works on the Talmud, whenever I have to speak of the fundamental principles of our religion, or to prove the existence of God, that I employ arguments which imply the eternity of the universe. I do not believe in that eternity, but I wish to establish the principle of the existence of God by an indisputable proof, and should not like to see this most important principle founded on a basis which every one could shake or attempt to demolish, and which others might consider as not being established at all ; especially when I see that the proofs of the philosophers are based on those visible properties of things, which can only be ignored by persons possessing certain preconceived notions, while the Mutakallemim establish their arguments on propositions which are to such an extent contrary to the actual state of things as to compel these arguers to deny altogether the existence of the laws of nature. When I shall have to treat of the creation, I shall in a special chapter prove my opinion to some extent, and shall attain the same end which every one of the Mutakallemim had in view, yet I shall not contradict the laws of nature, or reject any such part of the Aristotelean theory as has been proved to be correct. Even the most cogent of the proofs offered by the Mutakallemim respecting the act of creation, has only been obtained by reversing the whole order of things and by rejecting everything fully demonstrated by the philosophers. I, however, shall be able to give a similar proof without ignoring the laws of nature and without being forced to contradict facts which have been clearly perceived. I find it necessary to mention to you the general propositions of the Mutakallemim, by which they prove the act of creation, the Existence of God, His Unity and His Incorporeality. I intend to explain their method, and also to point out the inferences which are to be drawn from each proposition. After this, I shall describe those theories of the philosophers which are closely connected with our subject, and I shall then explain their method.

Do not ask me to prove in this work the propositions of the philosophers, which I shall briefly mention to you ; they form the principal part of Physics and Metaphysics. Nor must you expect that I should repeat the arguments of the Mutakallemim in support of their propositions, with which they wasted their time, with which the time of future generations will likewise be wasted, and on which numerous books have been written. Their propositions, with few exceptions, are contradicted by the visible properties of things, and beset with numerous objections. For this reason they were obliged to write many books and controversial works in defence of their theories, for the refutation of objections, and for the reconciliation of all apparent contradictions, although in reality this object cannot be attained by any sophistical contrivance. As to the propositions of the philosophers which I shall briefly explain, and which are indispensable for the demonstration of the three principles—the Existence, the Unity, and the Incorporeality of God, they will for the greater part be admitted by you as soon as you shall hear them and understand their meaning ; whilst in the discussion of other parts reference must be made for their proofs to works on Physics and Metaphysics, and if you direct your attention to such passages as will be pointed out to you, you will find everything verified that requires verification.

I have already told you that nothing exists except God and this universe, and that there is no other evidence for His Existence but this universe in its entirety and in its several parts. Consequently the universe must be examined as it is; the propositions must be derived from those properties of the universe which are clearly perceived, and hence you must know its visible form and its nature. Then only will you find in the universe evidence for the existence of a being not included therein. I have considered it, therefore, necessary to discuss first in a merely colloquial manner, in the next chapter, the totality of existing things, and to confine our remarks to such as have been fully proved and established beyond all doubt. In subsequent chapters I shall treat of the propositions of the Mutakallemim, and describe the method by which they explain the four fundamental principles. In the chapters which will follow, I propose to expound the propositions of the philosophers and the methods applied by them in verifying those principles. In the last place, I shall explain to you the method applied by me in proving those four principles, as I have stated to you.

CHAPTER LXXII

KNOW that this Universe, in its entirety, is nothing else but one individual being; that is to say, the outermost heavenly sphere, together with all included therein, is as regards individuality beyond all question a single being like Said and Omar. The variety of its substances—I mean the substances of that sphere and all its component parts—is like the variety of the substances of a human being: just as, e.g., Said is one individual, consisting of various solid substances, such as flesh, bones, sinews, of various humours, and of various spiritual elements; in like manner this sphere in its totality is composed of the celestial orbs, the four elements and their combinations; there is no vacuum whatever therein, but the whole space is filled up with matter. Its centre is occupied by the earth, earth is surrounded by water, air encompasses the water, fire envelopes the air, and this again is enveloped by the fifth substance (quintessence). These substances form numerous spheres, one being enclosed within another so that no intermediate empty space, no vacuum, is left. One sphere surrounds and closely joins the other. All the spheres revolve with constant uniformity, without acceleration or retardation; that is to say, each sphere retains its individual nature as regards its velocity and the peculiarity of its motion; it does not move at one time quicker, at another slower. Compared with each other, however, some of the spheres move with less, others with greater velocity. The outermost, all-encompassing sphere, revolves with the greatest speed; it completes its revolution in one day, and causes everything to participate in its motion, just as every particle of a thing moves when the entire body is in motion; for existing beings stand in the same relation to that sphere as a part of a thing stands to the whole. These spheres have not a common centre; the centres of some of them are identical with the centre of the Universe, while those of the rest are different from it. Some of the spheres have a motion independent of that of the whole Universe, constantly revolving from East to West, while other spheres move from West to East. The stars contained in those spheres are part of their respective orbits; they are fixed in them, and have no motion of their own, but participating in the motion of the sphere of which they are a part, they appear themselves to move. The entire substance of this revolving fifth element is unlike the substance of those bodies which consist of the other four elements, and are enclosed by the fifth element.

The number of these spheres encompassing the Universe cannot possibly be less than eighteen; it may even be larger; but this is a matter for further investigation. It also remains an open question whether there are spheres which, without moving round the centre of the Universe, have nevertheless a circular motion. Within that sphere which is nearest to us, a substance is contained which is different from the substance of the fifth element; it first received four primary forms, and then became in these four forms, four kinds of matter: earth, water, air, fire. Each of the four elements occupies a certain position of its own assigned to it by nature; it is not found in another place, so long as no other but its own natural force acts upon it; it is a dead body; it has no life, no perception, no spontaneous motion, and remains at rest in its natural place. When moved from its place by some external force, it returns towards its natural place as soon as that force ceases to operate. For the elements have the property of moving back to their place in a straight line, but they have no properties which would cause them to remain where they are, or to move otherwise than in a straight line. The rectilinear motions of these four elements when returning to their original place are of two kinds, either centrifugal, viz., the motion of the air and the fire; or centripetal, viz., the motion of the earth, and the water; and when the elements have reached their original place, they remain at rest.

The spherical bodies, on the other hand, have life, possess a soul by which they move spontaneously; they have no properties by which they could at any time come to a state of rest; in their perpetual rotations they are not subject to any change, except that of position. The question whether they are endowed with an intellect, enabling them to comprehend, cannot be solved without deep research. Through the constant revolution of the fifth element, with all contained therein, the four elements are forced to move and to change their respective positions, so that fire and air are driven into the water, and again these three elements enter the depth of the earth. Thus are the elements mixed together; and when they return to their respective places, parts of the earth, in quitting their places, move together with the water, the air and the fire. In this whole process the elements act and react upon each other. The elements intermixed, are then combined, and form at first various kinds of vapours; afterwards the several kinds of minerals, every species of plants, and many species of living beings, according to the relative proportion of the constituent parts. All transient beings have their origin in the elements, into which again they resolve when their existence comes to an end. The elements themselves are subject to being transformed from one into another; for although one substance is common to all, substance without form is in reality impossible, just as the physical form of these transient beings cannot exist without substance. The formation and the dissolution of the elements, together with the things composed of them, and resolving into them, follow each other in rotation. The changes of the finite substance, in successively receiving one form after the other, may therefore be compared to the revolution of the sphere in space, when each part of the sphere periodically reappears in the same position.

As the human body consists both of principal organs and of other members which depend on them and cannot exist without the control of those organs, so does the universe consist both of principal parts, viz., the quintessence, which encompasses the four elements and of other parts which are subordinated and require a leader, viz., the four elements and the things composed of them.

Again, the principal part in the human body, namely, the heart, is in constant motion, and is the source of every motion noticed in the body; it rules over the other members, and communicates to them through its own pulsations the force required for their functions. The outermost sphere by its motion rules in a similar way over all other parts of the universe, and supplies all things with their special properties. Every motion in the universe has thus its origin in the motion of that sphere; and the soul of every animated being derives its origin from the soul of that same sphere.

The forces which according to this explanation are communicated by the spheres to this sublunary world are four in number, viz., (*a*) the force which effects the mixture and the composition of the elements, and which undoubtedly suffices to form the minerals; (*b*) the force which supplies every growing thing with its vegetative functions; (*c*) the force which gives to each living being its vitality, and (*d*) the force which endows rational beings with intellect. All this is effected through the action of light and darkness, which are regulated by the position and the motion of the spheres round the earth.

When for one instant the beating of the heart is interrupted, man dies, and all his motions and powers come to an end. In a like manner would the whole universe perish, and everything therein cease to exist if the spheres were to come to a standstill.

The living being as such is one through the action of its heart, although some parts of the body are devoid of motion and sensation, as, e.g., the bones, the cartilage, and similar parts. The same is the case with the entire universe; although it includes many beings without motion and without life, it is a single being living through the motion of the sphere, which may be compared to the heart of an animated being. You must therefore consider the entire globe as one individual being which is endowed with life, motion, and a soul. This mode of considering the universe is, as will be explained, indispensable, that is to say, it is very useful for demonstrating the unity of God; it also helps to elucidate the principle that He who is One has created only *one* being.

Again, it is impossible that any of the members of a human body should exist by themselves, not connected with the body, and at the same time should actually be organic parts of that body, that is to say, that the liver should exist by itself, the heart by itself, or the flesh by itself. In like manner, it is impossible that one part of the Universe should exist independently of the other parts in the existing order of things as here considered, viz., that the fire should exist without the co-existence of the earth, or the earth without the heaven, or the heaven without the earth.

In man there is a certain force which unites the members of the body, controls them, and gives to each of them what it requires for the conservation of its condition, and for the repulsion of injury—the physicians distinctly call it the leading force in the body of the living being ; sometimes they call it " nature." The Universe likewise possesses a force which unites the several parts with each other, protects the species from destruction, maintains the individuals of each species as long as possible, and endows some individual beings with permanent existence. Whether this force operates through the medium of the sphere or otherwise remains an open question.

Again, in the body of each individual there are parts which are intended for a certain purpose, as the organs of nutrition for the preservation of the individual, the organs of generation for the preservation of the species, the hands and eyes for administering to certain wants, as to food, etc. ; there are also parts which, in themselves, are not intended for any purpose, but are mere accessories and adjuncts to the constitution of the other parts. The peculiar constitution of the organs, indispensable for the conservation of their particular forms and for the performance of their primary functions, produces, whilst it serves its special purpose, according to the nature of the substance, other things, such as the hair and the complexion of the body. Being mere accessories, they are not formed according to a fixed rule ; some are altogether absent in many individuals ; and vary considerably in others. This is not the case with the organs of the body. You never find that the liver of one person is ten times larger than that of another person, but you may find a person without a beard, or without hair on certain parts of his body, or with a beard ten times longer than that of another man. Instances of this phenomenon, viz., great variation as regards hair and colour, are not rare. The same differences occur in the constitution of the Universe. Some species exist as an integral part of the whole system ; these are constant and follow a fixed law ; though they vary as far as their nature permits, this variation is insignificant in quantity and quality. Other species do not serve any purpose ; they are the mere result of the general nature of transient things, as, e.g., the various insects which are generated in dunghills, the animals generated in rotten fruit, or in fetid liquids, and worms generated in the intestines, etc. In short, everything devoid of the power of generation belongs to this class. You will, therefore, find that these things do not follow a fixed law, although their entire absence is just as impossible as the absence of different complexions and of different kinds of hair amongst human beings.

In man there are substances the individual existence of which is permanent, and there are other substances which are only constant in the species not in the individuals, as, e.g., the four humours. The same is the case in the Universe ; there are substances which are constant in individuals, such as the fifth element, which is constant in all its formations, and other substances which are constant in the species, as, e.g., the four elements and all that is composed of them.

The same forces which operate in the birth and the temporal existence of the human being operate also in his destruction and death. This truth holds good with regard to this whole transient world. The causes of production are at the same time the causes of destruction. This may be illustrated by the following example. If the four forces which are present in every being sustained by food, viz., attraction, retention, digestion, and secretion, were, like intelligent forces, able to confine themselves to what is necessary, and to act at the proper time and within the proper limits, man would be exempt from those great sufferings and the numerous diseases [to which he is exposed]. Since, however, such is not the case, and since the forces perform their natural functions without thought and intelligence, without any consciousness of their action, they necessarily cause dangerous maladies and great pains, although they are the direct cause of the birth and the temporal existence of the human being. This fact is to be explained as follows : if the attractive force would absorb nothing but that which is absolutely beneficial, and nothing but the quantity which is required, man would be free from many such sufferings and disorders. But such is not the case ; the attractive force absorbs any humour that comes within the range of its action, although such humour be ill-adapted in quality or in quantity. It is, therefore, natural that sometimes a humour is absorbed which is too warm, too cold, too thick, or too thin, or that too much humour is absorbed, and thus the veins are choked, obstruction and decay ensue, the quality of the humour is deteriorated, its quantities altered, diseases are originated, such as scurvy, leprosy, abscess, or a dangerous illness, such as cancer, elephantiasis, gangrene, and at last the organ or organs are destroyed. The same is the case with every one of the four forces, and with all existing beings. The same force that originates all things, and causes them to exist for a certain time, namely, the combination of the elements which are moved and penetrated by the forces of the heavenly spheres, that same cause becomes throughout the world a source of calamities, such as devastating rain, showers, snow-storms, hail, hurricanes, thunder, lightning, malaria, or other terrible catastrophes by which a place or many places or an entire country may be laid waste, such as landslips, earthquakes, meteoric showers and floods issuing forth from the seas and from the interior of the earth.

Bear in mind, however, that in all that we have noticed about the similarity between the Universe and the human being, nothing would warrant us to assert that man is a microcosm ; for although the comparison in all its parts applies to the Universe and any living being in its normal state, we never heard that any ancient author called the ass or the horse a microcosm. This attribute has been given to man alone on account of his peculiar faculty of thinking, I mean the intellect, viz., the hylic intellect which appertains to no other living being. This may be explained as follows. An animal does not require for its sustenance any plan, thought or scheme ; each animal moves and acts by its nature, eats as much as it can find of suitable things, it makes its resting-place wherever it happens to be, cohabits with any mate it meets while in heat in the periods of its sexual excitement. In this manner does each individual conserve itself for a certain time, and perpetuates the existence of its species without requiring for its maintenance the assistance or support of any of its fellow creatures ; for all the things to which it has to attend it performs by itself. With man it is different ; if an individual had a solitary existence, and were, like an animal, left without guidance, he would soon perish, he would not endure even one day, unless it were by mere chance, unless he happened to find something upon which he might feed. For the food which man requires for his subsistence demands much work and preparation, which can only be accomplished by reflection and by plan ; many vessels must be used, and many individuals, each in his peculiar work, must be employed. It is therefore necessary that one person should organize the work and direct men in such a manner that they should properly co-operate, and that they should assist each other. The protection from heat in summer and from cold in winter, and shelter from rain, snow, and wind, require in the same manner the preparation of many things, none of which can properly be done without design and thought. For this reason man has been endowed with intellectual faculties, which enable him to think, con-sider, and act, and by various labours to prepare and procure for himself food, dwelling and clothing, and to control every organ of his body, causing both the principal and the secondary organs to perform their respective functions. Consequently, if a man, being deprived of his intellectual faculties, only possessed vitality, he would in a short time be lost. The intellect is the highest of all faculties of living creatures ; it is very difficult to comprehend, and its true character cannot be understood as easily as man's other faculties.

There also exists in the Universe a certain force which controls the whole, which sets in motion the chief and principal parts, and gives them the motive power for governing the rest. Without that force, the existence of this sphere, with its principal and secondary parts, would be impossible. It is the source of the existence of the Universe in all its, parts. That force is God ; blessed be His name ! It is on account of this force that man is called microcosm ; for he likewise possesses a certain principle which governs all the forces of the body, and on account of this comparison God is called " the life of the Universe " ; comp. " and he swore by the life of the Universe " (Dan. xii. 7).

You must understand that in the parallel which we have drawn between the whole universe, on the one hand, and the individual man, on the other, there is a complete harmony in all the points which we mentioned above ; only in the following three points a discrepancy may be noticed.

First, the principal organ of any living being which has a heart, derives a benefit from the organs under the control of the heart, and the benefits of the organs thus become the benefits of the heart. This is not the case in the constitution of the universe. That part which bestows authority or distributes power, does not receive in return any benefit from the things under its control ; whatever it grants, is granted in the manner of a generous benefactor, not from any selfish motive, but from a natural generosity and kindliness ; only for the sake of imitating the ways of the Most High.

Secondly, living creatures endowed with a heart have it within the body and in the midst thereof ; there it is surrounded by organs which it governs. Thus it derives a benefit from them, for they guard and protect it, and they do not allow that any injury from without should approach it. The reverse occurs in the case of the Universe. The superior part encompasses the in-ferior parts, it being certain that it cannot be affected by the action of any other being ; and even if it could be affected, there is nobody without it that could affect it. While it influences all that is contained within, it is not influenced by any act or force of any material being. There is, however, some similarity [between the universe and man] in this point. In the body of animals, the organs more distant from the principal organ are of less importance than those nearer to it. Also in the universe, the nearer the parts are to the centre, the greater is their turbidness, their solidity, their inertness, their dimness and darkness, because they are further away from the loftiest element, from the source of light and brightness, which moves by itself and the substance of which is the most rarefied and simplest : from the outermost sphere. At the same ratio at which a body is nearer this sphere, it derives properties from it, and rises above the spheres below it.

Thirdly. The faculty of thinking is a force inherent in the body, and is not separated from it, but God is not a force inherent in the body of the universe, but is separate from all its parts. How God rules the universe and provides for it is a complete mystery ; man is unable to solve it. For, on the one hand, it can be proved that God is separate from the universe, and in no contact whatever with it ; but, on the other hand, His rule and providence can be proved to exist in all parts of the universe, even in the smallest. Praised be He whose perfection is above our comprehension.

It is true, we might have compared the relation between God and the universe, to the relation between the absolute acquired intellect and man ; it is not a power inherent in the body, but a power which is absolutely separate from the body, and is from without brought into contact with the body. The rational faculty of man may be further compared to the intelligence of the spheres, which are, as it were, material bodies. But the intelligence of the spheres, purely spiritual beings, as well as man's absolute and acquired intellect, are subjects of deep study and research ; the proof of their existence, though correct, is abstruse, and includes arguments which present doubts, are exposed to criticism, and can be easily attacked by objectors. We have, therefore, preferred to illustrate the relation of God to the universe by a simile which is clear, and which will not be contradicted in any of the points which have been laid down by us without any qualification. The opposition can only emanate either from an ignorant man, who contradicts truths even if they are perfectly obvious, just as a person unacquainted with geometry rejects elementary propositions which have been clearly demonstrated, or from the prejudiced man who deceives himself. Those, however, who wish to study the subject must persevere in their studies until they are convinced that all our observations are true, and until they understand that our account of this universe unquestionably agrees with the existing order of things. If a man is willing to accept this theory from one who understands how to prove things which can be proved, let him accept it, and let him establish on it his arguments and proofs. If, on the other hand, he refuses to accept without proof even the foregoing principles, let him inquire for himself, and ultimately he will find that they are correct. "Lo this, we have searched it, so it is ; hear it, and know thou it for thy good" (Job v. 27).

After these preliminary remarks, we will treat of the subject which we promised to introduce and to explain.

CHAPTER LXXIII

THERE are twelve propositions common to all Mutakallemim, however different their individual opinions and methods may be ; the Mutakallemim require them in order to establish their views on the four principles.   I shall first enumerate these propositions, and then discuss each separately, together with the inferences which may be drawn from it.

PROPOSITION I. All things are composed of atoms.

PROPOSITION II. There is a vacuum.

PROPOSITION III. Time is composed of time-atoms.

PROPOSITION IV. Substance cannot exist without numerous accidents.

PROPOSITION V. Each atom is completely furnished with the accidents (which I will describe), and cannot exist without them.

PROPOSITION VI. Accidents do not continue in existence during two time-atoms.

PROPOSITION VII. Both positive and negative properties have a real existence, and are accidents which owe their existence to some *causa efficiens*.

PROPOSITION VIII. All existing things, i.e., all creatures, consist of substance and of accidents, and the physical form of a thing is likewise an accident.

PROPOSITION IX. No accident can form the substratum for another accident.

PROPOSITION X. The test for the possibility of an imagined object does not consist in its conformity with the existing laws of nature.

PROPOSITION XI. The idea of the infinite is equally inadmissible, whether the infinite be actual, potential, or accidental, i.e., there is no difference whether the infinite be formed by a number of co-existing things, or by a series of things, of which one part comes into existence when another has ceased to exist, in which case it is called accidental infinite ; in both cases the infinite is rejected by the Mutakallemim as fallacious.

PROPOSITION XII. The senses mislead, and are in many cases inefficient ; their perceptions, therefore, cannot form the basis of any law, or yield data for any proof.

FIRST PROPOSITION.

" The Universe, that is, everything contained in it, is composed of very small parts [atoms] which are indivisible on account of their smallness ; such an atom has no magnitude ; but when several atoms combine, the sum has a magnitude, and thus forms a body." If, therefore, two atoms were joined together, each atom would become a body, and they would thus form two bodies, a theory which in fact has been proposed by some Mutakellemim.   All these atoms are perfectly alike ; they do not differ from each other in any point.   The Mutakallemim further assert, that it is impossible to find a body that is not composed of such equal atoms which are placed side by side.   According to this view *genesis* and composition are identical ; destruction is the same as decomposition.   They do not use the term " destruction," for they hold that " genesis " implies composition and decomposition, motion and rest.   These atoms, they believe, are not, as was supposed by Epicurus and other Atomists numerically constant; but are created anew whenever it pleases the Creator; their annihilation is therefore not impossible. Now I will explain to you their opinion concerning the vacuum.

SECOND PROPOSITION.

On the vacuum. The original Mutakallemim also believe that there is a vacuum, i.e., one space, or several spaces which contain nothing, which are not occupied by anything whatsoever, and which are devoid of all substance. This proposition is to them an indispensable sequel to the first. For, if the Universe were full of such atoms, how could any of them move ? For it is impossible to conceive that one atom should move into another. And yet the composition, as well as the decomposition of things, can only be effected by the motion of atoms ! Thus the Mutakallemim are compelled to assume a vacuum, in order that the atoms may combine, separate, and move in that vacuum which does not contain any thing or any atom.

THIRD PROPOSITION.

" Time is composed of time-atoms," i.e., of many parts, which on account of their short duration cannot be divided. This proposition also is a logical consequence of the first. The Mutakallemim undoubtedly saw how Aristotle proved that time, space, and locomotion are of the same nature, that is to say, they can be divided into parts which stand in the same proportion to each other : if one of them is divided, the other is divided in the same proportion. They, therefore, knew that if time were continuous and divisible *ad infinitum*, their assumed atom of space would of necessity likewise be divisible. Similarly, if it were supposed that space is continuous, it would necessarily follow, that the time-element, which they considered to be indivisible, could also be divided. This has been shown by Aristotle in the treatise called *Acroasis*. Hence they concluded that space was not continuous, but was composed of elements that could not be divided; and that time could likewise be reduced to time-elements, which were indivisible. An hour is, e.g., divided into sixty minutes, the minute into sixty seconds, the second into sixty parts, and so on ; at last after ten or more successive divisions by sixty, time-elements are obtained, which are not subjected to division, and in fact are indivisible, just as is the case with space. Time would thus be an object of position and order.

The Mutakallemim did not at all understand the nature of time. This is a matter of course ; for if the greatest philosophers became embarrassed when they investigated the nature of time, if some of them were altogether unable to comprehend what time really was, and if even Galenus declared time to be something divine and incomprehensible, what can be expected of those who do not regard the nature of things ?

Now, mark what conclusions were drawn from these three propositions, and were accepted by the Mutakallemim as true. They held that locomotion consisted in the translation of each atom of a body from one point to the next one ; accordingly the velocity of one body in motion cannot be greater than that of another body. When, nevertheless, two bodies are observed to move during the same time through different spaces, the cause of this difference is not attributed by them to the fact that the body which has moved through a larger distance had a greater velocity, but to the circumstance that motion which in ordinary language is called slow, has been interrupted by more moments of rest, while the motion which ordinarily is called quick has been interrupted by fewer moments of rest. When it is shown that the motion of an arrow, which is shot from a powerful bow, is in contradiction to their theory, they declare that in this case too the motion is interrupted by moments of rest. They believe that it is the fault of man's senses if he believes that the arrow moves continuously, for there are many things which cannot be perceived by the senses, as they assert in the twelfth proposition. But we ask them : " Have you observed a complete revolution of a millstone ? Each point in the extreme circumference of the stone describes a large circle in the very same time in which a point nearer the centre describes a small circle ; the velocity of the outer circle is therefore greater than that of the inner circle. You cannot say that the motion of the latter was interrupted by more moments of rest ; for the whole moving body, i.e., the millstone, is one coherent body." They reply, " During the circular motion, the parts of the millstone separate from each other, and the moments of rest interrupting the motion of the portions nearer the centre are more than those which interrupt the motion of the outer portions." We ask again, " How is it that the millstone, which we perceive as one body, and which cannot be easily broken, even with a hammer, resolves into its atoms when it moves, and becomes again one coherent body, returning to its previous state as soon as it comes to rest, while no one is able to notice the breaking up [of the stone] ? " Again their reply is based on the twelfth proposition, which is to the effect that the perception of the senses cannot be trusted, and thus only the evidence of the intellect is admissible. Do not imagine that you have seen in the foregoing example the most absurd of the inferences which may be drawn from these three propositions : the proposition relating to the existence of a vacuum leads to more preposterous and extravagant conclusions. Nor must you suppose that the aforegoing theory concerning motion is less irrational than the proposition resulting from this theory, that the diagonal of a square is equal to one of its sides, and some of the Mutakallemim go so far as to declare that the square is not a thing of real existence. In short, the adoption of the first proposition would be tantamount to the rejection of all that has been proved in Geometry. The propositions in Geometry would, in this respect, be divided into two classes : some would be absolutely rejected ; e.g., those which relate to properties of the incommensurability and the commensurability of lines and planes, to rational and irrational lines, and all other propositions contained in the tenth book of Euclid, and in similar works. Other propositions would appear to be only partially correct ; e.g., the solution of the problem to divide a line into two equal parts, if the line consists of an odd number of atoms ; according to the theory of the Mutakallemim such a line cannot be bisected. Furthermore, in the well-known book of problems by the sons of Shakir are contained more than a hundred problems, all solved and practically demonstrated ; but if there really were a vacuum, not one of these problems could be solved, and many of the waterworks [described in that book] could not have been constructed. The refutation of such propositions is a mere waste of time. I will now proceed to treat of the other propositions mentioned above.

Fourth Proposition.

" The accidents of things have real existence ; they are elements superadded to the substance itself, and no material thing can be without them."
Had this proposition been left by the Mutakallemim in this form it would
have been correct, simple, clear, and indisputable. They have, however,
gone further, asserting that a substance which has not the attribute of life,
must necessarily have that of death ; for it must always have one of two con-
trasting properties. According to their opinion, colour, taste, motion or
rest, combination or separation, etc., can be predicated of all substances,
and, if a substance have the attribute of life, it must at the same time possess
such other kinds of accidents, as wisdom or folly, freewill or the reverse,
power or weakness, perception or any of its opposites, and, in short, the
substance must have the one or the other of all correlative accidents appertaining to a living being.

Fifth Proposition.

" The atom is fully provided with all these foregoing accidents, and cannot
exist if any be wanting." The meaning of the proposition is this : The
Mutakallemim say that each of the atoms created by God must have accidents, such as colour, smell, motion, or rest, except the accident of quantity :
for according to their opinion an atom has no magnitude ; and they do not
designate quantity as an accident, nor do they apply to it the laws of accidents. In accordance with this proposition, they do not say, when an accident is noticed in a body, that it is peculiar to the body as such, but that it
exists in each of the atoms which form the constituent elements of that body.
E.g., take a heap of snow ; the whiteness does not exist in that heap
as a whole, but each atom of the snow is white, and therefore the aggregate
of these atoms is likewise white. Similarly they say that when a body moves
each atom of it moves, and thus the whole body is in motion. Life likewise
exists, according to their view, in each atom of a living body. The same is
the case according to their opinion with the senses ; in each atom of the
aggregate they notice the faculty of perception. Life, sensation, intellect
and wisdom are considered by them as accidents, like blackness and whiteness,
as will be shown in the further discussion of their theory.

Concerning the soul, they do not agree. The view most predominant
among them is the following :—The soul is an accident existing in one of
the atoms of which, e.g., man is composed ; the aggregate is called a being
endowed with a soul, in so far as it includes that atom. Others are of opinion
that the soul is composed of ethereal atoms, which have a peculiar faculty
by virtue of which they constitute the soul, and that these atoms are mixed
with the atoms of the body. Consequently they maintain that the soul is
an accident.

As to the intellect, I found that all of them agreed in considering it to be
an accident joined to one of the atoms which constitute the whole of the
intelligent being. But there is a confusion among them about knowledge ;
they are uncertain whether it is an accident to each of the atoms which form
the knowing aggregate, or whether it belongs only to one atom. Both views
can be disproved by a *reductio ad absurdum,* when the following facts are
pointed out to them. Generally metals and stones have a peculiar colour,

which is strongly pronounced, but disappears when they are pulverised. Vitriol, which is intensely green, becomes white dust when pounded; this shows that that accident exists only in the aggregate, not in the atoms. This fact is more striking in the following instance: when parts of a living being are cut off they cease to live, a proof that the accident [of life] belongs to the aggregate of the living being, not to each atom. In order to meet this objection they say that the accident is of no duration, but is constantly renewed. In discussing the next proposition I shall explain their view on this subject.

Sixth Proposition.

" The accidents do not exist during two time-atoms."—The sense of the proposition is this: They believe that God creates a substance, and simultaneously its accidents; that the Creator is incapable of creating a substance devoid of an accident, for that is impossible; that the essential characteristic of an accident is its incapability of enduring for two periods, for two time-atoms; that immediately after its creation it is utterly destroyed, and another accident of the same kind is created; this again is destroyed and a third accident of the same kind is created, and so on, so long as God is pleased to preserve [in that substance] this kind of accident; but He can at His will create in the same substance an accident of a different kind, and if He were to discontinue the creation and not produce a new accident, that substance would at once cease to exist. This is one of the opinions held by the Mutakallemim; it has been accepted by most of them, and it is the so-called " theory of the creation of the accidents." Some of them, however, and they belong to the sect of the Mu'tazilah, say that there are accidents which endure for a certain period, and other accidents which do not endure for two atoms of time; they do not follow a fixed principle in deciding what class of accidents has and what class has not a certain duration. The object of this proposition is to oppose the theory that there exists a natural force from which each body derives its peculiar properties. They prefer to assume that God himself creates these properties without the intervention of a natural force or of any other agency: a theory which implies that no accident can have any duration. For suppose that certain accidents could endure for a certain period and then cease to exist, the question would naturally be asked, What is the cause of that non-existence? They would not be satisfied with the reply that God by His will brought about this non-existence, and non-existence does not at all require any *agens* whatever; for as soon as the *agens* leaves off acting, the product of the *agens* ceases likewise to exist. This is true to some extent. Having thus chosen to establish the theory that there does not exist any natural force upon which the existence or non-existence of a thing depends, they were compelled to assume that the properties of things were successively renewed. When God desires to deprive a thing of its existence, He, according to some of the Mutakallemim, discontinues the creation of its accidents, and *eo ipso* the body ceases to exist. Others, however, say that if it pleased the Almighty to destroy the world, He would create the accident of destruction, which would be without any substratum. The destruction of the Universe would be the correlative accident to that of existence.—In accordance with this [sixth] proposition they say, that the cloth which according to our belief we dyed red, has not been dyed by us at all, but God created that colour in the cloth when it came into contact with the red pigment; we believe that colour to have penetrated into the cloth, but they assert that this is not the case. They say that God generally acts in such a way, that, e.g., the black colour is not created unless the cloth is brought into contact with indigo; but this blackness, which God creates in the instant when the cloth touches the black pigment is of no duration, and another creation of blackness then takes place; they further say that after the blackness is gone, He does not create a red or green colour, but again a black colour.

According to this principle, the knowledge which we have of certain things to-day, is not the same which we had of them yesterday; that knowledge is gone, and another like it has been created. They positively believe that this does take place, knowledge being an accident. In like manner it would follow that the soul, according to those who believe that it is an accident, is renewed each moment in every animated being, say a hundred thousand times; for, as you know, time is composed of time-atoms. In accordance with this principle they assert that when man is perceived to move a pen, it is not he who has really moved it; the motion produced in the pen is an accident which God has created in the pen; the apparent motion of the hand which moves the pen is likewise an accident which God has created in the moving hand; but the creative act of God is performed in such a manner that the motion of the hand and the motion of the pen follow each other closely; but the hand does not act, and is not the cause of the pen's motion; for, as they say, an accident cannot pass from one thing to another. Some of the Mutakallemim accordingly contend that this white cloth, which is coloured when put into the vessel filled with indigo, has not been blackened by the indigo; for blackness being an attribute of indigo, does not pass from one object to another. There does not exist any thing to which an action could be ascribed; the real *agens* is God, and He has [in the foregoing instance] created the blackness in the substance of the cloth when it came into contact with the indigo, for this is the method adopted by Him. In short, most of the Mutakallemim believe that it must never be said that one thing is the cause of another; some of them who assumed causality were blamed for doing so. As regards, however, the acts of man their opinions are divided. Most of them, especially the sect of the Asha'ariyah, assume that when the pen is set in motion God has created four accidents, none of which is the cause of any of the rest, they are only related to each other as regards the time of their co-existence, and have no other relation to each other. The first accident is man's will to move the pen, the second is man's power to do so, the third is the bodily motion itself, i.e., the motion of the hand, and the fourth is the motion of the pen. They believe that when a man has the will to do a thing and, as he believes, does it, the will has been created for him, then the power to conform to the will, and lastly the act itself. The act is not accomplished by the power created in man; for, in reality, no act can be ascribed to that power. The Mu'tazilah contend that man acts by virtue of the power which has been created in him. Some of the Asha'ariyah assert that the power created in man participates in the act, and is connected with it, an opinion which has been rejected by the majority of them. The will and the power created in man, according to the concurrent belief of the Mutakal-lemim, together with the act created in him, according to some of them, are accidents without duration. In the instance of the pen, God continually creates one motion after the other so long as the pen is in motion ; it only then ceases to move when God has created in it the accident of rest ; and so long as the pen is at rest, God continually renews in it that accident. Consequently in every one of these moments, i.e., of the time-atoms, God creates some accident in every existing individual, e.g., in the angels, in the spheres and in other things ; this creation takes place continually and without interruption. Such is, according to their opinion, the right interpretation of the creed that God is the *causa efficiens*. But I, together with all rational persons, apply to those theories the words, " Will you mock at Him, as you mock at man ? " for their words are indeed nothing but mockery.

SEVENTH PROPOSITION.

" The absence of a property is itself a property that exists in the body, a something superadded to its substance, an actual accident, which is constantly renewed ; as soon as it is destroyed it is reproduced." The reason why they hold this opinion is this : they do not understand that rest is the absence of motion ; death the absence of life ; that blindness is the absence of sight, and that all similar negative properties are the absence of the positive corre-latives. The relation between motion and rest is, according to their theory, the same as the relation between heat and cold, namely, as heat and cold are two accidents found in two objects which have the properties of heat and cold, so motion is an accident created in the thing which moves, and rest an accident created in the thing which rests ; it does not remain in existence during two consecutive time-atoms, as we have stated in treating of the pre-vious proposition. Accordingly, when a body is at rest, God has created the rest in each atom of that body, and so long as the body remains at rest God continu-ally renews that property. The same, they believe, is the case with a man's wisdom and ignorance ; the latter is considered by them as an actual accident, which is subject to the constant changes of destruction and creation, so long as there remains a thing of which such a man is ignorant. Death and life are likewise accidents, and as the Mutakallemim distinctly state, life is con-stantly destroyed and renewed during the whole existence of a living being ; when God decrees its death, He creates in it the accident of death after the accident of life, which does not continue during two time-atoms, has ceased to exist. All this they state clearly.

The logical consequence of this proposition is that the accident of death created by God instantly ceases to exist, and is replaced by another death which again is created by God ; otherwise death could not continue. Death is thus continually created in the same manner as life is renewed every moment. But I should wish to know how long God continues to create death in a dead body. Does He do so whilst the form remains, or whilst one of the atoms exists ? For in each of the atoms of the body the accident of death which God creates is produced, and there are to be found teeth of persons who died thousands of years ago ; we see that those teeth have not been deprived of existence, and therefore the accident of death has during all these thousands of years been renewed, and according to the opinion prevailing amongst those theorists, death was continually replaced by death. Some of the Mu'tazilah hold that there are cases in which the absence of a physical property is not a real property, that weariness is the absence of strength, and ignorance the absence of knowledge ; but this cannot be said in every case of negative properties : it cannot be said that darkness is the mere absence of light, or that rest is the absence of motion. Some negative properties are thus considered by them as having a real existence, while other negative properties are considered as non-existing, just as suits their belief. Here they proceed in the same manner as they proceed respecting the duration of accidents, and they contend that some accidents exist a long time, and other accidents do not last two time-atoms. Their sole object is to fashion the Universe according to their peculiar opinions and beliefs.

Eighth Proposition.

" There exists nothing but substance and accident, and the physical form of things belong to the class of accidents." It is the object of this proposition to show that all bodies are composed of similar atoms, as we have pointed out in explaining the first proposition. The difference of bodies from each other is caused by the accidents, and by nothing else. Animality, humanity, sensibility, and speech, are denoted as accidents like blackness, whiteness, bitterness, and sweetness, and the difference between two individuals of two classes is the same as the difference of two individuals of the same class. Also the body of the heaven, the body of the angels, the body of the Divine Throne—such as it is assumed to be—the body of anything creeping on the earth, and the body of any plant, have one and the same substance ; they only differ in the peculiarity of the accidents, and in nothing else : the substance of all things is made up of equal atoms.

Ninth Proposition.

" None of the accidents form the substratum of another accident ; it cannot be said, This is an accident to a thing which is itself an accident to a substance. All accidents are directly connected with the substance." The Mutakallemim deny the indirect relation of the accident to the substance, because if such a relation were assumed it would follow that the second accident could only exist in the substance after another accident had preceded it, a conclusion to which they would object even with regard to some special accidents ; they prefer to show that these accidents can exist in every possible substance, although such substance is not determined by any other accident ; for they hold that all the accidents collectively determine the thing. They advance also another proof [in support of this proposition], namely : The substratum which is the bearer of certain attributes must continue to exist for a certain time ; how, then, could the accident; which—according to their opinion—does not remain in existence for two moments, become the substratum of something else ?

Tenth Proposition.

This proposition concerns the theory of "admissibility," which is mentioned by the Mutakallemim, and forms the principal support of their doctrine. Mark its purport : they observe that everything conceived by the imagination is admitted by the intellect as possible ; e.g., that the terrestrial globe should become the all-encompassing sphere, or that this sphere should become the terrestrial globe ; reason does not find here an impossibility ; or that the sphere of fire should move towards the centre, and the sphere of earth towards the circumference.   Human intellect does not perceive any reason why a body should be in a certain place instead of being in another. In the same manner they say that reason admits the possibility that an existing being should be larger or smaller than it really is, or that it should be different in form and position from what it really is ; e.g., a man might have the height of a mountain, might have several heads, and fly in the air ; or an elephant might be as small as an insect, or an insect as huge as an elephant. This method of admitting possibilities is applied to the whole Universe. Whenever they affirm that a thing belongs to this class of admitted possibilities, they say that it can have this form, and that it is also possible that it be found differently, and that the one form is not more possible than the other ; but they do not ask whether the reality confirms their assumption. They say that the thing which exists with certain constant and permanent forms, dimensions, and properties, only follows the direction of habit, just as the king generally rides on horseback through the streets of the city, and is never found departing from this habit; but reason does not find it impossible that he should walk on foot through the place ; there is no doubt that he may do so, and this possibility is fully admitted by the intellect.   Similarly, earth moves towards the centre, fire turns away from the centre ; fire causes heat, water causes cold, in accordance with a certain habit ; but it is logically not impossible that a deviation from this habit should occur, namely, that fire should cause cold, move downward, and still be fire ; that the water should cause heat, move upward, and still be water.   On this foundation their whole fabric is constructed.   They admit, however, the impossibility of two opposite properties coexisting at the same time in one substance.   This is impossible ; reason would not admit this possibility.   Again, reason does not admit the possibility of a substance existing without an accident, or an accident existing without a substance, a possibility admitted by some of the Mutakallemim.   It is also impossible that a substance should become an accident, that an accident should become a substance, or that one substance should penetrate another.   They admit that reason rejects all these things as impossible.   It is perfectly true that no notion whatever can be formed of those things which they describe as impossible ; whilst a notion can be formed of those things which they consider as possible.   The philosophers object to this method, and say, You call a thing impossible because it cannot be imagined, or possible because it can be imagined ; and thus you consider as possible that which is found possible by imagination, not by the intellect, consequently you determine that a thing is necessary, possible, or impossible in some instances, by the aid of the imagination—not by the intellect—and in other instances by the ordinary common sense, as Abu Nasr says in speaking of that which the Mutakallemim call intellect.   It is clear that they describe as possible that which can be imagined, whether the reality correspond to it or not, and as impossible that which cannot be imagined. This proposition can only be established by the nine aforementioned propositions, and no doubt these were exclusively required for the support of this proposition. This you will see clearly when I shall show and explain to you some important parts of this theory, which I shall now introduce in the form of a discussion supposed to have taken place between a Mutakallem and a philosopher.

The Mutakallem said to the philosopher : What is the reason that we find the substance of iron extremely hard and strong, with a dark colour ; the substance of cream, on the other hand, extremely soft and white ? The philosopher replied as follows : All physical bodies have two kinds of accidents : those which concern their substance, as, e.g., the health and the illness of a man ; and those which concern their form, as, e.g., the astonishment and laughter of a man. The substances of compound bodies differ very much in their ultimate form, according to the difference of the forms peculiar to each component substance. Hence the substance of iron has become in its properties the opposite of the substance of cream, and this difference is attended by the difference of accidents. You notice, therefore, hardness in the one, and softness in the other : two accidents, whose difference results from the difference which exists in the forms of the substances ; while the darkness and the whiteness are accidents whose divergence corresponds to that of the two substances in their ultimate condition. The Mutakallem refuted this reply by means of his propositions, as I am now going to state :—There does not exist a form which, as you believe, modifies the substance, and thus causes substances to be different from each other ; this difference is exclusively effected by the accidents—according to the theory of the Kalâm, which we mentioned in explaining the eighth proposition. He then continued thus : There is no difference between the substance of iron and that of cream ; all things are composed of the same kind of atoms.—We explained the view of the Mutakallemim on this point in treating of the first proposition, the logical consequences of which are, as we have shown, the second and the third propositions ; they further require the twelfth proposition, in order to establish the theory of atoms. Nor do they admit that any accidents determine the nature of a substance, or predispose it to receive certain other accidents ; for, according to their opinion, an accident cannot be the substratum of another accident, as we have shown in explaining the ninth proposition ; nor can it have any duration, according to the sixth proposition. When the Mutakallemim have established all that they wish to infer from these propositions, they arrive at the conclusion that the component atoms of cream and of iron are alike.—The relation of each atom to each of the accidents is the same ; one atom is not more adapted than another to receive a certain accident ; and as a certain atom is not more fitted to move than to rest, so one atom is not more apt than another to receive the accident of life, of reason, of sensation. It is here of no moment whether a thing contains a larger or smaller quantity of atoms, for, according to the view of the Mutakallemim, which we explained in treating of the fifth proposition, every accident [of a thing] exists in each of its atoms. All these propositions lead to the conclusion that a human being is not better constituted to become wise than the bat, and establish the theory of admissibility expressed in this [tenth] proposition. Every effort was made to demonstrate this proposition, because it is the best means for proving anything they like, as will be explained.

NOTE.—Mark, O reader, that if you know the nature of the soul and its properties, and if you have a correct notion of everything which concerns the soul, you will observe that most animals possess imagination. As to the higher class of animals, that is, those which have a heart, it is obvious that they have imagination. Man's distinction does not consist in the possession of imagination, and the action of imagination is not the same as the action of the intellect, but the reverse of it. For the intellect analyses and divides the component parts of things, it forms abstract ideas of them, represents them in their true form as well as in their causal relations, derives from one object a great many facts, which—for the intellect—totally differ from each other, just as two human individuals appear different to the imagination ; it distinguishes that which is the property of the *genus* from that which is peculiar to the individual,—and no proof is correct, unless founded on the former ; the intellect further determines whether certain qualities of a thing are essential or non-essential. Imagination has none of these functions. It only perceives the individual, the compound in that aggregate condition in which it presents itself to the senses ; or it combines things which exist separately, joins some of them together, and represents them all as one body or as a force of the body. Hence it is that some imagine a man with a horse's head, with wings, etc. This is called a fiction, a phantasm ; it is a thing to which nothing in the actual world corresponds. Nor can imagination in any way obtain a purely immaterial image of an object, however abstract the form of the image may be. Imagination yields therefore no test for the reality of a thing.

Hear what profit we derive from the preliminary disciplines, and how excellent the propositions are which we learn through them. Know that there are certain things, which would appear impossible, if tested by man's imagination, being as inconceivable as the co-existence of two opposite properties in one object ; yet the existence of those same things, which cannot be represented by imagination, is nevertheless established by proof, and attested by their reality. E.g., Imagine a large globe, of any magnitude you like, even as large as the all-encompassing sphere ; further an axis passing through the centre, and two persons standing on the two extremities of the axis in such a manner that their feet are in the same straight line with the axis, which may be either in the plane of the horizon or not ; in the first case both persons would fall, in the second case one, namely the one who stands on the lower extremity would fall, the other would remain standing, as far as our imagination can perceive. It has however, already been proved that the earth has the form of a globe, that it is inhabited on both extremities of a certain diameter, that both the inhabitants have their heads towards the heaven, and their legs towards each other, and yet neither can possibly fall, nor can it be imagined ; for it is incorrect to say that the one extremity is above, the other below ; but the term " above " and " below " apply to both of them as regards their relative position to each other. Similarly it has been proved in the second chapter of the book on Conic Sections, that two lines, which at first are at a certain distance from each other, may approach each other in the same proportion as they are produced further, and yet would never meet, even if they were produced to infinity, although they are observed to be constantly converging. This is a fact which cannot easily be conceived, and which does not come within the scope of imagination. Of these two lines the one is straight, the other curved, as stated in the aforementioned book. It has consequently been proved that things which cannot be perceived or imagined, and which would be found impossible if tested solely by imagination, are nevertheless in real existence. The non-existence of things which are represented by imagination as possible has likewise been established by proof, e.g., the corporeality of God, and His existence as a force residing in a body. Imagination perceives nothing except bodies, or properties inherent in bodies.

It has thus been clearly shown that in man exists a certain faculty which is entirely distinct from imagination, and by which the necessary, the possible, and the impossible can be distinguished from each other. This inquiry is most useful. It is of the greatest profit to him who desires to guard himself against the errors of men guided by imagination! Do not think that the Mutakallemim ignore this altogether; to some extent they do take it into consideration; they know it, and call that which can be imagined without having reality—as, e.g., the corporeality of God—a phantom and a fancy; they state frequently that such phantoms are not real. It is for this reason that they advance the first nine propositions and establish on them the proof of the tenth, according to which all those imaginable things which they wish to admit as possible are really possible, because of the similarity of all atoms and the equality of all accidents as regards their accidentality, as we have explained.

Consider, O reader, and bear in mind that this requires deep research. For there are certain notions which some believe to be founded on reason, while others regard them as mere fictions. In such cases it would be necessary to find something that could show the difference between conceptions of the intellect and mere imaginary fancies. When the philosopher, in his way of expressing himself, contends, " Reality is my evidence; by its guidance I examine whether a thing is necessary, possible, or impossible," the religionist replies, " This is exactly the difference between us; that which actually exists, has, according to my view, been produced by the will of the Creator, not by necessity; just as it has been created with that special property, it might have been created with any other property, unless the impossibility which you postulate be proved by a logical demonstration."

About this admissibility (of imaginable things) I shall have to say more, and I shall return to it in various parts of this treatise; for it is not a subject which should be rejected in haste and on the spur of the moment.

Eleventh Proposition.

" The existence of the infinite is in every respect impossible." The following is an explanation of this proposition. The impossibility of the existence of an infinite body has been clearly demonstrated; the same can be said of an infinite number of bodies, though each of them be finite, if these beings, infinite in number, exist at the same time; equally impossible is the existence of an infinite series of causes, namely, that a certain thing should be the cause of another thing, but itself the effect of another cause, which again is the result of another cause, and so on to infinity, or that things in an infinite series, either bodies or ideals, should be in actual existence, and in causal relation to each other. This causal relation is the essential order of nature, in which, as has been fully proved, the infinite is impossible. As regards the virtual and the accidental existence of the infinite, it has been established in some cases ; it has been proved, e.g., that a body can virtually be divided *ad infinitum*, also that time can be divided *ad infinitum* ; in other cases it is still an open question, as, e.g., the existence of the infinite in succession, which is called the accidental infinite, i.e., a series of things in which one thing comes forth when the other is gone, and this again in its turn succeeded a thing which had ceased to exist, and so on *ad infinitum*. This subject requires deep research.

Those who boast that they have proved the eternity of the Universe say that time is infinite ; an assertion which is not necessarily erroneous ; for only when one atom has ceased to exist, the other follows. Nor is it absolutely wrong, when they assert, that the accidents of the substance succeed each other in an infinite series, for these accidents do not co-exist, but come in succession one after the other, and the impossibility of the infinite in that case has not been proved. The Mutakallemim, however, make no difference between the existence of an infinite body and the divisibility of a body or of time *ad infinitum*, between the co-existence of an infinite number of things, as e.g., the individual human beings who exist at present, and the infinite number of beings successively existing, as, e.g., Reuben the son of Jacob, and Jacob the son of Isaac, and Isaac the son of Abraham, and so on to infinity. This is according to their opinion as inadmissible as the first case ; they believe these four forms of the infinite to be quite equal. Some of the Mutakallemim endeavour to establish their proposition concerning the last named form of the infinite, and to demonstrate its impossibility by a method which I shall explain in this treatise; others say that this impossibility is a self-evident axiom and requires no further proof. But if it were undoubtedly wrong to assume that an infinite number of things can exist in succession, although that link of the series which exists at present is finite, the inadmissibility of the eternity of the Universe would be equally self-evident, and would not require for its proof any other proposition. This, however, is not the place for investigating the subject.

Twelfth Proposition.

" The senses are not always to be trusted." For two reasons the Mutakallemim find fault with the perception of the senses. First, the senses are precluded from perceiving many objects, either on account of the smallness of the objects—this is the case with the atoms, as we have already stated— or on account of the remoteness of the objects from the person who desires to perceive them ; e.g., we cannot see, hear, or smell at a distance of many miles ; nor do we perceive the motion of the heavens. Secondly, the senses misapprehend the objects of their perception : a large object appears small from a distance ; a small object immersed in water appears larger ; a crooked thing appears straight when partly placed in water, and partly out of it ; things appear yellow to a person suffering from jaundice ; sweet things are bitter to him whose tongue has imbibed red gall ; and they mention many other things of this kind. Therefore they say, we cannot trust our senses so far as to establish any proof on their perceptions. You must not believe that the Mutakallemim had no purpose in agreeing upon this proposition, or as most of the later adherents of that school affirm, that the first Mutakallemim had no ulterior object in endeavouring to prove the existence of atoms. On the contrary, every proposition here mentioned is indispensable ; if one of these be rejected, the whole theory falls to the ground. The last-mentioned proposition is of particular importance ; for when our senses perceive things by which any of the foregoing propositions are confuted, the Mutakallemim say that no notice should be taken of the perception of the senses so long as the proposition is supported by the testimony of the intellect, and established (as they believe) by proof. Thus they say that the continuous motion is interrupted by moments of rest ; that the millstone in its motion is broken into atoms ; that the white colour of a garment ceases to exist, and another whiteness comes in its stead. All these theories are contrary to what the eye perceives, and many inferences are drawn from the assumed existence of a vacuum, all of which are contradicted by the senses. The Mutakallemim, however, meet these objections by saying, whenever they can do so, that the perception of these things is withheld from the senses ; in other instances they maintain that the contradiction has its source in the deceptive character of the senses. You know that this theory is very ancient, and was the pride of the sophists, who asserted that they themselves were its authors ; this is stated by Galenus in his treatise on natural forces ; and you know well what he says of those who will not admit the evidence of the senses.

Having discussed these propositions, I now proceed to explain the theory of the Mutakallemim concerning the above-mentioned four problems.

CHAPTER LXXIV

IN this chapter will be given an outline of the proofs by which the Mutakallemim attempt to demonstrate that the universe is not eternal. You must of course not expect that I shall quote their lengthy arguments *verbatim* ; I only intend to give an abstract of each proof, to show in what way it helps to establish the theory of the *creatio ex nihilo* or to confute the eternity of the universe, and briefly to notice the propositions they employed in support of their theory. If you were to read their well-known and voluminous writings, you would not discover any arguments with which they support their view left unnoticed in the present outline, but you might find there greater copiousness of words combined with more grace and elegance of style ; frequently they employ rhyme, rhythm, and poetical diction, and sometimes mysterious phrases which perhaps are intended to startle persons listening to their discourses, and to deter those who might otherwise criticize them. You would also find many repetitions ; questions propounded and, as they believe, answered, and frequent attacks on those who differ from their opinions.

The First Argument.

Some of the Mutakallemim thought that by proving the creation of one thing, they demonstrated the *creatio ex nihilo* in reference to the entire universe. E.g., Zaid, who from a small molecule had gradually been brought

to a state of perfection, has undoubtedly not effected this change and development by his own efforts, but owes it to an external agency. It is therefore clear that an agent is required for such organization and successive
transmutation. A palm-tree or any other object might equally be selected
to illustrate this idea. The whole universe, they argue, is analogous to these
instances. Thus you see how they believe that a law discovered in one thing
may equally be applied to everything.

The Second Argument.

This argument is likewise based on the belief that the proof by which the
creation of one thing is demonstrated, holds good for the *creatio ex nihilo*
in reference to the whole universe. E.g., a certain individual, called Zaid,
who one time was not yet in existence, subsequently came into existence;
and if it be assumed that Amr, his father, was the cause of his existence, Amr
himself must likewise have passed from non-existence into existence; suppose then that Zaid's father unquestionably owed his origin to Khaled, Zaid's
grandfather, it would be found that Khaled himself did not exist from
eternity, and the series of causes could thus be carried back to infinity. But
such an infinite series of beings is inadmissible according to the theory of the
Mutakallemim, as we have shown in our discussion of the eleventh proposition. In continuing this species of reasoning, you come to a first man, who
had no parent, viz. Adam. Then you will of course ask, whence came this
first man ? If, e.g., the reply be given that he was made out of earth, you
will again inquire, " Whence came that earth ? " " Out of water." " Whence
came the water ? " The inquiry would be carried on, either *ad infinitum*,
which is absurd, or until you meet with a something that came into existence
from absolute non-existence; in this latter case you would arrive at the real
truth; here the series of inquiries ends. This result of the question proves,
according to the opinion of the Mutakallemim, that the whole universe came
into existence from absolute non-existence.

The Third Argument.

The atoms of things are necessarily either joined together or separate, and
even the same atoms may at one time be united at another disunited. It is
therefore evident that the nature of the atoms does not necessitate either
their combination or their separation; for if they were separate by virtue of
their nature they would never join, and if they were joined by virtue of their
nature, they could never again be separated. Thus there is no reason
why atoms should rather be combined than separate, or *vice versâ*, why
rather in a state of separation than of combination. Seeing that some atoms
are joined, others separate, and again others subject to change, they being
combined at one time and separated at another, the fact may therefore be
taken as a proof that the atoms cannot combine or separate without an agent.
This argument, according to the opinion of the Mutakallemim, establishes
the theory that the universe has been created from nothing. You have
already been told, that those who employ this argument rely on the first
proposition of the Mutakallemim with its corollaries.

The Fourth Argument.

The whole Universe is composed of substance and accidents; every substance must possess one accident or more, and since the accidents are not eternal, the substance, the substratum of the accidents, cannot be eternal; for that which is joined to transient things and cannot exist without them is itself transient. Therefore the whole Universe has had a beginning. To the objection, that the substance may possibly be eternal while the accidents, though in themselves transient, succeed each other in an infinite series, they reply that, in this case, an infinite number of transient things would be in existence, an eventuality which, according to their theory, is impossible. This argument is considered by them the best and safest, and has been accepted by many of them as a strict proof. Its acceptance implies the admission of the following three propositions, the object of which is well understood by philosophers. (1) An infinite series of things, of which the one succeeds when the other has ceased to exist, is impossible. (2) All accidents have a beginning.—Our opponent, who defends the theory of the eternity of the universe, can refute this proposition by pointing to one particular accident, namely to the circular motion of the sphere; for it is held by Aristotle that this circular motion is eternal, and, therefore, the spheres which perform this motion are, according to his opinion, likewise eternal. It is of no use to prove that all other accidents have a beginning; for our opponent does not deny this; he says that accidents may supervene an object which has existed from eternity, and may follow each other in rotation. He contents himself with maintaining that this particular accident, viz., circular motion, the motion of the heavenly sphere, is eternal, and does not belong to the class of transient accidents. It is therefore necessary to examine this accident by itself, and to prove that it is not eternal. (3) The next proposition which the author of this argument accepts is as follows: Every material object consists of substance and accidents, that is to say, of atoms and accidents in the sense in which the Mutakallemim use the term. But if a material object were held to be a combination of matter and form, as has been proved by our opponent, it would be necessary to demonstrate that the primal matter and the primal form are transient, and only then the proof of the *creatio ex nihilo* would be complete.

The Fifth Argument.

This argument is based on the theory of Determination, and is made much of by the Mutakallemim. It is the same as the theory which I explained in discussing the tenth proposition. Namely, when they treat either of the Universe in general, or of any of its parts, they assume that it can have such properties and such dimensions as it actually has; that it may receive such accidents as in reality are noticed in it, and that it may exist in such a place and at such a time as in fact is the case; but it may be larger or smaller, may receive other properties and accidents, and come to existence at an earlier or a later period, or in a different place. Consequently, the fact that a thing has been determined in its composition, size, place, accident and time—a variation in all these points being possible—is a proof that a being exists which freely chooses and determines these divers relations; and the circumstance that the Universe or a part of it requires a being able to make this selection, proves that the Universe has been created *ex nihilo*. For there is no difference which of the following expressions is used : to determine, to make, to create, to produce, to originate, or to intend ; these verbs have all one and the same meaning. The Mutakallemim give a great many examples, both of a general and a special character. They say it is not more natural for earth to be under water than to be above water ; who then determined its actual position ? Or, is it more natural that the sun is round than that it should be square or triangular ; for all qualities have the same relation to a body capable of possessing them. Who then determined one particular quality ? In a similar way they treat of every individual being ; when, e.g., they notice flowers of different colours, they are unable to explain the phenomenon, and they take it as a strong proof in favour of their theory ; they say, " Behold, the earth is everywhere alike, the water is alike ; why then is this flower red and that one yellow ? Some being must have determined the colour of each, and that being is God. A being must therefore exist which determines everything, both as regards the Universe generally, and each of its parts individually. All this is the logical consequence of the tenth proposition. The theory of determination is moreover adopted by some of those who assume the eternity of the Universe, as will be explained below. In conclusion, I consider this to be the best argument ; and in another part I shall more fully acquaint you with the opinion I have formed concerning the theory of Determination.

The Sixth Argument.

One of the modern Mutakallemim thought that he had found a very good argument, much better than any advanced hitherto, namely, the argument based on the triumph of existence over non-existence. He says that, according to the common belief, the existence of the Universe is merely possible ; for if it were necessary, the Universe would be God—but he seems to forget that we are at issue with those who, whilst they believe in the existence of God, admit at the same time the eternity of the Universe.—The expression " A thing is possible " denotes that the thing may either be in existence or not in existence, and that there is not more reason why it should exist than why it should not exist. The fact that a thing, the existence of which is possible, actually does exist—although it bears the same relation to the state of existence as to that of non-existence—proves that there is a Being which gave the preference to existence over non-existence. This argument is very forcible ; it is a modified form of the foregoing argument which is based on the theory of determination. He only chose the term " preference " instead of " determination," and instead of applying it to the properties of the existing being he applies it to " the existence of the being itself." He either had the intention to mislead, or he misunderstood the proposition, that the existence of the Universe is possible. Our opponent who assumes the eternity of the Universe, employs the term " possible," and says, " the existence of the Universe is possible " in a sense different from that in which the Mutakallem applies it, as will be explained below. Moreover it may be doubted whether the conclusion, that the Universe owes its origin to a being which is able to give preference to existence over non-existence, is correct. For we may apply the terms " preference " and " determination " to anything capable of receiving either of two properties which are contrary or opposed to each other; and when we find that the thing actually possesses one property and not the other, we are convinced that there exists a determining agent. E.g., you say that a piece of copper could just as well be formed into a kettle as into a lamp; when we find that it is a lamp or a kettle, we have no doubt that a deciding and determining agent had advisedly chosen one of the two possible forms; for it is clear that the substance of copper existed, and that before the determination took place it had neither of the two possible forms which have just been mentioned. When, however, it is the question whether a certain existing object is eternal, or whether it has passed from non-existence into existence, this argument is inadmissible; for it cannot be asked who decided in favour of the existence of a thing, and rejected its non-existence, except when it has been admitted that it has passed from non-existence into existence; in the present case this is just the point under discussion. If we were to take the existence and the non-existence of a thing as mere objects of imagination, we should have to apply the tenth proposition which gives prominence to imagination and fiction, and ignores the things which exist in reality, or are conceived by the intellect. Our opponent, however, who believes in the eternity of the Universe, will show that we can imagine the non-existence of the universe as well as we can imagine any other impossibility. It is not my intention to refute their doctrine of the *creatio ex nihilo* : I only wish to show the incorrectness of their belief that this argument differs from the one which precedes; since in fact the two arguments are identical, and are founded on the well-known principle of determination.

The Seventh Argument.

One of the modern Mutakallemim says that he is able to prove the creation of the Universe from the theory put forth by the philosophers concerning the immortality of the soul. He argues thus : If the world were eternal the number of the dead would necessarily be infinite, and consequently an infinite number of souls would coexist, but it has long since been shown that the coexistence of an infinite number of things is positively impossible. This is indeed a strange argument! One difficulty is explained by another which is still greater ! Here the saying, well known among the Arameans, may be applied: " Your guarantee wants himself a guarantee." He rests his argument on the immortality of the soul, as though he understood this immortality, in what respect the soul is immortal, or what the thing is which is immortal ! If, however, he only meant to controvert the opinion of his opponent, who believed in the eternity of the Universe, and also in the immortality of the soul, he accomplished his task, provided the opponent admitted the correctness of the idea which that Mutakallem formed of the philosopher's view on the immortality of the soul. Some of the later philosophers explained this difficulty as follows : the immortal souls are not substances which occupy a locality or a space, and their existence in an infinite number is therefore not impossible. You must bear in mind that those abstract beings which are neither bodies nor forces dwelling in bodies, and which in fact are ideals—are altogether incapable of being represented as a plurality unless some ideals be the cause of the existence of others, and can be distinguished from each other by the specific difference that some are the efficient cause and others the effect ; but that which remains of Zaid [after his death] is neither the cause nor the effect of that which is left of Amr, and therefore the souls of all the departed form only one being as has been explained by Ibn Bekr Ibn Al-zaig, and others who ventured to speak on these profound subjects. In short, such intricate disciplines, which our mind can scarcely comprehend, cannot furnish any principles for the explanation of other subjects.—It should be noted that whoever endeavours to prove or to disprove the eternity of the Universe by these arguments of the Mutakallemim, must necessarily rely on one of the two following propositions, or on both of them ; namely on the tenth proposition, according to which the actual form of a thing is merely one of many equally possible forms, and which implies that there must be a being capable of making the special selection ; or on the eleventh proposition which rejects the existence of an infinite series of things coming successively into existence. The last-named proposition is demonstrated in various ways, e.g., they advert to a class of transient individuals, and to a certain particular date. From the theory which asserts the eternity of the Universe, it would follow that the individuals of that class up to that particular date are infinite in number ; a thousand years later the individuals of that class are likewise infinite in number ; the last number must exceed the previous one by the number of the individuals born in those thousand years, and consequently one infinite number would be larger than another. The same argument is applied to the revolutions of the heavenly sphere, and in like manner it is shown that one infinite number of revolutions would be larger than another ; the same result is obtained when revolutions of one sphere are compared with those of another moving more slowly ; the revolutions of both spheres [though unequal] would be infinite in number. Similarly they proceed with all those accidents which are subject to destruction and production ; the individual accidents that have passed into non-existence are counted and represented as though they were still in existence, and as though they were things with a definite beginning ; this imaginary number is then either increased or reduced. Yet all these things have no reality and are mere fictions. Abunazar Alfarabi in criticizing this proposition, has exposed all its weak points, as you will clearly perceive, when you study his book on the changeable beings earnestly and dispassionately. These are the principal arguments of the Mutakallemim in seeking to establish the *creatio ex nihilo*. Having thus proved that the Universe is not eternal, they necessarily infer that there is an *Agens* who created it in accordance with His intention, desire and will. They then proceed to prove the unity of that *Agens* as I am going to point out in the next chapter.

CHAPTER LXXV

In this chapter I shall explain to you how the Mutakallemim prove the Unity of God. They contend that the Maker and Creator of the Universe, the existence of whom is testified by all nature, is One. Two propositions are employed by them in demonstrating the Unity of God, viz., two deities or

more would neutralize each other, and if several deities existed they would
be distinguished from each other by a specific difference.

First Argument.

The first argument is that of mutual neutralization, and is employed by
the majority of the Mutakallemim. It is to the following effect :—If the
Universe had two Gods, it would necessarily occur that the atom—subject
to a combination with one or two opposite qualities—either remained without either of them, and that is impossible, or, though being only one atom,
included both qualities at the same time, and that is likewise impossible.
E.g., whilst one of the two deities determined that one atom or more should
be warm, the other deity might determine that the same should be cold ;
the consequence of the mutual neutralization of the two divine beings would
thus be that the atoms would be neither warm nor cold—a contingency
which is impossible, because all bodies must combine with one of two opposites ; or they would be at the same time both warm and cold. Similarly,
it might occur that whilst one of the deities desired that a body be in motion,
the other might desire that it be at rest ; the body would then be either
without motion and rest, or would both move and rest at the same time.
Proofs of this kind are founded on the atomic theory contained in the first
proposition of the Mutakallemim, on the proposition which refers to the
creation of the accidents, and on the proposition that negatives are properties
of actual existence and require for their production an *agens*. For if it were
assumed that the substance of this world which, according to the philosophers
is subject to successive production and destruction, is different from the substance of the world above, viz., from the substance of the spheres—a fact
established by proof—and that as the Dualists assert, there are two divine
beings, one of whom rules this world without influencing the spheres, whilst
the other governs the world above without interfering with this world—such
theory would not involve the mutual neutralization of the two deities. If
it were then objected, that the existence of two deities would necessitate an
imperfection in both of them, in so far as one deity would be unable to influence the province of the other, the objection would be met by the reply
that this inability need not be considered a defect in either of them ; for that
which is not included within the sphere of action of a being can of course not
be performed by that being, and an *agens* is not deficient in power, if it is
unable to perform what is intrinsically impossible. Thus we, Monotheists,
do not consider it a defect in God, that He does not combine two opposites
in one object, nor do we test His omnipotence by the accomplishment of
any similar impossibility. When the Mutakallemim noticed the weakness
of their argument, for which they had some apparent support, they had
recourse to another argument.

Second Argument.

If there were two Gods, there would necessarily be some element common
to both, whilst some element present in the one would be absent in the other,
and constitute the specific difference between them. This is a philosophic
and sound argument for those who are able to examine it, and to obtain a
clear insight into its premises, which will be further explained, in our ex-

position of the view of the philosophers on this point. But it cannot be accepted by those who admit the existence of divine attributes. For according to their opinion, the Primal Cause includes many different elements. They represent its wisdom and its omnipotence as two different things, and again the omnipotence as different from the will. Consequently it would not be impossible that either of the two divine beings possessed several properties, some of which would be common to both, and some peculiar to only one of them.

Third Argument.

This argument is likewise based on one of the Propositions of the Kalâm. For some of the Mutakallemim belonging to the old school assume, that when the Creator *wills* a thing, the will is not an element superadded to the essence of God : it is a will without a substratum. In accordance with the propositions which we have mentioned, and of which, as you will see, it is difficult to form a true conception, they say that *one* will, which is independent of any substratum, cannot be ascribed to *two* beings ; for, as they assert, *one* cause cannot be the source of two laws for two essences. This is, as I told you, the method of explaining one difficulty by means of another and still greater difficulty. For as they define the Will, it is inconceivable, and some have, therefore, considered it to be a mere non-entity ; others who admit its existence, meet with many insuperable difficulties. The Mutakallemim, nevertheless, establish on its existence one of the proofs for the unity of God.

Fourth Argument.

The existence of an action is necessarily positive evidence of the existence of an *agens*, but does not prove the existence of more than one *agens*. There is no difference whether the existence of one God be assumed or the existence of two, or three, or twenty, or any number. This is plain and clear. But the argument does not seem to prove the non-existence of a multitude of deities ; it only shows that their number is unknown ; the deity may be one sole being, but may also include several divine beings. The following supplemental argument has therefore been advanced : possibility is inapplicable to the existence of God, which is absolute ; the possibility of the existence of more than one God must therefore be denied. This is the whole essence of the proof, and its fallacy is self-evident ; for although the notion of possibility cannot be applied to the existence of God, it can be applied to our knowledge of God : for an alternative in our knowledge of a thing does not involve an alternative in the actual existence of the thing, and perhaps there is neither a tripartite deity as the Christians believe, nor an undivided Unity as we believe. This is clear to those who have been taught to notice the conclusions implied in given premises.

Fifth Argument.

One of the modern Mutakallemim thought that he found a proof of the Unity of God in the idea of requisiteness. Suppose there were two divine beings ; if one of them were able to create the universe, the second God would be superfluous, and there would be no need for his existence. If, on the other hand, the entire universe could not be created or governed except by both of them, each of them would be imperfect in so far as he would require the co-operation of another being, and would thus be limited in power. This argument is, in fact, only a variation of " the mutual neutralization of two deities." There is this difficulty in such proofs, that a certain degree of imperfection is ascribed to a Being which does not accomplish tasks beyond its sphere. We do not call a person weak because he cannot move a thousand hundredweights, and we do not say that God is imperfect because He cannot transform Himself into a body, or cannot create another being like Himself, or make a square whose diagonal should be equal to one of its sides. In the same manner we should not consider it an imperfection in God, if He were not the only Creator, and if it were absolutely necessary that there should be two Creators ; not because the one God required the assistance of the other, but because the existence of both of them was equally necessary, and because it was impossible that it should be otherwise. Further we do not say that the Almighty is imperfect, because He does not, according to the opinion of the Mutakallemim, produce a body otherwise than by the creation of atoms, and by their combination with accidents created in them. That inability is not called want or imperfection, since another process is impossible. In like manner the Dualist might say, that it is impossible for one Being to act alone, and that this circumstance constitutes no imperfection in either of the Deities, because the absolute existence of one Deity necessitates the co-existence of the other. Some of the Mutakallemim, weary of these arguments, declared that the Unity of God is a doctrine which must be received as a matter of faith, but most of them rejected this theory, and reviled its authors. I, however, hold, that those who accept this theory are right-minded, and shrink from admitting an erroneous opinion ; when they do not perceive any cogency in the arguments, and find that the proofs advanced in favour of the doctrine are inconclusive, they prefer to assume that it could only be received as a matter of faith. For the Mutakallemim do not hold that the Universe has any defined properties on which a true proof could be founded, or that man's intellect is endowed with any such faculty as would enable him to form correct conclusions. It is, however, not without a motive that they defend this theory ; they wish to assume such a form of the Universe, as could be employed to support a doctrine for which otherwise no proof could be found, and would lead us to neglect the investigation of that which in fact can be proved. We can only appeal to the Almighty and to those intelligent persons who confess their error when they discover it.

CHAPTER LXXVI

The reasonings and arguments of the Mutakallemim to demonstrate the Incorporeality of God are very weak, and indeed inferior to their arguments for the Unity of God. They treat the doctrine of the Incorporeality of God as if it were the logical sequence of the theory of His Unity, and they say that the attribute " one " cannot be applied to a corporeal object. Those who maintain that God is incorporeal because a corporeal object consists of substance and form—a combination known to be impossible in the Divine Being, are not in my opinion Mutakallemim, and such an argument is not founded on the propositions of the Kalâm ; on the contrary, it is a logical proof based on the theory of substance and form, and on a right conception of their properties. It has the character of a philosophical argument, and I shall fully explain it when treating of the arguments of the philosophers. Here we only propose to discuss the arguments by which the Mutakallemim desire to prove the Incorporeality of God in accordance with their propositions and the method of their reasoning.

First Argument.

If God were corporeal, His true essence would necessarily either exist entirely in every part of the body, that is to say, in each of its atoms, or would be confined to one of the atoms. In the latter alternative the other atoms would be superfluous, and the existence of the corporeal being [with the exception of the one atom] would be of no purpose. If, on the other hand, each atom fully represented the Divine Being, the whole body would not be *one* deity, but a complex of deities, and this would be contrary to the doctrine adopted by the *kalâm* that God is one. An examination of this argument shows that it is based on the first and fifth propositions. But there is room for the following objection : " God does not consist of atoms, that is to say, He is not, as you assert, composed of a number of elements created by Himself, but is one continuous body, and indivisible except in man's imagination, which affords no test ; for in man's imagination the substance of the heavens may be torn or rent asunder. The philosopher holds that such a possibility results from assuming a similarity and an analogy between the visible, i.e., the bodies which exist among us, and the invisible."

Second Argument.

This argument, they believe, is of great importance. Its main support is the impossibility of comparison, i.e., the belief that God cannot be compared to any of His creatures ; and that He would be comparable to other corporeal objects if He were corporeal. They put great stress on this argument, and say as follows : " If it were asserted that God is corporeal, but that His substance is not like that of other corporeal beings, it would be self-contradictory ; for all bodies are alike as regards their substance, and are distinguished from each other by other things, viz., the accidents." They also argue that if God were corporeal it would follow that He has created another being like Himself. This argument is refuted in two ways. First, the objector does not admit the impossibility of comparison ; he asks how it could be proved that God cannot be compared to any of His creatures. No doubt that, in support of their view, that a comparison between the Almighty and any other being is inadmissible, they would have to cite the words of the Prophets, and thus accept this doctrine by the authority of tradition, not by the authority of reason. The argument that God, if comparable to any of His creatures, would be found to have created beings like Himself, is refuted by the objector in the following way : " The created things are not like Him in every respect ; for I do not deny that God has many properties and peculiarities." For he who admits the corporeality of God does not deny the existence of properties in the divine Being. Another and more forcible argument is this : All who have studied philosophy, and have made themselves thoroughly acquainted with philosophical theories, assume as demonstrated facts, first that the term substance, when applied to the spheres above and to the corporeal objects here on earth is a perfect homonym, for the substance of the one is not the substance of the other ; and secondly that the forms of the things on this earth are different from the forms of the spheres ; the terms substance and form when applied both to things below and to the spheres above are homonyms ; although there is no doubt that the spheres have [like the things below, three] dimensions, they are corporeal because they consist of substance and form, not because they have dimensions. If this explanation is admitted with reference to the spheres, how much more is he who believes that God is corporeal justified in saying that God is a corporeal being which has dimensions, but which in its substance, its true nature and properties is very different from all created bodies, and that the term " substance " is applied to Him and to His creatures homonymously, in the same manner as the true believers, who have a correct conception of the divine idea, apply the term " existence " homonymously to Him and to His creatures. The Corporealists do not admit that all bodies consist of similar atoms ; they believe that God created all things, and that these differ from each other both in their substances and in their constituent properties ; and just as the substance of dung differs from the substance of the sun, so does, according to this theory, the substance of the spheres and the stars differ from the substance of the created light, i.e., the Divine Glory (*Shechinah*), and again the substance of the Divine Glory, or the pillar of cloud created [for the purpose], differ from the substance of the Most High ; for the substance of the latter is sublime, perfect, simple, constant and immutable. His absolute existence remains always the same, and He creates all things according to His will and desire. How could this argument, though it be weak, be refuted by these strange methods of the Mutakallemim, which I pointed out to you ?

Third Argument.

If God were corporeal, He would be finite, and so far this argument is correct ; if He were finite, He would have certain dimensions and a certain form ; this is also a correct conclusion. But they continue thus : Attribute to God any magnitude or form whatever : He might be either larger or smaller, and might also have a different form. The fact that He has one special magnitude and one special form presupposes the existence of a determining *agens*. I have heard that they attach great importance to this argument, but in truth it is the weakest of all the arguments mentioned above. It is founded on the tenth proposition, the feebleness of which in ignoring the actual properties of things, we have clearly shown in regard to ordinary beings and must be much more evident in regard to the Creator. There is no difference between this argument and their assertion that the fact of the existence of the Universe having been preferred to its non-existence proves the existence of an *agens* that preferred the existence of the Universe to its non-existence at a time when both were equally possible. If it were asked why this argument should not be applied to God—viz., that His mere existence proved the existence of an *agens* which determined His existence and rejected His non-existence—they would undoubtedly answer that this admission would only lead to a repetition of the same argument until at length a being be found whose existence is not merely potential but necessary, and which does not require a *causa efficiens*. But this same answer can also be applied to dimensions and to form. It can only be said in reference to all other forms and magnitudes, the existence of which is *pôssible*, that is to say which came into existence after a state of non-existence, that they might have been larger or smaller than they actually are, or that they might have had a form different from that which they actually possess, and require for this reason some determining *agens*. But the forms and dimensions of God (who is above all imperfection and similitude) ! did not come into existence according to the opinion of the Corporealist after a state of non-existence, and therefore no determining *agens* was necessary ; His substance with its dimensions and forms has a necessary existence ; no *agens* was required to decide upon His existence, and to reject His non-existence, since non-existence is altogether inadmissible in God. In like manner there was no force required to determine His magnitude and form, they were absolutely inseparable from His existence.

If you wish to go in search of truth, to cast aside your passions, your tradition, and your fondness of things you have been accustomed to cherish, if you wish to guard yourself against error : then consider the fate of these speculators and the result of their labours ; observe how they rushed, as it were, from the ashes into the fire. They denied the nature of the existing things, misrepresented the properties of heaven and earth, and thought that they were able, by their propositions, to prove the creation of the world, but in fact they were far from proving the *creatio ex nihilo*, and have weakened the arguments for the existence, the unity, and the incorporeality of God. The proofs of all these doctrines must be based on the well-known nature of the existing things, as perceived by the senses and the intellect.

Having thus discussed the arguments of the Mutakallemim, we shall now proceed to consider the propositions of the philosophers and their arguments for the existence of God, His Unity and His Incorporeality, and we shall for the present assume the Eternity of the Universe without finally accepting it. Next to this we shall develop our own method, which is the result of deep study, in demonstrating these three principles, and we shall then examine the theory of the Eternity of the Universe as assumed by the philosophers.

PART II

INTRODUCTION

Twenty-five of the propositions which are employed in the proof for the existence of God, or in the arguments demonstrating that God is neither corporeal nor a force connected with a material being, or that He is One, have been fully established, and their correctness is beyond doubt. Aristotle and the Peripatetics who followed him have proved each of these propositions. There is, however, one proposition which we do not accept—namely, the proposition which affirms the Eternity of the Universe, but we will admit it for the present, because by doing so we shall be enabled clearly to demonstrate our own theory.

Proposition I.

The existence of an infinite magnitude is impossible.

Proposition II.

The co-existence of an infinite number of finite magnitudes is impossible

Proposition III.

The existence of an infinite number of causes and effects is impossible, even if these were not magnitudes; if, e.g., one Intelligence were the cause of a second, the second the cause of a third, the third the cause of a fourth, and so on, the series could not be continued *ad infinitum*.

Proposition IV.

Four categories are subject to change :—

(*a.*) *Substance.*—Changes which affect the substance of a thing are called genesis and destruction.

(*b.*) *Quantity.*—Changes in reference to quantity are increase and decrease.

(*c.*) *Quality.*—Changes in the qualities of things are transformations.

(*d.*) *Place.*—Change of place is called motion.

The term " motion " is properly applied to change of place, but is also used in a general sense of all kinds of changes.

Proposition V.

Motion implies change and transition from potentiality to actuality.

Proposition VI.

The motion of a thing is either essential or accidental; or it is due to an external force, or to the participation of the thing in the motion of another thing. This latter kind of motion is similar to the accidental one. An instance of essential motion may be found in the translation of a thing from one place to another. The accident of a thing, as, e.g., its black colour, is said to move when the thing itself changes its place. The upward motion of a stone, owing to a force applied to it in that direction, is an instance of a motion due to an external force. The motion of a nail in a boat may serve to illustrate motion due to the participation of a thing in the motion of another thing; for when the boat moves, the nail is said to move likewise. The same is the case with everything composed of several parts : when the thing itself moves, every part of it is likewise said to move.

Proposition VII.

Things which are changeable are, at the same time, divisible. Hence everything that moves is divisible, and consequently corporeal; but that which is indivisible cannot move, and cannot therefore be corporeal.

Proposition VIII.

A thing that moves accidentally must come to rest, because it does not move of its own accord; hence accidental motion cannot continue for ever.

Proposition IX.

A corporeal thing that sets another corporeal thing in motion can only effect this by setting itself in motion at the time it causes the other thing to move.

Proposition X.

A thing which is said to be contained in a corporeal object must satisfy either of the two following conditions: it either exists through that object, as is the case with accidents, or it is the cause of the existence of that object; such is, e.g., its essential property. In both cases it is a force existing in a corporeal object.

Proposition XI.

Among the things which exist through a material object, there are some which participate in the division of that object, and are therefore accidentally divisible, as, e.g., its colour, and all other qualities that spread throughout its parts. On the other hand, among the things which form the essential elements of an object, there are some which cannot be divided in any way, as, e.g., the soul and the intellect.

Proposition XII.

A force which occupies all parts of a corporeal object is finite, that object itself being finite.

Proposition XIII.

None of the several kinds of change can be continuous, except motion from place to place, provided it be circular.

Proposition XIV.

Locomotion is in the natural order of the several kinds of motion the first and foremost. For genesis and corruption are preceded by transformation, which, in its turn, is preceded by the approach of the transforming agent to the object which is to be transformed. Also, increase and decrease are impossible without previous genesis and corruption.

Proposition XV.

Time is an accident that is related and joined to motion in such a manner that the one is never found without the other. Motion is only possible in time, and the idea of time cannot be conceived otherwise than in connexion with motion; things which do not move have no relation to time.

Proposition XVI.

Incorporeal bodies can only be numbered when they are forces situated in a body; the several forces must then be counted together with substances or objects in which they exist. Hence purely spiritual beings, which are neither corporeal nor forces situated in corporeal objects, cannot be counted, except when considered as causes and effects.

PROPOSITION XVII.

When an object moves, there must be some agent that moves it, from without, as, e.g., in the case of a stone set in motion by the hand ; or from within, e.g., when the body of a living being moves. Living beings include in themselves, at the same time, the moving agent and the thing moved ; when, therefore, a living being dies, and the moving agent, the soul, has left the body, i.e., the thing moved, the body remains for some time in the same condition as before, and yet cannot move in the manner it has moved previously. The moving agent, when included in the thing moved, is hidden from, and imperceptible to, the senses. This circumstance gave rise to the belief that the body of an animal moves without the aid of a moving agent. When we therefore affirm, concerning a thing in motion, that it is its own moving agent, or, as is generally said, that it moves of its own accord, we mean to say that the force which really sets the body in motion exists in that body itself.

PROPOSITION XVIII.

Everything that passes over from a state of potentiality to that of actuality, is caused to do so by some external agent ; because if that agent existed in the thing itself, and no obstacle prevented the transition, the thing would never be in a state of potentiality, but always in that of actuality. If, on the other hand, while the thing itself contained that agent, some obstacle existed, and at a certain time that obstacle was removed, the same cause which removed the obstacle would undoubtedly be described as the cause of the transition from potentiality to actuality, [and not the force situated within the body]. Note this.

PROPOSITION XIX.

A thing which owes its existence to certain causes has in itself merely the possibility of existence ; for only if these causes exist, the thing likewise exists. It does not exist if the causes do not exist at all, or if they have ceased to exist, or if there has been a change in the relation which implies the existence of that thing as a necessary consequence of those causes.

PROPOSITION XX.

A thing which has in itself the necessity of existence cannot have for its existence any cause whatever.

PROPOSITION XXI.

A thing composed of two elements has necessarily their composition as the cause of its present existence. Its existence is therefore not necessitated by its own essence ; it depends on the existence of its two component parts and their combination.

PROPOSITION XXII.

Material objects are always composed of two elements [at least], and are without exception subject to accidents. The two component elements of all bodies are substance and form. The accidents attributed to material objects are quantity, geometrical form, and position.

Proposition XXIII.

Everything that exists potentially, and whose essence includes a certain state of possibility, may at some time be without actual existence.

Proposition XXIV.

That which is potentially a certain thing is necessarily material, for the state of possibility is always connected with matter.

Proposition XXV.

Each compound substance consists of matter and form, and requires an agent for its existence, viz., a force which sets the substance in motion, and thereby enables it to receive a certain form. The force which thus prepares the substance of a certain individual being, is called the immediate motor.

Here the necessity arises of investigating into the properties of motion, the moving agent and the thing moved. But this has already been explained sufficiently; and the opinion of Aristotle may be expressed in the following proposition: Matter does not move of its own accord—an important proposition that led to the investigation of the Prime Motor (the first moving agent).

Of these foregoing twenty-five propositions some may be verified by means of a little reflection and the application of a few propositions capable of proof, or of axioms or theorems of almost the same force, such as have been explained by me. Others require many arguments and propositions, all of which, however, have been established by conclusive proofs partly in the Physics and its commentaries, and partly in the Metaphysics and its commentary. I have already stated that in this work it is not my intention to copy the books of the philosophers or to explain difficult problems, but simply to mention those propositions which are closely connected with our subject, and which we want for our purpose.

To the above propositions one must be added which enunciates that the universe is eternal, and which is held by Aristotle to be true, and even more acceptable than any other theory. For the present we admit it, as a hypothesis, only for the purpose of demonstrating our theory. It is the following proposition :—

Proposition XXVI

Time and motion are eternal, constant, and in actual existence.

In accordance with this proposition, Aristotle is compelled to assume that there exists actually a body with constant motion, viz., the fifth element. He therefore says that the heavens are not subject to genesis or destruction, because motion cannot be generated nor destroyed. He also holds that every motion must necessarily be preceded by another motion, either of the same or of a different kind. The belief that the locomotion of an animal is not preceded by another motion, is not true; for the animal is caused to move, after it had been in rest, by the intention to obtain those very things which bring about that locomotion. A change in its state of health, or some image, or some new idea can produce a desire to seek that which is conducive to its welfare and to avoid that which is contrary. Each of these three causes sets the living being in motion, and each of them is produced by various kinds of motion. Aristotle likewise asserts that everything which is created must, before its actual creation, have existed *in potentiâ*. By inferences drawn from this assertion he seeks to establish his proposition, viz., The thing that moves is finite, and its path finite; but it repeats the motion in its path an infinite number of times. This can only take place when the motion is circular, as has been stated in Proposition XIII. Hence follows also the existence of an infinite number of things which do not co-exist but follow one after the other.

Aristotle frequently attempts to establish this proposition; but I believe that he did not consider his proofs to be conclusive. It appeared to him to be the most probable and acceptable proposition. His followers, however, and the commentators of his books, contend that it contains not only a probable but a demonstrative proof, and that it has, in fact, been fully established. On the other hand, the Mutakallemim try to prove that the proposition cannot be true, as, according to their opinion, it is impossible to conceive how an infinite number of things could even come into existence successively. They assume this impossibility as an axiom. I, however, think that this proposition is admissible, but neither demonstrative, as the commentators of Aristotle assert, nor, on the other hand, impossible, as the Mutakallemim say. We have no intention to explain here the proofs given by Aristotle, or to show our doubts concerning them, or to set forth our opinions on the creation of the universe. I here simply desire to mention those propositions which we shall require for the proof of the three principles stated above. Having thus quoted and admitted these propositions, I will now proceed to explain what may be inferred from them.

CHAPTER I

ACCORDING to Proposition XXV., a moving agent must exist which has moved the substance of all existing transient things and enabled it to receive Form. The cause of the motion of that agent is found in the existence of another motor of the same or of a different class, the term " motion," in a general sense, being common to four categories (Prop. IV.). This series of motions is not infinite (Prop. III.); we find that it can only be continued till the motion of the fifth element is arrived at, and then it ends. The motion of the fifth element is the source of every force that moves and prepares any substance on earth for its combination with a certain form, and is connected with that force by a chain of intermediate motions. The celestial sphere [or the fifth element] performs the act of locomotion which is the first of the several kinds of motion (Prop. XIV.), and all locomotion is found to be the indirect effect of the motion of this sphere; e.g., a stone is set in motion by a stick, the stick by a man's hand, the hand by the sinews, the sinews by the muscles, the muscles by the nerves, the nerves by the natural heat of the body, and the heat of the body by its form. This is undoubtedly the immediate motive cause, but the action of this immediate cause is due to a certain design, e.g., to bring a stone into a hole by striking against it with a stick in order to prevent the draught from coming through the crevice. The motion of the air that causes the draught is the effect of the motion of the celestial sphere. Similarly it may be shown that the ultimate cause of all genesis and destruction can be traced to the motion of the sphere. But the motion of the sphere must likewise have been effected by an agent (Prop. XVII.) residing either without the sphere or within it ; a third case being impossible. In the first case, if the motor is without the sphere, it must either be corporeal or incorporeal ; if incorporeal, it cannot be said that the agent is *without* the sphere.; it can only be described as *separate* from it ; because an incorporeal object can only be said metaphorically to reside without a certain corporeal object. In the second case, if the agent resides within the sphere, it must be either a force distributed throughout the whole sphere so that each part of the sphere includes a part of the force, as is the case with the heat of fire ; or it is an indivisible force, e.g., the soul and the intellect (Props. X. and XI.). The agent which sets the sphere in motion must consequently be one of the following four things : a corporeal object without the sphere ; an incorporeal object separate from it ; a force spread throughout the whole of the sphere ; or an indivisible force [within the sphere].

The first case, viz., that the moving agent of the sphere is a corporeal object without the sphere, is impossible, as will be explained. Since the moving agent is corporeal, it must itself move while setting another object in motion (Prop. IX.), and as the sixth element would likewise move when imparting motion to another body, it would be set in motion by a seventh element, which must also move. An infinite number of bodies would thus be required before the sphere could be set in motion. This is contrary to Proposition II.

The third case, viz., that the moving object be a force distributed throughout the whole body, is likewise impossible. For the sphere is corporeal, and must therefore be finite (Prop. I.) ; also the force it contains must be finite (Prop. XII.), since each part of the sphere contains part of the force (Prop. XI.) : the latter can consequently not produce an infinite motion, such as we assumed according to Proposition XXVI., which we admitted for the present.

The fourth case is likewise impossible, viz., that the sphere is set in motion by an indivisible force residing in the sphere in the same manner as the soul resides in the body of man. For this force, though indivisible, could not be the cause of infinite motion by itself alone ; because if that were the case the prime motor would have an accidental motion (Prop.VI.). But things that move accidentally must come to rest (Prop. VIII.), and then the thing comes also to rest which is set in motion. (The following may serve as a further illustration of the nature of accidental motion. When man is moved by the soul, i.e., by his form, to go from the basement of the house to the upper storey, his body moves directly, while the soul, the really efficient cause of that motion, participates in it accidentally. For through the translation of the body from the basement to the upper storey, the soul has likewise changed its place, and when no fresh impulse for the motion of the body is given by the soul, the body which has been set in motion by such impulse comes to rest, and the accidental motion of the soul is discontinued). Consequently the motion of that supposed first motor must be due to some cause which does not form part of things composed of two elements, viz., a moving agent and an object moved ; if such a cause is present the motor in that compound sets the other element in motion ; in the absence of such a cause no motion takes place. Living beings do therefore not move continually, although each of them possesses an indivisible motive element ; because this element is not constantly in motion, as it would be if it produced motion of its own accord. On the contrary, the things to which the action is due are separate from the motor. The action is caused either by desire for that which is agreeable, or by aversion from that which is disagreeable, or by some image, or by some ideal when the moving being has the capacity of conceiving it. When any of these causes are present then the motor acts ; its motion is accidental, and must therefore come to an end (Prop. VIII.). If the motor of the sphere were of this kind the sphere could not move *ad infinitum.* Our opponent, however, holds that the spheres move continually *ad infinitum ;* if this were the case, and it is in fact possible (Prop. XIII.), the efficient cause of the motion of the sphere must, according to the above division, be of the second kind, viz., something incorporeal and separate from the sphere.

It may thus be considered as proved that the efficient cause of the motion of the sphere, if that motion be eternal, is neither itself corporeal nor does it reside in a corporeal object ; it must move neither of its own accord nor accidentally ; it must be indivisible and unchangeable (Prop. VII. and Prop. V.). This Prime Motor of the sphere is God, praised be His name !

The hypothesis that there exist two Gods is inadmissible, because absolutely incorporeal beings cannot be counted (Prop. XVI.), except as cause and effect ; the relation of time is not applicable to God (Prop. XV.), because motion cannot be predicated of Him.

The result of the above argument is consequently this : the sphere cannot move *ad infinitum* of its own accord ; the Prime Motor is not corporeal, nor a force residing within a body ; it is One, unchangeable, and in its existence independent of time. Three of our postulates are thus proved by the principal philosophers.

The philosophers employ besides another argument, based on the following proposition of Aristotle. If there be a thing composed of two elements, and the one of them is known to exist also by itself, apart from that thing, then the other element is likewise found in existence by itself separate from that compound. For if the nature of the two elements were such that they could only exist together—as, e.g., matter and form—then neither of them could in any way exist separate from the other. The fact that the one component is found also in a separate existence proves that the two elements are not indissolubly connected, and that the same must therefore be the case with the other component. Thus we infer from the existence of honey-vinegar and of honey by itself, that there exists also vinegar by itself. After having explained this Proposition Aristotle continues thus : We notice many objects consisting of a *motor* and a *motum*, i.e., objects which set other things in motion, and whilst doing so are themselves set in motion by other things ; such is clearly the case as regards all the middle members of a series of things in motion. We also see a thing that is moved, but does not itself move anything, viz., the last member of the series ; consequently a *motor* must exist without being at the same time a *motum*, and that is the Prime Motor, which, not being subject to motion, is indivisible, incorporeal, and independent of time, as has been shown in the preceding argument.

Third Philosophical Argument.—This is taken from the words of Aristotle, though he gives it in a different form. It runs as follows : There is no doubt that many things actually exist, as, e.g., things perceived with the senses. Now there are only three cases conceivable, viz., either all these things are without beginning and without end, or all of them have beginning and end, or some are with and some without beginning and end. The first of these three cases is altogether inadmissible, since we clearly perceive objects which come into existence and are subsequently destroyed. The second case is likewise inadmissible, for if everything had but a temporary existence all things might be destroyed, and that which is enunciated of a whole class of things as possible is necessarily actual. All things must therefore come to an end, and then nothing would ever be in existence, for there would not exist any being to produce anything. Consequently nothing whatever would exist [if all things were transient] ; but as we see things existing, and find ourselves in existence we conclude as follows :—Since there are undoubtedly beings of a temporary existence, there must also be an eternal being that is not subject to destruction, and whose existence is real, not merely possible.

It has been further argued that the existence of this being is necessary, either on account of itself alone or on account of some external force. In the latter case its existence and non-existence would be equally possible, because of its own properties, but its existence would be necessary on account of the external force. That force would then be the being that possesses absolute existence (Prop. XIX.). It is therefore certain that there must be a being which has absolutely independent existence, and is the source of the existence of all things, whether transient or permanent, if, as Aristotle assumes, there is in existence such a thing, which is the effect of an eternal cause, and must therefore itself be eternal. This is a proof the correctness of which is not doubted, disputed, or rejected, except by those who have no knowledge of the method of proof. We further say that the existence of anything that has independent existence is not due to any cause (Prop. X.), and that such a being does not include any plurality whatever (Prop. XXI.) ; consequently it cannot be a body, nor a force residing in a body (Prop. XXII.). It is now clear that there must be a being with absolutely independent existence, a being whose existence cannot be attributed to any external cause, and which does not include different elements ; it cannot therefore be corporeal, or a force residing in a corporeal object ; this being is God.

It can easily be proved that absolutely independent existence cannot be attributed to two beings. For, if that were the case, absolutely independent existence would be a property added to the substance of both ; neither of them would be absolutely independent on account of their essence, but only through a certain property, viz., that of this independent existence, which is common to both. It can besides be shown in many ways that independent existence cannot be reconciled with the principle of dualism by any means. It would make no difference, whether we imagine two beings of similar or of different properties. The reason for all this is to be sought in the absolute simplicity and in the utmost perfection of the essence of this being, which is the only member of its species, and does not depend on any cause whatever ; this being has therefore nothing in common with other beings.

Fourth Argument.—This is likewise a well-known philosophical argument. We constantly see things passing from a state of potentiality to that of actuality, but in every such case there is for that transition of a thing an agent separate from it (Prop. XVIII.). It is likewise clear that the agent has also passed from potentiality to actuality. It has at first been potential, because it could not be actual, owing to some obstacle contained in itself, or on account of the absence of a certain relation between itself and the object of its action ; it became an actual agent as soon as that relation was present. Whichever cause be assumed, an agent is again necessary to remove the obstacle or to create the relation. The same can be argued respecting this last-mentioned agent that creates the relation or removes the obstacle. This series of causes cannot go on *ad infinitum* ; we must at last arrive at a cause of the transition of an object from the state of potentiality to that of actuality, which is constant, and admits of no potentiality whatever. In the essence of this cause nothing exists potentially, for if its essence included any possibility of existence it would not exist at all (Prop. XXIII.) ; it cannot be corporeal, but it must be spiritual (Prop. XXIV.) ; and the immaterial being that includes no possibility whatever, but exists actually by its own essence, is God. Since He is incorporeal, as has been demonstrated, it follows that He is One (Prop. XVI.).

Even if we were to admit the Eternity of the Universe, we could by any of these methods prove the existence of God ; that He is One and incorporeal, and that He does not reside as a force in a corporeal object.

The following is likewise a correct method to prove the Incorporeality and the Unity of God : If there were two Gods, they would necessarily have one element in common by virtue of which they were Gods, and another element by which they were distinguished from each other and existed as two Gods ; the distinguishing element would either be in both different from the property common to both—in that case both of them would consist of different elements, and neither of them would be the First Cause, or have absolutely independent existence ; but their existence would depend on certain causes (Prop. XIX.)—or the distinguishing element would only in one of them be different from the element common to both : then that being could not have absolute independence.

Another proof of the Unity of God.—It has been demonstrated by proof that the whole existing world is one organic body, all parts of which are connected together ; also, that the influences of the spheres above pervade the earthly substance and prepare it for its forms. Hence it is impossible to assume that one deity be engaged in forming one part, and another deity in forming another part of that organic body of which all parts are closely connected together. A duality could only be imagined in this way, either that at one time the one deity is active, the other at another time, or that both act simultaneously, nothing being done except by both together. The first alternative is certainly absurd for many reasons ; if at the time the one deity be active the other *could* also be active, there is no reason why the one deity should then act and the other not ; if, on the other hand, it be impossible for the one deity to act when the other is at work, there must be some other cause [besides these deities] which [at a certain time] enables the one to act and disables the other. [Such difference would not be caused by time], since time is without change, and the object of the action likewise remains one and the same organic whole. Besides, if two deities existed in this way, both would be subject to the relations of time, since their actions would depend on time ; they would also in the moment of acting pass from potentiality to actuality, and require an agent for such transition ; their essence would besides include possibility [of existence]. It is equally absurd to assume that both together produce everything in existence, and that neither of them does anything alone ; for when a number of forces must be united for a certain result, none of these forces acts of its own accord, and none is by itself the immediate cause of that result, but their union is the immediate cause. It has, furthermore, been proved that the action of the absolute cannot be due to an [external] cause. The union is also an act which presupposes a cause effecting that union, and if that cause be one, it is un-doubtedly God ; but if it also consists of a number of separate forces, a cause is required for the combination of these forces, as in the first case. Finally, one simple being must be arrived at, that is the cause of the existence of the Universe, which is one whole ; it would make no difference whether we assumed that the First Cause had produced the Universe by *creatio ex nihilo,* or whether the Universe co-existed with the First Cause. It is thus clear how we can prove the Unity of God from the fact that this Universe is one whole.

Another argument concerning the Incorporeality of God.—Every corporeal object is composed of matter and form (Prop. XXII.) ; every compound of these two elements requires an agent for effecting their combination. Be-sides, it is evident that a body is divisible and has dimensions ; a body is thus undoubtedly subject to accidents. Consequently nothing corporeal can be a unity, either because everything corporeal is divisible or because it is a compound ; that is to say, it can logically be analysed into two elements ; because a body can only be said to be a certain body when the distinguishing element is added to the corporeal substratum, and must therefore include two elements ; but it has been proved that the Absolute admits of no dualism whatever.

Now that we have discussed these proofs, we will expound our own method in accordance with our promise.

CHAPTER II

The fifth essence, i.e., the heavenly spheres, must either be transient, and in this case motion would likewise be temporary, or, as our opponent assumes, it must be eternal. If the spheres are transient, then God is their Creator ; for if anything comes into existence after a period of non-existence, it is self-evident that an agent exists which has effected this result. It would be absurd to contend that the thing itself effected it. If, on the other hand, the heavenly spheres be eternal, with a regular perpetual motion, the cause of this perpetual motion, according to the Propositions enumerated in the Introduction, must be something that is neither a body, nor a force residing in a body, and that is God, praised be His name ! We have thus shown that whether we believe in the *Creatio ex Nihilo*, or in the Eternity of the Universe, we can prove by demonstrative arguments the existence of God, i.e., an absolute Being, whose existence cannot be attributed to any cause, or admit in itself any potentiality. The theory that God is One and Incorporeal has likewise been established by proof without any reference to the theory of the Creation or the Eternity of the Universe. This has been explained by us in the third philosophical argument [in support of the Existence of God], and also in our subsequent description of the methods of the philosophers in proving the Incorporeality and the Unity of God.

We deem it now convenient to continue with the theory of the philosophers, and to give their proofs for the existence of Intelligences. We will then show that their theory in this regard is in harmony with the teaching of Scripture concerning the existence of angels. After the full treatment of this subject we shall return to our task and discuss the theory of *creatio ex nihilo*. For the best arguments in favour of this theory cannot be fully comprehended unless the theory of the existence of Intelligences be well understood, and also the method which I adopt in proving their existence. We must, however, first give the following note, which will introduce you into the secrets of this whole subject, both of that which we have already given and of what will yet be given.

Note.—It was not my intention when writing this treatise to expound natural science or discuss metaphysical systems; it was not my object to prove truths which have already been demonstrated, or describe the number and the properties of the spheres: for the books written on these subjects serve their purpose, and if in some points they are not satisfactory, I do not think that what I could say would be better than what has already been explained by others. But my intention was, as has been stated in the Introduction, to expound Biblical passages which have been impugned, and to elucidate their hidden and true sense, which is above the comprehension of the multitude. When you therefore notice that I prove the existence and number of Intelligences or the number of the spheres, with the causes of their motion, or discuss the true relation of matter and form, the meaning of Divine manifestation, or similar subjects, you must not think that I intend merely to establish a certain philosophical proposition; for these subjects have been discussed in many books, and most of them have been demonstrated by proof. I only desire to mention that which might, when well understood, serve as a means of removing some of the doubts concerning anything taught in Scripture; and indeed many difficulties will disappear when that which I am about to explain is taken into consideration. From the Introduction to this treatise you may learn that its principal object is to expound, as far as can be done, the account of the Creation (Gen. i.–iii.), and of the Divine Chariot (Ezek. i.), and to answer questions raised in respect to Prophecy and to the knowledge of God. You will sometimes notice that I am rather explicit on truths already ascertained; some of them Natural Philosophy has established as facts; others Metaphysics has either fully demonstrated, or at least shown to be worthy of belief; others Mathematics have made plain. But you will invariably find that my exposition includes the key for the understanding of some allegorical passage of Holy Writ and its esoteric interpretation, and that I have mentioned, explained, and demonstrated the subject only because it furthers the knowledge of the " Divine Chariot," or " the Creation," or explains some principle with respect to Prophecy, or to the belief in any of the truths taught in Scripture. Now, having made this statement, we return to the subject of which we began to treat.

CHAPTER III

THE theory of Aristotle in respect to the causes of the motion of the spheres led him to assume the existence of Intelligences. Although this theory consists of assertions which cannot be proved, yet it is the least open to doubt, and is more systematic than any other, as has been stated by Alexander in the book called *The Origin of the Universe*. It includes maxims which are identical with those taught in Scripture, and it is to a still greater extent in harmony with doctrines contained in well-known genuine Midrashim, as will be explained by me. For this reason I will cite his views and his proofs, and collect from them what coincides with the teachings of Scripture, and agrees with the doctrine held by our Sages.

CHAPTER IV

THE enunciation that the heavenly sphere is endowed with a soul will appear reasonable to all who sufficiently reflect on it ; but at first thought they may find it unintelligible or even objectionable ; because they wrongly assume that when we ascribe a soul to the heavenly spheres we mean something like the soul of man, or that of an ass, or ox. We merely intend to say that the locomotion of the sphere undoubtedly leads us to assume some inherent principle by which it moves ; and this principle is certainly a soul. For it would be absurd to assume that the principle of the circular motion of the spheres was like that of the rectilinear motion of a stone downward or of fire upwards, for the cause of the latter motion is a natural property and not a soul ; a thing set in motion by a natural property moves only as long as it is away from the proper place of its element, but when it has again arrived there, it comes to rest ; whilst the sphere continues its circular motion in its own place. It is, however, not because the sphere has a soul, that it moves in this manner ; for animate beings move either by instinct or by reason. By " instinct " I mean the intention of an animal to approach something agreeable, or to retreat from something disagreeable ; e.g., to approach the water it seeks because of thirst, or to retreat from the sun because of its heat. It makes no difference whether that thing really exists or is merely imaginary, since the imagination of something agreeable or of something disagreeable likewise causes the animal to move. The heavenly sphere does not move for the purpose of withdrawing from what is bad or approaching what is good. For in the first instance it moves toward the same point from which it has moved away, and *vice versâ* it moves away from the same point towards which it has moved. Secondly, if this were the object of the motion, we should expect that the sphere would move towards a certain point, and would then rest ; for if it moved for the purpose of avoiding something, and never obtained that object, the motion would be in vain. The circular motion of the sphere is consequently due to the action of some idea which produces this particular kind of motion; but as ideas are only possible in intellectual beings, the heavenly sphere is an intellecual being. But even a being that is endowed with the faculty of forming an idea, and possesses a soul with the faculty of moving, does not change its place on each occasion that it forms an idea; for an idea alone does not produce motion, as has been explained in [Aristotle's] Metaphysics. We can easily understand this, when we consider how often we form ideas of certain things, yet do not move towards them, though we are able to do so; it is only when a desire arises for the thing imagined, that we move in order to obtain it. We have thus shown that both the soul, the principle of motion, and the intellect, the source of the ideas, would not produce motion without the existence of a desire for the object of which an idea has been formed. It follows that the heavenly sphere must have a desire for the ideal which it has comprehended, and that ideal, for which it has a desire, is God, exalted be His name! When we say that God moves the spheres, we mean it in the following sense: the spheres have a desire to become similar to the ideal comprehended by them. This ideal, however, is simple in the strictest sense of the word, and not subject to any change or alteration, but constant in producing everything good, whilst the spheres are corporeal; the latter can therefore not be like this ideal in any other way, except in the production of circular motion; for this is the only action of corporeal beings that can be perpetual; it is the most simple motion of a body; there is no change in the essence of the sphere, nor in the beneficial results of its motion.

When Aristotle had arrived at this result, he further investigated the subject, and found, by proof, that there were many spheres, and that all moved in circles, but each with its peculiar motion as regards velocity and direction. He naturally argued that the ideal comprehended by the one sphere, which completes its circuit in one day, is different from that of another sphere which completes its circuit in thirty years; he thus arrived at the conclusion that there were as many ideals as there were spheres; each sphere has a desire for that ideal which is the source of its existence, and that desire is the cause of its individual motion, so that in fact the ideal sets the sphere in motion. Aristotle does not say, nor does any other authority, that there are ten or a hundred ideals; he simply states that their number agrees with that of the spheres. When, therefore, some of his contemporaries held that the number of spheres was fifty, he said, if that was true, the number of ideals must likewise be fifty. For the scholars in his time were few and possessed but imperfect learning; they thought that there must be a separate sphere for each movement, because they did not know that what appear to be several distinct movements can be explained as resulting from the inclination of one sphere as is, e.g., the case with the change in the longitude of a star, its declination and the places of its rising and setting noticed in the circle of the horizon. This point, however, does not concern us at present; let us therefore return to our subject.

The later philosophers assumed ten Intelligences, because they counted the spheres containing stars and the all-encompassing sphere, although some of the spheres included several distinct orbits. There are altogether nine spheres, viz., the all-encompassing sphere, that of the fixed stars, and those of the seven planets; nine Intelligences correspond to the nine spheres;

the tenth Intelligence is the Active Intellect.   The existence of the latter is proved by the transition of our intellect from a state of potentiality to that of actuality, and by the same transition in the case of the forms of all transient beings.   For whatever passes from potentiality into actuality, requires for that transition an external agent of the same kind as itself.   Thus the builder does not build the storehouse in his capacity of workman, but in that of a person that has the form of the storehouse in his mind ; and that form of the building which exists in the mind of the builder caused the transition of the potential form of the storehouse into actuality, and impressed it on the material of the building.   As that which gives form to matter must itself be pure form, so the source of intellect must itself be pure intellect, and this source is the Active Intellect.   The relation of the latter to the elements and their compounds is the same as that of the Intelligences to their respective spheres ;   and our intellect in action, which originates in the Active Intellect, and enables us to comprehend that intellect, finds a parallel in the intellect of each of the spheres which originates in the Intelligence corresponding to that sphere, and enables the sphere to comprehend that Intelligence, to form an idea of it, and to move in seeking to become similar to it.

Aristotle further infers, what has already been explained, that God does not act by means of direct contact.   When, e.g., He destroys anything with fire, the fire is set in motion through the movement of the spheres, and the spheres by the Intelligences ; the latter, which are identical with " the angels," and act by direct influence, are consequently, each in its turn, the cause of the motion of the spheres ; as however, purely spiritual beings do not differ in their essence, and are by no means discrete quantities, he (Aristotle) came to the following conclusion : God created the first Intelligence, the motive agent of the first sphere ; the Intelligence which causes the second sphere to move has its source and origin in the first Intelligence, and so on ; the Intelligence which sets the sphere nearest to the earth in motion is the source and origin of the Active Intellect, the last in the series of purely spiritual beings.   The series of material bodies similarly begins with the uppermost sphere, and ends with the elements and their compounds.   The Intelligence which moves the uppermost sphere cannot be the Absolute Being, for there is an element common to all Intelligences, namely, the property of being the motive agent of a sphere, and there is another element by which each of them is distinguished from the rest ; each of the ten Intelligences includes, therefore, two elements, and consequently another being must be the First Cause.

This is the theory and opinion of Aristotle on these questions, and his proofs, where proof is possible, are given in various works of the Aristotelian school.   In short, he believes that the spheres are animated and intellectual beings, capable of fully comprehending the *principia* of their existence ; that there exist purely spiritual beings (Intelligences), which do not reside in corporeal objects, and which derive existence from God ; and that these form the intermediate element between God and this material world.

In the chapters which follow I will show how far the teaching of Scripture is in harmony with these views, and how far it differs from them.

CHAPTER V

Scripture supports the theory that the spheres are animate and intellectual, i.e., capable of comprehending things ; that they are not, as ignorant persons believe, inanimate masses like fire and earth, but are, as the philosophers assert, endowed with life, and serve their Lord, whom they mightily praise and glorify ; comp. " The heavens declare the glory of God," etc. (Ps. xix. 2). It is a great error to think that this is a mere figure of speech ; for the verbs " to declare " and " to relate," when joined together, are, in Hebrew, only used of intellectual beings. That the Psalmist really means to describe the heavens' own doing, in other words, what the spheres actually do, and not what man thinks of them, may be best inferred from the words, " There is no speech, nor language, their voice is not heard " (ver. 4). Here he clearly shows that he describes the heavens themselves as in reality praising God, and declaring His wonders without words of lip and tongue. When man praises God in words actually uttered, he only relates the ideas which he has conceived, but these ideas form the real praise. The reason why he gives expression to these ideas is to be found in his desire to communicate them to others, or to make himself sure that he has truly conceived them. There- fore it is said, " Commune with your own heart upon your bed, and be still " (Ps. iv. 5). Only ignorant or obstinate persons would refuse to admit this proof taken from Scripture.

As to the opinion of our Sages, I do not see any necessity for expounding or demonstrating it. Consider only the form they gave to the blessing recited on seeing the new moon, the ideas repeatedly occurring in the prayers and the remarks in the Midrash on the following and similar passages :— " And the host of heaven worshippeth thee " (Neh. ix. 6) ; " When the morning stars sang together, and all the sons of God shouted for joy " (Job xxxviii. 7). In *Bereshit Rabba*, on the passage—" And the earth was empty and formless " (Gen. i. 2), our Sages remark as follows : " The words *tohu* and *bohu* mean mourning and crying ; the earth mourned and cried on account of her evil lot, saying, ' I and the heavens were created together, and yet the beings above live for ever, and we are mortal.' " Our Sages, by this remark, indicate their belief that the spheres are animated beings, and not inanimate matter like the elements.

The opinion of Aristotle, that the spheres are capable of comprehension and conception, is in accordance with the words of our prophets and our theologians or Sages. The philosophers further agree that this world below is governed by influences emanating from the spheres, and that the latter comprehend and have knowledge of the things which they influence. This theory is also met with in Scripture ; comp. [the stars and all the host of heaven] " which the Lord thy God hath divided unto all nations " (Deut. iv. 19), that is to say, the stars, which God appointed to be the means of governing His creatures, and not the objects of man's worship. It has there- fore been stated clearly : " And to rule over the day and over the night " (Gen. i. 18). The term " ruling " here refers to the power which the spheres possess of governing the earth, in addition to the property of giving light and darkness. The latter property is the direct cause of genesis and destruction ; it is described in the words, " And to divide the light from the darkness " (*ibid.*). It is impossible to assume that those who rule a thing are ignorant of that very thing which they rule, if we take " to rule " in its proper sense. We will add another chapter on this subject.

CHAPTER VI

As for the existence of angels, there is no necessity to cite any proof from Scripture, where the fact is frequently mentioned. The term *elohim* signifies " judges " ; comp. " The cause of both parties shall come before the ' judges ' " (*ha-elohim* ; Exod. xxii. 8). It has been figuratively applied to angels, and to the Creator as being Judge over the angels. When God says, " I am the Lord your God," the pronoun " your " refers to all mankind; but in the phrase *elohe ha-elohim,* He is described as the God of the angels, and in *adone ha-adonim,* as the Lord of the spheres and the stars, which are the masters of the rest of the corporeal creation. The nouns *elohim* and *adonim* in these phrases do not refer to human judges or masters, because these are in rank inferior to the heavenly bodies ; much less do they refer to mankind in general, including masters and servants, or to objects of stone and wood worshipped by some as gods ; for it is no honour or greatness to God to be superior to stone, wood, or a piece of metal. The phrases therefore admit of no other meaning than this : God is the Judge over the judges ; i.e., over the angels, and the Lord over the spheres.

We have already stated above that the angels are incorporeal. This agrees with the opinion of Aristotle : there is only this difference in the names employed—he uses the term " Intelligences," and we say instead " angels." His theory is that the Intelligences are intermediate beings between the Prime Cause and existing things, and that they effect the motion of the spheres, on which motion the existence of all things depends. This is also the view we meet with in all parts of Scripture ; every act of God is described as being performed by angels. But " angel " means " messenger " ; hence every one that is intrusted with a certain mission is an angel. Even the movements of the brute creation are sometimes due to the action of an angel, when such movements serve the purpose of the Creator, who endowed it with the power of performing that movement ; e.g., " God hath sent His angel, and hath shut the lions' mouths that they have not hurt me " (Dan. vi. 22). Another instance may be seen in the movements of Balaam's ass, described as caused by an angel. The elements are also called angels. Comp. " Who maketh winds His angels, flaming fire His ministers " (Ps. civ. 4). There is no doubt that the word " angel " is used of a messenger sent by man ; e.g., " And Jacob sent angels " (Gen. xxxii. 4) ; of a prophet, e.g., " And an angel of the Lord came up from Gilgal to Bochim " (Judges ii. 1) ; " And He sent an angel, and hath brought us out of Egypt " (Num. xx. 16). It is also used of ideals, perceived by prophets in prophetic visions, and of man's animal powers, as will be explained in another place.

When we assert that Scripture teaches that God rules this world through angels, we mean such angels as are identical with the Intelligences. In some passages the plural is used of God, e.g., " Let us make man in our image " (Gen. i. 26) ; " Go to, let us go down, and there confound their language " (*ibid.* xi. 7). Our Sages explain this in the following manner : God, as it were, does nothing without contemplating the host above. I wonder at the

expression " contemplating," which is the very expression used by Plato :
God, as it were, " contemplates the world of ideals, and thus produces the
existing beings." In other passages our Sages expressed it more decidedly :
" God does nothing without consulting the host above " (the word *familia*,
used in the original, is a Greek noun, and signifies " host "). On the words,
" what they have already made " (Eccles. ii. 12), the following remark is
made in *Bereshit Rabba* and in *Midrash Koheleth* : " It is not said ' what
He has made,' but ' what they have made ' ; hence we infer that He, as it
were, with His court, have agreed upon the form of each of the limbs of man
before placing it in its position, as it is said, ' He hath made thee and established thee ' " (Deut. xxxii. 6). In *Bereshit Rabba* (chap. li.) it is also stated,
that wherever the term " *and* the Lord " occurred in Scripture, the Lord
with His court is to be understood. These passages do not convey the idea
that God spoke, thought, reflected, or that He consulted and employed the
opinion of other beings, as ignorant persons have believed. How could the
Creator be assisted by those whom He created ! They only show that all
parts of the Universe, even the limbs of animals in their actual form, are produced through angels ; for natural forces and angels are identical. How
bad and injurious is the blindness of ignorance ! Say to a person who is
believed to belong to the wise men of Israel that the Almighty sends His
angel to enter the womb of a woman and to form there the fœtus, he will be
satisfied with the account ; he will believe it, and even find in it a description
of the greatness of God's might and wisdom ; although he believes that the
angel consists of burning fire, and is as big as a third part of the Universe, yet
he considers it possible as a divine miracle. But tell him that God gave the
seed a formative power which produces and shapes the limbs, and that this
power is called " angel," or that all forms are the result of the influence of
the Active Intellect, and that the latter is the angel, the Prince of the world,
frequently mentioned by our Sages, and he will turn away ; because he cannot comprehend the true greatness and power of creating forces that act in
a body without being perceived by our senses. Our Sages have already
stated—for him who has understanding—that all forces that reside in a body
are angels, much more the forces that are active in the Universe. The theory
that each force acts only in one particular way, is expressed in *Bereshit Rabba*
(chap. l.) as follows : " One angel does not perform two things, and two
angels do not perform one thing " ; this is exactly the property of all forces.
We may find a confirmation of the opinion that the natural and psychical
forces of an individual are called angels in a statement of our Sages which is
frequently quoted, and occurs originally in *Bereshit Rabba* (chap. lxxviii.) :
" Every day God creates a legion of angels ; they sing before Him, and disappear." When, in opposition to this statement, other statements were quoted
to the effect that angels are eternal—and, in fact, it has repeatedly been shown
that they live permanently—the reply has been given that some angels live
permanently, others perish ; and this is really the case ; for individual forces
are transient, whilst the genera are permanent and imperishable. Again, we
read (in *Bereshit Rabba*, chap. lxxxv.), in reference to the relation between
Judah and Tamar : " R. Jochanan said that Judah was about to pass by
[without noticing Tamar], but God caused the angel of lust, i.e., the libidi-
nous disposition, to present himself to him." Man's disposition is here called

an angel. Likewise we frequently meet with the phrase " the angel set over a certain thing." In Midrash-Koheleth (on Eccles. x. 7) the following passage occurs : " When man sleeps, his soul speaks to the angel, the angel to the cherub." The intelligent reader will find here a clear statement that man's imaginative faculty is also called " angel," and that " cherub " is used for man's intellectual faculty. How beautiful must this appear to him who understands it ; how absurd to the ignorant !

We have already stated that the forms in which angels appear form part of the prophetic vision. Some prophets see angels in the form of man, e.g., " And behold three men stood by him " (Gen. xviii. 2) ; others perceive an angel as a fearful and terrible being, e.g., " And his countenance was as the countenance of an angel of God, very terrible " (Judges xiii. 6) ; others see them as fire, e.g., " And the angel of the Lord appeared to him in a flame of fire " (Exod. iii. 2). In *Bereshit Rabba* (chap. l.) the following remark occurs : " To Abraham, whose prophetic power was great, the angels appeared in the form of men ; to Lot, whose power was weak, they appeared as angels." This is an important principle as regards Prophecy ; it will be fully discussed when we treat of that subject (chap. xxxii. *sqq.*). Another passage in *Bereshit Rabba* (*ibid.*) runs thus : " Before the angels have accomplished their task they are called men, when they have accomplished it they are angels." Consider how clearly they say that the term " angel " signifies nothing but a certain action, and that every appearance of an angel is part of a prophetic vision, depending on the capacity of the person that perceives it.

There is nothing in the opinion of Aristotle on this subject contrary to the teaching of Scripture. The whole difference between him and ourselves is this : he believes all these beings to be eternal, co-existing with the First Cause as its necessary effect ; but we believe that they have had a beginning, that God created the Intelligences, and gave the spheres the capacity of seeking to become like them ; that in creating the Intelligences and the spheres, He endowed them with their governing powers. In this point we differ from him.

In the course of this treatise we shall give his theory as well as the theory of *Creatio ex nihilo* taught in Scripture.

CHAPTER VII

WE have already explained that the term " angel " is a homonym, and is used of the intellectual beings, the spheres, and the elements ; for all these are engaged in performing a divine command. But do not imagine that the Intelligences and the spheres are like other forces which reside in bodies and act by the laws of nature without being conscious of what they do. The spheres and the Intelligences are conscious of their actions, and select by their own free will the objects of their influence, although not in the same manner as we exercise free will and rule over other things, which only concern temporary beings. I have been led to adopt this theory by certain passages in Scripture ; e.g., an angel says to Lot : " For I cannot do anything," etc. (Gen. xix. 21) ; and telling him to deliver himself, the angel says : " Behold I have accepted thee concerning this thing " (ver. 21).

Again : " Take heed before him, and listen to his voice," etc. (Exod. xxiii. 21). These passages show that angels are conscious of what they do, and have free will in the sphere of action intrusted to them, just as we have free will within our province, and in accordance with the power given to us with our very existence. The difference is that what we do is the lowest stage of excellence, and that our influence and actions are preceded by non-action ; whilst the Intelligences and the spheres always perform that which is good, they contain nothing except what is good and perfect, as will be shown further on, and they have continually been active from the beginning.

CHAPTER VIII

IT is one of the ancient beliefs, both among the philosophers and other people, that the motions of the spheres produced mighty and fearful sounds. They observed how little objects produced by rapid motion a loud, shrilling, and terrifying noise, and concluded that this must to a far higher degree be the case with the bodies of the sun, the moon and the stars, considering their greatness and their velocity. The Pythagoreans believed that the sounds were pleasant, and, though loud, had the same proportions to each other as the musical notes. They also explained why these mighty and tremendous sounds are not heard by us. This belief is also widespread in our nation. Thus our Sages describe the greatness of the sound produced by the sun in the daily circuit in its orbit. The same description could be given of all heavenly bodies. Aristotle, however, rejects this, and holds that they produce no sounds. You will find his opinion in the book *The Heavens and the World* (De Cœlo). You must not find it strange that Aristotle differs here from the opinion of our Sages. The theory of the music of the spheres is connected with the theory of the motion of the stars in a fixed sphere, and our Sages have, in this astronomical question, abandoned their own theory in favour of the theory of others. Thus, it is distinctly stated, " The wise men of other nations have defeated the wise men of Israel." It is quite right that our Sages have abandoned their own theory ; for speculative matters every one treats according to the results of his own study, and every one accepts that which appears to him established by proof.

CHAPTER IX

WE have stated above that in the age of Aristotle the number of spheres was not accurately known ; and that those who at present count nine spheres consider a sphere containing several rotating circles as one, a fact well known to all who have a knowledge of astronomy. We need, therefore, not reject the opinion of those who assume two spheres in accordance with the words of Scripture : " Behold the heaven and the heaven of heavens are the Lord's " (Deut. x. 14). They reckon all the spheres with stars, i.e., with all the circles in which the stars move, as one ; the all-encompassing sphere in which there are no stars, is regarded by them as the second ; hence they maintain that there are two spheres.

I will here introduce an explanation which is necessary for the understanding of our view on the present subject. There is a difference among ancient astronomers whether the spheres of Mercury and Venus are above or below the sun, because no proof can be given for the position of these two spheres. At first it was generally assumed that they were above the sun— note this well ; later on Ptolemy maintained that they were below the sun ; because he believed that in this manner the whole arrangement of the spheres would be most reasonable ; the sun would be in the middle, having three stars below and three above itself. More recently some Andalusian scholars concluded, from certain principles laid down by Ptolemy, that Venus and Mercury were above the sun. Ibn Aflaḥ of Seville, with whose son I was acquainted, has written a famous book on the subject ; also the excellent philosopher Abu-Bekr ibn-Alzaig, one of whose pupils was my fellow-student, has treated of this subject and offered certain proofs—which we have copied —of the improbability of Venus and Mercury being above the sun. The proofs given by Abu-Bekr show only the improbability, not the impossibility. In short, whether it be so or not, the ancients placed Venus and Mercury above the sun, and had, therefore, the following five spheres : that of the moon, which is undoubtedly the nearest to us ; that of the sun, which is, of course, above the former ; then that of the five planets, the sphere of the fixed stars, and the outermost sphere, which does not contain any star. Consequently there are four spheres containing figures, i.e., stars, which were called figures by the ancients in their well-known works—viz., the spheres of the fixed stars, of the five planets, of the sun, and of the moon ; above these there is one sphere which is empty, without any star. This number is for me of great importance in respect to an idea which none of the philosophers clearly stated, though I was led to it by various utterances of the philosophers and of our Sages. I will now state the idea and expound it.

CHAPTER X

It is a well-known fact that the philosophers, when they discuss in their works the order of the Universe, assume that the existing order of things in this sublunary world of transient beings depends on forces which emanate from the spheres. We have mentioned this several times. In like manner our Sages say, " There is no single herb below without its corresponding star above, that beats upon it and commands it to grow." Comp. " Knowest thou the ordinances of heaven ? Canst thou set the dominion thereof in the earth ? " (Job xxxviii. 33). The term mazzal, literally meaning a constellation in the Zodiac, is also used of every star, as may be in- ferred from the following passage in the beginning of Bereshit Rabba (chap. x.) : " While one star (mazzal) completes its circuit in thirty days, another completes it in thirty years." They have thus clearly expressed it, that even each individual being in this world has its corresponding star. Although the influences of the spheres extend over all beings, there is besides the influence of a particular star directed to each particular species ; a fact noticed also in reference to the several forces in one organic body ; for the whole Universe is like one organic body, as we have stated above. Thus the philosophers speak of the peculiar influence of the moon on the particular element water. That this is the case is proved by the increase and decrease of the water in the seas and rivers according to the increase and decrease of the moon ; also by the rising and the falling of the seas according to the advance or return of the moon, i.e., her ascending and her descending in the several quarters of her course. This is clear to every one who has directed his attention to these phenomena. The influence of the sun's rays upon fire may easily be noticed in the increase of heat or cold on earth, according as the sun approaches the earth or recedes or is concealed from it. All this is so clear that I need not explain it further. Now it occurred to my mind that the four spheres which contain stars exercise influence upon all beings on earth that come into existence, and, in fact, are the cause of their existence ; but each of the four spheres is the exclusive source of the properties of one only of the four elements, and becomes by its own motion the cause of the motion and changes of that element. Thus water is set in motion by the moon-sphere, fire by the sun-sphere, air by the other planets, which move in many and different courses with retrogressions, progressions, and stations, and therefore produce the various forms of the air with its frequent changes, contractions, and expansions ; the sphere of the other stars, namely, the fixed stars, sets earth in motion ; and it may be that on this account, viz., on account of the slow motion of the fixed stars, earth is but slowly set in motion to change and to combine with other elements. The particular influence which the fixed stars exercise upon earth is implied in the saying of our Sages, that the number of the species of plants is the same as that of the individuals included in the general term " stars."

The arrangement of the Universe may therefore be assumed to be as follows : there are four spheres, four elements set in motion by them, and also four principal properties which earthly beings derive from them, as has been stated above. Furthermore, there are four causes of the motion of every sphere, namely, the following four essential elements in the sphere ; its spherical shape, its soul, its intellect, by which the sphere is capable of forming ideas, and the Intelligence, which the sphere desires to imitate. Note this well. The explanation of what I said is this : the sphere could not have been continuously in motion, had it not this peculiar form ; continuity of motion is only possible when the motion is circular. Rectilinear motion, even if frequently repeated in the same moment, cannot be continuous ; for when a body moves successively in two opposite directions, it must pass through a moment of rest, as has been demonstrated in its proper place. The necessity of a continuous motion constantly repeated in the same path implies the necessity of a circular form. The spheres must have a soul ; for only animate beings can move freely. There must be some cause for the motion, and as it does not consist in the fear of that which is injurious, or the desire of that which is profitable, it must be found in the notion which the spheres form of a certain being, and in the desire to approach that being. This formation of a notion demands, in the first place, that the spheres possess intellect ; it demands further that something exists which corresponds to that notion, and which the spheres desire to approach. These are the four causes of the motion of the spheres. The following are the four principal forces directly derived from the spheres : the nature of minerals, the properties peculiar to plants, the animal faculties, and the intellect. An examination of these forces shows that they have two functions, namely, to produce things and to perpetuate them ; that is to say, to preserve the species perpetually, and the individuals in each species for a certain time. These are also the functions ascribed to Nature, which is said to be wise, to govern the Universe, to provide, as it were, by plan for the production of living beings, and to provide also for their preservation and perpetuation. Nature creates formative faculties, which are the cause of the production of living beings, and nutritive faculties as the source of their temporal existence and preservation. It may be that by Nature the Divine Will is meant, which is the origin of these two kinds of faculties through the medium of the spheres.

As to the number four, it is strange, and demands our attention. In *Midrash Tanḥuma* the following passage occurs : " How many steps were in Jacob's ladder ?—Four." The question refers to the verse, " And behold a ladder set upon the earth," etc. (Gen. xxviii. 12). In all the Midrashim it is stated that there were four hosts of angels ; this statement is frequently repeated. Some read in the above passage : " How many steps were in the ladder ?—Seven." But all readings and all Midrashim unanimously express that the angels whom Jacob saw ascending the ladder, and descending, were only four ; two of whom were going up and two coming down. These four angels, the two that went up and the two that came down, occupied one step of the ladder, standing in one line. Hence it has been inferred that the breadth of the ladder in this vision was four-thirds of the world. For the breadth of an angel in a prophetic vision is equal to one-third of the world ; comp. " And his body was like *tarshish* (two-sixths) " (Dan. x. 6) ; the four angels therefore occupied four-thirds of the world.—Zechariah, in describing the allegorical vision of " the four chariots that came out from between two mountains, which mountains were mountains of brass " (Zech. vi. 1), adds the explanation, " These are the four spirits of the heavens which go forth from standing before the Lord of all the earth" (*ibid.* ver. 5). By these four spirits the causes are meant which produce all changes in the Universe. The term " brass " (*neḥoshet*), employed here, and the phrase " burnished brass " (*neḥoshet kalal*), used by Ezekiel (i. 7), are to some extent homonymous, and will be discussed further on.

The saying of our Sages, that the angel is as broad as the third part of the Universe, or, in the words of *Bereshit Rabba* (chap. x.), that the angel is the third part of the world, is quite clear ; we have already explained it in our large work on the Holy Law. The whole creation consists of three parts, (1) the pure intelligences, or angels ; (2) the bodies of the spheres ; and (3) the *materia prima*, or the bodies which are below the spheres, and are subject to constant change.

In this manner may those understand the dark sayings of the prophets who desire to understand them, who awake from the sleep of forgetfulness, deliver themselves from the sea of ignorance, and raise themselves upward nearer the higher beings. But those who prefer to swim in the waters of their ignorance, and to " go down very low," need not exert the body or heart ; they need only cease to move, and they will go down by the law of nature. Note and consider well all we have said.

CHAPTER XI

WHEN a simple mathematician reads and studies these astronomical discussions, he believes that the form and the number of the spheres are facts established by proof. But this is not the case ; for the science of astronomy does not aim at demonstrating them, although it includes subjects that can be proved ; e.g., it has been proved that the path of the sun is inclined against the equator ; this cannot be doubted. But it has not yet been decided whether the sphere of the sun is excentric or contains a revolving epicycle, and the astronomer does not take notice of this uncertainty, for his object is simply to find an hypothesis that would lead to a uniform and circular motion of the stars without acceleration, retardation, or change, and which is in its effects in accordance with observation. He will, besides, endeavour to find such an hypothesis which would require the least complicated motion and the least number of spheres ; he will therefore prefer an hypothesis which would explain all the phenomena of the stars by means of three spheres to an hypothesis which would require four spheres. From this reason we adopt, in reference to the circuit of the sun, the theory of excentricity, and reject the epicyclic revolution assumed by Ptolemy. When we therefore perceive that all fixed stars move in the same way uniformly, without the least difference, we conclude that they are all in one sphere. It is, however, not impossible that the stars should have each its own sphere, with a separate centre, and yet move in the same way. If this theory be accepted, a number of Intelligences must be assumed, equal to that of the stars, and therefore Scripture says in reference to them, " Is there any number of his armies ? " (Job xxv. 3) ; for the Intelligences, the heavenly bodies, and the natural forces, are called the armies of God. Nevertheless the species of the stars can be numbered, and therefore we would still be justified in counting the spheres of the fixed stars collectively as one, just as the five spheres of the planets, together with the numerous spheres they contain, are regarded by us as one. Our object in adopting this number is, as you have noticed, to divide the influences which we can trace in the Universe according to their general character, without desiring to fix the number of the Intelligences and the spheres. All we wish to point out is this : in the first place, that the whole Creation is divided into three parts, viz. (1) the pure Intelligences ; (2) the bodies of the spheres endowed with permanent forms—(the forms of these bodies do not pass from one substratum to another, nor do their substrata undergo any change whatever) ; and (3) the transient earthly beings, all of which consist of the same substance. Furthermore, we desire to show that the ruling power emanates from the Creator, and is received by the Intelligences according to their order ; from the Intelligences part of the good and the light bestowed upon them is communicated to the spheres, and the latter, being in possession of the abundance obtained of the Intelligences, transmit forces and properties unto the beings of this transient world. We must, however, add that the part which benefits the part below it in the order described does not exist for the sole purpose of producing that benefit. For if this were the case it would lead to the paradox that the higher, better, and nobler beings existed for the sake of beings lower in rank, whilst in reality the object should be of greater importance than the means applied for attaining it. No intelligent person will admit that this is possible. The nature of the influence which one part of the Creation exercises upon another must be explained as follows : A thing perfect in a certain way is either perfect only in itself, without being able to communicate that perfection to another being, or it is so perfect that it is capable of imparting perfection to another being. A person may possess wealth sufficient for his own wants without being able to spare anything for another, or he may have wealth enough to benefit also other people, or even to enrich them to such an extent as would enable them to give part of their property to others. In the same manner the creative act of the Almighty in giving existence to pure Intelligences endows the first of them with the power of giving existence to another, and so on, down to the Active Intellect, the lowest of the purely spiritual beings. Besides producing other Intelligences, each Intelligence gives existence to one of the spheres, from the highest down to the lowest, which is the sphere of the moon. After the latter follows this transient world, i.e., the *materia prima*, and all that has been formed of it. In this manner the elements receive certain properties from each sphere, and a succession of genesis and destruction is produced.

We have already mentioned that these theories are not opposed to anything taught by our Prophets or by our Sages. Our nation is wise and perfect, as has been declared by the Most High, through Moses, who made us perfect : " Surely this great nation is a wise and understanding people " (Deut. iv. 6). But when wicked barbarians have deprived us of our possessions, put an end to our science and literature, and killed our wise men, we have become ignorant ; this has been foretold by the prophets, when they pronounced the punishment for our sins : " The wisdom of their wise men shall perish, and the understanding of their prudent men shall be hid " (Isa. xxix. 14). We are mixed up with other nations ; we have learnt their opinions, and followed their ways and acts. The Psalmist, deploring this imitation of the actions of other nations, says, " They were mingled among the nations, and learned their works " (Ps. cvi. 35). Isaiah likewise complains that the Israelites adopted the opinions of their neighbours, and says, " And they please themselves in the children of strangers " (Isa. ii. 6) ; or, according to the Aramaic version of Jonathan, son of Uzziel, " And they walk in the ways of the nations." Having been brought up among persons untrained in philosophy, we are inclined to consider these philosophical opinions as foreign to our religion, just as uneducated persons find them foreign to their own notions. But, in fact, it is not so.

Since we have repeatedly spoken of the influence emanating from God and the Intelligences, we will now proceed to explain what is the true meaning of this influence, and after that I will discuss the theory of the Creation.

CHAPTER XII

It is clear that whenever a thing is produced, an efficient cause must exist for the production of the thing that has not existed previously. This immediate efficient cause is either corporeal or incorporeal ; if corporeal, it is not the efficient cause on account of its corporeality, but on account of its being an individual corporeal object, and therefore by means of its form. I will speak of this subject later on. The immediate efficient cause of a thing may again be the effect of some cause, and so on, but not *ad infinitum*. The series of causes for a certain product must necessarily conclude with a First Cause, which is the true cause of that product, and whose existence is not due to another cause. The question remains, Why has this thing been produced now and not long before, since the cause has always been in existence ? The answer is, that a certain relation between cause and product has been absent, if the cause be corporeal ; or, that the substance has not been sufficiently prepared, if the cause be incorporeal. All this is in accordance with the teachings of natural science. We ignore for the present the question whether to assume the Eternity of the Universe, or the *Creatio ex nihilo*. We do not intend to discuss the question here.

In Physics it has been shown that a body in acting upon another body must either directly be in contact with it, or indirectly through the medium of other bodies. E.g., a body that has been heated has been in contact with fire, or the air that surrounds the body has been heated by the fire, and has communicated the heat to the body ; the immediate cause of the heat in this body is the corporeal substance of the heated air. The magnet attracts iron from a distance through a certain force communicated to the air round the iron. The magnet does therefore not act at all distances, just as fire does not act at every distance, but only as long as the air between the fire and the object is affected by the fire. When the air is no longer affected by the fire which is under a piece of wax, the latter does not melt. The same is the case with magnetism. When an object that has previously not been warm has now become warm, the cause of its heat must now have been created ; either some fire has been produced, or the distance of the fire from the object has been changed, and the altered relation between the fire and the object is the cause now created. In a similar manner we find the causes of all changes in the Universe to be changes in the combination of the elements that act upon each other when one body approaches another or separates from it. There are, however, changes which are not connected with the combination of the elements, but concern only the forms of the things ; they require likewise an efficient cause ; there must exist a force that produces the various forms. This cause is incorporeal, for that which produces form must itself be abstract form, as has been shown in its proper place. I have also indicated the proof of this theorem in previous chapters. The following may, in addition, serve to illustrate it : All combinations of the elements are subject to increase and decrease, and this change takes place gradually. It is different with forms ; they do not change gradually, and are therefore without motion ; they appear and disappear instantaneously, and are consequently not the result of the combination of corporeal elements. This combination merely prepares matter for receiving a certain form. The efficient cause which produces the form is indivisible, because it is of the same kind as the thing produced. Hence it may be concluded that the agent that has produced a certain form, or given it to a certain substance, must itself be an abstract form. The action of this incorporeal agent cannot depend on a certain relation to the corporeal product ; being incorporeal, it cannot approach a body, or recede from it ; nor can a body approach the incorporeal agent, or recede from it, because there is no relation of distance between corporeal and incorporeal beings. The reason why the action has not taken place before must be sought in the circumstance that the substance has not been prepared for the action of the abstract form.

It is now clear that the action of bodies upon each other, according to their forms, prepares the substance for receiving the action of an incorporeal being, or Form. The existence of actions of purely incorporeal beings, in every case of change that does not originate in the mere combination of elements, is now firmly established. These actions do not depend on impact, or on a certain distance. They are termed "influence" (or "emanation"), on account of their similarity to a water-spring. The latter sends forth water in all directions, has no peculiar side for receiving or spending its contents; it springs forth on all sides, and continually waters both neighbouring and distant places. In a similar manner incorporeal beings, in receiving power and imparting it to others, are not limited to a particular side, distance, or time. They act continually; and whenever an object is sufficiently prepared, it receives the effect of that continuous action, called "influence" (or "emanation"). God being incorporeal, and everything being the work of Him as the efficient cause, we say that the Universe has been created by the Divine influence, and that all changes in the Universe emanate from Him. In the same sense we say that He caused wisdom to emanate from Him and to come upon the prophets. In all such cases we merely wish to express that an incorporeal Being, whose action we call "influence," has produced a certain effect. The term "influence" has been considered applicable to the Creator on account of the similarity between His actions and those of a spring. There is no better way of describing the action of an incorporeal being than by this analogy; and no term can be found that would accurately describe it. For it is as difficult to form an idea of that action as to form an idea of the incorporeal being itself. As we imagine only bodies or forces residing in bodies, so we only imagine actions possible when the agent is near, at a certain distance, and on a particular side. There are therefore persons who, on learning that God is incorporeal, or that He does not approach the object of His action, believe that He gives commands to angels, and that the latter carry them out by approach or direct contact, as is the case when we produce something. These persons thus imagine also the angels as bodies. Some of them, further, believe that God commands an action in words consisting, like ours, of letters and sound, and that thereby the action is done. All this is the work of the imagination, which is, in fact, identical with "evil inclination." For all our defects in speech or in character are either the direct or the indirect work of imagination. This is not the subject of the present chapter, in which we only intended to explain the term "influence" in so far as it is applied to incorporeal beings, namely, to God and to the Intelligences or angels. But the term is also applied to the forces of the spheres in their effects upon the earth; and we speak of the "influence" of the spheres, although the spheres are corporeal, and the stars, being corporeal, only act at certain distances, i.e., at a smaller or a greater distance from the centre, or at a definite distance from each other, a circumstance which led to Astrology.

As to our assertion that Scripture applies the notion of "influence" to God, compare "They have forsaken me, the fountain of living waters" (Jer. ii. 13), i.e., the Divine influence that gives life or existence, for the two are undoubtedly identical. Further, "For with Thee is the fountain of life" (Ps. xxxvi. 10), i.e., the Divine influence that gives existence. The concluding words of this verse, " in Thy light we see light," express exactly what we said, namely, that by the influence of the intellect which emanates from God we become wise, by it we are guided and enabled to comprehend the Active Intellect. Note this.

CHAPTER XIII

AMONG those who believe in the existence of God, there are found three different theories as regards the question whether the Universe is eternal or not.

First Theory.—Those who follow the Law of Moses, our Teacher, hold that the whole Universe, i.e., everything except God, has been brought by Him into existence out of non-existence. In the beginning God alone existed, and nothing else; neither angels, nor spheres, nor the things that are contained within the spheres existed. He then produced from nothing all existing things such as they are, by His will and desire. Even time itself is among the things created; for time depends on motion, i.e., on an accident in things which move, and the things upon whose motion time depends are themselves created beings, which have passed from non-existence into existence. We say that God *existed* before the creation of the Universe, although the verb *existed* appears to imply the notion of time; we also believe that He existed an infinite space of time before the Universe was created; but in these cases we do not mean time in its true sense. We only use the term to signify something analogous or similar to time. For time is undoubtedly an accident, and, according to our opinion, one of the created accidents, like blackness and whiteness; it is not a quality, but an accident connected with motion. This must be clear to all who understand what Aristotle has said on time and its real existence.

The following remark does not form an essential part of our present research; it will nevertheless be found useful in the course of this discussion. Many scholars do not know what time really is, and men like Galen were so perplexed about it that they asked whether time has a real existence or not; the reason for this uncertainty is to be found in the circumstance that time is an accident of an accident. Accidents which are directly connected with material bodies, e.g., colour and taste, are easily understood, and correct notions are formed of them. There are, however, accidents which are connected with other accidents, e.g., the splendour of colour, or the inclination and the curvature of a line; of these it is very difficult to form a correct notion, especially when the accident which forms the substratum for the other accident is not constant but variable. Both difficulties are present in the notion of time: it is an accident of motion, which is itself an accident of a moving object; besides, it is not a fixed property; on the contrary, its true and essential condition is, not to remain in the same state for two consecutive moments. This is the source of ignorance about the nature of time.

We consider time a thing created; it comes into existence in the same manner as other accidents, and the substances which form the substratum for the accidents. For this reason, viz., because time belongs to the things created, it cannot be said that God produced the Universe *in the beginning*.

Consider this well; for he who does not understand it is unable to refute forcible objections raised against the theory of *Creatio ex nihilo*. If you admit the existence of time before the Creation, you will be compelled to accept the theory of the Eternity of the Universe. For time is an accident and requires a substratum. You will therefore have to assume that something [beside God] existed before this Universe was created, an assumption which it is our duty to oppose.

This is the first theory, and it is undoubtedly a fundamental principle of the Law of our teacher Moses; it is next in importance to the principle of God's unity. Do not follow any other theory. Abraham, our father, was the first that taught it, after he had established it by philosophical research. He proclaimed, therefore, " the name of the Lord the God of the Universe " (Gen. xxi. 33); and he had previously expressed this theory in the words, " The Possessor of heaven and earth " (*ibid.* xiv. 22).

Second Theory.—The theory of all philosophers whose opinions and works are known to us is this: It is impossible to assume that God produced anything from nothing, or that He reduces anything to nothing; that is to say, it is impossible that an object consisting of matter and form should be produced when that matter is absolutely absent, or that it should be destroyed in such a manner that that matter be absolutely no longer in existence. To say of God that He can produce a thing from nothing or reduce a thing to nothing is, according to the opinion of these philosophers, the same as if we were to say that He could cause one substance to have at the same time two opposite properties, or produce another being like Himself, or change Himself into a body, or produce a square the diagonal of which be equal to its side, or similar impossibilities. The philosophers thus believe that it is no defect in the Supreme Being that He does not produce impossibilities, for the nature of that which is impossible is constant—it does not depend on the action of an agent, and for this reason it cannot be changed, Similarly there is, according to them, no defect in the greatness of God, when He is unable to produce a thing from nothing, because they consider this as one of the impossibilities. They therefore assume that a certain substance has co-existed with God from eternity in such a manner that neither God existed without that substance nor the latter without God. But they do not hold that the existence of that substance equals in rank that of God; for God is the cause of that existence, and the substance is in the same relation to God as the clay is to the potter, or the iron to the smith; God can do with it what He pleases; at one time He forms of it heaven and earth, at another time He forms some other thing. Those who hold this view also assume that the heavens are transient, that they came into existence, though not from nothing, and may cease to exist, although they cannot be reduced to nothing. They are transient in the same manner as the individuals among living beings which are produced from some existing substance, and are again reduced to some substance that remains in existence. The process of genesis and destruction is, in the case of the heavens, the same as in that of earthly beings.

The followers of this theory are divided into different schools, whose opinions and principles it is useless to discuss here; but what I have mentioned is common to all of them. Plato holds the same opinion. Aristotle says in his *Physics*, that according to Plato the heavens are transient. This view is also stated in Plato's *Timæus*. His opinion, however, does not agree with our belief; only superficial and careless persons wrongly assume that Plato has the same belief as we have. For whilst we hold that the heavens have been created from absolutely nothing, Plato believes that they have been formed out of something.—This is the second theory.

Third Theory.—viz., that of Aristotle, his followers, and commentators. Aristotle maintains, like the adherents of the second theory, that a corporeal object cannot be produced without a corporeal substance. He goes, however, farther, and contends that the heavens are indestructible. For he holds that the Universe in its totality has never been different, nor will it ever change : the heavens, which form the permanent element in the Universe, and are not subject to genesis and destruction, have always been so ; time and motion are eternal, permanent, and have neither beginning nor end ; the sublunary world, which includes the transient elements, has always been the same, because the *materia prima* is itself eternal, and merely combines successively with different forms ; when one form is removed, another is assumed. This whole arrangement, therefore, both above and here below, is never disturbed or interrupted, and nothing is produced contrary to the laws or the ordinary course of Nature. He further says—though not in the same terms—that he considers it impossible for God to change His will or conceive a new desire ; that God produced this Universe in its totality by His will, but not from nothing. Aristotle finds it as impossible to assume that God changes His will or conceives a new desire, as to believe that He is non-existing, or that His essence is changeable. Hence it follows that this Universe has always been the same in the past, and will be the same eternally.

This is a full account of the opinions of those who consider that the existence of God, the First Cause of the Universe, has been established by proof. But it would be quite useless to mention the opinions of those who do not recognize the existence of God, but believe that the existing state of things is the result of accidental combination and separation of the elements, and that the Universe has no Ruler or Governor. Such is the theory of Epicurus and his school, and similar philosophers, as stated by Alexander [Aphrodisiensis] ; it would be superfluous to repeat their views, since the existence of God has been demonstrated whilst their theory is built upon a basis proved to be untenable. It is likewise useless to prove the correctness of the followers of the second theory in asserting that the heavens are transient, because they at the same time believe in the Eternity of the Universe, and so long as this theory is adopted, it makes no difference to us whether it is believed that the heavens are transient, and that only their substance is eternal, or the heavens are held to be indestructible, in accordance with the view of Aristotle. All who follow the Law of Moses, our Teacher, and Abraham, our Father, and all who adopt similar theories, assume that nothing is eternal except God, and that the theory of *Creatio ex nihilo* includes nothing that is impossible, whilst some thinkers even regard it as an established truth.

After having described the different theories, I will now proceed to show how Aristotle proved his theory, and what induced him to adopt it.

CHAPTER XIV

IT is not necessary to repeat in every chapter that I write this treatise with the full knowledge of what you have studied ; that I therefore need not quote the exact words of the philosophers ; it will suffice to give an abstract of their views. I will, however, point out the methods which they employ, in the same manner as I have done when I discussed the theories of the Mutakallemim. No notice will be taken of the opinion of any philosopher but that of Aristotle ; his opinions alone deserve to be criticized, and if our objections or doubts with regard to any of these be well founded, this must be the case in a far higher degree in respect to all other opponents of our fundamental principles.

I now proceed to describe the methods of the philosophers.

First Method.—According to Aristotle, motion, that is to say, motion *par excellence,* is eternal. For if the motion had a beginning, there must already have been some motion when it came into existence, for transition from potentiality into actuality, and from non-existence into existence, always implies motion ; then that previous motion, the cause of the motion which follows, must be eternal, or else the series would have to be carried back *ad infinitum.* On the same principle he maintains that time is eternal, for time is related to and connected with motion : there is no motion except in time, and time can only be perceived by motion, as has been demonstrated by proof. By this argument Aristotle proves the eternity of the Universe.

Second Method.—The First Substance common to the four elements is eternal. For if it had a beginning it would have come into existence from another substance ; it would further be endowed with a form, as coming into existence is nothing but receiving Form. But we mean by " First Substance " a formless substance ; it can therefore not have come into existence from another substance, and must be without beginning and without end ; hence it is concluded that the Universe is eternal.

Third Method.—The substance of the spheres contains no opposite elements ; for circular motion includes no such opposite directions as are found in rectilinear motion. Whatever is destroyed, owes its destruction to the opposite elements it contains. The spheres contain no opposite elements ; they are therefore indestructible, and because they are indestructible they are also without beginning. Aristotle thus assumes the axiom that everything that has had a beginning is destructible, and that everything destructible has had a beginning ; that things without beginning are indestructible, and indestructible things are without beginning. Hence follows the Eternity of the Universe.

Fourth Method.—The actual production of a thing is preceded in time by its possibility. The actual change of a thing is likewise preceded in time by its possibility. From this proposition Aristotle derives the eternity of the circular motion of the spheres. The Aristotelians in more recent time employ this proposition in demonstrating the Eternity of the Universe. They argue thus : When the Universe did not yet exist, its existence was either possible or necessary, or impossible. If it was necessary, the Universe could never have been non-existing ; if impossible, the Universe could never have been in existence ; if possible, the question arises, What was the substratum of that possibility ?   for there must be in existence something of which that possibility can be predicated.   This is a forcible argument in favour of the Eternity of the Universe.   Some of the later schools of the Mutakallemim imagined that they could confute this argument by objecting that the possibility rests with the agent, and not with the production.   But this objection is of no force whatever ; for there are two distinct possibilities, viz., the thing produced has had the possibility of being produced before this actually took place ;   and the agent has had the possibility of producing it before he actually did so.   There are, therefore, undoubtedly two possibilities—that of the substance to receive a certain form, and that of the agent to perform a certain act.

These are the principal methods, based on the properties of the Universe, by which Aristotle proves the Eternity of the Universe.   There are, however, other methods of proving the Eternity of the Universe.   They are based on the notions formed of God, and philosophers after Aristotle derived them from his philosophy.   Some of them employed the following argument :—

Fifth Method.—If God produced the Universe from nothing, He must have been a potential agent before He was an actual one, and must have passed from a state of potentiality into that of actuality—a process that is merely possible, and requires an agent for effecting it.   This argument is likewise a source of great doubts, and every intelligent person must examine it in order to refute it and to expose its character.

Sixth Method.—An agent is active at one time and inactive at another, according as favourable or unfavourable circumstances arise.   The unfavourable circumstances cause the abandonment of an intended action.   The favourable ones, on the other hand, even produce a desire for an action for which there has not been a desire previously.   As, however, God is not subject to accidents which could bring about a change in His will, and is not affected by obstacles and hindrances that might appear or disappear, it is impossible, they argue, to imagine that God is active at one time and inactive at another.   He is, on the contrary, always active in the same manner as He is always in actual existence.

Seventh Method.—The actions of God are perfect ; they are in no way defective, nor do they contain anything useless or superfluous.   In similar terms Aristotle frequently praises Him, when he says that Nature is wise and does nothing in vain, but makes everything as perfect as possible.   The philosophers therefore contend that this existing Universe is so perfect that it cannot be improved, and must be permanent ; for it is the result of God's wisdom, which is not only always present in His essence, but is identical with it.

All arguments in favour of the Eternity of the Universe are based on the above methods, and can be traced to one or other of them.   The following objection is also raised against *Creatio ex nihilo* :   How could God ever have been inactive without producing or creating anything in the infinite past ?   How could He have passed the long infinite period which preceded the Creation without producing anything, so as to commence, as it were, only yesterday, the Creation of the Universe ?   For even if you said, e.g., that God created previously as many successive worlds as the outermost sphere could contain grains of mustard, and that each of these worlds existed as many years : considering the infinite existence of God, it would be the same as if He had only yesterday commenced the Creation. For when we once admit the beginning of the existence of things after their non-existence, it makes no difference whether thousands of centuries have passed since the beginning, or only a short time. Those who defend the Eternity of the Universe find both assumptions equally improbable.

Eighth Method.—The following method is based on the circumstance that the theory implies a belief which is so common to all peoples and ages, and so universal, that it appears to express a real fact and not merely an hypothesis. Aristotle says that all people have evidently believed in the permanency and stability of the heavens ; and thinking that these were eternal, they declared them to be the habitation of God and of the spiritual beings or angels. By thus attributing the heavens to God, they expressed their belief that the heavens are indestructible. Several other arguments of the same kind are employed by Aristotle in treating of this subject in order to support the results of his philosophical speculation by common sense.

CHAPTER XV

In this chapter I intend to show that Aristotle was well aware that he had not proved the Eternity of the Universe. He was not mistaken in this respect. He knew that he could not prove his theory, and that his arguments and proofs were only apparent and plausible. They are the least objectionable, according to Alexander ; but, according to the same authority, Aristotle could not have considered them conclusive, after having himself taught us the rules of logic, and the means by which arguments can be refuted or confirmed.

The reason why I have introduced this subject is this : Later philosophers, disciples of Aristotle, assume that he has proved the Eternity of the Universe, and most of those who believe that they are philosophers blindly follow him in this point, and accept all his arguments as conclusive and absolute proofs. They consider it wrong to differ from Aristotle, or to think that he was ignorant or mistaken in anything. For this reason, taking their standpoint, I show that Aristotle himself did not claim to have proved the Eternity of the Universe. He says in his book *Physics* (viii., chap. i.) as follows : " All the Physicists before us believed that motion is eternal, except Plato, who holds that motion is transient ; according to his opinion the heavens are likewise transient." Now if Aristotle had conclusive proofs for his theory, he would not have considered it necessary to support it by citing the opinions of preceding Physicists, nor would he have found it necessary to point out the folly and absurdity of his opponents. For a truth, once established by proof, does neither gain force nor certainty by the consent of all scholars, nor lose by the general dissent. We further find that Aristotle, in the book *The Heavens and the World*, introduces his theory of the Eternity of the Universe in the following manner : " Let us inquire into the nature of the heavens, and see whether they are the product of something or not, destructible or not." After this statement of the problem, he proceeds to cite the views of those who hold that the heavens have had a beginning, and continues thus : " By doing this, our theory will be most plausible and acceptable in the

opinion of profound thinkers ; and it will be the more so, when, as we propose, the arguments of our opponents are first heard.   For if we were to state
our opinion and our arguments without mentioning those of our opponents,
our words would be received less favourably.   He who desires to be just
must not show himself hostile to his opponent ; he must have sympathy with
him, and readily acknowledge any truth contained in his words ; he must
admit the correctness of such of his opponent's arguments as he would admit
if they were in his own favour."   This is the contents of the words of Aristotle.   Now, I ask you, men of intelligence, can we have any complaint
against him after this frank statement ?   Or can any one now imagine that
a real proof has been given for the Eternity of the Universe ?   Or can
Aristotle, or any one else, believe that a theorem, though fully proved, would
not be acceptable unless the arguments of the opponents were fully refuted ?
We must also take into consideration that Aristotle describes this theory as
his *opinion*, and his proofs as *arguments*.   Is Aristotle ignorant of the difference between argument and proof? between opinions, which may be received
more or less favourably, and truths capable of demonstration ? or would rhetorical appeal to the impartiality of opponents have been required for the
support of his theory if a real proof had been given ?   Certainly not.   Aristotle only desires to show that his theory is better than those of his opponents,
who hold that philosophical speculation leads to the conviction that the
heavens are transient, but have never been entirely without existence ; or
that the heavens have had a beginning, but are indestructible ; or to defend
any of the other views mentioned by him.   In this he is undoubtedly right ;
for his opinion is nearer the truth than theirs, so far as a proof can be taken
from the nature of existing things ; we differ from him, as will be explained.
Passion, that exercises great influence in most of the different sects, must have
influenced even the philosophers who wished to affirm that Aristotle demonstrated his theory by proof.   Perhaps they really believe it, and assume that
Aristotle himself was not aware of it, as it was only discovered after his death !
My conviction is, that what Aristotle says on the Eternity of the Universe, the
cause of the variety in the motion of the spheres and the order of the Intelligences, cannot be proved, and that Aristotle never intended to prove these
things.   I agree with him that the ways of proving this theory have their
gates closed before us, there being no foundation on which to build up the
proof.   His words on this subject are well known.   He says, " There are
things concerning which we are unable to reason, or which we find too high
for us ; to say why these things have a certain property is as difficult as to
decide whether the Universe is eternal or not."   So far Aristotle.   The
interpretation which Abu-nasr offers of this parallel is well known.   He
denies that Aristotle had any doubt about the Eternity of the Universe, and
is very severe upon Galen, who maintains that this theory is still doubtful,
and that no proof has been offered.   According to Abu-nasr, it is clear and
demonstrable by proof that the heavens are eternal, but all that is enclosed
within the heavens is transient.   We hold, that by none of the methods
mentioned in this chapter can a theory be established, refuted, or shaken.

We have mentioned these things only because we know that the majority
of those who consider themselves wise, although they know nothing of
science, accept the theory of the Eternity of the Universe on the authority

of famous scholars. They reject the words of the prophets, because the latter do not employ any scientific method by which only a few persons would be instructed who are intellectually well prepared, but simply communicate the truth as received by Divine inspiration.

In the chapters which follow we will expound the theory of the Creation in accordance with the teaching of Scripture.

CHAPTER XVI

In this chapter I will first expound my view on this question, and then support it by argument—not by such arguments as those of the Mutakallemim, who believe that they have proved the *Creatio ex nihilo*. I will not deceive myself, and consider dialectical methods as proofs ; and the fact that a certain proposition has been proved by a dialectical argument will never induce me to accept that proposition, but, on the contrary, will weaken my faith in it, and cause me to doubt it. For when we understand the fallacy of a proof, our faith in the proposition itself is shaken. It is therefore better that a proposition which cannot be demonstrated be received as an axiom, or that one of the two opposite solutions of the problem be accepted on authority. The methods by which the Mutakallemim proved the *Creatio ex nihilo* have already been described by me, and I have exposed their weak points. As to the proofs of Aristotle and his followers for the Eternity of the Universe, they are, according to my opinion, not conclusive ; they are open to strong objections, as will be explained. I intend to show that the theory of the Creation, as taught in Scripture, contains nothing that is impossible ; and that all those philosophical arguments which seem to disprove our view contain weak points which make them inconclusive, and render the attacks on our view untenable. Since I am convinced of the correctness of my method, and consider either of the two theories—viz., the Eternity of the Universe, and the Creation—as admissible, I accept the latter on the authority of Prophecy, which can teach things beyond the reach of philosophical speculation. For the belief in prophecy is, as will be shown in the course of this treatise, consistent even with the belief in the Eternity of the Universe. When I have established the admissibility of our theory, I will, by philosophical reasoning, show that our theory of the Creation is more acceptable than that of the Eternity of the Universe ; and although our theory includes points open to criticism, I will show that there are much stronger reasons for the rejection of the theory of our opponents.

I will now proceed to expound the method by which the proofs given for the Eternity of the Universe can be refuted.

CHAPTER XVII

Everything produced comes into existence from non-existence ; even when the substance of a thing has been in existence, and has only changed its form, the thing itself, which has gone through the process of genesis and development, and has arrived at its final state, has now different properties from those which it possessed at the commencement of the transition from potentiality to reality, or before that time. Take, e.g., the human ovum as contained in the female's blood when still included in its vessels; its nature is different from what it was in the moment of conception, when it is met by the semen of the male and begins to develop; the properties of the semen in that moment are different from the properties of the living being after its birth when fully developed. It is therefore quite impossible to infer from the nature which a thing possesses after having passed through all stages of its development, what the condition of the thing has been in the moment when this process commenced; nor does the condition of a thing in this moment show what its previous condition has been. If you make this mistake, and attempt to prove the nature of a thing in potential existence by its properties when actually existing, you will fall into great confusion; you will reject evident truths and admit false opinions. Let us assume, in our above instance, that a man born without defect had after his birth been nursed by his mother only a few months; the mother then died, and the father alone brought him up in a lonely island, till he grew up, became wise, and acquired knowledge. Suppose this man has never seen a woman or any female being; he asks some person how man has come into existence, and how he has developed, and receives the following answer: " Man begins his existence in the womb of an individual of his own class, namely, in the womb of a female, which has a certain form. While in the womb he is very small; yet he has life, moves, receives nourishment, and gradually grows, till he arrives at a certain stage of development. He then leaves the womb and continues to grow till he is in the condition in which you see him." The orphan will naturally ask: " Did this person, when he lived, moved, and grew in the womb, eat and drink, and breathe with his mouth and his nostrils? Did he excrete any substance?" The answer will be, " No." Undoubtedly he will then attempt to refute the statements of that person, and to prove their impossibility, by referring to the properties of a fully developed person, in the following manner: " When any one of us is deprived of breath for a short time he dies, and cannot move any longer: how then can we imagine that any one of us has been inclosed in a bag in the midst of a body for several months and remained alive, able to move? If any one of us would swallow a living bird, the bird would die immediately when it reached the stomach, much more so when it came to the lower part of the belly; if we should not take food or drink with our mouth, in a few days we should undoubtedly be dead: how then can man remain alive for months without taking food? If any person would take food and would not be able to excrete it, great pains and death would follow in a short time, and yet I am to believe that man has lived for months without that function! Suppose by accident a hole were formed in the belly of a person, it would prove fatal, and yet we are to believe that the navel of the fœtus has been open! Why should the fœtus not open the eyes, spread forth the hands and stretch out the legs, if, as you think, the limbs are all whole and perfect." This mode of reasoning would lead to the conclusion that man cannot come into existence and develop in the manner described.

If philosophers would consider this example well and reflect on it, they would find that it represents exactly the dispute between Aristotle and ourselves. We, the followers of Moses, our Teacher, and of Abraham, our Father, believe that the Universe has been produced and has developed in a certain manner, and that it has been created in a certain order.   The Aristotelians oppose us, and found their objections on the properties which the things in the Universe possess when in actual existence and fully developed. We admit the existence of these properties, but hold that they are by no means the same as those which the things possessed in the moment of their production; and we hold that these properties themselves have come into existence from absolute non-existence.   Their arguments are therefore no objection whatever to our theory; they have demonstrative force only against those who hold that the nature of things as at present in existence proves the Creation.   But this is not my opinion.

I will now return to our theme, viz., to the description of the principal proofs of Aristotle, and show that they prove nothing whatever against us, since we hold that God brought the entire Universe into existence from absolute non-existence, and that He caused it to develop into the present state.   Aristotle says that the *materia prima* is eternal, and by referring to the properties of transient beings he attempts to prove this statement, and to show that the *materia prima* could not possibly have been produced.   He is right; we do not maintain that the *materia prima* has been produced in the same manner as man is produced from the ovum, and that it can be destroyed in the same manner as man is reduced to dust.   But we believe that God created it from nothing, and that since its creation it has its own properties, viz., that all things are produced of it and again reduced to it, when they cease to exist; that it does not exist without Form; and that it is the source of all genesis and destruction.   Its genesis is not like that of the things produced from it, nor its destruction like theirs; for it has been created from nothing, and if it should please the Creator, He might reduce it to absolutely nothing.   The same applies to motion.   Aristotle founds some of his proofs on the fact that motion is not subject to genesis or destruction. This is correct; if we consider motion as it exists at present, we cannot imagine that in its totality it should be subject, like individual motions, to genesis and destruction.   In like manner Aristotle is correct in saying that circular motion is without beginning, in so far as seeing the rotating spherical body in actual existence, we cannot conceive the idea that that rotation has ever been absent.   The same argument we employ as regards the law that a state of potentiality precedes all actual genesis.   This law applies to the Universe as it exists at present, when everything produced originates in another thing; but nothing perceived with our senses or comprehended in our mind can prove that a thing created from nothing must have been previously in a state of potentiality.   Again, as regards the theory that the heavens contain no opposites [and are therefore indestructible], we admit its correctness; but we do not maintain that the production of the heavens has taken place in the same way as that of a horse or ass, and we do not say that they are like plants and animals, which are destructible on account of the opposite elements they contain.   In short, the properties of things when fully developed contain no clue as to what have been the properties of the things before their perfection.   We therefore do not reject as impossible the opinion of those who say that the heavens were produced before the earth, or the reverse, or that the heavens have existed without stars, or that certain species of animals have been in existence, and others not.   For the state of the whole Universe when it came into existence may be compared with that of animals when their existence begins ; the heart evidently precedes the testicles, the veins are in existence before the bones ; although, when the animal is fully developed, none of the parts is missing which is essential to its existence. This remark is not superfluous, if the Scriptural account of the Creation be taken literally ; in reality, it cannot be taken literally, as will be shown when we shall treat of this subject.

The principle laid down in the foregoing must be well understood ; it is a high rampart erected round the Law, and able to resist all missiles directed against it. Aristotle, or rather his followers, may perhaps ask us how we know that the Universe has been created ; and that other forces than those it has at present were acting in its Creation, since we hold that the properties of the Universe, as it exists at present, prove nothing as regards its creation ? We reply, there is no necessity for this according to our plan ; for we do not desire to prove the Creation, but only its possibility ; and this possibility is not refuted by arguments based on the nature of the present Universe, which we do not dispute. When we have established the admissibility of our theory, we shall then show its superiority. In attempting to prove the inadmissibility of *Creatio ex nihilo*, the Aristotelians can therefore not derive any support from the nature of the Universe ; they must resort to the notion our mind has formed of God. Their proofs include the three methods which I have mentioned above, and which are based on the notion conceived of God. In the next chapter I will expose the weak points of these arguments, and show that they really prove nothing.

CHAPTER XVIII

THE first method employed by the philosophers is this : they assume that a transition from potentiality to actuality would take place in the Deity itself, if He produced a thing only at a certain fixed time. The refutation of this argument is very easy. The argument applies only to bodies composed of substance—the element that possesses the possibility [of change]—and form ; for when such a body does not act for some time, and then acts by virtue of its form, it must undoubtedly have possessed something *in potentia* that hath now become actual, and the transition can only have been effected by some external agent. As far as corporeal bodies are concerned, this has been fully proved. But that which is incorporeal and without substance does not include anything merely possible ; everything it contains is always in existence. The above argument does not apply to it, and it is not impossible that such a being acts at one time and does not act at another. This does not imply a change in the incorporeal being itself nor a transition from potentiality to actuality. The Active Intellect may be taken as an illustration. According to Aristotle and his school, the Active Intellect, an incorporeal being, acts at one time and does not act at another, as has been shown by Abu-nasr in his treatise on the Intellect. He says there quite correctly as follows : " It is an evident fact that the Active Intellect does not act continually, but only at times." And yet he does not say that the Active Intellect is changeable, or passes from a state of potentiality to that of actuality, although it produces at one time something which it has not produced before.   For there is no relation or comparison whatever between corporeal and incorporeal beings, neither in the moment of action nor in that of inaction.   It is only by homonymity that the term " action " is used in reference to the forms residing in bodies, and also in reference to absolutely spiritual beings.   The circumstance that a purely spiritual being does not effect at one time that which it effects at another, does not necessitate a transition from potentiality to actuality ; such a transition is necessary in the case of forces connected with bodies.   It might, perhaps, be objected that our argument is, to some extent, a fallacy ; since it is not due to anything contained in the Active Intellect itself, but to the absence of substances sufficiently prepared for its action, that at times it does not act ; it does act always when substances sufficiently prepared are present, and, when the action does not continue, it is owing to the absence of substance sufficiently prepared, and not to any change in the Intellect.   I answer that it is not our intention to state the reason why God created at one time and not at another ; and, in referring to the Active Intellect as a parallel, we do not mean to assert that God acts at one time and not at another, in the same manner as the Active Intellect, an absolutely spiritual being, acts intermittently.   We do not make this assertion, and, if we did, the conclusion would be fallacious. What we infer, and what we are justified in inferring, is this : the Active Intellect is neither a corporeal object nor a force residing in a body ; it acts intermittently, and yet whatever the cause may be why it does not always act, we do not say that the Active Intellect has passed from a state of potentiality to that of actuality ; or that it implies the possibility [of change], or that an agent must exist that causes the transition from potentiality to actuality.   We have thus refuted the strong objection raised by those who believe in the Eternity of the Universe ; since we believe that God is neither a corporeal body nor a force residing in a body, we need not assume that the Creation, after a period of inaction, is due to a change in the Creator Himself.

The second method employed in proving the Eternity of the Universe is based on the theory that all wants, changes, and obstacles are absent from the Essence of God.   Our refutation of this proof, which is both difficult and profound, is this.   Every being that is endowed with free will and performs certain acts in reference to another being, necessarily interrupts those acts at one time or another, in consequence of some obstacles or changes. E.g., a person desires to have a house, but he does not build one, because he meets with some obstacles : he has not the material, or he has the material, but it is not prepared for the purpose on account of the absence of proper instruments ; or he has material and instruments, and yet does not build a house, because he does not desire to build it ; since he feels no want for a refuge.   When changed circumstances, as heat or cold, impel him to seek a refuge, then he desires to build a house.   Thus changed circumstances change his will, and the will, when it meets with obstacles, is not carried into effect.   This, however, is only the case when the causes of the actions are external ; but when the action has no other purpose whatever than to fulfil the will, then the will does not depend on the existence of favourable circumstances.   The being endowed with this will need not act continually even in the absence of all obstacles, because there does not exist anything for the sake of which it acts, and which, in the absence of all obstacles, would necessitate the action : the act simply follows the will. But, some might ask, even if we admit the correctness of all this, is not change imputed in the fact that the will of the being exists at one time and not at another ? I reply thus : The true essence of the will of a being is simply the faculty of conceiving a desire at one time and not conceiving it at another. In the case of corporeal beings, the will which aims at a certain external object changes according to obstacles and circumstances. But the will of an absolutely spiritual being which does not depend on external causes is unchangeable, and the fact that the being desires one thing one day and another thing another day, does not imply a change in the essence of that being, or necessitate the existence of an external cause [for this change in the desire]. Similarly it has been shown by us that if a being acted at one time and did not act at another, this would not involve a change in the being itself. It is now clear that the term " will " is homonymously used of man's will and of the will of God, there being no comparison whatever between God's will and that of man. The objection is refuted, and our theory is not shaken by it. This is all we desire to establish.

The third method employed in proving the Eternity of the Universe is this : whatever the wisdom of God finds necessary to produce is produced *eo ipso* ; but this wisdom, being His Essence, is eternal, and that which results from His wisdom must be eternal. This is a very weak argument. As we do not understand why the wisdom of God produced nine spheres, neither more nor less, or why He fixed the number and size of the stars exactly as they are ; so we cannot understand why His wisdom at a certain time caused the Universe to exist, whilst a short time before it had not been in existence. All things owe their existence to His eternal and constant wisdom, but we are utterly ignorant of the ways and methods of that wisdom, since, according to our opinion [that God has no attributes], His will is identical with His wisdom, and all His attributes are one and the same thing, namely, His Essence or Wisdom. More will be said on this question in the section on Providence. Thus this objection to our theory falls likewise to the ground.

There is no evidence for the theory of the Eternity of the Universe, neither in the fact cited by Aristotle of the general consent of the ancient peoples when they describe the heavens as the habitation of the angels and of God, nor in the apparent concurrence of Scriptural texts with this belief. These facts merely prove that the heavens lead us to believe in the existence of the Intelligences, i.e., ideals and angels, and that these lead us to believe in the existence of God ; for He sets them in motion, and rules them. We will explain and show that there is no better evidence for the existence of a Creator, as we believe, than that furnished by the heavens ; but also according to the opinion of the philosophers, as has been mentioned by us, they give evidence that a being exists that sets them in motion, and that this being is neither a corporeal body nor a force residing in a body.

Having proved that our theory is admissible, and not impossible, as those who defend the Eternity of the Universe assert, I will, in the chapters which follow, show that our theory is preferable from a philosophical point of view, and expose the absurdities implied in the theory of Aristotle.

CHAPTER XIX

It has been shown that according to Aristotle, and according to all that defend his theory, the Universe is inseparable from God ; He is the cause, and the Universe the effect ; and this effect is a necessary one ; and as it cannot be explained why or how God exists in this particular manner, namely, being One and incorporeal, so it cannot be asked concerning the whole Universe why or how it exists in this particular way. For it is necessary that the whole, the cause as well as the effect, exist in this particular manner, it is impossible for them not to exist, or to be different from what they actually are. This leads to the conclusion that the nature of everything remains constant, that nothing changes its nature in any way, and that such a change is impossible in any existing thing. It would also follow that the Universe is not the result of design, choice, and desire ; for if this were the case, they would have been non-existing before the design had been conceived.

We, however, hold that all things in the Universe are the result of design, and not merely of necessity ; He who designed them may change them when He changes His design. But not every design is subject to change ; for there are things which are impossible, and their nature cannot be altered, as will be explained. Here, in this chapter, I merely wish to show by arguments almost as forcible as real proofs, that the Universe gives evidence of design ; but I will not fall into the error in which the Mutakallemim have so much distinguished themselves, namely, of ignoring the existing nature of things or assuming the existence of atoms, or the successive creation of accidents, or any of their propositions which I have tried to explain, and which are intended to establish the principle of Divine selection. You must not, however, think that they understood the principle in the same sense as we do, although they undoubtedly aimed at the same thing, and mentioned the same things which we also will mention, when they treated of Divine Selection. For they do not distinguish between selection in the case of a plant to make it red and not white, or sweet and not bitter, and determination in the case of the heavens which gave them their peculiar geometrical form and did not give them a triangular or quadrilateral shape. The Mutakallemim established the principle of determination by means of their propositions, which have been enumerated above (Part I., chap. lxxiii.). I will establish this principle only as far as necessary, and only by philosophical propositions based on the nature of things. But before I begin my argument, I will state the following facts : Matter is common to things different from each other ; there must be either one external cause which endows this matter partly with one property, partly with another, or there must be as many different causes as there are different forms of the matter common to all things. This is admitted by those who assume the Eternity of the Universe. After having premised this proposition, I will proceed with the discussion of our theme from an Aristotelian point of view, in form of a dialogue.

We.—You have proved that all things in the sublunary world have one common substance ; why then do the species of things vary ? why are the *individuals* in each species different from each other ?

Aristotelian.—Because the composition of the things formed of that substance varies. For the common substance at first received four different
forms, and each form was endowed with two qualities, and through these
four qualities the substance was turned into the elements of which all things
are formed. The composition of the elements takes place in the following
manner :—First they are mixed in consequence of the motion of the spheres,
and then they combine together ; a cause for variation arises then in the
variation of the degree of heat, cold, moisture, and dryness of the elements
which form the constituent parts of the things. By these different combinations things are variously predisposed to receive different forms ; and
these in their turn are again prepared to receive other forms, and so on.
Each generic form finds a wide sphere in its substance both as regards quality
and quantity ; and the individuals of the classes vary accordingly. This is
fully explained in Natural Science. It is quite correct and clear to every
one that readily acknowledges the truth, and does not wish to deceive
himself.

We.—Since the combination of the elements prepares substances and
enables them to receive different forms, what has prepared the first substance
and caused one part of it to receive the form of fire, another part the form
of earth, and the parts between these two the forms of water and of air,
since one substance is common to all ? Through what has the substance of
earth become more fit for the form of earth, and the substance of fire more
fit for that of fire ?

Ar.—The difference of the elements was caused by their different position ;
for the different places prepared the same substance differently, in the
following way : the portion nearest the surrounding sphere became more
rarified and swifter in motion, and thus approaching the nature of that
sphere, it received by this preparation the form of fire. The farther the
substance is away from the surrounding sphere towards the centre, the denser,
the more solid, and the less luminous it is ; it becomes earth ; the same is
the cause of the formation of water and air. This is necessarily so ; for it
would be absurd to deny that each part of the substance is in a certain place ;
or to assume that the surface is identical with the centre, or the centre with
the surface. This difference in place determined the different forms, i.e.,
predisposed the substance to receive different forms.

We.—Is the substance of the surrounding sphere, i.e., the heavens, the
same as that of the elements ?

Ar.—No ; the substance is different, and the forms are different. The
term " body " is homonymously used of these bodies below and of the heavens, as has been shown by modern philosophers. All this has been demonstrated by proof.

But let now the reader of this treatise hear what I have to say. Aristotle
hass proved that the difference of forms becomes evident by the difference
of actions. Since, therefore, the motion of the elements is rectilinear, and
that of the spheres circular, we infer that the substances are different. This
inference is supported by Natural Science. When we further notice that
substances with rectilinear motion differ in their directions, that some move
upward, some downward, and that substances which move in the same direction have different velocities, we infer that their forms must be different.

Thus we learn that there are four elements. In the same way we come to the conclusion that the substance of all the spheres is the same, since they all have circular motion. Their forms, however, are different, since one sphere moves from east to west, and another from west to east; and their motions have also different velocities. We can now put the following question to Aristotle: There is one substance common to all spheres; each one has its own peculiar form. Who thus determined and predisposed these spheres to receive different forms? Is there above the spheres any being capable of determining this except God? I will show the profundity and the extraordinary acumen which Aristotle displayed when this question troubled him. He strove very hard to meet this objection with arguments, which, however, were not borne out by facts. Although he does not mention this objection, it is clear from his words that he endeavours to show the nature of the spheres, as he has shown that of the things in the sublunary world. Everything is, according to him, the result of a law of Nature, and not the result of the design of a being that designs as it likes, or the determination of a being that determines as it pleases. He has not carried out the idea consistently, and it will never be done. He tries indeed to find the cause why the sphere moves from east and not from west; why some spheres move with greater velocity, others with less velocity, and he finds the cause of these differences in their different positions in reference to the uppermost sphere. He further attempts to show why there are several spheres for each of the seven planets, while there is only one sphere for the large number of fixed stars. For all this he endeavours to state the reason, so as to show that the whole order is the necessary result of the laws of Nature. He has not attained his object. For as regards the things in the sublunary world, his explanations are in accordance with facts, and the relation between cause and effect is clearly shown. It can therefore be assumed that everything is the necessary result of the motions and influences of the spheres. But when he treats of the properties of the spheres, he does not clearly show the causal relation, nor does he explain the phenomena in that systematic way which the hypothesis of natural laws would demand. For let us consider the spheres: in one case a sphere with greater velocity is above a sphere with less velocity, in another case we notice the reverse; in a third case there are two spheres with equal velocities, one above the other. There are, besides, other phenomena which speak strongly against the hypothesis that all is regulated by the laws of Nature, and I will devote a special chapter to the discussion of these phenomena. In short, there is no doubt that Aristotle knew the weakness of his arguments in tracing and describing the cause of all these things, and therefore he prefaces his researches on these things as follows :—" We will now thoroughly investigate two problems, which it is our proper duty to investigate and to discuss according to our capacity, wisdom, and opinion. This our attempt must not be attributed to presumption and pride, but to our extraordinary zeal in the study of philosophy ; when we attempt the highest and grandest problems, and endeavour to offer some proper solution, every one that hears it should rejoice and be pleased." So far Aristotle. This shows that he undoubtedly knew the weakness of his theory. How much weaker must it appear when we bear in mind that the science of Astronomy was not yet fully developed, and that in the days of Aristotle the motions of the spheres were not known so well as they are at present. I think that it was the object of Aristotle in attributing in his *Metaphysics* one Intelligence to every sphere, to assume the existence of something capable of determining the peculiar course of each sphere. Later on I will show that he has not gained anything thereby; but now I will explain the words, "according to our capacity, wisdom, and opinion," occurring in the passage which we quoted. I have not noticed that any of the commentators explain them. The term "our opinion" refers to the principle that everything is the result of natural laws, or to the theory of the Eternity of the Universe. By "our wisdom" he meant the knowledge of that which is clear and generally accepted, viz., that the existence of every one of these things is due to a certain cause, and not to chance. By "our capacity" he meant the insufficiency of our intellect to find the causes of all these things. He only intended to trace the causes for a few of them; and so he did. For he gives an excellent reason why the sphere of the fixed stars moves slowly, while the other spheres move with greater velocity, namely, because its motion is in a different direction [from the uppermost sphere]. He further says that the more distant a sphere is from the eighth sphere the greater is its velocity. But this rule does not hold good in all cases, as I have already explained (p. 174). More forcible still is the following objection: There are spheres below the eighth that move from east to west. Of these each upper one, according to this rule, would have a greater velocity than the lower one; and the velocity of these spheres would almost equal that of the ninth sphere. But Astronomy had, in the days of Aristotle, not yet developed to the height it has reached at present.

According to our theory of the Creation, all this can easily be explained; for we say that there is a being that determines the direction and the velocity of the motion of each sphere; but we do not know the reason why the wisdom of that being gave to each sphere its peculiar property. If Aristotle had been able to state the cause of the difference in the motion of the spheres, and show that it corresponded as he thought to their relative positions, this would have been excellent, and the variety in their motions would be explained in the same way as the variety of the elements, by their relative position between the centre and the surface; but this is not the case, as I said before.

There is a phenomenon in the spheres which more clearly shows the existence of voluntary determination; it cannot be explained otherwise than by assuming that some being designed it: this phenomenon is the existence of the stars. The fact that the sphere is constantly in motion, while the stars remain stationary, indicates that the substance of the stars is different from that of the spheres. Abu-nasr has already mentioned the fact in his additions to the *Physics* of Aristotle. He says: "There is a difference between the stars and the spheres; for the spheres are transparent, the stars are opaque; and the cause of this is that there is a difference, however small it may be, between their substances and forms." So far Abu-nasr. But I do not say that there is a small difference, but a very great difference; because I do not infer it from the transparency of the spheres, but from their motions. I am convinced that there are three different kinds of substance, with three different forms, namely:—(1) Bodies which never move of their own accord; such are the bodies of the stars ; (2) bodies which always move, such are the bodies of the spheres ; (3) bodies which both move and rest, such are the elements. Now, I ask, what has united these two bodies, which, according to my opinion, differ very much from each other, though, according to Abu-nasr, only a little ? Who has prepared the bodies for this union ? In short, it would be strange that, without the existence of design, one of two different bodies should be joined to the other in such a manner that it is fixed to it in a certain place but does not combine with it. It is still more difficult to explain the existence of the numerous stars in the eighth sphere ; they are all spherical ; some of them are large, some small ; here we notice two stars apparently distant from each other one cubit ; there a group of ten close together ; whilst in another place there is a large space without any star. What determined that the one small part should have ten stars, and the other portion should be without any star ? and the whole body of the sphere being uniform throughout, why should a particular star occupy the one place and not another? The answer to these and similar questions is very difficult, and almost impossible, if we assume that all emanates from God as the necessary result of certain permanent laws, as Aristotle holds. But if we assume that all this is the result of design, there is nothing strange or improbable ; and the only question to be asked is this : What is the cause of this design ? The answer to this question is that all this has been made for a certain purpose, though we do not know it ; there is nothing that is done in vain, or by chance. It is well known that the veins and nerves of an individual dog or ass are not the result of chance ; their magnitude is not determined by chance ; nor is it by chance, but for a certain purpose, that one vein is thick, another thin ; that one nerve has many branches, another has none ; that one goes down straight, whilst another is bent ; it is well known that all this must be just as it is. How, then, can any reasonable person imagine that the position, magnitude, and number of the stars, or the various courses of their spheres, are purposeless, or the result of chance ? There is no doubt that every one of these things is necessary and in accordance with a certain design ; and it is extremely improbable that these things should be the necessary result of natural laws, and not that of design.

The best proof for design in the Universe I find in the different motions of the spheres, and in the fixed position of the stars in the spheres. For this reason you find all the prophets point to the spheres and stars when they want to prove that there must exist a Divine Being. Thus Abraham reflected on the stars, as is well known ; Isaiah (xl. 26) exhorts to learn from them the existence of God, and says, " Lift up your eyes on high, and behold who hath created these things ? " Jeremiah [calls God] " The Maker of the heavens " ; Abraham calls Him " The God of the heavens " (Gen. xxiv. 7) ; [Moses], the chief of the Prophets, uses the phrase explained by us (Part I., chap. lxx.), " He who rideth on the heavens " (Deut. xxxiii. 26). The proof taken from the heavens is convincing ; for the variety of things in the sublunary world, though their substance is one and the same, can be explained as the work of the influences of the spheres, or the result of the variety in the position of the substance in relation to the spheres, as has been shown by Aristotle. But who has determined the variety in the spheres and the stars, if not the Will of God ? To say that the Intelligences have determined it is of no use whatever ; for the Intelligences are not corporeal, and have no local relation to the spheres. Why then should the one sphere in its desire to approach the Intelligence, move eastward, and another westward ? Is the one Intelligence in the east, the other in the west ? or why does one move with great velocity, another slowly ? This difference is not in accordance with their distances from each other, as is well known. We must then say that the nature and essence of each sphere necessitated its motion in a certain direction, and in a certain manner, as the consequence of its desire to approach its Intelligence. Aristotle clearly expresses this opinion. We thus have returned to the part from which we started ; and we ask, Since the substance of all things is the same, what made the nature of one portion different from another ? Why has this sphere a desire which produces a motion different from that which the desire of another sphere produces ? This must have been done by an agent capable of determining. We have thus been brought to examine two questions :—(1) Is it necessary to assume that the variety of the things in the Universe is the result of Design, and not of fixed laws of Nature, or is it not necessary ? (2) Assuming that all this is the result of Design, does it follow that it has been created after not having existed, or does *Creatio ex nihilo* not follow, and has the Being which has determined all this done always so ? Some of those who believe in the Eternity of the Universe hold the last opinion. I will now begin the examination of these two questions, and explain them as much as necessary in the following chapters.

CHAPTER XX

ACCORDING to Aristotle, none of the products of Nature are due to chance. His proof is this : That which is due to chance does not reappear constantly nor frequently, but all products of Nature reappear either constantly or at least frequently. The heavens, with all that they contain, are constant ; they never change, as has been explained, neither as regards their essence nor as regards their place. But in the sublunary world we find both things which are constant and things which reappear frequently [though not constantly]. Thus, e.g., the heat of fire and the downward tendency of a stone are constant properties, whilst the form and life of the individuals in each species are the same in most cases. All this is clear. If the parts of the Universe are not accidental, how can the whole Universe be considered as the result of chance ? Therefore the existence of the Universe is not due to chance. The following is, in short, the objection which Aristotle raises against one of the earlier philosophers who assumed that the Universe is the result of chance, and that it came into existence by itself, without any cause Some assume that the heavens and the whole Universe came into existence spontaneously, as well as the rotation and motion [of the spheres], which has produced the variety of things and established their present order. This opinion implies a great adsurdity. They admit that animals and plants do not owe their existence or production to chance, but to a certain cause, be that cause Nature, or reason, or the like ; e.g., they do not assume that everything might be formed by chance of a certain seed or semen, but that of a certain seed only an olive-tree is produced, and of a certain semen only a human being is developed. And yet they think that the heavens, and those bodies which appear divine among the rest of bodies, came into existence spontaneously, without the action of any such cause as produces plants and animals. Having thus examined this theory, Aristotle then proceeds to refute it at greater length. It is therefore clear that Aristotle believes and proves that things in real existence are not accidental; they cannot be accidental, because they are essential, i.e., there is a cause which necessitates that they should be in their actual condition, and on account of that cause they are just as they in reality are. This has been proved, and it is the opinion of Aristotle. But I do not think that, according to Aristotle, the rejection of the spontaneous origin of things implies the admission of Design and Will. For as it is impossible to reconcile two opposites, so it is impossible to reconcile the two theories, that of necessary existence by causality, and that of Creation by the desire and will of a Creator. For the necessary existence assumed by Aristotle must be understood in this sense, that for everything that is not the product of work there must be a certain cause that produces it with its properties; for this cause there is another cause, and for the second a third, and so on. The series of causes ends with the Prime Cause, from which everything derives existence, since it is impossible that the series should continue *ad infinitum*. He nevertheless does not mean to say that the existence of the Universe is the necessary product of the Creator, i.e., the Prime Cause, in the same manner as the shadow is caused by a body, or heat by fire, or light by the sun. Only those who do not comprehend his words attribute such ideas to him. He uses here the term necessary in the same sense as we use the term when we say that the existence of the *intellectus* necessarily implies that of the *intellectum*, for the former is the efficient cause of the latter in so far as *intellectum*. Even Aristotle holds that the Prime Cause is the highest and most perfect Intellect; he therefore says that the First Cause is pleased, satisfied, and delighted with that which necessarily derives existence from Him, and it is impossible that He should wish it to be different. But we do not call this " design," and it has nothing in common with design. E.g., man is pleased, satisfied, and delighted that he is endowed with eyes and hands, and it is impossible that he should desire it to be otherwise, and yet the eyes and hands which a man has are not the result of his design, and it is not by his own determination that he has certain properties and is able to perform certain actions. The notion of design and determination applies only to things not yet in existence, when there is still the possibility of their being in accordance with the design or not. I do not know whether the modern Aristotelians understood his words to imply that the existence of the Universe presupposes some cause in the sense of design and determination, or whether, in opposition to him, they assumed design and determination, in the belief that this does not conflict with the theory of the Eternity of the Universe.

Having explained this, I will now proceed to examine the opinions of the modern philosophers.

CHAPTER XXI

SOME of the recent philosophers who adhere to the theory of the Eternity of the Universe hold that God produces the Universe, that He by His will designs and determines its existence and form ; they reject, however, the theory that this act took place at one certain time, and assume that this always has been the case, and will always be so.　The circumstance that we cannot imagine an agent otherwise than preceding the result of its action, they explain by the fact that this is invariably the case in all that *we* produce ; because for agents of the same kind as we are, there are some moments in which they are not active, and are only agents *in potentia ;* they become agents when they act.　But as regards God there are no moments of non-action, or of potentiality in any respect ; He is not before His work, He is always an actual agent.　And as there is a great difference between His essence and ours, so is also a great difference between the relation of His work to Him and the relation of our work to us.　They apply the same argument to will and determination ; for there is no difference in this respect whether we say He acts, wills, designs, or determines.　They further assume that change in His action or will is inadmissible.　It is therefore clear that these philosophers abandoned the term " necessary result," but retained the theory of it ; they perhaps sought to use a better expression, or to remove an objectionable term.　For it is the same thing, whether we say in accordance with the view of Aristotle that the Universe is the result of the Prime Cause, and must be eternal as that Cause is eternal, or in accordance with these philosophers that the Universe is the result of the act, design, will, selection, and determination of God, but it has always been so, and will always be so ; in the same manner as the rising of the sun undoubtedly produces the day, and yet it does not precede it.　But when we speak of design we do not mean it in this sense ; we mean to express by it that the Universe is not the " necessary result " of God's existence, as the effect is the necessary result of the efficient cause ; in the latter case the effect cannot be separated from the cause ; it cannot change unless the cause changes entirely, or at least in some respect.　If we accept this explanation we easily see how absurd it is to say that the Universe is in the same relation to God as the effect is to the efficient cause, and to assume at the same time that the Universe is the result of the action and determination of God.

Having fully explained this subject, we come to the question whether the cause, which must be assumed for the variety of properties noticed in the heavenly beings, is merely an efficient cause, that must necessarily produce that variety as its effect, or whether that variety is due to a determining agent, such as we believe, in accordance with the theory of Moses our Teacher. Before I discuss this question I will first explain fully what Aristotle means by " necessary result " ; after that I will show by such philosophical arguments as are free from every fallacy why I prefer the theory of *Creatio ex nihilo.*　It is clear that when he says that the first Intelligence is the necessary result of the existence of God, the second Intelligence the result of the existence of the first, the third of the second [and so on], and that the spheres are the necessary result of the existence of the Intelligences, and so forth, in the well-known order which you learnt from passages dealing with it, and of which we have given a *résumé* in this part (ch. iv.)—he does not mean that the one thing was first in existence, and then the second came as the necessary result of the first ; he denies that any one of these beings has had a beginning.   By " necessary result " he merely refers to the causal relation ; he means to say that the first Intelligence is the cause of the existence of the second ; the second of the third, and so on to the last of the Intelligences ; and the same is also the case as regards the spheres and the *materia prima ;* none of these preceded another, or has been in existence without the existence of that other.   We say, e.g., that the necessary result of the primary qualities are roughness [and] smoothness, hardness [and] softness, porosity and solidity ; and no person doubts that heat, cold, moisture, and dryness are the causes of smoothness and roughness, of hardness and softness, porosity and solidity, and similar qualities, and that the latter are the necessary result of those four primary qualities. And yet it is impossible that a body should exist with the primary qualities without the secondary ones ; for the relation between the two sets of qualities is that of causality, not that of agent and its product.   Just in the same way the term " necessary result " is used by Aristotle in reference to the whole Universe, when he says that one portion is the result of the other, and continues the series up to the First Cause as he calls it, or first Intellect, if you prefer this term.   For we all mean the same, only with this difference, that according to Aristotle everything besides that Being is the necessary result of the latter, as I have already mentioned ; whilst, according to our opinion, that Being created the whole Universe with design and will, so that the Universe which had not been in existence before, has by His will come into existence.   I will now begin in the following chapters my proofs for the superiority of our theory, that of *Creatio ex nihilo.*

CHAPTER XXII

Aristotle and all philosophers assume as an axiom that a simple element can only produce one simple thing, whilst a compound can produce as many things as it contains simple elements ; e.g., fire combines in itself two properties, heat and dryness ; it gives heat by the one property, and produces dryness by the other : an object composed of matter and form produces certain things on account of its matter, and others on account of its form, if [both matter and form] consist of several elements.   In accordance with this axiom, Aristotle holds that the direct emanation from God must be one simple Intelligence, and nothing else.

A second axiom assumed by him is this : Things are not produced by other things at random ; there must be some relation between cause and effect. Thus accidents are not produced by accidents promiscuously ; quality cannot be the origin of quantity, nor quantity that of quality ; a form cannot emanate from matter, nor matter from form.

A third axiom is this : A single agent that acts with design and will, and not merely by the force of the laws of Nature, can produce different objects.

A fourth axiom is as follows : An object, whose several elements are only connected by juxtaposition, is more properly a compound than an object whose different elements have entirely combined ; e.g., bone, flesh, veins, or nerves, are more simple than the hand or the foot, that are a combination of bone, flesh, veins, and nerves.   This is very clear, and requires no further explanation.

Having premised these axioms, I ask the following question : Aristotle holds that the first Intelligence is the cause of the second, the second of the third, and so on, till the thousandth, if we assume a series of that number. Now the first Intellect is undoubtedly simple. How then can the compound form of existing things come from such an Intellect by fixed laws of Nature, as Aristotle assumes ? We admit all he said concerning the Intelligences, that the further they are away from the first, the greater is the variety of their compounds, in consequence of the larger number of the objects comprehensible by the Intelligences ; but even after admitting this, the question remains, By what law of Nature did the spheres emanate from the Intelligences ? What relation is there between material and immaterial beings ? Suppose we admit that each sphere emanates from an Intelligence of the form mentioned ; that the Intelligence, including, as it were, two elements, in so far as it comprehends itself and another thing, produces the next Intelligence by the one element, and a sphere by the other ; but the question would then be, how the one simple element could produce the sphere, that contains two substances and two forms, namely, the substance and the form of the sphere, and also the substance and the form of the star fixed in that sphere. For, according to the laws of Nature, the compound can only emanate from a compound. There must therefore be one element, from which the body of the sphere emanates, and another element, from which the body of the star emanates. This would be necessary even if the substance of all stars were the same ; but it is possible that the luminous stars have not the same substance as the non-luminous stars ; it is besides well known that each body has its own matter and its own form. It must now be clear that this emanation could not have taken place by the force of the laws of Nature, as Aristotle contends. Nor does the difference of the motions of the spheres follow the order of their positions ; and therefore it cannot be said that this difference is the result of certain laws of Nature. We have already mentioned this (ch. xix.).

There is in the properties of the spheres another circumstance that is opposed to the assumed laws of Nature ; namely, if the substance of all spheres is the same, why does it not occur that the form of one sphere combines with the substance of another sphere, as is the case with things on earth, simply because their substance is fit [for such changes] ? If the substance of all spheres is the same, if it is not assumed that each of them has a peculiar substance, and if, contrary to all principles, the peculiar motion of each sphere is no evidence for the special character of its substance, why then should a certain form constantly remain united with a certain substance ? Again, if the stars have all one substance, by what are they distinguished from each other ? is it by forms ? or by accidents ? Whichever be the case, the forms or the accidents would interchange, so that they would successively unite with every one of the stars, so long as their substance [being the same] admits the combinations [with every one of the forms or the accidents]. This shows that the term substance, when used of the spheres or the stars, does not mean the same as it signifies when used of the substance of earthly things, but is applied to the two synonymously. It further shows that every one of the bodies of the spheres has its own peculiar form of existence different from that of all other beings.   Why then is circular motion common to all spheres, and why is the fixed position of the stars in their respective spheres common to all stars ? If we, however, assume design and determination of a Creator, in accordance with His incomprehensible wisdom, all these difficulties disappear.   They must arise when we consider the whole Universe, not as the result of free will, but as the result of fixed laws of Nature : a theory which, on the one hand, is not in harmony with the existing order of things, and does not offer for it a sufficient reason or argument ; and, on the other hand, implies many and great improbabilities.   For, according to this theory, God, whose perfection in every respect is recognised by all thinking persons, is in such a relation to the Universe that He cannot change anything ; if He wished to make the wing of a fly longer, or to reduce the number of the legs of a worm by one, He could not accomplish it.   According to Aristotle, He does not try such a thing, and it is wholly impossible for Him to desire any change in the existing order of things ; if He could, it would not increase His perfection ; it might, on the contrary, from some point of view, diminish it.

Although I know that many partial critics will ascribe my opinion concerning the theory of Aristotle to insufficient understanding, or to intentional opposition, I will not refrain from stating in short the results of my researches, however poor my capacities may be.   I hold that the theory of Aristotle is undoubtedly correct as far as the things are concerned which exist between the sphere of the moon and the centre of the earth.   Only an ignorant person rejects it, or a person with preconceived opinions of his own, which he desires to maintain and to defend, and which lead him to ignore clear facts.   But what Aristotle says concerning things above the sphere of the moon is, with few exceptions, mere imagination and opinion ; to a still greater extent this applies to his system of Intelligences, and to some of his metaphysical views ;   they include great improbabilities, [promote] ideas which all nations consider as evidently corrupt, and cause views to spread which cannot be proved.

It may perhaps be asked why I have enumerated all the doubts which can be raised against the theory of Aristotle ; whether by mere doubts a theory can be overthrown, or its opposite established ?   This is certainly not the case.   But we treat this philosopher exactly as his followers tell us to do. For Alexander stated that when a theory cannot be established by proof, the two most opposite views should be compared as to the doubts entertained concerning each of them, and that view which admits of fewer doubts should be accepted.   Alexander further says that this rule applies to all those opinions of Aristotle in *Metaphysics* for which he offered no proof. For those that followed Aristotle believed that his opinions are far less subject to doubt than any other opinion.   We follow the same rule.   Being convinced that the question whether the heavens are eternal or not cannot be decided by proof, neither in the affirmative nor in the negative, we have enumerated the objections raised to either view, and shown how the theory of the Eternity of the Universe is subject to stronger objections, and is more apt to corrupt the notions concerning God [than the other].   Another argument can be drawn from the fact that the theory of the Creation was held by our Father Abraham, and by our Teacher Moses.

Having mentioned the method of testing the two theories by the objections raised against them, I find it necessary to give some further explanation of the subject.

CHAPTER XXIII

IN comparing the objections raised against one theory with those raised against the opposite theory, in order to decide in favour of the least objectionable, we must not consider the number of the objections, but the degree of improbability and of deviation from real facts [pointed out by the objections]; for one objection may sometimes have more weight than a thousand others. But the comparison cannot be trustworthy unless the two theories be considered with the same interest, and if you are predisposed in favour of one of them, be it on account of your training or because of some advantage, you are too blind to see the truth. For that which can be demonstrated you cannot reject, however much you may be inclined against it; but in questions like those under consideration you are apt to dispute [in consequence of your inclination]. You will, however, be able to decide the question, as far as necessary, if you free yourself from passions, ignore customs, and follow only your reason. But many are the conditions which must be fulfilled. First you must know your mental capacities and your natural talents; you will find this out when you study all mathematical sciences, and are well acquainted with Logic. Secondly, you must have a thorough knowledge of Natural Science, that you may be able to understand the nature of the objections. Thirdly, you must be morally good. For if a person is voluptuous or passionate, and, loosening the reins, allows his anger to pass the just limits, it makes no difference whether he is so from nature or from habit, he will blunder and stumble in his way, he will seek the theory which is in accordance with his inclinations. I mention this lest you be deceived; for a person might some day, by some objection which he raises, shake your belief in the theory of the Creation, and then easily mislead you; you would then adopt the theory [of the Eternity of the Universe] which is contrary to the fundamental principles of our religion, and leads to " speaking words that turn away from God." You must rather have suspicion against your own reason, and accept the theory taught by two prophets who have laid the foundation for the existing order in the religious and social relations of mankind. Only demonstrative proof should be able to make you abandon the theory of the Creation; but such a proof does not exist in Nature.

You will not find it strange that I introduce into this discussion historical matter in support of the theory of the Creation, seeing that Aristotle, the greatest philosopher, in his principal works, introduces histories in support of the theory of the Eternity of the Universe. In this regard we may justly quote the saying: " Should not our perfect Law be as good as their gossip ? " (B. T. Baba batra, 115 b). When he supports his view by quoting Sabean stories, why should we not support our view by that which Moses and Abraham said, and that which follows from their words ?

I have before promised to describe in a separate chapter the strong objections which must occur to him who thinks that human wisdom comprehends fully the nature of the spheres and their motions ; that these are subject to fixed laws, and capable of being comprehended as regards order and relation. I will now explain this.

CHAPTER XXIV

You know of Astronomy as much as you have studied with me, and learnt from the book Almagest; we had not sufficient time to go beyond this. The theory that [the spheres] move regularly, and that the assumed courses of the stars are in harmony with observation, depends, as you are aware, on two hypotheses: we must assume either epicycles, or excentric spheres, or a combination of both. Now I will show that each of these two hypotheses is irregular, and totally contrary to the results of Natural Science. Let us first consider an epicycle, such as has been assumed in the spheres of the moon and the five planets, rotating on a sphere, but not round the centre of the sphere that carries it. This arrangement would necessarily produce a revolving motion; the epicycle would then revolve, and entirely change its place; but that anything in the spheres should change its place is exactly what Aristotle considers impossible. For that reason Abu-bekr ibn-Alzaig, in an astronomical treatise which he wrote, rejects the existence of epicycles. Besides this impossibility, he mentions others, showing that the theory of epicycles implies other absurd notions. I will here explain them :—(1) It is absurd to assume that the revolution of a cycle has not the centre of the Universe for its centre; for it is a fundamental principle in the order of the Universe that there are only three kinds of motion—from the centre, towards the centre, and round the centre; but an epicycle does not move away from the centre, nor towards it, nor round it. (2) Again, according to what Aristotle explains in Natural Science, there must be something fixed round which the motion takes place; this is the reason why the earth remains stationary. But the epicycle would move round a centre which is not stationary. I have heard that Abu-bekr discovered a system in which no epicycles occur; but excentric spheres are not excluded by him. I have not heard it from his pupils; and even if it be correct that he discovered such a system, he has not gained much by it; for excentricity is likewise as contrary as possible to the principles laid down by Aristotle. For it seems to me that an excentric sphere does not move round the centre of the Universe, but round an imaginary point distant from the centre, and therefore round a point which is not fixed. A person ignorant of astronomy might think that the motion of the excentric spheres may still be considered as taking place round something fixed, since their centre is apparently within the sphere of the moon. I would admit this if the centre were situated in the region of fire or air, although the spheres would not move round a stable point. But I will show that the amount of excentricity has, in a certain way, been described in the Almagest; and later scholars have calculated the exact amount of excentricity in terms of radii of the earth, and have proved the result. The same measure has been used in astronomy in describing all distances and magnitudes. It has thu been shown that the point round which the sun moves lies undoubtedly beyond the sphere of the moon, and below the superficies of the sphere of Mercury. The centre for the circuit of Mars, that is, the centre of the excentric sphere of Mars, is beyond the sphere of Mercury, and below the sphere of Venus. The centre of Jupiter has the same distance; it lies between the sphere of Venus and that of Mercury, whilst the centre of Saturn lies between the spheres of Mars and Jupiter. Now, consider how improbable all this appears according to the laws of Natural Science. You will find it out when you consider the known distances and magnitudes of each sphere and each star, all expressed in terms of the radii of the earth. There is a uniform measure for all, and the excentricity of each sphere is not determined by units proportionate to its own magnitude.

It is still more improbable and more objectionable to assume that there are two spheres, the one within the other; that these are closely joined from all sides, and have, nevertheless, different centres. For in this case the smaller sphere might move whilst the larger be at rest; but the smaller cannot be at rest when the larger moves, and must move with the larger when the latter rotates round any other axis than that which passes through the two centres. Now we have this proposition which can be proved; and, further, the established theory that there is no vacuum, and also the assumed excentricity of the spheres; from all this it follows that in every two spheres the motion of the upper one should cause the lower sphere to move in the same way, and round the same centre. But this is not the case; the outer and the inner spheres do not move in the same way, and not round the same centre or the same axis; each of them has its peculiar motion. For this reason it has been assumed that between every two spheres there are substances different from those of the spheres. It may be very much doubted whether this is the case; for where should the centres of these intermediate substances be placed? have these substances likewise their own peculiar motion? Thabith has explained the above-mentioned theory in one of his treatises, and proved that we must assume a substance of a spherical form intermediate between one sphere and the other. All this is part of that which I have not explained to you when you studied with me, for I was afraid you might become confused and would not understand even those things which I wished to show you. But as to the inclination and the deviation assumed in respect to the latitude of the paths of Venus and Mercury, I have already clearly shown you *vivâ voce* that it is impossible to imagine material beings under such conditions. You have seen that Ptolemy has already pointed out this difficulty. He says as follows: " Let no one think that these and similar principles are improbable. If any one considers what we have here expounded in the same light as he considers things produced by skill and subtle work, he will find it improbable; but it is not right to compare human things to divine things." This is, as you know, what Ptolemy says, and I have already pointed out to you the passages by which you can verify all I said, except what I stated about the position of the centres of the excentric spheres; for I have not heard that any one has paid attention to this question. But you will understand it when you know the length of the diameter of each sphere, and .the extent of its excentricity in terms of radii of the earth, according to the facts which Kabici has established in his treatise on the distances. When you notice these distances you will confirm my words.

Consider, therefore, how many difficulties arise if we accept the theory which Aristotle expounds in Physics. For, according to that theory, there are no epicycles, and no excentric spheres, but all spheres rotate round the centre of the earth! How then can the different courses of the stars be explained? how is it possible to assume a uniform perfect rotation with the phenomena which we perceive, except by admitting one of the two hypotheses or both of them ?   The difficulty is still more apparent when we find that admitting what Ptolemy said as regards the epicycle of the moon, and its inclination towards a point different both from the centre of the Universe and from its own centre, the calculations according to these hypotheses are perfectly correct, within one minute ; that their correctness is confirmed by the most accurate calculation of the time, duration, and extent of the eclipses, which is always based on these hypotheses.   Furthermore, how can we reconcile, without assuming the existence of epicycles, the apparent re-trogression of a star with its other motions ?   How can rotation or motion take place round a point which is not fixed ?   These are real difficulties.

I have explained to you already *vivâ voce*, that these difficulties do not concern the astronomer ; for he does not profess to tell us the existing pro-perties of the spheres, but to suggest, whether correctly or not, a theory in which the motion of the stars is circular and uniform, and yet in agreement with our observation.   You know that Abu-bekr al-Zaig, in his treatise on Physics, expresses a doubt whether Aristotle knew the excentricity of the sun but ignored it, and only discussed the effect of the inclination, because he saw that the effect of the excentricity was identical with that of the inclination ; or whether he did not perceive it.   The truth is that he did not notice it or hear of it ; the science was not perfect in his age.   If he had heard of it, he would have strongly opposed it ; if he had been convinced of its correctness, he would have been greatly embarrassed as regards all that he said on the question.   What I said before (ch. xxii.) I will repeat now, namely, that the theory of Aristotle, in explaining the phenomena in the sublunary world, is in accordance with logical inference ; here we know the causal relation between one phenomenon and another ; we see how far science can investigate them, and the manage-ment of nature is clear and intelligible.   But of the things in the heavens man knows nothing except a few mathematical calculations, and you see how far these go.   I say in the words of the poet, " The heavens are the Lord's, but the earth He hath given to the sons of man " (Ps. cxv. 16) ; that is to say, God alone has a perfect and true knowledge of the heavens, their nature, their essence, their form, their motions, and their causes ; but He gave man power to know the things which are under the heavens ; here is man's world, here is his home, into which he has been placed, and of which he is himself a portion.   This is in reality the truth.   For the facts which we require in proving the existence of heavenly beings are withheld from us ; the heavens are too far from us, and too exalted in place and rank.   Man's faculties are too deficient to comprehend even the general proof the heavens contain for the existence of Him who sets them in motion.   It is in fact ignorance or a kind of madness to weary our minds with finding out things which are beyond our reach, without having the means of approaching them.   We must con-tent ourselves with that which is within our reach, and that which cannot be approached by logical inference let us leave to him who has been endowed with that great and divine influence, expressed in the words : " Mouth to mouth do I speak with Him " (Num. xii. 8).

This is all I can say on this question ; another person may perhaps be able to establish by proof what appears doubtful to me.   It is on account of my great love of truth that I have shown my embarrassment in these matters, and I have not heard, nor do I know that any of these theories have been established by proof.

CHAPTER XXV

WE do not reject the Eternity of the Universe, because certain passages in Scripture confirm the Creation; for such passages are not more numerous than those in which God is represented as a corporeal being; nor is it impossible or difficult to find for them a suitable interpretation. We might have explained them in the same manner as we did in respect to the Incorporeality of God. We should perhaps have had an easier task in showing that the Scriptural passages referred to are in harmony with the theory of the Eternity of the Universe if we accepted the latter, than we had in explaining the anthropomorphisms in the Bible when we rejected the idea that God is corporeal. For two reasons, however, we have not done so, and have not accepted the Eternity of the Universe. First, the Incorporeality of God has been demonstrated by proof; those passages in the Bible, which in their literal sense contain statements that can be refuted by proof, must and can be interpreted otherwise. But the Eternity of the Universe has not been proved; a mere argument in favour of a certain theory is not sufficient reason for rejecting the literal meaning of a Biblical text, and explaining it figuratively, when the opposite theory can be supported by an equally good argument.

Secondly, our belief in the Incorporeality of God is not contrary to any of the fundamental principles of our religion; it is not contrary to the words of any prophet. Only ignorant people believe that it is contrary to the teaching of Scripture; but we have shown that this is not the case; on the contrary, Scripture teaches the Incorporeality of God. If we were to accept the Eternity of the Universe as taught by Aristotle, that everything in the Universe is the result of fixed laws, that Nature does not change, and that there is nothing supernatural, we should necessarily be in opposition to the foundation of our religion, we should disbelieve all miracles and signs, and certainly reject all hopes and fears derived from Scripture, unless the miracles are also explained figuratively. The Allegorists amongst the Mohammedans have done this, and have thereby arrived at absurd conclusions. If, however, we accepted the Eternity of the Universe in accordance with the second of the theories which we have expounded above (ch. xxiii.), and assumed, with Plato, that the heavens are likewise transient, we should not be in opposition to the fundamental principles of our religion; this theory would not imply the rejection of miracles, but, on the contrary, would admit them as possible. The Scriptural text might have been explained accordingly, and many expressions might have been found in the Bible and in other writings that would confirm and support this theory. But there is no necessity for this expedient, so long as the theory has not been proved. As there is no proof sufficient to convince us, this theory need not be taken into consideration, nor the other one; we take the text of the Bible literally, and say that it teaches us a truth which we cannot prove; and the miracles are evidence for the correctness of our view.

Accepting the Creation, we find that miracles are possible, that Revelation is possible, and that every difficulty in this question is removed. We might be asked, Why has God inspired a certain person and not another? why has He revealed the Law to one particular nation, and at one particular time? why has He commanded this, and forbidden that? why has He shown through a prophet certain particular miracles? what is the object of these laws? and — why has He not made the commandments and the prohibitions part of our nature, if it was His object that we should live in accordance with them? We answer to all these questions: He willed it so; or, His wisdom decided so. Just as He created the world according to His will, at a certain time, in a certain form, and as we do not understand why His will or His wisdom decided upon that peculiar form, and upon that peculiar time, so we do not know why His will or wisdom determined any of the things mentioned in the preceding questions. But if we assume that the Universe has the present form as the result of fixed laws, there is occasion for the above questions; and these could only be answered in an objectionable way, implying denial and rejection of the Biblical texts, the correctness of which no intelligent person doubts. Owing to the absence of all proof, we reject the theory of the Eternity of the Universe; and it is for this very reason that the noblest minds spent and will spend their days in research. For if the Creation had been demonstrated by proof, even if only according to the Platonic hypothesis, all arguments of the philosophers against us would be of no avail. If, on the other hand, Aristotle had a proof for his theory, the whole teaching of Scripture would be rejected, and we should be forced to other opinions. I have thus shown that all depends on this question. Note it.

CHAPTER XXVI

In the famous chapters known as the Chapters of Rabbi Eliezer, I find R. Eliezer the Great saying something more extraordinary than I have ever seen in the utterances of any believer in the Law of Moses. I mean the following passage: "Whence were the heavens created? He took part of the light of His garment, stretched it like a cloth, and thus the heavens were extending continually, as it is said: He covereth Himself with light as with a garment, He stretcheth the heavens like a curtain" (Ps. civ. 2). "Whence was the earth created? He took of the snow under the throne of glory, and threw it; according to the words: He saith to the snow, Be thou earth" (Job xxxvii. 6). These are the words given there; and I, in my surprise, ask, What was the belief of this sage? did he think that nothing can be produced from nothing, and that a substance must have existed of which the things were formed? and did he for this reason ask whence were the heavens and the earth created? What has he gained by the answer? We might ask him, Whence was the light of His garment created? or the snow under the throne of His glory? or the throne of glory itself? If the terms "the light of His garment" and "the throne of glory" mean something eternal, they must be rejected; the words would imply an admission of the Eternity of the Universe, though only in the form taught by Plato. The creation of the throne of glory is mentioned by our Sages, though in a strange way; for they say that it has been created before the creation of the Universe. Scripture, however, does not mention the creation of the throne, except in

the words of David, " The Lord hath established his throne in the heavens "
(Ps. ciii. 19), which words admit of figurative interpretation ; but the eternity of the throne is distinctly described, " Thou, O Lord, dwellest for ever,
thy throne for ever and ever " (Lam. v. 19). Now, if R. Eliezer had believed that the throne was eternal, so that the word " throne " expressed an
attribute of God, and not something created, how could anything be produced of a mere attribute ? Stranger still is his expression " of the light of
His garment."

In short, it is a passage that greatly confuses the notions of all intelligent
and religious persons. I am unable to explain it sufficiently. I quoted it
in order that you may not be misled by it. One important thing R. Eliezer
taught us here, that the substance of the heavens is different from that of the
earth ; that there are two different substances : the one is described as
belonging to God, being the light of His garment, on account of its superiority ; and the other, the earthly substance, which is distant from His
splendour and light, as being the snow under the throne of His glory. This
led me to explain the words, " And under his feet as the work of the whiteness of the sapphire " (Exod. xxiv. 10), as expressing that the nobles of the
children of Israel comprehended in a prophetical vision the nature of the
earthly *materia prima*. For, according to Onkelos, the pronoun in the
phrase, " His feet," refers to " throne," as I have shown ; this indicates that
the whiteness under the throne signifies the earthly substance. R. Eliezer
has thus repeated the same idea, and told us that there are two substances—
a higher one, and a lower one ; and that there is not one substance common
to all things. This is an important subject, and we must not think light of
the opinion which the wisest men in Israel have held on this point. It concerns an important point in explaining the existence of the Universe, and
one of the mysteries of the Law. In *Bereshit Rabba* (chap. xii.) the following passage occurs : " R. Eliezer says, The things in the heavens have been
created of the heavens, the things on earth of the earth." Consider how
ingeniously this sage stated that all things on earth have one common substance ; the heavens and the things in them have one substance, different
from the first. He also explains in the Chapters [of R. Eliezer], in addition
to the preceding things, the superiority of the heavenly substance, and its
proximity to God ; and, on the other hand, the inferiority of the earthly
substance and its position. Note it.

CHAPTER XXVII

WE have already stated that the belief in the Creation is a fundamental principle of our religion ; but we do not consider it a principle of our faith that
the Universe will again be reduced to nothing. It is not contrary to the
tenets of our religion to assume that the Universe will continue to exist for
ever. It might be objected that everything produced is subject to destruction, as has been shown ; consequently the Universe, having had a beginning,
must come to an end. This axiom cannot be applied according to our views.
We do not hold that the Universe came into existence, like all things in
Nature, as the result of the laws of Nature. For whatever owes its existence
to the action of physical laws is, according to the same laws, subject to de-

struction : the same law which caused the existence of a thing after a period
of non-existence, is also the cause that the thing is not permanent ; since
the previous non-existence proves that the nature of that thing does not
necessitate its permanent existence. According to our theory, taught in
Scripture, the existence or non-existence of things depends solely on the
will of God and not on fixed laws, and, therefore, it does not follow that God
must destroy the Universe after having created it from nothing. It depends
on His will. He may, according to His desire, or according to the decree of
His wisdom, either destroy it, or allow it to exist, and it is therefore possible
that He will preserve the Universe for ever, and let it exist permanently as
He Himself exists. It is well known that our Sages never said that the throne
of glory will perish, although they assumed that it has been created. No
prophet or sage ever maintained that the throne of glory will be destroyed
or annihilated ; but, on the contrary, the Scriptural passages speak of its
permanent existence. We are of opinion that the souls of the pious have
been created, and at the same time we believe that they are immortal.
Some hold, in accordance with the literal meaning of the Midrashim, that
the bodies of the pious will also enjoy everlasting happiness. Their notion
is like the well-known belief of certain people, that there are bodily enjoyments in Paradise. In short, reasoning leads to the conclusion that the destruction of the Universe is not a certain fact. There remains only the
question as to what the prophets and our Sages say on this point ; whether
they affirm that the world will certainly come to an end, or not. Most
people amongst us believe that such statements have been made, and that
the world will at one time be destroyed. I will show you that this is not the
case ; and that, on the contrary, many passages in the Bible speak of the
permanent existence of the Universe. Those passages which, in the literal
sense, would indicate the destruction of the Universe, are undoubtedly to
be understood in a figurative sense, as will be shown. If, however, those
who follow the literal sense of the Scriptural texts reject our view, and assume
that the ultimate certain destruction of the Universe is part of their faith,
they are at liberty to do so. But we must tell them that the belief in the
destruction is not necessarily implied in the belief in the Creation ; they
believe it because they trust the writer, who used a figurative expression,
which they take literally. Their faith, however, does not suffer by it.

CHAPTER XXVIII

MANY of our coreligionists thought that King Solomon believed in the
Eternity of the Universe. This is very strange. How can we suppose that
any one that adheres to the Law of Moses, our Teacher, should accept that
theory ? if we were to assume that Solomon has on this point, God forbid,
deviated from the Law of Moses, the question would be asked, Why did most
of the Prophets and of the Sages accept it of him ?   Why have they not
opposed him, or blamed him for holding that opinion, as he has been blamed
for having married strange women, and for other things ?   The reason why
this has been imputed to him is to be found in the following passage : " They
desired to suppress the book Koheleth, because its words incline towards
scepticism." It is undoubtedly true that certain passages in this book in-

clude, when taken literally, opinions different from those taught in the Law, and they must therefore be explained figuratively. But the theory of the Eternity of the Universe is not among those opinions, the book does not even contain any passage that implies this theory; much less a passage in which it is clearly set forth. There are, however, in the book, some passages which imply the indestructibility of the Universe, a doctrine that is true; and from the fact that the indestructibility of the Universe is taught in this book, some persons wrongly inferred that the author believed in the Eternity of the Universe. The following are the words that refer to the indestructibility of the Universe : " And the earth remaineth for ever." And those who do not agree with me as regards the above distinction [between the indestructibility and the Eternity of the Universe], are compelled to explain the term *le-'olam* (lit., " for ever "), to mean "the time fixed for the existence of the earth." Similarly they explain the words of God, " Yet all the days of the earth " (Gen. viii. 22) to signify the days fixed for its existence. But I wonder how they would explain the words of David : " He laid the foundations of the earth, that it should not be moved for ever " (Ps. civ. 5). If they maintain here also that the term *le-'olam va-'ed* (lit. " for ever ") does not imply perpetuity, they must come to the conclusion that God exists only for a fixed period, since the same term is employed in describing the perpetuity of God, " The Lord will reign (*le-'olam*) for ever " (Exod. xv. 18, or Ps. x. 16). We must, however, bear in mind that *'olam* only signifies perpetuity when it is combined with *'ad ;* it makes no difference whether *'ad* follows, as in *'olam va-'ed*, or whether it precedes, as in *'ad 'olam*. The words of Solomon which only contain the word *le-'olam*, have therefore less force than the words of David, who uses the term *'olam va-'ed*. David has also in other passages clearly spoken of the incorruptibility of the heavens, the perpetuity and immutability of their laws, and of all the heavenly beings. He says, " Praise ye the Lord from the heavens, etc. For He commanded, and they were created. He hath also stablished them for ever and ever ; he hath made a decree which shall not pass " (Ps. cxlviii. 1–6) ; that is to say, there will never be a change in the decrees which God made, or in the sources of the properties of the heavens and the earth, which the Psalmist has mentioned before. But he distinctly states that they have been created. For he says, " He hath commanded, and they were created." Jeremiah (xxxi. 35) likewise says, " He giveth the sun for a light by day, and the ordinances of the moon and of the stars for a light by night," etc. " If these ordinances depart from before me, saith the Lord, then the seed of Israel also shall cease from being a nation before me for ever." He thus declares, that these decrees will never be removed, although they had a beginning. We therefore find this idea, when we search for it, expressed not only by Solomon but also by others. Solomon himself has stated that these works of God, the Universe, and all that is contained in it, remain with their properties for ever, although they have been created. For he says, " Whatsoever God doeth, it shall be for ever ; nothing can be put to it, nor anything taken away from it " (Eccles. iii. 14). He declares in these words that the world has been created by God and remains for ever. He adds the reason for it by saying, " Nothing can be put to it, nor anything taken from it ; " for this is the reason for the perpetuity, as if he meant to say that things are changed in order to supply that which is wanting, or in order to take away what is superfluous. The works of God being most perfect, admitting no addition or deduction, must remain the same for ever. It is impossible that anything should exist that could cause a change in them. In the conclusion of the verse, Solomon, as it were describes the purpose of exceptions from the laws of Nature, or an excuse for changes in them, when he says, " And God doeth it (viz., He performs miracles) that men should fear before him." The words which follow, " That which hath been is now; and that which is to be hath already been, and God seeketh that which is pursued," contain the idea that God desires the perpetuity and continuity of the Universe. The fact that the works of God are perfect, admitting of no addition or diminution, has already been mentioned by Moses, the wisest of all men, in the words : " The rock, His work is perfect " (Deut. xxxii. 14). All His works or creations are most perfect, containing no defect whatever, nothing superfluous, nor anything unnecessary. Also whatever God decrees for those created things, and whatever He effects through them, is perfectly just, and is the result of His wisdom, as will be explained in some chapters of this treatise.

CHAPTER XXIX

IF we hear a person speaking whose language we do not understand, we undoubtedly know that he speaks, but do not know what his words mean; it may even happen that we hear some words which mean one thing in the tongue of the speaker, and exactly the reverse in our language, and taking the words in the sense which they have in our language, we imagine that the speaker employed them in that sense. Suppose, e.g., an Arab hears of a Hebrew the word *abah*, he thinks that the Hebrew relates how a man despised and refused a certain thing, whilst the Hebrew in reality says that the man was pleased and satisfied with it. The very same thing happens to the ordinary reader of the Prophets ; some of their words he does not understand at all, like those to whom the prophet says (Isa. xxix. 11), " the vision of all is become unto you as the words of a book that is sealed "; in other passages he finds the opposite or the reverse of what the prophet meant ; to this case reference is made in the words, " Ye have perverted the words of the living God " (Jer. xxiii. 36). Besides, it must be borne in mind that every prophet has his own peculiar diction, which is, as it were, his language, and it is in that language that the prophecy addressed to him is communicated to those who understand it. After this preliminary remark you will understand the metaphor frequently employed by Isaiah, and less frequently by other prophets, when they describe the ruin of a kingdom or the destruction of a great nation in phrases like the following :—" The stars have fallen," " The heavens are overthrown," " The sun is darkened," " The earth is waste, and trembles," and similar metaphors. The Arabs likewise say of a person who has met with a serious accident, " His heavens, together with his earth, have been covered " ; and when they speak of the approach of a nation's prosperity, they say, " The light of the sun and moon has increased," " A new heaven and a new earth has been created," or they use similar phrases. So also the prophets, in referring to the ruin of a person, of a nation, or of a country, describe it as the result of God's great anger and wrath, whilst the prosperity of a nation is the result of God's pleasure and satisfaction. In the former case the prophets employ such phrases as " He came forth," " came down," " roared," " thundered," or " caused his voice to be heard " ; also " He commanded," " said," " did," " made," and the like, as will be shown. Sometimes the prophets use the term " mankind " instead of " the people of a certain place," whose destruction they predict ; e.g., Isaiah speaking of the destruction of Israel says, " And the Lord will remove man far away " (Isa. vi. 12). So also Zephaniah (i. 3, 4), " And I will cut off man from off the earth. I will also stretch out mine hand upon Judah." Note this likewise.

Having spoken of the language of the prophets in general, I will now verify and prove my statement. When Isaiah received the divine mission to prophesy the destruction of the Babylonian empire, the death of Sennacherib and that of Nebuchadnezzar, who rose after the overthrow of Sennacherib, he commences in the following manner to describe their fall and the end of their dominion, their defeat, and such evils as are endured by all who are vanquished and compelled to flee before the victorious sword [of the enemy] : " For the stars of heaven, and the constellations thereof, shall not give their light : the sun is darkened in his going forth, and the moon shall not cause her light to shine " (xiii. 10) ; again, " Therefore I will shake the heavens, and the earth shall remove out of her place, in the wrath of the Lord of hosts, and in the day of his fierce anger " (xiii. 13). I do not think that any person is so foolish and blind, and so much in favour of the literal sense of figurative and oratorical phrases, as to assume that at the fall of the Babylonian kingdom a change took place in the nature of the stars of heaven, or in the light of the sun and moon, or that the earth moved away from its centre. For all this is merely the description of a country that has been defeated ; the inhabitants undoubtedly find all light dark, and all sweet things bitter : the whole earth appears too narrow for them, and the heavens are changed in their eyes. He speaks in a similar manner when he describes the poverty and humiliation of the people of Israel, their captivity and their defeat, the continuous misfortunes caused by the wicked Sennacherib when he ruled over all the fortified places of Judah, or the loss of the entire land of Israel when it came into the possession of Sennacherib. He says (xxiv. 17) : " Fear, and the pit, and the snare, are upon thee, O inhabitant of the earth. And it shall come to pass, that he who fleeth from the noise of the fear shall fall into the pit ; and he that cometh out of the midst of the pit shall be taken in the snare : for the windows from on high are open, and the foundations of the earth do shake. The earth is utterly broken down, the earth is clean dissolved, the earth is moved exceedingly. The earth shall reel to and fro like a drunkard." At the end of the same prophecy, when Isaiah describes how God will punish Sennacherib, destroy his mighty empire, and reduce him to disgrace, he uses the following figure (xxiv. 23) : " Then the moon shall be confounded, and the sun ashamed, when the Lord of hosts shall reign," etc. This verse is beautifully explained by Jonathan, the son of Uzziel ; he says that when Sennacherib will meet with his fate because of Jerusalem, the idolaters will understand that this is the work of God ; they will faint and be confounded. He therefore translates the verse thus : " Those who worship the moon will be ashamed, and those who bow down to the sun will be humbled, when the kingdom of God shall reveal itself," etc.　The prophet then pictures the peace of the children of Israel after the death of Sennacherib, the fertility and the cultivation of their land, and the increasing power of their kingdom through Hezekiah.　He employs here the figure of the increase of the light of the sun and moon.　When speaking of the defeated, he says that for them the light of the sun and moon will be diminished and darkened ; in the same sense their light is said to increase for the victorious.　We can frequently notice the correctness of this figure of speech.　When great troubles befall us, our eyes become dim, and we cannot see clearly because the *spiritus visus* is made turbid by the prevailing vapours, and is weakened and diminished by great anxiety and straits of the soul ; whilst in a state of gladness and comfort of the soul the *spiritus visus* becomes clear, and man feels as if the light had increased.　Thus the good tidings that the people shall dwell in Zion, and in Jerusalem, and shall weep no more, etc., conclude in the following manner : " Moreover, the light of the moon shall be as the light of the sun, and the light of the sun shall be sevenfold, as the light of seven days, in the day that the Lord bindeth up the breaches of his people, and healeth the stroke of their wound " (Isa. xxx. 19, 26) ; that is to say, when God will raise them up again after they had fallen through the wicked Sennacherib.　The phrase " as the light of seven days " signifies, according to the commentators, " very great light " : for in this same sense the number " seven " is frequently used in Hebrew.　I think that reference is made by this phrase to the seven days of the dedication of the temple in the reign of Solomon ; for there was never a nation so great, prosperous, and happy in every respect, as Israel was at that time, and therefore the prophet says, that Israel's greatness and happiness will be the same as it was in those seven days.　Speaking of wicked Edom, Israel's oppressor, Isaiah says : " Their slain also shall be cast out, and their stink shall come up out of their carcases, and the mountains shall be melted with their blood.　And all the host of heaven shall be dissolved, and the heavens shall be rolled together as a scroll : and all their host shall fall down, as a leaf falleth off from the vine, and as a fig falleth from the fig-tree.　For my sword shall be bathed in heaven ; behold, I shall come down upon Idumea, and upon the people of my curse, to judgment," etc. (Isa. xxxiv. 3–5).　Will any person who has eyes to see find in these verses any expression that is obscure, or that might lead him to think that they contain an account of what will befall the heavens ?　or anything but a figurative description of the ruin of the Edomites, the withdrawal of God's protection from them, their decline, and the sudden and rapid fall of their nobles ?　The prophet means to say that the individuals, who were like stars as regards their permanent, high, and undisturbed position, will quickly come down, as a leaf falleth from the vine, and as a fig falling from the fig-tree.　This is self-evident ; and there would be no need to mention it, much less to speak on it at length, had it not become necessary, owing to the fact that the common people, and even persons who are considered as distinguished scholars, quote this passage without regarding its context or its purpose, [in support of their view of the future destruction of the heavens].　They believe that Scripture describes here what will, in future, happen to the heavens, in the same manner as it informs us how the heavens have come into existence.　Again, when Isaiah told the Israelites— what afterwards became a well-known fact—that Sennacherib, with his allied nations and kings, would perish, and that the Israelites would be helped by God alone, he employed figurative language, and said : " See how the heavens decay and the earth withers away, and all beings on the earth die, and you are saved " ; that is to say, those who have filled the earth, and have been considered, to use an hyperbole, as permanent and stable as the heavens, will quickly perish and disappear like smoke ; and their famous power, that has been as stable as the earth, will be destroyed like a garment. The passage to which I refer begins : " For the Lord hath comforted Zion ; He hath comforted all her waste places," etc. " Hearken unto me, my people," etc. " My righteousness is near : my salvation is gone forth," etc. It continues thus : " Lift up your eyes to the heavens, and look upon the earth beneath ; for the heavens shall vanish like smoke, and the earth shall wax old like a garment, and they that dwell therein shall die in like manner ; for my salvation shall be for ever, and my righteousness shall not be abolished " (Isa. li. 3–6). The restoration of the kingdom of Israel, its stability and permanence, is described as a creation of heaven and earth. For Isaiah frequently speaks of the land of a king as if it were the whole Universe, as if heaven and earth belonged to him. He therefore comforts Israel and says : " I, even I, am he that comforteth you," etc. " And I have put my words in thy mouth, and I have covered thee in the shadow of mine hand, that I may plant the heavens, and lay the foundations of the earth, and say unto Zion, Thou art my people " (li. 12–16). In the following verses, Isaiah declares that the dominion of Israel will continue, whilst that of the renowned and mighty people will cease : " For the mountains shall depart," etc. (liv. 10). In order to express that the kingdom of the Messiah will be permanent, and that the kingdom of Israel will not be destroyed any more, he says, " Thy sun shall no more go down," etc. (lx. 20). In metaphors like these, which are intelligible to those who understand the context, Isaiah continues to describe the details of the exile, the restoration, and the removal of all sorrow, and says figuratively as follows : " I will create new heavens and a new earth ; for the first shall be forgotten, and their memory shall be blotted out." He explains this in the course of the speech, by pointing out that by the phrase, " I will create," he means that God will give them perpetual gladness and joy in place of the previous grief and mourning, which shall no longer be remembered. I will now describe the sequence of the ideas, and the order of the verses in which these ideas are contained. The prophet begins as follows : " I will mention the loving-kindnesses of the Lord," etc. (lxiii. 7). He then gives (1) an account of God's past kindness to us, concluding with the words, " And he bare them and carried them all the days of old " (ver. 9). (2) Next follows our rebellion : " But they rebelled, and vexed his holy spirit," etc. (ver. 10) ; (3) the dominion of our enemies over us : " Our adversaries have trodden down thy sanctuary ; we are like those over whom thou hast never ruled," etc. (vers. 18, 19) ; (4) and the prophet's prayer on our account : " Be not wroth very sore," etc. (lxiv. 9). (5) The prophet then describes how we deserved these punishments, and how we were called to the truth but did not respond : " I offered myself to be sought of them that asked not for me," etc. (lxv. 1) ; (6) promises mercy and pardon : " Thus saith the Lord, As the new wine is found in the cluster," etc. (ver. 8) ; (7) predicts evil for our oppressors : " Behold, my servant shall eat, but ye shall be hungry," etc. (ver. 13); (8) and moral improvement of our nation to such a degree that we shall be a blessing on the earth, and the previous troubles will be forgotten: "And he shall call his servants by another name: that he who blesseth himself in the earth, shall bless himself in the God of truth; and he that sweareth in the earth, shall swear by the God of truth; because the former troubles are forgotten, and because they are hid from mine eyes. For, behold, I create new heavens, and a new earth: and the former shall not be remembered, nor come into mind. But be ye glad and rejoice for ever in that which I create: for, behold, I create Jerusalem a rejoicing, and her people a joy. And I will rejoice in Jerusalem, and joy in my people," etc. (lxv. 15–19). The whole subject must now be clear and evident; for the words, "I create new heavens, and a new earth," etc., are followed by the explanation, "I create Jerusalem a rejoicing, and her people a joy," etc. The prophet then adds that the seed and name of Israel will be as permanent as their faith and as the rejoicing in it, which God promised to create and to spread over the whole earth: for faith in God and rejoicing in it are two possessions which, once obtained, are never lost or changed. This is expressed in the words: "For as the new heavens and the new earth, which I will make, remain before me, saith the Lord, so shall your seed and your name remain" (lxvi. 22). But of other nations, in some instances, the seed remains, whilst the name has perished; so, e.g., many people are of the seed of the Persians or Greeks, without being known by that special name; they bear the names of other nations, of which they form part. According to my opinion, we have here a prophecy that our religion, which gives us our special name, will remain permanently.

As these figures are frequent in Isaiah, I explained all of them. But we meet with them also in the words of other prophets. Jeremiah, in describing the destruction of Jerusalem in consequence of our sins, says (iv. 23): "I beheld the earth, and, lo, it was without form, and void," etc. Ezekiel (xxxii. 7, 8) foretells the destruction of the kingdom of Egypt, and the death of Pharaoh, through Nebuchadnezzar, in the following words: "And when I shall put thee out, I will cover the heaven, and make the stars thereof dark; I will cover the sun with a cloud, and the moon shall not give her light. All the bright lights of heaven will I make dark over thee, and set darkness upon thy land, saith the Lord." Joel, the son of Pethuel (ii. 10), describes the multitude of locusts that came in his days as follows: "The earth shall quake before them: the heavens shall tremble: the sun and the moon shall be dark, and the stars shall withdraw their shining." Amos (viii. 9, 10), speaking of the destruction of Samaria, says: "I will cause the sun to go down at noon, and I will darken the earth in the clear day; and I will turn your feasts," etc. Micah (i. 3, 4), in relating the fall of Samaria, uses the following well-known rhetorical figures: "For, behold, the Lord cometh forth out of his place, and will come down, and tread upon the high places of the earth. And the mountains shall be molten," etc. Similarly Haggai (ii. 6, 7), in describing the destruction of the kingdom of the Medes and Persians: "I will shake the heavens and the earth, and the sea, and the dry land; and I will shake all nations," etc. When [David] (Ps. lx. 4) describes how, during the expedition of Joab against the Edomites, the nation was low and weak, and how he prayed to God for His assistance, he says: "Thou hast made the earth to tremble; thou hast broken it: heal the breaches thereof; for it shaketh." In another instance he expresses the idea that we need not fear when we see other nations die and perish, because we rely on God's support, and not on our sword and strength, in accordance with the words: "A people saved by the Lord, the shield of thy help" (Deut. xxxiii. 29); he says (Ps. xlvi. 2): "Therefore will we not fear, though the earth be removed, and though the mountains be shaken in the midst of the sea."

The following figurative language is employed in Scripture in referring to the death of the Egyptians in the Red Sea: "The waters saw thee; they were afraid: the depths also were troubled, etc. The voice of thy thunder was in the heaven: the lightnings lightened the world; the earth trembled and shook" (Ps. lxxvii. 17-19). "Was the Lord displeased against the rivers?" etc. (Hab. iii. 8). "There went up a smoke out of his nostrils," etc. (Ps. xviii. 9). "The earth trembled," etc. (Judges v. 4, in the Song of Deborah). There are many other instances; but those which I have not quoted can be explained in accordance with those which I have cited.

Let us now consider the words of Joel (iii. 3-5): "And I will show wonders in the heavens and in the earth, blood and fire, and pillars of smoke. The sun shall be turned into darkness, and the moon into blood, before the great and terrible day of the Lord come. And it shall come to pass, that whosoever shall call on the name of the Lord shall be delivered, for in Mount Zion and in Jerusalem shall be deliverance," etc. I refer them to the defeat of Sennacherib near Jerusalem; but they may be taken as an account of the defeat of Gog and Magog near Jerusalem in the days of the Messiah, if this appears preferable, although nothing is mentioned in this passage but great slaughter, destruction, fire, and the diminution of the light of the two luminaries. You may perhaps object: How can the day of the fall of Sennacherib, according to our explanation, be called "the great and the terrible day of the Lord?" But you must know that a day of great salvation or of great distress is called "the great and terrible day of the Lord." Thus Joel (ii. 11) says of the day on which the locusts came over the land, "For the day of the Lord is great and terrible, and who can abide it?"

Our opinion, in support of which we have quoted these passages, is clearly established, namely, that no prophet or sage has ever announced the destruction of the Universe, or a change of its present condition, or a permanent change of any of its properties. When our Sages say, "The world remains six thousand years, and one thousand years it will be waste," they do not mean a complete cessation of existing things; the phrase "one thousand years it will be waste" distinctly shows that *time* will continue; besides, this is the individual opinion of one Rabbi, and in accordance with one particular theory. But on the other hand the words, "There is nothing new under the sun" (Eccles. i. 9), in the sense that no new creation takes place in any way and under any circumstances, express the general opinion of our Sages, and include a principle which every one of the doctors of the Mishnah and the Talmud recognises and makes use of in his arguments. Even those who understand the words "new heavens and a new earth" in their literal sense hold that the heavens, which will in future be formed, have already been created and are in existence, and that for this reason the present tense "remain" is used, and not the future "will remain." They support their view by citing the text, " There is nothing new under the sun." Do not imagine that this is opposed to our opinion. They mean, perhaps, to say that the natural laws, by which the promised future condition of Israel will be effected, have been in existence since the days of the Creation, and in that they are perfectly correct. When I, however, said that no prophet ever announced " a *permanent* change of any of its properties," I intended to except miracles. For although the rod was turned into a serpent, the water into blood, the pure and noble hand into a leprous one, without the existence of any natural cause that could effect these or similar phenomena, these changes were *not permanent*, they have not become a physical property. On the contrary, the Universe since continues its regular course. This is my opinion; this should be our belief. Our Sages, however, said very strange things as regards miracles; they are found in *Bereshit Rabba*, and in *Midrash Koheleth*, namely, that the miracles are to some extent also natural; for they say, when God created the Universe with its present physical properties, He made it part of these properties, that they should produce certain miracles at certain times, and the sign of a prophet consisted in the fact that God told him to declare when a certain thing will take place, but the thing itself was effected according to the fixed laws of Nature. If this is really the meaning of the passage referred to, it testifies to the greatness of the author, and shows that he held it to be impossible that there should be a change in the laws of Nature, or a change in the will of God [as regards the physical properties of things] after they have once been established. He therefore assumes, e.g., that God gave the waters the property of joining together, and of flowing in a downward direction, and of separating only at the time when the Egyptians were drowned, and only in a particular place. I have already pointed out to you the source of this passage, and it only tends to oppose the hypothesis of a new creation. It is said there : R. Jonathan said, God made an agreement with the sea that it should divide before the Israelites ; thus it is said, " And the sea returned to its strength when the morning appeared " (Exod. xiv. 27). R. Jeremiah, son of Elazar, said : Not only with the sea, but with all that has been created in the six days of the beginning [was the agreement made] ; this is referred to in the words, " I, even my hands have stretched out the heavens, and all their host have I commanded " (Isa. xlv. 12) ; i.e., I have commanded the sea to divide, the fire not to hurt Hananiah, Mishael, and Azariah, the lions not to harm Daniel, and the fish to spit out Jonah. The same is the case with the rest of the miracles.

We have thus clearly stated and explained our opinion, that we agree with Aristotle in one half of his theory. For we believe that this Universe remains perpetually with the same properties with which the Creator has endowed it, and that none of these will ever be changed except by way of miracle in some individual instances, although the Creator has the power to change the whole Universe, to annihilate it, or to remove any of its properties. The Universe, had, however, a beginning and commencement, for when nothing was as yet in existence except God, His wisdom decreed that the Universe be brought into existence at a certain time, that it should not be annihilated or changed as regards any of its properties, except in some instances ; some of these are known to us, whilst others belong to the future, and are therefore unknown to us. This is our opinion and the basis of our religion. The opinion of Aristotle is that the Universe, being permanent and indestructible, is also eternal and without beginning. We have already shown that this theory is based on the hypothesis that the Universe is the necessary result of causal relation, and that this hypothesis includes a certain amount of blasphemy. Having come thus far we will make in the next chapter a few remarks on passages in the first chapters of Genesis. For the primary object in this treatise has been to expound as much as possible of the Scriptural account of the Creation (*ma'aseh bereshit*), and the description of the heavenly chariot (*ma'aseh mercabah*). But let us premise two general observations.

First, the account given in Scripture of the Creation is not, as is generally believed, intended to be in all its parts literal. For if this were the case, wise men would not have kept its explanation secret, and our Sages would not have employed figurative speech [in treating of the Creation] in order to hide its true meaning, nor would they have objected to discuss it in the presence of the common people. The literal meaning of the words might lead us to conceive corrupt ideas and to form false opinions about God, or even entirely to abandon and reject the principles of our Faith. It is therefore right to abstain and refrain from examining this subject superficially and unscientifically. We must blame the practice of some ignorant preachers and expounders of the Bible, who think that wisdom consists in knowing the explanation of words, and that greater perfection is attained by employing more words and longer speech. It is, however, right that we should examine the Scriptural texts by the intellect, after having acquired a knowedge of demonstrative science, and of the true hidden meaning of prophecies. But if one has obtained some knowledge in this matter he must not preach on it, as I stated in my Commentary on the Mishnah (Ḥagigah, ii. 7), and our Sages said distinctly : From the beginning of the book to this place—after the account of the sixth day of the Creation—it is " the glory of God to conceal a thing " (Prov. xxv. 2).

We have thus clearly stated our opinion. It is, however, part of the Divine plan that every one who has obtained some perfection transmit it to some other persons, as will be shown in the chapter on Prophecy. It is, therefore, impossible for a scholar to possess knowledge of these problems, whether it be through his own researches or through his master's teaching, without communicating part of that knowledge to others ; it cannot be done in clear words ; it must be done sparingly by way of hints. We find in the words of some of our Sages numerous hints and notes of this kind, but mixed up with the words of others and with other subjects. In treating of these mysteries, as a rule, I quote as much as contains the principal idea, and leave the rest for those who are worthy of it.

Secondly, the prophets employ homonymous terms and use words which are not meant to be understood in their ordinary signification, but are only used because of some other meaning which they admit, e.g., " a rod of an almond-tree (*shaked*)," because of the words which follow, " for I will hasten (*shaked*) " (Jer. i. 11, 12), as will be shown in the chapter on Prophecy. According to the same principle Ezekiel in the account of the Divine Chariot employs, as we have stated the term *ḥashmal* (Ezek. i. 4) ; also *regel egel* (v. 7), *neḥoshet kalal* (v. 7), and similar terms ; Zechariah (vi. 1) likewise adopts this method, and says : " And the mountains were mountains of *neḥoshet* (brass)," and the like.

After these two remarks I will proceed to the chapter which I have promised.

CHAPTER XXX

THERE is a difference between *first* and *beginning* (or principle). The latter exists in the thing of which it is the beginning, or co-exists with it ; it need not precede it ; e.g., the heart is the beginning of the living being ; the element is the beginning of that of which it is the basis. The term " *first* " is likewise applied to things of this kind ; but is also employed in cases where precedence in time alone is to be expressed, and the thing which precedes is not the beginning (or the cause) of the thing that follows. E.g., we say A. was the first inhabitant of this house, after him came B ; this does not imply that A is the cause of B inhabiting the house. In Hebrew, *teḥillah* is used in the sense of " first " ; e.g., when God first (*teḥillat*) spake to Hosea (Hos. i. 1), and the " beginning " is expressed by *reshith*, derived from *rosh*, " head," the principal part of the living being as regards position. The Universe has not been created out of an element that preceded it in time, since time itself formed part of the Creation. For this reason Scripture employs the term " *bereshit* " (in a principle), in which the *beth* is a preposition denoting " in." The true explanation of the first verse of Genesis is as follows : " In [creating] a principle God created the beings above and the things below." This explanation is in accordance with the theory of the Creation. We find that some of our Sages are reported to have held the opinion that time existed before the Creation. But this report is very doubtful, because the theory that time cannot be imagined with a beginning, has been taught by Aristotle, as I showed you, and is objectionable. Those who have made this assertion have been led to it by a saying of one of our Sages in reference to the terms " one day," " a second day." Taking these terms literally, the author of that saying asked, What determined " the first day," since there was no rotating sphere, and no sun ? and continues as follows : Scripture uses the term " one day " ; R. Jehudah, son of R. Simon, said : " Hence we learn that the divisions of time have existed previously." R. Abahu said, " Hence we learn that God built worlds and again destroyed them." This latter exposition is still worse than the former. Consider the difficulty which these two Rabbis found in the statement that time existed before the creation of the sun. We shall undoubtedly soon remove this difficulty, unless these two Rabbis intended to infer from the Scriptural text that the divisions of time must have existed before the Creation, and thus adopted the theory of the Eternity of the Universe. But every religious man rejects this. The above saying is, in my opinion, certainly of the same character as that of R. Eliezer, " Whence were the heavens created," etc., (chap. xxvi.). In short, in these questions, do not take notice of the utterances of any person. I told you that the foundation of our faith is the belief that God created the Universe from nothing ; that time did not exist previously, but was created ; for it depends on the motion of the sphere, and the sphere has been created.

You must know that the particle *et* in the phrase *et ha-shamayim ve-et ha-arez* ("the heavens and the earth") signifies "together with"; our Sages have explained the word in the same sense in many instances. Accordingly they assume that God created with the heavens everything that the heavens contain, and with the earth everything the earth includes. They further say that the simultaneous Creation of the heavens and the earth is implied in the words, "I call unto them, they stand up together" (Ps. xlviii.). Consequently, all things were created together, but were separated from each other successively. Our Sages illustrated this by the following simile: We sow various seeds at the same time; some spring forth after one day, some after two, and some after three days, although all have been sown at the same time. According to this interpretation, which is undoubtedly correct, the difficulty is removed, which led R. Jehudah, son of R. Simon, to utter the above saying, and consisted in the doubt as to the thing by which the first day, the second, and the third were determined. In *Bereshit Rabba*, our Sages, speaking of the light created on the first day according to the Scriptural account, say as follows: these lights [of the luminaries mentioned in the Creation of the fourth day] are the same that were created on the first day, but were only fixed in their places on the fourth day. The meaning [of the first verse] has thus been clearly stated.

We must further consider that the term *erez* is a homonym, and is used in a general and a particular sense. It has a more general signification when used of everything within the sphere of the moon, i.e., of all the four elements; and is used in particular of one of them, of the lowest, viz., earth. This is evident from the passage: "And the earth was without form and void, and darkness was on the surface of the deep. And the wind of God moved upon the face of the waters." The term "earth" [mentioned here, and in the first verse] includes all the four elements, whilst further on it is said, "And God called the dry land Earth" (Gen. i. 10).

It is also important to notice that the words, "And God called a certain thing a certain name," are invariably intended to distinguish one thing from others which are called by the same common noun. I explain, therefore, the first verse in Genesis thus: In creating the principle God created the things above and those below. *Erez* in this verse denotes "the things below," or "the four elements," and in the verse, "And God called the dry land Earth" (*erez*), it signifies the element earth. This subject is now made clear.

The four elements indicated, according to our explanation, in the term *erez* "earth," in the first verse, are mentioned first after the heavens; for there are named *erez* (earth), *ruaḥ* (air), *mayim* (water), and *ḥoshek* (fire). By *ḥoshek* the element fire is meant, nothing else; comp. "And thou heardest his words out of the midst of *the fire*" (Deut. iv. 36); and, "When ye heard the voice out of the midst of the *ḥoshek*" (darkness) (*ibid.* v. 2); again, "All *ḥoshek* (darkness) shall be hid in his secret places: a *fire* not blown shall consume him" (Job xx. 26). The element fire is called *ḥoshek* because it is not luminous, it is only transparent; for if it were luminous we should see at night the whole atmosphere in flames. The order of the four elements, according to the natural position is here described; namely, first earth, above it water, air close to water, and fire above air; for by placing air over water, *hoshek* (fire), which is " upon the face of the deep," is undoubtedly above air. It was here necessary to use the term *ruah elohim*, because air is described here as in motion (*merahefet*), and the motion of the air is, as a rule, ascribed to God ; comp. " And there went forth a wind from the Lord " (Num. xi. 31) ; " Thou didst blow with thy wind " (Exod. xv. 10) ; " And the Lord turned a mighty strong west wind " (*ibid*. x. 19), and the like. As the first *hoshek*, which denotes the element fire, is different from the *hoshek* mentioned further on in the sense of " darkness," the latter is explained and distinguished from the former, according to our explanation, in the words, " And darkness he called Night." This is now clear.

The phrase, " And he divided between the waters," etc., does not describe a division in space, as if the one part were merely above the other, whilst the nature of both remained the same, but a distinction as regards their nature or form. One portion of that which was first called water was made one thing by certain properties it received, and another portion received a different form, and this latter portion is that which is commonly called water and of this it is said, " And the gathering of the waters he called Seas." Scripture even indicates that the first *mayim* (" water ") in the phrase, " On the face of the waters," does not refer to the waters which form the seas ; and that part of the element " water," having received a particular form, and being above the air, is distinguished from the other part which has received the form of ordinary water. For the words, " And he divided between the waters which are beneath the firmament and the waters which are above the firmament," are similar in meaning to the phrase, " And God divided between the light and the darkness," and refer to a distinction by a separate form. The firmament itself was formed of water ; and in the words of our Sages (*Bereshit Rabba* ; cap. iv.), " The middle drop congealed and formed the heavens."

Here likewise Scripture says, in accordance with what I said above, " And God called the firmament Heaven " (Gen. i. 8), in order to explain the homonymity of the term *shamayim* (heaven), and to show that *shamayim* in the first verse is not the firmament which is also called *shamayim* (heaven). The difference is more clearly expressed in the words, " In the open firmament of heaven " (*ibid*. i. 20) ; here it is shown that " firmament " (*raki·a*), and " heaven " (*shamayim*), are two different things. In consequence of this homonymity of the term *shamayim* the term *raki·a* (firmament) is also used of the true heaven, just as the real firmament is sometimes called *shamayim* (heaven) ; comp. " And God set them in the *raki·a* (firmament) of the heaven " (*ibid*. i. 17).

This verse shows clearly that the stars, the sun, and the moon are not, as people believe, on the surface of the spheres, but they are fixed in the spheres, and this has been proved satisfactorily, there being no vacuum in the Universe ; for it is said, " *in* the firmament of the heaven," and not " *upon* the firmament of the heaven."

It is therefore clear that there has been one common element called water, which has been afterwards distinguished by three different forms ; one part forms the seas, another the firmament, and a third part is over the firmament, and all this is separate from the earth. The Scriptural text follows here a peculiar method in order to indicate some extraordinary mysteries. It has also been declared by our Sages that the portion above the firmament is only water by name, not in reality, for they say (Babyl. Talmud, Ḥagigah 14b) "Four entered the paradise," etc. R. Akiba said to them, "When you come to the stores of pure marble, do not say, Water, water, for it is written, 'He that telleth lies shall not tarry in my sight'" (Ps. ci. 7). Consider, if you belong to the class of thinking men, how clearly and distinctly this passage explains the subject for those who reflect on it! Understand that which has been proved by Aristotle in his book *On Meteorology*, and note whatever men of science have said on meteorological matters.

It is necessary to inquire into the reason why the declaration " that it was good " is not found in the account of the second day of the Creation. The various Midrashic sayings of our Sages on this point are well known ; the best of them is the explanation that the creation of the water was not completed on that day. According to my opinion the reason is likewise clear, and is as follows : When the creation of any part of the Universe is described that is permanent, regular, and in a settled order, the phrase " that it is good " is used. But the account of the firmament, with that which is above it and is called water, is, as you see, of a very mysterious character. For if taken literally the firmament would appear at first thought to be merely an imaginary thing, as there is no other substance but the elements between us and the lowest of the heavenly spheres, and there is no water above the air ; and if the firmament, with that which is over it, be supposed to be above the heavens, it would *a fortiori* seem to be unreal and uncomprehensible. But if the account be understood in a figurative sense and according to its true meaning, it is still more mysterious, since it was considered necessary to make this one of the most hidden secrets, in order to prevent the multitude from knowing it. This being the case, how could it be said [of the creation of the second day] " that it was good " ? This phrase would tell us that it is perfectly clear what share the thing to which it refers takes in the permanent existence of the Universe. But what good can people find in a thing whose real nature is hidden, and whose apparent nature is not real ? Why, therefore, should it be said in reference to it, " that it was good " ? I must, however, give the following additional explanation. Although the result of the second day's creation forms an important element among the existing things, the firmament was not its primary object in the organization of the Universe, and therefore it could not be said " that it was good " ; it was only the means for the uncovering of the earth. Note this. Our Sages have already explained that the herbs and trees, which God caused to spring forth from the ground, were caused by God to grow, after He had sent down rain upon them ; and the passage beginning, " And there went up a mist from the earth " (ii. 6), refers to that which took place before the creative act, related in the words, " Let the earth bring forth grass," etc. (i. ii.). Therefore Onkelos translates it : " And there *had* gone up a mist from the earth." It is also evident from the text itself, where it is distinctly said, " And every plant in the field before it was in the earth," etc. (ii. 5). This question is now explained.

It is well known to every philosopher that the principal causes of production and destruction, after the influence of the spheres, are light and darkness, in so far as these are accompanied by heat and cold.   For by the motion of the spheres the elements intermix, and by light and darkness their constitution changes.   The first change consists in the formation of two kinds of mist; these are the first causes of meteorological phenomena, such as rain; they also caused the formation of minerals, of plants, of animals, and at last of man.   It is likewise known that darkness is the natural property of all things on earth; in them light is accidental, coming from an external cause, and therefore everything remains in a state of rest in the absence of light.   The Scriptural account of the Creation follows in every respect exactly the same order, without any deviation.

Note also the saying of our Sages: " When the Universe was created, all things were created with size, intellect, and beauty fully developed, i.e., everything was created perfect in magnitude and form, and endowed with the most suitable properties; the word *zibyonam* (their beauty) used here has the same meaning as *zebi*, ' glory ' " (Ezek. xx. 6).   Note this likewise, for it includes a principle fully established.

The following point now claims our attention.   The account of the six days of creation contains, in reference to the creation of man, the statement : " Male and female created he them " (i. 27), and concludes with the words : " Thus the heavens and the earth were finished, and all the host of them " (ii. 1), and yet the portion which follows describes the creation of Eve from Adam, the tree of life, and the tree of knowledge, the history of the serpent and the events connected therewith, and all this as having taken place after Adam had been placed in the Garden of Eden.   All our Sages agree that this took place on the sixth day, and that nothing new was created after the close of the six days.   None of the things mentioned above is therefore impossible, because the laws of Nature were then not yet permanently fixed.   There are, however, some utterances of our Sages on this subject [which apparently imply a different view].   I will gather them from their different sources and place them before you, and I will refer also to certain things by mere hints, just as has been done by the Sages.   You must know that their words, which I am about to quote, are most perfect, most accurate, and clear to those for whom they were said.   I will therefore not add long explanations, lest I make their statements plain, and I might thus become " a revealer of secrets," but I will give them in a certain order, accompanied with a few remarks, which will suffice for readers like you.

One of these utterances is this : " Adam and Eve were at first created as one being, having their backs united; they were then separated, and one half was removed and brought before Adam as Eve."   The term *mi-zal·otav* (lit. " of his ribs ") signifies " of his sides."   The meaning of the word is proved by referring to *zel·a*, " the side " of the tabernacle (Exod. xxvi. 20), which Onkelos renders *setar* (" side "), and so also *mi-zal·otav* is rendered by him " *mi-sitrohi* " (of his sides).   Note also how clearly it has been stated that Adam and Eve were two in some respects, and yet they remained one, according to the words, " Bone of my bones, and flesh of my flesh " (Gen. ii. 23).   The unity of the two is proved by the fact that both have the same name, for she is called *ishshah* (woman), because she was taken out of *ish* (man), also by the words, " And shall cleave unto his wife, and they shall be one flesh " (ii. 24).   How great is the ignorance of those who do not see that all this necessarily includes some [other] idea [besides the literal meaning of the words]. This is now clear.

Another noteworthy Midrashic remark of our Sages is the following : " The serpent had a rider, the rider was as big as a camel, and it was the rider that enticed Eve ; this rider was Samaël." Samaël is the name generally applied by our Sages to Satan. Thus they say in several places that Satan desired to entice Abraham to sin, and to abstain from binding Isaac, and he desired also to persuade Isaac not to obey his father. At the same time they also say, in reference to the same subject, viz., the *Akedah* (" the binding of Isaac "), that *Samaël* came to Abraham and said to him, " What ! hast thou, being an old man, lost thy senses ? " etc. This shows that Samaël and Satan are identical. There is a meaning in this name [Samaël], as there is also in the name *naḥash* (" serpent "). In describing how the serpent came to entice Eve, our Sages say : " Samaël was riding on it, and God was laughing at both the camel and its rider." It is especially of importance to notice that the serpent did not approach or address Adam, but all his attempts were directed against Eve, and it was through her that the serpent caused injury and death to Adam. The greatest hatred exists between the serpent and Eve, and between his seed and her seed ; her seed being undoubtedly also the seed of man. More remarkable still is the way in which the serpent is joined to Eve, or rather his seed to her seed ; the head of the one touches the heel of the other. Eve defeats the serpent by crushing its head, whilst the serpent defeats her by wounding her heel. This is likewise clear.

The following is also a remarkable passage, most absurd in its literal sense ; but as an allegory it contains wonderful wisdom, and fully agrees with real facts, as will be found by those who understand all the chapters of this treatise. When the serpent came to Eve he infected her with poison ; the Israelites, who stood at Mount Sinai, removed that poison ; idolaters, who did not stand at Mount Sinai, have not got rid of it. Note this likewise. Again they said : " The tree of life extends over an area of five hundred years' journey, and it is from beneath it that all the waters of the creation sprang forth " ; and they added the explanation that this measure referred to the thickness of its body, and not to the extent of its branches, for they continue thus : " Not the extent of the branches thereof, but the stem thereof [*korato*, lit., ' its beam,' signifying here ' its stem '] has a thickness of five hundred years' journey." This is now sufficiently clear. Again : " God has never shown the tree of knowledge [of good and evil] to man, nor will He ever show it." This is correct, for it must be so according to the nature of the Universe. Another noteworthy saying is this : " And the Lord God took the man, i.e., raised him, and placed him in the Garden of Eden," i.e., He gave him rest. The words " He took him," " He gave him," have no reference to position in space, but they indicate his position in rank among transient beings, and the prominent character of his existence. Remarkable and noteworthy is the great wisdom contained in the names of Adam, Cain, and Abel, and in the fact that it was Cain who slew Abel in the field, that both of them perished, although the murderer had some respite, and that the existence of mankind is due to Seth alone. Comp. " For God has appointed me another seed " (iv. 25). This has proved true.

It is also necessary to understand and consider the words, " And Adam gave names " (ii. 20); here it is indicated that languages are conventional, and that they are not natural, as has been assumed by some. We must also consider the four different terms employed in expressing the relations of the heavens to God, *bore* (Creator), *'oseh* (Maker), *koneh* (Possessor), and *el* (God). Comp. " God *created* the heaven and the earth " (i. 1); " In the day that God *made* the earth and the heavens " (ii. 4); " *Possessor* of heaven and earth " (xiv. 19); " *God* of the Universe " (xxi. 31); " The God of heaven and the God of the earth " (xxiv. 3). As to the verbs, *konen*, " he established," *tafaḥ*, " he spanned," and *natah*, " he stretched out," occurring in the following passages, " Which thou hast *established* " (Ps. viii. 4), " My right hand hath *spanned* the heavens " (Isa. xviii. 13), " Who *stretchest out* the heavens " (Ps. civ. 2), they are included in the term *'asah* (" he made "); the verb *yazar*, " he formed," does not occur in reference to the heavens. According to my opinion the verb *yazar* denotes to make a form, a shape, or any other accident (for form and shape are likewise accidents). It is therefore said, *yozer or*, " Who formeth the light " (Isa. xiv. 7), light being an accident; *yozer harim*, " That formeth the mountains " (Amos iv. 13), i.e., that gave them their shape. In the same sense the verb is used in the passage, " And the Lord God formed (*va-yizer*) all the beasts," etc. (Gen. ii. 7). But in reference to the Universe, viz., the heavens and the earth, which comprises the totality of the Creation, Scripture employs the verb *bara*, which we explain as denoting he produced something from nothing; also *'asah* (" he made "), on account of the general forms or natural properties of the things which were given to them; *kanah*, " he possessed," because God rules over them like a master over his servants. For this reason He is also called, " The Lord of the whole earth " (Jos. iii. 11-13); *ha-adon*, " the Lord " (Exod. xx., iii. 17). But although none can be a master unless there exists something that is in his possession, this attribute cannot be considered to imply the belief in the eternal existence of a *materia prima*, since the verbs *bara*, " he created," and *'asah*, " he made," are also employed in reference to the heavens. The Creator is called the God of the heavens and the God of the Universe, on account of the relations between Him and the heavens; He governs, and they are governed; the word *elohim* does not signify " master " in the sense of " owner "; it expresses the relation between His position in the totality of existing beings, and the position of the heavens or the Universe; He is God, not they, i.e., not the heavens. Note this.

This, together with those explanations which we have given, and which we intend to give, in reference to this subject, may suffice, considering the object of this treatise and the capacity of the reader.

CHAPTER XXXI

It is perhaps clear why the laws concerning Sabbath are so severe, that their transgression is visited with death by stoning, and that the greatest of the prophets put a person to death for breaking the Sabbath. The commandment of the Sabbath is the third from the commandment concerning the existence and the unity of God. For the commandment not to worship any other being is merely an explanation of the first. You know already from what I have said, that no opinions retain their vitality except those which are confirmed, published, and by certain actions constantly revived among the people. Therefore we are told in the Law to honour this day; in order to confirm thereby the principle of Creation which will spread in the world, when all peoples keep Sabbath on the same day. For when the question is asked, why this is done, the answer is given: " For in six days the Lord hath made," etc. (Exod. xx. 11). Two different reasons are given for this commandment, because of two different objects. In the Decalogue in Exodus, the following reason is given for distinguishing the Sabbath: " For in six days," etc. But in Deuteronomy (chap. v. 15) the reason is given: " And thou shalt remember that thou hast been a slave in the land of Egypt, etc., therefore the Lord thy God commanded thee," etc. This difference can easily be explained. In the former, the cause of the honour and distinction of the day is given; comp. " Therefore the Lord hath blessed the day of the Sabbath and sanctified it " (Exod. xx. 10), and the cause for this is, " For in six days," etc. But the fact that God has given us the law of the Sabbath and commanded us to keep it, is the consequence of our having been slaves; for then our work did not depend on our will, nor could we choose the time for it; and we could not rest. Thus God commanded us to abstain from work on the Sabbath, and to rest, for two purposes; namely, (1) That we might confirm the true theory, that of the Creation, which at once and clearly leads to the theory of the existence of God. (2) That we might remember how kind God has been in freeing us from the burden of the Egyptians.—The Sabbath is therefore a double blessing: it gives us correct notions, and also promotes the well-being of our bodies.

CHAPTER XXXII

THERE are as many different opinions concerning Prophecy as concerning the Eternity or Non-Eternity of the Universe. For we have shown that those who assume the existence of God as proved may be divided into three classes, according to the view they take of the question, whether the Universe is eternal or not. Similarly there are three different opinions on Prophecy. I will not notice the view of the Atheist; he does not believe in the Existence of God, much less in Prophecy; but I will content myself with discussing the various opinions [on Prophecy] held by those who believe in God.

1. Among those who believe in Prophecy, and even among our coreligionists, there are some ignorant people who think as follows: God selects any person He pleases, inspires him with the spirit of Prophecy, and entrusts him with a mission. It makes no difference whether that person be wise or stupid, old or young; provided he be, to some extent, morally good. For these people have not yet gone so far as to maintain that God might also inspire a wicked person with His spirit. They admit that this is impossible, unless God has previously caused him to improve his ways.

2. The philosophers hold that prophecy is a certain faculty of man in a state of perfection, which can only be obtained by study. Although the faculty is common to the whole race, yet it is not fully developed in each individual, either on account of the individual's defective constitution, or on account of some other external cause. This is the case with every faculty common to a class. It is only brought to a state of perfection in some indi-

viduals, and not in all ; but it is impossible that it should not be perfect in some individual of the class ; and if the perfection is of such a nature that it can only be produced by an agent, such an agent must exist. Accordingly, it is impossible that an ignorant person should be a prophet ; or that a person being no prophet in the evening, should, unexpectedly on the following morning, find himself a prophet, as if prophecy were a thing that could be found unintentionally. But if a person, perfect in his intellectual and moral faculties, and also perfect, as far as possible, in his imaginative faculty, pre- pares himself in the manner which will be described, he must become a prophet ; for prophecy is a natural faculty of man. It is impossible that a man who has the capacity for prophecy should prepare himself for it without attaining it , just as it is impossible that a person with a healthy constitution should be fed well, and yet not properly assimilate his food ; and the like.

3. The third view is that which is taught in Scripture, and which forms one of the principles of our religion. It coincides with the opinion of the philosophers in all points except one. For we believe that, even if one has the capacity for prophecy, and has duly prepared himelf, it may yet happen that he does not actually prophesy. It is in that case the will of God [that withholds from him the use of the faculty]. According to my opinion, this fact is as exceptional as any other miracle, and acts in the same way. For the laws of Nature demand that every one should be a prophet, who has a proper physical constitution, and has been duly prepared as regards educa- tion and training. If such a person is not a prophet, he is in the same position as a person who, like Jeroboam (1 Kings xiii. 4), is deprived of the use of his hand, or of his eyes, as was the case with the army of Syria, in the history of Elisha (2 Kings vi. 18). As for the principle which I laid down, that pre- paration and perfection of moral and rational faculties are the *sine quâ non*, our Sages say exactly the same : "The spirit of prophecy only rests upon persons who are wise, strong, and rich." We have explained these words in our Commentary on the Mishnah, and in our large work. We stated there that the Sons of the Prophets were constantly engaged in preparation. That those who have prepared themselves may still be prevented from being pro- phets, may be inferred from the history of Baruch, the son of Nerijah ; for he followed Jeremiah, who prepared and instructed him ; and yet he hoped in vain for prophecy ; comp., "I am weary with my sighing, and rest have I not found." He was then told through Jeremiah, "Thus saith the Lord, Thus shalt thou say to him, Thou seekest for thee great things, do not seek " (Jer. xlv. 5). It may perhaps be assumed that prophecy is here described as a thing "too great " for Baruch. So also the fact that "her prophets did not find visions from the Lord " (Lam. ii. 4), may be considered as the result of the exile of her prophets, as will be explained (chap. xxxvi.). There are, however, numerous passages in Scripture as well as in the writings of our Sages, which support the principle that it depends chiefly on the will of God who is to prophesy, and at what time ; and that He only selects the best and the wisest. We hold that fools and ignorant people are unfit for this dis- tinction. It is as impossible for any one of these to prophesy as it is for an ass or a frog ; for prophecy is impossible without study and training ; when these have created the possibility, then it depends on the will of God whether the possibility is to be turned into reality. We must not be misled by the

words of Jeremiah (i. 5), " Before I formed thee in the womb I knew thee, and before thou camest forth from the womb I have sanctified thee " ; for this is the case with all prophets ; there must be a physical preparation from the beginning of their existence, as will be explained. As to the words, " For I am young " (*ibid.* ver. 6), it is well known that the pious Joseph, when he was thirty years old, is called by the Hebrew " young " (*na·ar*) ; also Joshua, when he was nearly sixty years old. For the statement, " and his minister Joshua, the son of Nun, was young," occurs in the account of the Golden Calf (Exod. xxxiii. 11). Moses was then eighty-one years old, he lived one hundred and twenty years ; Joshua, who survived him fourteen years, lived one hundred and ten years and must consequently have been at least fifty-seven years old at the time when the Golden Calf was made, and yet he is called *na·ar*, " young." Nor must we be misled by prophecies like the following : " I will pour out my spirit over all flesh, and your sons and your daughters shall prophesy " ; since it is distinctly stated what is meant by " prophesy " in this place, viz., " Your old men will dream dreams, your young men shall see visions." For we call also prophets all those who reveal something unknown by surmises, or conjectures, or correct inferences. Thus " prophets of Baal " and " of Asherah " are mentioned in Scripture. And God says, " If there arise among you a prophet or a dreamer of dreams," etc. (Deut. xiii. 1). As to the revelation on Mount Sinai, all saw the great fire, and heard the fearful thunderings, that caused such an extraordinary terror ; but only those of them who were duly qualified were prophetically inspired, each one according to his capacities. Therefore it is said, " Come up unto the Lord, thou and Aaron, Nadab and Abihu." Moses rose to the highest degree of prophecy, according to the words, " And Moses alone shall come near the Lord." Aaron was below him, Nadab and Abihu below Aaron, and the seventy elders below Nadab and Abihu, and the rest below the latter, each one according to his degree of perfection. Similarly our Sages wrote : Moses had his own place and Aaron his own. Since we have touched upon the revelation on Mount Sinai, we will point out in a separate chapter what may be inferred as regards the nature of that event, both from the Scriptural text, in accordance with reasonable interpretation, and from the words of our Sages.

CHAPTER XXXIII

IT is clear to me that what Moses experienced at the revelation on Mount Sinai was different from that which was experienced by all the other Israelites, for Moses alone was addressed by God, and for this reason the second person singular is used in the Ten Commandments ; Moses then went down to the foot of the mount and told his fellow-men what he had heard. Comp., " I stood between the Lord and you at that time to tell you the word of the Lord " (Deut. v. 5). Again, " Moses spake, and God answered him with a loud voice " (Exod. xix. 19). In the Mechilta our Sages say distinctly that he brought to them every word as he had heard it. Furthermore, the words, " In order that the people hear when I speak with thee " (Exod. xix. 9), show that God spoke to Moses, and the people only heard the mighty sound, not distinct words. It is to the perception of this mighty sound that Scripture refers in the passage, "When ye hear the sound" (Deut. v. 20); again it is stated, "You heard a sound of w rds" (*ibid.* iv. 12), and it is not said "You heard words"; and even where the hearing of the words is mentioned, only the perception of the sound is meant. It was only Moses that heard the words, and he reported them to the people. This is apparent from Scripture, and from the utterances of our Sages in general. There is, however, an opinion of our Sages frequently expressed in the Midrashim, and found also in the Talmud, to this effect: The Israelites heard the first and the second commandments from God, i.e., they learnt the truth of the principles contained in these two commandments in the same manner as Moses, and not through Moses. For these two principles, the existence of God and His Unity, can be arrived at by means of reasoning, and whatever can be established by proof is known by the prophet in the same way as by any other person; he has no advantage in this respect. These two principles were not known through prophecy alone. Comp., "Thou hast been shown to know that," etc. (Deut. iv. 34). But the rest of the commandments are of an ethical and authoritative character, and do not contain [truths] perceived by the intellect. Notwithstanding all that has been said by our Sages on this subject, we infer from Scripture as well as from the words of our Sages, that the Israelites heard on that occasion a certain sound which Moses understood to proclaim the first two commandments, and through Moses all other Israelites learnt them when he in intelligible sounds repeated them to the people. Our Sages mention this view, and support it by the verse, "God hath spoken once; twice have I heard this" (Ps. lxii. 11). They state distinctly, in the beginning of *Midrash Ḥazita*, that the Israelites did not hear any other command directly from God; comp. "A loud voice, and it was not heard again" (Deut. v. 19). It was after this first sound was heard that the people were seized with the fear and terror described in Scripture, and that they said, "Behold the Lord our God has shown us, etc., and now why shall we die, etc. Come thou near," etc. Then Moses, the most distinguished of all mankind, came the second time, received successively the other commandments, and came down to the foot of the mountain to proclaim them to the people, whilst the mighty phenomena continued; they saw the fire, they heard the sounds, which were those of thunder and lightning during a storm, and the loud sound of the shofar; and all that is said of the many sounds heard at that time, e.g., in the verse, "and all the people perceived the sounds," etc., refers to the sound of the shofar, thunder, and similar sounds. But the voice of the Lord, that is, the voice created for that purpose, which was understood to include the diverse commandments, was only heard once, as is declared in the Law, and has been clearly stated by our Sages in the places which I have indicated to you. When the people heard this voice their soul left them; and in this voice they perceived the first two commandments. It must, however, be noticed that the people did not understand the voice in the same degree as Moses did. I will point out to you this important fact, and show you that it was a matter of tradition with the nation, and well known by our Sages. For, as a rule, Onkelos renders the word *va-yedabber* by *u-mallel* ("and God spake"); this is also the case with this word in the beginning of the twentieth chapter of Exodus, but the words *ve-al yedabber immanu elohim*, "let not God speak to us"

(Exod. xx. 19), addressed by the people to Moses, is rendered *vela yitmallel immanu min kodam adonai* (" Let not aught be spoken to us by the Lord "). Onkelos makes thus the same distinction which we made. You know that according to the Talmud Onkelos received all these excellent interpretations directly from R. Eliezer and R. Joshua, the wisest men in Israel. Note it, and remember it, for it is impossible for any person to expound the revelation on Mount Sinai more fully than our Sages have done, since it is one of the secrets of the Law. It is very difficult to have a true conception of the events, for there has never been before, nor will there ever be again, anything like it. Note it.

CHAPTER XXXIV

THE meaning of the Scriptural passage, " Behold I will send an angel before thee," etc. (Exod. xxiii. 20), is identical with the parallel passage in Deuteronomy which God is represented to have addressed to Moses at the revelation on Mount Sinai, namely, " I will raise them up a prophet from among their brethren," etc. (Deut. xviii. 18). The words, " Beware of him, and obey his voice," etc., said in reference to the angel, prove [that this passage speaks of a prophet]. For there is no doubt that the commandment is given to the ordinary people, to whom angels do not appear with commandments and exhortations, and it is therefore unnecessary to tell them not to disobey him. The meaning of the passage quoted above is this : God informs the Israelites that He will raise up for them a prophet, to whom an angel will appear in order to speak to him, to command him, and to exhort him ; he therefore cautions them not to rebel against this angel, whose word the prophet will communicate to them. Therefore it is expressly said in Deuteronomy, " Unto him ye shall hearken " (Deut. xviii. 15) ; " And it shall come to pass that whosoever shall not hearken unto my words which he shall speak in my name," etc. (*ibid.* 19). This is the explanation of the words, " for my name is in him " (Exod. xxiv. 21). The object of all this is to say to the Israelites, This great sight witnessed by you, the revelation on Mount Sinai, will not continue for ever, nor will it ever be repeated. Fire and cloud will not continually rest over the tabernacle, as they are resting now on it ; but the towns will be conquered for you, peace will be secured for you in the land, and you will be informed of what you have to do, by an angel whom I will send to your prophets ; he will thus teach you what to do, and what not to do. Here a principle is laid down which I have constantly expounded, viz., that all prophets except Moses receive the prophecy through an angel. Note it.

CHAPTER XXXV

I HAVE already described the four points in which the prophecy of Moses our Teacher was distinguished from that of other prophets, in books accessible to every one, in the Commentary on the Mishnah (Sanhedrin x. 1) and in Mishneh-torah (S. Madd‹a I. vii. 6) ; I have also adduced evidence for my explanation, and shown the correctness thereof. I need not repeat the subject here, nor is it included in the theme of this work. For I must tell you that whatever I say here of prophecy refers exclusively to the form of the prophecy of all prophets before and after

Moses. But as to the prophecy of Moses I will not discuss it in this work with one single word, whether directly or indirectly, because, in my opinion, the term prophet is applied to Moses and other men homonymously. A similar distinction, I think, must be made between the miracles wrought by Moses and those wrought by other prophets, for his signs are not of the same class as the miracles of other prophets. That his prophecy was distinguished from that of all his predecessors is proved by the passage, " And I appeared to Abraham, etc., but by my name, the Lord, I was not known unto them " (Exod. vi. 3). We thus learn that his prophetic perception was different from that of the Patriarchs, and excelled it; *a fortiori* it must have excelled that of other prophets before Moses. As to the distinction of Moses' prophecy from that of succeeding prophets, it is stated as a fact, " And there arose not a prophet since in Israel like unto Moses, whom the Lord knew face to face " (Deut. xxxiv. 10). It is thus clear that his prophetic perception was above that of later prophets in Israel, who are " a kingdom of priests and a holy nation," and " in whose midst is the Lord " ; much more is it above that of prophets among other nations.

The general distinction between the wonders of Moses and those of other prophets is this : The wonders wrought by prophets, or for them, are witnessed by a few individuals, e.g., the wonders wrought by Elijah and Elisha ; the king of Israel is therefore surprised, and asked Gehazi to describe to him the miracles wrought by Elisha : " Tell me, I pray thee, all the great things that Elisha hath done. And it came to pass as he was telling, etc. And Gehazi said : ' My lord, O king, this is the woman, and this is her son, whom Elisha restored to life ' " (2 Kings viii. 4, 5). The same is the case with the signs of every other prophet, except Moses our Teacher. Scripture, therefore, declares that no prophet will ever, like Moses, do signs publicly in the presence of friend and enemy, of his followers and his opponents ; this is the meaning of the words : " And there arose not a prophet since in Israel like unto Moses, etc., in all the signs and the wonders, etc., in the sight of all Israel." Two things are here mentioned together ; namely, that there will not arise a prophet that will perceive as Moses perceived, or a prophet that will do as he did ; then it is pointed out that the signs were made in the presence of Pharaoh, all his servants and all his land, the opponents of Moses, and also in the presence of all the Israelites, his followers. Comp. " In the sight of all Israel." This is a distinction not possessed by any prophet before Moses ; nor, as is correctly foretold, will it ever be possessed by another prophet. We must not be misled by the account that the light of the sun stood still certain hours for Joshua, when " he said in the sight of Israel," etc. (Josh. x. 12) ; for it is not said there " in the sight of *all* Israel," as is said in reference to Moses. So also the miracle of Elijah, at Mount Carmel, was witnessed only by a few people. When I said above that the sun stood still *certain hours*, I explain the words " *ka-jom tamim* " to mean " the longest possible day," because *tamim* means " perfect," and indicates that that day appeared to the people at Gibeon as their longest day in the summer. Your mind must comprehend the distinction of the prophecy and the wonders of Moses, and understand that his greatness in prophetic perception was the same as his power of producing miracles. If you further assume that we are unable fully to comprehend the nature of this greatness, you will understand that when I speak, in the chapters which follow this, on prophecy and the different classes of prophets, I only refer to the prophets which have not attained the high degree that Moses attained. This is what I desired to explain in this chapter.

CHAPTER XXXVI

Prophecy is, in truth and reality, an emanation sent forth by the Divine Being through the medium of the Active Intellect, in the first instance to man's rational faculty, and then to his imaginative faculty; it is the highest degree and greatest perfection man can attain; it consists in the most perfect development of the imaginative faculty. Prophecy is a faculty that cannot in any way be found in a person, or acquired by man, through a culture of his mental and moral faculties; for even if these latter were as good and perfect as possible, they would be of no avail, unless they were combined with the highest natural excellence of the imaginative faculty. You know that the full development of any faculty of the body, such as the imagination, depends on the condition of the organ, by means of which the faculty acts. This must be the best possible as regards its temperament and its size, and also as regards the purity of its substance. Any defect in this respect cannot in any way be supplied or remedied by training. For when any organ is defective in its temperament, proper training can in the best case restore a healthy condition to some extent, but cannot make such an organ perfect. But if the organ is defective as regards size, position, or as regards the substance and the matter of which the organ is formed, there is no remedy. You know all this, and I need not explain it to you at length.

Part of the functions of the imaginative faculty is, as you well know, to retain impressions by the senses, to combine them, and chiefly to form images. The principal and highest function is performed when the senses are at rest and pause in their action, for then it receives, to some extent, divine inspiration in the measure as it is predisposed for this influence. This is the nature of those dreams which prove true, and also of prophecy, the difference being one of quantity, not of quality. Thus our Sages say, that dream is the sixtieth part of prophecy; and no such comparison could be made between two things of different kinds, for we cannot say the perfection of man is so many times the perfection of a horse. In *Bereshit Rabba* (sect. xvii.) the following saying of our Sages occurs, "Dream is the *nobelet* (the unripe fruit) of prophecy." This is an excellent comparison, for the unripe fruit (*nobelet*) is really the fruit to some extent, only it has fallen from the tree before it was fully developed and ripe. In a similar manner the action of the imaginative faculty during sleep is the same as at the time when it receives a prophecy, only in the first case it is not fully developed, and has not yet reached its highest degree. But why need I quote the words of our Sages, when I can refer to the following passage of Scripture: " If there be among you a prophet, I, the Lord, will make myself known unto him in a vision, in a dream will I speak to him " (Num. xii. 6). Here the Lord tells us what the real essence of prophecy is, that it is a perfection acquired in a dream or in a vision (the original *mareh* is a noun derived from the verb *raah*) ; the imaginative faculty acquires such an efficiency in its action that it sees the thing as if it came from without, and perceives it as if through the medium of bodily senses. These two modes of prophecy, vision and dream, include all its different degrees. It is a well-known fact that the thing which engages greatly and earnestly man's attention whilst he is awake and in the full possession of his senses forms during his sleep the object of the action of his imaginative faculty. Imagination is then only influenced by the intellect in so far as it is predisposed for such influence. It would be quite useless to illustrate this by a simile, or to explain it fully, as it is clear, and every one knows it. It is like the action of the senses, the existence of which no person with common sense would ever deny. After these introductory remarks you will understand that a person must satisfy the following conditions before he can become a prophet: The substance of the brain must from the very beginning be in the most perfect condition as regards purity of matter, composition of its different parts, size and position; no part of his body must suffer from ill-health; he must in addition have studied and acquired wisdom, so that his rational faculty passes from a state of potentiality to that of actuality; his intellect must be as developed and perfect as human intellect can be; his passions pure and equally balanced; all his desires must aim at obtaining a knowledge of the hidden laws and causes that are in force in the Universe; his thoughts must be engaged in lofty matters; his attention directed to the knowledge of God, the consideration of His works, and of that which he must believe in this respect. There must be an absence of the lower desires and appetites, of the seeking after pleasure in eating, drinking, and cohabitation; and, in short, every pleasure connected with the sense of touch. (Aristotle correctly says that this sense is a disgrace to us, since we possess it only in virtue of our being animals; and it does not include any specifically human element, whilst enjoyments connected with other senses, as smell, hearing, and sight, though likewise of a material nature, may sometimes include [intellectual] pleasure, appealing to man as man, according to Aristotle. This remark, although forming no part of our subject, is not superfluous, for the thoughts of the most renowned wise men are to a great extent affected by the pleasures of this sense, and filled with a desire for them. And yet people are surprised that these scholars do not prophesy, if prophesying be nothing but a certain degree in the natural development of man.) It is further necessary to suppress every thought or desire for unreal power and dominion; that is to say, for victory, increase of followers, acquisition of honour, and service from the people without any ulterior object. On the contrary, the multitude must be considered according to their true worth; some of them are undoubtedly like domesticated cattle, and others like wild beasts, and these only engage the mind of the perfect and distinguished man in so far as he desires to guard himself from injury, in case of contact with them, and to derive some benefit from them when necessary. A man who satisfies these conditions, whilst his fully developed imagination is in action, influenced by the Active Intellect according to his mental training, —such a person will undoubtedly perceive nothing but things very extraordinary and divine, and see nothing but God and His angels. His knowledge will only include that which is real knowledge, and his thought will only be directed to such general principles as would tend to improve the social relations between man and man.

We have thus described three kinds of perfection: mental perfection acquired by training, perfection of the natural constitution of the imaginative faculty, and moral perfection produced by the suppression of every thought of bodily pleasures, and of every kind of foolish or evil ambition. These qualities are, as is well known, possessed by the wise men in different degrees, and the degrees of prophetic faculty vary in accordance with this difference. Faculties of the body are, as you know, at one time weak, wearied, and corrupted, at others in a healthy state. Imagination is certainly one of the faculties of the body. You find, therefore, that prophets are deprived of the faculty of prophesying when they mourn, are angry, or are similarly affected. Our Sages say, Inspiration does not come upon a prophet when he is sad or languid. This is the reason why Jacob did not receive any revelation during the period of his mourning, when his imagination was engaged with the loss of Joseph. The same was the case with Moses, when he was in a state of depression through the multitude of his troubles, which lasted from the murmurings of the Israelites in consequence of the evil report of the spies, till the death of the warriors of that generation. He received no message of God, as he used to do, even though he did not receive prophetic inspiration through the medium of the imaginative faculty, but directly through the intellect. We have mentioned it several times that Moses did not, like other prophets, speak in similes. This will be further explained (chap. xlv.), but it is not the subject of the present chapter. There were also persons who prophesied for a certain time and then left off altogether, something occurring that caused them to discontinue prophesying. The same circumstance, prevalence of sadness and dulness, was undoubtedly the direct cause of the interruption of prophecy during the exile ; for can there be any greater misfortune for man than this : to be a slave bought for money in the service of ignorant and voluptuous masters, and powerless against them as they unite in themselves the absence of true knowledge and the force of all animal desires ? Such an evil state has been prophesied to us in the words, " They shall run to and fro to seek the word of God, but shall not find it " (Amos viii. 12) ; " Her king and her princes are among the nations, the law is no more, her prophets also find no vision from the Lord " (Lam. ii. 9). This is a real fact, and the cause is evident ; the pre-requisites [of prophecy] have been lost. In the Messianic period—may it soon commence—prophecy will therefore again be in our midst, as has been promised by God.

CHAPTER XXXVII

It is necessary to consider the nature of the divine influence, which enables us to think, and gives us the various degrees of intelligence. For this influence may reach a person only in a small measure, and in exactly the same proportion would then be his intellectual condition, whilst it may reach another person in such a measure that, in addition to his own perfection, he can be the means of perfection for others. The same relation may be observed throughout the whole Universe. There are some beings so perfect that they can govern other beings, but there are also beings that are only perfect in so far as they can govern themselves and cannot influence other beings. In some cases the influence of the [Active] Intellect reaches only the logical and not the imaginative faculty; either on account of the insufficiency of that influence, or on account of a defect in the constitution of the imaginative faculty, and the consequent inability of the latter to receive that influence : this is the condition of wise men or philosophers. If, however, the imaginative faculty is naturally in the most perfect condition, this influence may, as has been explained by us and by other philosophers, reach both his logical and his imaginative faculties : this is the case with prophets. But it happens sometimes that the influence only reaches the imaginative faculty on account of the insufficiency of the logical faculty, arising either from a natural defect, or from a neglect in training. This is the case with statesmen, lawgivers, diviners, charmers, and men that have true dreams, or do wonderful things by strange means and secret arts, though they are not wise men ; all these belong to the third class. It is further necessary to understand that some persons belonging to the third class perceive scenes, dreams, and confused images, when awake, in the form of a prophetic vision. They then believe that they are prophets ; they wonder that they perceive visions, and think that they have acquired wisdom without training. They fall into grave errors as regards important philosophical principles, and see a strange mixture of true and imaginary things. All this is the consequence of the strength of their imaginative faculty, and the weakness of their logical faculty, which has not developed, and has not passed from potentiality to actuality.

It is well known that the members of each class differ greatly from each other. Each of the first two classes is again subdivided, and contains two sections, namely, those who receive the influence only as far as is necessary for their own perfection, and those who receive it in so great a measure that it suffices for their own perfection and that of others. A member of the first class, the wise men, may have his mind influenced either only so far, that he is enabled to search, to understand, to know, and to discern, without attempting to be a teacher or an author, having neither the desire nor the capacity ; but he may also be influenced to such a degree that he becomes a teacher and an author. The same is the case with the second class. A person may receive a prophecy enabling him to perfect himself but not others ; but he may also receive such a prophecy as would compel him to address his fellowmen, teach them, and benefit them through his perfection. It is clear that, without this second degree of perfection, no books would have been written, nor would any prophets have persuaded others to know the truth. For a scholar does not write a book with the object to teach himself what he already knows. But the characteristic of the intellect is this : what the intellect of one receives is transmitted to another, and so on, till a person is reached that can only himself be perfected by such an influence, but is unable to communicate it to others, as has been explained in some chapters of this treatise (chap. xi.). It is further the nature of this element in man that he who possesses an additional degree of that influence is compelled to address his fellowmen, under all circumstances, whether he is listened to or not, even if he injures himself thereby. Thus we find prophets that did not leave off speaking to the people until they were slain ; it is this divine influence that moves them, that does not allow them to rest in any way, though they might bring upon themselves great evils by their action. E.g., when Jeremiah was despised, like other teachers and scholars of his age, he could not, though he desired it, withhold his prophecy, or cease from reminding the people of the truths which they rejected. Comp. " For the Word of the Lord was unto me a reproach and a mocking all day, and I said, I will not mention it, nor will I again speak in His name ; but it was in mine heart as a burning fire, enclosed in my bones, and I was wearied to keep it, and did not prevail " (Jer. xx. 8, 9). This is also the meaning of the words of another prophet, " The Lord God hath spoken, who shall not prophesy ? " (Amos iii. 8) Note it.

CHAPTER XXXVIII

EVERY man possesses a certain amount of courage, otherwise he would not stir to remove anything that might injure him. This psychical force seems to me analogous to the physical force of repulsion. Energy varies like all other forces, being great in one case and small in another. There are, there-fore, people who attack a lion, whilst others run away at the sight of a mouse. One attacks a whole army and fights, another is frightened and terrified by the threat of a woman. This courage requires that there be in a man's con-stitution a certain disposition for it. If man, in accordance with a certain view, employs it more frequently, it develops and increases, but, on the other hand, if it is employed, in accordance with the opposite view, more rarely, it will diminish. From our own youth we remember that there are different degrees of energy among boys.

The same is the case with the intuitive faculty ; all possess it, but in differ-ent degrees. Man's intuitive power is especially strong in things which he has well comprehended, and in which his mind is much engaged. Thus you may yourself guess correctly that a certain person said or did a certain thing in a certain matter. Some persons are so strong and sound in their imagi-nation and intuitive faculty that, when they assume a thing to be in existence, the reality either entirely or partly confirms their assumption. Although the causes of this assumption are numerous, and include many preceding, succeed-ing, and present circumstances, by means of the intuitive faculty the intellect can pass over all these causes, and draw inferences from them very quickly, almost instantaneously. This same faculty enables some persons to foretell important coming events. The prophets must have had these two forces, courage and intuition, highly developed, and these were still more strength-ened when they were under the influence of the Active Intellect. Their courage was so great that, e.g., Moses, with only a staff in his hand, dared to address a great king in his desire to deliver a nation from his service. He was not frightened or terrified, because he had been told, " I will be with thee " (Exod. iii. 12). The prophets have not all the same degree of courage, but none of them have been entirely without it. Thus Jeremiah is told : " Be not afraid of them," etc. (Jer. i. 8), and Ezekiel is exhorted, " Do not fear them or their word " (Ezek. ii. 6). In the same manner, you find that all prophets possessed great courage. Again, through the excellence of their intuitive faculty, they could quickly foretell the future, but this excellence, as is well known, likewise admits of different degrees.

The true prophets undoubtedly conceive ideas that result from premisses which human reason could not comprehend by itself; thus they tell things which men could not tell by reason and ordinary imagination alone; for [the action of the prophets' mental capacities is influenced by] the same agent that causes the perfection of the imaginative faculty, and that enables the prophet thereby to foretell a future event with such clearness as if it was a thing already perceived with the senses, and only through them conveyed to his imagination. This agent perfects the prophet's mind, and influences it in such a manner that he conceives ideas which are confirmed by reality, and are so clear to him as if he deduced them by means of syllogisms.

This should be the belief of all who choose to accept the truth. For [all things are in a certain relation to each other, and] what is noticed in one thing may be used as evidence for the existence of certain properties in another, and the knowledge of one thing leads us to the knowledge of other things But [what we said of the extraordinary powers of our imaginative faculty] applies with special force to our intellect, which is directly influenced by the Active Intellect, and caused by it to pass from potentiality to actuality. It is through the intellect that the influence reaches the imaginative faculty. How then could the latter be so perfect as to be able to represent things not previously perceived by the senses, if the same degree of perfection were withheld from the intellect, and the latter could not comprehend things otherwise than in the usual manner, namely, by means of premiss, conclusion, and inference? This is the true characteristic of prophecy, and of the disciplines to which the preparation for prophecy must exclusively be devoted. I spoke here of true prophets in order to exclude the third class, namely, those persons whose logical faculties are not fully developed, and who do not possess any wisdom, but are only endowed with imaginative and inventive powers. It may be that things perceived by these persons are nothing but ideas which they had before, and of which impressions were left in their imaginations together with those of other things; but whilst the impressions of other images are effaced and have disappeared, certain images alone remain, are seen and considered as new and objective, coming from without. The process is analogous to the following case: A person has with him in the house a thousand living individuals; all except one of them leave the house: when the person finds himself alone with that individual, he imagines that the latter has entered the house now, contrary to the fact that he has only not left the house. This is one of the many phenomena open to gross misinterpretations and dangerous errors, and many of those who believed that they were wise perished thereby.

There were, therefore, men who supported their opinion by a dream which they had, thinking that the vision during sleep was independent of what they had previously believed or heard when awake. Persons whose mental capacities are not fully developed, and who have not attained intellectual perfection, must not take any notice of these [dreams]. Those who reach that perfection may, through the influence of the divine intellect, obtain knowledge independent of that possessed by them when awake. They are true prophets, as is distinctly stated in Scripture, *ve-nabi lebab ḥokmah* (Ps. xc. 12), " And the true prophet possesseth a heart of wisdom." This must likewise be noticed.

CHAPTER XXXIX

WE have given the definition of prophecy, stated its true characteristics, and shown that the prophecy of Moses our Teacher was distinguished from that of other prophets; we will now explain that this distinction alone qualified him for the office of proclaiming the Law, a mission without a parallel in the history from Adam to Moses, or among the prophets who came after him; it is a principle in our faith that there will never be revealed another Law. Consequently we hold that there has never been, nor will there ever be, any other divine Law but that of Moses our Teacher. According to what is written in Scripture and handed down by tradition, the fact may be explained in the following way: There were prophets before Moses, as the patriarchs Shem, Eber, Noah, Methushelah, and Enoch, but of these none said to any portion of mankind that God sent him to them and commanded him to convey to them a certain message or to prohibit or to command a certain thing. Such a thing is not related in Scripture, or in authentic tradition. Divine prophecy reached them as we have explained. Men like Abraham, who received a large measure of prophetic inspiration, called their fellow-men together and led them by training and instruction to the truth which they had perceived. Thus Abraham taught, and showed by philosophical arguments that there is one God, that He has created everything that exists beside Him, and that neither the constellations nor anything in the air ought to be worshipped; he trained his fellow-men in this belief, and won their attention by pleasant words as well as by acts of kindness. Abraham did not tell the people that God had sent him to them with the command concerning certain things which should or should not be done. Even when it was commanded that he, his sons, and his servants should be circumcised, he fulfilled that commandment, but he did not address his fellow-men prophetically on this subject. That Abraham induced his fellow-men to do what is right, telling them only his own will [and not that of God], may be learnt from the following passage of Scripture: "For I know him, because he *commands* his sons and his house after him, to practise righteousness and judgment" (Gen. xix. 19). Also Isaac, Jacob, Levi, Kohath, and Amram influenced their fellow-men in the same way. Our Sages, when speaking of prophets before Moses, used expressions like the following: The *bet-din* (court of justice) of Eber, the *bet-din* of Methushelah, and in the college of Methushelah; although all these were prophets, yet they taught their fellow-men in the manner of preachers, teachers, and pedagogues, but did not use such phrases as the following: "And God said to me, Speak to certain people so and so." This was the state of prophecy before Moses. But as regards Moses, you know what [God] said to him, what he said [to the people], and the words addressed to him by the whole nation: "This day we have seen that God doth talk with man, and that he liveth" (Deut. v. 21). The history of all our prophets that lived after Moses is well known to you; they performed, as it were, the function of warning the people and exhorting them to keep the Law of Moses, threatening evil to those who would neglect it, and announcing blessings to those who would submit to its guidance. This we believe will always be the case. Comp. "It is not in the heavens that one might say," etc. (*ibid.* xxx. 12); "For us and for our children for ever " (*ibid.* xxix. 28). It is but natural that it should be so. For if one individual of a class has reached the highest perfection possible in that class, every other individual must necessarily be less perfect, and deviate from the perfect measure either by surplus or deficiency. Take, e.g., the normal constitution of a being, it is the most proper composition possible in that class ; any constitution that deviates from that norm contains something too much or too little. The same is the case with the Law. It is clear that the Law is normal in this sense ; for it contains " Just statutes and judgments " (Deut. iv. 8) ; but " just " is here identical with " equibalanced." The statutes of the Law do not impose burdens or excesses as are implied in the service of a hermit or pilgrim, and the like ; but, on the other hand, they are not so deficient as to lead to gluttony or lewdness, or to prevent, as the religious laws of the heathen nations do, the development of man's moral and intellectual faculties. We intend to discuss in this treatise the reasons of the commandments, and we shall then show, as far as necessary, the justice and wisdom of the Law, on account of which it is said : " The Law of God is perfect, refreshing the heart " (Ps. xix. 8). There are persons who believe that the Law commands much exertion and great pain, but due consideration will show them their error. Later on I will show how easy it is for the perfect to obey the Law. Comp. " What does the Lord thy God ask of thee ? " etc. (Deut. x. 12) ; " Have I been a wilderness to Israel ? " (Jer. ii. 31). But this applies only to the noble ones ; whilst wicked, violent, and pugnacious persons find it most injurious and hard that there should be any divine authority tending to subdue their passion. To low-minded, wanton, and passionate persons it appears most cruel that there should be an obstacle in their way to satisfy their carnal appetite, or that a punishment should be inflicted for their doings. Similarly every godless person imagines that it is too hard to abstain from the evil he has chosen in accordance with his inclination. We must not consider the Law easy or hard according as it appears to any wicked, lowminded, and immoral person, but as it appears to the judgment of the most perfect, who, according to the Law, are fit to be the example for all mankind. This Law alone is called divine ; other laws, such as the political legislations among the Greeks, or the follies of the Sabeans, are the works of human leaders, but not of prophets, as I have explained several times.

CHAPTER XL

It has already been fully explained that man is naturally a social being, that by virtue of his nature he seeks to form communities ; man is therefore different from other living beings that are not compelled to combine into communities. He is, as you know, the highest form in the creation, and he therefore includes the largest number of constituent elements ; this is the reason why the human race contains such a great variety of individuals, that we cannot discover two persons exactly alike in any moral quality, or in external appearance. The cause of this is the variety in man's temperament, and in accidents dependent on his form ; for with every physical form there are connected certain special accidents different from those which are connected with the substance. Such a variety among the individuals of a class does not exist in any other class of living beings; for the variety in any other species is limited; only man forms an exception; two persons may be so different from each other in every respect that they appear to belong to two different classes. Whilst one person is so cruel that he kills his youngest child in his anger, another is too delicate and faint-hearted to kill even a fly or worm. The same is the case with most of the accidents. This great variety and the necessity of social life are essential elements in man's nature. But the well-being of society demands that there should be a leader able to regulate the actions of man; he must complete every shortcoming, remove every excess, and prescribe for the conduct of all, so that the natural variety should be counterbalanced by the uniformity of legislation, and the order of society be well established. I therefore maintain that the Law, though not a product of Nature, is nevertheless not entirely foreign to Nature. It being the will of God that our race should exist and be permanently established, He in His wisdom gave it such properties that men can acquire the capacity of ruling others. Some persons are therefore inspired with theories of legislation, such as prophets and lawgivers; others possess the power of enforcing the dictates of the former, and of compelling people to obey them, and to act accordingly. Such are kings, who accept the code of lawgivers, and [rulers] who pretend to be prophets, and accept, either entirely or partly, the teaching of the prophets. They accept one part while rejecting another part, either because this course appears to them more convenient, or out of ambition, because it might lead people to believe that the rulers themselves had been prophetically inspired with these laws, and did not copy them from others. For when we like a certain perfection, find pleasure in it, and wish to possess it, we sometimes desire to make others believe that we possess that virtue, although we are fully aware that we do not possess it. Thus people, e.g., adorn themselves with the poems of others, and publish them as their own productions. It also occurs in the works of wise men on the various branches of Science, that an ambitious, lazy person sees an opinion expressed by another person, appropriates it, and boasts that he himself originated it. The same [ambition] occurs also with regard to the faculty of prophecy. There were men who, like Zedekiah, the son of Chenaanah (1 Kings xxii. 11, 24) boasted that they received a prophecy, and declared things which have never been prophesied. Others, like Hananiah, son of Azzur (Jer. xxviii. 1–5), claim the capacity of prophecy, and proclaim things which, no doubt, have been said by God, that is to say, that have been the subject of a divine inspiration, but not to them. They nevertheless say that they are prophets, and adorn themselves with the prophecies of others. All this can easily be ascertained and recognized. I will, however, fully explain this to you, so that no doubt be left to you on this question, and that you may have a test by which you may distinguish between the guidance of human legislation, of the divine law, and of teachings stolen from prophets. As regards those who declare that the laws proclaimed by them are their own ideas, no further test is required; the confession of the defendant makes the evidence of the witness superfluous. I only wish to instruct you about laws which are proclaimed as prophetic. Some of these are truly prophetic, originating in divine inspiration, some are of non-prophetic character, and some, though prophetic originally, are the result of plagiarism. You will find that the sole object of certain laws, in accordance with the intention of their author, who well considered their effect, is to establish the good order of the state and its affairs, to free it from all mischief and wrong ; these laws do not deal with philosophic problems, contain no teaching for the perfecting of our logical faculties, and are not concerned about the existence of sound or unsound opinions. Their sole object is to arrange, under all circumstances, the relations of men to each other, and to secure their well-being, in accordance with the view of the author of these laws. These laws are political, and their author belongs, as has been stated above, to the third class, viz., to those who only distinguish themselves by the perfection of their imaginative faculties. You will also find laws which, in all their rules, aim, as the law just mentioned, at the improvement of the material interests of the people ; but, besides, tend to improve the state of the faith of man, to create first correct notions of God, and of angels, and to lead then the people, by instruction and education, to an accurate knowledge of the Universe : this education comes from God ; these laws are divine. The question which now remains to be settled is this : Is the person who proclaimed these laws the same perfect man that received them by prophetic inspiration, or a plagiarist, who has stolen these ideas from a true prophet ? In order to be enabled to answer this question, we must examine the merits of the person, obtain an accurate account of his actions, and consider his character. The best test is the rejection, abstention, and contempt of bodily pleasures ; for this is the first condition of men, and *a fortiori* of prophets ; they must especially disregard pleasures of the sense of touch, which, according to Aristotle, is a disgrace to us ; and, above all, restrain from the pollution of sensual intercourse. Thus God exposes thereby false prophets to public shame, in order that those who really seek the truth may find it, and not err or go astray ; e.g., Zedekiah, son of Maasiah, and Ahab, son of Kolaiah, boasted that they had received a prophecy. They persuaded the people to follow them, by proclaiming utterances of other prophets ; but all the time they continued to seek the low pleasures of sensual intercourse, committing even adultery with the wives of their companions and followers. God exposed their falsehood as He has exposed that of other false prophets. The king of Babylon burnt them, as Jeremiah distinctly states : " And of them shall be taken up a curse by all the captivity of Judah, which are in Babylon, saying, The Lord make thee like Zedekiah, and like Ahab, whom the king of Babylon roasted in the fire. Because they have committed villany in Israel, and have committed adultery with their neighbours' wives, and have spoken lying words in my name, which I have not commanded them " (Jer. xxix. 22, 23). Note what is meant by these words,

CHAPTER XLI

I NEED not explain what a dream is, but I will explain the meaning of the term *mareh*, " vision," which occurs in the passage : " In a vision (*be-mareh*) do I make myself known unto him " (Num. xii. 6). The term signifies that which is also called *mareh ha-nebuah*, " prophetic vision," *yad ha-shem*, " the hand of God," and *mahazeh*, " a vision." It is something terrible and fearful which the prophet feels while awake, as is distinctly stated by

Daniel: " And I saw this great vision, and there remained no strength in me, for my comeliness was turned in me into corruption, and I retained no strength " (Dan. x. 8). He afterwards continues, " Thus was I in deep sleep on my face, and my face toward the ground " (*ibid.* ver. 9). But it was in a prophetic vision that the angel spoke to him and " set him upon his knees." Under such circumstances the senses cease to act, and the [Active Intellect] influences the rational faculties, and through them the imaginative faculties, which become perfect and active. Sometimes the prophecy begins with a prophetic vision, the prophet greatly trembles, and is much affected in consequence of the perfect action of the imaginative faculty; and after that the prophecy follows. This was the case with Abraham. The commencement of the prophecy is, " The word of the Lord came to Abraham in a vision " (Gen. xv. 1); after this, " a deep sleep fell upon Abraham "; and at last, " he said unto Abraham," etc. When prophets speak of the fact that they received a prophecy, they say that they received it from an angel, or from God; but even in the latter case it was likewise received through an angel. Our Sages, therefore, explain the words, " And the Lord said unto her " that He spake through an angel. You must know that whenever Scripture relates that the Lord or an angel spoke to a person, this took place in a dream or in a prophetic vision.

There are four different ways in which Scripture relates the fact that a divine communication was made to the prophet. (1) The prophet relates that he heard the words of an angel in a dream or vision; (2) He reports the words of the angel without mentioning that they were perceived in a dream or vision, assuming that it is well known that prophecy can only originate in one of the two ways, " In a vision I will make myself known unto him, in a dream I will speak unto him " (Num. xii. 6). (3) The prophet does not mention the angel at all; he says that God spoke to him, but he states that he received the message in a dream or a vision. (4) He introduces his prophecy by stating that God spoke to him, or told him to do a certain thing, or speak certain words, but he does not explain that he received the message in a dream or vision, because he assumes that it is well known, and has been established as a principle that no prophecy or revelation originates otherwise than in a dream or vision, and through an angel. Instances of the first form are the following :—" And the angel of the Lord said unto me in a dream, Jacob " (Gen. xxxi. 11); " And an angel said unto Israel in a vision of night " (*ibid.* xlvi. 2); " And an angel came to Balaam by night "; " And an angel said unto Balaam " (Num. xxii. 20-22). Instances of the second form are these : " And Elohim (an angel), said unt Jacob, Rise, go up to Bethel " (Gen. xxxv. 1); " And Elohim said unto him, Thy name is Jacob," etc. (*ibid.* xxxv. 10); " And an angel of the Lord called unto Abraham out of heaven the second time " (*ibid.* xxii. 15); " And Elohim said unto Noah " (*ibid.* vi. 13). The following is an instance of the third form : " The word of the Lord came unto Abraham in a vision " (*ibid.* xv. 1). Instances of the fourth form are : " And the Lord said unto Abraham " (*ibid.* xviii. 13); " And the Lord said unto Jacob, Return," etc. (*ibid.* xxxi. 3); " And the Lord said unto Joshua " (Josh. v. 9); " And the Lord said unto Gideon " (Judges vii. 2). Most of the prophets speak in a similar manner : " And the Lord said unto me " (Deut. ii. 2); " And the word of the Lord came unto me "

(Ezek. xxx. 1); "And the word of the Lord came" (2 Sam. xxiv. 11); "And behold, the word of the Lord came unto him" (1 Kings xix. 9); "And the word of the Lord came expressly" (Ezek. i. 3); "The beginning of the word of the Lord by Hosea" (Hos. i. 2); "The hand of the Lord was upon me" (Ezek. xxxvii. 1). There are a great many instances of this class. Every passage in Scripture introduced by any of these four forms is a prophecy proclaimed by a prophet; but the phrase, "And Elohim (an angel) came to a certain person in the dream of night," does not indicate a prophecy, and the person mentioned in that phrase is not a prophet; the phrase only informs us that the attention of the person was called by God to a certain thing, and at the same time that this happened at night. For just as God may cause a person to move in order to save or kill another person, so He may cause, according to His will, certain things to rise in man's mind in a dream by night. We have no doubt that the Syrian Laban was a perfectly wicked man, and an idolater; likewise Abimelech, though a good man among his people, is told by Abraham concerning his land [Gerar] and his kingdom, "Surely there is no fear of God in this place" (Gen. xx. 11). And yet concerning both of them, viz., Laban and Abimelech, it is said [that an angel appeared to them in a dream]. Comp. "And Elohim (an angel) came to Abimelech in a dream by night" (*ibid.* ver. 3); and also, "And Elohim came to the Syrian Laban in the dream of the night" (*ibid.* xxxi. 24). Note and consider the distinction between the phrases, "And Elohim came," and "Elohim said," between "in a dream by night," and "in a vision by night." In reference to Jacob it is said, "And an angel said to Israel in the visions by night" (Gen. xlvi. 2), but in reference to Laban and Abimelech, "And Elohim came," etc. Onkelos makes the distinction clear; he translates, in the last two instances, *ata memar min kodam adonai*, "a word came from the Lord," and not *ve-itgeli*, "and the Lord appeared." The phrase, "And the Lord said to a certain person," is employed even when this person was not really addressed by the Lord, and did not receive any prophecy, but was informed of a certain thing through a prophet. E.g., "And she went to inquire of the Lord" (Gen. xxv. 22); that is, according to the explanation of our Sages, she went to the college of Eber, and the latter gave her the answer; and this is expressed by the words, "And the Lord said unto her" (*ibid.* ver. 23). These words have also been explained thus, God spoke to her through an angel; and by "angel" Eber is meant here, for a prophet is sometimes called "angel," as will be explained; or the angel that appeared to Eber in this vision is referred to, or the object of the Midrash explanation is merely to express that wherever God is introduced as directly speaking to a person, i.e., to any of the ordinary prophets, He speaks through an angel, as has been set forth by us (chap. xxxiv.).

CHAPTER XLII

WE have already shown that the appearance or speech of an angel mentioned in Scripture took place in a vision or dream; it makes no difference whether this is expressly stated or not, as we have explained above. This is a point of considerable importance. In some cases the account begins by stating that the prophet saw an angel; in others, the account apparently introduces a human being, who ultimately is shown to be an angel; but it makes no difference, for if the fact that an angel has been heard is only mentioned at the end, you may rest satisfied that the whole account from the beginning describes a prophetic vision. In such visions, a prophet either sees God who speaks to him, as will be explained by us, or he sees an angel who speaks to him, or he hears some one speaking to him without seeing the speaker, or he sees a man who speaks to him, and learns afterwards that the speaker was an angel. In this latter kind of prophecies, the prophet relates that he saw a man who was doing or saying something, and that he learnt afterwards that it was an angel.

This important principle was adopted by one of our Sages, one of the most distinguished among them, R. Ḥiya the Great (*Bereshit Rabba*, xlviii.), in the exposition of the Scriptural passage commencing, " And the Lord appeared unto him in the plain of Mamre " (Gen. xviii.). The general statement that the Lord appeared to Abraham is followed by the description in what manner that appearance of the Lord took place; namely, Abraham saw first three men; he ran and spoke to them. R. Ḥiya, the author of the explanation, holds that the words of Abraham, " My Lord, if now I have found grace in thy sight, do not, I pray thee, pass from thy servant," were spoken by him in a prophetic vision to one of the men; for he says that Abraham addressed these words to the chief of these men. Note this well, for it is one of the great mysteries [of the Law]. The same, I hold, is the case when it is said in reference to Jacob, " And a man wrestled with him " (Gen. xxxii. 25); this took place in a prophetic vision, since it is expressly stated in the end (ver. 31) that it was an angel. The circumstances are here exactly the same as those in the vision of Abraham, where the general statement, " And the Lord appeared to him," etc., is followed by a detailed description. Similarly the account of the vision of Jacob begins, " And the angels of God met him " (Gen. xxxii. 2); then follows a detailed description how it came to pass that they met him; namely, Jacob sent messengers, and after having prepared and done certain things, " he was left alone," etc., " and a man wrestled with him " (*ibid.* ver. 24). By this term " *man* " [one of] the angels of God is meant, mentioned in the phrase, " And angels of God met him "; the wrestling and speaking was entirely a prophetic vision. That which happened to Balaam on the way, and the speaking of the ass, took place in a prophetic vision, since further on, in the same account, an angel of God is introduced as speaking to Balaam. I also think that what Joshua perceived, when " he lifted up his eyes and saw, and behold a man stood before him " (Josh. v. 13) was a prophetic vision, since it is stated afterwards (ver. 14) that it was " the prince of the host of the Lord." But in the passages, " And an angel of the Lord came up from Gilgal " (Judges ii. 1); " And it came to pass that the angel of the Lord spake these words to all Israel " (*ibid.* ver. 2); the " angel " is, according to the explanation of our Sages, Phineas. They say, The angel is Phineas, for, when the Divine Glory rested upon him, he was " like an angel." We have already shown (chap. vi.) that the term " angel " is homonymous, and denotes also " prophet," as is the case in the following passages :—" And He sent an angel, and He hath brought us up out of Egypt " (Num. xx. 16); " Then spake Haggai, the angel of the Lord, in the Lord's message " (Hagg. i. 13); " But they mocked the angels of

God " (2 Chron. xxxvi. 16).—Comp. also the words of Daniel, " And the man Gabriel, whom I had seen in the vision at the beginning, being caused to fly swiftly, touched me about the time of the evening oblation " (Dan. ix. 11). All this passed in a prophetic vision. Do not imagine that an angel is seen or his word heard otherwise than in a prophetic vision or prophetic dream, according to the principle laid down :—" I make myself known unto him in a vision, and speak unto him in a dream " (Num. xii. 6). The instances quoted may serve as an illustration of those passages which I do not mention. From the rule laid down by us that prophecy requires preparation, and from our interpretation of the homonym " angel," you will infer that Hagar, the Egyptian woman, was not a prophetess ; also Manoah and his wife were no prophets ; for the speech they heard, or imagined they heard, was like the *bat-kol* (prophetic echo), which is so frequently mentioned by our Sages, and is something that may be experienced by men not prepared for prophecy. The homonymity of the word " angel " misleads in this matter. This is the principal method by which most of the difficult passages in the Bible can be explained. Consider the words, " And an angel of the Lord found her by the well of water " (Gen. xvi. 7), which are similar to the words referring to Joseph—" And a man found him, and behold, he was erring in the field " (*ibid.* xxxvii. 15). All the Midrashim assume that by *man* in this passage an angel is meant.

CHAPTER XLIII

WE have already shown in our work that the prophets sometimes prophesy in allegories ; they use a term allegorically, and in the same prophecy the meaning of the allegory is given. In our dreams, we sometimes believe that we are awake, and relate a dream to another person, who explains the meaning, and all this goes on while we dream. Our Sages call this " a dream interpreted in a dream." In other cases we learn the meaning of the dream after waking from sleep. The same is the case with prophetic allegories. Some are interpreted in the prophetic vision. Thus it is related in Zechariah, after the description of the allegorical vision—" And the angel that talked with me came again and waked me as a man that is awakened from his sleep. And he said unto me, ' What dost thou see ? ' " etc. (Zech. iv. 1-2), and then the allegory is explained (ver. 6, *sqq.*).

Another instance we find in Daniel. It is first stated there : " Daniel had a dream and visions of his head upon his bed " (Dan. vii. 1). The whole allegory is then given, and Daniel is described as sighing that he did not know its interpretation. He asks the angel for an explanation, and he received it in a prophetic vision. He relates as follows : " I came near unto one of those that stood by, and asked him the truth of all this. So he told me, and made me know the interpretation of the things " (*ibid.* ver. 16). The whole scene is called *ḥazon* (vision), although it was stated that Daniel had a dream, because an angel explained the dream to him in the same manner as is mentioned in reference to a prophetic dream. I refer to the verse : " A vision appeared to me Daniel, after that which appeared to me at the first " (*ibid.* viii. 1). This is clear, for *ḥazon* (vision) is derived from *ḥaza*, " to see," and *mareh*, " vision," from *raah*, " to see " ; and *ḥaza* and *raah* are synonymous. There is therefore no difference whether we use *mareh*, or *maḥazeh*, or *ḥazon*, there is no other mode of revelation but the two mentioned in Scripture : " In a vision I make myself known to him, in a dream I will speak unto him " (Num. xii. 6). There are, however, different degrees [of prophetic proficiency], as will be shown (chap. xlv.).

There are other prophetic allegories whose meaning is not given in a prophetic vision. The prophet learns it when he awakes from his sleep. Take, e.g., the staves which Zechariah took in a prophetic vision.

You must further know that the prophets see things shown to them allegorically, such as the candlesticks, horses, and mountains of Zechariah (Zech. iv. 2 ; vi. 1–7), the scroll of Ezekiel (Ezek. ii. 9), the wall made by a plumb-line (Amos vii. 7), which Amos saw, the animals of Daniel (Dan. vii. and viii.), the seething pot of Jeremiah (Jer. i. 13), and similar allegorical objects shown to represent certain ideas. The prophets, however, are also shown things which do not illustrate the object of the vision, but indicate it by their name through its etymology or homonymity. Thus the imaginative faculty forms the image of a thing, the name of which has two meanings, one of which denotes something different [from the image]. This is likewise a kind of allegory. Comp. *Makkal shaked*, " almond staff," of Jeremiah (i. 11–12). It was intended to indicate by the second meaning of *shaked* the prophecy, " For I will watch " (*shoked*), etc., which has no relation whatever to the staff or to almonds. The same is the case with the *kelub ḳayiẓ*, " a basket of summer fruit," seen by Amos, by which the completion of a certain period was indicated, " the end (*ha-ḳeẓ*) having come " (Amos viii. 2). Still more strange is the following manner of calling the prophet's attention to a certain object. He is shown a different object, the name of which has neither etymologically nor homonymously any relation to the first object, but the names of both contain the same letters, though in a different order, Take, e.g., the allegories of Zechariah (chap. xi. 7, *sqq.*). He takes in a prophetic vision staves to lead the flock ; he calls the one *Noʻam* (pleasure), the other *ḥobelim*. He indicates thereby that the nation was at first in favour with God, who was their leader and guide. They rejoiced in the service of God, and found happiness in it, while God was pleased with them, and loved them, as it is said, " Thou hast avouched the Lord thy God," etc., and " the Lord hath avouched thee," etc. (Deut. xxvi. 17, 18). They were guided and directed by Moses and the prophets that followed him. But later a change took place. They rejected the love of God, and God rejected them, appointing destroyers like Jeroboam and Manasse as their rulers. Accordingly, the word *ḥobelim* has the same meaning [viz., destroying] as the root *ḥabal* has in *Meḥabbelim keramim*, " destroying vineyards " (Song of Sol. ii. 15). But the prophet found also in this name *Ḥobelim* the indication that the people despised God, and that God despised them. This is, however, not expressed by the word *ḥabal*, but by a transposition of the letters *Ḥet*, *Bet*, and *Lamed*, the meaning of despising and rejecting is obtained. Comp. " My soul loathed them, and their soul also abhorred me " [*baḥalah*] (Zech. xi. 8). The prophet had therefore to change the order of the letters in *ḥabal* into that of *Baḥal*. In this way we find very strange things and also mysteries (*Sodot*) in the words *neḥoshet*, *Kalal*, *regel*, *ʻegel*, and *ḥashmal* of the *Mercabah*, and in other terms in other passages. After the above explanation you will see the mysteries in the meaning of these expressions if you examine them thoroughly.

CHAPTER XLIV

PROPHECY is given either in a vision or in a dream, as we have said so many times, and we will not constantly repeat it. We say now that when a prophet is inspired with a prophecy he may see an allegory, as we have shown frequently, or he may in a prophetic vision perceive that God speaks to him, as is said in Isaiah (vi. 8), "And I heard the voice of the Lord saying, Whom shall I send, and who will go for us ? " or he hears an angel addressing him, and sees him also. This is very frequent, e.g., " And the angel of God spake unto me," etc. (Gen. xxxi. 11); "And the angel that talked with me answered and said unto me, Dost thou not know what these are " (Zech. iv. 5); " And I heard one holy speaking " (Dan. viii. 13). Instances of this are innumerable. The prophet sometimes sees a man that speaks to him. Comp., " And behold there was a man, whose appearance was like the appearance of brass, and the man said to me," etc. (Ezek. xl. 3, 4), although the passage begins, " The hand of the Lord was upon me " (*ibid.* ver. 1). In some cases the prophet sees no figure at all, only hears in the prophetic vision the words addressed to him ; e.g., " And I heard the voice of a man between the banks of Ulai " (Dan. viii. 16) ; " There was silence, and I heard a voice " (in the speech of Eliphaz, Job iv. 16); "And I heard a voice of one that spake to me " (Ezek. i. 28). The being which Ezekiel perceived in the prophetic vision was not the same that addressed him ; for at the conclusion of the strange and extraordinary scene which Ezekiel describes expressly as having been perceived by him, the object and form of the prophecy is introduced by the words, " And I heard a voice of a man that spake to me." After this remark on the different kinds of prophecy, as suggested by Scripture, I say that the prophet may perceive that which he hears with the greatest possible intensity, just as a person may hear thunder in his dream, or perceive a storm or an earthquake ; such dreams are frequent. The prophet may also hear the prophecy in ordinary common speech, without anything unusual. Take, e.g., the account of the prophet Samuel. When he was called in a prophetic vision, he believed that the priest Eli called him ; and this happened three times consecutively. The text then explains the cause of it, saying that Samuel naturally believed that Eli had called him, because at that time he did not yet know that God addressed the prophet in this form, nor had that secret as yet been revealed to him. Comp., " And Samuel did not yet know the Lord, and the word of the Lord was not yet revealed to him," i.e., he did not yet know, and it had not yet been revealed to him, that the word of God is communicated in this way. The words, " He did not yet know the Lord," may perhaps mean that Samuel had not yet received any prophecy ; for in reference to a prophet's receiving divine communication it is said, " I make myself known to him in a vision, I speak to him in a dream " (Num. xii. 6). The meaning of the verse accordingly is this, Samuel had not yet received any prophecy, and therefore did not know that this was the form of prophecy. Note it.

CHAPTER XLV

AFTER having explained prophecy in accordance with reason and Scripture, I must now describe the different degrees of prophecy from these two points of view. Not all the degrees of prophecy which I will enumerate qualify a person for the office of a prophet. The first and the second degrees are only steps leading to prophecy, and a person possessing either of these two degrees does not belong to the class of prophets whose merits we have been discussing. When such a person is occasionally called prophet, the term is used in a wider sense, and is applied to him because he is almost a prophet. You must not be misled by the fact that according to the books of the Prophets, a certain prophet, after having been inspired with one kind of prophecy, is reported to have received prophecy in another form. For it is possible for a prophet to prophesy at one time in the form of one of the degrees which I am about to enumerate, and at another time in another form. In the same manner, as the prophet does not prophesy continuously, but is inspired at one time and not at another, so he may at one time prophesy in the form of a higher degree, and at another time in that of a lower degree; it may happen that the highest degree is reached by a prophet only once in his lifetime, and afterwards remains inaccessible to him, or that a prophet remains below the highest degree until he entirely loses the faculty; for ordinary prophets must cease to prophesy a shorter or longer period before their death. Comp. " And the word of the Lord ceased from Jeremiah " (Ezra i. 1); " And these are the last words of David " (2 Sam. xxiii. 1). From these instances it can be inferred that the same is the case with all prophets. After this introduction and explanation, I will begin to enumerate the degrees of prophecy to which I have referred above.

(1) The first degree of prophecy consists in the divine assistance which is given to a person, and induces and encourages him to do something good and grand, e.g., to deliver a congregation of good men from the hands of evil-doers; to save one noble person, or to bring happiness to a large number of people; he finds in himself the cause that moves and urges him to this deed. This degree of divine influence is called " the spirit of the Lord "; and of the person who is under that influence we say that the spirit of the Lord came upon him, clothed him, or rested upon him, or the Lord was with him, and the like. All the judges of Israel possessed this degree, for the following general statement is made concerning them :—" The Lord raised up judges for them; and the Lord was with the judge, and he saved them " (Judges ii. 18). Also all the noble chiefs of Israel belonged to this class. The same is distinctly stated concerning some of the judges and the kings :—" The spirit of the Lord came upon Jephthah " (*ibid.* xi. 29); of Samson it is said, " The spirit of the Lord came upon him " (*ibid.* xiv. 19); " And the spirit of the Lord came upon Saul when he heard those words " (1 Sam. xi. 6). When Amasa was moved by the holy spirit to assist David, " A spirit clothed Amasa, who was chief of the captains, and he said, Thine are we, David," etc. (1 Chron. xii. 18). This faculty was always possessed by Moses from the time he had attained the age of manhood; it moved him to slay the Egyptian, and to prevent evil from the two men that quarrelled; it was so strong that, after he had fled from Egypt out of fear, and arrived in Midian, a trembling

stranger, he could not restrain himself from interfering when he saw wrong being done; he could not bear it. Comp. "And Moses rose and saved them" (Exod. ii. 17). David likewise was filled with this spirit, when he was anointed with the oil of anointing. Comp. "And the spirit of God came upon David from that day and upward" (1 Sam. xvi. 13). He thus conquered the lion and the bear and the Philistine, and accomplished similar tasks, by this very spirit. This faculty did not cause any of the above-named persons to speak on a certain subject, for it only aims at encouraging the person who possesses it to action; it does not encourage him to do every-thing, but only to help either a distinguished man or a whole congregation when oppressed, or to do something that leads to that end. Just as not all who have a true dream are prophets, so it cannot be said of every one who is assisted in a certain undertaking, as in the acquisition of property, or of some other personal advantage, that the spirit of the Lord came upon him, or that the Lord was with him, or that he performed his actions by the holy spirit. We only apply such phrases to those who have accomplished something very good and grand, or something that leads to that end; e.g., the success of Joseph in the house of the Egyptian, which was the first cause leading evidently to great events that occurred subsequently.

(2) The second degree is this: A person feels as if something came upon him, and as if he had received a new power that encourages him to speak. He treats of science, or composes hymns, exhorts his fellow-men, discusses political and theological problems; all this he does while awake, and in the full possession of his senses. Such a person is said to speak by the holy spirit. David composed the Psalms, and Solomon the Book of Proverbs, Ecclesiastes, and the Song of Solomon by this spirit; also Daniel, Job, Chronicles, and the rest of the Hagiographa were written in this holy spirit; therefore they are called *ketubim* (Writings, or Written), i.e., written by men inspired by the holy spirit. Our Sages mention this expressly concerning the Book of Esther. In reference to such holy spirit, David says: "The spirit of the Lord spoke in me, and his word is on my tongue" (2 Sam. xxiii. 2); i.e., the spirit of the Lord caused him to utter these words. This class includes the seventy elders of whom it is said, "And it came to pass when the spirit rested upon them, that they prophesied, and did not cease" (Num. xi. 25); also Eldad and Medad (*ibid.* ver. 26); furthermore, every high priest that inquired [of God] by the Urim and Tummim; on whom, as our Sages say, the divine glory rested, and who spoke by the holy spirit; Yahaziel, son of Zechariah, belongs likewise to this class. Comp. "The spirit of the Lord came upon him in the midst of the assembly, and he said, Listen, all Judah and inhabitants of Jerusalem, thus saith the Lord unto you," etc. (2 Chron. xx. 14, 15); also Zechariah, son of Jehoiada the priest. Comp. "And he stood above the people and said unto them, Thus saith God" (*ibid.* xxiv. 20); furthermore, Azariah, son of Oded; comp. "And Azariah, son of Oded, when the spirit of the Lord came upon him, went forth before Asa," etc. (*ibid.* xv. 1, 2); and all who acted under similar circumstances. You must know that Balaam likewise belonged to this class, when he was good; this is indicated by the words, "And God put a word in the mouth of Balaam" (Num. xxiii. 5), i.e., Balaam spoke by divine inspiration; he there-fore says of himself, "Who heareth the words of God," etc. (*ibid.* xxiv. 4).

We must especially point out that David, Solomon, and Daniel belonged to this class, and not to the class of Isaiah, Jeremiah, Nathan the prophet, Ahijah the Shilonite, and those like them.   For David, Solomon, and Daniel spoke and wrote inspired by the holy spirit, and when David says, " The God of Israel spoke and said unto me, the rock of Israel " (2 Sam. xxiii. 3), he meant to say that God promised him happiness through a prophet, through Nathan or another prophet.   The phrase must here be interpreted in the same manner as in the following passages, " And God said to her " (Gen. xxv. 26) ; " And God said unto Solomon, Because this hath been in thy heart, and thou hast not kept my covenant," etc. (1 Kings xi. 11).   The latter passage undoubtedly contains a prophecy of Ahijah the Shilonite, or another prophet, who foretold Solomon that evil would befall him.   The passage, " God appeared to Solomon at Gibeon in a dream by night, and God said " (*ibid.* iii.-5), does not contain a real prophecy, such as is introduced by the words : " The word of the Lord came to Abram in a vision, saying " (Gen. xv. 1) ; or, " And God said to Israel in the visions of the night " (*ibid.* xlvi. 2), or such as the prophecies of Isaiah and Jeremiah contain ; in all these cases the prophets, though receiving the prophecy in a prophetic dream, are told that it is a prophecy, and that they have received prophetic inspiration.   But in the case of Solomon, the account concludes, " And Solomon awoke, and behold it was a dream " (1 Kings iii. 15) ; and in the account of the second divine appearance, it is said, " And God appeared to Solomon a second time, as he appeared to him at Gibeon " (*ibid.* ix. 2) ; it was evidently a dream. This kind of prophecy is a degree below that of which Scripture says, " In a dream I will speak to him " (Num. xii. 6).   When prophets are inspired in a dream, they by no means call this a dream, although the prophecy reached them in a dream, but declare it decidedly to be a prophecy.   Thus Jacob, our father, when awaking from a prophetic dream, did not say it was a dream, but declared, " Surely there is the Lord in this place," etc. (Gen. xxviii. 16) ; " God the Almighty appeared to me in Luz, in the land of Canaan " (*ibid.* xlviii. 3), expressing thereby that it was a prophecy.   But in reference to Solomon we read :—" And Solomon awoke, and behold it was a dream " (1 Kings iii. 15).   Similarly Daniel declares that he had a dream ; although he sees an angel and hears his word, he speaks of the event as of a dream ; even when he had received the information [concerning the dreams of Nebuchadnezzar], he speaks of it in the following manner—" Then was the secret revealed to Daniel in a night vision " (Dan. ii. 19).   On other occasions it is said, " He wrote down the dream " ; " I saw in the visions by night," etc. ; " And the visions of my head confused me " (Dan. vii. 1, 2, 15) ; " I was surprised at the vision, and none noticed it " (*ibid.* viii. 27).   There is no doubt that this is one degree below that form of prophecy to which the words, " In a dream I will speak to him," are applied.   For this reason the nation desired to place the book of Daniel among the Hagiographa, and not among the Prophets.   I have, therefore, pointed out to you, that the prophecy revealed to Daniel and Solomon, although they saw an angel in the dream, was not considered by them as a perfect prophecy, but as a dream containing correct information.   They belonged to the class of men that spoke, inspired by the *ruaḥ ha-kodesh*, " the holy spirit."   Also in the order of the holy writings, no distinction is made between the books of Proverbs,

Ecclesiastes, Daniel, Psalms, Ruth, and Esther; they are all written by divine inspiration. The authors of all these books are called prophets in the more general sense of the term.

(3) The third class is the lowest [class of actual prophets, i.e.] of those who introduce their speech by the phrase, " And the word of the Lord came unto me," or a similar phrase. The prophet sees an allegory in a dream—under those conditions which we have mentioned when speaking of real prophecy—and in the prophetic dream itself the allegory is interpreted. Such are most of the allegories of Zechariah.

(4) The prophet hears in a prophetic dream something clearly and distinctly, but does not see the speaker. This was the case with Samuel in the beginning of his prophetic mission, as has been explained (chap. xliv.).

(5) A person addresses the prophet in a dream, as was the case in some of the prophecies of Ezekiel. Comp. " And the man spake unto me, Son of man," etc. (Ezek. xl. 4).

(6) An angel speaks to him in a dream; this applies to most of the prophets; e.g., " And an angel of God said to me in a dream of night " (Gen. xxxi. 11).

(7) In a prophetic dream it appears to the prophet as if God spoke to him. Thus Isaiah says, " And I saw the Lord, and I heard the voice of the Lord saying, Whom shall I send, and who will go for us ? " (Isa. vi. 1, 8). Micaiah, son of Imla, said likewise, " I saw the Lord " (1 Kings xxii. 19).

(8) Something presents itself to the prophet in a prophetic vision; he sees allegorical figures, such as were seen by Abraham in the vision " between the pieces " (Gen. xv. 9, 10); for it was in a vision by daytime, as is distinctly stated.

(9) The prophet hears words in a prophetic vision; as, e.g., is said in reference to Abraham, " And behold, the word came to him, saying, This shall not be thine heir " (*ibid.* xv. 4).

(10) The prophet sees a man that speaks to him in a prophetic vision; e.g., Abraham in the plain of Mamre (*ibid.* xviii. 1), and Joshua in Jericho (Josh. v. 13).

(11) He sees an angel that speaks to him in the vision, as was the case when Abraham was addressed by an angel at the sacrifice of Isaac (Gen. xxii. 15). This I hold to be—if we except Moses—the highest degree a prophet can attain according to Scripture, provided he has, as reason demands, his rational faculties fully developed. But it appears to me improbable that a prophet should be able to perceive in a prophetic vision God speaking to him; the action of the imaginative faculty does not go so far, and therefore we do not notice this in the case of the ordinary prophets; Scripture says expressly, " In a *vision* I will make myself known, in a *dream* I will speak to him "; the speaking is here connected with *dream*, the influence and the action of the intellect is connected with *vision*; comp. " In a vision I will make myself known to him " (*etvadda'*, hitpael of *yada'*, " to know "), but it is not said here that in a vision anything is heard from God. When I, therefore, met with statements in Scripture that a prophet heard words spoken to him, and that this took place in a vision, it occurred to me that the case in which God appears to address the prophet seems to be the only difference between a vision and a dream, according to the literal sense of the Scriptural

text. But it is possible to explain the passages in which a prophet is reported to have heard in the course of a vision words spoken to him, in the following manner : at first he has had a vision, but subsequently he fell into a deep sleep, and the vision was changed into a dream. Thus we explained the words, " And a deep sleep fell upon Abram " (Gen. xv. 12) ; and our Sages remark thereon, " This was a deep sleep of prophecy." According to this explanation, it is only in a dream that the prophet can hear words addressed to him ; it makes no difference in what manner words are spoken. Scripture supports this theory, " In a dream I will speak to him." But in a prophetic vision only allegories are perceived, or rational truths are obtained, that lead to some knowledge in science, such as can be arrived at by reasoning. This is the meaning of the words, " In a vision I will make myself *known* unto him." According to this second explanation, the degrees of prophecy are reduced to eight, the highest of them being the prophetic vision, including all kinds of vision, even the case in which a man appears to address the prophet, as has been mentioned. You will perhaps ask this question : among the different degrees of prophecy there is one in which prophets, e.g., Isaiah, Micaiah, appear to hear God addressing them ; how can this be reconciled with the principle that all prophets are prophetically addressed through an angel, except Moses our Teacher, in reference to whom Scripture says, " Mouth to mouth I speak to him " (Num. xii. 8) ? I answer, this is really the case, the medium here being the imaginative faculty that hears in a prophetic dream God speaking ; but Moses heard the voice addressing him " from above the covering of the ark from between the two cherubim " (Exod. xxv. 22) without the medium of the imaginative faculty. In *Mishne-torah* we have given the characteristics of this kind of prophecy, and explained the meaning of the phrases, " Mouth to mouth I speak to him " ; " As man speaketh to his neighbour " (Exod. xxxiii. 11), and the like. Study it there, and I need not repeat what has already been said.

CHAPTER XLVI

ONE individual may be taken as an illustration of the individuals of the whole species. From its properties we learn those of each individual of the species. I mean to say that the form of one account of a prophecy illustrates all accounts of the same class. After this remark you will understand that a person may sometimes dream that he has gone to a certain country, married there, stayed there for some time, and had a son, whom he gave a certain name, and who was in a certain condition [though nothing of all this has really taken place] ; so also in prophetic allegories certain objects are seen, acts performed—if the style of the allegory demands it—things are done by the prophet, the intervals between one act and another determined, and journeys undertaken from one place to another ; but all these things are only processes of a prophetic vision, and not real things that could be perceived by the senses of the body. Some of the accounts simply relate these incidents [without premising that they are part of a vision], because it is a well-known fact that all these accounts refer to prophetic visions, and it was not necessary to repeat in each case a statement to this effect.

Thus the prophet relates : " And the Lord said unto me," and need not add the explanation that it was in a dream. The ordinary reader believes that the acts, journeys, questions, and answers of the prophets really took place, and were perceived by the senses, and did not merely form part of a prophetic vision. I will mention here an instance concerning which no person will entertain the least doubt. I will add a few more of the same kind, and these will show you how those passages must be understood which I do not cite. The following passage in Ezekiel (viii. 1, 3) is clear, and admits of no doubt: "I sat in mine house, and the elders of Judah ʳⁿᵗ before me, etc., and a spirit lifted me up between the earth and the heaven, and brought me in the visions of God to Jerusalem," etc.; also the passage, "Thus I arose and went into the plain" (iii. 2, 3), refers to a prophetic vision; just as the words, "And he brought him forth abroad, and said, Look now toward heaven and tell the stars, if thou be able to number them" (Gen. xv. 5) describe a vision. The same is the case with the words of Ezekiel (xxxvii. 1), "And set me down in the midst of the valley." In the description of the vision in which Ezekiel is brought to Jerusalem, we read as follows: "And when I looked, behold a hole in the wall. Then said he unto me, Son of man, dig now in the wall; and when I had digged in the wall, behold a door" (ibid. viii. 7–8), etc. It was thus in a vision that he was commanded to dig in the wall, to enter and to see what people were doing there, and it was in the same vision that he digged, entered through the hole, and saw certain things, as is related. Just as all this forms part of a vision, the same may be said of the following passages: "And thou take unto thee a tile," etc., "and lie thou also on thy left side," etc.; "Take thou also wheat and barley," etc., "and cause it to pass over thine head and upon thy beard" (chaps. iv. and v.) It was in a prophetic vision that he saw that he did all these actions which he was commanded to do. God forbid to assume that God would make his prophets appear an object of ridicule and sport in the eyes of the ignorant, and order them to perform foolish acts. We must also bear in mind that the command given to Ezekiel implied disobedience to the Law, for he, being a priest, would, in causing the razor to pass over every corner of the beard and of the head, have been guilty of transgressing two prohibitions in each case. But it was only done in a prophetic vision. Again, when it is said, "As my servant Isaiah went naked and barefoot" (Isa. xx. 3), the prophet did so in a prophetic vision. Weak-minded persons believe that the prophet relates here what he was commanded to do, and what he actually did, and that he describes how he was commanded to dig in a wall on the Temple mount although he was in Babylon, and relates how he obeyed the command, for he says, "And I digged in the wall." But it is distinctly stated that all this took place in a vision.

It is analogous to the description of the vision of Abraham which begins, "The word of the Lord came to Abram in a vision, saying" (Gen. xv. 1); and contains at the same time the passage, "He brought him forth abroad, and said, Look now to the heaven and count the stars" (ibid. ver. 6). It is evident that it was in a vision that Abraham saw himself brought forth from his place looking towards the heavens and being told to count the stars. This is related [without repeating the statement that it was in a vision]. The same I say in reference to the command given to Jeremiah, to conceal the girdle in the Euphrates, and the statement that he concealed it, examined it after a long time, and found it rotten and spoiled (Jér. xiii. 4–7). All this was allegorically shown in a vision; Jeremiah did not go from Palestine to Babylon, and did not see the Euphrates. The same applies to the account of the commandment given to Hosea (i.–iii.): " Take unto thee a wife of whoredom, and children of whoredom," to the birth of the children and to the giving of names to them. All this passed in a prophetic vision. When once stated that these are allegories, there is left no doubt that the events related had no real existence, except in the minds of those of whom the prophet says : " And the vision of every one was unto them like the words of a sealed book " (Isa. xxix. 11). I believe that the trial of Gideon (Judges vi. 21, 27) with the fleece and other things was a vision. I do not call it a prophetic vision, as Gideon had not reached the degree of prophets, much less that height which would enable him to do wonders. He only rose to the height of the Judges of Israel, and he has even been counted by our Sages among persons of little importance, as has been pointed out by us.

The same can be said of the passage in Zechariah (xi. 7), " And I fed the flock of slaughter," and all the incidents that are subsequently described ; the graceful asking for wages, the acceptance of the wages, the wanting of the money, and the casting of the same into the house of the treasure ; all these incidents form part of the vision. He received the commandment and carried it out in a prophetic vision or dream.

The correctness of this theory cannot be doubted, and only those do not comprehend it who do not know to distinguish between that which is possible, and that which is impossible. The instances quoted may serve as an illustration of other similar Scriptural passages not quoted by me. They are all of the same kind, and in the same style. Whatever is said in the account of a vision, that the prophet heard, went forth, came out, said, was told, stood, sat, went up, went down, journeyed, asked, or was asked, all is part of the prophetic vision ; even when there is a lengthened account, the details of which are well connected as regards the time, the persons referred to, and the place. After it has once been stated that the event described is to be understood figuratively, it must be assumed for certain that the whole is a prophetic vision.

CHAPTER XLVII

It is undoubtedly clear and evident that most prophecies are given in images, for this is the characteristic of the imaginative faculty, the organ of prophecy. We find it also necessary to say a few words on the figures, hyperboles, and exaggerations that occur in Scripture. They would create strange ideas if we were to take them literally without noticing the exaggeration which they contain, or if we were to understand them in accordance with the original meaning of the terms, ignoring the fact that these are used figuratively. Our Sages say distinctly Scripture uses hyperbolic or exaggerated language ; and quote as an instance, " cities walled and fortified, rising up to heaven " (Deut. i. 28). As a hyperbole our Sages quote, " For the bird of heaven carries the voice " (Eccles. x. 20) ; in the same sense it is said, " Whose height is like that of cedar trees " (Amos ii. 9). Instances of this kind are frequent in the language of all prophets ; what they say is frequently hyperbolic or exaggerated, and not precise or exact. What Scripture says about Og, " Behold, his bedstead was an iron bedstead, nine cubits its length," etc. (Deut.), does not belong to this class of figures, for the bedstead (*eres*, comp. *arsenu*, Song of Sol. i. 16) is never exactly of the same dimensions as the person using it; it is not like a dress that fits round the body; it is always greater than the person that sleeps therein; as a rule, is it by a third longer. If, therefore, the bed of Og was nine cubits in length, he must, according to this proportion, have been six cubits high, or a little more. The words, " by the cubit of a man," mean, by the measure of an ordinary man, and not by the measure of Og; for men have the limbs in a certain proportion. Scripture thus tells us that Og was double as long as an ordinary person, or a little less. This is undoubtedly an exceptional height among men, but not quite impossible. As regards the Scriptural statement about the length of man's life in those days, I say that only the persons named lived so long, whilst other people enjoyed the ordinary length of life. The men named were exceptions, either in consequence of different causes, as e.g., their food or mode of living, or by way of miracle, which admits of no analogy.

We must further discuss the figurative language employed in Scripture. In some cases this is clear and evident, and doubted by no person; e.g., " The mountains and hills shall break forth in song before you, and all the trees of the wood clap their hands " (Isa. lv. 12); this is evidently figurative language; also the following passage—" The fir-trees rejoice at thee," etc. (*ibid.* xiv. 8), which is rendered by Jonathan, son of Uzziel, " The rulers rejoice at thee, who are rich in possessions." This figure is similar to that used in the phrase, " Butter of kine and milk of sheep," etc. (Deut. xxxii. 14).

And these figures are very frequent in the books of the prophets. Some are easily recognised by the ordinary reader as figures, others with some difficulty. Thus nobody doubts that the blessing, " May the Lord open to thee his good treasure, the heavens," must be taken figuratively; for God has no treasure in which He keeps the rain. The same is the case with the following passage—" He opened the doors of heaven, he rained upon them manna to eat " (Ps. lxxviii. 23, 24). No person assumes that there is a door or gate in heaven, but every one understands that this is a simile and a figurative expression. In the same way must be understood the following passages— " The heavens were opened " (Ezek. i. 1); " If not, blot me out from thy book which thou hast written " (Exod. xxxii. 32); " I will blot him out from the book of life " (*ibid.* ver. 33). All these phrases are figurative; and we must not assume that God has a book in which He writes, or from which He blots out, as those generally believe that do not find figurative speech in these passages. They are all of the same kind. You must explain passages not quoted by me by those which I have quoted in this chapter. Employ your reason, and you will be able to discern what is said allegorically, figuratively, or hyperbolically, and what is meant literally, exactly according to the original meaning of the words. You will then understand all prophecies, learn and retain rational principles of faith, pleasing in the eyes of God who is most pleased with truth, and most displeased with falsehood; your mind and heart will not be so perplexed as to believe or accept as law what is untrue or improbable, whilst the Law is perfectly true when properly understood. Thus Scripture says, " Thy testimonies are righteousness for ever "

(Ps. cxix. 144) ; and " I the Lord speak righteousness " (Isa. xlv. 19). If you adopt this method, you will not imagine the existence of things which God has not created, or accept principles which might partly lead to atheism, or to a corruption of your notions of God so as to ascribe to Him corporeality, attributes, or emotions, as has been shown by us, nor will you believe that the words of the prophets are false ; for the cause of this disease is ignorance of what we have explained. These things belong likewise to the mysteries of the Law ; and although we have treated them in a general manner, they can easily be understood in all their details in accordance with the above remarks.

CHAPTER XLVIII

It is clear that everything produced must have an immediate cause which produced it ; that cause again a cause, and so on, till the First Cause, viz., the will and decree of God is reached. The prophets therefore omit some- times the intermediate causes, and ascribe the production of an individual thing directly to God, saying that God has made it. This method is well known, and we, as well as others of those who seek the truth, have explained it ; it is the belief of our co-religionists.

After having heard this remark, listen to what I will explain in this chapter ; direct your special attention to it more than you have done to the other chapters of this part. It is this : As regards the immediate causes of things produced, it makes no difference whether these causes consist in substances, physical properties, freewill, or chance—by freewill I mean that of man—or even in the will of another living being. The prophets [omit them and] ascribe the production directly to God and use such phrases as, God has done it, commanded it, or said it ; in all such cases the verbs " to say," " to speak," " to command," " to call," and " to send " are employed. What I desired to state in this chapter is this : According to the hypothesis and theory accepted, it is God that gave will to dumb animals, freewill to the human being, and natural properties to everything ; and as accidents originate in the redundancy of some natural force, as has been explained [by Aristotle], and are mostly the result of the combined action of nature, desire, and freewill : it can con- sequently be said of everything which is produced by any of these causes, that God commanded that it should be made, or said that it should be so. I will give you instances, and they will guide you in the interpretation of passages which I do not mention. As regards phenomena produced regularly by natural causes, such as the melting of the snow when the atmosphere becomes warm, the roaring of the sea when a storm rages [I quote the following passages], " He sendeth his word and melteth them " (Ps. cxlvii. 18) ; " And he saith, and a storm-wind riseth, and lifteth up its waves " (*ibid.* cvii. 25). In reference to the rain we read : " I will command the clouds that they shall not rain," etc. (Isa. v. 6). Events caused by man's freewill, such as war, the dominion of one nation over another, the attempt of one person to hurt another, or to insult him, [are ascribed to God, as] e.g., in reference to the dominion of Nebuchadnezzar and his host, " I have commended my holy ones, also I have called my heroes for my anger " (Isa. xiii. 3) ; and " I will send him against a hypocrite nation " (*ibid.* x. 6) ; in reference to Shimei, son of Gera, " For God said to him, Curse David " (2 Sam. xvi. 10) ; in reference to the deliverance of Joseph, the righteous, from prison, " He sent an angel and loosed him " (Ps. cv. 20) ; in reference to the victory of the Persians over the Chaldees, " I will send to Babylon scatterers, and they shall scatter it " (Jer. li. 2) ; in reference to the providing of food to Eliah, " I have commanded there a woman, a widow, to maintain thee " (1 Kings xvii. 9) ; and Joseph, the righteous, says : " Not ye have sent me hither," etc. (Gen. xlv. 8). The case that the will of an animal or its desire for some of its natural wants is the cause of some event, may be illustrated by the following instance : " And God spake unto the fish, and it vomited out Jonah " (ii. 11). The act is ascribed to God, because He gave the fish the will, and not because He made it a prophet or endowed it with a prophetical spirit. Similarly it is said of the locusts that appeared in the days of Joel, son of Pethuel, " Mighty is he that accomplishes his word " (Joel ii. 11) ; or of the beasts that took possession of the land of Edom when destroyed in the days of Sennacherib, " He cast lot for them, and his hand divided it unto them by a line " (Isa. xxxiv. 17). Although here the verbs " to say," " to command," " to send," are not used, the meaning is evidently the same, and you must explain all passages that are analogous to it in a similar manner. Events evidently due to chance are ascribed to God ; e.g., in reference to Rebecca, " Let her be a wife to the son of thy master, as the Lord spake " (Gen. xxiv. 51) ; in reference to David and Jonathan, " Go, for the Lord has sent thee." (1 Sam. xx. 22) ; in reference to Joseph, " God sent me before you " (Gen. xlv. 7). You see clearly that the providing of a cause, in whatever manner this may take place, by substance, accident, freewill, or will, is always expressed by one of the five terms, commanding, saying, speaking, sending, or calling. Note this, and apply it everywhere according to the context. Many difficulties will thereby be removed, and passages apparently containing things far from truth will prove to be true. This is the conclusion of the treatise on Prophecy, its allegories and language. It is all I intend to say on this subject in this treatise. We will now commence to treat of other subjects, with the help of the Most High.

PART   III

INTRODUCTION

WE have stated several times that it is our primary object in this treatise to expound, as far as possible, the Biblical account of the Creation (*Ma'aseh bereshit*) and the description of the Divine Chariot (*Ma'aseh mercabah*) in a manner adapted to the training of those for whom this work is written.

We have also stated that these subjects belong to the mysteries of the Law. You are well aware how our Sages blame those who reveal these mysteries, and praise the merits of those who keep them secret, although they are perfectly clear to the philosopher. In this sense they explain the passage, " Her merchandise shall be for them that dwell before the Lord, to eat sufficiently " (Isa. xxiii. 18), which concludes in the original with the words *ve-li-me-kasseh 'atik*, i.e., that these blessings are promised to him who hides things which the Eternal has revealed [to him], viz., the mysteries of the Law (Babyl. Talmud, *Pesaḥim* 119a). If you have understanding you will comprehend that which our Sages pointed out. They have clearly stated that the Divine Chariot includes matters too deep and too profound for the ordinary intellect. It has been shown that a person favoured by Providence with reason to understand these mysteries is forbidden by the Law to teach them except *vivâ voce*, and on condition that the pupil possess certain qualifications, and even then only the heads of the sections may be communicated. This has been the cause why the knowledge of this mystery has entirely disappeared from our nation, and nothing has remained of it. This was unavoidable, for the explanation of these mysteries was always communicated *vivâ voce*, it was never committed to writing. Such being the case, how can I venture to call your attention to such portions of it as may be known, intelligible, and perfectly clear to me ? But if, on the other hand, I were to abstain from writing on this subject, according to my knowledge of it, when I die, as I shall inevitably do, that knowledge would die with me, and I would thus inflict great injury on you and all those who are perplexed [by these theological problems]. I would then be guilty of withholding the truth from those to whom it ought to be communicated, and of jealously depriving the heir of his inheritance. I should in either case be guilty of gross misconduct.

To give a full explanation of the mystic passages of the Bible is contrary to the Law and to reason ; besides, my knowledge of them is based on reasoning, not on divine inspiration [and is therefore not infallible]. I have not received my belief in this respect from any teacher, but it has been formed by what I learnt from Scripture and the utterances of our Sages, and by the philosophical principles which I have adopted. It is therefore possible that my view is wrong, and that I misunderstood the passages referred to. Correct thought and divine help have suggested to me the proper method, viz., to explain the words of the prophet Ezekiel in such a manner that those who will read my interpretation will believe that I have not added anything to the contents of the text, but only, as it were, translated from one language into another, or given a short exposition of plain things. Those, however, for whom this treatise has been composed, will, on reflecting on it and thoroughly examining each chapter, obtain a perfect and clear insight into all that has been clear and intelligible to me. This is the utmost that can be done in treating this subject so as to be useful to all without fully explaining it.

After this introductory remark I ask you to study attentively the chapters which follow on this sublime, important, and grand subject, which is the pin upon which everything hangs, and the pillar upon which everything rests.

CHAPTER I

It is well known that there are men whose face is like that of other animals ; thus the face of some person is like that of a lion, that of another person like that of an ox, and so on ; and man's face is described according as the form of his face resembles the form of the face of other animals. By the expressions, " the face of an ox," " the face of a lion," " the face of an eagle " (Ezek. i. 10), the prophet describes a human face inclining towards the forms of these various species. This interpretation can be supported by two proofs. First, the prophet says of the *Ḥayyot* in general that " their appearance is this, they have the form of man " (ver. 5), and then in describing each of the *Ḥayyot* he attributes to them the face of a man, that of an ox, that of a lion, and that of an eagle. Secondly, in the second description of the Chariot, which is intended as a supplement to the first, the prophet says, Each hath four faces ; the one is the face of a cherub, the second a man's face, the third a lion's face, and the fourth that of an eagle (*ibid.* x. 14). He thus clearly indicates that the terms " the face of an ox " and " the face of a cherub " are identical. But cherub designates " a youth." By analogy we explain the two other terms—" the face of a lion " and " the face of an eagle " in the same manner. " The face of the ox " has been singled out on account of the etymology of the Hebrew term *shor* (ox), as has been indicated by me. It is impossible to assume that this second description refers to the perception of another prophetic vision, because it concludes thus : " This is the *Ḥayyah* which I saw at the river Chebar " (*ibid.* ver. 15). What we intended to explain is now clear.

CHAPTER II

The prophet says that he saw four *Ḥayyot ;* each of them had four faces, four wings, and two hands, but on the whole their form was human. Comp. " They had the likeness of a man " (Ezek. i. 5). The hands are also described as human hands, because these have undoubtedly, as is well known, such a form as enables them to perform all manner of cunning work. Their feet are straight; that is to say, they are without joints. This is the meaning of the phrase "a straight foot," taken literally. Similarly our Sages say, the words, "And their feet were straight feet" (*ibid.* i. 7), show that the beings above do not sit. Note this likewise. The soles of the feet of the *Ḥayyot*, the organs of walking, are described as different from the feet of man, but the hands are like human hands. The feet are round, for the prophet says, "like the sole of a round foot." The four *Ḥayyot* are closely joined together, there is no space or vacuum left between them. Comp. "They were joined one to another" (*ibid.* i. 9). "But although they were thus joined together, their faces and their wings were separated above" (*ibid.* ver. 11). Consider the expression "above" employed here, although the bodies were closely joined, their faces and their wings were separated, but only above. The prophet then states that they are transparent; they are "like burnished brass" (*ibid.* ver. 7). He also adds that they are luminous. Comp. "Their appearance was like burning coals of fire" (*ibid.* ver. 13). This is all that has been said as regards the form, shape, face, figure, wings, hands, and feet of the *Ḥayyot*. The prophet then begins to describe the motions of these *Ḥayyot*, namely, that they have a uniform motion, without any curvature, deviation, or deflexion: "They turned not when they went" (ver. 17). Each of the *Ḥayyot* moves in the direction of its face. Comp. "They went every one in the direction of his face" (ver. 9). Now, it is here clearly stated that each *Ḥayyah* went in the direction of its face, but since each *Ḥayyah* has several faces, I ask, in the direction of which face? In short, the four *Ḥayyot* do not move in the same direction; for, if this were the case, a special motion would not have been ascribed to each of them; it would not have been said, "They went each one towards the side of his face." The motion of these *Ḥayyot* is further described as a running, so also their returning is described as a running. Comp. "And the *Ḥayyot* ran, and returned as the appearance of a flash of lightning" (ver. 14), *raẓoh* being the infinitive of *ruẓ*, "to run," and *shob* the infinitive instead of *shub*, "to return." The ordinary words, *haloch* and *bo*, "to go" and "to come," are not used, but such words as indicate running to and fro; and these are further explained by the phrase, "As the appearance of a flash of lightning" (*bazak*, used by the prophet, is identical with *barak*), for the lightning appears to move very quickly; it seems to hasten and to run from a certain place, and then to turn back and to come again to the place from which it had started. This is repeated several times with the same velocity. Jonathan, the son of Uzziel, renders the phrase *raẓo vashob* thus: They move round the world and return at once, and are as swift as the appearance of lightning. This quick movement and return the *Ḥayyah* does not perform of its own accord, but through something outside of it, viz., the Divine Will; for "to whichever side it is the Divine Will that the *Ḥayyah* should move, thither the *Ḥayyah* moves," in that quick manner which is expressed by "running and returning." This is implied in the words, "Whithersoever the spirit was to go they went" (ver. 20); "They turned not when they went" (ver. 17). By "the spirit" (*ruaḥ*), the prophet does not mean "the wind," but "the intention," as we have explained when discussing the homonym *ruaḥ* (spirit). The meaning of the phrase is, that whithersoever it is the Divine Will that the *Hayyah* shall go, thither it runs. Jonathan, the son of Uzziel, gives a similar explanation : Towards the place whither it is the will to go, they go; they do not turn when they go. The employment of the future tense of the verbs *yihyeh* and *yeleku* in this passage seems to imply that sometimes it will be the will of God that the *Hayyah* should move in one direction, in which it will in fact move, and at other times it will be His will that the *Hayyah* should move in the opposite direction, in which it will then move. An explanation is, however, added, which is contrary to/this conclusion, and shows that the future form (*yihyeh*) of the verb has here the meaning of the preterite, as is frequently the case in Hebrew. The direction in which God desires the *Hayyah* to move has already been determined and fixed, and the *Hayyah* moves in that direction which His will has determined long ago, without having ever changed. The prophet, therefore, in explaining, and at the same time concluding [this description of the *Hayyot*], says, " Whithersoever the spirit was to go they go, thither *was* the spirit to go " (ver. 20). Note this wonderful interpretation. This passage forms likewise part of the account of the motion of the four *Hayyot* which follows the description of their form.

Next comes the description of another part; for the prophet relates that he saw a body beneath the *Hayyot*, but closely joining them. This body, which is connected with the earth, consists likewise of four bodies, and has also four faces. But no distinct form is ascribed to it ; neither that of man nor that of any other living being. The [four bodies] are described as great, tremendous, and terrible ; no form is given to them, except that they are covered with eyes. These are the bodies called *Ofannim* (lit. wheels). The prophet therefore says : " Now, as I beheld the *Hayyot*, behold one wheel upon the earth beside the living creatures, with his four faces " (ver. 15). He thus distinctly states that the *Ofannim* form a body, of which the one part touches the *Hayyot*, and the other part the earth ; and that the *Ofan* has four faces. But he continues—" The appearance of the *Ofannim* (wheels) and their work was like unto the colour of a beryl : and they four had one likeness " (ver. 16). By speaking of four *Ofannim*, after having mentioned only one *Ofan*, the prophet indicates that the " four faces " and the " four *Ofannim* " are identical. These four *Ofannim* have the same form ; comp., " And they four had one likeness." The *Ofannim* are then described as partly inter-joined ; for " their appearance and their work was as it were a wheel in the middle of a wheel " (ver. 16). In the description of the *Hayyot* such a phrase, with the term " in the middle of " (*tok*) is not employed. The *Hayyot* are partly joined, according to the words, " they were joined one to another " (ver. 11) ; whilst in reference to the *Ofannim* it is stated that they are partly intermixed, " as it were a wheel in the middle of a wheel." The body of the *Ofannim* is described as being covered with eyes ; it is possible that a body covered with real eyes is here meant, or a body with different colours [*ayin* denoting " eye, " also " colour "], as in the phrase " the colour thereof [*eno*] as the colour (*ke'en*) of bdellium " (Num. xi. 7) ; or a body filled with likenesses of things. In this latter sense the term *ayin* is used by our Sages in phrases like the following :—Like that [*ke'en*] which he has stolen, like that [*ke'en*] which he has robbed ; or different properties and qualities are meant, according to the meaning of the word *'ayin* in the passage, " It may be that the Lord will look (*be'enai*) on my condition " (2 Sam. xvi. 12). So much for the form of the *Ofannim*. Their motion is described as being without curvature and deviation; as being straight, without any change. This is expressed in the words, " When they went, they went upon their four sides : and they turned not when they went " (E. ; ver. 17). The four *Ofannim* do not move of their own accord, as the *Ḥayyot*, and have no motion whatever of their own ; they are set in motion by other beings, as is emphatically stated twice. The *Ḥayyot* are the moving agents of the *Ofannim*. The relation between the *Ofan* and the *Ḥayyah* may be compared to the relation between a lifeless body tied to the hand or the leg of a living animal ; whithersoever the latter moves, thither moves also the piece of wood, or the stone, which is tied to the named limb of the animal. This is expressed in the following words :—" And when the *Ḥayyot* went, the *Ofannim* went by them ; and when the living creatures were lifted up from the earth, the *Ofannim* were lifted up " (ver. 19) ; " and the *Ofannim* were lifted up over against them " (ver. 20). And the cause of this is explained thus :—" The spirit of the *Ḥayyah* was in the *Ofannim* " (*ibid.*). For the sake of emphasis and further explanation the prophet adds, " When those went, these went ; and when those stood, these stood ; and when those were lifted up from the earth, the *Ofannim* were lifted up over against them ; for the spirit of the *Ḥayyah* was in the *Ofannim* " (ver. 21). The order of these movements is therefore as follows :—Whithersoever it is the will of God that the *Ḥayyot* should move, thither they move of their own accord. When the *Ḥayyot* move the *Ofannim* necessarily follow them, because they are tied to them, and not because they move of their own accord in the direction in which the *Ḥayyot* move. This order is expressed in the words, " Whithersoever the spirit was to go, they went, thither was the spirit to go ; and the *Ofannim* were lifted up over against them ; for the spirit of the *Ḥayyah* was in the *Ofannim* " (ver. 20). I have told you that Jonathan, the son of Uzziel, translates the verse thus, " to the place whither it was the will that the *Ḥayyot* should go," etc.

After having completed the account of the *Ḥayyot*, with their form and motion, and of the *Ofannim*, which are beneath the *Ḥayyot*, connected with them and forced to move when the *Ḥayyot* move, the prophet begins to describe a third object which he perceived prophetically, and gives the account of a new thing, viz., of that which is above the *Ḥayyot*. He says that the firmament is above the four *Ḥayyot*, above the firmament is the likeness of a throne, and over the throne the likeness of the appearance of man. This is the whole account of what the prophet perceived at first at the river Chebar.

CHAPTER III

Wʜᴇɴ Ezekiel recalled to memory the form of the Chariot, which he described in the beginning of the book, the same vision presented itself to him a second time ; in this vision he was borne to Jerusalem. He explains in describing it things which have not been made clear at first, e.g., he substitutes the term " cherubim " for *Ḥayyot*, whereby he expresses that the

Ḥayyot of the first vision are likewise angels like the cherubim. He says, therefore: " Where the cherubims went, the Ofannim went by them: and when the cherubims lifted up their wings to mount up from the earth, the same Ofannim also turned not from beside them " (x. 16). By these words he shows how closely connected the two motions are [viz., that of the Ḥayyot and that of the Ofannim]. The prophet adds, " This is the Ḥayyah that I saw under the God of Israel by the river of Chebar; and I knew that they were cherubims " (ver. 20). He thus describes the same forms and the same motions, and states that the Ḥayyot and the cherubim are identical. A second point is then made clear in this second description, namely, that the Ofannim are spherical; for the prophet says, " As for the Ofannim, it was cried unto them in my hearing, O sphere " (ver. 13). A third point concerning the Ofannim is illustrated here in the following words: " To the place whither the head looked they followed it: they turned not as they went " (ver. 11). The motion of the Ofannim is thus described as involuntary, and directed " to the place whither the head looketh "; and of this it is stated that it moves " whither the spirit is to go " (i. 20). A fourth point is added concerning the Ofannim, namely, "And the Ofannim were full of eyes round about, even the Ofannim that they four had " (x. 12). This has not been mentioned before. In this second description there are further mentioned " their flesh, and their backs, and their hands, and their wings " (ibid.), whilst in the first account none of these is mentioned; and it is only stated that they are bodies. Though they are endowed in the second account with flesh, hands, and wings, no form is given to them. In the second account each ofan is attributed to a cherub, " one ofan by one cherub, and another ofan by another cherub." The four Ḥayyot are then described as one Ḥayyah on account of their interjoining: " This is the Ḥayyah that I saw under the God of Israel by the river of Chebar " (ver. 20). Also the Ofannim, though being four in number, as has been mentioned, are called " one ofan upon the earth " (ver. 15), because they interjoin, and " they four have one likeness " (ver. 16). This is the additional explanation which the second vision gives of the form of the Ḥayyot and the Ofannim.

CHAPTER IV

It is necessary to call your attention to an idea expressed by Jonathan, the son of Uzziel. When he saw that the prophet says in reference to the Ofannim, " It was cried unto them in my hearing, O gilgal " (" sphere ") (x. 13), he assumed that by Ofannim the heavens are meant, and rendered ofan by gilgal, " sphere," and ofannim by gilgelaya, " spheres." I have no doubt that he found a confirmation of his opinion in the words of the prophet that the Ofannim were like unto the colour of tarshish (ver. 16), a colour ascribed to the heavens, as is well known. When he, therefore, noticed the passage, " Now as I beheld the Ḥayyot, behold one Ofan upon the earth " (i. 15), which clearly shows that the Ofannim were upon the earth, he had a difficulty in explaining it in accordance with his opinion. Following, however, his interpretation, he explains the terms erez, employed here as denoting the inner surface of the heavenly sphere, which may be considered as erez (" earth " or " below "), in relation to all that is above that surface. He therefore translates the words *ofan ehad ba-arez* as follows: "One *ofan* was below the height of the heavens." Consider what his explanation of the passage must be. I think that he gave this explanation because he thought that *gilgal* denotes in its original meaning " heaven." My opinion is that *gilgal* means originally "anything rolling "; comp. "And I will roll thee (*ve-gilgaltika*) down from the rocks" (Jer. li. 25); " and rolled (*va-yagel*) the stone " (Gen. xxix. 10); the same meaning the word has in the phrase: "Like a rolling thing (*galgal*) before the whirlwind" (Isa. xvii. 13). The poll of the head, being round, is therefore called *gulgolet;* and because everything round rolls easily, every spherical thing is called *gilgal;* also the heavens are called *gilgallim* on account of their spherical form. Thus our Sages use the phrase, "It is a wheel (*gilgal*) that moves round the world "; and a wooden ball, whether small or large, is called *gilgal*. If so, the prophet merely intended by the words, "As for the *Ofannim*, it is cried to them in my hearing, O sphere " (*gilgal*), to indicate the shape of the *Ofannim*, as nothing has been mentioned before respecting their form and shape; but he did not mean to say that the *Ofannim* are the same as the heavens. The term "like *tarshish* " is explained in the second account, in which it is said of the *Ofannim :* "And the appearance of the *ofannim* was like the colour of *tarshish*." This latter passage is translated by Jonathan, the son of Uzziel, "like the colour of a precious stone," exactly in the same manner as Onkelos translates the phrase *ke-ma'ase libnat ha-sappir*, "like the work of the whiteness of sapphire " (Exod. xxix. 10). Note this. You will not find it strange that I mention the explanation of Jonathan, son of Uzziel, whilst I gave a different explanation myself; for you will find many of the wise men and the commentators differ sometimes from him in the interpretation of words and in many things respecting the prophets. Why should it be otherwise in these profound matters ? Besides, I do not decide in favour of my interpretation. It is for you to learn both—the whole of his explanation, from what I have pointed out to you, and also my own opinion. God knoweth which of the two explanations is in accordance with that which the prophet intended to say.

CHAPTER V

IT is necessary to notice that the plural *marot elohim*, "visions of God," is here used, and not the singular *mareh*, "vision," for there were several things, of different kinds, that were perceived by the prophet. The following three things were perceived by him: the *Ofannim*, the *Hayyot*, and the man above the *Hayyot*. The description of each of these visions is introduced by the word *va-ereh*, "and I beheld." For the account of the *Hayyot*, begins, "And I looked (*va-ereh*), and behold a whirlwind," etc. (Ezek. i. 4). The account of the *Ofannim* begins : "Now as I beheld (*va-ereh*) the *Hayyot*, behold one *Ofan* upon the earth" (ver. 15). The vision of that which is above the *Hayyot* in order and rank begins : "And I saw (*va-ereh*) as the colour of the amber, etc., from the appearance of his loins even upward " (ver. 27). The word *va-ereh*, "and I beheld," only occurs these three times in the description of the Mercabah. The doctors of the Mishnah have already explained this fact, and my attention was called to it by their remarks. For they said that only the two first visions, namely, that of the *Hayyot* and the *Ofannim,* might be interpreted to others ; but of the third vision, viz., that of the *hashmal* and all that is connected with it, only the heads of the sections may be taught. Rabbi [Jehudah], the Holy, is of opinion that all the three visions are called *ma'aseh mercabah,* and nothing but the heads of the sections could be communicated to others. The exact words of the discussion are as follows :—Where does *maaseh mercabbah* end ? Rabbi says, with the last *va-ereh ;* Rabbi Yizhak says it ends at the word *hashmal* (ver. 27). The portion from *va-ereh* to *hashmal* may be fully taught ; of that which follows, only the heads of the sections ; according to some it is the passage from *va-ereh* to *hashmal,* of which the heads of the sections may be taught, but that which follows may only be studied by those who possess the capacity, whilst those that cannot study it by themselves must leave it.—It is clear from the words of our Sages that different visions are described, as may also be inferred from the repetition of the word *va-ereh,* and that these visions are different from each other in degree ; the last and highest of them is the vision commencing, " And I saw as the colour of *hashmal* " ; that is to say, the divided figure of the man, described as " the appearance of fire, etc., from the appearance of his loins even upward, and from the appearance of his loins even downward," etc. There is a difference of opinion among our Sages whether it is permitted to give by way of hints an exposition of any part of this third vision, or whether it is prohibited even to teach of it the heads of the sections, so that only the wise can arrive at understanding it by their own studies. You will also notice a difference of opinion among our Sages in reference to the two first visions, viz., that of the *Hayyot* and that of the *Ofannim* whether these may be taught explicitly or only by way of hints, dark sayings, and heads of sections. You must also notice the order of these three visions. First comes the vision of the *Hayyot,* because they are first in rank and in the causal relation, as it is said, " For the spirit of the *Hayyah* was in the *Ofannim,*" and also for other reasons. The vision of the *Ofannim* [comes next, and] is followed by one which is higher than the *Hayyot,* as has been shown. The cause of this arrangement is, that in study the first two must necessarily precede the third, and in fact they lead to it.

CHAPTER VI

THE sublime and great subject which Ezekiel by prophetic impulse began to teach us in the description of the Mercabah, is exactly the same which Isaiah taught us in general outlines, because he did not require all the detail. Isaiah says, " I saw the Lord sitting upon a throne, high and lifted up, and his train filled the temple. Above it stood seraphims," etc. (Isa. vi. 1 *seq.*). Our Sages have already stated all this clearly, and called our attention to it. For they say that the vision of Ezekiel is the same as that of Isaiah, and illustrate their view by the following simile :—Two men saw the king riding, the one a townsman, the other a countryman. The former, seeing that his neighbours know well how the king rides, simply tells them that he saw the king ; but the villager, wishing to tell his friends things which they do not know, relates in detail how the king was riding, describes his followers, and the officers who execute his order and command. This remark is a most useful hint; it is contained in the following passage (*Ḥagigah*, 13 b): " Isaiah saw all that has been seen by Ezekiel; Isaiah is like a townsman that sees the king, Ezekiel like a countryman that sees the king." These words can be explained in the manner which I have just mentioned, viz., the generation of Isaiah did not require the detailed description; his account, " I saw the Lord," etc., sufficed. The generation of the Babylonian exile wanted to learn all the details. It is, however, possible that the author of this saying held Isaiah as more perfect than Ezekiel, so that the vision might have over-awed Ezekiel and appeared fearful to him; but Isaiah was so familiar with it that he did not consider it necessary to communicate it to others as a new thing, especially as it was well known to the intelligent.

CHAPTER VII

ONE of the points that require investigation is the connexion between the vision of the *mercabah* and the year, month, and day, and also the place of the vision. A reason must be found for this connexion, and we must not think that it is an indifferent element in the vision. We must consider the words, " the heavens were opened " (Ezek. i. 1); they give the key to the understanding of the whole. The figure of opening, also that of opening the gates, occurs frequently in the books of the prophets; e.g., " Open ye the gates that the righteous nation may enter in " (Isa. xxvi. 2); " He opened the doors of heaven " (Ps. lxxviii. 23); " Lift them up, ye everlasting doors " (*ibid.* xxiv. 9); " Open to me the gates of righteousness, I will go into them, and I will praise the Lord " (*ibid.* cxviii. 19). There are many other instances of this kind. You must further notice that the whole de-scription refers undoubtedly to a prophetic vision, as it is said, " And the hand of the Lord was there upon him " (Ezek. i. 3); and yet there is a very great difference between the various parts of the description, for in the account of the *Ḥayyot* the prophet does not say four *Ḥayyot*, but " the likeness of the four *Ḥayyot* " (*ibid.* ver. 5); similarly he says, " And the likeness of a firmament was over the heads of the *Ḥayyot* " ver. 22); " as the appear-ance of a sapphire stone, the likeness of a throne," and " the likeness of the appearance of man above it " (ver. 26). In all these instances the word " likeness " is used, whilst in the account of the *Ofannim* the phrases, " the likeness of *Ofannim*," the " likeness of an *Ofan*," are not employed, but they are described in a positive manner as beings in actual existence, with their real properties. The sentence " they four had one likeness " must not mislead you, for here the word " likeness " is not used in the same connexion or in the same sense as indicated above. In the description of the last vision the prophet confirms and explains this view. When he commences to de-scribe the firmament in detail, he says, " the firmament," without adding the words " the likeness of," for he says, " And I looked, and behold, in the firmament that was above the head of the cherubims there appeared over them as it were a sapphire stone, as the appearance of the likeness of a throne " (x. 1). Here the prophet speaks of " the firmament " and not of " the like-ness of the firmament," as he does when he connects the firmament with the heads of the likeness of the *Hayyot* (i. 22). But, as regards the throne, he says, " the likeness of a throne appeared over them," in order to indicate that the firmament was first perceived and then the likeness of the throne was seen over it. Consider this well.

You must further notice that in the description of the first vision the *Hayyot* have wings and at the same time human hands, whilst in the second vision, in which the term cherubim is substituted for *Hayyot*, at first only wings were perceived, and later on human hands were seen. Comp. " And there appeared in the cherubims the form of a man's hand under their wings " (x. 8). Here " form " (*tabnit*) is used instead of " likeness " (*demut*) ; and the hands are placed under the wings. Note this.

Consider that in reference to the *ofannim*, the prophet says, *le-ʻummatam*, " over against them," although he does not ascribe to them any form.

He further says, " As the appearance of the bow that is in the cloud in the day of rain, so was the appearance of the brightness round about. This was the appearance of the likeness of the glory," etc. (i. 28). The substance and true essence of the bow described here is well known. The simile and comparison is in this case very extraordinary, and is undoubtedly part of the prophecy ; and note it well.

It is also noteworthy that the likeness of man above the throne is divided, the upper part being like the colour of *hashmal*, the lower part like the appearance of fire. As regards the word *hashmal*, it has been explained to be a compound of two words *hash* and *mal*, including two different notions, viz., *hash* signifying " swiftness," and *mal* denoting " pause." The two different notions are here joined in one word in order to indicate figuratively the two different parts, —the upper part and the lower. We have already given a second explanation, namely, that *hashmal* includes the two notions of speech and silence ; in accordance with the saying of our Sages, " At times they are silent, at times they speak," thus deriving *hash* of the same root as *heheshethi*, " I have been silent " (Isa. xlii. 14) ; the word *hashmal* thus includes two notions, and indicates " speech without sound." There is no doubt that the words, " at times they are silent, at times they speak," refer to a created object. Now consider how they clearly stated that the divided likeness of man over the throne does not represent God, who is above the whole chariot, but represents a part of the creation. The prophet likewise says " that is the likeness of the glory of the Lord " ; but " the glory of the Lord " is different from " the Lord " Himself, as has been shown by us several times. All the figures in this vision refer to the glory of the Lord, to the chariot, and not to Him who rides upon the chariot ; for God cannot be compared to anything. Note this. I have thus given you also in this chapter as much of the heads of the sections as will be useful to you for the comprehension of this subject, if you fill out [the sections of] these heads. If you consider all that has been said in this part up to this chapter, the greater part of this subject or the whole of it will be clear to you, except a few points and some repetitions the meaning of which is unknown. Perhaps further study will help to reveal even these things so that nothing will remain unintelligible.

Do not expect or hope to hear from me after this chapter a word on this subject, either explicitly or implicitly, for all that could be said on it has been said, though with great difficulty and struggle.   I will now begin to treat of some of the other subjects which I hope to elucidate in this treatise.

CHAPTER VIII

Transient bodies are only subject to destruction through their substance and not through their form, nor can the essence of their form be destroyed ; in this respect they are permanent.   The generic forms, as you know, are all permanent and stable.   Form can only be destroyed accidentally, i.e., on account of its connexion with substance, the true nature of which consists in the property of never being without a disposition to receive form.   This is the reason why no form remains permanently in a substance ; a constant change takes place, one form is taken off and another is put on.   How wonderfully wise is the simile of King Solomon, in which he compares matter to a faithless wife ; for matter is never found without form, and is therefore always like such a wife who is never without a husband, never single ; and yet, though being wedded, constantly seeks another man in the place of her husband ; she entices and attracts him in every possible manner till he obtains from her what her husband has obtained.   The same is the case with matter. Whatever form it has, it is disposed to receive another form ; it never leaves off moving and casting off the form which it has in order to receive another.   The same takes place when this second form is received.   It is therefore clear that all corruption, destruction, or defect comes from matter. Take, e.g., man ; his deformities and unnatural shape of limbs ; all weakness, interruption, or disorder of his actions, whether innate or not, originate in the transient substance, not in the form.   All other living beings likewise die or become ill through the substance of the body and not through its form. Man's shortcomings and sins are all due to the substance of the body and not to its form ; while all his merits are exclusively due to his form.   Thus the knowledge of God, the formation of ideas, the mastery of desire and passion, the distinction between that which is to be chosen and that which is to be rejected, all these man owes to his form ; but eating, drinking, sexual intercourse, excessive lust, passion, and all vices, have their origin in the substance of his body.   Now it was clear that this was the case,—it was impossible, according to the wisdom of God, that substance should exist without form, or any of the forms of the bodies without substance, and it was necessary that the very noble form of man, which is the image and likeness of God, as has been shown by us, should be joined to the substance of dust and darkness, the source of all defect and loss.   For these reasons the Creator gave to the form of man power, rule, and dominion over the substance ;—the form can subdue the substance, refuse the fulfilment of its desires, and reduce them, as far as possible, to a just and proper measure.   The station of man varies according to the exercise of this power.   Some persons constantly strive to choose that which is noble, and to seek perpetuation in accordance with the direction of their nobler part,—their form ; their thoughts are engaged in the formation of ideas, the acquisition of true knowledge about everything, and the union with the divine intellect which flows down upon them, and which is the source of man's form.   Whenever they are led by the wants of the body to that which is low and avowedly disgraceful, they are grieved at their position, they feel ashamed and confounded at their situation. They try with all their might to diminish this disgrace, and to guard against it in every possible way. They feel like a person whom the king in his anger ordered to remove refuse from one place to another in order to put him to shame; that person tries as much as possible to hide himself during the time of his disgrace; he perhaps removes a small quantity a short distance in such a manner that his hands and garments remain clean, and he himself be unnoticed by his fellow-men. Such would be the conduct of a free man, whilst a slave would find pleasure in such work;—he would not consider it a great burden, but throw himself into the refuse, smear his face and his hands, carry the refuse openly, laughing and singing. This is exactly the difference in the conduct of different men. Some consider, as we just said, all wants of the body as shame, disgrace, and defect to which they are compelled to attend; this is chiefly the case with the sense of touch, which is a disgrace to us according to Aristotle, and which is the cause of our desire for eating, drinking, and sensuality. Intelligent persons must, as much as possible, reduce these wants, guard against them, feel grieved when satisfying them, abstain from speaking of them, discussing them, and attending to them in company with others. Man must have control over all these desires, reduce them as much as possible, and only retain of them as much as is indispensable. His aim must be the aim of man as man, viz., the formation of ideas, and nothing else. The best and sublimest among them is the idea which man forms of God, angels, and the rest of the creation according to his capacity. Such men are always with God, and of them it is said, " Ye are princes, and all of you are children of the Most High " (Ps. lxxxii. 6). This is man's task and purpose. Others, however, that are separated from God form the multitude of fools, and do just the opposite. They neglect all thought and all reflection on ideas, and consider as their task the cultivation of the sense of touch,—that sense which is the greatest disgrace; they only think and reason about eating and love. Thus it is said of the wicked who are drowned in eating, drinking, and love, " They also have erred through wine, and through strong drink are out of the way," etc. (Isa. xxviii. 7), " for all tables are full of vomit and filthiness, so that there is no place clean " (ver. 8); again, "And women rule over them " (*ibid.* iii. 2),—the opposite of that which man was told in the beginning of the creation, " And for thy husband shall thy desire be, and he shall rule over thee " (Gen. iii. 16). The intensity of their lust is then described thus, " Every one neighed after his neighbour's wife," etc. (Jer. v. 8); " they are all adulterers, an assembly of treacherous men " (*ibid.* ix. 2). The whole book of the Proverbs of Solomon treats of this subject, and exhorts to abstain from lust and intemperance. These two vices ruin those that hate God and keep far from Him; to them the following passages may be applied, " They are not the Lord's " (*ibid.* v. 10); " Cast them out of my sight, and let them go forth " (*ibid.* xv. 1). As regards the portion beginning, " Who can find a virtuous woman ? " it is clear what is meant by the figurative expression, " a virtuous woman." When man possesses a good sound body that does not overpower him nor disturb the equilibrium in him, he possesses a divine gift. In short, a good constitution facilitates the rule of the soul over the body, but it is not impossible to conquer a bad constitution by training. For this reason King

Solomon and others wrote the moral lessons; also all the commandments and exhortations in the Pentateuch aim at conquering the desires of the body. Those who desire to be men in truth, and not brutes, having only the appearance and shape of men, must constantly endeavour to reduce the wants of the body, such as eating, love, drinking, anger, and all vices originating in lust and passion; they must feel ashamed of them and set limits to them for themselves. As for eating and drinking in so far as it is indispensable, they will eat and drink only as much as is useful and necessary as food, and not for the purpose of pleasure. They will also speak little of these things, and rarely congregate for such purposes. Thus our Sages, as is well known, kept aloof from a banquet that was not part of a religious act, and pious men followed the example of R. Phinehas, son of Jair, who never dined with other persons, and even refused to accept an invitation of R. Jehudah, the Holy. Wine may be treated as food, if taken as such, but to form parties for the purpose of drinking wine together must be considered more disgraceful than the unrestrained conduct of persons who in daylight meet in the same house undressed and naked. For the natural action of the digestive organ is indispensable to man, he cannot do without it; whilst drunkenness depends on the free will of an evil man. To appear naked in the presence of other people is misconduct only according to public opinion, not according to the dictates of reason, whilst drunkenness, which ruins the mind and the body of man, reason stamps as a vice. You, therefore, who desire to act as human beings must keep away from it, and even from speaking of it. On sexual intercourse, I need not add anything after I have pointed out in the commentary on *Abot* (i. 17) how it is treated by our Law, which is the teaching of pure wisdom—no excuse whatever should induce us to mention it or to speak of it. Thus our Sages said, that Elisha the prophet is called holy, because he did not think of it, and consequently never found himself polluted with semen. In a similar manner they say that Jacob had the first issue of semen for the conception of Reuben. All these traditional stories have the object of teaching the nation humane conduct. There is a well-known saying of our Sages, " The thoughts about the sin are more dangerous than the sin itself." I can offer a good explanation of this saying: When a person is disobedient, this is due to certain accidents connected with the corporeal element in his constitution; for man sins only by his animal nature, whereas thinking is a faculty of man connected with his form,—a person who thinks sinfully sins therefore by means of the nobler portion of his self; and he who wrongly causes a foolish slave to work does not sin as much as he who wrongly causes a noble and free man to do the work of a slave. For this specifically human element, with all its properties and powers, should only be employed in suitable work, in attempts to join higher beings, and not in attempts to go down and reach the lower creatures. You know how we condemn lowness of speech, and justly so, for speech is likewise peculiar to man and a boon which God granted to him that he may be distinguished from the rest of living creatures. Thus God says, " Who gave a mouth to man ? " (Exod. iv. 11); and the prophet declares, " The Lord God hath given me a learned tongue " (Isa. l. 4). This gift, therefore, which God gave us in order to enable us to perfect ourselves, to learn and to teach, must not be employed in doing that which is for us most degrading and perfectly disgraceful; we must not imitate the songs and tales of ignorant and lascivious people. It may be suitable to them, but is not fit for those who are told, " And ye shall be unto me a kingdom of priests and a holy nation " (Exod. xix. 6). Those who employ the faculty of thinking and speaking in the service of that sense which is no honour to us, who think more than necessary of drink and love, or even sing of these things ; they employ and use the divine gift in acts of rebellion against the Giver, and in the transgression of His commandments. To them the following words may be applied : " And I multiplied her silver and gold, which they pre- pared for Baal " (Hos. ii. 10). I have also a reason and cause for calling our language the holy language—do not think it is exaggeration or error on my part, it is perfectly correct—the Hebrew language has no special name for the organ of generation in females or in males, nor for the act of generation itself, nor for semen, nor for secretion. The Hebrew has no original ex- pressions for these things, and only describes them in figurative language and by way of hints, as if to indicate thereby that these things should not be men- tioned, and should therefore have no names ; we ought to be silent about them, and when we are compelled to mention them, we must manage to employ for that purpose some suitable expressions, although these are gener- ally used in a different sense. Thus the organ of generation in males is called in Hebrew *gid*, which is a figurative term, reminding of the words, " And thy neck is an iron sinew " (*gid*) (Isa. xlviii. 4). It is also called *shupka*, " pouring out " (Deut. xxiii. 2), on account of its function. The female organ is called *kobah* (Num. xxv. 8), from *kebah* (Deut. xviii. 3), which denotes " stomach " ; *reḥem*," womb," is the inner organ in which the fœtus develops; *zoah* (Isa. xxviii. 8), " refuse," is derived from the verb *yaza*, " he went out"; for "urine" the phrase *meme raglayim*, " the water of the feet " (2 Kings. xviii. 17), is used ; semen is expressed by *shikbat zera*ʿ, " a layer of seed." For the act of generation there is no expression whatever in Hebrew ; it is described by the following words only : *baʿal*, " he was master"; *shakab*, " he lay "; *lakaḥ*, " he took " ; *gillah ʿervah*, " he uncovered the nakedness." Be not misled by the word *yishgalennah* (Deut. xxviii. 30), to take it as denoting that act ; this is not the case, for *shegal* denotes a female ready for cohabitation. Comp. " Upon thy right hand did stand the maiden " (*shegal*) " in gold of Ophir " (Ps. xlv. 10). *Yishgalennah*, according to the *Kethib*, denotes therefore " he will take the female for the purpose of cohabitation."

We have made in the greater part of this chapter a digression from the theme of this treatise, and introduced some moral and religious matter, although they do not entirely belong to the subject of this treatise, but the course of the discussion has led to it.

CHAPTER IX

THE corporeal element in man is a large screen and partition that prevents him from perfectly perceiving abstract ideals; this would be the case even if the corporeal element were as pure and superior as the substance of the spheres ; how much more must this be the case with our dark and opaque body. However great the exertion of our mind may be to comprehend the Divine Being or any of the ideals, we find a screen and partition between Him and ourselves. Thus the prophets frequently hint at the existence of a partition between God and us. They say He is concealed from us in vapours, in darkness, in mist, or in a thick cloud ; or use similar figures to express that on account of our bodies we are unable to comprehend His essence. This is the meaning of the words, " Clouds and darkness are round about Him " (Ps. xcvii. 2). The prophets tell us that the difficulty consists in the grossness of our substance ; they do not imply, as might be gathered from the literal meaning of their words, that God is corporeal, and is invisible because He is surrounded by thick clouds, vapours, darkness, or mist. This figure is also expressed in the passage, " He made darkness His secret place " (Ps. xviii. 12). The object of God revealing Himself in thick clouds, darkness, vapours, and mist was to teach this lesson ; for every prophetic vision contains some lesson by means of allegory ; that mighty vision, therefore, though the greatest of all visions, and above all comparison, viz., His revelation in a thick cloud, did not take place without any purpose, it was intended to indicate that we cannot comprehend Him on account of the dark body that surrounds us. It does not surround God, because He is incorporeal. A tradition is current among our people that the day of the revelation on Mount Sinai was misty, cloudy, and a little rainy. Comp. " Lord, when thou wentest forth from Seir, when thou marchedst out of the field of Edom, the earth trembled, and the heavens dropped water " (Judges v. 4). The same idea is expressed by the words " darkness, clouds, and thick darkness " (Deut. iv. 11). The phrase does not denote that darkness surrounds God, for with Him there is no darkness, but the great, strong, and permanent light, which, emanating from Him, illuminates all darkness, as is expressed by the prophetic simile, " And the earth shined with His glory " (Ezek. xliii. 2).

CHAPTER X

The Mutakallemim, as I have already told you, apply the term non-existence only to absolute non-existence, and not to the absence of properties. A property and the absence of that property are considered by them as two opposites, they treat, e.g., blindness and sight, death and life, in the same way as heat and cold. Therefore they say, without any qualification, non-existence does not require any agent, an agent is required when *something* is produced. From a certain point of view this is correct. Although they hold that non-existence does not require an agent, they say in accordance with their principle that God causes blindness and deafness, and gives rest to anything that moves, for they consider these negative conditions as positive properties. We must now state our opinion in accordance with the results of philosophical research. You know that he who removes the obstacle of motion is to some extent the cause of the motion, e.g., if one removes the pillar which supports the beam he causes the beam to move, as has been stated by Aristotle in his *Physics* (VIII., chap. iv.) ; in this sense we say of him who removed a certain property that he produced the absence of that property, although absence of a property is nothing positive. Just as we say of him who puts out the light at night that he has produced darkness, so we say of him who destroyed the sight of any being that he produced blindness, although darkness and blindness are negative properties, and require no agent.

In accordance with this view we explain the following passage of Isaiah :
" I form the light and create (*bore*) darkness : I make peace, and create (*bore*)
evil " (Isa. xlv. 7), for darkness and evil are non-existing things. Consider
that the prophet does not say, I make (*'oseh*) darkness, I make (*'oseh*) evil, because darkness and evil are not things in positive existence to which the verb
" to make " would apply ; the verb *bara* " he created " is used, because in
Hebrew this verb is applied to non-existing things, e.g., " In the beginning
God created " (*bara*), etc. ; here the creation took place from nothing.
Only in this sense can non-existence be said to be produced by a certain action
of an agent.   In the same way we must explain the following passage :
" Who hath made man's mouth ? or who maketh the dumb, or the deaf, or
the seeing," etc. (Exod. iv. 11).   The passage can also be explained as follows :
Who has made man able to speak ? or can create him without the capacity
of speaking, i.e., create a substance that is incapable of acquiring this property ? for he who produces a substance that cannot acquire a certain property may be called the producer of that privation.   Thus we say, if any one
abstains from delivering a fellow-man from death, although he is able to do
so, that he killed him.   It is now clear that according to all these different
views the action of an agent cannot be directly connected with a thing that
does not exist ; only indirectly is non-existence described as the result of
the action of an agent, whilst in a direct manner an action can only influence
a thing really in existence ; accordingly, whoever the agent may be, he can
only act upon an existing thing.

After this explanation you must recall to memory that, as has been proved,
the [so-called] evils are evils only in relation to a certain thing, and that which
is evil in reference to a certain existing thing, either includes the non-existence
of that thing or the non-existence of some of its good conditions.   The proposition has therefore been laid down in the most general terms, " All evils
are negations."   Thus for man death is evil ; death is his non-existence.
Illness, poverty, and ignorance are evils for man ; all these are privations
of properties.   If you examine all single cases to which this general proposition applies, you will find that there is not one case in which the proposition
is wrong except in the opinion of those who do not make any distinction between negative and positive properties, or between two opposites, or do not
know the nature of things,—who, e.g., do not know that health in general
denotes a certain equilibrium, and is a relative term.   The absence of that
relation is illness in general, and death is the absence of life in the case of any
animal.   The destruction of other things is likewise nothing but the absence
of their form.

After these propositions, it must be admitted as a fact that it cannot be
said of God that He directly creates evil, or He has the direct intention to
produce evil ; this is impossible.   His works are all perfectly good.   He
only produces existence, and all existence is good ; whilst evils are of a
negative character, and cannot be acted upon.   Evil can only be attributed
to Him in the way we have mentioned.   He creates evil only in so far as He
produces the corporeal element such as it actually is ; it is always connected
with negatives, and is on that account the source of all destruction and all evil.
Those beings that do not possess this corporeal element are not subject to
destruction or evil ; consequently the true work of God is all good, since it

is existence. The book which enlightened the darkness of the world says therefore, "And God saw everything that He had made, and, behold, it was very good" (Gen. i. 31). Even the existence of this corporeal element, low as it in reality is, because it is the source of death and all evils, is likewise good for the permanenee of the Universe and the continuation of the order of things, so that one thing departs and the other succeeds. Rabbi Meir therefore explains the words "and behold it was very good" (*tob me'od*); that even death was good in accordance with what we have observed in this chapter. Remember what I said in this chapter, consider it, and you will understand all that the prophets and our Sages remarked about the perfect goodness of all the direct works of God. In *Bereshit Rabba* (chap. i.) the same idea is expressed thus : " No evil comes down from above."

CHAPTER XI

ALL the great evils which men cause to each other because of certain intentions, desires, opinions, or religious principles, are likewise due to non-existence, because they originate in ignorance, which is absence of wisdom. A blind man, for example, who has no guide, stumbles constantly, because he cannot see, and causes injury and harm to himself and others. In the same manner various classes of men, each man in proportion to his ignorance, bring great evils upon themselves and upon other individual members of the species. If men possessed wisdom, which stands in the same relation to the form of man as the sight to the eye, they would not cause any injury to themselves or to others ; for the knowledge of truth removes hatred and quarrels, and prevents mutual injuries. This state of society is promised to us by the prophet in the words : " And the wolf shall dwell with the lamb," etc. ; " and the cow and the bear shall feed together," etc. ; and " the sucking child shall play on the hole of the asp," etc. (Isa. xi. 6 *seq.*). The prophet also points out what will be the cause of this change ; for he says that hatred, quarrel, and fighting will come to an end, because men will then have a true knowledge of God. " They shall not hurt nor destroy in all my holy mountain : for the earth shall be full of the knowledge of the Lord, as the waters cover the sea " (*ibid.* ver. 9). Note it.

CHAPTER XII

MEN frequently think that the evils in the world are more numerous than the good things ; many sayings and songs of the nations dwell on this idea. They say that a good thing is found only exceptionally, whilst evil things are numerous and lasting. Not only common people make this mistake, but even many who believe that they are wise. Al-Razi wrote a well-known book *On Metaphysics* [or Theology]. Among other mad and foolish things, it contains also the idea, discovered by him, that there exists more evil than good. For if the happiness of man and his pleasure in the times of prosperity be compared with the mishaps that befall him,—such as grief, acute pain, defects, paralysis of the limbs, fears, anxieties, and troubles,—it would seem as if the existence of man is a punishment and a great evil for him. This author commenced to verify his opinion by counting all the evils one by one ; by this means he opposed those who hold the correct view of the benefits bestowed by God and His evident kindness, viz., that God is perfect goodness, and that all that comes from Him is absolutely good. The origin of the error is to be found in the circumstance that this ignorant man, and his party among the common people, judge the whole universe by examining one single person. For an ignorant man believes that the whole universe only exists for him; as if nothing else required any consideration. If, therefore, anything happens to him contrary to his expectation, he at once concludes that the whole universe is evil. If, however, he would take into consideration the whole universe, form an idea of it, and comprehend what a small portion he is of the Universe, he will find the truth. For it is clear that persons who have fallen into this widespread error as regards the multitude of evils in the world, do not find the evils among the angels, the spheres and stars, the elements, and that which is formed of them, viz., minerals and plants, or in the various species of living beings, but only in some individual instances of mankind. They wonder that a person, who became leprous in consequence of bad food, should be afflicted with so great an illness and suffer such a misfortune; or that he who indulges so much in sensuality as to weaken his sight, should be struck with blindness! and the like. What we have, in truth, to consider is this :—The whole mankind at present in existence, and *a fortiori*, every other species of animals, form an infinitesimal portion of the permanent universe. Comp. " Man is like to vanity " (Ps. cxliv. 4) ; " How much less man, that is a worm ; and the son of man, which is a worm " (Job xxv. 6) ; " How much less in them who dwell in houses of clay " (*ibid.* iv. 19) ; " Behold, the nations are as a drop of the bucket " (Isa. xl. 15). There are many other passages in the books of the prophets expressing the same idea. It is of great advantage that man should know his station, and not erroneously imagine that the whole universe exists only for him. We hold that the universe exists because the Creator wills it so; that mankind is low in rank as compared with the uppermost portion of the universe, viz., with the spheres and the stars ; but, as regards the angels, there cannot be any real comparison between man and angels, although man is the highest of all beings on earth ; i.e., of all beings formed of the four elements. Man's existence is nevertheless a great boon to him, and his distinction and perfection is a divine gift. The numerous evils to which individual persons are exposed are due to the defects existing in the persons themselves. We complain and seek relief from our own faults ; we suffer from the evils which we, by our own free will, inflict on ourselves and ascribe them to God, who is far from being connected with them! Comp. " Is destruction his [work] ? No. Ye [who call yourselves] wrongly his sons, you who are a perverse and crooked generation " (Deut. xxxii. 5). This is explained by Solomon, who says, " The foolishness of man perverteth his way, and his heart fretteth against the Lord " (Prov. xix. 3).

I explain this theory in the following manner. The evils that befall man are of three kinds :—

(1) The first kind of evil is that which is caused to man by the circumstance that he is subject to genesis and destruction, or that he possesses a body. It is on account of the body that some persons happen to have great deformities or paralysis of some of the organs. This evil may be part of the natural con-

stitution of these persons, or may have developed subsequently in consequence of changes in the elements, e.g., through bad air, or thunderstorms,
or landslips. We have already shown that, in accordance with the divine
wisdom, genesis can only take place through destruction, and without the
destruction of the individual members of the species the species themselves
would not exist permanently. Thus the true kindness, and beneficence,
and goodness of God is clear. He who thinks that he can have flesh and
bones without being subject to any external influence, or any of the accidents
of matter, unconsciously wishes to reconcile two opposites, viz., to be at the
same time subject and not subject to change. If man were never subject
to change there could be no generation ; there would be one single being,
but no individuals forming a species. Galen, in the third section of his book,
The Use of the Limbs, says correctly that it would be in vain to expect to see
living beings formed of the blood of menstruous women and the semen virile,
who will not die, will never feel pain, or will move perpetually, or will shine
like the sun. This dictum of Galen is part of the following more general proposition :—Whatever is formed of any matter receives the most perfect form
possible in that species of matter ; in each individual case the defects are in
accordance with the defects of that individual matter. The best and most
perfect being that can be formed of the blood and the semen is the species of
man, for as far as man's nature is known, he is living, reasonable, and mortal.
It is therefore impossible that man should be free from this species of evil.
You will, nevertheless, find that the evils of the above kind which befall man
are very few and rare ; for you find countries that have not been flooded or
burned for thousands of years ; there are thousands of men in perfect health,
deformed individuals are a strange and exceptional occurrence, or say few
in number if you object to the term exceptional,—they are not one-hun-
dredth, not even one-thousandth part of those that are perfectly normal.

(2) The second class of evils comprises such evils as people cause to each
other, when, e.g., some of them use their strength against others. These
evils are more numerous than those of the first kind ; their causes are numerous and known ; they likewise originate in ourselves, though the sufferer
himself cannot avert them. This kind of evil is nevertheless not widespread
in any country of the whole world. It is of rare occurrence that a man plans
to kill his neighbour or to rob him of his property by night. Many persons
are, however, afflicted with this kind of evil in great wars ; but these are not
frequent, if the whole inhabited part of the earth is taken into consideration.

(3) The third class of evils comprises those which every one causes to himself by his own action. This is the largest class, and is far more numerous
than the second class. It is especially of these evils that all men complain,—
only few men are found that do not sin against themselves by this kind of
evil. Those that are afflicted with it are therefore justly blamed in the
words of the prophet, " This hath been by your means " (Mal. i. 9) ; the
same is expressed in the following passage, " He that doeth it destroyeth his
own soul " (Prov. vi. 32). In reference to this kind of evil, Solomon says,
" The foolishness of man perverteth his way " (*ibid.* xix. 3). In the following passage he explains also that this kind of evil is man's own work, " Lo,
this only have I found, that God hath made man upright, but they have
thought out many inventions " (Eccles. vii. 29), and these inventions bring the

evils upon him.   The same subject is referred to in Job (v. 6), " For affliction cometh not forth of the dust, neither doth trouble spring out of the ground." These words are immediately followed by the explanation that man himself is the author of this class of evils, " But man is born unto trouble."   This class of evils originates in man's vices, such as excessive desire for eating, drinking, and love ; indulgence in these things in undue measure, or in improper manner, or partaking of bad food.   This course brings diseases and afflictions upon body and soul alike.   The sufferings of the body in consequence of these evils are well known ; those of the soul are twofold :—First, such evils of the soul as are the necessary consequence of changes in the body, in so far as the soul is a force residing in the body ; it has therefore been said that the properties of the soul depend on the condition of the body.   Secondly, the soul, when accustomed to superfluous things, acquires a strong habit of desiring things which are neither necessary for the preservation of the individual nor for that of the species.   This desire is without a limit, whilst things which are necessary are few in number and restricted within certain limits ; but what is superfluous is without end—e.g., you desire to have your vessels of silver, but golden vessels are still better : others have even vessels of sapphire, or perhaps they can be made of emerald or rubies, or any other substance that could be suggested.   Those who are ignorant and perverse in their thought are constantly in trouble and pain, because they cannot get as much of superfluous things as a certain other person possesses.   They as a rule expose themselves to great dangers, e.g., by sea-voyage, or service of kings, and all this for the purpose of obtaining that which is superfluous and not necessary.   When they thus meet with the consequences of the course which they adopt, they complain of the decrees and judgments of God ; they begin to blame the time, and wonder at the want of justice in its changes ; that it has not enabled them to acquire great riches, with which they could buy large quantities of wine for the purpose of making themselves drunk, and numerous concubines adorned with various kind of ornaments of gold, embroidery, and jewels, for the purpose of driving themselves to voluptuousness beyond their capacities, as if the whole Universe existed exclusively for the purpose of giving pleasure to these low people. The error of the ignorant goes so far as to say that God's power is insufficient, because He has given to this Universe the properties which they imagine cause these great evils, and which do not help all evil-disposed persons to obtain the evil which they seek, and to bring their evil souls to the aim of their desires, though these, as we have shown, are really without limit. The virtuous and wise, however, see and comprehend the wisdom of God displayed in the Universe.   Thus David says, " All the paths of the Lord are mercy and truth unto such as keep His covenant and His testimonies " (Ps. xxv. 10).   For those who observe the nature of the Universe and the commandments of the Law, and know their purpose, see clearly God's mercy and truth in everything ; they seek, therefore, that which the Creator intended to be the aim of man, viz., comprehension.   Forced by the claims of the body, they seek also that which is necessary for the preservation of the body, " bread to eat and garment to clothe," and this is very little ; but they seek nothing superfluous ; with very slight exertion man can obtain it, so long as he is contented with that which is indispensable.   All the difficulties and troubles we meet in this respect are due to the desire for superfluous things ; when we seek unnecessary things, we have difficulty even in finding that which is indispensable. For the more we desire to have that which is superfluous, the more we meet with difficulties; our strength and possessions are spent in unnecessary things, and are wanting when required for that which is necessary. Observe how Nature proves the correctness of this assertion. The more necessary a thing is for living beings, the more easily it is found and the cheaper it is ; the less necessary it is, the rarer and dearer it is. E.g., air, water, and food are indispensable to man : air is most necessary, for if man is without air a short time he dies; whilst he can be without water a day or two. Air is also undoubtedly found more easily and cheaper [than water]. Water is more necessary than food ; for some people can be four or five days without food, provided they have water; water also exists in every country in larger quantities than food, and is also cheaper. The same proportion can be noticed in the different kinds of food; that which is more necessary in a certain place exists there in larger quantities and is cheaper than that which is less necessary. No intelligent person, I think, considers musk, amber, rubies, and emerald as very necessary for man except as medicines ; and they, as well as other like substances, can be replaced for this purpose by herbs and minerals. This shows the kindness of God to His creatures, even to us weak beings. His righteousness and justice as regards all animals are well known ; for in the transient world there is among the various kinds of animals no individual being distinguished from the rest of the same species by a peculiar property or an additional limb. On the contrary, all physical, psychical, and vital forces and organs that are possessed by one individual are found also in the other individuals. If any one is somehow different it is by accident, in consequence of some exception, and not by a natural property ; it is also a rare occurrence. There is no difference between individuals of a species in the due course of Nature ; the difference originates in the various dispositions of their substances. This is the necessary consequence of the nature of the substance of that species ; the nature of the species is not more favourable to one individual than to the other. It is no wrong or injustice that one has many bags of finest myrrh and garments embroidered with gold, while another has not those things, which are not necessary for our maintenance ; he who has them has not thereby obtained control over anything that could be an essential addition to his nature, but has only obtained something illusory or deceptive. The other, who does not possess that which is not wanted for his maintenance, does not miss anything indispensable : " He that gathered much had nothing over, and he that gathered little had no lack : they gathered every man according to his eating " (Exod. xvi. 18). This is the rule at all times and in all places ; no notice should be taken of exceptional cases, as we have explained.

In these two ways you will see the mercy of God toward His creatures, how He has provided that which is required, in proper proportions, and treated all individual beings of the same species with perfect equality. In accordance with this correct reflection the chief of the wise men says, " All his ways are judgment " (Deut. xxxii. 4); David likewise says : " All the paths of the Lord are mercy and truth " (Ps. xxv. 10); he also says expressly, " The Lord is good to all ; and his tender mercies are over all his works " (*ibid.* cxlv. 9) ; for it is an act of great and perfect goodness that He gave us existence ; and the creation of the controlling faculty in animals is a proof of His mercy towards them, as has been shown by us.

CHAPTER XIII

INTELLIGENT persons are much perplexed when they inquire into the purpose of the Creation.   I will now show how absurd this question is, according to each one of the different theories [above-mentioned]. An agent that acts with intention must have a certain ulterior object in that which he performs. This is evident, and no philosophical proof is required.   It is likewise evident that that which is produced with intention has passed over from non-existence to existence.   It is further evident, and generally agreed upon, that the being which has absolute existence, which has never been and will never be without existence, is not in need of an agent.   We have explained this before.   The question, " What is the purpose thereof ? " cannot be asked about anything which is not the product of an agent ; therefore we cannot ask what is the purpose of the existence of God.   He has not been created. According to these propositions it is clear that the purpose is sought for everything produced intentionally by an intelligent cause ; that is to say, a final cause must exist for everything that owes its existence to an intelligent being : but for that which is without a beginning, a final cause need not be sought, as has been stated by us.   After this explanation you will understand that there is no occasion to seek the final cause of the whole Universe, neither according to our theory of the Creation, nor according to the theory of Aristotle, who assumes the Eternity of the Universe.   For according to Aristotle, who holds that the Universe has not had a beginning, an ultimate final cause cannot be sought even for the various parts of the Universe.   Thus it cannot be asked, according to his opinion, What is the final cause of the existence of the heavens ?   Why are they limited by this measure or by that number ?   Why is matter of this description ?   What is the purpose of the existence of this species of animals or plants ?   Aristotle considers all this as the result of a permanent order of things.   Natural Philosophy investigates into the object of everything in Nature, but it does not treat of the ultimate final cause, of which we speak in this chapter.   It is a recognized fact in Natural Philosophy that everything in Nature has its object, or its final cause, which is the most important of the four causes, though it is not easily recognized in most species.   Aristotle repeatedly says that Nature produces nothing in vain, for every natural action has a certain object.   Thus, Aristotle says that plants exist for animals ; and similarly he shows of other parts of the Universe for what purpose they exist.   This is still more obvious in the case of the organs of animals.   The existence of such a final cause in the various parts of Nature has compelled philosophers to assume the existence of a primal cause apart from Nature ; it is called by Aristotle the intellectual or divine cause, and this cause creates one thing for the purpose of another. Those who acknowledge the truth will accept as the best proof for the Creation the fact that everything in Nature serves a certain purpose, so that one thing exists for the benefit of another ; this fact is supported by numerous instances, and shows that there is design in Nature ; but the existence of design in Nature cannot be imagined unless it be assumed that Nature has been produced.

I will now return to the subject of this chapter, viz., the final cause. Aristotle has already explained that in Nature the efficient cause of a thing, its form, and its final cause are identical; that is to say, they are one thing in relation to the whole species. E.g., the form of Zeid produces the form of his son Amr; its action consists in imparting the form of the whole species [of man] to the substance of Amr, and the final cause is Amr's possession of human form. The same argument is applied by Aristotle to every individual member of a class of natural objects which is brought to existence by another individual member. The three causes coincide in all such cases. All this refers only to the immediate purpose of a thing; but the existence of an ultimate purpose in every species, which is considered as absolutely necessary by every one who investigates into the nature of things, is very difficult to discover: and still more difficult is it to find the purpose of the whole Universe. I infer from the words of Aristotle that according to his opinion the ultimate purpose of the genera is the preservation of the course of genesis and destruction; and this course is absolutely necessary [in the first instance] for the successive formation of material objects, because individual beings formed of matter are not permanent; [secondly], for the production of the best and the most perfect beings that can be formed of matter, because the ultimate purpose [in these productions] is to arrive at perfection. Now it is clear that man is the most perfect being formed of matter; he is the last and most perfect of earthly beings, and in this respect it can truly be said that all earthly things exist for man, i.e., that the changes which things undergo serve to produce the most perfect being that can be produced. Aristotle, who assumes the Eternity of the Universe, need therefore not ask to what purpose does man exist, for the immediate purpose of each individual being is, according to his opinion, the perfection of its specific form. Every individual thing arrives at its perfection fully and completely when the actions that produce its form are complete. The ultimate purpose of the species is the perpetuation of this form by the repeated succession of genesis and destruction, so that there might always be a being capable of the greatest possible perfection. It seems therefore clear that, according to Aristotle, who assumes the Eternity of the Universe, there is no occasion for the question what is the object of the existence of the Universe. But of those who accept our theory that the whole Universe has been created from nothing, some hold that the inquiry after the purpose of the Creation is necessary, and assume that the Universe was only created for the sake of man's existence, that he might serve God. Everything that is done they believe is done for man's sake; even the spheres move only for his benefit, in order that his wants might be supplied. The literal meaning of some passages in the books of the prophets greatly support this idea. Comp. " He formed it (viz., the earth) to be inhabited " (Isa. xlv. 18); " If my covenant of day and night were not," etc. (Jer. xxxiii. 25); "And spreadeth them out as a tent to dwell in" (Isa. xl. 22). If the sphere existed for the sake of man, how much more must this be the case with all other living beings and the plants. On examining this opinion as intelligent persons ought to examine all different opinions, we shall discover the errors it includes. Those who hold this view, namely, that the existence of man is the object of the whole creation, may be asked whether God could have created man without those previous creations, or whether man could only have come into existence after the creation of all other things. If they answer in the affirmative, that man could have been created even if, e.g., the heavens did not exist, they will be asked what is the object of all these things, since they do not exist for their own sake but for the sake of something that could exist without them ? Even if the Universe existed for man's sake and man existed for the purpose of serving God, as has been mentioned, the question remains, What is the end of serving God ? He does not become more perfect if all His creatures serve Him and comprehend Him as far as possible ; nor would He lose anything if nothing existed beside Him. It might perhaps be replied that the service of God is not intended for God's perfection ; it is intended for our own perfection,—it is good for us, it makes us perfect. But then the question might be repeated, What is the object of our being perfect ?   We must in continuing the inquiry as to the purpose of the creation at last arrive at the answer, It was the Will of God, or His Wisdom decreed it ; and this is the correct answer.   The wise men in Israel have, therefore, introduced in our prayers (for Ne'ilah of the Day of Atonement) the following passage :— " Thou hast distinguished man from the beginning, and chosen him to stand before Thee ; who can say unto Thee, What dost Thou ? And if he be righteous, what does he give Thee ? " They have thus clearly stated that it was not a final cause that determined the existence of all things, but only His will.   This being the case, we who believe in the Creation must admit that God could have created the Universe in a different manner as regards the causes and effects contained in it, and this would lead to the absurd conclusion that everything except man existed without any purpose, as the principal object, man, could have been brought into existence without the rest of the creation.   I consider therefore the following opinion as most correct according to the teaching of the Bible, and best in accordance with the results of philosophy ; namely, that the Universe does not exist for man's sake, but that each being exists for its own sake, and not because of some other thing.   Thus we believe in the Creation, and yet need not inquire what purpose is served by each species of the existing things, because we assume that God created all parts of the Universe by His will ; some for their own sake, and some for the sake of other beings, that include their own purpose in themselves.   In the same manner as it was the will of God that man should exist, so it was His will that the heavens with their stars should exist, that there should be angels, and each of these beings is itself the purpose of its own existence.   When anything can only exist provided some other thing has previously existed, God has caused the latter to precede it ; as, e.g., sensation precedes comprehension.   We meet also with this view in Scripture : " The Lord hath made everything (*la-ma'anehu*) for its pur- pose " (Prov. xvi. 4).   It is possible that the pronoun in *la-maanehu* refers to the object ; but it can also be considered as agreeing with the subject ; in which case the meaning of the word is, for the sake of Himself, or His will which is identical with His self [or essence], as has been shown in this treatise. We havê also pointed out that His essence is also called His glory.   The words, " The Lord hath made everything for Himself," express therefore the

same idea as the following verse, " Everything that is called by my name : I
have created it for my glory, I have formed it ; yea, I have made it " (Isa.
xliii. 7) ; that is to say, everything that is described as My work has been
made by Me for the sake of My will and for no other purpose.   The words,
" I have formed it," " I have made it," express exactly what I pointed out
to you, that there are things whose existence is only possible after certain
other things have come into existence.   To these reference is made in the
text, as if to say, I have formed the first thing which must have preceded the
other things, e.g., matter has been formed before the production of material
beings ; I have then made out of that previous creation, or after it, what I
intended to produce, and there was nothing but My will.   Study the book
which leads all who want to be led to the truth, and is therefore called *Torah*
(Law or Instruction), from the beginning of the account of the Creation to
its end, and you will comprehend the opinion which we attempt to expound.
For no part of the creation is described as being in existence for the sake of
another part, but each part is declared to be the product of God's will, and
to satisfy by its existence the intention [of the Creator].   This is expressed
by the phrase, " And God saw that it was good " (Gen. i. 4, etc.).   You
know our interpretation of the saying of our Sages, " Scripture speaks the
same language as is spoken by man."   But we call " good " that which is in
accordance with the object we seek.   When therefore Scripture relates in
reference to the whole creation (Gen. i. 31), " And God saw all that He had
made, and behold it was exceedingly good," it declares thereby that everything created was well fitted for its object, and would never cease to act, and
never be annihilated.   This is especially pointed out by the word " exceedingly " ; for sometimes a thing is temporarily good ; it serves its purpose,
and then it fails and ceases to act.   But as regards the Creation it is said that
everything was fit for its purpose, and able continually to act accordingly.
You must not be misled by what is stated of the stars [that God put them in
the firmament of the heavens] to give light upon the earth, and to rule by
day and by night.   You might perhaps think that here the purpose of their
creation is described.   This is not the case ; we are only informed of the
nature of the stars, which God desired to create with such properties that
they should be able to give light and to rule.   In a similar manner we must
understand the passage, " And have dominion over the fish of the sea " (*ibid.*
i. 28).   Here it is not meant to say that man was created for this purpose,
but only that this was the nature which God gave man.   But as to the
statement in Scripture that God gave the plants to man and other living
beings, it agrees with the opinion of Aristotle and other philosophers.   It is
also reasonable to assume that the plants exist only for the benefit of the
animals, since the latter cannot live without food.   It is different with the
stars, they do not exist only for our sake, that we should enjoy their good
influence ; for the expressions " to give light " and " to rule " merely describe, as we have stated above, the benefit which the creatures on earth
derive from them.   I have already explained to you the character of that
influence that causes continually the good to descend from one being to another.   To those who receive the good flowing down upon them, it may
appear as if the being existed for them alone that sends forth its goodness
and kindness unto them.   Thus some citizen may imagine that it was for

the purpose of protecting his house by night from thieves that the king was chosen. To some extent this is correct; for when his house is protected, and he has derived this benefit through the king whom the country had chosen, it appears as if it were the object of the king to protect the house of that man. In this manner we must explain every verse, the literal meaning of which would imply that something superior was created for the sake of something inferior, viz., that it is part of the nature of the superior thing [to influence the inferior in a certain manner]. We remain firm in our belief that the whole Universe was created in accordance with the will of God, and we do not inquire for any other cause or object. Just as we do not ask what is the purpose of God's existence, so we do not ask what was the object of His will, which is the cause of the existence of all things with their present properties, both those that have been created and those that will be created.

You must not be mistaken and think that the spheres and the angels were created for our sake. Our position has already been pointed out to us, " Behold, the nations are as a drop of a bucket " (Isa. xl. 15). Now compare your own essence with that of the spheres, the stars, and the Intelligences, and you will comprehend the truth, and understand that man is superior to everything formed of earthly matter, but not to other beings; he is found exceedingly inferior when his existence is compared with that of the spheres, and *a fortiori* when compared with that of the Intelligences. Comp. " Behold, he putteth no trust in his servants : and his messengers he charged with folly : how much less in them that dwell in houses of clay, whose foundation is in the dust, which are crushed before the moth ? " (Job iv. 18, 19). The expression " his servants," occurring in this passage, does not denote human beings; this may be inferred from the words, " How much less in them that dwell in houses of clay ? " The " servants " referred to in this place are the angels; whilst by the term " his messengers " the spheres are undoubtedly meant. Eliphas himself, who uttered the above words, explains this [in the second speech] when he refers to it in one of his replies in other words, saying, " Behold, he putteth no trust in his holy ones; yea, the heavens are not clean in his sight, how much more abominable and filthy is man, who drinketh iniquity like water " (*ibid.* xv. 15, 16). He thus shows that " his servants " and " his holy ones " are identical, and that they are not human beings; also that " his messengers," mentioned in the first passage, are the same as " the heavens." The term " folly " is explained by the phrase " they are not clean in his sight," i.e., they are material; although their substance is the purest and the most luminous, compared with the Intelligences it appears dark, turbid, and impure. The phrase, " Behold, he putteth no trust in his servants," is employed in reference to the angels, indicating that these do not possess perpetual existence, since, as we believe, they have had a beginning; and even according to those who assume the Eternity of the Universe, the existence of the angels is at all events dependent on and therefore inferior to, the absolute existence of God. The words, " How much more abominable and filthy is man," in the one passage, correspond to the phrase " How much less in those who dwell in houses of clay " in the other passage. Their meaning is this : How much less in man who is abominable and filthy, in whose person crookedness or corporeality is mixed up and spread through all his parts. " Iniquity " (*'avlah*) is identical with

" crookedness," as may be inferred from the passage, " In the land of up-rightness he will act with iniquity " (Isa. xxvi. 10), and *ish*, " man," is here used in the same sense as *adam*, " human being " ; for " man " in a general sense is sometimes expressed in Scripture by *ish*. Comp. " He who smiteth a man (*ish*) and he die " (Exod. xxi. 12).

This must be our belief when we have a correct knowledge of our own self, and comprehend the true nature of everything ; we must be content, and not trouble our mind with seeking a certain final cause for things that have none, or have no other final cause but their own existence, which depends on the Will of God, or, if you prefer, on the Divine Wisdom.

CHAPTER XIV

In order to obtain a correct estimate of ourselves, we must reflect on the results of the investigations which have been made into the dimensions and the distances of the spheres and the stars. The distances are clearly stated in radii of the earth, and are well known, since the circumference and the radius of the earth are known. It has been proved that the distance between the centre of the earth and the outer surface of the sphere of Saturn is a journey of nearly eight thousand seven hundred solar years. Suppose a day's journey to be forty legal miles of two thousand ordinary cubits, and consider the great and enormous distance ! or in the words of Scripture, " Is not God in the height of heaven ? and behold the height of the stars, how high they are ! " (Job xxii. 12) ; that is to say, learn from the height of the heavens how far we are from comprehending God, for there is an enor-mous distance between ourselves and these corporeal objects, and the latter are greatly distinguished from us by their position, and hidden from us as regards their essence and most of their actions. How much more incom-prehensible therefore is their Maker, who is incorporeal ! The great dis-tance which has been proved is, in fact, the least that can be assumed. The distance between the centre of the earth and the surface of the sphere of the fixed stars can by no means be less, but it may possibly be many times as great ; for the measure of the thickness of the body of the spheres has not been proved, and the least possible has been assumed, as appears from the treatises *On the Distances*. The same is the case with the substances which are between every two spheres. According to logical inference, as has been mentioned by Thabit, the thickness of these substances cannot be accurately stated, since they do not contain any star, which might serve as a means of obtaining it. As to the thickness of the sphere of the fixed stars, it is at least four years' journey, as may be inferred from the measure of the stars con-tained in the sphere. The body of each of these stars is more than ninety times as big as the globe of the earth, and it is possible that the thickness of the sphere is still greater. Of the ninth sphere, that causes the daily revolu-tion of the whole system of spheres, we do not know the dimensions ; it contains no stars, and therefore we have no means of finding out its magni-tude. Now consider the enormous dimensions and the large number of these material beings. If the whole earth is infinitely small in comparison with the sphere of the stars, what is man compared with all these created beings ! How, then, could any one of us imagine that these things exist for his sake

and benefit, and that they are his tools ! This is the result of an examination
of the corporeal beings : how much more so will this be the result of an
examination into the nature of the Intelligences !

The following question may be asked against the opinion of philosophers
on this subject : There is no doubt that from a philosophical point of view
it would be a mistake to assume that the spheres exist for the purpose of
regulating the fate of one individual person or community ; but it is not
absurd to think that they serve to regulate the affairs of mankind, since these
mighty individual beings would serve to give existence to the individual
members of the species, the number of which, according to the philosophers,
will never come to an end. We can best illustrate this by the following
simile : An artisan makes iron tools of a hundred-weight for the purpose of
making a small needle of the weight of a grain. If only one needle had to be
produced, we admit that it would certainly be bad management, though it
would not be entirely a failure ; but if with those enormous tools needle
after needle is produced, even many hundred-weights of needles, the preparation of those tools would be a wise act and excellent management. In
a similar manner the object of the spheres may be the continuance of successive genesis and destruction ; and the succession of genesis and destruction
serves, as has already been said, to give existence to mankind. This idea is
supported by Biblical texts and sayings [of our Sages]. The philosopher
replies thus : If the difference between the heavenly bodies and the transient individual members of the species consisted in their different sizes,
this opinion could be maintained ; but as the difference consists in their
essence, it remains improbable that the superior beings should be the means
of giving existence to the lower ones. In short, this question supports our
belief in the Creation ; and this is the principal object of this chapter. [It
serves] besides [a second purpose]. I frequently hear from those who know
something about astronomy, that our Sages exaggerated the distances [of
the heavenly bodies] when they said that the thickness of each sphere is five
hundred years' journey ; the distance of the seven spheres from each other
five hundred years' journey, so that the distance of the outer surface of the
seventh sphere from the centre of the earth is seven thousand years' journey.
Those who hear such statements consider them [at first thought] as exaggeration, and believe that the distance is not so great. But you may ascertain
from the data proved in scientific treatises on the distances, that the centre
of the earth is distant from the inner surface of the seventh sphere, that of
Saturn, nearly seven thousand and twenty-four years' journey. The number
eight thousand and seven hundred given by us, refers to the distance of the
centre of the earth from the inner surface of the eighth sphere. The distance of the spheres from each other, mentioned by astronomers, is identical
with the thickness of the substance that intervenes between one sphere and
the other, and does not imply that there is a vacuum. You must, however,
not expect that everything our Sages say respecting astronomical matters
should agree with observation, for mathematics were not fully developed in
those days ; and their statements were not based on the authority of the
Prophets, but on the knowledge which they either themselves possessed or
derived from contemporary men of science. But I will not on that account
denounce what they say correctly in accordance with real fact, as untrue or

accidentally true. On the contrary, whenever the words of a person can be interpreted in such a manner that they agree with fully established facts, it is the duty of every educated and honest man to do so.

CHAPTER XV

THAT which is impossible has a permanent and constant property, which is not the result of some agent, and cannot in any way change, and consequently we do not ascribe to God the power of doing what is impossible. No thinking man denies the truth of this maxim ; none ignore it, but such as have no idea of Logic. There is, however, a difference of opinion among philosophers with reference to the existence of any particular thing. Some of them consider its existence to be impossible, and hold that God cannot produce the thing in question, whilst others think that it is possible, and that God can create it if He pleases to do so. E.g., all philosophers consider that it is impossible for one substratum to have at the same moment two opposite properties, or for the elementary components of a thing, substance and accident, to interchange, so that the substance becomes accident, and the accident becomes substance, or for a material substance to be without accident. Likewise it is impossible that God should produce a being like Himself, or annihilate, corporify, or change Himself. The power of God is not assumed to extend to any of these impossibilities. But the existence of accidents independent of substance is possible according to one class of philosophers, the Mutazilah, whilst according to others it is impossible ; it must, however, be added that those who admit the existence of an accident independent of substance, have not arrived at this conclusion by philosophical research alone ; but it was mainly by the desire to defend certain religious principles, which speculation had greatly shaken, that they had recourse to this theory. In a similar manner the creation of corporeal things, otherwise than from a substance, is possible according to our view, whilst the philosophers say that it is impossible. Again, whilst philosophers say that it is impossible to produce a square with a diagonal equal to one of the sides, or a solid angle that includes four right angles, or similar things, it is thought possible by some persons who are ignorant of mathematics, and who only know the words of these propositions, but have no idea of that which is expressed by them. I wonder whether this gate of research is open, so that all may freely enter, and whilst one imagines a thing and considers it possible, another is at liberty to assert that such a thing is impossible by its very nature ; or whether the gate is closed and guarded by certain rules, so that we are able to decide with certainty whether a thing is physically impossible. I should also like to know, in the latter case, whether imagination or reason has to examine and test objects as to their being possible or not ; likewise how things imagined, and things conceived intellectually, are to be distinguished from each other. For it occurs that we consider a thing as physically possible, and then some one objects, or we ourselves fear that our opinion is only the result of imagination, and not that of reason. In such a case it would be desirable to ascertain whether there exists some faculty to distinguish between imagination and intellect, [and if so,] whether this faculty is different from both, or whether it is part of the intellect itself to distinguish between intellectual and imaginary objects. All this requires investigation, but it does not belong to the theme of this chapter.

We have thus shown that according to each one of the different theories there are things which are impossible, whose existence cannot be admitted, and whose creation is excluded from the power of God, and the assumption that God does not change their nature does not imply weakness in God, or a limit to His power. Consequently things impossible remain impossible, and do not depend on the action of an agent. It is now clear that a difference of opinion exists only as to the question to which of the two classes a thing belongs ; whether to the class of the impossible, or to that of the possible. Note it.

CHAPTER XVI

THE philosophers have uttered very perverse ideas as regards God's Omniscience of everything beside Himself ; they have stumbled in such a manner that they cannot rise again, nor can those who adopt their views. I will further on tell you the doubts that led them to these perverse utterances on this question; and I will also tell you the opinion which is taught by our religion, and which differs from the evil and wrong principles of the philosophers as regards God's Omniscience.

The principal reason that first induced the philosophers to adopt their theory is this : at first thought we notice an absence of system in human affairs. Some pious men live a miserable and painful life, whilst some wicked people enjoy a happy and pleasant life. On this account the philosophers assumed as possible the cases which you will now hear. They said that only one of two things is possible, either God is ignorant of the individual or particular things on earth, and does not perceive them, or He perceives and knows them. These are all the cases possible. They then continued thus : If He perceives and knows all individual things, one of the following three cases must take place : (1) God arranges and manages human affairs well, perfectly and faultlessly ; (2) He is overcome by obstacles, and is too weak and powerless to manage human affairs ; (3) He knows [all things] and can arrange and manage them, but leaves and abandons them, as too base, low, and vile, or from jealousy ; as we may also notice among ourselves some who are able to make another person happy, well knowing what he wants for his happiness, and still in consequence of their evil disposition, their wickedness and jealousy against him, they do not help him to his happiness.—This is likewise a complete enumeration of all possible cases. For those who have a knowledge of a certain thing necessarily either (1) take care of the thing which they know, and manage it, or (2) neglect it (as we, e.g., neglect and forget the cats in our house, or things of less importance) ; or (3) while taking care of it, have not sufficient power and strength for its management, although they have the will to do so. Having enumerated these different cases, the philosophers emphatically decided that of the three cases possible [as regards the management of a thing] by one who knows that thing], two are inadmissible in reference to God — viz., want of power, or absence of will ; because they imply either evil disposition or weakness, neither of which can by any means be attributed to

Him. Consequently there remains only the alternative that God is altogether ignorant of human affairs, or that He knows them and manages them well. Since we, however, notice that events do not follow a certain order, that they cannot be determined by analogy, and are not in accordance with what is wanted, we conclude that God has no knowledge of them in any way or for any reason. This is the argument which led the philosophers to speak such blasphemous words. In the treatise *On Providence*, by Alexander Aphrodisiensis, you will find the same as I have said about the different views of the philosophers, and as I have stated as to the source of their error.

You must notice with surprise that the evil into which these philosophers have fallen is greater than that from which they sought to escape, and that they ignore the very thing which they constantly pointed out and explained to us. They have fallen into a greater evil than that from which they sought to escape, because they refuse to say that God neglects or forgets a thing, and yet they maintain that His knowledge is imperfect, that He is ignorant of what is going on here on earth, that He does not perceive it. They also ignore, what they constantly point out to us, in as much as they judge the whole universe by that which befalls individual men, although, according to their own view, frequently stated and explained, the evils of man originate in himself, or form part of his material nature. We have already discussed this sufficiently. After having laid this foundation, which is the ruin of all good principles, and destroys the majesty of all true knowledge, they sought to remove the opprobrium by declaring that for many reasons it is impossible that God should have a knowledge of earthly things, for the individual members of a species can only be perceived by the senses, and not by reason ; but God does not perceive by means of any of the senses. Again, the individuals are infinite, but knowledge comprehends and circumscribes the object of its action, and the infinite cannot be comprehended or circumscribed ; furthermore, knowledge of individual beings, that are subject to change, necessitates some change in him who possesses it, because this knowledge itself changes constantly. They have also raised the following two objections against those who hold, in accordance with the teaching of Scripture, that God knows things before they come into existence. First, this theory implies that there can be knowledge of a thing that does not exist at all ; secondly, it leads to the conclusion that the knowledge of an object *in potentia* is identical with the knowledge of that same object in reality. They have indeed come to very evil conclusions, and some of them assumed that God only knows the species, not the individual beings, whilst others went as far as to contend that God knows nothing beside Himself, because they believe that God cannot have more than one knowledge.

Some of the great philosophers who lived before Aristotle agree with us, that God knows everything, and that nothing is hidden from Him. Alexander also refers to them in the above-mentioned treatise ; he differs from them, and says that the principal objection against this theory is based on the fact that we clearly see evils befalling good men, and wicked men enjoying happiness.

In short, you see that if these philosophers would find human affairs managed according to rules laid down by the common people, they would not venture or presume to speak on this subject. They are only led to this speculation because they examine the affairs of the good and the wicked, and consider them as being contrary to all rule, and say in the words of the foolish in our nation, " The way of the Lord is not right " (Ezek. xxxiii. 17).

After having shown that knowledge and Providence are connected with each other, I will now proceed to expound the opinions of thinkers on Providence, and then I shall attempt to remove their doubts as to God's knowledge of individual beings.

CHAPTER XVII

THERE are four different theories concerning Divine Providence; they are all ancient, known since the time of the Prophets, when the true Law was revealed to enlighten these dark regions.

First Theory.—There is no Providence at all for anything in the Universe; all parts of the Universe, the heavens and what they contain, owe their origin to accident and chance; there exists no being that rules and governs them or provides for them. This is the theory of Epicurus, who assumes also that the Universe consists of atoms, that these have combined by chance, and have received their various forms by mere accident. There have been atheists among the Israelites who have expressed the same view; it is reported of them : " They have denied the Lord, and said he is not " (Jer. v. 12). Aristotle has proved the absurdity of the theory, that the whole Universe could have originated by chance; he has shown that, on the contrary, there is a being that rules and governs the Universe. We have already touched upon this subject in the present treatise.

Second Theory.—Whilst one part of the Universe owes its existence to Providence, and is under the control of a ruler and governor, another part is abandoned and left to chance. This is the view of Aristotle about Providence, and I will now explain to you his theory. He holds that God controls the spheres and what they contain : therefore the individual beings in the spheres remain permanently in the same form. Alexander has also expressed it in his writings that Divine Providence extends down to, and ends with, the sphere of the moon. This view results from his theory of the Eternity of the Universe; he believes that Providence is in accordance with the nature of the Universe : consequently in the case of the spheres with their contents, where each individual being has a permanent existence, Providence gives permanency and constancy. From the existence of the spheres other beings derive existence, which are constant in their species but not in their individuals : in the same manner it is said that Providence sends forth [from the spheres to the earth] sufficient influence to secure the immortality and constancy of the species, without securing at the same time permanence for the individual beings of the species. But the individual beings in each species have not been entirely abandoned, that portion of the *materia prima* which has been purified and refined, and has received the faculty of growth, is endowed with properties that enable it to exist a certain time, to attract what is useful and to repel what is useless. That portion of the *materia prima* which has been subject to a further development, and has received the faculty of sensation, is endowed with other properties for its protection and preservation; it has a new faculty of moving freely toward that which is conducive to, and away from that which is contrary to its well-being. Each individual being received besides such properties as are required for the preservation of the species to which it belongs. The portion of the *materia prima* which is still more refined, and is endowed with the intellectual faculty, possesses a special property by which each individual, according to the degree of his perfection, is enabled to manage, to calculate, and to discover what is conducive both to the temporary existence of the individual and to the preservation of the species. All other movements, however, which are made by the individual members of each species are due to accident; they are not, according to Aristotle, the result of rule and management; e.g., when a storm or gale blows, it causes undoubtedly some leaves of a tree to drop, breaks off some branches of another tree, tears away a stone from a heap of stones, raises dust over herbs and spoils them, and stirs up the sea so that a ship goes down with the whole or part of her contents. Aristotle sees no difference between the falling of a leaf or a stone and the death of the good and noble people in the ship; nor does he distinguish between the destruction of a multitude of ants caused by an ox depositing on them his excrement and the death of worshippers killed by the fall of the house when its foundations give way; nor does he discriminate between the case of a cat killing a mouse that happens to come in her way, or that of a spider catching a fly, and that of a hungry lion meeting a prophet and tearing him. In short, the opinion of Aristotle is this: Everything is the result of management which is constant, which does not come to an end and does not change any of its properties, as e.g., the heavenly beings, and everything which continues according to a certain rule, and deviates from it only rarely and exceptionally, as is the case in objects of Nature. All these are the result of management, i.e., in a close relation to Divine Providence. But that which is not constant, and does not follow a certain rule, as e.g., incidents in the existence of the individual beings in each species of plants or animals, whether rational or irrational, is due to chance and not to management; it is in no relation to Divine Providence. Aristotle holds that it is even impossible to ascribe to Providence the management of these things. This view is closely connected with his theory of the Eternity of the Universe, and with his opinion that everything different from the existing order of things in Nature is impossible. It is the belief of those who turned away from our Law, and said: "God hath forsaken the earth" (Ezek. ix. 9).

Third Theory.—This theory is the reverse of the second. According to this theory, there is nothing in the whole Universe, neither a class nor an individual being, that is due to chance; everything is the result of will, intention, and rule. It is a matter of course that he who rules must know [that which is under his control]. The Mohammedan Ashariyah adhere to this theory, notwithstanding evident absurdities implied in it; for they admit that Aristotle is correct in assuming one and the same cause [viz., the wind] for the fall of leaves [from the tree] and for the death of a man [drowned in the sea]. But they hold at the same time that the wind did not blow by chance; it is God that caused it to move; it is not therefore the wind that caused the leaves to fall; each leaf falls according to the Divine decree; it is God who caused it to fall at a certain time and in a certain place; it could not have fallen before or after that time or in another place, as this has previously been decreed. The Ashariyah were therefore compelled to assume that motion and rest of living beings are predestined, and that it is not in the power of man to do a certain thing or to leave it undone. The theory further implies a denial of possibility in these things; they can only be either necessary or impossible. The followers of this theory accepted also the last-mentioned proposition, and say, that we call certain things possible, as e.g., the facts that Zeid stands, and that Amr is coming; but they are only possible for us, whilst in their relation to God they cannot be called possible; they are either necessary or impossible. It follows also from this theory, that precepts are perfectly useless, since the people to whom any law is given are unable to do anything: they can neither do what they are commanded nor abstain from what they are forbidden. The supporters of this theory hold that it was the will of God to send prophets, to command, to forbid, to promise, and to threaten, although we have no power [over our actions]. A duty would thus be imposed upon us which is impossible for us to carry out, and it is even possible that we may suffer punishment when obeying the command and receive reward when disobeying it. According to this theory, it must also be assumed that the actions of God have no final cause. All these absurdities are admitted by the Ashariyah for the purpose of saving this theory. When we see a person born blind or leprous, who could not have merited a punishment for previous sins, they say, It is the will of God; when a pious worshipper is tortured and slain, it is likewise the will of God; and no injustice can be asserted to Him for that, for according to their opinion it is proper that God should afflict the innocent and do good to the sinner. Their views on these matters are well known.

Fourth Theory.—Man has free will; it is therefore intelligible that the Law contains commands and prohibitions, with announcements of reward and punishment. All acts of God are due to wisdom; no injustice is found in Him, and He does not afflict the good. The Mu'tazila profess this theory, although they do not believe in man's absolute free will. They hold also that God takes notice of the falling of the leaf and the destruction of the ant, and that His Providence extends over all things. This theory likewise implies contradictions and absurdities. The absurdities are these: The fact that some persons are born with defects, although they have not sinned previously, is ascribed to the wisdom of God, it being better for those persons to be in such a condition than to be in a normal state, though we do not see why it is better; and they do not suffer thereby any punishment at all, but, on the contrary, enjoy God's goodness. In a similar manner the slaughter of the pious is explained as being for them the source of an increase of reward in future life. They go even further in their absurdities. We ask them why is God only just to man and not to other beings, and how has the irrational animal sinned, that it is condemned to be slaughtered? and they reply it is good for the animal, for it will receive reward for it in the world to come; also the flea and the louse will there receive compensation for their untimely death: the same reasoning they apply to the mouse torn by a cat or vulture; the wisdom of God decreed this for the mouse, in order to reward it after death for the mishap. I do not consider it proper to blame the followers of any of the [last named] three theories on Providence, for they have been driven to accept them by weighty considerations. Aristotle was guided by that which appears to be the nature of things. The Ashariyah refused to ascribe to God ignorance about anything, and to say that God whilst knowing one individual being or one portion of the Universe is ignorant of another portion; they preferred to admit the above-mentioned absurdities. The Mu'tazilites refused to assume that God does what is wrong and unjust; on the other hand, they would not contradict common sense and say that it was not wrong to inflict pain on the guiltless, or that the mission of the Prophets and the giving of the Law had no intelligible reason. They likewise preferred to admit the above-named absurdities. But they even contradicted themselves, because they believe on the one hand that God knows everything, and on the other that man has free will. By a little consideration we discover the contradiction.

Fifth Theory.—This is our theory, or that of our Law. I will show you [first] the view expressed on this subject in our prophetical books, and generally accepted by our Sages. I will then give the opinion of some later authors among us, and lastly, I will explain my own belief. The theory of man's perfectly free will is one of the fundamental principles of the Law of our Teacher Moses, and of those who follow the Law. According to this principle man does what is in his power to do, by his nature, his choice, and his will; and his action is not due to any faculty created for the purpose. All species of irrational animals likewise move by their own free will. This is the Will of God; that is to say, it is due to the eternal divine will that all living beings should move freely, and that man should have power to act according to his will or choice within the limits of his capacity. Against this principle we hear, thank God, no opposition on the part of our nation. Another fundamental principle taught by the Law of Moses is this: Wrong cannot be ascribed to God in any way whatever; all evils and afflictions as well as all kinds of happiness of man, whether they concern one individual person or a community, are distributed according to justice; they are the result of strict judgment that admits no wrong whatever. Even when a person suffers pain in consequence of a thorn having entered into his hand, although it is at once drawn out, it is a punishment that has been inflicted on him [for sin], and the least pleasure he enjoys is a reward [for some good action]; all this is meted out by strict justice; as is said in Scripture, " all his ways are judgment " (Deut. xxxii. 4); we are only ignorant of the working of that judgment.

The different theories are now fully explained to you; everything in the varying human affairs is due to chance, according to Aristotle, to the Divine Will alone according to the Ashariyah, to Divine Wisdom according to the Mu'tazilites, to the merits of man according to our opinion. It is therefore possible, according to the Ashariyah, that God inflicts pain on a good and pious man in this world, and keeps him for ever in fire, which is assumed to rage in the world to come; they simply say it is the Will of God. The Mu'tazilites would consider this as injustice, and therefore assume that every being, even an ant, that is stricken with pain [in this world], has compensation for it, as has been mentioned above; and it is due to God's Wisdom that a being is struck and afflicted in order to receive compensation. We, however, believe that all these human affairs are managed with justice; far be it from God to do wrong, to punish any one unless the punishment is necessary and merited. It is distinctly stated in the Law, that all is done in accordance with justice ; and the words of our Sages generally express the same idea. They clearly say : " There is no death without sin, no sufferings without transgression." (B. T. Shabbath, 55a.) Again, " The deserts of man are meted out to him in the same measure which he himself employs." (Mish. Sotah, i. 7.) These are the words of the Mishnah. Our Sages declare it wherever opportunity is given, that the idea of God necessarily implies justice ; that He will reward the most pious for all their pure and upright actions, although no direct commandment was given them through a prophet ; and that He will punish all the evil deeds of men, although they have not been prohibited by a prophet, if common sense warns against them, as e.g., injustice and violence. Thus our Sages say : " God does not deprive any being of the full reward [of its good deed] " (B. T. Pes. 118a) again, " He who says that God remits part of a punishment, will be punished severely ; He is long-suffering, but is sure to exact payment." (B. T. Baba K. 50a.) Another saying is this : " He who has received a command-ment and acts accordingly is not like him who acts in the same manner without being commanded to do so " (B. T. Kidd. 31a) ; and it is distinctly added that he who does a good thing without being commanded, receives neverthe-less his reward. The same principle is expressed in all sayings of our Sages. But they contain an additional doctrine which is not found in the Law ; viz., the doctrine of " afflictions of love," as taught by some of our Sages. According to this doctrine it is possible that a person be afflicted without having previously committed any sin, in order that his future reward may be increased ; a view which is held by the Mu'tazilites, but is not supported by any Scriptural text. Be not misled by the accounts of trials, such as " God tried Abraham " (Gen. xxii. 1) ; " He afflicted thee and made thee hungry," etc. (Deut. viii. 3) ; for you will hear more on this subject later on (chap. xxiv.). Our Law is only concerned with the relations of men ; but the idea that irrational living beings should receive a reward, has never before been heard of in our nation ; the wise men mentioned in the Talmud do not notice it ; only some of the later Geonim were pleased with it when they heard it from the sect of the Mu'tazilites, and accepted it.

My opinion on this principle of Divine Providence I will now explain to you. In the principle which I now proceed to expound I do not rely on demonstrative proof, but on my conception of the spirit of the Divine Law, and the writings of the Prophets. The principle which I accept is far less open to objections, and is more reasonable than the opinions mentioned before. It is this : In the lower or sublunary portion of the Universe Divine Provi-dence does not extend to the individual members of species except in the case of mankind. It is only in this species that the incidents in the existence of the individual beings, their good and evil fortunes, are the result of justice, in accordance with the words, " For all His ways are judgment." But I agree with Aristotle as regards all other living beings, and *à fortiori* as regards plants and all the rest of earthly creatures. For I do not believe that it is through the interference of Divine Providence that a certain leaf drops [from a tree], nor do I hold that when a certain spider catches a certain fly, that this is the direct result of a special decree and will of God in that moment ; it is not by a particular Divine decree that the spittle of a certain person moved, fell on a certain gnat in a certain place, and killed it ; nor is it by the direct will of God that a certain fish catches and swallows a certain worm on the surface of the water. In all these cases the action is, according to my opinion, entirely due to chance, as taught by Aristotle. Divine Providence is connected with Divine intellectual influence, and the same beings which are benefited by the latter so as to become intellectual, and to comprehend things comprehensible to rational beings, are also under the control of Divine Providence, which examines all their deeds in order to reward or punish them. It may be by mere chance that a ship goes down with all her contents, as in the above-mentioned instance, or the roof of a house falls upon those within ; but it is not due to chance, according to our view, that in the one instance the men went into the ship, or remained in the house in the other instance ; it is due to the will of God, and is in accordance with the justice of His judgments, the method of which our mind is incapable of understanding. I have been induced to accept this theory by the circumstance that I have not met in any of the prophetical books with a description of God's Providence otherwise than in relation to human beings. The prophets even express their surprise that God should take notice of man, who is too little and too unimportant to be worthy of the attention of the Creator ; how, then, should other living creatures be considered as proper objects for Divine Providence ! Comp. " What is man, that thou takest knowledge of him ? " (Ps. cxliv. 3) ; " What is man, that thou art mindful of him ? " (*ibid.* viii. 8). It is clearly expressed in many Scriptural passages that God provides for all men, and controls all their deeds—e.g., " He fashioneth their hearts alike, he considereth all their works " (*ibid.* xxxiii. 15) ; " For thine eyes are open upon all the ways of the sons of men, to give every one according to his ways " (Jer. xxxii. 19). Again : " For his eyes are upon the ways of man, and he seeth all his goings " (Job xxxii. 21). In the Law there occur instances of the fact that men are governed by God, and that their actions are examined by him. Comp. " In the day when I visit I will visit their sin upon them " (Exod. xxxii. 34) ; " I will even appoint over you terror " (Lev. xxvi. 16) ; " Whosoever hath sinned against me, him will I blot out of my book " (Exod. xxxii. 33) ; " The same soul will I destroy " (Lev. xxiii. 30) ; " I will even set my face against that soul " (*ibid.* xx. 6). There are many instances of this kind. All that is mentioned of the history of Abraham, Isaac, and Jacob is a perfect proof that Divine Providence extends to every man individually. But the condition of the individual beings of other living creatures is undoubtedly the same as has been stated by Aristotle. On that account it is allowed, even commanded, to kill animals ; we are permitted to use them according to our pleasure. The view that other living beings are only governed by Divine Providence in the way described by Aristotle, is supported by the words of the Prophet Habakkuk. When he perceived the victories of Nebuchadnezzar, and saw the multitude of those slain by him, he said, " O God, it is as if men were abandoned, neglected, and unprotected like fish and like worms of the earth." He thus shows that these classes are abandoned. This is expressed in the following passage : " And makest men as the fishes of the sea, as the creeping things, that have no ruler over them. They take up all of them with the angle," etc. (Hab. i. 14, 15). The prophet then declares that such is not the case ; for the events referred to are not the result of abandonment, forsaking, and absence of Providence, but are intended as a punishment for the people, who well deserved all that befell them. He therefore says : " O Lord, Thou hast ordained them for judgment, and O mighty God, Thou hast established them for correction " (*ibid.* ver. 12). Our opinion is not contradicted by Scriptural passages like the following : " He giveth to the beast his food " (Ps. cxlvii. 9) ; " The young lions roar after their prey, and seek their meat from God " (*ibid.* civ. 21) ; " Thou openest thine hand, and satisfiest the desire of every living thing " (*ibid.* cxlv. 16) ; or by the saying of our Sages : " He sitteth and feedeth all, from the horns of the unicorns even unto the eggs of insects." There are many similar sayings extant in the writings of our Sages, but they imply nothing that is contrary to my view. All these passages refer to Providence in relation to species, and not to Providence in relation to individual animals. The acts of God are as it were enumerated ; how He provides for every species the necessary food and the means of subsistence. This is clear and plain. Aristotle likewise holds that this kind of Providence is necessary, and is in actual existence. Alexander also notices this fact in the name of Aristotle, viz., that every species has its nourishment prepared for its individual members ; otherwise the species would undoubtedly have perished. It does not require much consideration to understand this. There is a rule laid down by our Sages that it is directly prohibited in the Law to cause pain to an animal, and is based on the words : " Wherefore hast thou smitten thine ass ? " etc. (Num. xxii. 32). But the object of this rule is to make us perfect ; that we should not assume cruel habits ; and that we should not uselessly cause pain to others ; that, on the contrary, we should be prepared to show pity and mercy to all living creatures, except when necessity demands the contrary : " When thy soul longeth to eat flesh," etc. (Deut. xii. 20). We should not kill animals for the purpose of practising cruelty, or for the purpose of play. It cannot be objected to this theory, Why should God select mankind as the object of His special Providence, and not other living beings ? For he who asks this question must also inquire, Why has man alone, of all species of animals, been endowed with intellect ? The answer to this second question must be, according to the three afore-mentioned theories : It was the Will of God, it is the decree of His Wisdom, or it is in accordance with the laws of Nature. The same answers apply to the first question. Understand thoroughly my theory, that I do not ascribe to God ignorance of anything or any kind of weakness ; I hold that Divine Providence is related and closely connected with the intellect, because Providence can only proceed from an intelligent being, from a being that is itself the most perfect Intellect. Those creatures, therefore, which receive part of that intellectual influence, will become subject to the action of Providence in the same proportion as they are acted upon by the Intellect. This theory is in accordance with reason and with the teaching of Scripture, whilst the other theories previously mentioned either exaggerate Divine Providence or detract from it. In the former case they lead to confusion and entire nonsense, and cause us to deny reason and to contradict that which is perceived with the senses. The latter case, viz., the theory that Divine Providence does not extend to man, and that there is no difference between man and other animals, implies very bad notions about God ; it disturbs all social order, removes and destroys all the moral and intellectual virtues of man.

CHAPTER XVIII

HAVING shown in the preceding chapter that of all living beings mankind alone is directly under the control of Divine Providence, I will now add the following remarks : It is an established fact that species have no existence except in our own minds. Species and other classes are merely ideas formed in our minds, whilst everything in real existence is an individual object, or an aggregate of individual objects. This being granted, it must further be admitted that the result of the existing Divine influence, that reaches mankind through the human intellect, is identical with individual intellects really in existence, with which, e.g., Zeid, Amr, Kaled and Bekr, are endowed. Hence it follows, in accordance with what I have mentioned in the preceding chapter, that the greater the share is which a person has obtained of this Divine influence, on account of both his physical predisposition and his training, the greater must also be the effect of Divine Providence upon him, for the action of Divine Providence is proportional to the endowment of intellect, as has been mentioned above. The relation of Divine Providence is therefore not the same to all men ; the greater the human perfection a person has attained, the greater the benefit he derives from Divine Providence. This benefit is very great in the case of prophets, and varies according to the degree of their prophetic faculty ; as it varies in the case of pious and good men according to their piety and uprightness. For it is the intensity of the Divine intellectual influence that has inspired the prophets, guided the good in their actions, and perfected the wisdom of the pious. In the same proportion as ignorant and disobedient persons are deficient in that Divine influence, their condition is inferior, and their rank equal to that of irrational beings ; and they are " like unto the beasts " (Ps. xlix. 21). For this reason it was not only considered a light thing to slay them, but it was even directly commanded for the benefit of mankind. This belief that God provides for every individual human being in accordance with his merits is one of the fundamental principles on which the Law is founded.

Consider how the action of Divine Providence is described in reference to every incident in the lives of the patriarchs, to their occupations, and even to their passions, and how God promised to direct His attention to them. Thus God said to Abraham, " I am thy shield " (Gen. xv. 1) ; to Isaac, " I will be with thee, and I will bless thee " (*ibid.* xxvi. 3) ; to Jacob, " I am with thee, and will keep thee " (*ibid.* xxviii. 15) ; to [Moses] the chief of the Prophets, " Certainly I will be with thee, and this shall be a token unto thee " (Exod. iii. 12) ; to Joshua, " As I was with Moses, so I shall be with thee " (Josh. i. 5). It is clear that in all these cases the action of Providence has been proportional to man's perfection. The following verse describes how Providence protects good and pious men, and abandons fools ; " He will keep the feet of his saints, and the wicked shall be silent in darkness ; for by strength shall no man prevail " (1 Sam. ii. 9). When we see that some men escape plagues and mishaps, whilst others perish by them, we must not attribute this to a difference in the properties of their bodies, or in their physical constitution, " for by strength shall no man prevail " ; but it must be attributed to their different degrees of perfection, some approaching God, whilst others moving away from Him. Those who approach Him are best protected, and " He will keep the feet of his saints " ; but those who keep far away from Him are left exposed to what may befall them ; there is nothing that could protect them from what might happen ; they are like those who walk in darkness, and are certain to stumble.   The protection of the pious by Providence is also expressed in the following passages :—" He keepeth all his bones," etc. (Ps. xxxiv. 21) ; " The eyes of the Lord are upon the right-eous " (ibid. ver. 16) ; " He shall call upon me and I shall answer him " (ibid. xci. 15).   There are in Scripture many more passages expressing the prin-ciple that men enjoy Divine protection in proportion to their perfection and piety.   The philosophers have likewise discussed this subject.   Abu-nasr, in the Introduction to his Commentary on Aristotle's Nikomachean Ethics, says as follows :—Those who possess the faculty of raising their souls from virtue to virtue obtain, according to Plato, Divine protection to a higher degree.

Now consider how by this method of reasoning we have arrived at the truth taught by the Prophets, that every person has his individual share of Divine Providence in proportion to his perfection.   For philosophical re-search leads to this conclusion, if we assume, as has been mentioned above, that Divine Providence is in each case proportional to the person's intellectual development.   It is wrong to say that Divine Providence extends only to the species, and not to individual beings, as some of the philosophers teach. For only individual beings have real existence, and individual beings are endowed with Divine Intellect ; Divine Providence acts, therefore, upon these individual beings.

Study this chapter as it ought to be studied ; you will find in it all the fundamental principles of the Law ; you will see that these are in conformity with philosophical speculation, and all difficulties will be removed ; you will have a clear idea of Divine Providence.

After having described the various philosophical opinions on Providence, and on the manner how God governs the Universe, I will briefly state the opinion of our co-religionists on the Omniscience of God, and what I have to remark on this subject.

CHAPTER XIX

IT is undoubtedly an innate idea that God must be perfect in every respect and cannot be deficient in anything.   It is almost an innate idea that ignor-ance in anything is a deficiency, and that God can therefore not be ignorant of anything.   But some thinkers assume, as I said before, haughtily and ex-ultingly, that God knows certain things and is ignorant of certain other things.   They did so because they imagined that they discovered a certain absence of order in man's affairs, most of which are not only the result of physical properties, but also of those faculties which he possesses as a being endowed with free will and reason.   The Prophets have already stated the proof which ignorant persons offer for their belief that God does not know our actions ; viz., the fact that wicked people are seen in happiness, ease, and peace.   This fact leads also righteous and pious persons to think that it is of no use for them to aim at that which is good and to suffer for it through the opposition of other people.   But the Prophets at the same time relate how their own thoughts were engaged on this question, and how they were at last

convinced that in the instances to which these arguments refer, only the end
and not the beginning ought to be taken into account. The following is a
description of these reflections (Ps. lxxiii. 11, *seq.*) : " And they say, How
does God know ? and is there knowledge in the Most High ? Behold, these
are the ungodly who prosper in the world ; they increase in riches. Verily
I have cleansed my heart in vain, and washed my hands in innocency." He
then continues, " When I thought to know this, it was too painful for me,
until I went into the sanctuary of God ; then understood I their end. Surely
thou didst set them in slippery places ; thou castedst them down into destruction. How are they brought into desolation, as in a moment ! They
are utterly consumed with terrors." The very same ideas have also been
expressed by the prophet Malachi, for he says thus (Mal. iii. 13–18) : " Your
words have been stout against me, saith the Lord. As you have said, It is vain
to serve God ; and what profit is it that we have kept his ordinance, and that
we have walked mournfully before the Lord of hosts ? And now we call the
proud happy ; yea, they that work wickedness are set up ; yea, they that
tempt God are even delivered. Then they that feared the Lord spake often
one to another, etc. Then shall ye return and discern between the righteous
and the wicked, between him that serveth God and him that serveth him
not." David likewise shows how general this view was in his time, and how
it led and caused people to sin and to oppress one another. At first he
argues against this theory, and then he declares that God is omniscient. He
says as follows :—" They slay the widow and the stranger, and murder the
fatherless. Yet they say, The Lord shall not see, neither shall the God of
Jacob regard it. Understand, ye brutish among the people, and ye fools,
when will you be wise ? He that planted the ear, shall he not hear ? He
that formed the eye, shall he not see ? He that chastiseth nations, shall
not he correct ? or he that teacheth man knowledge ? " I will now show
you the meaning of these arguments, but first I will point out how the
opponents to the words of the Prophets misunderstood this passage. Many
years ago some intelligent co-religionists—they were physicians—told me
that they were surprised at the words of David ; for it would follow from
his arguments that the Creator of the mouth must eat and the Creator of the
lungs must cry ; the same applies to all other organs of our body. You who
study this treatise of mine, consider how grossly they misunderstood David's
arguments. Hear now what its true meaning is : He who produces a vessel
must have had in his mind an idea of the use of that instrument, otherwise
he could not have produced it. If, e.g., the smith had not formed an idea
of sewing and possessed a knowledge of it, the needle would not have had the
form so indispensable for sewing. The same is the case with all instruments.
When some philosopher thought that God, whose perception is purely intellectual, has no knowledge of individual things, which are perceivable only
by the senses, David takes his argument from the existence of the senses, and
argues thus :—If the sense of sight had been utterly unknown to God, how
could He have produced that organ of the sense of sight ? Do you think
that it was by chance that a transparent humour was formed, and then
another humour with certain similar properties, and besides a membrane
which by accident had a hole covered with a hardened transparent substance ? in short, considering the humour of the eye, its membranes and

nerves, with their well-known functions, and their adaptation to the purpose of sight, can any intelligent person imagine that all this is due to chance ? Certainly not ; we see here necessarily design in nature, as has been shown by all physicians and philosophers ; but as nature is not an intellectual being, and is not capable of governing [the universe], as has been accepted by all philosophers, the government [of the universe], which shows signs of design, originates, according to the philosophers, in an intellectual cause, but is according to our view the result of the action of an intellectual being, that endows everything with its natural properties. If this intellect were in-capable of perceiving or knowing any of the actions of earthly beings, how could He have created, or, according to the other theory, caused to emanate from Himself, properties that bring about those actions of which He is sup-posed to have no knowledge ? David correctly calls those who believe in this theory brutes and fools. He then proceeds to explain that the error is due to our defective understanding ; that God endowed us with the intellect which is the means of our comprehension, and which on account of its in-sufficiency to form a true idea of God has become the source of great doubts ; that He therefore knows what our defects are, and how worthless the doubts are which originate in our faulty reasoning. The Psalmist therefore says : " He who teaches man knowledge, the Lord, knoweth the thoughts of man that they are vanity " (*ibid.* xciv. 10–11).

My object in this chapter was to show how the belief of the ignorant, that God does not notice the affairs of man because they are uncertain and un-systematic, is very ancient. Comp. " And the Israelites uttered things that were not right against the Lord " (2 Kings xvii. 9). In reference to this passage the Midrash says : " What have they uttered ? This Pillar [i.e., God] does not see, nor hear, nor speak " ; i.e., they imagine that God takes no notice of earthly affairs, that the Prophets received of God neither affirma-tive nor negative precepts ; they imagine so, simply because human affairs are not arranged as every person would think it desirable. Seeing that these are not in accordance with their wish, they say, " The Lord does not see us " (Ezek. viii. 12). Zephaniah (i. 12) also describes those ignorant persons " who say in their heart the Lord will not do good, neither will he do evil." I will tell you my own opinion as regards the theory that God knows all things on earth, but I will before state some propositions which are generally adopted, and the correctness of which no intelligent person can dispute.

CHAPTER XX

It is generally agreed upon that God cannot at a certain time acquire know-ledge which He did not possess previously ; it is further impossible that His knowledge should include any plurality, even according to those who admit the Divine attributes. As these things have been fully proved, we, who assert the teaching of the Law, believe that God's knowledge of many things does not imply any plurality ; His knowledge does not change like ours when the objects of His knowledge change. Similarly we say that the various events are known to Him before they take place ; He constantly knows them, and therefore no fresh knowledge is acquired by Him. E.g., He knows that a certain person is non-existent at present, will come to existence at a certain time, will continue to exist for some time, and will then cease to exist. When this person, in accordance with God's foreknowledge concerning him, comes into existence, God's knowledge is not increased ; it contains nothing that it did not contain before, but something has taken place that was known previously exactly as it has taken place. This theory implies that God's knowledge extends to things not in existence, and includes also the infinite. We nevertheless accept it, and contend that we may attribute to God the knowledge of a thing which does not yet exist, but the existence of which God foresees and is able to effect. But that which never exists cannot be an object of His knowledge ; just as our knowledge does not comprise things which we consider as non-existing. A doubt has been raised, however, whether His knowledge includes the infinite. Some thinkers assume that knowledge has the species for its object, and therefore extends at the same time to all individual members of the species. This view is taken by every man who adheres to a revealed religion and follows the dictates of reason. Philosophers, however, have decided that the object of knowledge cannot be a non-existing thing, and that it cannot comprise that which is infinite. Since, therefore, God's knowledge does not admit of any increase, it is impossible that He should know any transient thing. He only knows that which is constant and unchangeable. Other philosophers raised the following objection : God does not know even things that remain constant ; for His knowledge would then include a plurality according to the number of objects known ; the knowledge of every thing being distinguished by a certain peculiarity of the thing. God therefore only knows His own essence.

My opinion is this : the cause of the error of all these schools is their belief that God's knowledge is like ours ; each school points to something withheld from our knowledge, and either assumes that the same must be the case in God's knowledge, or at least finds some difficulty how to explain it. We must blame the philosophers in this respect more than any other persons, because they demonstrated that there is no plurality in God, and that He has no attribute that is not identical with His essence ; His knowledge and His essence are one and the same thing ; they likewise demonstrated, as we have shown, that our intellect and our knowledge are insufficient to comprehend the true idea of His essence. How then can they imagine that they comprehend His knowledge, which is identical with His essence ; seeing that our incapacity to comprehend His essence prevents us from understanding the way how He knows objects ? for His knowledge is not of the same kind as ours, but totally different from it and admitting of no analogy. And as there is an Essence of independent existence, which is, as the philosophers' call it, the Cause of the existence of all things, or, as we say, the Creator of everything that exists beside Him, so we also assume that this Essence knows everything, that nothing whatever of all that exists is hidden from it, and that the knowledge attributed to this essence has nothing in common with our knowledge, just as that essence is in no way like our essence. The homonymity of the term " knowledge " misled people ; [they forgot that] only the words are the same, but the things designated by them are different ; and therefore they came to the absurd conclusion that that which is required for our knowledge is also required for God's knowledge.

Besides, I find it expressed in various passages of Scripture that the fact that God knows things while in a state of possibility, when their existence belongs to the future, does not change the nature of the possible in any way ; that nature remains unchanged ; and the knowledge of the realization of one of several possibilities does not yet effect that realization.   This is likewise one of the fundamental principles of the Law of Moses, concerning which there is no doubt nor any dispute.   Otherwise it would not have been said, " And thou shalt make a battlement for thy roof," etc. (Deut. xxii. 8), or " Lest he die in the battle, and another man take her " (*ibid.* xx. 7).   The fact that laws were given to man, both affirmative and negative, supports the principle, that God's knowledge of future [and possible] events does not change their character.   The great doubt that presents itself to our mind is the result of the insufficiency of our intellect.   Consider in how many ways His knowledge is distinguished from ours according to all the teaching of every revealed religion.   First, His knowledge is one, and yet embraces many different kinds of objects.   Secondly, it is applied to things not in existence. Thirdly, it comprehends the infinite.   Fourthly, it remains unchanged, though it comprises the knowledge of changeable things ; whilst it seems [in reference to ourselves] that the knowledge of a thing that is to come into existence is different from the knowledge of the thing when it has come into existence ;   because there is the additional knowledge of its transition from a state of potentiality into that of reality.   Fifthly, according to the teaching of our Law, God's knowledge of one of two eventualities does not determine it, however certain that knowledge may be concerning the future occurrence of the one eventuality.—Now I wonder what our knowledge has in common with God's knowledge, according to those who treat God's knowledge as an attribute.   Is there anything else common to both besides the mere name ? According to our theory that God's knowledge is not different from His essence, there is an essential distinction between His knowledge and ours, like the distinction between the substance of the heavens and that of the earth.   The Prophets have clearly expressed this.   Comp. " For my thoughts are not your thoughts, neither are your ways my ways, saith the Lord.   For as the heavens are higher than the earth, so are my ways higher than your ways " (Isa. lv. 8–9).   In short, as we cannot accurately comprehend His essence, and yet we know that His existence is most perfect, free from all admixture of deficiency, change, or passiveness, so we have no correct notion of His knowledge, because it is nothing but His essence, and yet we are convinced that He does not at one time obtain knowledge which He had not before ;   i.e., He obtains no new knowledge, He does not increase it, and it is not finite ;   nothing of all existing things escapes His knowledge, but their nature is not changed thereby ;   that which is possible remains possible. Every argument that seems to contradict any of these statements is founded on the nature of our knowledge, that has only the name in common with God's knowledge.   The same applies to the term intention ;   it is homonymously employed to designate our intention towards a certain thing, and the intention of God.   The term " management " (Providence) is likewise homonymously used of our management of a certain thing, and of God's management.   In fact management, knowledge, and intention are not the same when ascribed to us and when ascribed to God.   When these three terms are taken in both cases in the same sense, great difficulties must arise ;   but when it is noticed that there is a great difference whether a thing is predicated of God or of us, the truth will become clear. The difference between that which is ascribed to God and that which is ascribed to man is expressed in the words above mentioned, " And your ways are not my ways."

CHAPTER XXI

THERE is a great difference between the knowledge which the producer of a thing possesses concerning it, and the knowledge which other persons possess concerning the same thing. Suppose a thing is produced in accordance with the knowledge of the producer, the producer was then guided by his knowledge in the act of producing the thing. Other people, however, who examine this work and acquire a knowledge of the whole of it, depend for that knowledge on the work itself. E.g., An artisan makes a box in which weights move with the running of the water, and thus indicate how many hours have passed of the day and of the night. The whole quantity of the water that is to run out, the different ways in which it runs, every thread that is drawn, and every little ball that descends—all this is fully perceived by him who makes the clock ; and his knowledge is not the result of observing the movements as they are actually going on ; but, on the contrary, the movements are produced in accordance with his knowledge. But another person who looks at that instrument will receive fresh knowledge at every movement he perceives ; the longer he looks on, the more knowledge does he acquire ; he will gradually increase his knowledge till he fully understands the machinery. If an infinite number of movements were assumed for this instrument, he would never be able to complete his knowledge. Besides, he cannot know any of the movements before they take place, since he only knows them from their actual occurrence. The same is the case with every object, and its relation to our knowledge and God's knowledge of it. Whatever we know of the things is derived from observation ; on that account it is impossible for us to know that which will take place in future, or that which is infinite.

Our knowledge is acquired and increased in proportion to the things known by us. This is not the case with God. His knowledge of things is not derived from the things themselves ; if this were the case, there would be change and plurality in His knowledge ; on the contrary, the things are in accordance with His eternal knowledge, which has established their actual properties, and made part of them purely spiritual, another part material and constant as regards its individual members, a third part material and changeable as regards the individual beings according to eternal and constant laws. Plurality, acquisition, and change in His knowledge is therefore impossible. He fully knows His unchangeable essence, and has thus a knowledge of all that results from any of His acts. If we were to try to understand in what manner this is done, it would be the same as if we tried to be the same as God, and to make our knowledge identical with His knowledge. Those who seek the truth, and admit what is true, must believe that nothing is hidden from God ; that everything is revealed to His knowledge, which is identical with His essence ; that this kind of knowledge cannot be comprehended by us ; for if we knew its method, we would possess that intellect by which such knowledge could be acquired. Such intellect does not exist except in God, and is at the same time His essence. Note this well, for I think that this is an excellent idea, and leads to correct views; no error will be found in it; no dialectical argument; it does not lead to any absurd conclusion, nor to ascribing any defect to God. These sublime and profound themes admit of no proof whatever, neither according to our opinion who believe in the teaching of Scripture, nor according to the philosophers who disagree and are much divided on this question. In all questions that cannot be demonstrated, we must adopt the method which we have adopted in this question about God's Omniscience. Note it.

CHAPTER XXII

THE strange and wonderful Book of Job treats of the same subject as we are discussing; its basis is a fiction, conceived for the purpose of explaining the different opinions which people hold on Divine Providence. You know that some of our Sages clearly stated Job has never existed, and has never been created, and that he is a poetic fiction. Those who assume that he has existed, and that the book is historical, are unable to determine when and where Job lived. Some of our Sages say that he lived in the days of the Patriarchs; others hold that he was a contemporary of Moses; others place him in the days of David, and again others believe that he was one of those who returned from the Babylonian exile. This difference of opinion supports the assumption that he has never existed in reality. But whether he has existed or not, that which is related of him is an experience of frequent occurrence, is a source of perplexity to all thinkers, and has suggested the above-mentioned opinions on God's Omniscience and Providence. This perplexity is caused by the account that a simple and perfect person, who is upright in his actions, and very anxious to abstain from sin, is afflicted by successive misfortunes, namely, by loss of property, by the death of his children, and by bodily disease, though he has not committed any sin. According to both theories, viz., the theory that Job did exist, and the theory that he did not exist, the introduction to the book is certainly a fiction; I mean the portion which relates to the words of the adversary, the words of God to the former, and the handing over of Job to him. This fiction, however, is in so far different from other fictions that it includes profound ideas and great mysteries, removes great doubts, and reveals the most important truths. I will discuss it as fully as possible; and I will also tell you the words of our Sages that suggested to me the explanation of this great poem.

First, consider the words: "There was a man in the land Uz." The term Uz has different meanings; it is used as a proper noun. Comp. "Uz, his first-born" (Gen. xxii. 21); it is also imperative of the verb *Uz*, "to take advice." Comp. *uzu*, "take counsel" (Isa. viii. 10). The name *Uz* therefore expresses the exhortation to consider well this lesson, study it, grasp its ideas, and comprehend them, in order to see which is the right view. "The sons of God then came to present themselves before the Lord, and the adversary came also among them and in their number" (chap. i. 6, ii. 1). It is not said: "And the sons of God and the adversary came to present themselves before the Lord"; this sentence would have implied that the existence of all that came was of the same kind and rank. The words used are these : " And the sons of God came to present themselves before the Lord, and the adversary came also among them." Such a phrase is only used in reference to one that comes without being expected or invited ; he only comes among others whose coming has been sought. The adversary is then described as going to and fro on the earth, and walking up and down thereon. He is in no relation to the beings above, and has no place among them. For this reason it is said, " from going to and fro on the earth, and walking up and down on it," for his " going " and " walking " can only take place on the earth. [Job], the simple and righteous man, is given and handed over to the adversary ; whatever evils and misfortunes befell Job as regards his property, children, and health, were all caused by this adversary. When this idea is sufficiently indicated, the author begins to reflect on it ; one opinion Job is represented to hold, whilst other opinions are defended by his friends. I will further on expound these opinions which formed the substance of the discussion on the misfortunes of Job, caused by the adversary alone. Job, as well as his friends, were of opinion that God Himself was the direct agent of what happened, and that the adversary was not the intermediate cause. It is remarkable in this account that wisdom is not ascribed to Job. The text does not say he was an intelligent, wise, or clever man ; but virtues and uprightness, especially in actions, are ascribed to him. If he were wise he would not have any doubt about the cause of his suffering, as will be shown later on. Besides, his misfortunes are enumerated in the same order as they rank in man's estimation. There are some who are not perplexed or discouraged by loss of property, thinking little of it ; but are terrified when they are threatened with the death of their children and are killed by their anxiety. There are others who bear without shock or fainting even the loss of their children, but no one endowed with sensation is able to bear bodily pain. We generally extol God in words, and praise Him as righteous and benevolent, when we prosper and are happy, or when the grief we have to bear is moderate. But [it is otherwise] when such troubles as are described in Job come over us. Some of us deny God, and believe that there is no rule in the Universe, even if only their property is lost. Others retain their faith in the existence of justice and order, even when suffering from loss of property, whereas loss of children is too much affliction for them. Others remain firm in their faith, even with the loss of their children ; but there is no one who can patiently bear the pain that reaches his own person ; he then murmurs and complains of injustice either in his heart or with his tongue.

Now consider that the phrase, " to present themselves before the Lord," is used in reference to the sons of God, both the first and the second times, but in reference to the adversary, who appeared on either occasion among them and in their number, this phrase is not used the first time, whilst in his second appearance " the adversary also came among them to present himself before the Lord." Consider this, and see how very extraordinary it is !—These ideas presented themselves like an inspiration to me.—The phrase, " to present themselves before the Lord," implies that they are beings who are forced by God's command to do what He desires. This may be inferred from the words of the prophet Zechariah concerning the four chariots that came forth. He says : " And the angel answered and said to me, These four winds of the heavens come forth from presenting themselves before the Lord of the whole earth " (Zech. vi. 5). It is clear that the relation of the sons of God to the Universe is not the same as that of the adversary. The relation of the sons of God is more constant and more permanent. The adversary has also some relation to the Universe, but it is inferior to that of the sons of God. It is also remarkable in this account that in the description of the adversary's wandering about on the earth, and his performing certain actions, it is distinctly stated that he has no power over the soul; whilst power has been given to him over all earthly affairs, there is a partition between him and the soul; he has not received power over the soul. This is expressed in the words, "But keep away from his soul" (Job. ii. 6). I have already shown you the homonymous use of the term "soul" (*nefesh*) in Hebrew (Part I., chap. xli.). It designates that element in man that survives him; it is this portion over which the adversary has no power.—After these remarks of mine listen to the following useful instruction given by our Sages, who in truth deserve the title of " wise men "; it makes clear that which appears doubtful, and reveals that which has been hidden, and discloses most of the mysteries of the Law. They said in the Talmud as follows : R. Simeon, son of Lakish, says: " The adversary (*satan*), evil inclination (*yezer ha-ra*'), and the angel of death, are one and the same being." Here we find all that has been mentioned by us in such a clear manner that no intelligent person will be in doubt about it. It has thus been shown to you that one and the same thing is designated by these three different terms, and that actions ascribed to these three are in reality the actions of one and the same agent. Again, the ancient doctors of the Talmud said : " The adversary goes about and misleads, then he goes up and accuses, obtains permission, and takes the soul." You have already been told that when David at the time of the plague was shown the angel " with the sword drawn in his hand stretched out over Jerusalem " (2 Sam. xxiv. 17), it was done for the purpose of conveying a certain idea to him. The same idea was also expressed in the vision concerning the sins of the sons of Joshua, the high priest, by the words, " And the adversary stood on his right hand to accuse him " (Zech. iii. 1). The vision then reveals that [the adversary] is far from God, and continues thus : " The Lord will rebuke thee, O adversary, the Lord who hath chosen Jerusalem will rebuke thee " (*ibid.* ver. 2). Balaam saw prophetically the same vision in his journey, addressing him with the words, " Behold I have come forth to be a hindrance to thee " (Num. xxii. 32). The Hebrew, *satan*, is derived from the same root as *séteh*, " turn away " (Prov. iv. 15); it implies the notion of turning and moving away from a thing; he undoubtedly turns us away from the way of truth, and leads us astray in the way of error. The same idea is contained in the passage, " And the imagination of the heart of man is evil from his youth " (Gen. viii. 21). The theory of the good and the evil inclinations (*yezer ha-tob, ve-yezer ha-ra*') is frequently referred to in our religion. Our Sages also say, " Serve God with your good and your evil inclinations." (B. T. Ber. 57*a*.) They also say that the evil inclination we receive at our birth; for " at the door sin croucheth " (Gen. iv. 7), as is distinctly said in the Law, " And the imagination of the heart of man is evil from his youth " (*ibid.* viii. 21). The good inclination, however, comes when the mind is developed. In explaining the allegory representing the body of man and his different faculties, our Sages (B. T. Ned. 32*b*) said : " The evil inclination is called a great king, whilst the good inclination is a child, poor, though wise " (Eccles. ix. 14). All these sayings of our Sages are contained in their writings, and are well known. According to our Sages the evil inclination, the adversary (*satan*), and the angel [of death], are undoubtedly identical ; and the adversary being called " angel," because he is among the sons of God, and the good inclination being in reality an angel, it is to the good and the evil inclinations that they refer in their well-known words, " Every person is accompanied by two angels, one being on his right side, one on his left." In the Babylonian Gemara (Shabbath 119*b*), they say distinctly of the two angels that one is good and one bad. See what extraordinary ideas this passage discloses, and how many false ideas it removes.

I believe that I have fully explained the idea contained in the account of Job ; but I will now show the character of the opinion attributed to Job, and of the opinions attributed to his friends, and support my statement by proofs gathered from the words of each of them. We need not take notice of the remaining passages which are only required for the context, as has been explained to you in the beginning of this treatise.

CHAPTER XXIII

ASSUMING the first part of the history of Job as having actually taken place, the five, viz., Job and his friends, agreed that the misfortune of Job was known to God, and that it was God that caused Job's suffering. They further agree that God does no wrong, and that no injustice can be ascribed to Him. You will find these ideas frequently repeated in the words of Job. When you consider the words of the five who take part in the discussion, you will easily notice that things said by one of them are also uttered by the rest. The arguments are repeated, mixed up, and interrupted by Job's description of his acute pain and troubles, which had come upon him in spite of his strict righteousness, and by an account of his charity, humane disposition, and good acts. The replies of the friends to Job are likewise interrupted by exhortations to patience, by words of comfort, and other speeches tending to make him forget his grief. He is told by them to be silent ; that he ought not to let loose the bridle of his tongue, as if he were in dispute with another man ; that he ought silently to submit to the judgments of God. Job replies that the intensity of his pains did not permit him to bear patiently, to collect his thoughts and to say what he ought to say. The friends, on the other hand, contend that those who act well receive reward, and those who act wickedly are punished. When a wicked and rebellious person is seen in prosperity, it may be assumed for certain that a change will take place ; he will die, or troubles will afflict him and his house. When we find a worshipper of God in misfortune, we may be certain that God will heal the stroke of his wound. This idea is frequently repeated in the words of the three friends, Eliphaz, Bildad, and Zofar, who agree in this opinion. It is, however, not the object of this chapter to describe in what they agree, but to define the distinguishing characteristic of each of them, and to elucidate the opinion of each as regards the question why the most simple and upright man is afflicted with the greatest and acutest pain. Job found in this fact a proof that the righteous and the wicked are equal before God, who holds all mankind in contempt. Job therefore says (ix. 22, 23) : " This is one thing, therefore I said it, He destroyeth the perfect and the wicked. If the scourge slay suddenly, he will laugh at the trial of the innocent." He thus declares that when a scourge comes suddenly, killing and destroying all it meets, God laughs at the trial of the innocent. He further confirms this view in the following passage : " One dieth in his full strength, being wholly at ease and quiet. His vessels are full of milk, etc. And another dieth in the bitterness of his soul, and never eateth with pleasure. They shall lie down alike in the dust, and the worms shall cover them " (*ibid.* xxi. 23–26). In a similar manner he shows the good condition and prosperity of wicked people ; and is even very explicit on this point. He speaks thus : " Even when I remember I am afraid, and trembling taketh hold on my flesh. Wherefore do the wicked live, become old, yea, are mighty in power ? Their seed is established in their sight with them," etc. (*ibid.* 6–8). Having thus described their prosperity, he addresses his opponents, and says to them : " Granted that as you think, the children of this prosperous atheist will perish after his death, and their memory will be blotted out, what harm will the fate of his family cause him after his death ? For what pleasure hath he in his house after him, when the number of his months is cut off in the midst ? " (*ibid.* 21). Job then explains that there is no hope after death, so that the cause [of the misfortune of the righteous man] is nothing else but entire neglect on the part of God. He is therefore surprised that God has not abandoned the creation of man altogether ; and that after having created him, He does not take any notice of him. He says in his surprise : " Hast thou not poured me out as milk, and curdled me like cheese ? " etc. (*ibid.* x. 10, *seq.*). This is one of the different views held by some thinkers on Providence. Our Sages (B. T. Baba B. 16*a*) condemned this view of Job as mischievous, and expressed their feeling in words like the following : " dust should have filled the mouth of Job " ; " Job wished to upset the dish " ; " Job denied the resurrection of the dead " ; " He commenced to blaspheme." When, however, God said to Eliphaz and his colleagues, " You have not spoken of me the thing that is right, as my servant Job hath " (xlii. 7), our Sages assume as the cause of this rebuke, the maxim " Man is not punished for that which he utters in his pain " ; and that God ignored the sin of Job [in his utterances], because of the acuteness of his suffering. But this explanation does not agree with the object of the whole allegory. The words of God are justified, as I will show, by the fact that Job abandoned his first very erroneous opinion, and himself proved that it was an error. It is the opinion which suggests itself as plausible at first thought, especially in the minds of those who meet with mishaps, well knowing that they have not merited them through sins. This is admitted by all, and therefore this opinion was assigned to Job. But he is represented to hold this view only so long as he was without wisdom, and knew God only by tradition, in the same manner as religious people generally know Him. As soon as he had acquired a true knowledge of God, he confessed that there is undoubtedly true felicity in the knowledge of God ; it is attained by all who acquire that knowledge, and no earthly trouble can disturb it. So long as Job's knowledge of God was based on tradition and communication, and not on research, he believed that such imaginary good as is possessed in health, riches, and children, was the utmost that men can attain ; this was the reason why he was in perplexity, and why he uttered the above-mentioned opinions, and this is also the meaning of his words : " I have heard of thee by the hearing of the ear ; but now mine eye seeth thee. Wherefore I abhor myself, and repent because of dust and ashes " (xlii. 5, 6) ; that is to say, he abhorred all that he had desired before, and that he was sorry that he had been in dust and ashes ; comp. " and he sat down among the ashes " (ii. 8). On account of this last utterance, which implies true perception, it is said afterwards in reference to him, " for you have not spoken of me the thing that is right, as my servant Job hath."

The opinion set forth by Eliphaz in reference to Job's suffering is likewise one of the current views on Providence. He holds that the fate of Job was in accordance with strict justice. Job was guilty of sins for which he deserved his fate. Eliphaz therefore says to Job : " Is not thy wickedness great, and thine iniquities infinite ? " (xxii. 5). He then points out to him that his upright actions and his good ways, on which he relies, need not be so perfect in the eyes of God that no punishment should be inflicted on him. " Behold, he putteth no trust in his servants ; and his angels he chargeth with folly : how much less in them that dwell in houses of clay," etc. (iv. 17–18). Eliphaz never abandoned his belief that the fate of man is the result of justice, that we do not know all our shortcomings for which we are punished, nor the way how we incur the punishment through them.

Bildad the Shuhite defends in this question the theory of reward and compensation. He therefore tells Job that if he is innocent and without sin, his terrible misfortunes will be the source of great reward, will be followed by the best compensation, and will prove a boon to him as the cause of great bliss in the future world. This idea is expressed in the words : " If thou be pure and upright, surely now he will awake for thee, and make the habitation of thy righteousness prosperous. Though thy beginning was small, yet thy latter end will greatly increase " (viii. 6–8). This opinion concerning Providence is widespread, and we have already explained it.

Zofar the Naamathite holds that the Divine Will is the source of everything that happens ; no further cause can be sought for His actions, and it cannot be asked why He has done this and why He has not done that. That which God does can therefore not be explained by the way of justice or the result of wisdom. His true Essence demands that He does what He wills ; we are unable to fathom the depth of His wisdom, and it is the law and rule of this wisdom that whatever He does is done because it is His will and for no other cause. Zofar therefore says to Job : " But oh that God would speak, and open his lips against thee ; and that he would show thee the secrets of wisdom, for wisdom hath two portions ! Know, therefore, that God exacteth of thee less than thine iniquity deserveth. Canst thou by searching find out God ? canst thou find out the Almighty unto perfection ? " (xi. 6–7).

In this manner consider well how the Book of Job discusses the problem, which has perplexed many people, and led them to adopt in reference to Divine Providence some one of the theories which I have explained above ; all possible different theories are mentioned therein. The problem is described either by way of fiction or in accordance with real fact, as having manifested itself in a man famous for his excellency and wisdom. The view ascribed to Job is the theory of Aristotle. Eliphaz holds the opinion taught in Scripture, Bildad's opinion is identical with that of the Mu'tazilah, whilst Zofar defends the theory of the Asha'riyah. These were the ancient views on Providence; later on a new theory was set forth, namely, that ascribed to Elihu. For this reason he is placed above the others, and described as younger in years but greater in wisdom. He censures Job for his foolishly exalting himself, expressing surprise at such great troubles befalling a good man, and dwelling on the praises of his own deeds. He also tells the three friends that their minds have been weakened by great age. A profound and wonderful discourse then follows. Reflecting on his words we may at first thought be surprised to find that he does not add anything to the words of Eliphaz, Bildad, and Zofar; and that he only repeats their ideas in other terms and more explicitly. For he likewise censures and rebukes Job, attributes justice to God, relates His wonders in nature, and holds that God is not affected by the service of the worshipper, nor by the disobedience of the rebellious. All this has already been said by His colleagues. But after due consideration we see clearly the new idea introduced by Elihu, which is the principal object of his speech, an idea which has not been uttered by those who spoke before him. In addition to this he mentions also other things set forth by the previous speakers, in the same manner as each of the rest, viz., Job and his three friends, repeat what the others have said. The purpose of this repetition is to conceal the opinion peculiar to each speaker, and to make all appear in the eyes of the ordinary reader to utter one and the same view, although in reality this is not the case. The new idea, which is peculiar to Elihu and has not been mentioned by the others, is contained in his metaphor of the angel's intercession. It is a frequent occurrence, he says, that a man becomes ill, approaches the gates of death, and is already given up by his neighbours. If then an angel, of any kind whatever, intercedes on his behalf and prays for him, the intercession and prayers are accepted; the patient rises from his illness, is saved, and returns to good health. This result is not always obtained; intercession and deliverance do not always follow each other; it happens only twice, or three times. Elihu therefore says: " If there be an angel with him, an interpreter, one among a thousand, to show unto man his uprightness," etc. (xxxiii. 29). He then describes man's condition when convalescent and the rejoicing at his recovery, and continues thus: " Lo, all these things worketh God twice, three times with man " (*ibid.* 29). This idea occurs only in the words of Elihu. His description of the method of prophecy in preceding verses is likewise new. He says: " Surely God speaketh in one way, yea in two ways, yet man perceiveth it not. In a dream, in a vision of the night, when deep sleep falleth upon man, in slumberings upon the bed " (*ibid.* 14, 15). He afterwards supports and illustrates his theory by a description of many natural phenomena, such as thunder, lightning, rain, and winds; with these are mixed up accounts of various incidents of life, e.g., an account of pestilence contained in the following passage: " In a moment they die, and at midnight; the people become tumultuous and pass away " (xxxiv. 20). Great wars are described in the following verse: " He breaketh in pieces mighty men without number, and setteth others in their stead " (*ibid.* 24).

There are many more passages of this kind. In a similar manner the Revelation that reached Job (chap. xxxviii., chap. xli.), and explained to him the error of his whole belief, constantly describes natural objects, and nothing else; it describes the elements, meteorological phenomena, and peculiarities of various kinds of living beings. The sky, the heavens, Orion and Pleiades are only mentioned in reference to their influence upon our atmosphere, so that Job's attention is in this prophecy only called to things below the lunar sphere. Elihu likewise derives instruction from the nature of various kinds of animals. Thus he says: " He teacheth us through the beasts of the earth, and maketh us wise through the fowls of heaven " (xxxv. 11). He dwells longest on the nature of the Leviathan, which possesses a combination of bodily peculiarities found separate in different animals, in those that walk, those that swim, and those that fly. The description of all these things serves to impress on our minds that we are unable to comprehend how these transient creatures come into existence, or to imagine how their natural properties commenced to exist, and that these are not like the things which we are able to produce. Much less can we compare the manner in which God rules and manages His creatures with the manner in which we rule and manage certain beings. We must content ourselves with this, and believe that nothing is hidden from God, as Elihu says: " For his eyes are upon the ways of man, and he seeth all his goings. There is no darkness nor shadow of death, where the workers of iniquity may hide themselves " (xxxiv. 21, 22). But the term management, when applied to God, has not the same meaning which it has when applied to us; and when we say that He rules His creatures we do not mean that He does the same as we do when we rule over other beings. The term " rule " has not the same definition in both cases; it signifies two different notions, which have nothing in common but the name. In the same manner, as there is a difference between works of nature and productions of human handicraft, so there is a difference between God's rule, providence, and intention in reference to all natural forces, and our rule, providence, and intention in reference to things which are the objects of our rule, providence, and intention. This lesson is the principal object of the whole Book of Job; it lays down this principle of faith, and recommends us to derive a proof from nature, that we should not fall into the error of imagining His knowledge to be similar to ours, or His intention, providence, and rule similar to ours. When we know this we shall find everything that may befall us easy to bear; mishap will create no doubts in our hearts concerning God, whether He knows our affairs or not, whether He provides for us or abandons us. On the contrary, our fate will increase our love of God; as is said in the end of this prophecy: " Therefore I abhor myself and repent concerning the dust and ashes " (xlii. 6); and as our Sages say: " The pious do everything out of love, and rejoice in their own afflictions." (B. T. Shabb. 88*b*.) If you pay to my words the attention which this treatise demands, and examine all that is said in the Book of Job, all will be clear to you, and you will find that I have grasped and taken hold of the whole subject; nothing has been left unnoticed, except such portions as are only introduced because of the context and the whole plan of the allegory. I have explained this method several times in the course of this treatise.

CHAPTER XXIV

THE doctrine of trials is open to great objections ; it is in fact more exposed to objections than any other thing taught in Scripture. It is mentioned in Scripture six times, as I will show in this chapter. People have generally the notion that trials consist in afflictions and mishaps sent by God to man, not as punishments for past sins, but as giving opportunity for great reward. This principle is not mentioned in Scripture in plain language, and it is only in one of the six places referred to that the literal meaning conveys this notion. I will explain the meaning of that passage later on. The principle taught in Scripture is exactly the reverse ; for it is said : " He is a God of faithfulness, and there is no iniquity in him " (Deut. xxxii. 4).

The teaching of our Sages, although some of them approve this general belief [concerning trials], is on the whole against it. For they say, " There is no death without sin, and no affliction without transgression." (See p. 285.) Every intelligent religious person should have this faith, and should not ascribe any wrong to God, who is far from it ; he must not assume that a person is innocent and perfect and does not deserve what has befallen him. The trials mentioned in Scripture in the [six] passages, seem to have been tests and experiments by which God desired to learn the intensity of the faith and the devotion of a man or a nation. [If this were the case] it would be very difficult to comprehend the object of the trials, and yet the sacrifice of Isaac seems to be a case of this kind, as none witnessed it, but God and the two concerned [Abraham and Isaac]. Thus God says to Abraham, " For now I know that thou fearest God," etc. (Gen. xxii. 12). In another passage it is said : " For the Lord your God proveth you to know whether ye love," etc. (Deut. xiii. 4). Again, " And to prove thee to know what was in thine heart," etc. (*ibid.* viii. 2). I will now remove all the difficulties.

The sole object of all the trials mentioned in Scripture is to teach man what he ought to do or believe ; so that the event which forms the actual trial is not the end desired ; it is but an example for our instruction and guidance. Hence the words " to know (*la-da'at*) whether ye love," etc., do not mean that God desires to know whether they loved God ; for He already knows it ; but *la-da'at*, " to know," has here the same meaning as in the phrase " to know (*la-da'at*) that I am the Lord that sanctifieth you " (Exod. xxxi. 13), i.e., that all nations shall know that I am the Lord who sanctifieth you. In a similar manner Scripture says :—If a man should rise, pretend to be a prophet, and show you his signs by which he desired to convince you that his words are true, know that God intends thereby to prove to the nations how firmly you believe in the truth of God's word, and how well you have comprehended the true Essence of God ; that you cannot be misled by any tempter to corrupt your faith in God. Your religion will then afford a guidance to all who seek the truth, and of all religions man will choose that which is so firmly established that it is not shaken by the performance of a miracle. For a miracle cannot prove that which is impossible ; it is useful only as a confirmation of that which is possible, as we have explained in our Mishneh-torah. (Yesode ha-torah vii. f. viii. 3.)

Having shown that the term " to know" means "that all people may know," we apply this interpretation to the following words said in reference to the manna : " To humble thee, and to prove thee, to know what was in thine heart, whether thou wouldst keep his commandments, or not " (Deut. viii. 2). All nations shall know, it shall be published throughout the world, that those who devote themselves to the service of God are supported beyond their expectation. In the same sense it was said when the manna commenced to come down, " that I may prove them whether they will walk in my law or no " (Exod. xvi. 4) ; i.e., let every one who desires try and see whether it is useful and sufficient to devote himself to the service of God. It is, however, said a third time in reference to the manna : " Who fed thee in the wilderness with manna, which thy fathers knew not, that he might humble thee, and that he might prove thee, to do thee good at thy latter end " (Deut. viii. 16). This might induce us to think that God sometimes afflicts man for the purpose of increasing his reward. But in truth this is not the case. We may rather assume one of the two following explanations ; either this passage expresses the same idea as is expressed in the first and second passages, viz., to show [to all people] whether faith in God is sufficient to secure man's maintenance and his relief from care and trouble, or not. Or the Hebrew term *le-nassoteka* means " to accustom thee " ; the word is used in this sense in the following passage : " She has not *accustomed* (*nisseta*) the sole of her foot to set it upon the ground " (*ibid.* xxviii. 56). The meaning of the above passage would then be : " God has first trained you in the hardships of the wilderness, in order to increase your welfare when you enter the land of Canaan." It is indeed a fact that the transition from trouble to ease gives more pleasure than continual ease. It is also known that the Israelites would not have been able to conquer the land and fight with its inhabitants, if they had not previously undergone the trouble and hardship of the wilderness. Scripture says in reference to this : " For God said, Lest peradventure the people repent when they see war, and they return to Egypt. But God led the people about, through the way of the wilderness of the Red Sea ; and the children of Israel went up harnessed out of the land of Egypt " (Exod. xiii. 17, 18). Ease destroys bravery, whilst trouble and care for food create strength ; and this was [also for the Israelites] the good that ultimately came out of their wanderings in the wilderness. The passage, " For God is come to *prove* you, and that his fear may be before your faces, that ye sin not " (*ibid.* xx. 20), expresses the same idea as is expressed in Deuteronomy (xiii. 4) in reference to a person who prophesies in the name of idols, namely in the words : " For the Lord your God *proveth* you to know whether ye love the Lord." We have already explained the meaning of the latter passage. In the same sense Moses said to the Israelites when they stood round Mount Sinai : " Do not fear ; the object of this great sight which you perceived is that you should see the truth with your own eyes. When the Lord your God, in order to show your faithfulness to Him, will prove you by a false prophet, who will tell you the reverse of what you have heard, you will remain firm and your steps will not slide. If I had come as a messenger as you desired, and had told you that which had been said unto me and which you had not heard, you would perhaps consider as true what another might tell you in opposition to that which you heard from me. But it is different now, as you have heard it in the midst of the great sight."

The account of Abraham our father binding his son, includes two great ideas or principles of our faith.   First, it shows us the extent and limit of the fear of God.   Abraham is commanded to perform a certain act, which is not equalled by any surrender of property or by any sacrifice of life, for it surpasses everything that can be done, and belongs to the class of actions which are believed to be contrary to human feelings.   He had been without child, and had been longing for a child ; he had great riches, and was ex- pecting that a nation should spring from his seed.   After all hope of a son had already been given up, a son was born unto him.   How great must have been his delight in the child !   how intensely must he have loved him !   And yet because he feared God, and loved to do what God commanded, he thought little of that beloved child, and set aside all his hopes concerning him, and consented to kill him after a journey of three days.   If the act by which he showed his readiness to kill his son had taken place immediately when he received the commandment, it might have been the result of con- fusion and not of consideration.   But the fact that he performed it three days after he had received the commandment, proves the presence of thought, proper consideration, and careful examination of what is due to the Divine command and what is in accordance with the love and fear of God.   There is no necessity to look for the presence of any other idea or of anything that might have affected his emotions.   For Abraham did not hasten to kill Isaac out of fear that God might slay him or make him poor, but solely because it is man's duty to love and to fear God, even without hope of reward or fear of punishment.   We have repeatedly explained this.   The angel, therefore, says to him, " For now I know," etc. (*ibid.* ver. 12), that is, from this action, for which you deserve to be truly called a God-fearing man, all people shall learn how far we must go in the fear of God.   This idea is confirmed in Scrip- ture ; it is distinctly stated that one sole thing, fear of God, is the object of the whole Law with its affirmative and negative precepts, its promises and its historical examples, for it is said, " If thou wilt not observe to do all the words of this Law that are written in this book, that thou mayest fear this glorious and fearful name, the Lord thy God," etc. (Deut. xxviii. 58).   This is one of the two purposes of the *'akedah* (sacrifice or binding of Isaac).

The second purpose is to show how the prophets believed in the truth of that which came to them from God by way of inspiration.   We shall not think that what the prophets heard or saw in allegorical figures may at times have included incorrect or doubtful elements, since the Divine communi- cation was made to them, as we have shown, in a dream or a vision and through the imaginative faculty.   Scripture thus tells us that whatever the Prophet perceives in a prophetic vision, he considers as true and correct and not open to any doubt ; it is in his eyes like all other things perceived by the senses or by the intellect.   This is proved by the consent of Abraham to slay "his only son whom he loved," as he was commanded, although the command- ment was received in a dream or a vision.   If the Prophets had any doubt or suspicion as regards the truth of what they saw in a prophetic dream or perceived in a prophetic vision, they would not have consented to do what is unnatural, and Abraham would not have found in his soul strength enough to perform that act, if he had any doubt [as regards the truth of the com- mandment].   It was just the right thing that this lesson derived from the *'akedah* ("sacrifice") should be taught through Abraham and a man like Isaac. For Abraham was the first to teach the Unity of God, to establish the faith [in Him], to cause it to remain among coming generations, and to win his fellow-men for his doctrine; as Scripture says of him: "I know him, that he will command," etc. (Gen. viii. 19). In the same manner as he was followed by others in his true and valuable opinions when they were heard from him, so also the principles should be accepted that may be learnt from his actions; especially from the act by which he confirmed the principle of the truth of prophecy, and showed how far we must go in the fear and the love of God.

This is the way how we have to understand the accounts of trials; we must not think that God desires to examine us and to try us in order to know what He did not know before. Far is this from Him; He is far above that which ignorant and foolish people imagine concerning Him, in the evil of their thoughts. Note this.

CHAPTER XXV

[MAN'S] actions are divided as regards their object into four classes; they are either *purposeless, unimportant, in vain,* or *good.* An action is *in vain* if the object which is sought by it is not obtained on account of some obstacles. Thus people frequently use the phrase "thou hast worked in vain" in reference to a person who looks out for some one and cannot find him; or who undertakes the troubles of a journey for his business without profit. Our endeavours and exertions are *in vain* as regards a patient that is not cured. This applies to all actions which are intended for certain purposes that are not realized. *Purposeless* are such actions, which serve no purpose at all. Some persons, e.g., do something with their hands whilst thinking of something else. The actions of the insane and confused are of this kind. *Unimportant* are such actions by which a trivial object is sought, an object that is not necessary and is not of great use. This is the case when a person dances without seeking to benefit his digestion by that exercise, or performs certain actions for the purpose of causing laughter. Such actions are certainly mere pastimes. Whether an action belongs to this class or not depends on the intention of those who perform it, and on the degree of their perfection. For many things are necessary or very useful in the opinion of one person and superfluous in the opinion of another. E.g., bodily exercise, in its different kinds, is necessary for the proper preservation of health in the opinion of him who understands the science of medicine; writing is considered as very useful by scholars. When people take exercise by playing with the ball, wrestling, stretching out the hands or keeping back the breathing, or do certain things as preparation for writing, shape the pen and get the paper ready, such actions are mere pastimes in the eyes of the ignorant, but the wise do not consider them as unimportant. *Useful* are such actions as serve a proper purpose; being either necessary or useful for the purpose which is to be attained. This division [of man's actions] is, as I believe, not open to any objection. For every action is either intended for a certain purpose or is not intended; and if intended for a certain purpose, that purpose may be important or unimportant, is sometimes attained and some-times missed. This division is therefore complete.

After having explained this division, I contend that no intelligent person can assume that any of the actions of God can be in vain, purposeless, or un-important. According to our view and the view of all that follow the Law of Moses, all actions of God are "exceedingly good." Thus Scripture says, "And God saw everything that he had made, and behold, it was very good" (Gen. i. 31). And that which God made for a certain thing is necessary or [at least] very useful for the existence of that thing. Thus food is necessary for the existence of living beings; the possession of eyes is very useful to man during his life, although food only serves to sustain living beings a certain time, and the senses are only intended to procure to animals the advantages of sensation. The philosophers likewise assume that in Nature there is nothing in vain, so that everything that is not the product of human industry serves a certain purpose, which may be known or unknown to us. There are thinkers that assume that God does not create one thing for the sake of another, that existing things are not to each other in the relation of cause and effect; that they are all the direct result of the Will of God, and do not serve any purpose. According to this opinion we cannot ask why has He made this and not that; for He does what pleases Him, without following a fixed system. Those who defend this theory must consider the actions of God as purposeless, and even as inferior to purposeless actions; for when we perform purposeless actions, our attention is engaged by other things and we do not know what we are doing; but God, according to these theorists, knows what He is doing, and knowingly does it for no purpose or use what-ever. The absurdity of assuming that some of God's actions are trivial, is appar-ent even at first sight, and no notice need be taken of the nonsensical idea that monkeys were created for our pastime. Such opinions originate only in man's ignorance of the nature of transient beings, and in his overlooking the principle that it was intended by the Creator to produce in its present form everything whose existence is possible; a different form was not decreed by the Divine Wisdom, and the existence [of objects of a different form] is there-fore impossible, because the existence of all things depends on the decree of God's wisdom. Those who hold that God's works serve no purpose what-ever believe that an examination of the totality of existing things compels them to adopt this theory. They ask what is the purpose of the whole Universe? they necessarily answer, like all those who believe in the Cre-ation, that it was created because God willed it so, and for no other purpose. The same answer they apply to all parts of the Universe, and do not admit that the hole in the uvea and the transparency of the cornea are intended for the purpose of allowing the *spiritus visus* to pass and to perceive certain objects; they do not assume that these circumstances are causes for the sight; the hole in the uvea and the transparent matter over it are not there because of the sight, but because of the Will of God, although the sense of sight could have been created in a different form. There are passages in the Bible which at first sight we might understand to imply this theory. E.g., "The Lord hath done whatever he pleased" (Ps. cxxxv. 6); "His soul desired it and he made it" (Job xxiii. 13); "Who will say unto thee, What doest thou?" (Eccles. viii. 4). The meaning of these and similar verses is this : whatever God desires to do is necessarily done ; there is no-thing that could prevent the realization of His will.   The object of His will is only that which is possible, and of the things possible only such as His wisdom decrees upon.   When God desires to produce the best work, no obstacle or hindrance intervenes between Him and that work.   This is the opinion held by all religious people, also by the philosophers ; it is also our opinion.   For although we believe that God created the Universe from nothing, most of our wise and learned men believe that the Creation was not the exclusive result of His will ; but His wisdom, which we are unable to comprehend, made the actual existence of the Universe necessary.   The same unchangeable wisdom found it as necessary that non-existence should precede the existence of the Universe.   Our Sages frequently express this idea in the explanation of the words, " He hath made everything beautiful in his time " (Eccles. iii. 11), only in order to avoid that which is objectionable, viz., the opinion that God does things without any purpose whatever.   This is the belief of most of our Theologians ; and in a similar manner have the Prophets ex-pressed the idea that all parts of natural products are well arranged, in good order, connected with each other, and stand to each other in the relation of cause and effect ; nothing of them is purposeless, trivial, or in vain ; they are all the result of great wisdom.   Comp. " O Lord, how manifold are thy works ! in wisdom hast thou made them all : the earth is full of thy riches " (Ps. civ. 24) ; " And all his works are done in truth " (*ibid.* xxxiii. 4) ; " The Lord by wisdom hath founded the earth " (Prov. iii. 19).   This idea occurs frequently ; there is no necessity to believe otherwise ; philo-sophic speculation leads to the same result ; viz., that in the whole of Nature there is nothing purposeless, trivial, or unnecessary, especially in the Nature of the spheres, which are in the best condition and order, in accordance with their superior substance.

Know that the difficulties which lead to confusion in the question what is the purpose of the Universe or of any of its parts, arise from two causes : first, man has an erroneous idea of himself, and believes that the whole world exists only for his sake ; secondly, he is ignorant both about the nature of the sublunary world, and about the Creator's intention to give existence to all beings whose existence is possible, because existence is undoubtedly good. The consequences of that error and of the ignorance about the two things named, are doubts and confusion, which lead many to imagine that some of God's works are trivial, others purposeless, and others in vain.   Those who adopt this absurd idea that God's actions are utterly purposeless, and refuse to consider them as the result of His wisdom, are afraid they might otherwise be compelled to admit the theory of the Eternity of the Universe, and guard themselves against it by the above theory.   I have already told you the view which is set forth in Scripture on this question, and which it is proper to accept.   It is this : it is not unreasonable to assume that the works of God, their existence and preceding non-existence, are the result of His wisdom, but we are unable to understand many of the ways of His wisdom in His works.   On this principle the whole Law of Moses is based ; it begins with this principle : " And God saw all that He had made, and, behold, it was very good " (Gen. i. 31) ; and it ends with this principle : " The Rock, perfect is His work " (Deut. xxxii. 4).   Note it.   When you examine this view and that of the philosophers, taking into consideration all preceding chapters which are connected with this subject, you will find that there is no other difference of opinion as regards any portions of the Universe, except that the philosophers believe in the Eternity of the Universe and we believe in the Creation.   Note this.

CHAPTER XXVI

As Theologians are divided on the question whether the actions of God are the result of His wisdom, or only of His will without being intended for any purpose whatever, so they are also divided as regards the object of the commandments which God gave us.   Some of them hold that the commandments have no object at all; and are only dictated by the will of God. Others are of opinion that all commandments and prohibitions are dictated by His wisdom and serve a certain aim; consequently there is a reason for each one of the precepts; they are enjoined because they are useful.   All of us, the common people as well as the scholars, believe that there is a reason for every precept, although there are commandments the reason of which is unknown to us, and in which the ways of God's wisdom are incomprehensible.   This view is distinctly expressed in Scripture; comp. "righteous statutes and judgments" (Deut. iv. 8); "the judgments of the Lord are true, and righteous altogether" (Ps. xix. 10).   There are commandments which are called *ḥuḳḳim*, "ordinances," like the prohibition of wearing garments of wool and linen (*sha'atnez*), boiling meat and milk together, and the sending of the goat [into the wilderness on the Day of Atonement]. Our Sages use in reference to them phrases like the following: "These are things which I have fully ordained for thee; and you dare not criticize them"; "Your evil inclination is turned against them"; and "non-Jews find them strange."   But our Sages generally do not think that such precepts have no cause whatever, and serve no purpose; for this would lead us to assume that God's actions are purposeless.   On the contrary, they hold that even these ordinances have a cause, and are certainly intended for some use, although it is not known to us; owing either to the deficiency of our knowledge or the weakness of our intellect.   Consequently there is a cause for every commandment; every positive or negative precept serves a useful object; in some cases the usefulness is evident, e.g., the prohibition of murder and theft; in others the usefulness is not so evident, e.g., the prohibition of enjoying the fruit of a tree in the first three years (Lev. xix. 23), or of a vineyard in which other seeds have been growing (Deut. xxii. 9). Those commandments, whose object is generally evident, are called "judgments" (*mishpatim*); those whose object is not generally clear are called "ordinances" (*ḥuḳḳim*).   Thus they say [in reference to the words of Moses]: *Ki lo dabar reḳ hu mi-kem* (lit. "for it is not a vain thing for you," Deut. xxxii. 74); "It is not in vain, and if it is in vain, it is only so through you." That is to say, the giving of these commandments is not a vain thing and without any useful object; and if it appears so to you in any commandment, it is owing to the deficiency in your comprehension.   You certainly know the famous saying that Solomon knew the reason for all commandments except that of the "red heifer."   Our Sages also said that God concealed the causes of commandments, lest people should despise them, as Solomon did in respect to three commandments, the reason for which is clearly stated. In this sense they always speak; and Scriptural texts support the idea. I have, however, found one utterance made by them in *Bereshit-rabba* (sect. xliv.), which might at first sight appear to imply that some commandments have no other reason but the fact that they are commanded, that no other object is intended by them, and that they do not serve any useful object. I mean the following passage : What difference does it make to God whether a beast is killed by cutting the neck in front or in the back ? Surely the commandments are only intended as a means of trying man ; in accordance with the verse, " The word of God is a test" (lit. tried) (Ps. xviii. 31). Although this passage is very strange, and has no parallel in the writings of our Sages, I explain it, as you shall soon hear, in such a manner that I remain in accord with the meaning of their words and do not depart from the principle which we agreed upon, that the commandments serve a useful object ; " for it is not a vain thing for you " ; " I have not said to the seed of Jacob, seek me in vain. I the Lord speak righteousness, declare that which is right " (Isa. xlv. 19). I will now tell you what intelligent persons ought to believe in this respect ; namely, that each commandment has necessarily a cause, as far as its general character is concerned, and serves a certain object ; but as regards its details we hold that it has no ulterior object. Thus killing animals for the purpose of obtaining good food is certainly useful, as we intend to show (below, ch. xlviii.) ; that, however, the killing should not be performed by *neḥirah* (poleaxing the animal), but by *sheḥitah* (cutting the neck), and by dividing the œsophagus and the windpipe in a certain place ; these regulations and the like are nothing but tests for man's obedience. In this sense you will understand the example quoted by our Sages [that there is no difference] between killing the animal by cutting its neck in front and cutting it in the back. I give this instance only because it has been mentioned by our Sages ; but in reality [there is some reason for these regulations]. For as it has become necessary to eat the flesh of animals, it was intended by the above regulations to ensure an easy death and to effect it by suitable means ; whilst decapitation requires a sword or a similar instrument, the *sheḥitah* can be performed with any instrument ; and in order to ensure an easy death our Sages insisted that the knife should be well sharpened.

A more suitable instance can be cited from the detailed commandments concerning sacrifices. The law that sacrifices should be brought is evidently of great use, as will be shown by us (*infra*, chap. xlvi.) ; but we cannot say why one offering should be a lamb, whilst another is a ram ; and why a fixed number of them should be brought. Those who trouble themselves to find a cause for any of these detailed rules, are in my eyes void of sense ; they do not remove any difficulties, but rather increase them. Those who believe that these detailed rules originate in a certain cause, are as far from the truth as those who assume that the whole law is useless. You must know that Divine Wisdom demanded it—or, if you prefer, say that circumstances made it necessary—that there should be parts [of His work] which have no certain object ; and as regards the Law, it appears to be impossible that it should not include some matter of this kind. That it cannot be avoided may be seen from the following instance. You ask why must a lamb be sacrificed and not a ram ? but the same question would be asked, why a ram had been commanded instead of a lamb, so long as one particular kind is required. The same is to be said as to the question why were seven lambs sacrificed and not eight ; the same question might have been asked if there were eight, ten, or twenty lambs, so long as some definite number of lambs were sacrificed. It is almost similar to the nature of a thing which can receive different forms, but actually receives one of them. We must not ask why it has this form and not another which is likewise possible, because we should have to ask the same question if instead of its actual form the thing had any of the other possible forms. Note this, and understand it. The repeated assertion of our Sages that there are reasons for all commandments, and the tradition that Solomon knew them, refer to the general purpose of the commandments, and not to the object of every detail. This being the case, I find it convenient to divide the six hundred and thirteen precepts into classes ; each class will include many precepts of the same kind, or related to each other by their character. I will [first] explain the reason of each class, and show its undoubted and undisputed object, and then I shall discuss each commandment in the class, and expound its reason. Only very few will be left unexplained, the reason for which I have been unable to trace unto this day. I have also been able to comprehend in some cases even the object of many of the conditions and details as far as these can be discovered. You will hear all this later on. But in order to fully explain these reasons I must premise several chapters ; in these I will discuss principles which form the basis of my theory. I will now begin these chapters.

CHAPTER XXVII

The general object of the Law is twofold : the well-being of the soul, and the well-being of the body. The well-being of the soul is promoted by correct opinions communicated to the people according to their capacity. Some of these opinions are therefore imparted in a plain form, others allegorically ; because certain opinions are in their plain form too strong for the capacity of the common people. The well-being of the body is established by a proper management of the relations in which we live one to another. This we can attain in two ways : first by removing all violence from our midst ; that is to say, that we do not do every one as he pleases, desires, and is able to do ; but every one of us does that which contributes towards the common welfare. Secondly, by teaching every one of us such good morals as must produce a good social state. Of these two objects, the one, the well-being of the soul, or the communication of correct opinions, comes undoubtedly first in rank, but the other, the well-being of the body, the government of the state, and the establishment of the best possible relations among men, is anterior in nature and time. The latter object is required first ; it is also treated [in the Law] most carefully and most minutely, because the well-being of the soul can only be obtained after that of the body has been secured. For it has already been found that man has a double perfection : the first perfection is that of the body, and the second perfection is that of the soul. The first consists in the most healthy condition of his material relations, and this is only possible when man has all his wants supplied, as they arise; if he has his food, and other things needful for his body, e.g., shelter, bath, and the like. But one man alone cannot procure all this; it is impossible for a single man to obtain this comfort; it is only possible in society, since man, as is well known, is by nature social.

The second perfection of man consists in his becoming an actually intelligent being; i.e., he knows about the things in existence all that a person perfectly developed is capable of knowing. This second perfection certainly does not include any action or good conduct, but only knowledge, which is arrived at by speculation, or established by research.

It is clear that the second and superior kind of perfection can only be attained when the first perfection has been acquired; for a person that is suffering from great hunger, thirst, heat, or cold, cannot grasp an idea even if communicated by others, much less can he arrive at it by his own reasoning. But when a person is in possession of the first perfection, then he may possibly acquire the second perfection, which is undoubtedly of a superior kind, and is alone the source of eternal life. The true Law, which as we said is one, and beside which there is no other Law, viz., the Law of our teacher Moses, has for its purpose to give us the twofold perfection. It aims first at the establishment of good mutual relations among men by removing injustice and creating the noblest feelings. In this way the people in every land are enabled to stay and continue in one condition, and every one can acquire his first perfection. Secondly, it seeks to train us in faith, and to impart correct and true opinions when the intellect is sufficiently developed. Scripture clearly mentions the twofold perfection, and tells us that its acquisition is the object of all the divine commandments. Comp. " And the Lord commanded us to do all these statutes, to fear the Lord our God, for our good always, that he might preserve us alive as it is this day " (Deut. vi. 24). Here the second perfection is first mentioned because it is of greater importance, being, as we have shown, the ultimate aim of man's existence. This perfection is expressed in the phrase, " for our good always." You know the interpretation of our Sages, " ' that it may be well with thee ' (*ibid*. xxii. 7), namely, in the world that is all good, ' and that thou mayest prolong thy days ' (*ibid*.), i.e., in the world that is all eternal." In the same sense I explain the words, " for our good always," to mean that we may come into the world that is all good and eternal, where we may live permanently; and the words, " that he might preserve us alive as it is this day," I explain as referring to our first and temporal existence, to that of our body, which cannot be in a perfect and good condition except by the co-operation of society, as has been shown by us.

CHAPTER XXVIII

It is necessary to bear in mind that Scripture only teaches the chief points of those true principles which lead to the true perfection of man, and only demands in general terms faith in them. Thus Scripture teaches the Existence, the Unity, the Omniscience, the Omnipotence, the Will, and the Eternity of God. All this is given in the form of final results, but they cannot be understood fully and accurately except after the acquisition of many kinds of knowledge. Scripture further demands belief in certain truths, the belief in which is indispensable in regulating our social relations ; such is the belief that God is angry with those who disobey Him, for it leads us to the fear and dread of disobedience [to the will of God]. There are other truths in reference to the whole of the Universe which form the substance of the various and many kinds of speculative sciences, and afford the means of verifying the above-mentioned principles as their final result. But Scripture does not so distinctly prescribe the belief in them as it does in the first case ; it is implied in the commandment, " to love the Lord " (Deut. xi. 13). It may be inferred from the words, " And thou shalt love the Lord thy God with all thy heart, and with all thy soul, and with all thy might " (*ibid.* vi. 5), what stress is laid on this commandment to love God. We have already shown in the Mishneh-torah (*Yes. ha-torah* ii. 2) that this love is only possible when we comprehend the real nature of things, and understand the divine wisdom displayed therein. We have likewise mentioned there what our Sages remark on this subject.

The result of all these preliminary remarks is this : The reason of a commandment, whether positive or negative, is clear, and its usefulness evident, if it directly tends to remove injustice, or to teach good conduct that furthers the well-being of society, or to impart a truth which ought to be believed either on its own merit or as being indispensable for facilitating the removal of injustice or the teaching of good morals. There is no occasion to ask for the object of such commandments ; for no one can, e.g., be in doubt as to the reason why we have been commanded to believe that God is one ; why we are forbidden to murder, to steal, and to take vengeance, or to retaliate, or why we are commanded to love one another. But there are precepts concerning which people are in doubt, and of divided opinions, some believing that they are mere commands, and serve no purpose whatever, whilst others believe that they serve a certain purpose, which, however, is unknown to man. Such are those precepts which in their literal meaning do not seem to further any of the three above-named results : to impart some truth, to teach some moral, or to remove injustice. They do not seem to have any influence upon the well-being of the soul by imparting any truth, or upon the well-being of the body by suggesting such ways and rules as are useful in the government of a state, or in the management of a household. Such are the prohibitions of wearing garments containing wool and linen ; of sowing divers seeds, or of boiling meat and milk together ; the commandment of covering the blood [of slaughtered beasts and birds], the ceremony of breaking the neck of a calf [in case of a person being found slain, and the murderer being unknown] ; the law concerning the first-born of an ass, and the like. I am prepared to tell you my explanation of all these commandments, and to assign for them a true reason supported by proof, with the exception of some minor rules, and of a few commandments, as I have mentioned above. I will show that all these and similar laws must have some bearing upon one of the following three things, viz., the regulation of our opinions, or the improvement of our social relations, which implies two things, the removal of injustice, and the teaching of good morals. Consider what we said of the opinions [implied in the laws] ; in some cases the law contains a truth which is itself the only

object of that law, as e.g., the truth of the Unity, Eternity, and Incorporeality of God ; in other cases, that truth is only the means of securing the
removal of injustice, or the acquisition of good morals ; such is the belief
that God is angry with those who oppress their fellow-men, as it is said,
" Mine anger will be kindled, and I will slay," etc. (Exod. xxii. 23) ; or the
belief that God hears the crying of the oppressed and vexed, to deliver them
out of the hands of the oppressor and tyrant, as it is written, " And it shall
come to pass, when he will cry unto me, that I will hear, for I am gracious "
(Exod. xxii. 25).

CHAPTER XXIX

It is well known that the Patriarch Abraham was brought up in the religion
and the opinion of the Sabeans, that there is no divine being except the stars.
I will tell you in this chapter their works which are at present extant in
Arabic translations, and also in their ancient chronicles ; and I will show you
their opinion and their practice according to these books. You will then
see clearly that they consider the stars as deities, and the sun as the chief
deity. They believe that all the seven stars are gods, but the two luminaries
are greater than all the rest. They say distinctly that the sun governs the
world, both that which is above and that which is below ; these are exactly
their expressions. In these books, and in their chronicles, the history of
Abraham our father is given in the following manner. Abraham was brought
up in Kutha ; when he differed from the people and declared that there is a
Maker besides the sun, they raised certain objections, and mentioned in their
arguments the evident and manifest action of the sun in the Universe.
" You are right," said Abraham ; " [the sun acts in the same manner] as
' the axe in the hand of him that hews with it.' " Then some of his arguments against his opponents are mentioned. In short, the king put him in
prison ; but he continued many days, while in prison, to argue against them.
At last the king was afraid that Abraham might corrupt the kingdom, and
turn the people away from their religion ; he therefore expelled Abraham
into Syria, after having deprived him of all his property.

This is their account which you find clearly stated in the book called
The Nabatean Agriculture. Nothing is said there of the account given in
our trustworthy books, nor do they mention what he learnt by way of prophecy ; for they refused to believe him, because he attacked their evil doctrine. I do not doubt that when he attacked the doctrine of all his fellow-
men, he was cursed, despised, and scorned by these people who adhered to
their erroneous opinions. When he submitted to this treatment for the
sake of God, as ought to be done for the sake of His glory, God said to him,
" And I will bless them that bless thee, and curse them that curse thee "
(Gen. xii. 3). The result of the course which Abraham took, is the fact that
most people, as we see at present, agree in praising him, and being proud of
him ; so that even those who are not his descendants call themselves by his
name. No one opposes him, and no one ignores his merits, except some
ignoble remnants of the nations left in the remote corners of the earth, like
the savage Turks in the extreme North, and the Indians in the extreme
South. These are remnants of the Sabeans, who once filled the earth.

Those who were able to think, and were philosophers in those days, could only raise themselves to the idea that God is the spirit of the spheres ; the spheres with their stars being the body, and God the spirit. Abu-becr al-Zaig mentions this in his Commentary on the book of Physics.

All the Sabeans thus believed in the eternity of the Universe, the heavens being in their opinion God. Adam was in their belief a human being born from male and female, like the rest of mankind ; he was only distinguished from his fellow-men by being a prophet sent by the moon ; he accordingly called men to the worship of the moon, and he wrote several works on agriculture. The Sabeans further relate that Noah was an agriculturist, and that he was not pleased with the worship of idols ; they blame him for that, and say that he did not worship any image. In their writings we meet even with the statement that Noah was rebuked and imprisoned because he worshipped God, and with many other accounts about him. The Sabeans contend that Seth differed from his father Adam, as regards the worship of the moon. They manufactured ridiculous stories, which prove that their authors were very deficient in knowledge, that they were by no means philosophers, but on the contrary were extremely ignorant persons. Adam, they say, left the torrid zone near India and entered the region of Babylon, bringing with him wonderful things, such as a golden tree, that was growing, and had leaves and branches ; a stone tree of the same kind, and a fresh leaf of a tree proof against fire. He related that there was a tree which could shelter ten thousand men, although it had only the height of a man ; two leaves he brought with him, each of which was sufficient to cover two men. Of these stories the Sabeans have a wonderful abundance. I am surprised that persons who think that the Universe is eternal, can yet believe in these things which nature cannot produce, as is known to every student of Natural Science. They only mention Adam, and relate the above stories about him, in order to support their theory of the Eternity of the Universe ; from this theory they then derive the doctrine that the stars and the spheres are deities. When [Abraham] the " Pillar of the World " appeared, he became convinced that there is a spiritual Divine Being, which is not a body, nor a force residing in a body, but is the author of the spheres and the stars ; and he saw the absurdity of the tales in which he had been brought up. He therefore began to attack the belief of the Sabeans, to expose the falsehood of their opinions, and to proclaim publicly in opposition to them, " the name of the Lord, the God of the Universe " (Gen. xxi. 33), which proclamation included at the same time the Existence of God, and the Creation of the Universe by God.

In accordance with the Sabean theories images were erected to the stars, golden images to the sun, images of silver to the moon, and they attributed the metals and the climates to the influence of the planets, saying that a certain planet is the god of a certain zone. They built temples, placed in them images, and assumed that the stars sent forth their influence upon these images, which are thereby enabled (to speak) to understand, to comprehend, to inspire human beings, and to tell them what is useful to them. They apply the same to trees which fall to the lot of these stars. When, namely, a certain tree, which is peculiar to a certain star, is dedicated to the name of this star, and certain things are done for the tree and to the tree, the spiritual force of that star which influences that tree, inspires men, and speaks to them when they are asleep. All this is written in their works, to which I will call your attention. It applies to the " prophets of Baal," and the " prophets of Asherah," mentioned in Scripture, in whose hearts the Sabean theories had taken root, who forsook God, and called, " Baal, hear us " (1 Kings xviii. 26) ; because these theories were then general, ignorance had spread, and the madness with which people adhered to this kind of imaginations had increased in the world. When such opinions were adopted among the Israelites, they had observers of clouds, enchanters, witches, charmers, consulters with familiar spirits, wizards, and necromancers.

We have shown in our large work, Mishneh-torah (Hilkot,'*Abodah-zarah*, i. 3), that Abraham was the first that opposed these theories by arguments and by soft and persuasive speech. He induced these people, by showing kindness to them, to serve God. Afterwards came the chief of the prophets, and completed the work by the commandment to slay those unbelievers, to blot out their name, and to uproot them from the land of the living. Comp. " Ye shall destroy their altars," etc. (Exod. xxxiv. 13). He forbade us to follow their ways ; he said, "Ye shall not walk in the manners of the heathen," etc. (Lev. xx. 23). You know from the repeated declarations in the Law that the principal purpose of the whole Law was the removal and utter destruction of idolatry, and all that is connected therewith, even its name, and everything that might lead to any such practices, e.g., acting as a consulter with familiar spirits, or as a wizard, passing children through the fire, divining, observing the clouds, enchanting, charming, or inquiring of the dead. The law prohibits us to imitate the heathen in any of these deeds, and *a fortiori* to adopt them entirely. It is distinctly said in the Law that everything which idolaters consider as service to their gods, and a means of approaching them, is rejected and despised by God ; comp. " for every abomination to the Lord, which he hateth, have they done unto their gods " (Deut. xii. 31). In the books which I shall name to you later on, it is stated that on certain occasions they offered to the sun, their greatest god, seven beetles, and seven mice, and seven bats. This alone suffices to show how disgusting their practice must be to human nature. Thus all precepts cautioning against idolatry, or against that which is connected therewith, leads to it, or is related to it, are evidently useful. They all tend to save us from the evil doctrines that deprive us of everything useful for the acquisition of the twofold perfection of man, by leading to those absurd practices in which our fathers and ancestors have been brought up. Comp. " And Joshua said unto all the people, Thus saith the Lord God of Israel, your fathers dwelt on the other side of the river in old time, even Terah, the father of Abraham, and the father of Nahor, and they served other gods " (Josh. xxiv. 2). It is in reference to these [idolatrous ideas] that the true prophets exclaim, " They walked after [vain] things, which do not profit." How great is the usefulness of every precept that delivers us from this great error, and leads us back to the true faith : that God, the Creator of all things, rules the Universe ; that He must be served, loved, and feared, and not those imaginary deities. According to this faith we approach the true God, and obtain His favour without having recourse to burdensome means ; for nothing else is required but to love and fear Him ; this is the aim in serving

God, as will be shown. Comp. " And now, Israel, what doth the Lord thy God require of thee but to fear the Lord " ? etc. (Deut. x. 12). I shall complete this subject later on ; now let us return to the theme [of this chapter].

I say that my knowledge of the belief, practice, and worship of the Sabeans has given me an insight into many of the divine precepts, and has led me to know their reason. You will confirm it when I shall give the reason of commandments which are seemingly purposeless. I will mention to you the works from which you may learn all that I know of the religion and the opinions of the Sabeans ; you will thereby obtain a true knowledge of my theory as regards the purpose of the divine precepts.

The great book on this subject is the book *On the Nabatean Agriculture*, translated by Ibn Wahshiya. In a succeeding chapter I shall explain why the Sabeans had their religious doctrines written in a work on agriculture. The book is full of the absurdities of idolatrous people, and with those things to which the minds of the multitude easily turn and adhere [perseveringly] ; it speaks of talismans, the means of directing the influence [of the stars] ; witchcraft, spirits, and demons that dwell in the wilderness. There occur also in this book great absurdities, which are ridiculous in the eyes of intelligent people. They were intended as a criticism and an attack on the evident miracles by which all people learnt that there exists a God who is judge over all people. Comp. " That thou mayest know how that the earth is the Lord's " (Exod. ix. 29), " That I am the Lord in the midst of the earth " (*ibid.* viii. 18).

The book describes things as having been mentioned by Adam in his book ; a tree which is found in India, and has the peculiarity that any branch taken from it and thrown to the ground creeps along and moves like serpents ; it also mentions a tree which in its root resembles a human being, utters a loud sound, and speaks a word or words ; a plant is mentioned which has this peculiarity, that a leaf of it put on the neck of a person conceals that person from the sight of men, and enables him to enter or leave a place without being seen, and if any part of it is burnt in open air a noise and terrible sounds are heard whilst the smoke ascends. Numerous fables of this kind are introduced in the description of the wonders of plants and the properties of agriculture. This leads the author to argue against the [true] miracles, and to say that they were the result of artifice.

Among other fables we read there that the plant althea, one of the Asherot, which they made, as I told you, stood in Nineveh twelve thousand years. This tree had once a quarrel with the mandragora, which wanted to take the place of the former. The person who had been inspired by this tree ceased to receive inspiration ; when after some time the prophetical power had returned to him, he was told by the althea that the latter had been engaged in a dispute with the mandragora. He was then commanded to write to the magicians that they should decide whether the althea or the mandragora was better and more effective in witchcraft. It is a long story, and you may learn from it, when you read it, the opinions and the wisdom of the men of that time. Such were in those days of darkness the wise men of Babel, to whom reference is made in Scripture, and such were the beliefs in which they were trained. And were it not that the theory of the Existence of God is at present generally accepted, our days would now have been darker than those days, though in other respects. I return now to my subject.

In that book the following story is also related : One of the idolatrous prophets, named Tammuz, called upon the king to worship the seven planets and the twelve constellations of the Zodiac ; whereupon the king killed him in a dreadful manner. The night of his death the images from all parts of the land came together in the temple of Babylon which was devoted to the image of the Sun, the great golden image. This image, which was suspended between heaven and earth, came down into the midst of the temple, and surrounded by all other images commenced to mourn for Tammuz, and to relate what had befallen him. All other images cried and mourned the whole night ; at dawn they flew away and returned to their temples in every corner of the earth. Hence the regular custom arose for the women to weep, lament, mourn, and cry for Tammuz on the first day of the month of Tammuz.

Consider what opinions people had in these days. The legend of Tammuz is very old among the Sabeans. This book will disclose to you most of the perverse ideas and practices of the Sabeans, including their feasts. But you must be careful and must not be misled to think that we have real incidents in the life of Adam, or of any other person, or any real fact in the stories which they relate about Adam, the serpent, the tree of knowledge of good and evil, and the allusion to the garment of Adam which he had not been accustomed to wear. A little consideration will lay open the falsehood of all these accounts ; it will show that they have been invented in imitation of the Pentateuch when it became known among the nations. The account of the Creation was heard, and it was taken entirely in its literal sense. They have done this in order that the ignorant may hear it, and be persuaded to assume the Eternity of the Universe, and to believe that the Scriptural account contained facts which happened in the manner as has been assumed by the Sabeans.

It is by no means necessary to point this out to men like you. You have acquired sufficient knowledge to keep your mind free from the absurdities of the Kasdim, Chaldeans, and Sabeans, who are bare of every true science. But I wish to exhort you that you should caution others, for ordinary people are very much inclined to believe these fables.

To the same class of books we count the book Istimachis, attributed to Aristotle, who can by no means have been its author ; also the books on Talismans, such as the book of Tomtom ; the book al-Sarb ; the book on the degrees of the sphere and the constellations rising with each degree ; a book on Talismans attributed to Aristotle, a book ascribed to Hermes, a book of the Sabean Isḥak in defence of the Sabean religion, and his large work on Sabean customs, details of their religion, ceremonies, festivals, offerings, prayers and other things relating to their faith.

All these books which I have mentioned are works on idolatry translated into Arabic ; there is no doubt that they form a very small portion in comparison to that which has not been translated, and that which is no longer extant, but has been lost in the course of time. But those works which are at present extant, include most of the opinions of the Sabeans and their practices, which are to some degree still in vogue in the world.

They describe how temples are built and images of metal and stone placed in them, altars erected and sacrifices and various kinds of food are offered thereon, festivals celebrated, meetings held in the temples for prayer and other kinds of service ; how they select certain very distinguished places and call them temples of Intellectual Images (or Forms) ; how they make images " on the high mountains " (Deut. xii. 2), rear *asherot*, erect pillars, and do many other things which you can learn from the books mentioned by us. The knowledge of these theories and practices is of great importance in explaining the reasons of the precepts. For it is the principal object of the Law and the axis round which it turns, to blot out these opinions from man's heart and make the existence of idolatry impossible. As regards the former Scripture says : " Lest your heart be persuaded," etc. (Deut. xi. 16), " whose heart turneth away to-day," etc. (*ibid.* xxix. 17). The actual abolition of idolatry is expressed in the following passage : " Ye shall destroy their altars, and burn their groves in fire " (Deut. vii. 5), " and ye shall destroy their name," etc. (xii. 3). These two things are frequently repeated ; they form the principal and first object of the whole Law, as our Sages distinctly told us in their traditional explanation of the words " all that God commanded you by the hand of Moses " (Num. xv. 23) ; for they say, " Hence we learn that those who follow idolatry deny as it were their adhesion to the whole Law, and those who reject idolatry follow as it were the whole Law." (B. T. Kidd, 40*a*.) Note it.

CHAPTER XXX

ON examining these old and foolish doctrines we find that it was most generally believed by the people that by the worship of stars the earth will become inhabited, and the ground fertilized. The wise, pious, and sin-fearing men among them reproved the people and taught them that agriculture, on which the preservation of mankind depended, would become perfect and satisfy man's wishes, when he worshipped the sun and the stars. If man provoked these beings by his rebelliousness, the towns would become empty and waste. In the above-named books it is stated that Mars was angry with [lands, that form now] deserts and wastes, and in consequence of that anger they were deprived of water and trees, and have become the habitation of demons. Tillers of the ground and husbandmen are praised in those books, because they are engaged with the cultivation of the land in accordance with the will and desire of the stars. The idolaters also held cattle in esteem on account of their use in agriculture, and went even so far as to say, that it is not allowed to slay them, because they combine in themselves strength and willingness to do the work of man in tilling the ground. The oxen, notwithstanding their great strength, do this, and submit to man, because it is the will of God that they should be employed in agriculture. When these views became generally known, idolatry was connected with agriculture, because the latter is indispensable for the maintenance of man, and of most animals. The idolatrous priests then preached to the people who met in the temples, and taught them that by certain religious acts, rain would come down, the trees of the field would yield their fruit, and the land would be fertile and inhabited. See what is said in the

Nabatean Agriculture in the chapter on vineyards. The following words of the Sabeans are quoted there : " All ancient wise men advised, and prophets likewise commanded and enjoined to play before the images on certain instruments during the festivals. They also said—and what they said is true—that the deities are pleased with it, and reward those who do it. They promise, indeed, very great reward for these things ; e.g., length of life, protection from illness, exemption from great bodily deformities, plenty of the produce of the earth, and of the fruits of the trees." These are the words of the Sabeans. When these ideas spread, and were considered as true, God, in His great mercy for us, intended to remove this error from our minds, and to protect our bodies from trouble ; and therefore desired us to discontinue the practice of these useless actions. He gave us His Law through Moses, our teacher, who told us in the name of God, that the worship of stars and other corporeal beings would effect that rain would cease, the land be waste, and would not produce anything, and the fruit of the trees would wither ; calamities would befall the people, their bodies would be deformed, and life would be shortened. These are the contents of " the words of the covenant which God made " (Deut. xxviii. 6–9). It is frequently expressed in all parts of Scripture, that the worship of the stars would be followed by absence of rain, devastation of the land, bad times, diseases, and shortness of life. But abandonment of that worship, and the return to the service of God, would be the cause of the presence of rain, fertility of the ground, good times, health and length of life. Thus Scripture teaches, in order that man should abandon idolatry, the reverse of that which idolatrous priests preached to the people, for, as has been shown by us, the principal object of the Law is to remove this doctrine, and to destroy its traces.

CHAPTER XXXI

THERE are persons who find it difficult to give a reason for any of the commandments, and consider it right to assume that the commandments and prohibitions have no rational basis whatever. They are led to adopt this theory by a certain disease in their soul, the existence of which they perceive, but which they are unable to discuss or to describe. For they imagine that these precepts, if they were useful in any respect, and were commanded because of their usefulness, would seem to originate in the thought and reason of some intelligent being. But as things which are not objects of reason and serve no purpose, they would undoubtedly be attributed to God, because no thought of man could have produced them. According to the theory of those weak-minded persons, man is more perfect than his Creator. For what man says or does has a certain object, whilst the actions of God are different ; He commands us to do what is of no use to us, and forbids us to do what is harmless. Far be this ! On the contrary, the sole object of the Law is to benefit us. Thus we explained the Scriptural passage, " for our good always, that He might preserve us alive, as it is this day " (Deut. vi. 24). Again, " which shall hear all those statutes (*ḥukkim*), and say, surely this great nation is a wise and understanding people " (*ibid.* iv. 6). He thus says that even every one of these " statutes " convinces all nations of the wisdom and understanding it includes. But if no reason could be found for these statutes, if they produced no advantage and removed no evil, why then should he who believes in them and follows them be wise, reasonable, and so excellent as to raise the admiration of all nations ? But the truth is undoubtedly as we have said, that every one of the six hundred and thirteen precepts serves to inculcate some truth, to remove some erroneous opinion, to establish proper relations in society, to diminish evil, to train in good manners, or to warn against bad habits. All this depends on three things : opinions, morals, and social conduct. We do not count words, because precepts, whether positive or negative, if they relate to speech, belong to those precepts which regulate our social conduct, or to those which spread truth, or to those which teach morals. Thus these three principles suffice for assigning a reason for every one of the Divine commandments.

CHAPTER XXXII

On considering the Divine acts, or the processes of Nature, we get an insight into the prudence and wisdom of God as displayed in the creation of animals, with the gradual development of the movements of their limbs and the relative positions of the latter, and we perceive also His wisdom and plan in the successive and gradual development of the whole condition of each individual. The gradual development of the animals' movements and the relative position of the limbs may be illustrated by the brain. The front part is very soft, the back part is a little hard, the spinal marrow is still harder, and the farther it extends the harder it becomes. The nerves are the organs of sensation and motion. Some nerves are only required for sensation, or for slight movements, as, e.g., the movement of the eyelids or of the jaws ; these nerves originate in the brain. The nerves which are required for the movements of the limbs come from the spinal marrow. But nerves, even those that come directly from the spinal cord, are too soft to set the joints in motion ; therefore God made the following arrangement : the nerves branch out into fibres which are covered with flesh, and become muscles ; the nerves that come forth at the extremities of the muscles and have already commenced to harden, and to combine with hard pieces of ligaments, are the sinews which are joined and attached to the limbs. By this gradual development the nerves are enabled to set the limbs in motion. I quote this one instance because it is the most evident of the wonders described in the book On the use of the limbs ; but the use of the limbs is clearly perceived by all who examine them with a sharp eye. In a similar manner did God provide for each individual animal of the class of mammalia. When such an animal is born it is extremely tender, and cannot be fed with dry food. Therefore breasts were provided which yield milk, and the young can be fed with moist food which corresponds to the condition of the limbs of the animal, until the latter have gradually become dry and hard.

Many precepts in our Law are the result of a similar course adopted by the same Supreme Being. It is, namely, impossible to go suddenly from one extreme to the other ; it is therefore according to the nature of man impossible for him suddenly to discontinue everything to which he has been accustomed. Now God sent Moses to make [the Israelites] a kingdom of priests and a holy nation (Exod. xix. 6) by means of the knowledge of God.

Comp. " Unto thee it was showed that thou mightest know that the Lord is God " (Deut. iv. 35) ; " Know therefore this day, and consider it in thine heart, that the Lord is God " (*ibid.* v. 39). The Israelites were commanded to devote themselves to His service ; comp. " and to serve him with all your heart " (*ibid.* xi. 13) ; " and you shall serve the Lord your God " (Exod. xxiii. 25) ; " and ye shall serve him " (Deut. xiii. 5). But the custom which was in those days general among all men, and the general mode of worship in which the Israelites were brought up, consisted in sacrificing animals in those temples which contained certain images, to bow down to those images, and to burn incense before them ; religious and ascetic persons were in those days the persons that were devoted to the service in the temples erected to the stars, as has been explained by us. It was in accordance with the wisdom and plan of God, as displayed in the whole Creation, that He did not command us to give up and to discontinue all these manners of service ; for to obey such a commandment it would have been contrary to the nature of man, who generally cleaves to that to which he is used ; it would in those days have made the same impression as a prophet would make at present if he called us to the service of God and told us in His name, that we should not pray to Him, not fast, not seek His help in time of trouble ; that we should serve Him in thought, and not by any action. For this reason God allowed these kinds of service to continue ; He transferred to His service that which had formerly served as a worship of created beings, and of things imaginary and unreal, and commanded us to serve Him in the same manner ; viz., to build unto Him a temple ; comp. " And they shall make unto me a sanctuary " (Exod. xxv. 8) ; to have the altar erected to His name ; comp. " An altar of earth thou shalt make unto me " (*ibid.* xx. 21) ; to offer the sacrifices to Him ; comp. " If any man of you bring an offering unto the Lord " (Lev. i. 2), to bow down to Him and to burn incense before Him. He has forbidden to do any of these things to any other being ; comp. " He who sacrificeth unto any God, save the Lord only, he shall be utterly destroyed " (Exod. xxii. 19) ; " For thou shalt bow down to no other God " (*ibid.* xxxiv. 14). He selected priests for the service in the temple ; comp. " And they shall minister unto me in the priest's office " (*ibid.* xxviii. 41). He made it obligatory that certain gifts, called the gifts of the Levites and the priests, should be assigned to them for their maintenance while they are engaged in the service of the temple and its sacrifices. By this Divine plan it was effected that the traces of idolatry were blotted out, and the truly great principle of our faith, the Existence and Unity of God, was firmly established ; this result was thus obtained without deterring or confusing the minds of the people by the abolition of the service to which they were accustomed and which alone was familiar to them. I know that you will at first thought reject this idea and find it strange ; you will put the following question to me in your heart : How can we suppose that Divine commandments, prohibitions, and important acts, which are fully explained, and for which certain seasons are fixed, should not have been commanded for their own sake, but only for the sake of some other thing ; as if they were only the means which He employed for His primary object ? What prevented Him from making His primary object a direct commandment to us, and to give us the capacity of obeying it ? Those precepts which in your opinion are only the means and not the object would then have been unnecessary. Hear my answer, which will cure your heart of this disease and will show you the truth of that which I have pointed out to you. There occurs in the Law a passage which contains exactly the same idea; it is the following: " God led them not through the way of the land of the Philistines, although that was near; for God said, Lest peradventure the people repent when they see war, and they return to Egypt; but God led the people about, through the way of the wilderness of the Red Sea," etc. (Exod. xiii. 17). Here God led the people about, away from the direct road which He originally intended, because He feared they might meet on that way with hardships too great for their ordinary strength; He took them by another road in order to obtain thereby His original object. In the same manner God refrained from prescribing what the people by their natural disposition would be incapable of obeying, and gave the above-mentioned commandments as a means of securing His chief object, viz., to spread a knowledge of Him [among the people], and to cause them to reject idolatry. It is contrary to man's nature that he should suddenly abandon all the different kinds of Divine service and the different customs in which he has been brought up, and which have been so general, that they were considered as a matter of course; it would be just as if a person trained to work as a slave with mortar and bricks, or similar things, should interrupt his work, clean his hands, and at once fight with real giants. It was the result of God's wisdom that the Israelites were led about in the wilderness till they acquired courage. For it is a well-known fact that travelling in the wilderness, and privation of bodily enjoyments, such as bathing, produce courage, whilst the reverse is the source of faint-heartedness; besides, another generation rose during the wanderings that had not been accustomed to degradation and slavery. All the travelling in the wilderness was regulated by Divine commands through Moses; comp. " At the commandment of the Lord they rested, and at the commandment of the Lord they journeyed; they kept the charge of the Lord and the commandment of the Lord by the hand of Moses " (Num. ix. 23). In the same way the portion of the Law under discussion is the result of divine wisdom, according to which people are allowed to continue the kind of worship to which they have been accustomed, in order that they might acquire the true faith, which is the chief object [of God's commandments]. You ask, What could have prevented God from commanding us directly, that which is the chief object, and from giving us the capacity of obeying it ? This would lead to a second question, What prevented God from leading the Israelites through the way of the land of the Philistines, and endowing them with strength for fighting ? The leading about by a pillar of cloud by day and a pillar of fire by night would then not have been necessary. A third question would then be asked in reference to the good promised as reward for the keeping of the commandments, and the evil foretold as a punishment for sins. It is the following question: As it is the chief object and purpose of God that we should believe in the Law, and act according to that which is written therein, why has He not given us the capacity of continually believing in it, and following its guidance, instead of holding out to us reward for obedience, and punishment for disobedience, or of actually giving all the predicted reward and punishment ? For [the promises and the threats] are but the means of leading to this chief object. What prevented Him from giving us, as part of our nature, the will to do that which He desires us to do, and to abandon the kind of worship which He rejects ? There is one general answer to these three questions, and to all questions of the same character ; it is this : Although in every one of the signs [related in Scripture] the natural property of some individual being is changed, the nature of man is never changed by God by way of miracle. It is in accordance with this important principle that God said, " O that there were such an heart in them, that they would fear me," etc. (Deut. v. 26). It is also for this reason that He distinctly stated the commandments and the prohibitions, the reward and the punishment. This principle as regards miracles has been frequently explained by us in our works ; I do not say this because I believe that it is difficult for God to change the nature of every individual person ; on the contrary, it is possible, and it is in His power, according to the principles taught in Scripture ; but it has never been His will to do it, and it never will be. If it were part of His will to change [at His desire] the nature of any person, the mission of prophets and the giving of the Law would have been altogether superfluous.

I now return to my theme. As the sacrificial service is not the primary object [of the commandments about sacrifice], whilst supplications, prayers, and similar kinds of worship are nearer to the primary object, and indispensable for obtaining it, a great difference was made in the Law between these two kinds of service. The one kind, which consists in offering sacrifices, although the sacrifices are offered to the name of God, has not been made obligatory for us to the same extent as it had been before. We were not commanded to sacrifice in every place, and in every time, or to build a temple in every place, or to permit any one who desires to become priest and to sacrifice. On the contrary, all this is prohibited unto us. Only one temple has been appointed, " in the place which the Lord shall choose " (Deut. xii. 26) ; in no other place is it allowed to sacrifice ; comp. " Take heed to thyself, that thou offer not thy burnt-offerings in every place that thou seest " (*ibid.* v. 13) ; and only the members of a particular family were allowed to officiate as priests. All these restrictions served to limit this kind of worship, and keep it within those bounds within which God did not think it necessary to abolish sacrificial service altogether. But prayer and supplication can be offered everywhere and by every person. The same is the case with the commandment of ziẓit (Num. xv. 38) ; *mezuzah* (Deut. vi. 9 ; xi. 20) ; *tefillin* (Exod. xiii. 9, 16) ; and similar kinds of divine service.

Because of this principle which I explained to you, the Prophets in their books are frequently found to rebuke their fellow-men for being over-zealous and exerting themselves too much in bringing sacrifices ; the prophets thus distinctly declared that the object of the sacrifices is not very essential, and that God does not require them. Samuel therefore said, " Hath the Lord as great delight in burnt-offerings and sacrifices as in obeying the voice of the Lord " (1 Sam. xv. 22) ? Isaiah exclaimed, " To what purpose is the multitude of your sacrifices unto me ? saith the Lord " (Isa. i. 11) ; Jeremiah declared : " For I spake not unto your fathers, nor commanded them in the day that I brought them out of the land of Egypt, concerning burnt-offerings or sacrifices. But this thing commanded I them, saying, Obey my voice, and

I will be your God, and ye shall be my people " (Jer. vii. 22, 23). This passage has been found difficult in the opinion of all those whose words I read or heard ; they ask, How can Jeremiah say that God did not command us about burnt-offering and sacrifice, seeing so many precepts refer to sacrifice ? The sense of the passage agrees with what I explained to you. Jeremiah says [in the name of God] the primary object of the precepts is this, Know me, and serve no other being ; " I will be your God, and ye shall be my people " (Lev. xxvi. 12). But the commandment that sacrifices shall be brought and that the temple shall be visited has for its object the success of that principle among you ; and for its sake I have transferred these modes of worship to my name ; idolatry shall thereby be utterly destroyed, and Jewish faith firmly established. You, however, have ignored this object, and taken hold of that which is only the means of obtaining it ; you have doubted my existence, " ye have denied the Lord, and said he is not " (Jer. v. 12) ; ye served idols ; " burnt incense unto Baal, and walked after other gods whom ye know not. And come and stand before me in this house " (*ibid.* vii. 9–10) ; i.e., you do not go beyond attending the temple of the Lord, and offering sacrifices ; but this is not the chief object.—I have another way of explaining this passage with exactly the same result. For it is distinctly stated in Scripture, and handed down by tradition, that the first commandments communicated to us did not include any law at all about burnt-offering and sacrifice. You must not see any difficulty in the Passover which was commanded in Egypt ; there was a particular and evident reason for that, as will be explained by me (chap. xlvi.). Besides it was revealed in the land of Egypt ; whilst the laws to which Jeremiah alludes in the above passage are those which were revealed after the departure from Egypt. For this reason it is distinctly added, " in the day that I brought them out from the land of Egypt." The first commandment after the departure from Egypt was given at Marah, in the following words, " If thou wilt diligently hearken to the voice of the Lord thy God, and wilt do that which is right in His sight, and wilt give ear to His commandments " (Exod. xv. 26). " There he made for them a statute and an ordinance, and there he proved them " (*ibid.* ver. 25). According to the true traditional explanation, Sabbath and civil laws were revealed at Marah ; " statute " alludes to Sabbath, and " ordinance " to civil laws, which are the means of removing injustice. The chief object of the Law, as has been shown by us, is the teaching of truths ; to which the truth of the *creatio ex nihilo* belongs. It is known that the object of the law of Sabbath is to confirm and to establish this principle, as we have shown in this treatise (Part. II. chap. xxxi.). In addition to the teaching of truths the Law aims at the removal of injustice from mankind. We have thus proved that the first laws do not refer to burnt-offering and sacrifice, which are of secondary importance. The same idea which is contained in the above passage from Jeremiah is also expressed in the Psalms, where the people are rebuked that they ignore the chief object, and make no distinction between chief and subsidiary lessons. The Psalmist says : " Hear, O my people, and I will speak ; O Israel, and I will testify against thee : I am God, even thy God. I will not reprove thee for thy sacrifices or thy burnt-offerings, they have been continually before me. I will take no bullock out of thy house, nor he-goats out of thy folds " (Ps. l.

29).—Wherever this subject is mentioned, this is its meaning. Consider it well, and reflect on it.

CHAPTER XXXIII

IT is also the object of the perfect Law to make man reject, despise, and reduce his desires as much as is in his power. He should only give way to them when absolutely necessary. It is well known that it is intemperance in eating, drinking, and sexual intercourse that people mostly rave and indulge in; and these very things counteract the ulterior perfection of man, impede at the same time the development of his first perfection, and generally disturb the social order of the country and the economy of the family. For by following entirely the guidance of lust, in the manner of fools, man loses his intellectual energy, injures his body, and perishes before his natural time; sighs and cares multiply; there is an increase of envy, hatred, and warfare for the purpose of taking what another possesses. The cause of all this is the circumstance that the ignorant considers physical enjoyment as an object to be sought for its own sake. God in His wisdom has therefore given us such commandments as would counteract that object, and prevent us altogether from directing our attention to it, and has debarred us from everything that leads only to excessive desire and lust. This is an important thing included in the objects of our Law. See how the Law commanded to slay a person from whose conduct it is evident that he will go too far in seeking the enjoyment of eating and drinking. I mean "the rebellious and stubborn son"; he is described as "a glutton and a drunkard" (Deut. xxi. 20). The Law commands to stone him and to remove him from society lest he grow up in this character, and kill many, and injure the condition of good men by his great lust.

Politeness is another virtue promoted by the Law. Man shall listen to the words of his neighbour; he shall not be obstinate, but shall yield to the wish of his fellow-men, respond to their appeal, act according to their desire, and do what they like. Thus the Law commands, "Circumcise therefore the foreskin of your heart, and be no more stiff-necked" (Deut. x. 16); "Take heed and hearken" (*ibid.* xxvii. 9). "If you be willing and obedient" (Isa. i. 19). Those who listen [to the words of others] and accept as much as is right are represented as saying, "We will hear and do" (Deut. v. 24), or in a figurative style, "Draw me, we will run after thee" (Song i. 4).

The Law is also intended to give its followers purity and holiness; by teaching them to suppress sensuality, to guard against it and to reduce it to a minimum, as will be explained by us. For when God commanded [Moses] to sanctify the people for the receiving of the Law, and said, "Sanctify them to-day and to-morrow" (Exod. xix. 10), Moses [in obedience to this command] said to the people, "Come not at your wives" (*ibid.* ver. 15). Here it is clearly stated that sanctification consists in absence of sensuality. But abstinence from drinking wine is also called holiness; in reference to the Nazarite it is therefore said, "He shall be holy" (Num. vi. 5). According to Siphra the words, "sanctify yourselves and be ye holy" (Lev. xx. 7), refer to the sanctification effected by performing the divine commands. As the obedience to such precepts as have been mentioned above is called by the Law sanctification and purification, so is defilement applied to the trans-gression of these precepts and the performance of disgraceful acts, as will be shown.   Cleanliness in dress and body by washing and removing sweat and dirt is included among the various objects of the Law, but only if connected with purity of action, and with a heart free from low principles and bad habits.   It would be extremely bad for man to content himself with a purity obtained by washing and cleanliness in dress, and to be at the same time voluptuous and unrestrained in food and lust.   These are described by Isaiah as follows : " They that sanctify themselves and purify themselves in the gardens, but continue their sinful life, when they are in the innermost [of their houses], eating swine's flesh, and the abomination, and the mouse " (Isa. lxvi. 17) : that is to say, they purify and sanctify themselves outwardly as much as is exposed to the sight of the people, and when they are alone in their chambers and the inner parts of their houses, they continue their rebelliousness and disobedience, and indulge in partaking of forbidden food, such as [the flesh of] swine, worms, and mice.   The prophet alludes perhaps in the phrase " behind one tree in the midst " to indulgence in forbidden lust.   The sense of the passage is therefore this : They appear outwardly clean, but their heart is bent upon their desires and bodily enjoyments, and this is contrary to the spirit of the Law.   For the chief object of the Law is to [teach man to] diminish his desires, and to cleanse his outer appearance after he has purified his heart.   Those who wash their body and cleanse their garments whilst they remain dirty by bad actions and principles, are de-scribed by Solomon as " a generation that are pure in their own eyes, and yet are not washed from their filthiness ; a generation, oh how lofty are their eyes ! " etc. (Prov. xxx. 12–13).   Consider well the principles which we mentioned in this chapter as the final causes of the Law ; for there are many precepts, for which you will be unable to give a reason unless you possess a knowledge of these principles, as will be explained further on.

CHAPTER XXXIV

IT is also important to note that the Law does not take into account excep-tional circumstances ; it is not based on conditions which rarely occur. Whatever the Law teaches, whether it be of an intellectual, a moral, or a practical character, is founded on that which is the rule and not on that which is the exception ; it ignores the injury that might be caused to a single person through a certain maxim or a certain divine precept.   For the Law is a divine institution, and [in order to understand its operation] we must con-sider how in Nature the various forces produce benefits which are general, but in some solitary cases they cause also injury.   This is clear from what has been said by ourselves as well as by others.   We must consequently not be surprised when we find that the object of the Law does not fully appear in every individual ; there must naturally be people who are not perfected by the instruction of the Law, just as there are beings which do not receive from the specific forms in Nature all that they require.   For all this comes from one God, is the result of one act ; " they are all given from one shep-herd " (Eccles. xii. 11).   It is impossible to be otherwise ; and we have al-ready explained (chap. xv.) that that which is impossible always remains impossible and never changes. From this consideration it also follows that the laws cannot like medicine vary according to the different conditions of persons and times ; whilst the cure of a person depends on his particular constitution at the particular time, the divine guidance contained in the Law must be certain and general, although it may be effective in some cases and ineffective in others. If the Law depended on the varying conditions of man, it would be imperfect in its totality, each precept being left indefinite. For this reason it would not be right to make the fundamental principles of the Law dependent on a certain time or a certain place ; on the contrary, the statutes and the judgments must be definite, unconditional, and general, in accordance with the divine words : " As for the congregation, one ordinance shall be for you and for the stranger " (Num. xv. 15) ; they are intended, as has been stated before, for all persons and for all times.

After having premised these introductory remarks I will now proceed to the exposition of that which I intended to explain

CHAPTER XXXV

In accordance with this intention I find it convenient to divide all precepts into fourteen classes.

The first class comprises those precepts which form fundamental principles, such as we have enumerated in *Hilkot yesode ha-torah*. Repentance and fasts belong also to this class, as will be shown.

The second class comprises the precepts which are connected with the prohibition of idolatry, and which have been described by us in *Hilkot a·bodah-zarah*. The laws concerning garments of linen and wool, concerning the fruit of trees in the first three years after they have been planted, and concerning divers seeds in a vineyard, are likewise contained in this class. The object of these precepts is to establish certain true principles and to perpetuate them among the people.

The third class is formed by commandments which are connected with the improvement of the moral condition [of mankind] ; these are mentioned in *Hilkot de·ot*. It is known that by a good moral state those social relations, which are indispensable for the well-being of mankind, are brought to perfection.

The fourth class includes precepts relating to charity, loans, gifts, and the like, e.g., the rules respecting " valuations," (scil., of things devoted to sacred purposes, Lev. xxvii. 1–27) ; " things devoted " (*ibid*. ver. 28) ; laws concerning loans and servants, and all the laws enumerated in the section *Zera·im*, except the rules of " mixtures " and " the fruit of trees in the first three years." The object of these precepts is clear ; their benefit concerns all people by turns ; for he who is rich to-day may one day be poor—either he himself or his descendants ; and he who is now poor, he himself or his son may be rich to-morrow.

The fifth class contains those precepts which relate to the prevention of wrong and violence ; they are included in our book in the section *Nezikin*. Their beneficial character is evident.

The sixth class is formed of precepts respecting fines, e.g., the laws on theft and robbery, on false witnesses, and most of the laws contained in the section *Shofetim* belong to this class. Their benefit is apparent; for if sinners and robbers were not punished, injury would not be prevented at all : and persons scheming evil would not become rarer. They are wrong who suppose that it would be an act of mercy to abandon the laws of compensation for injuries ; on the contrary, it would be perfect cruelty and injury to the social state of the country. It is an act of mercy that God commanded "judges and officers thou shalt appoint to thee in all thy gates " (Deut. xvi. 18).

The seventh class comprises those laws which regulate the business transactions of men with each other ; e.g., laws about loans, hire, trust, buying, selling, and the like ; the rules about inheritance belong to this class. We have described these precepts in the sections *Kinyan* and *Mishpatim*. The object of these precepts is evident, for monetary transactions are necessary for the peoples of all countries, and it is impossible to have these transactions without a proper standard of equity and without useful regulations.

The eighth class includes those precepts which relate to certain days, as Sabbaths and holydays ; they are enumerated in the section *Zemannim*. The Law states clearly the reason and object of each of these precepts ; they are to serve as a means for establishing a certain principle among us, or securing bodily recreation, or effecting both things at the same time, as will be shown by me.

The ninth class comprises the general laws concerning religious rites and ceremonies, e.g., laws concerning prayers, the reading of Shema', and the other rules given in the section *Ahabah*, with the exception of the law concerning circumcision. The object of these laws is apparent ; they all prescribe actions which firmly establish the love of God in our minds, as also the right belief concerning Him and His attributes.

The tenth class is formed of precepts which relate to the Sanctuary, its vessels, and its ministers ; they are contained in the section *'Abodah*. The object of these precepts has already been mentioned by us (*supra*, chap. xxxii.).

The eleventh class includes those precepts which relate to Sacrifices. Most of these laws we have mentioned in the sections *'Abodah* and *Korbanot*. We have already shown the general use of the sacrificial laws, and their necessity in ancient time.

The twelfth class comprises the laws concerning things unclean and clean. The general object of these laws is, as will be explained by me, to discourage people from [frequently] entering the Sanctuary ; in order that their minds be impressed with the greatness of the Sanctuary, and approach it with respect and reverence.

The thirteenth class includes the precepts concerning forbidden food and the like ; we have given them in *Hilkot maakalot asurot* ; the laws about vows and temperance belong also to this class. The object of all these laws is to restrain the growth of desire, the indulgence in seeking that which is pleasant, and the disposition to consider the appetite for eating and drinking as the end [of man's existence]. We have explained this in our Commentary on the Mishnah, in the Introduction (chap. iv.) to *The Sayings of the Fathers*.

The fourteenth class comprises the precepts concerning forbidden sexual intercourse ; they are given in the section *Nashim* and *Hilkot issure-biah*.

The laws concerning the intermixture of cattle belong to this class. The object of these precepts is likewise to diminish sexual intercourse, to restrain as much as possible indulgence in lust, and [to teach] that this enjoyment is not, as foolish people think, the final cause of man's existence. We have explained this in our Commentary on *The Sayings of the Fathers* (Introd., chap. viii.). The laws about circumcision belong to this class.

As is well known, the precepts are also divided into two classes, viz., precepts concerning the relation between man and God, and precepts concerning the relation between man and man. Of the classes into which we divide the precepts and which we have enumerated, the fifth, sixth, and seventh, and part of the third, include laws concerning the relation of man to man. The other classes contain the laws about the relation of man tô God, i.e., positive or negative precepts, which tend to improve the moral or intellectual condition of mankind, or to regulate such of each man's actions which [directly] only concern him and lead him to perfection. For these are called laws concerning man's relation to God, although in reality they lead to results which concern also his fellow-men; because these results become only apparent after a long series of intermediate links, and from a general point of view; whilst directly these laws are not intended to prevent man from injuring his fellow-man. Note this.

Having described the laws of these classes, I will now again consider the precepts of each class, and explain the reason and use of those which are believed to be useless or unreasonable, with the exception of a few, the object of which I have not yet comprehended.

CHAPTER XXXVI

THE reason of all precepts of the first class, viz., of the principles enumerated by us in the *Hilkot yesode ha-torah*, is obvious. Consider them one by one, and you will find that the lesson which every one of them contains is correct and demonstrable. It is also evident that the precepts which exhort and command us to learn and to teach are useful; for without wisdom there cannot be any good act or any true knowledge. The law which prescribes to honour the teachers of the Law is likewise useful; for if they were not considered by the people as great and honourable men, they would not be followed as guides in their principles and actions. The Law demands also that we be humble and modest [in their presence]. "Thou shalt rise up before the hoary head" (Lev. xix. 32). This class includes also the commandment to swear by the name of God and the prohibition of swearing falsely or in vain. The reason for all these precepts is evident; they aim at the glorification of God; they prescribe acts which lead to the belief in God's greatness. Likewise the commandment to cry to God in time of trouble, "to blow an alarm with the trumpets" (Num. x. 9), belongs to this class. We are told to offer up prayers to God, in order to establish firmly the true principle that God takes notice of our ways, that He can make them successful if we worship Him, or disastrous if we disobey Him, that [success and failure] are not the result of chance or accident. In this sense we must understand the passage, "If ye walk with me by chance" (*beḳeri*, Lev. xxvi. 21); i.e., if I bring troubles upon you for punishment, and you consider them as mere accidents, I will again send you some of these accidents as you call them, but of a more serious and troublesome character. This is expressed in the words : " If ye walk with me by chance : then I will walk with you also in the fury of chance " (*ibid.* vers. 27, 28). For the belief of the people that their troubles are mere accidents causes them to continue in their evil principles and their wrong actions, and prevents them from abandoning their evil ways. Comp. " Thou hast stricken them, but they have not grieved " (Jer. v. 3). For this reason God commanded us to pray to Him, to entreat Him, and to cry before Him in time of trouble. It is clear that repentance is likewise included in this class ; that is to say, it is one of those principles which are an indispensable element in the creed of the followers of the Law. For it is impossible for man to be entirely free from error and sin ; he either does not know the opinion which he has to choose, or he adopts a principle, not for its own merits, but in order to gratify his desire or passion. If we were convinced that we could never make our crooked ways straight, we should for ever continue in our errors, and perhaps add other sins to them since we did not see that any remedy was left to us. But the belief in the effect of repentance causes us to improve, to return to the best of the ways, and to become more perfect than we were before we sinned. For this reason many things are prescribed for the promotion of this very useful principle ; e.g., confessions and sacrifices for sins committed unknowingly, and in some cases even for sins committed intentionally, and fasts, and that which is common to all cases of repentance from sin, the resolve to discontinue sinning. For that is the aim of this principle. Of all these precepts the use is obvious.

CHAPTER XXXVII

THE precepts of the second class are those which we have enumerated in the section " On idolatry." It is doubtless that they all tend to save man from the error of idolatry and the evil practices connected with it ; e.g., observing the times, enchantment, witchcraft, incantation, consulting with familiar spirits, and the like. When you read the books which I mentioned to you, you will find that witchcraft, which will be described to you, is part of the customs of the Sabeans, Kasdim, Chaldeans, and to a higher degree of the Egyptians and Canaanites. They caused others to believe, or they themselves believed, that by means of these arts they would perform wonderful things in reference to an individual person, or to the inhabitants of a whole country, although no analogy and no reasoning can discover any relation between these performances of the witches and the promised result. Thus they are careful to collect certain plants at a particular time, and to take a definite number of certain objects. There are many things comprised by witchcraft ; they may be divided into three classes : first, witchcraft connected with objects in Nature, viz., plants, animals, or minerals. Secondly, witchcraft dependent for its performance on a certain time ; and thirdly, witchcraft dependent on the performance of certain acts of man, such as dancing, clapping, laughing, jumping with one leg, lying on the ground with the face upward, burning a thing, fumigating with a certain material, or speaking intelligible or unintelligible words.

These are the various kinds of witchcraft. In some cases all these various performances are required. Thus the witches sometimes order : take a leaf of a certain plant, when the moon is seen in a certain degree [of the Zodiac] in the east point or in one of the other cardinal points [of the horizon], also a certain quantity of the horn, the sweat, the hair and the blood of a certain animal when the sun is, e.g., in the middle of the sky, or in some other definite place ; and a portion of a certain mineral or minerals, melted at a certain conjunction of sun and moon, and at a definite position of the stars ; speak then, and say certain words, and fumigate with those leaves or similar ones to that molten image, and such and such a thing will happen. In other instances of witchcraft it is assumed that one of the above performances suffices. In most cases the condition is added that women must perform these actions. Thus it is stated in reference to the means of obtaining rain, that ten virgins dressed with diadems and red garments should dance, push each other, moving backwards and forwards, and make signs to the sun : the result of this long process was believed [by the idolaters] to be a downpour of rain.

It is further stated that if four women lay on their back, with their feet spread and lifted up, said certain words and did certain things whilst in this disgraceful position, hail would discontinue coming down in that place. The number of these stupid and mad things is great ; in all of them without exception women are required to be the agent. Witchcraft is intimately connected with astrology ; those that practise it assign each plant, animal, or mineral to a certain star, and believe that the above processes of witchcraft are different forms of worship offered to that star, which is pleased with that act, word, or offering of incense, and fulfils their wishes.

After this remark, which you will understand when you have read such of their works as are at present extant, and have been mentioned by me, hear what I will tell you. It is the object and centre of the whole Law to abolish idolatry and utterly uproot it, and to overthrow the opinion that any of the stars could interfere for good or evil in human matters, because it leads to the worship of stars. It was therefore necessary to slay all witches as being undoubtedly idolaters, because every witch is an idolater ; they only have their own strange ways of worship, which are different from the common mode of worship offered to those deities. But in all performances of witchcraft it is laid down as a rule that women should be employed in the chief operation ; and therefore the Law says, " Thou shalt not suffer a witch to live " (Exod. xxii. 17). Another reason is the natural reluctance of people to slay women. This is also the cause why in the law of idolatry it is said " man or woman " (Deut. xvii. 2), and again repeated a second time, " the man or the woman " (*ibid*. ver. 5)—a phrase which does not occur in the law about the breaking of Sabbath, or in any other law ; for great sympathy is naturally shown to women. Now the witches believed that they produced a certain result by their witchcraft ; that they were able through the above-mentioned actions to drive such dangerous animals as lions, serpents, and the like out of the cities, and to remove various kinds of damage from the products of the earth. Thus they imagine that they are able by certain acts to prevent hail from coming down, and by certain other acts to kill the worms in the vineyards, whereby the latter are protected from injury ; in fact, the killing of the worms in vineyards, and other superstitions mentioned in the *Nabatean Agriculture*, are fully described by the Sabeans. They likewise imagine that they know certain acts by which they can prevent the dropping of leaves from the trees and the untimely falling of their fruit. On account of these ideas, which were general in those days, the Law declares in " the words of the covenant " as follows : The same idolatry and superstitious perfor- mances which, in your belief, keep certain misfortunes far from you, will cause those very misfortunes to befall you. " I will also send wild beasts among you " (Lev. xxvi. 22) ; " I will also send the teeth of wild beasts upon them, with the poison of those that creep in dust " (Deut. xxxii. 24). " The fruit of thy land, and all thy labours, shall a nation, which thou knowest not, eat up " (*ibid.* xxviii. 33). " Thou shalt plant vineyards and dress them, but shalt neither drink of the wine nor gather the grapes, etc. Thou shalt have olive trees throughout all thy coasts, but thou shalt not anoint thyself with the oil " (Deut. xxviii. 39, 40). In short, in spite of the schemes of idolaters to support and firmly establish their doctrine, and to make people believe that by idolatry certain misfortunes could be averted and certain benefits gained, worship of idols will, on the contrary, as is stated in " the words of the covenant," prevent the advantages and bring the troubles. The reader will now understand why, of all kinds of curses and blessings, those mentioned in " the words of the covenant " have been selected by the Law, and particularly pointed out. Note also the greatness of the benefit [of these laws].

In order that we may keep far from all kinds of witchcraft, we are warned not to adopt any of the practices of the idolaters, even such as are connected with agriculture, the keeping of cattle, and similar work. [The Law pro- hibits] everything that the idolaters, according to their doctrine, and con- trary to reason, consider as being useful and acting in the manner of certain mysterious forces. Comp. " Neither shall ye walk in their ordinances " (Lev. xviii. 3). " And ye shall not walk in the manners of the nation which I cast out before you " (*ibid.* xx. 23). Our Sages call such acts " the ways of the Amorite " ; they are kinds of witchcraft, because they are not arrived at by reason, but are similar to the performances of witchcraft, which is necessarily connected with the influences of the stars ; thus [" the manners of the nations "] lead people to extol, worship, and praise the stars. Our Sages say distinctly, " whatever is used as medicine " does not come under the law of " the ways of the Amorite " ; for they hold that only such cures as are recommended by reason are permitted, and other cures are prohibited. When, therefore, the dictum was quoted : a tree that casts off its fruit may be laden with stone or dyed with red colour, the following objection was raised : The loading of the tree with stones may be justified on the plea that it serves to weaken the strength of the tree, but why should it be permitted to dye the tree with red colour ? This question shows that the dyeing of the tree with red colour, and all similar things which are not explained by analogy from nature, are prohibited as " ways of the Amorite." For the same reason our Sages said, " The uterus of animals which have been selected for the Sanctuary must be buried ; it must not be suspended from a tree, and not buried in the cross-road, because this is one of ' the ways of the Amorite.' " Hence you may learn how to treat similar cases.

It is not inconsistent that a nail of the gallows and the tooth of a fox have been permitted to be used as cures ; for these things have been considered in those days as facts established by experiment. They served as cures, in the same manner as the hanging of the peony over a person subject to epileptic fits, or the application of a dog's refuse to the swellings of the throat, and of the vapours of vinegar and marcasite to the swelling of hard tumours. For the Law permits as medicine everything that has been verified by experiment, although it cannot be explained by analogy. The above-named cures are permitted in the same way as the application of purgatives. Learn, reader, these noteworthy lessons from this my work, and keep them ; " for they are a diadem of grace for thy head " (Prov. iv.).

We have explained in our large work that it is prohibited to round the corners of the head, and to mar the corners of the beard, because it was the custom of idolatrous priests. For the same reason, the wearing of garments made of linen and wool is prohibited ; the heathen priests adorned themselves with garments containing vegetable and animal material, whilst they held in their hand a seal made of a mineral. This you find written in their books. The same is also the reason of the precept, " The woman shall not wear that which pertaineth unto a man " (Deut. xxii. 5). You find it in the book Tomtom, that a male person should wear coloured woman's dress when he stands before Venus, and a female, when standing before Mars, should wear a buckler and other armour. I think that this precept has also another reason ; namely, that the interchange of dress creates lust and leads to immorality.

It is easily understood why it is prohibited to derive any benefit whatever from an idol. For sometimes a person buys it with the intention to break it, but keeps it, and it becomes a snare to him. Even if he broke it, recast it, and sold it to a heathen, he must not use the money which he received in exchange for the idol ; because people frequently mistake accidental circumstances for essential causes ; thus most people say of a certain person that he has become rich and wealthy after having dwelt in a certain house, or bought a certain animal or vessel ; and that these things were a blessing to him. In the same way a person may be successful and make a good profit on the business in which he employed the money received for the idol ; he might then think that the idol was the cause of his success, and that the blessing of the money received for it brought him the profit ; he would then believe in the idol ; a belief which is just the reverse of the chief object of the Law, as is clearly seen in every word of it. For this same reason, we are forbidden to turn to our use the covering of the idol, its offerings and vessels. We are thus guarded against the idea [of ascribing our success to idols]. In those days the belief in the stars was very strong ; it was generally assumed that life and death, good and evil, depended on the stars. The Law employed therefore strong means, as covenant, witnesses, great oaths, and the above-mentioned [blessings and] curses, in order to overthrow that belief. We are thus commanded to abstain from taking any portion of the idol, and deriving any benefit from it ; and God tells us that if money received for idols be mixed with any person's property, it will bring loss and ruin to that property. This warning is contained in the words : " Neither shalt thou bring an abomination into thine house, lest thou be a cursed thing like it " (Deut.

vii. 26). How much more wrong must it be to believe that there is a blessing in idols. When you examine all the precepts that relate to idolatry, you will find that their reason is obvious, and that they serve to make us abandon this evil belief, and keep at the greatest possible distance from it.

We must also point out that originators of false, baseless, and useless principles scheme and plan for the firm establishment of their faith; and tell their fellow-men that a certain plague will befall those who will not perform the act by which that faith is supported and confirmed for ever; this plague may one day accidentally befall a person, who will then direct his attention to the performance of that act, and adopt idolatry. It being well known that people are naturally most in fear and dread of the loss of their property and their children, the worshippers of fire spread the tale, that if any one did not pass his son and daughter through the fire, he will lose his children by death. There is no doubt that on account of this absurd menace every one at once obeyed, out of pity and sympathy for the child; especially as it was a trifling and a light thing that was demanded, in passing the child over the fire. We must further take into account that the care of young children is intrusted to women, who are generally weak-minded, and ready to believe everything, as is well known. The Law makes, therefore, an earnest stand against this practice, and uses in reference to it stronger terms than in any other kind of idolatry; namely, " he defileth my sanctuary, and profaneth my holy name " (Lev. xx. 3). The true prophet then declares in the name of God that the very act which is performed for the purpose of keeping the child alive, will bring death upon him who performs it, and destruction upon his seed. Comp. " And I will set my face against that man and against his family," etc. (*ibid.* xx. 5). Know that traces of this practice have survived even to the present day, because it was widespread in the world. You can see how midwives take a young child wrapped in its swaddling-clothes, and after having placed incense of a disagreeable smell on the fire, swing the child in the smoke over that fire. This is certainly a kind of passing children through the fire, and we must not do it. Reflect on the evil cunning of the author of this doctrine; how people continued to adhere to this doctrine, and how, in spite of the opposition of the Law during thousands of years, its name is not blotted out, and its traces are still in existence.

Idolaters have acted similarly in reference to property. They made it a law that a certain tree, the *asherah*, should be worshipped, and that of its fruit one part should be offered, and the rest consumed in the temple of the idol; this is stated in the regulations concerning the *asherah*. In the same manner, they made it a rule, that the first-fruit of every fruit-tree should be partly offered as a sacrifice and partly consumed in the idol's temple. It was also a widespread belief that if the first-fruit of any tree was not treated in this manner, the tree would dry up, its fruit would be cast off, its increase would be diminished, or some disease would come over it; just as they spread the belief that every child, that was not passed through the fire, must die. People in their anxiety for their property obeyed also this precept unhesitatingly. The Law, in opposition to this doctrine, commanded us to burn the produce of fruit-trees the first three years; for some trees bear fruit after one year, whilst some begin to yield fruit after two, and others after three years. The law is based upon the nature of trees grown in an ordinary way, namely, in one of the three well-known methods : planting, propagation, and inoculation (*neti'ah, habrakah,* and *harcabah*). The Law does not take notice of the case that a kernel or stone is sown ; for the ordinances of the Law are based on the usual condition of things, and as a rule a young tree in Palestine bears fruit for the first time not later than the third year after it has been planted. According to the divine promise, the waste and destruction of this first-fruit of the tree will be followed by years of plenty of fruit ; for it is said, " that it may increase unto you the fruit thereof " (Lev. xix. 25). The fruit of the fourth year we are commanded to eat before God, instead of [the heathen custom of] eating *'orlah,* " the fruit of the preceding years," in the temples of the idols, as has been described by us.

It is further mentioned in the *Nabatean Agriculture* that the ancient idolaters caused certain things named in that work to rot, waited till the sun stood in a certain degree [of the ecliptic], and then they performed many acts of witchcraft. They believed that that substance should be kept ready by every one, and when a fruit-tree is planted, a portion of that rotten substance should be scattered round the tree or under it ; the tree would then grow quicker and produce more fruit than is generally the case. They say that this process is very extraordinary ; it acts like a talisman, and is more efficient than any kind of witchcraft in accelerating the productiveness of fruit-trees. I have already shown and explained to you how the Law opposes all kinds of witchcraft. The Law, therefore, prohibits us to use the fruit yielded by a tree in the first three years after it has been planted, so that there should be no opportunity for accelerating, according to their imagination, the productiveness of any tree. After three years most fruit-trees in Palestine yield fruit by the ordinary course of nature, without the application of those magical performances which were very general in those days. Note this remarkable fact.

Another belief which was very common in those days, and survived the Sabeans, is this : When a tree is grafted into another in the time of a certain conjunction of sun and moon, and is fumigated with certain substances whilst a formula is uttered, that tree will produce a thing that will be found exceedingly useful. More general than anything mentioned by the heathen writers was the ceremony of grafting an olive branch upon a citron tree, as described in the beginning of the *Nabatean Agriculture.* I am of opinion that the book of medicines which Hezekiah put away (B. T. Pes. 56*a*) was undoubtedly of this kind. They also said that when one species is grafted upon another, the branch which is to be grafted must be in the hand of a beautiful damsel, whilst a male person has disgraceful and unnatural sexual intercourse with her ; during that intercourse the woman grafts the branch into the tree. There is no doubt that this ceremony was general, and that nobody refused to perform it, especially as the pleasure of love was added to the (supposed) future results of the grafting. The Law, therefore, prohibits us to mix different species together, i.e., to graft one tree into another, because we must keep away from the opinions of idolaters and the abominations of their unnatural sexual intercourse. In order to guard against the grafting of trees, we are forbidden to sow any two kinds of seed together or near each other. When you study the traditional explanation of this precept, you will find that the prohibition of grafting, the principal element in this commandment, holds good for all countries, and is punishable by forty stripes; but the sowing of seeds one near the other is only prohibited in Palestine. In the *Nabatean Agriculture* it is further distinctly stated that it was the custom of the people in those days to sow barley and stones of grapes together, in the belief that the vineyard could only prosper in this way. Therefore the Law prohibits us to use seed that has grown in a vineyard, and commands us to burn both the barley and the produce of the vineyard. For the practices of the heathen, which they considered as of a magic and talismanic character, even if not containing any idolatrous element, are prohibited, as we have stated above (p. 334) in reference to the dictum of our Sages, " We must not hang upon a tree the fœtus of an animal belonging to the Sanctuary." The Law prohibits all heathen customs, called by our Sages " the ways of the Amorite," because they are connected with idolatry. On considering the customs of the heathen in their worship, you will find that in certain kinds of worship they turn toward stars, in others to the two great luminaries ; frequently they choose the rise of signs in the Zodiac for sowing and fumigating ; and as to the circuits made by those who plant or sow, some complete five circles, corresponding to the five planets, with the exclusion of the two luminaries ; others go seven times round, according to the number of the planets, when including sun and moon. They believe that all these practices are magic charms of great efficiency in agriculture. Thus those practices lead to the worship of stars ; and therefore all practices of those nations have been prohibited, in the words, " Ye shall not walk in the manners of the nation which I cast out before you " (Lev. xx. 23). Those practices which were more general and common, or were distinctly connected with idolatry, are particularly pointed out as prohibited ; e.g., eating the fruit of a tree during the first three years, intermixing of species and the mixed species sown in a vineyard. I am surprised as the dictum of Rabbi Joshiyah, which has been adopted as legally binding, in reference to the mixed seed in a vineyard, viz., that the law is only transgressed when wheat, barley, and the stone of a grape are sown simultaneously. He must undoubtedly have seen the source of that kind of the ways of the Amorite. It must now be clear to you, and no room can be left for any doubt, that the prohibition of wearing garments of wool and linen, of using the fruit of a tree in the first three years, and of mixing divers species, are directed against idolatry, and that the prohibition against adopting heathen manners serves to remove anything which leads to idolatry, as has been shown by us.

CHAPTER XXXVIII

THE precepts of the third class are identical with those which we have enumerated in *Hilkot de'ot*. Their use is evident ; they are rules concerning moral conduct by which the social relations of men are regulated. This is sufficiently clear, and I need not dwell long on it. Know that some precepts prescribe certain acts which are considered as arbitrary decrees without any purpose, but are nevertheless the means of acquiring some moral principle. We shall explain every one of them in its proper place. But of all those precepts which are mentioned in *Hilkot de'ot*, it is distinctly stated that their object is to inculcate good moral principles.

CHAPTER XXXIX

THE precepts in the fourth class include the laws which in our work are contained in the section Zera'im, excepting the laws on the mixture of species ; the rules about things to be " valued " and things " devoted " (*Hilkot 'erekin va-ḥaramim*), and those concerning lender and borrower (*Hilkot malveh ve-loveh*) and slaves (*Hilkot 'abadim*). When you examine these precepts you will clearly see the use of every one of them : they teach us to have sympathy with the poor and infirm, to assist the needy in various ways ; not to hurt the feelings of those who are in want, and not to vex those who are in a helpless condition [viz., the widow, the orphan, and the like]. The purpose of the laws concerning the portions which are to be given to the poor is likewise obvious ; the reason of the laws concerning the heave-offerings and the tithe is distinctly stated : " for he hath no portion and inheritance with thee " (Deut. xiv. 29). You certainly know that the Levites had no portion, because their whole tribe was to be exclusively engaged in the service of God and the study of the Law. They shall not plow or cut the corn, but shall only minister to God. " They shall teach Jacob thy judgments and Israel thy law : they shall put incense before thee " (Deut. xxxiii. 10). In the Law we meet frequently with the phrase, " the Levite, the stranger, and the orphan and the widow " ; for the Levite is reckoned among the poor because he had no property. The second tithe was commanded to be spent on food in Jerusalem ; in this way the owner was compelled to give part of it away as charity. As he was not able to use it otherwise than by way of eating and drinking, he must have easily been induced to give it gradually away. This rule brought multitudes together in one place, and strengthened the bond of love and brotherhood among the children of men. The law concerning the fruit of a tree in its fourth year has some relation to idolatrous customs, as has been stated by us (chap. xxxvii.), and is connected with the law concerning the fruit of a tree in its first three years. But it has in addition the same object as the law concerning the heave-offering (Deut. xviii. 4), the dough-offering (*ḥallah*) (Num. xv. 20), the first-fruit (Exod. xxiii. 19), and the first of the shearing (Deut. xviii. 4). For the first of everything is to be devoted to the Lord ; and by doing so man accustoms himself to be liberal, and to limit his appetite for eating and his desire for property. The same is the reason why the priest took the shoulder, the two cheeks, and the maw (Deut. xviii. 3) ; the cheek being the first part of the body of animals, the right shoulder the first of the extremities of the body, and the maw the first of all inwards.

The reciting of a certain portion of the Law when the first-fruits are brought to the temple, tends also to create humility. For he who brings the first-fruits takes the basket upon his shoulders and proclaims the kindness and goodness of God. This ceremony teaches man that it is essential in the service of God to remember the times of trouble and the history of past distress, in days of comfort. The Law lays stress on this duty in several places ; comp. " And thou shalt remember that thou hast been a slave," etc. (Deut. v. 15). For it is to be feared that those who become great in riches and comfort might, as is generally the case, fall into the vices of insolence and haughtiness, and abandon all good principles. Comp. " Lest thou eat and be full, etc., and thine heart be lifted up and thou forget the Lord " (*ibid.* viii. 12–14); "And Jeshurun waxed fat and kicked" (*ibid.* xxx. 15). On account of this fear the Law commanded us to read each year a certain portion before the Lord and His glory, when we offer the first-fruit. You know how much the Law insists that we shall always remember the plagues that have befallen the Egyptians; comp. "That thou mayest remember the day when thou camest forth out of the land of Egypt all the days of thy life" (*ibid.* xvi. 3); "That thou mayest tell in the ears of thy son what things I have wrought in Egypt" (Exod. x. 2). Such a law was necessary in order to perpetuate the memory of the departure from Egypt; because such events verify prophecy and the doctrine of reward and punishment. The benefit of every commandment that serves to keep certain miracles in remembrance, or to perpetuate true faith, is therefore obvious.

In reference to the law concerning the first-born of man and cattle it is distinctly said, "And it came to pass, when Pharaoh would hardly let us go, that the Lord slew all the first-born in the land of Egypt, etc., therefore I sacrifice to the Lord," etc. (Exod. xiii. 15). But it can easily be explained why only cattle, sheep, and asses are mentioned in this law; these are kept as domestic animals, and are found in most places, especially in Palestine, where the Israelites were shepherds, they, their fathers, and forefathers; comp. "Thy servants are shepherds, both we and also our fathers" (Gen. xlvii. 3). Horses and camels, however, are not wanted by shepherds, and are not found in all places; thus in the booty of Midian (Num. xxxi.) no other animals are mentioned but oxen, sheep, and asses. But asses alone are indispensable to all people, especially to those who are engaged in the field or in the forest. Thus Jacob says, "I have oxen and asses" (Gen. xxxii. 5). Camels and horses are not possessed by many people, but only by a few, and are only found in a few places. The law that the first-born of an ass was to have its neck broken [in case it is not redeemed], will only ensure the redemption of the ass. It has, therefore, been said that the act of redeeming the ass is to be preferred to that of breaking its neck.

As to the precepts enumerated in the laws concerning the year of release and the jubilee (*Hilkot shemittah ve-yobel*) some of them imply sympathy with our fellow-men, and promote the well-being of mankind; for in reference to these precepts it is stated in the Law, "That the poor of thy people may eat" (Exod. xxiii. 11); and besides, the land will also increase its produce and improve when it remains fallow for some time. Other precepts of this class prescribe kindness to servants and to the poor, by renouncing all claims to debts [in the year of release], and relieving the slaves of their bondage [in the seventh year]. There are some precepts in this class that serve to secure for the people a permanent source of maintenance and support by providing that the land should remain the permanent property of its owners, and that it could not be sold. "And the land shall not be sold for ever" (Lev. xxv. 23). In this way the property of a person remains intact for him and his heirs, and he can only enjoy the produce thereof. I have thus explained the reason of all precepts contained in our work in the Section *Zera'im*, with the exception of the laws concerning the intermixture of different species of beasts the reason of which will be given (chap. xlix.).

In the same manner we find that all the precepts comprised in "the laws on valuations," and on " things devoted " are based on the principle of charity ; some of them prescribe what should be given to the priests ; others tell us what must be devoted to the repairs of the temple. The practice of all these things accustoms man to act liberally and to spend money unhesitatingly to the glory of God. For it is in the nature of man to strive to gain money and to increase it ; and his great desire to add to his wealth and honour is the chief source of misery for man. Also the precepts contained in " the laws concerning the relation between lender and borrower " (*Hilkot malveh veloveh*) will be found, on being carefully examined, to be nothing but commands to be lenient, merciful and kind to the needy, not to deprive them of the use of anything indispensable in the preparation of food. " No man shall take the nether or the upper millstone to pledge : for he taketh a man's life to pledge " (Deut. xxiv. 6).

The precepts contained in " the laws concerning slaves " (*Hilkot 'abadim*), likewise prescribe only acts of pity, mercy and kindness to the poor. It is an act of mercy to give liberty to a Canaanite servant for the loss of one of his limbs (Exod. xxi. 26, 27), in order that he should not suffer from slavery and illness at the same time. The law applies even to the case that a tooth of a slave has been knocked out, much more to the mutilation of other limbs. He could only be corrected with a rod or reed or the like, as we have stated in *Mishneh-torah*. Besides, if the master strikes the slave too hard and kills him, he is punished with death as for ordinary murder. Mercy is also the object of the law, " Thou shalt not deliver unto his master the servant that is escaped from his master " (Deut. xxiii. 15) ; but it teaches besides a very useful lesson, namely, that we must always practise this virtue, help and protect those who seek our help, and not deliver them unto those from whom they flee ; and it is not sufficient to give assistance to those who are in need of our help ; we must look after their interests, be kind to them, and not hurt their feeling by words. Thus the Law says : " He shall dwell with thee, even among you, in that place which he shall choose in one of thy gates, where it liketh him best : thou shalt not vex him " (*ibid.* ver. 16). This we owe to the lowest among men, to the slave ; how much more must we do our duty to the freeborn, when they seek our assistance ? But, on the other hand, when sinners and evildoers seek our help, it must not be granted ; no mercy must be shown to them, and the course of justice must not be interfered with, even if they claim the protection of that which is noblest and highest ; for " Thou shalt take him from mine altar that he may die " (Exod. xxi. 14). Here a person comes to seek the help of God, and claims the protection of that which is devoted to his name ; God, however, does not help him, and commands that he be delivered up to the prosecutor, from whom he fled. Much less need any one of us help or pity his fellow-men [under such circumstances] ; because mercy on sinners is cruelty to all creatures. These are undoubtedly the right ways designated " righteous statutes and judgments " (Deut. iv. 8), and different from the ways of the fools, who consider a person praiseworthy when he helps and protects his fellow-men, without discriminating between the oppressor and the oppressed. This is well known from their words and songs.

The reason and usefulness of every precept of this class has thus been clearly demonstrated.

CHAPTER XL

The precepts of the fifth class, enumerated in the Section " On Damages "
(*Sepher nezikin*), aim at the removal of wrong and the prevention of injury.
As we are strongly recommended to prevent damage, we are responsible for
every damage caused by our property or through our work in so far as it is in
our power to take care and to guard it from becoming injurious.   We are,
therefore, responsible for all damage caused by our cattle ; we must guard
them.   The same is the case with fire and pits ; they are made by man, and
he can be careful that they do not cause damage.   I will point out the equity
of the various laws in this respect.   No compensation is enforced for damage
caused by the mouth or the foot of an animal in a public thoroughfare ; because this cannot be guarded against, and the damage caused there is not
very large.   Those who place their things in a public place are themselves
guilty of neglect, and expose their property to injury.   But compensation
is given for damage caused to the property of a person in his own field by the
tooth or the foot of an animal.   It is different in the case of damage caused
by the horn of animals or the like.   The animal can be guarded everywhere
[and prevented from causing injury], whilst those who pass public thorough-
fares cannot sufficiently take care against accidents of this kind.   In this case
the law is the same for all places ; but there is a difference whether the owner
of the animal has been warned concerning it or not (*mu'ad* or *tam*).   If the
animal has not been in the habit of causing damage, the owner need only
pay half the damage ; but damage caused by an animal which has been in
the habit of doing so, and has been known as savage, must be paid in full.
The compensation for a slave is uniformly estimated at half the value fixed
for a free man.   For in the law concerning the valuation of man you find
the highest valuation at sixty shekels, whilst the money to be paid for a slave
is fixed at thirty shekels silver.   The killing of an animal that has killed a
human being (Exod. xxi. 28, 29) is not a punishment to the animal, as the
dissenters insinuate against us, but it is a fine imposed on the owner
of that animal.   For the same reason the use of its flesh is prohibited.   The
owner of an animal will, therefore, take the greatest possible care in guarding
it ; he will know that if any person is killed by the animal, whether that person
be grown up or young, free or in bondage, he forfeits at least the animal ;
and in case he has already received a warning concerning it, he will have to
pay a ransom in addition to the loss of the animal.   This is also the reason
why a beast is killed that has been used by a human being for an immoral
purpose (Lev. xx. 15, 16) ; its owner will be more careful as regards his beast,
will guard it, and never lose sight of it, just as he watches his household :
for people fear the loss of their property as much as that of their own life ;
some even more, but most people hold both in the same estimation.
Comp. " and to take us for bondmen, and our asses " (Gen. xliii. 18).

This class includes also the duty of killing him who pursues another person ; that is to say, if a person is about to commit a crime we may prevent it
by killing him.   Only in two cases is this permitted ; viz., when a person runs
after another in order to murder him, or in order to commit fornication ;
because in these two cases the crime, once committed ; cannot be remedied.
In the case of other sins, punished with death by the court of law, such as

idolatry and profanation of the Sabbath, by which the sinner does no harm to another person, and which concern only his own principles, no person may be killed for the mere intention, if he has not carried it out.

It is known that desire is denounced because it leads to coveting, and the latter is prohibited because it leads to robbery, as has been said by our Sages.

The object of the law of restoring lost property to its owner (Deut. xxii. 1–3) is obvious. In the first instance, it is in itself a good feature in man's character. Secondly, its benefit is mutual ; for if a person does not return the lost property of his fellow-man, nobody will restore to him what he may lose, just as those who do not honour their parents cannot expect to be honoured by their children.

A person who killed another person unknowingly must go into exile (Exod. xxi. 13; Num. xxxv. 11–28); because the anger of "the avenger of the blood" (Num. xxxv. 19) cools down while the cause of the mischief is out of sight. The chance of returning from the exile depends on the death of [the high-priest], the most honoured of men, and the friend of all Israel. By his death the relative of the slain person becomes reconciled (*ibid*. ver. 25) ; for it is a natural phenomenon that we find consolation in our misfortune when the same misfortune or a greater one has befallen another person. Amongst us no death causes more grief than that of the high-priest.

The beneficial character of the law concerning "the breaking of the neck of a heifer" (Deut. xxi. 1–8) is evident. For it is the city that is nearest to the slain person that brings the heifer, and in most cases the murderer comes from that place. The elders of the place call upon God as their witness, according to the interpretation of our Sages, that they have always kept the roads in good condition, have protected them, and have directed every one that asked his way ; that the person has not been killed because they were careless in these general provisions, and they do not know who has slain him. As a rule the investigation, the procession of the elders, the measuring, and the taking of the heifer, make people talk about it, and by making the event public, the murderer may be found out, and he who knows of him, or has heard of him, or has discovered him by any clue, will now name the person that is the murderer, and as soon as a man, or even a woman or handmaid, rises up and names a certain person as having committed the murder, the heifer is not killed. It is well known that it is considered great wickedness and guilt on the part of a person who knows the murderer, and is silent about him whilst the elders call upon God as witness that they know nothing about the murderer. Even a woman will, therefore, communicate whatever knowledge she has of him. When the murderer is discovered, the benefit of the law is apparent. If the court of justice cannot sentence him to death, the king may find him guilty, who has the power to sentence to death on circumstantial evidence ; and if the king does not put him to death, the avenger of blood may scheme and plan his death, and at last kill him. We have thus shown the use of the law concerning the breaking of the neck of the heifer in discovering the murderer   Force is added to the law by the rule that the place in which the neck of the heifer is broken should never be cultivated or sown. The owner of the land will therefore use all means in his power to search and to find the murderer, in order that the heifer be not killed and his land be not made useless to him.

CHAPTER XLI

THE precepts of the sixth class comprise the different ways of punishing the sinner. Their general usefulness is known and has also been mentioned by us. I will here describe them one by one and point out their nature in detail.

The punishment of him who sins against his neighbour consists in the general rule that there shall be done unto him exactly as he has done : if he injured any one personally, he must suffer personally ; if he damaged the property of his neighbour, he shall be punished by loss of property. But the person whose property has been damaged should be ready to resign his claim totally or partly. Only to the murderer we must not be lenient because of the greatness of his crime ; and no ransom must be accepted of him. " And the land cannot be cleansed of the blood that is shed therein but by the blood of him that shed it " (Num. xxxi. 33). Hence even if the murdered person continued to live after the attack for an hour or for days, was able to speak and possessed complete consciousness, and if he himself said, " Pardon my murderer, I have pardoned and forgiven him," he must not be obeyed. We must take life for life, and estimate equally the life of a child and that of a grown-up person, of a slave and of a freeman, of a wise man and of a fool. For there is no greater sin than this. And he who mutilated a limb of his neighbour, must himself lose a limb. " As he hath caused a blemish in a man, so shall it be done to him again " (Lev. xxiv. 20). You must not raise an objection from our practice of imposing a fine in such cases. For we have proposed to ourselves to give here the reason for the precepts mentioned in the Law, and not for that which is stated in the Talmud. I have, however, an explanation for the interpretation given in the Talmud, but it will be communicated *vivâ voce*. Injuries that cannot be reproduced exactly in another person, are compensated for by payment ; " only he shall pay for the loss of his time, and shall cause him to be thoroughly healed " (Exod. xxi. 19). If any one damaged the property of another, he must lose exactly as much of his own property : " whom the judges shall condemn he shall pay double unto his neighbour " (Exod. xxii. 8); namely, he restores that which he has taken, and adds just as much [to it] of his own property. It is right that the more frequent transgressions and sins are, and the greater the probability of their being committed, the more severe must their punishment be, in order to deter people from committing them ; but sins which are of rare occurrence require a less severe punishment. For this reason one who stole a sheep had to pay twice as much as for other goods, i.e., four times the value of the stolen object ; but this is only the case when he has disposed of it by sale or slaughter (Exod. xxi. 37). As a rule, the sheep remained always in the fields, and could therefore not be watched so carefully as things kept in town. The thief of a sheep used therefore to sell it quickly before the theft became known, or to slaughter it and thereby change its appearance. As such theft happened frequently, the punishment was severe. The compensation for a stolen ox is still greater by one-fourth, because the theft is easily carried out. The sheep keep together when they feed, and can be watched by the shepherd, so that theft when it is committed can only take place by night. But oxen when feeding are very widely scattered, as is also mentioned in the *Nabatean Agriculture*, and a shepherd cannot watch them properly; theft of oxen is therefore a more frequent occurrence.

The law concerning false witnesses (Deut. xix. 19) prescribes that they shall suffer exactly the same loss which they intended to inflict upon another. If they intended to bring a sentence of death against a person, they are killed; if they aimed at the punishment of stripes, they receive stripes; and if they desire to make a person pay money, they are sentenced to pay exactly the same sum. The object of all these laws is to make the punishment equal to the crime; and it is also on this account that the judgments are " righteous " (Deut. iv. 8). A robber with violence is not ordered to pay anything as fine (Lev. v. 24); the additional fifth part [of the value of the robbed goods] is only an atonement-offering for his perjury. The reason of this rule is to be found in the rare occurrence of robbery; theft is committed more frequently than robbery, for theft can be committed everywhere; robbery is not possible in towns, except with difficulty; besides, the thief takes things exposed as well as things hidden away; robbery applies only to things exposed; against robbery we can guard and defend ourselves; we cannot do so against theft; again, the robber is known, can be sought, and forced to return that which he has robbed, whilst the thief is not known. On account of all these circumstances the law fines the thief and not the robber.

Preliminary Remark.—Whether the punishment is great or small, the pain inflicted intense or less intense, depends on the following four conditions.

1. The greatness of the sin. Actions that cause great harm are punished severely, whilst actions that cause little harm are punished less severely.

2. The frequency of the crime. A crime that is frequently committed must be put down by severe punishment; crimes of rare occurrence may be suppressed by a lenient punishment considering that they are rarely committed.

3. The amount of temptation. Only fear of a severe punishment restrains us from actions for which there exists a great temptation, either because we have a great desire for these actions, or are accustomed to them, or feel unhappy without them.

4. The facility of doing the thing secretly, and unseen and unnoticed. From such acts we are deterred only by the fear of a great and terrible punishment.

After this preliminary remark, I say that the precepts of the Law may be divided into the following four classes with respect to the punishment for their transgression :—(1) Precepts whose transgression is followed by sentence of death pronounced by a court of law. (2) Precepts whose transgression is punished with excision, such transgression being held to be a very great sin. (3) In some cases the transgression is punished by stripes administered with a strap (such transgression not being considered a grievous sin, as it concerns only a simple prohibition); or by " death by Heaven." (4) Precepts the transgression of which is not punished [even] by stripes. Prohibitions of this kind are all those that involve no act. But there are the following exceptions : [First], Swearing falsely, because it is gross neglect of man's duty, who ought to bear constantly in mind the greatness of God. [Secondly], Changing an animal devoted to the sanctuary for another (Lev. xxvii. 10), because this change leads to contemning sacrifices devoted to the name of God. [Thirdly], Cursing a person by the name of God (*ibid.* xix. 14); because many dread the effect of a curse more than bodily harm. The transgression of other negative commandments that involve no act causes little harm, and cannot always be avoided, as it consists in mere words; moreover, man's back would be inflicted with stripes all the year round if he were to be punished with stripes for each transgression of this kind. Besides, previous warning is impossible in this case. There is also wisdom in the number of stripes; for although the number of their maximum is given, there is no fixed number how many are to be applied to each person; each man receives only as many stripes as he can bear, but not more than forty (Deut. xxv. 3), even if he be strong enough for a hundred.

The "death by the court of law" is not inflicted for the transgression of any of the dietary laws; because in such a case no great harm is done, and the temptation of man to transgress these laws is not so great as the temptation to the enjoyment of sexual intercourse. In some of the dietary laws the punishment is excision. This is the case with the prohibition of eating blood (Lev. xvii. 26). For in ancient days people were very eager and anxious to eat blood as a kind of idolatrous ceremony, as is explained in the book Tomtom, and therefore the prohibition of eating blood is made very stringent. Excision is also the punishment for eating fat; because people enjoy it, and because it was distinguished and sanctified by its use in the offerings. The eating of leavened bread on Passover (Exod. xii. 15), and breaking the fast on the Day of Atonement (Lev. xxiii. 29), are likewise punished with excision: [first] on account of the great discomfort which the obedience to the law causes in these cases; [secondly] on account of the principles of faith which the laws of Passover and of the Day of Atonement inculcate: they confirm fundamental principles of the Law, viz., the belief in the wonderful departure [of Israel] from Egypt, and in the effect of repentance, according to the words, "For on this day will he forgive you" (Lev. xvi. 31). Just as in the case of eating fat, so is excision also announced as a punishment when a person eats that which is left [of a sacrifice beyond its limited time], or partakes of a sacrifice which has been made abominable; or when an unclean person eats of holy things (*ibid.* vii. 16–21). The object of this severity is to increase the estimation of the offering in the eyes of the people, as has been shown.

Death by the court of law is decreed in important cases: when faith is undermined, or a great crime is committed, viz., idolatry, incest, murder, or actions that lead to these crimes. It is further decreed for breaking the Sabbath (Exod. xxxi. 15); because the keeping of Sabbath is a confirmation of our belief in the Creation; a false prophet and a rebellious elder are put to death on account of the mischief which they cause; he who strikes his father or his mother is killed on account of his great audacity, and because he undermines the constitution of the family, which is the foundation of the state. A rebellious and disobedient son is put to death (Deut. xxi. 18 *seq.*) on account of what he might become, because he will likely be a murderer; he who steals a human being is killed, because he is also prepared to kill him whom he steals (Exod. xxi. 16). Likewise he who is found breaking into a house is prepared for murder (*ibid.* xxii. 1), as our Sages stated. These three, the rebellious and disobedient son, he who steals and sells a human being, and he who breaks into a house, become murderers in the course of time, as is well known. Capital punishment is only decreed for these serious crimes, and in no other case. Not all forbidden sexual intercourse is visited with the penalty of death, but only in those cases in which the criminal act can easily be done, is of frequent occurrence, is base and disgraceful, and of a tempting character; otherwise excision is the punishment. Likewise not all kinds of idolatry are capital crimes, but only the principal acts of idolatry, such as praying to an idol, prophesying in its name, passing a child through the fire, consulting with familiar spirits, and acting as a wizard or witch.

As punishments and judgments are evidently indispensable, it was necessary to appoint judges throughout the country in every town; witnesses must be heard; and a king is required whom all fear and respect, who is able to restrain the people by various means, and who can strengthen and support the authority of the judges. Although I have shown the reason of all the laws contained in "the Section of Judges" (*Sefer Shofetim*), I find it necessary, in accordance with the object of this treatise, to explain a few of these laws, e.g., the laws concerning a rebellious elder.

God knew that the judgments of the Law will always require an extension in some cases and curtailment in others, according to the variety of places, events, and circumstances. He therefore cautioned against such increase and diminution, and commanded, "Thou shalt not add thereto nor diminish from it" (Deut. xiii. 1); for constant changes would tend to disturb the whole system of the Law, and would lead people to believe that the Law is not of Divine origin. But permission is at the same time given to the wise men, i.e., the great court (Synhedrion) of every generation to make fences round the judgments of the Law for their protection, and to introduce bye-laws (fences) in order to ensure the keeping of the Law. Such fences once erected remain in force for ever. The Mishnah therefore teaches : "And make a fence round the Law" (Abot i. 1). In the same manner they have the power temporarily to dispense with some religious act prescribed in the Law, or to allow that which is forbidden, if exceptional circumstances and events require it; but none of the laws can be abrogated permanently, as has been explained by us in the Introduction to the Commentary on the Mishnah in treating of temporary legislation. By this method the Law will remain perpetually the same, and will yet admit at all times and under all circumstances such temporary modifications as are indispensable. If every scholar had the power to make such modifications, the multitude of disputes and differences of opinion would have produced an injurious effect. Therefore it was commanded that of the Sages only the great Synhedrion, and none else, should have this power; and whoever would oppose their decision should be killed. For if any critic were allowed to dispute the decision of the Synhedrion, the object of this law would not be attained; it would be useless.

Transgressions may be divided into four classes, viz.—(1) involuntary transgressions, (2) sins committed in ignorance, (3) sins done knowingly, and (4) sins done spitefully. He who sins involuntarily is, according to the distinct declaration of the Law, exempt from punishment, and free from all blame; comp. "Unto the damsel thou shalt do nothing; there is in the damsel no sin worthy of death" (Deut. xxii. 26). If a person sins in ignorance, he is blamable; for if he had been more considerate and careful, he would not have erred. Although he is not punished, his sin must be atoned for, and for this reason he brings a sin-offering. The Law distinguishes in this respect between a private person and a king, a high-priest or Teacher of Halakah. Hence we conclude that a person who acts wrongly, or who teaches wrongly, guided by his own reasoning—except in the case of the great Synhedrion or the high-priest—is treated as *mezid* (as one who sins knowingly), and does not belong to the category of *shogegim* (of those who sin by error). A rebellious elder is therefore put to death, although he acted and taught according to his view. But the great Synhedrion must teach according to its opinion, and if the opinion is wrong, the sin is considered as due to error. In reference to such a case the Law says, "And if the whole congregation of Israel *err*," etc. (Lev. iv. 13). It is on this principle that our Sages say, "The error in learning amounts to intentional sin" (Abot iv. 13); he who has studied insufficiently, and teaches and acts according to his defective knowledge, is to be considered as if he sinned knowingly. For if a person eats of the fat of the kidneys in the belief that it is the fat of the rump, his error is not so grave as the error of him who, eating of the fat of the kidneys, knows that it is that fat, but is ignorant of the fact that it is prohibited. The latter brings a sin-offering although he is almost an intentional transgressor. But this is only the case as far as he *acts* according to his knowledge; but if he decides a religious question [wrongly], he is undoubtedly an intentional sinner. The Law admits the plea of error in a religious decision only in the case of the great Synhedrion.

He who has sinned knowingly must pay the penalty prescribed in the Law; he is put to death or receives stripes, or—for transgression of prohibitions not punishable by stripes—other corporal punishment, or pays a fine. There are some sins for which the punishment is the same, whether they have been committed knowingly or unknowingly; because they are frequent, and are easily done, consisting only in the utterance of words, and involving no action besides; e.g., false swearing by witnesses, or by trustees. Intercourse with a betrothed handmaid is likewise easy and frequent; she is exposed unprotected, being in reality neither handmaid nor a free person, nor a married woman, according to the traditional interpretation of this precept.

If a person sins presumptuously, so that in sinning he shows impudence and seeks publicity, if he does not sin only to satisfy his appetite, if he does what is prohibited by the Law, not only because of his evil inclinations, but in order to oppose and resist the Law, he "reproacheth the Lord" (Num. xv. 30), and must undoubtedly be put to death. None will act in such a manner but such as have conceived the idea to act contrary to the Law. According to the traditional interpretation, therefore, the above passage speaks of an idolater who opposes the fundamental principles of the Law; for no one worships a star unless he believes [—contrary to the teachings of Scripture—] that the star is eternal, as we have frequently stated in our work. I think that the same punishment [viz., sentence of death] applies to every sin which involves the rejection of the Law, or opposition to it. Even if an Israelite eats meat [boiled] in milk, or wears garments of wool and linen, or rounds the corners of his head, out of spite against the Law, in order to show clearly that he does not believe in its truth, I apply to him the words, " he reproacheth the Lord," and [I am of opinion] that he must suffer death as an unbeliever, though not for a punishment, but in the same manner as the inhabitants of a " city misled to idolatry " are slain for their unbelief, and not by way of punishment for crime ; wherefore their property is destroyed by fire, and is not given to their heirs, as is the case with the property of other criminals condemned to death. According to my opinion, all the members of an Israelitish community which has insolently and presumptuously trans-gressed any of the divine precepts, must be put to death. This is proved by the history of " the sons of Reuben and the sons of Gad " (Josh. xxii.), against whom the whole congregation of Israel decided to make war. When warning was given to the supposed offenders, it was explained to them that they had relinquished their faith, because by agreeing to transgress one par-ticular law they rejected the truth of the whole Law. For they were ad-dressed as follows : " What trespass is this that ye have committed against the God of Israel, to turn away this day from following the Lord ? " (Josh. xxii. 16) ; and they replied : " The Lord knoweth, etc., if it be in rebellion, or if in transgression against the Lord," etc. (*ibid.* 22). Take well notice of these principles in respect to punishments.

The Section on Judges includes also the commandment to blot out the memory of Amalek (Deut. xxv. 17–19). In the same way as one individual person is punished, so must also a whole family or a whole nation be pun-ished, in order that other families shall hear it and be afraid, and not accustom themselves to practise mischief. For they will say, we may suffer in the same way as those people have suffered ; and if there be found among them a wicked, mischievous man, who cares neither for the evil he brings upon himself nor for that which he causes to others, he will not find in his family any one ready to help him in his evil designs. As Amalek was the first to attack Israel with the sword (Exod. xvii. 8–16), it was commanded to blot out his name by means of the sword; whilst Ammon and Moab, who have not been friendly simply from meanness, and have caused them injury by cunning, were only punished by exclusion from intermarriage with the Israelites, and from their friendship. All these things which God has commanded as a punishment are not excessive nor inadequate, but, as is distinctly stated, " according to the fault " (Deut. xxv. 2).

This section contains also the law concerning preparing " a place without the camp," and " having a paddle upon the weapon " (Deut. xxiii. 12, 13). As I have told you, it is one of the objects of the Law to train Israel to clean-liness ; that they should keep free from dirt and filth, and that men should not be degraded to the condition of cattle. Another object of this law is to confirm by these preparations the belief of the warriors that God dwells in their midst. The reason of the law is therefore stated thus : " For the Lord thy God walketh in the midst of thy camp " (*ibid.* ver. 14). The mention of this reason gave occasion to add another lesson : " That he see no unclean thing in thee and turn away from thee " (*ibid.*). These words warn and caution us against the usual inclination of soldiers to fornication, when they are away from their homes a long time. God therefore commanded us to do certain things which remind us that He is in our midst ; we will thereby

be saved from those evil practices ; as it is said, " and thy camp shall be holy'
that he see no unclean thing in thee " (*ibid.*).   Even those who are unclean
by pollution were compelled to stop outside the camp till the evening, and
" then he shall come into the camp again."   It will thus be confirmed in
the heart of every one of the Israelites that their camp must be like a sanctuary of the Lord, and it must not be like the camps of the heathen, whose
sole object is corruption and sin ; who only seek to cause injury to others
and to take their property ; whilst our object is to lead mankind to the service of God, and to a good social order.   I have told you already that I only
propose to give here such reasons as are apparent from the text of the Law.

To the same class belongs also the law concerning " the marriage of a
captive woman " (Deut. xxi. 10 *seq*.).   There is a well-known saying of our
Sages : " This law is only a concession to human weakness."   This law
contains, nevertheless, even for the nobler class of people, some moral lessons
to which I will call your attention.   For although the soldier may be overcome by his desire which he is unable to suppress or to restrain, he must take
the object of his lust to a private place, " into the inner of his house " (Deut.
xxi. 12), and he is not permitted to force her in the camp.   Similarly our
Sages say, that he may not cohabit with her a second time before she leaves
off her mourning, and is at ease about her troubles.   She must not be prevented from mourning and crying, and she must be permitted to abstain
from bathing, in accordance with the words, " and she shall weep for her
father and for her mother " (*ibid.*) ; for mourners find comfort in crying
and in excitement till the body has not sufficient strength to bear the inner
emotions ; in the same manner as happy persons find rest in various kinds of
play.   Thus the Lord is merciful to her and gives her permission to continue
her mourning and weeping till she is worn out.   You know certainly that he
married her as a heathen, and that during the thirty days she openly keeps
her religion and even continues her idolatrous practices ; no interference
with her faith was allowed during that time ; and after all that she could not
be sold, nor treated as a handmaid, if she could not be induced to accept the
statutes of the Law.   Thus the Law does not ignore the cohabitation of the
Israelite with the captive woman, although it involved disobedience to God
to some extent, having taken place when she was still a heathen.   The Law
prescribes : " Thou shalt not make merchandise of her, because thou hast
humbled her " (*ibid.* 14).   We have thus shown the moral lessons contained
in these laws, and we have explained the reason of every precept of this
section.

CHAPTER XLII

THE precepts of the seventh class are the civil laws enumerated in the Section
on Judgments, and part of the Section on Property.   The object of these
precepts is obvious.   They define the ways of equity in the various transactions which must take place between man and man.   Those that are engaged in such transactions must mutually promote each other's interests ;
neither of the parties must strive to increase only his own profit, and that he
alone should enjoy the whole benefit of the transaction.   In the first place,
no overcharge is permitted ; only the ordinary and known rate of profit may

be taken. The law fixes the limits of profits within which the transaction is valid. Even imposition in mere words [where no material harm is inflicted] is forbidden, as is well known. Next comes the law of the four kinds of bailees; the fairness of the law is evident. If one keeps the property of his neighbour for nothing, without deriving therefrom any benefit for himself, and is only obliging his neighbour, he is free from all responsibility, and if any injury is done to the property, the owner alone must bear the loss. He who borrows a thing keeps it only for his own advantage, whilst the owner lends it to him to oblige him; he is therefore responsible for everything; any loss in the property must be borne by the borrower. If one takes wages for keeping the property or pays for using it, he as well as the owner profit thereby; the losses must therefore be divided between them. It is done in this manner; the bailee pays for any loss caused through want of care, namely, when the property is stolen or lost; for this happens only when the bailee does not take sufficient precaution. The owner, on the other hand, bears such losses as cannot be prevented; namely, if by accident the animal falls and breaks its limbs, or is carried away by armed men as booty, or if it dies. The Law further ordains merciful conduct towards hired workmen because of their poverty. Their wages should be paid without delay, and they must not be wronged in any of their rights; they must receive their pay according to their work. Another instance of kindness to workmen is this: according to the regulations of this law, workmen, and even animals, must be permitted to partake of the food in the preparation of which they have been engaged. The laws which relate to property include laws concerning inheritance. They are based on the sound principle that man must not " withhold good from those to whom it is due " (Prov. iii. 27), and when he is about to die, he must not conceive ill-will against his heirs, by squandering his property, but leave it to the one who has the greatest claim on it, that is, to him who is his nearest relation, " unto his kinsman that is next to him of his family " (Num. xxvii. 11). It is clearly stated that the son has the first claim, then comes the daughter, then the brother, and then the father's brothers, as is well known. The father must leave the right of the first-born to his eldest son, because his love for this son came first; he must not be guided by his inclination. He may not make the son of the beloved first-born before the son of the hated (Deut. xxi. 16). Thus our highly equitable Law preserves and strengthens the virtue of respecting all kinsmen, and doing well unto them, as the prophet says: " He that is cruel troubleth his own flesh " (Prov. xi. 17). The Law correctly says, " Thou shalt open thine hand wide unto thy brother, unto thy poor " (Deut. xv. 11). Our Sages bestow much praise upon him who is kind to his relatives, and him who marries the daughter of his sister. The Law has taught us how far we have to extend this principle of favouring those who are near to us, and of treating kindly every one with whom we have some relationship, even if he offended or wronged us; even if he is very bad, we must have some consideration for him. Thus the Law says: " Thou shalt not abhor an Edomite, for he is thy brother " (*ibid.* xxiii. 7). Again, if we find a person in trouble, whose assistance we have once enjoyed, or of whom we have received some benefit, even if that person has subsequently done evil to us, we must bear in mind his previous [good] conduct. Thus the Law tells us: " Thou shalt not abhor an Egyptian, because thou wast a stranger in his land " (*ibid.*), although the Egyptians have subsequently oppressed us very much, as is well-known. See how many moral lessons we have derived from these precepts. The last two precepts do not belong to the seventh class; but the discussion of the preference due to relatives as regards inheritance led us to speak of the Egyptians and the Edomites.

CHAPTER XLIII

THE precepts of the eighth class are enumerated in "the Section on Seasons" (*Sefer zemannim*). With a few exceptions, the reasons for all of them are stated in the Law. The object of Sabbath is obvious, and requires no explanation. The rest it affords to man is known; one-seventh of the life of every man, whether small or great, passes thus in comfort, and in rest from trouble and exertion. This the Sabbath effects in addition to the perpetuation and confirmation of the grand doctrine of the Creation. The object of the Fast of Atonement is evident. The Fast creates the sense of repentance; it is the same day on which the chief of all prophets came down [from Mount Sinai] with the second tables, and announced to the people the divine pardon of their great sin; the day was therefore appointed for ever as a day devoted to repentance and true worship of God. For this reason all material enjoyment, all trouble and care for the body, are interdicted, no work may be done; the day must be spent in confession; everʸ one shall confess his sins and abandon them.

Other holy days are appointed for rejoicing and for such pleasant gathering as people generally need. They also promote the good feeling that men should have to each other in their social and political relations. The appointment of the special days for such purposes has its cause. The reason for the Passover is well known. It is kept seven days, because the period of seven days is the unit of time intermediate between a day and a month. It is also known how great is the importance of this period in Nature, and in many religious duties. For the Law always follows Nature, and in some respects brings it to perfection; for Nature is not capable of designing and thinking, whilst the Law is the result of the wisdom and guidance of God, who is the author of the intellect of all rational beings. This, however, is not the theme of the present chapter; let us return to our subject.

The Feast of Weeks is the anniversary of the Revelation on Mount Sinai. In order to raise the importance of this day, we count the days that pass since the preceding festival, just as one who expects his most intimate friend on a certain day counts the days and even the hours. This is the reason why we count the days that pass since the offering of the Omer, between the anniversary of our departure from Egypt and the anniversary of the Lawgiving. The latter was the aim and object of the exodus from Egypt, and thus God said, " I brought you unto myself " (Exod. xix. 4). As that great revelation took place only on one day, so we keep its anniversary only one day; but if the eating of unleavened bread on Passover were only commanded for one day, we should not have noticed it, and its object would not have been manifest. For it frequently happens that we take the same kind of food for two or three days. But by our continuing for a whole period [of seven days] to eat unleavened bread, its object becomes clear and evident.

New-Year is likewise kept for one day; for it is a day of repentance, on which we are stirred up from our forgetfulness. For this reason the shofar is blown on this day, as we have shown in Mishneh-torah. The day is, as it were, a preparation for and an introduction to the day of the Fast, as is obvious from the national tradition about the days between New-Year and the Day of Atonement.

The Feast of Tabernacles, which is a feast of rejoicing and gladness, is kept seven days, in order that the idea of the festival may be more noticeable. The reason why it is kept in the autumn is stated in the Law, " When thou hast gathered in thy labours out of the field " (Exod. xxiii. 16); that is to say, when you rest and are free from pressing labours. Aristotle, in the ninth book of his Ethics, mentions this as a general custom among the nations. He says: " In ancient times the sacrifices and assemblies of the people took place after the ingathering of the corn and the fruit, as if the sacrifices were offered on account of the harvest." Another reason is this—in this season it is possible to dwell in tabernacles, as there is neither great heat nor troublesome rain.

The two festivals, Passover and the Feast of Tabernacles, imply also the teaching of certain truths and certain moral lessons. Passover teaches us to remember the miracles which God wrought in Egypt, and to perpetuate their memory; the Feast of Tabernacles reminds us of the miracles wrought in the wilderness. The moral lessons derived from these feasts is this: man ought to remember his evil days in his days of prosperity. He will thereby be induced to thank God repeatedly, to lead a modest and humble life. We eat, therefore, unleavened bread and bitter herbs on Passover in memory of what has happened unto us, and leave [on Succoth] our houses in order to dwell in tabernacles, as inhabitants of deserts do that are in want of comfort. We shall thereby remember that this has once been our condition; [comp.] " I made the children of Israel to dwell in booths " (Lev. xxiii. 43); although we dwell now in elegant houses, in the best and most fertile land, by the kindness of God, and because of His promises to our forefathers, Abraham, Isaac, and Jacob, who were perfect in their opinions and in their conduct. This idea is likewise an important element in our religion; that whatever good we have received and ever will receive of God, is owing to the merits of the Patriarchs, who " kept the way of the Lord to do justice and judgment " (Gen. xviii. 19). We join to the Feast of Tabernacles the Feast of the Eighth Day, in order to complete our rejoicings, which cannot be perfect in booths, but in comfortable and well-built houses. As regards the four species [the branches of the palm tree, the citron, the myrtle, and the willows of the brook] our Sages gave a reason for their use by way of Agadic interpretation, the method of which is well known to those who are acquainted with the style of our Sages. They use the text of the Bible only as a kind of poetical language [for their own ideas], and do not intend thereby to give an interpretation of the text. As to the value of these Midrashic interpretations, we meet with two different opinions. For some think that the Midrash contains the real explanation of the text, whilst others, finding that it cannot be reconciled with the words quoted, reject and ridicule it. The former struggle and fight to prove and to confirm such interpretations according to their opinion, and to keep them as the real meaning of the text; they consider them in the same light as traditional laws. Neither of the two classes understood it, that our Sages employ biblical texts merely as poetical expressions, the meaning of which is clear to every reasonable reader. This style was general in ancient days; all adopted it in the same way as poets [adopt a certain style]. Our Sages say, in reference to the words, " and a paddle (*yated*) thou shalt have upon thy weapon " [*azeneka*, Deut. xxiii. 14]: Do not read *azeneka*, " thy weapon," but *ozneka*, " thy ear." You are thus told, that if you hear a person uttering something disgraceful, put your fingers into your ears. Now, I wonder whether those ignorant persons [who take the Midrashic interpretations literally] believe that the author of this saying gave it as the true interpretation of the text quoted, and as the meaning of this precept; that in truth *yated*, " the paddle," is used for " the finger," and *azeneka* denotes " thy ear." I cannot think that any person whose intellect is sound can admit this. The author employed the text as a beautiful poetical phrase, in teaching an excellent moral lesson, namely this: It is as bad to listen to bad language as it is to use it. This lesson is poetically connected with the above text. In the same sense you must understand the phrase, " Do not read so, but so," wherever it occurs in the Midrash. I have departed from my subject, but it was for the purpose of making a remark useful to every intellectual member of the Rabbanites. I now return to our theme. I believe that the four species are a symbolical expression of our rejoicing that the Israelites changed the wilderness, " no place of seed, or of figs, or of vines, or of pomegranates, or of water to drink " (Num. xx. 5), with a country full of fruit-trees and rivers. In order to remember this we take the fruit which is the most pleasant of the fruit of the land, branches which smell best, most beautiful leaves, and also the best of herbs, i.e., the willows of the brook. These four kinds have also those three purposes: First, they were plentiful in those days in Palestine, so that every one could easily get them. Secondly, they have a good appearance, they are green; some of them, viz., the citron and the myrtle, are also excellent as regards their smell, the branches of the palm-tree and the willow having neither good nor bad smell. Thirdly, they keep fresh and green for seven days, which is not the case with peaches, pomegranates, asparagus, nuts, and the like.

CHAPTER XLIV

THE precepts of the ninth class are those enumerated in the Section on Love. Their reason is obvious. The actions prescribed by them serve to remind us continually of God, and of our duty to fear and to love Him, to keep all His commandments, and to believe concerning God that which every religious person must believe. This class includes the laws of Prayer, Reading of Shema, Grace, and duties connected with these, Blessing of the priests, Tefillin, Mezuzah, Zizit, acquiring a scroll of the Law, and reading in it at certain times. The performance of all these precepts inculcates into our heart useful lessons. All this is clear, and a further explanation is superfluous, as being a mere repetition and nothing else.

CHAPTER XLV

THE precepts of the tenth class are those enumerated in the laws on the Temple (*Hilkot bet ha-beḥirah*), the laws on the vessels of the temple and on the ministers in the temple [*Hilkot kele ha-miḳdash veha-'obedim bo*]. The use of these precepts we have stated in general terms. It is known that idolaters selected the highest possible places on high mountains where to build their temples and to place their images. Therefore Abraham, our father, chose Mount Moriah, being the highest mount in that country, and proclaimed there the Unity of God. He selected the west of the mount as the place toward which he turned during his prayers, because [he thought that] the most holy place was in the West; this is the meaning of the saying of our Sages, " The *Shekinah* " (the Glory of God) is in the West " (B. T. Baba B 25*a*); and it is distinctly stated in the Talmud Yoma that our father Abraham chose the west side, the place where the Most Holy was built. I believe that he did so because it was then a general rite to worship the sun as a deity. Undoubtedly all people turned then to the East [worshipping the Sun]. Abraham turned therefore on Mount Moriah to the West, that is, the site of the Sanctuary, and turned his back toward the sun; and the Israelites, when they abandoned their God and returned to the early bad principles, stood " with their backs toward the Temple of the Lord and their faces toward the East, and they worshipped the sun toward the East " (Ezek. viii. 16). Note this strange fact. I do not doubt that the spot which Abraham chose in his prophetical spirit, was known to Moses our Teacher, and to others; for Abraham commanded his children that on this place a house of worship should be built. Thus the Targum says distinctly, " And Abraham worshipped and prayed there in that place, and said before God, ' Here shall coming generations worship the Lord ' " (Gen. xxii. 14). For three practical reasons the name of the place is not distinctly stated in the Law, but indicated in the phrase " To the place which the Lord will choose " (Deut. xii. 11, etc.). First, if the nations had learnt that this place was to be the centre of the highest religious truths, they would occupy it, or fight about it most perseveringly. Secondly, those who were then in posses- sion of it might destroy and ruin the place with all their might. Thirdly, and chiefly, every one of the twelve tribes would desire to have this place in its borders and under its control; this would lead to divisions and discord, such as were caused by the desire for the priesthood. Therefore it was commanded that the Temple should not be built before the election of a king who would order its erection, and thus remove the cause of discord. We have explained this in the Section on Judges (ch. xli.).

It is known that the heathen in those days built temples to stars, and set up in those temples the image which they agreed upon to worship; because it was in some relation to a certain star or to a portion of one of the spheres. We were, therefore, commanded to build a temple to the name of God, and to place therein the ark with two tables of stone, on which there were written the commandments " I am the Lord," etc., and " Thou shalt have no other God before me," etc. Naturally the fundamental belief in prophecy pre- cedes the belief in the Law, for without the belief in prophecy there can be no belief in the Law. But a prophet only receives divine inspiration through the agency of an angel. Comp. " The angel of the Lord called " (Gen. xxii. 15) ; " The angel of the Lord said unto her " (*ibid.* xvi. 11) ; and other innumerable instances. Even Moses our Teacher received his first prophecy through an angel. " And an angel of the Lord appeared to him in the flame of fire " (Exod. iii.). It is therefore clear that the belief in the existence of angels precedes the belief in prophecy, and the latter precedes the belief in the Law. The Sabeans, in their ignorance of the existence of God, believed that the spheres with their stars were beings without beginning and without end, that the images and certain trees, the Asherot, derived certain powers from the spheres, that they inspired the prophets, spoke to them in visions, and told them what was good and what bad. I have explained their theory when speaking of the prophets of the Ashera. But when the wise men discovered and proved that there was a Being, neither itself corporeal nor residing as a force in a corporeal body, viz., the true, one God, and that there existed besides other purely incorporeal beings which God endowed with His goodness and His light, namely, the angels, and that these beings are not included in the sphere and its stars, it became evident that it was these angels and not the images or *Asherot* that charged the prophets. From the preceding remarks it is clear that the belief in the existence of angels is connected with the belief in the Existence of God ; and the belief in God and angels leads to the belief in Prophecy and in the truth of the Law. In order to firmly establish this creed, God commanded [the Israelites] to make over the ark the form of two angels. The belief in the existence of angels is thus inculcated into the minds of the people, and this belief is in importance next to the belief in God's Existence ; it leads us to believe in Prophecy and in the Law, and opposes idolatry. If there had only been one figure of a cherub, the people would have been misled and would have mistaken it for God's image which was to be worshipped, in the fashion of the heathen ; or they might have assumed that the angel [represented by the figure] was also a deity, and would thus have adopted a Dualism. By making two cherubim and distinctly declaring " the Lord is our God, the Lord is One," Moses clearly proclaimed the theory of the existence of a number of angels ; he left no room for the error of considering those figures as deities, since [he declared that] God is one, and that He is the Creator of the angels, who are more than one.

A candlestick was then put in front of the curtain, as a sign of honour and distinction for the Temple. For a chamber in which a continual light burns, hidden behind a curtain, makes a great impression on man, and the Law lays great stress on our holding the Sanctuary in great estimation and regard, and that at the sight of it we should be filled with humility, mercy, and softheartedness. This is expressed in the words, " And ye shall reverence my sanctuary " (Lev. xix. 30), and in order to give these words more weight, they are closely joined to the command to keep the Sabbath.

The use of the altar for incense and the altar for burnt-offering and their vessels is obvious ; but I do not know the object of the table with the bread upon it continually, and up to this day I have not been able to assign any reason to this commandment.

The commandment that the stones of the altar shall not be hewn and that no iron tool shall be lifted up upon them (Deut. xxvii. 5), has been explained by our Sages as follows : It is not right that the tool that shortens man's life should be lifted up upon that which gives length of life. As an Agadic explanation this is good ; but the real reason is this : the heathen used to build their altars with hewn stones ; we ought not to imitate them. For this reason we have to make an altar of earth : " Thou shalt make unto me an altar of earth " (Exod. xx. 24) ; if it should be impossible to dispense altogether with stones, they must not be hewn, but employed in their natural state. Thus the Law also prohibits from worshipping over painted stones (Lev. xxvi. 1), or from planting any tree near the altar of the Lord (Deut. xvi. 21). The object of all these commandments is the same, namely, that we shall not employ in the worship of God anything which the heathen employed in the worship of their idols. In general terms this is repeated in the following passage : " Take heed, that thou inquire not after their gods, saying, How did these nations serve their gods ? even so will I do likewise " (Deut. xii. 30) ; the Israelites shall not do this, because—as is expressly added—" every abomination unto the Lord,which he hateth,have they done unto their gods."

The mode of worshipping Peor, then very general among the heathen, consisted in uncovering the nakedness. The priests were therefore commanded to make breeches for themselves to cover their nakedness during the service, and, besides, no steps were to lead up to the altar, " that thy nakedness be not discovered thereon " (Exod. xx. 23).

The Sanctuary was constantly guarded and surrounded [by Levites] as a mark of respect and honour ; and at the same time the layman, the unclean, and mourners, were prevented from entering the Sanctuary, as will be explained. Among other things that tend to display the greatness and the glory of the Temple and to inspire us with awe, is the rule that none shall approach it in a state of drunkenness or uncleanness, or in a disorderly state, i.e., the hair undressed and the garments rent ; and that every one who officiated as priest should first wash his hands and his feet.

In order to raise the estimation of the Temple, those who ministered therein received great honour ; and the priests and Levites were therefore distinguished from the rest. It was commanded that the priests should be clothed properly with beautiful and good garments, " holy garments for glory and for beauty " (Exod. xxviii. 2). A priest that had a blemish was not allowed to officiate ; and not only those that had a blemish were excluded from the service, but also—according to the Talmudic interpretation of this precept—those that had an abnormal appearance ; for the multitude does not estimate man by his true form but by the perfection of his bodily limbs and the beauty of his garments, and the Temple was to be held in great reverence by all.

The Levites did not sacrifice ; they were not considered as being agents in the atonement of sins, for it was only the priest who was commanded " to make atonement for him " (Lev. iv. 26) and " to make atonement for her " (Lev. xii. 8). The duty of the Levites was the performance of vocal music ; and a Levite became therefore disabled for service when he lost his voice. The object of the singing is to produce certain emotions ; this object can only be attained by pleasing sounds and melodies accompanied by music, as was always the case in the Temple.

Again, the priests, even when fit for service, and actually officiating in the

Temple, were not allowed to sit down, or enter it whenever they liked ; the Most Holy was only entered by the high-priest four times on the Day of Atonement, and on no other occasion.   The object of all these rules was to raise the estimation of the Sanctuary in the eyes of the people.

Since many beasts were daily slaughtered in the holy place, the flesh cut in pieces and the entrails and the legs burnt and washed, the smell of the place would undoubtedly have been like the smell of slaughter-houses, if nothing had been done to counteract it.   They were therefore commanded to burn incense there twice every day, in the morning and in the evening (Exod. xxx. 7, 8), in order to give the place and the garments of those who officiated there a pleasant odour.   There is a well-known saying of our Sages, " In Jericho they could smell the incense " [burnt in the Temple].   This pro-vision likewise tended to support the dignity of the Temple.   If there had not been a good smell, let alone if there had been a stench, it would have produced in the minds of the people the reverse of respect ; for our heart generally feels elevated in the presence of good odour, and is attracted by it, but it abhors and avoids bad smell.

The anointing oil (Exod. xxx. 22–33) served a double purpose : to give the anointed object a good odour, and to produce the impression that it was something great, holy, and distinguished, and better than other objects of the same species ; it made no difference whether that object was a human being, a garment, or a vessel.   All this aimed at producing due respect to-wards the Sanctuary, and indirectly fear of God.   When a person enters the Temple, certain emotions are produced in him ; and obstinate hearts are softened and humbled.   These plans and indirect means were devised by the Law, to soften and humble man's heart at entering the holy place, in order that he might entrust himself to the sure guidance of God's commandments. This is distinctly said in the Law : " And thou shalt eat before the Lord thy God, in the place which he shall choose to place his name there, the tithe of thy corn, of thy wine, and of thine oil, and the firstlings of thy herds and of thy flocks ; that thou mayest learn to fear the Lord thy God always " (Deut. xiv. 23).   The object of all these ceremonies is now clear.   The reason why we are not allowed to prepare [for common use] the anointing oil and the incense (*ibid*. ver. 32, 38) is obvious ; for when the odour [of the oil and incense] is perceived only in the Sanctuary, the desired effect is great ; be-sides [if it were allowed for every one to prepare the anointing oil], people might anoint themselves therewith and imagine themselves distinguished ; much disorder and dissension would then follow.

It is clear that when the ark was carried on the shoulder, and was not put on a waggon, it was done out of respect towards it, and also to prevent its being damaged in its form and shape ; even the staves were not moved out of the rings, for this reason.   In order that the form of the ephod and the breastplate should not be spoiled, they were never separated.   The garments were also entirely woven and not cut, in order not to spoil the work of the weaving.

Those that ministered in the Temple were strictly prohibited to interfere with each other's work ; for if in public duties and offices, each one would not have assigned to him his particular task, general carelessness and neglect would soon be noticed.

It is evident that the object of giving different degrees of sanctity to the different places, to the Temple mount, the place between the two walls, to the Hall of women, to the Hall, and so on up to the Most Holy, was to raise the respect and reverence of the Temple in the heart of every one that approached it.

We have thus described the reason of all precepts of this class.

CHAPTER XLVI

THE precepts of the eleventh class are enumerated in the Section on Divine Service (*Sefer 'abodah*) and the Section on Sacrifices (*Sefer ha-korbanot*). We have described their use in general terms (chap. xxxii.). I will now proceed to give the reason of each precept separately.

Scripture tells us, according to the Version of Onkelos, that the Egyptians worshipped Aries, and therefore abstained from killing sheep, and held shepherds in contempt. Comp. " Behold we shall sacrifice the abomination of the Egyptians," etc. (Exod. viii. 26) ; " For every shepherd is an abomination to the Egyptians " (Gen. xlvi. 34). Some sects among the Sabeans worshipped demons, and imagined that these assumed the form of goats, and called them therefore " goats " [*se'irim*]. This worship was widespread. Comp. " And they shall no more offer their sacrifices unto demons, after whom they have gone a whoring " (Lev. xvii. 7). For this reason those sects abstained from eating goats' flesh. Most idolaters objected to killing cattle, holding this species of animals in great estimation. Therefore the people of Hodu [Indians] up to this day do not slaughter cattle even in those countries where other animals are slaughtered. In order to eradicate these false principles, the Law commands us to offer sacrifices only of these three kinds : " Ye shall bring your offering of the cattle [viz.], of the herd and of the flock " (Lev. i. 2). Thus the very act which is considered by the heathen as the greatest crime, is the means of approaching God, and obtaining His pardon for our sins. In this manner, evil principles, the diseases of the human soul, are cured by other principles which are diametrically opposite.

This is also the reason why we were commanded to kill a lamb on Passover, and to sprinkle the blood thereof outside on the gates. We had to free ourselves of evil doctrines and to proclaim the opposite, viz., that the very act which was then considered as being the cause of death would be the cause of deliverance from death. Comp. " And the Lord will pass over the door, and will not suffer the destroyer to come unto your houses to s nite you " (Exod. xii. 23). Thus they were rewarded for performing openly a service every part of which was objected to by the idolaters.

To the above reason for the exclusive selection of the three kinds of animals for sacrifices, we may add the following, namely, that these species are animals which can be got very easily, contrary to the practice of idolaters that sacrifice lions, bears, and wild beasts, as is stated in the book Tomtom. As, however, many could not afford to offer a beast, the Law commanded that birds also should be sacrificed, but only of those species which are found abundantly in Palestine, are suitable, and can easily be obtained, namely, turtledoves and pigeons. Those who are too poor to offer a bird, may bring bread of any of the kinds then in use : baked in the oven, baked in a pan, or in a frying-pan. If the baking of the bread is too much trouble for a person, he may bring flour. All this concerns only those who desire to sacrifice; for we are distinctly told that the omission of the sacrificial service on our part will not be reckoned to us a sin: " If thou shalt forbear to vow, it shall be no sin in thee " (Deut. xxiii. 22). The idolaters did not offer any other bread but leavened, and chose sweet things for their sacrifices, which they seasoned with honey, as is fully described in the books which I named before ; but salt is not mentioned in any of their sacrifices. Our Law therefore forbade us to offer leaven or honey, and commanded us to have salt in every sacrifice : " With all thine offerings thou shalt offer salt " (Lev. ii. 13). It is further ordained that the offerings must all be perfect and in the best condition, in order that no one should slight the offering or treat with contempt that which is offered to God's name : " Offer it now unto thy governor ; will he be pleased with thee ? " (Mal. i. 8). This is the reason why no animal could be brought that was not yet seven days old (Lev. xxii. 26) ; it is imperfect and contemptible, like an untimely birth. Because of their degraded character it was prohibited to bring " the hire of a harlot and the price of a dog " (Deut. xxiii. 18) into the Sanctuary. In order to bring the offering in the best condition, we choose the old of the turtle-doves and the young of the pigeons, the old pigeons being less agreeable. The oblation must likewise be mingled with oil, and must be of fine flour (Lev. ii. 1), for in this condition it is good and pleasant. Frankincense is prescribed (*ibid.*) because its fumes are good in places filled with the odour of burnt flesh. The burnt-offering was flayed (Lev. i. 16), and its inwards and legs, although they were entirely burnt, had to be previously washed (*ibid.* ver. 9), in order that due respect should be shown to the sacrifice, and it should not appear despicable and contemptible. This object is constantly kept in view, and is often taught, " Ye say, The table of the Lord is polluted ; and the fruit thereof, even his meat, is contemptible " (Mal. i. 12). For the same reason no body uncircumcised, or unclean (Lev. xxii. 4), was allowed to partake of any offering ; nor could any offering be eaten that had become unclean (Lev. vii. 19), or was left till after a certain time (*ibid.* vii. 15–17), or concerning which an illegal intention had been conceived ; and it had also to be consumed in a particular place. Of the burnt-offering, which is entirely devoted to God, nothing at all was eaten. Those sacrifices which are brought for a sin, viz., sin-offering and guilt-offering, must be eaten within the court of the Sanctuary (*azarah*), and only on the day of their slaughtering and the night following, whilst peace-offerings, which are next in sanctity, being sacrifices of the second degree, may be eaten in the whole of Jerusalem, on the day they have been offered and on the following day, but not later. After that time the sacrifices would become spoiled, and be unfit for food.

In order that we may respect the sacrifices and all that is devoted to the name of God, we are told that whosoever takes part of a holy thing for common use has committed a trespass, must bring a sin-offering, and restore what he has taken with an addition of the fifth part of its value, although he may have committed the trespass in ignorance. For the same reason animals reserved for holy purposes must not be employed in work ; nor is the shearing of such animals permitted (Deut. xv. 19). The law concerning the change of a sacrifice must be considered as a preventive ; for if it were permitted to substitute a good animal for a bad one, people would substitute a bad animal for a good one, and say that it was better than the original ; it was therefore the rule that, if any such change had taken place, both the " original sacrifice and the exchange thereof should be holy " (Lev. xxvii. 9). When a person redeems a thing devoted by him to the Sanctuary, he must likewise add one-fifth (Lev. xxvii. 13, 15) ; the reason for this is plain. Man is usually selfish, and is naturally inclined to keep and save his property. He would therefore not take the necessary trouble in the interest of the Sanctuary ; he would not expose his property sufficiently to the sight of the valuer, and its true value would not be fixed. Therefore the owner had to add one-fifth, whilst a stranger paid only the exact value. These rules were laid down in order that people should not despise that with which the name of God is connected, and which serves as a means of approaching God. The oblation of the priest was entirely burnt (Lev. vi. 16), because the priest offered up his oblation by himself, and if he were to offer it, and at the same time to eat it, it would appear as if he had not performed any service. For nothing was offered upon the altar of the ordinary oblations of any person except the frankin-cense and a handful of the flour or cake ; and if, in addition to the fact that the offering was small, he who offered it were himself to eat it, nothing of a sacrificial service would be noticed. It is therefore entirely burnt (Lev. vi. 16).

The reason of the particular laws concerning the Passover lamb is clear. It was eaten roasted by fire (Exod. xii. 8–9) in one house, and without breaking the bones thereof (*ibid.* ver. 46). In the same way as the Israelites were commanded to eat unleavened bread, because they could prepare it hastily, so they were commanded, for the sake of haste, to roast the lamb, because there was not sufficient time to boil it, or to prepare other food ; even the delay caused by breaking the bones and to extract their marrow was pro-hibited ; the one principle is laid down for all these rules, " Ye shall eat it in haste " (Exod. xii. 11). But when haste is necessary the bones cannot be broken, nor parts of it sent from house to house ; for the company could not wait with their meal till he returned. Such things would lead to laxity and delay, whilst the object of these rules was to make a show of the hurry and haste, in order that none should be too late to leave Egypt with the main body of the people, and be thus exposed to the attacks and the evil [designs of the enemy]. These temporary commandments were then made perma-nent, in order that we may remember what was done in those days. " And thou shalt keep this ordinance in his season from year to year " (Exod. xiii. 10). Each Passover lamb was only eaten by those who had previously agreed to consume it together, in order that people should be anxious to procure it, and should not rely on friends, relations, or on chance, without themselves taking any trouble about it before Passover. The reason of the prohibition that the uncircumcised should not eat of it (Exod. xii. 48) is explained by our Sages as follows :—The Israelites neglected circumcision during their long stay in Egypt, in order to make themselves appear like the Egyptians. When God gave them the commandment of the Passover, and ordered that no one should kill the Passover lamb unless he, his sons, and all the male per-sons in his household were circumcised, that only " then he could come near and keep it " (*ibid.* xii. 48), all performed this commandment, and the number of the circumcised being large the blood of the Passover and that of the circumcision flowed together. The Prophet Ezekiel (xvi. 6), referring to this event, says, "When I saw thee sprinkled with thine own blood I said unto thee, Live because of thy [two kinds of] blood," i.e., because of the blood of the Passover and that of the circumcision.

Although blood was very unclean in the eyes of the Sabeans, they nevertheless partook of it, because they thought it was the food of the spirits ; by eating it man has something in common with the spirits, which join him and tell him future events, according to the notion which people generally have of spirits. There were, however, people who objected to eating blood, as a thing naturally disliked by man ; they killed a beast, received the blood in a vessel or in a pot, and ate of the flesh of that beast, whilst sitting round the blood. They imagined that in this manner the spirits would come to partake of the blood which was their food, whilst the idolaters were eating the flesh ; that love, brotherhood, and friendship with the spirits were established, because they dined with the latter at one place and at the same time ; that the spirits would appear to them in dreams, inform them of coming events, and be favourable to them. Such ideas people liked and accepted in those days ; they were general, and their correctness was not doubted by any one of the common people. The Law, which is perfect in the eyes of those who know it, and seeks to cure mankind of these lasting diseases, forbade the eating of blood, and emphasized the prohibition exactly in the same terms as it emphasizes idolatry : "I will set my face against that soul that eateth blood" (Lev. xvii. 10). The same language is employed in reference to him "who giveth of his seed unto Molech"; "then I will set my face against that man" (*ibid.* xx. 5). There is, besides idolatry and eating blood, no other sin in reference to which these words are used. For the eating of blood leads to a kind of idolatry, to the worship of spirits. Our Law declared the blood as pure, and made it the means of purifying other objects by its touch. "And thou shalt take of the blood . . . and sprinkle it upon Aaron, and upon his garments, and upon his sons, and upon the garments of his sons with him. And he shall be hallowed, and his garments, and his sons," etc. (Exod. xxix. 21). Furthermore, the blood was sprinkled upon the altar, and in the whole service it was insisted upon pouring it out, and not upon collecting it. Comp. "And he shall pour out all the blood at the bottom of the altar" (Lev. iv. 18) ; "And the blood of thy sacrifices shall be poured out upon the altar of the Lord thy God" (Deut. xii. 27). Also the blood of those beasts that were killed for common use, and not for sacrifices, must be poured out, "Thou shalt pour it upon the earth as water" (*ibid.* ver. 24). We are not allowed to gather and have a meal round the blood, "You shall not eat round the blood" (Lev. xix. 26). As the Israelites were inclined to continue their rebellious conduct, to follow the doctrines in which they had been brought up, and which were then general, and to assemble round the blood in order to eat there and to meet the spirits, God forbade the Israelites to eat ordinary meat during their stay in the wilderness ; they could only partake of the meat of peace-offerings. The reason of this precept is distinctly stated, viz., that the blood shall be poured out upon the altar, and the people do not assemble round about. Comp. "To the end that the children of Israel may bring their sacrifices, which they offer in the open field, even that they may bring them unto the Lord. . . . And the priest shall sprinkle the blood upon the altar, . . . and they shall no more offer their sacrifices unto the spirits " (Lev. xvii. 5–7). Now there remained to provide for the slaughtering of the beasts of the field and birds, because those beasts were never sacrificed, and birds did never serve as peace-offerings (Lev. iii.). The commandment was therefore given that whenever a beast or a bird that may be eaten is killed, the blood thereof must be covered with earth (Lev. xvii. 13), in order that the people should not assemble round the blood for the purpose of eating there. The object was thus fully gained to break the connexion between these fools and their spirits. This belief flourished about the time of our Teacher Moses. People were attracted and misled by it. We find it in the Song of Moses (Deut. xxxii.): " They sacrificed unto spirits, not to God " (*ibid.* 17). According to the explanation of our Sages, the words *lo eloha* imply the following idea : They have not only not left off worshipping things in existence ; they even worship imaginary things. This is expressed in Sifri as follows : " It is not enough for them to worship the sun, the moon, the stars ; they even worship their *babuah*. The word *babuah* signifies " shadow." Let us now return to our subject. The prohibition of slaughtering cattle for common use applied only to the wilderness, because as regards the " spirits " it was then the general belief that they dwelt in deserts, that there they spoke and were visible, whilst in towns and in cultivated land they did not appear. In accordance with this belief those inhabitants of a town who wanted to perform any of those stupid practices, left the town and went to woods and waste places. The use of cattle for common food was therefore allowed when the Israelites entered Palestine. Besides, there were great hopes that the disease would become weakened, and the followers of the doctrines would decrease. Furthermore, it was almost impossible that every one who wanted to eat meat should come to Jerusalem. For these reasons the above restriction was limited to the stay of the Israelites in the wilderness.

The greater the sin which a person had committed, the lower was the species from which the sin-offering was brought. The offering for worshipping idols in ignorance was only a she-goat, whilst for other sins an ordinary person brought either a ewe-lamb or a she-goat (Lev. iv. 27–35), the females bring, as a rule, in every species, inferior to the males. There is no greater sin than idolatry, and also no inferior species than a she-goat. The offering of a king for sins committed ignorantly was a he-goat (*ibid.* vers. 22–26), as a mark of distinction. The high priest and the Synhedrion, who only gave a wrong decision in ignorance, but have not actually committed a sin, brought a bull for their sin-offering (*ibid.* ver. 3–21), or a he-goat, when the decision referred to idolatry (Num. xv. 22–26). The sins for which guilt-offerings were brought were not as bad as transgressions that required a sin-offering. The guilt-offering was therefore a ram, or a lamb, so that the species as well as the sex were superior in this latter case, for the guilt-offering was a male sheep. For the same reason we see the burnt-offering, which was entirely burnt upon the altar, was selected from the superior sex ; for only male animals were admitted as burnt-offerings. It is in accordance with the same principle that luxury and incense were absent from the oblations of a sinner (Lev. v. 11), and of a *sotah*, i.e., a woman suspected of adultery (Num. v. 15). In these cases the oil and the frankincense were not added; this luxury was absent, because the persons that brought the oblation were not good and proper in their deeds, and they are, as it were, to be reminded by their offerings that they ought to repent; as if they were told, " Your offering is without any ornamental addition on account of the wickedness of your deeds." As the *sotah* acted more disgracefully than any person who sins in ignorance, her offering consisted of the lowest kind, viz., of barley flour (*ibid.*). Thus the reasons of all these particular laws are well connected, and show that the precepts are wonderful in their significance.

Our Sages say that the offering for the eighth day of dedication was " a calf, a young bullock, for a sin-offering " (Lev. xi. 2), in order to atone for the sin of the Israelites in making a golden calf. The sin-offering, which was brought on the Day of Atonement (*ibid.* xvi. 3), was likewise explained as being an atonement for that sin. From this argument of our Sages I deduce that he-goats were always brought as sin-offerings, by individual persons and also by the whole congregation, viz., on the Festivals, New-moon, Day of Atonement, and for idolatry, because most of the transgressions and sins of the Israelites were sacrifices to spirits (*se'irim*, lit., goats), as is clearly stated, " They shall no more offer their sacrifices unto spirits " (Lev. xvii. 7). Our Sages, however, explained the fact that goats were always the sin-offer-ings of the congregation, as an allusion to the sin of the whole congregation of Israel; for in the account of the selling of the pious Joseph we read, " And they killed a kid of the goats " (Gen. xxxvii. 31). Do not consider this as a weak argument; for it is the object of all these ceremonies to impress on the mind of every sinner and transgressor the necessity of continually remem-bering and mentioning his sins. Thus the Psalmist says, " And my sin is ever before me " (Ps. li. 3). The above-mentioned sin-offerings further show us that when we commit a sin, we, our children, and the children of our children, require atonement for that sin by some kind of service analogous to the sin committed. If a person has sinned in respect to property he must liberally spend his property in the service of God; if he indulged in sinful bodily enjoyments he must weary his body and trouble it by a service of privation and fasting, and rising early before daybreak. If he went astray in respect to his moral conduct he must oppose his failings by keeping to the opposite extreme, as we have pointed out in Mishneh-torah *Hilkot De'ot* (chap. ii.) *et passim.* If his intellectual faculties have been concerned in the sin, if he has believed something false on account of the insufficiency of his intellect, and his neglect of research and proper study, he must remedy his fault by turning his thoughts entirely away from worldly affairs, and directing them exclusively to intellectual exercise, and by carefully reflecting on that which ought to form the subject of his belief. Comp. " And my heart hath been secretly enticed, but my hand touched my mouth " (Job xxxi. 27). These words express figuratively the lesson that we should pause and stop at that which appears doubtful, as has been pointed out by us in the begin-ning of this treatise. The same we notice in the case of Aaron. He had his share in the sin of the golden calf, and therefore a bullock and a calf were brought by him and his successors as an offering. Similarly, the sin connected with a kid of goats was atoned for by a kid of goats. When this theory has been well established in the minds of the people, they must certainly be led by it to consider disobedience to God as a disgraceful thing. Every one will then be careful that he should not sin, and require a protracted and burdensome atonement; he will be afraid he might not be able to complete it, and will therefore altogether abstain from sinning, and avoid it. This object [of the laws under discussion] is very clear, and note it likewise.

I will here call your attention to a very remarkable thing, although it does not seem at first thought to belong to our subject. It is only the goat brought on New-moon as a sin-offering that the law calls " a sin-offering unto the Lord " (Num. xxviii. 15). The sin-offerings brought on the three festivals (*ibid.* vers. 22, 30; xxix. 5, 11, etc.) are not called so, nor are any other sin-offerings. The reason thereof is, according to my opinion, undoubtedly this: The additional offerings brought by the congregation at certain periods were all burnt-offerings; only " one kid of goats to make an atonement " was offered on every one of these exceptional days. The latter was eaten [by the priests], whilst the burnt-offerings were entirely consumed by fire, and are called " an offering made by fire unto the Lord." The phrases " a sin-offering unto the Lord " and " a peace-offering unto the Lord " do not occur in the law, because these were eaten by man; but even those sin-offerings that were entirely burnt (Lev. iv. 12, 21) cannot be called " an offering made by fire unto the Lord," as will be explained in the course of this chapter. It is therefore impossible that the goats which are eaten [by the priests], and are not entirely burnt, should be called " sin-offerings unto the Lord." But as it was found that the kid offered on New-moon might be mistaken as an offering brought to the moon, in the manner of the Egyptians, who sacrificed to the moon on the days of New-moon, it was distinctly stated that this goat is offered in obedience to God's command, and not in honour of the moon. This fear did not apply to the sin-offerings on the Festivals, nor to any other sin-offering, because they were not offered on the days of New-moon, or on any other day marked out by Nature, but on such days as were selected by the Divine Will. Not so the days of New-moon; they are not fixed by the Law [but by Nature]. On the New-moon the idolaters sacrificed to the moon, in the same manner as they sacrificed to the sun when it rose and set in certain particular degrees. This is described in the works [mentioned above]. On this account the extraordinary phrase " A sin-offering unto the Lord " is exceptionally introduced in reference to the goat brought on New-moon, in order to remove the idolatrous ideas that were still lingering in the sorely diseased hearts. Note this exception likewise. A sin-offering which is brought in the hope to atone for one or more great sins, as, e.g., the sin-offering [of the Synhedrion or the high-priest] for a sin committed in ignorance, and the like, are not burnt upon the altar, but without the camp; upon the altar only the burnt-offering, and the like, are burnt, wherefore it was called the altar of the burnt-offering. The burning of the holocaust, and of every " memorial," is called " a sweet savour unto the Lord "; and so it undoubtedly is, since it serves to remove idolatrous doctrines from our hearts, as we have shown. But the burning of these sin-offerings is a symbol that the sin [for which the offering is brought] is utterly removed and destroyed, like the body that is being burnt; of the sinful seed no trace shall remain, as no trace is left of the sin-offering, which is entirely destroyed by fire; the smoke thereof is not " a sweet savour unto the Lord," but, on the contrary, a smoke despised and abhorred. For this reason the burning took place without the camp. Similarly we notice that the oblations of a *sotah* is called " an offering of memorial, bringing iniquity to remembrance " (Num. v. 15); it is not a pleasing thing [to the Lord]. The goat [of the Day of Atonement] that was sent [into the wilderness] (Lev. xvi. 20, *seq.*) served as an atonement for all serious transgressions more than any other sin-offering of the congregation. As it thus seemed to carry off all sins, it was not accepted as an ordinary sacrifice to be slaughtered, burnt, or even brought near the Sanctuary; it was removed as far as possible, and sent forth into a waste, uncultivated, uninhabited land. There is no doubt that sins cannot be carried like a burden, and taken off the shoulder of one being to be laid on that of another being. But these ceremonies are of a symbolic character, and serve to impress men with a certain idea, and to induce them to repent; as if to say, we have freed ourselves of our previous deeds, have cast them behind our backs, and removed them from us as far as possible.

As regards the offering of wine (Num. xv. 5, *seq.*), I am at a loss to find a reason why God commanded it, since idolaters brought wine as an offering. But though I am unable to give a reason, another person suggested the following one : Meat is the best nourishment for the appetitive faculty, the source of which is the liver; wine supports best the vital faculty, whose centre is the heart; music is most agreeable to the psychic faculty, the source of which is in the brain. Each one of our faculties approaches God with that which it likes best. Thus the sacrifice consists of meat, wine, and music.

The use of keeping festivals is plain. Man derives benefit from such assemblies : the emotions produced renew the attachment to religion; they lead to friendly and social intercourse among the people. This is especially the object of the commandment to gather the people together on the Feast of Tabernacles, as is plainly stated : " that they may hear, and that they may learn and fear the Lord " (Deut. xxxi. 12). The same is the object of the rule that the money for the second tithe must be spent by all in one place (*ibid.* xiv. 22–26), as we have explained (chap. xxxix. p. 184). The fruit of trees in their fourth year, and the tithe of the cattle, had to be brought to Jerusalem. There would therefore be in Jerusalem the meat of the tithes, the wine of the fruit of the fourth year, and the money of the second tithe. Plenty of food would always be found there. Nothing of the above things could be sold ; nothing could be set aside for another year ; the Law orders that they should be brought " year by year " (Deut. xiv. 22); the owner was thus compelled to spend part of them in charity. As regards the Festivals it is especially enjoined : " And thou shalt rejoice in thy feast, thou, and thy son, and thy daughter, and thy man-servant, and thy maid-servant, and the Levite, the stranger, and the fatherless, and the widow " (*ibid.* xvi. 14). We have thus explained the reason of every law belonging to this class, and even many details of the laws.

CHAPTER XLVII

THE precepts of the twelfth class are those which we have enumerated in the section on " Purity " (*Sefer tohorah*). Although we have mentioned their use in general, we will here offer an additional explanation, and [first] fully discuss the object of the whole class, and then show the reason of each single commandment, as far as we have been able to discover it. I maintain that the Law which was revealed to Moses, our Teacher, and which is called by his name, aims at facilitating the service and lessening the burden, and if a person complains that certain precepts cause him pain and great trouble, he cannot have thought of the habits and doctrines that were general in those days. Let him consider the difference between a man burning his own son in serving his god, and our burning a pigeon to the service of our God. Scripture relates, " for even their sons and their daughters they burn in the fire to their gods " (Deut. xii. 31). This was the way in which the heathen worshipped their gods, and instead of such a sacrifice we have the burning of a pigeon or a handful of flour in our worship. In accordance with this fact, the Israelites, when disobedient, were rebuked by God as follows : " O My people, what have I done unto thee ? and wherein have I wearied thee ? Testify against me " (Mic. vi. 3). Again, " Have I been a wilderness unto Israel ? a land of darkness ? Wherefore say my people, We are miserable ; we will come no more unto thee " (Jer. ii. 31) ; that is to say, Through which of the commandments has the Law become burdensome to the Israelites, that they renounce it ? In the same manner God asks the people, " What iniquity have your fathers found in me, that they are gone far from me ? " etc. (*ibid.* ii. 5). All these passages express one and the same idea.

This is the great principle which you must never lose sight of. After having stated this principle, I repeat that the object of the Sanctuary was to create in the hearts of those who enter it certain feelings of awe and reverence, in accordance with the command, " You shall reverence my sanctuary " (Lev. xix. 30). But when we continually see an object, however sublime it may be, our regard for that object will be lessened, and the impression we have received of it will be weakened. Our Sages, considering this fact, said that we should not enter the Temple whenever we liked, and pointed to the words : " Make thy foot rare in the house of thy friend " (Prov. xxv. 17). For this reason the unclean were not allowed to enter the Sanctuary, although there are so many kinds of uncleanliness, that [at a time] only a few people are clean. For even if a person does not touch a beast that died of its own accord (Lev. xi. 27), he can scarcely avoid touching one of the eight kinds of creeping animals (*ibid.* 29, *seq.*), the dead bodies of which we find at all times in houses, in food and drink, and upon which we frequently tread wherever we walk ; and, if he avoids touching these, he may touch a woman in her separation (*ibid.* xv. 18), or a male or female that have a running issue (*ibid.* ver. 1, *seq.* and 25, *seq.*), or a leper (*ibid.* xiii. 46), or their bed (*ibid.* xv. 5). Escaping these, he may become unclean by cohabitation with his wife, or by pollution (*ibid.* 15), and even when he has cleansed himself from any of these kinds of uncleanliness, he cannot enter the Sanctuary till after sunset ; but not being enabled to enter the Sanctuary at night time, although he is clean after sunset, as may be inferred from *Middot* and *Tamid*, he is again, during the night, subject to becoming unclean either by cohabiting with his wife or by some other source of uncleanliness, and may rise in the morning in the same condition as the day before. All this serves to keep people away from the Sanctuary, and to prevent them from entering it whenever they liked. Our Sages, as is well known, said, " Even a clean person may not enter the

Sanctuary for the purpose of performing divine service, unless he takes previously a bath." By such acts the reverence [for the Sanctuary] will continue, the right impression will be produced which leads man, as is intended, to humility.

The easier the diffusion of uncleanliness is, the more difficult and the more retarded is its purification. Most easily is uncleanliness communicated by the dead body to those who are under the same roof, especially to relatives. The purification can only be completed by means of the ashes of the red heifer, however scarce it may be, and only in seven days (Num. xix. 11). The uncleanness caused by a woman having running issue or during her separation is more frequent than that caused by contact with unclean objects ; seven days are therefore required for their purification (Lev. xv. 19, 28), whilst those that touch them are only unclean one day (*ibid.* vii. 18). Males or females that are unclean through running issue, and a woman after childbirth, must in addition bring a sacrifice, because their uncleanness occurs less frequently than that of women in their separation. All these cases of uncleanliness, viz., running issue of males or females, menstruations, leprosy, dead bodies of human beings, carcases of beasts and creeping things, and issue of semen, are sources of dirt and filth. We have thus shown that the above precepts are very useful in many respects. First, they keep us at a distance from dirty and filthy objects ; secondly, they guard the Sanctuary ; thirdly, they pay regard to an established custom (for the Sabeans submitted to very troublesome restrictions when unclean, as you will soon hear) ; fourthly, they lightened that burden for us ; for we are not impeded through these laws in our ordinary occupations by the distinction the Law makes between that which is unclean and that which is clean. For this distinction applies only in reference to the Sanctuary and the holy objects connected with it ; it does not apply to other cases. " She shall touch no hallowed thing, nor come into the Sanctuary " (Lev. xii. 4). Other persons [that do not intend to enter the Sanctuary or touch any holy thing], are not guilty of any sin if they remain unclean as long as they like, and eat, according to their pleasure, ordinary food that has been in contact with unclean things. But the practice of the Sabeans, even at present general in the East, among the few still left of the Magi, was to keep a menstruous woman in a house by herself, to burn that upon which she treads, and to consider as unclean every one that speaks with her ; even if a wind passed over her and a clean person, the latter was unclean in the eyes of the Sabeans. See the difference between this practice and our rule, that " whatever services a wife generally does to her husband, she may do to him in her separation " ; only cohabitation is prohibited during the days of her uncleanness. Another custom among the Sabeans, which is still widespread, is this : whatever is separated from the body, as hair, nail, or blood, is unclean ; every barber is therefore unclean in their estimation, because he touches blood and hair ; whenever a person passes a razor over his skin he must take a bath in running water. Such burdensome practices were numerous among the Sabeans, whilst we apply the laws that distinguish between the unclean and the clean only with regard to hallowed things and to the Sanctuary. The divine words, " And ye shall sanctify yourselves, and ye shall be holy " (Lev. xi. 44), do not refer to these laws at all. According to Sifra, they refer to sanctity by obedience to God's commandments. The same interpretation is given in Sifra of the words, " Ye shall be holy," i.e. obedient to His commandments (xix. 2). Hence the transgression of commandments is also called uncleanliness or defilement. This term is especially used of the chief and principal crimes, which are idolatry, adultery, and murder. In reference to idolatry it is said, " He hath given of his seed unto Molech to defile my sanctuary, and to profane my holy name " (*ibid.* xx. 3). In reference to adultery we read, " Defile not ye yourselves in any of these things " (*ibid.* xviii. 24), and " Defile not the land " (Num. xxxv. 34) in reference to murder. It is therefore clear that the term " defilement " [or uncleanliness] is used homonymously of three things : 1. Of man's violation and transgression of that which he is commanded as regards his actions and his opinions. 2. Of dirt and filth ; comp. " Her filthiness in her skirts " (Lam. i. 9). 3. Of the above-named imaginary defilement such as touching and carrying certain objects, or being with them under the same roof. In reference to the third kind, our Sages said, The words of the Law are not subject to becoming unclean (B. T. Ber. 22*a*). In the same manner the term " holiness " is used homonymously of three things corresponding to the three kinds of uncleanness. As uncleanness caused by a dead body could only be removed after seven days, by means of the ashes of the red heifer, and the priests had constantly occasion to enter the Sanctuary, the Law exceptionally forbids them to defile themselves by a dead body (Lev. xxi. 1), except in cases where defilement is necessary, and the contrary would be unnatural. For it would be unnatural to abstain from approaching the dead body of a parent, child, or brother. As it was very necessary that the high-priest should *always* be in the Sanctuary, in accordance with the Divine command, " And it shall always be on his forehead " (Exod. xxviii. 38), he was not permitted to defile himself by any dead body whatever, even of the above-named relatives (Lev. xxi. 10–12). Women were not engaged in sacrificial service ; the above law consequently does not apply to women ; it is addressed to " the sons of Aaron," and not to " the daughters of Aaron." It was, however, impossible to assume that none of the Israelites made a mistake, by entering the Sanctuary, or eating hallowed things in a state of uncleanliness. It was even possible that there were persons who did this knowingly, since there are wicked people who commit knowingly even the greatest crimes ; for this reason certain sacrifices were commanded as an atonement for the defilement of the Sanctuary and its hallowed things. They were of different kinds ; some of them atoned for defilement caused ignorantly, others for defilement caused knowingly. For this purpose were brought the goats on the Festivals and the New-moon days (Num. xxviii. 15, 22, etc.), and the goat sent away on the Day of Atonement (Lev. xvi. 16), as is explained in its place (Mishnah Shebnot, i. 4). These sacrifices serve to prevent those who defiled the Sanctuary of the Lord knowingly from thinking that they had not done a great wrong ; they should know that they obtained atonement by the sacrifice of the goat, as the Law says, " That they die not in their uncleanness " (Lev. xv. 31) ; " That Aaron may bear the iniquity of the holy things " (Exod. xxviii. 38). This idea is frequently repeated.

The uncleanness through leprosy we have already explained. Our Sages have also clearly stated the meaning thereof. All agree that leprosy is a punishment for slander. The disease begins in the walls of the houses (Lev. xiv. 33, *seq.*). If the sinner repents, the object is attained ; if he remains in his disobedience, the disease affects his bed and house furniture ; if he still continues to sin, the leprosy attacks his own garments, and then his body. This is a miracle received in our nation by tradition, in the same manner as the effect of the trial of a faithless wife (Num. v. 11, *seq.*). The good effect of this belief is evident. Leprosy is besides a contagious disease, and people almost naturally abhor it, and keep away from it. The purification was effected by cedar-wood, hyssop, scarlet thread, and two birds (Lev. xiv. 4) ; their reason is stated in various Midrashic sayings, but the explanation does not agree with our theory. I do not know at present the reason of any of these things ; nor why cedar-wood, hyssop, and scarlet were used in the sacrifice of the red heifer (Num. xix. 6) ; nor why a bundle of hyssop was commanded for the sprinkling of the blood of the Passover-lamb (Exod. xii. 22). I cannot find any principle upon which to found an explanation why these particular things have been chosen.

The red heifer is called a sin-offering, because it effects the purification of persons that have become unclean through the dead body of a human being, and enables them to enter the Sanctuary [and to eat of hallowed things]. The idea taught by this law is this : Those who have defiled themselves would never be allowed to enter the Sanctuary, or to partake of holy things, were it not for the sacrifice of the red heifer, by which this sin is removed ; in the same manner as the plate [which the high-priest wears on his forehead] atones for uncleanness, and as a similar object is attained by the goats that are burnt. For this reason those were unclean who were engaged in the sacrifice of the heifer or the goats which were burnt, and even their garments were unclean. The same was the law in the case of the goat that was sent away [on the Day of Atonement] ; for it was believed that it made unclean those who touched it, because it carried off so many sins.

We have now mentioned the reasons for those commandments of this class, for which we were able to give a satisfactory reason according to our view.

CHAPTER XLVIII

The precepts of the thirteenth class are those which we have enumerated in the " Laws concerning forbidden food " (*Hilkot maakalot asurot*), " Laws concerning killing animals for food " (*Hilkot shehitah*), and " Laws concerning vows and Nazaritism " (*Hilkot nedarim u-nezirot*). We have fully and very explicitly discussed the object of this class in this treatise, and in our Commentary on the Sayings of the Fathers. We will here add a few remarks in reviewing the single commandments which are mentioned there.

I maintain that the food which is forbidden by the Law is unwholesome. There is nothing among the forbidden kinds of food whose injurious character is doubted, except pork (Lev. xi. 7), and fat (*ibid.* vii. 23). But also in these cases the doubt is not justified. For pork contains more moisture than necessary [for human food], and too much of superfluous matter. The principal reason why the Law forbids swine's flesh is to be found in the circumstance that its habits and its food are very dirty and loathsome. It has already been pointed out how emphatically the Law enjoins the removal of the sight of loathsome objects, even in the field and in the camp; how much more objectionable is such a sight in towns. But if it were allowed to eat swine's flesh, the streets and houses would be more dirty than any cesspool, as may be seen at present in the country of the Franks. A saying of our Sages declares: " The mouth of a swine is as dirty as dung itself " (B.T. Ber. 25*a*).

The fat of the intestines makes us full, interrupts our digestion, and produces cold and thick blood; it is more fit for fuel [than for human food].

Blood (Lev. xvii. 12), and *nebelah*, i.e., the flesh of an animal that died of itself (Deut. xiv. 21), are indigestible, and injurious as food; *Trefah*, an animal in a diseased state (Exod. xxii. 30), is on the way of becoming a *nebelah*.

The characteristics given in the Law (Lev. xi., and Deut. xiv.) of the permitted animals, viz., chewing the cud and divided hoofs for cattle, and fins and scales for fish, are in themselves neither the cause of the permission when they are present, nor of the prohibition when they are absent; but merely signs by which the recommended species of animals can be discerned from those that are forbidden.

The reason why the sinew that shrank is prohibited is stated in the Law (Gen. xxxii. 33).

It is prohibited to cut off a limb of a living animal and eat it, because such act would produce cruelty, and develop it; besides, the heathen kings used to do it; it was also a kind of idolatrous worship to cut off a certain limb of a living animal and to eat it.

Meat boiled in milk is undoubtedly gross food, and makes overfull; but I think that most probably it is also prohibited because it is somehow connected with idolatry, forming perhaps part of the service, or being used on some festival of the heathen. I find a support for this view in the circumstance that the Law mentions the prohibition twice after the commandment given concerning the festivals " Three times in the year all thy males shall appear before the Lord God " (Exod. xxiii. 17, and xxxiv. 23), as if to say, " When you come before me on your festivals, do not seethe your food in the manner as the heathen used to do." This I consider as the best reason for the prohibition; but as far as I have seen the books on Sabean rites, nothing is mentioned of this custom.

The commandment concerning the killing of animals is necessary, because the natural food of man consists of vegetables and of the flesh of animals; the best meat is that of animals permitted to be used as food. No doctor has any doubts about this. Since, therefore, the desire of procuring good food necessitates the slaying of animals, the Law enjoins that the death of the animal should be the easiest. It is not allowed to torment the animal by cutting the throat in a clumsy manner, by poleaxing, or by cutting off a limb whilst the animal is alive.

It is also prohibited to kill an animal with its young on the same day (Lev. xxii. 28), in order that people should be restrained and prevented from killing the two together in such a manner that the young is slain in the sight of the mother; for the pain of the animals under such circumstances is very great. There is no difference in this case between the pain of man and the pain of other living beings, since the love and tenderness of the mother for her young ones is not produced by reasoning, but by imagination, and this faculty exists not only in man but in most living beings. This law applies only to ox and lamb, because of the domestic animals used as food these alone are permitted to us, and in these cases the mother recognises her young.

The same reason applies to the law which enjoins that we should let the mother fly away when we take the young. The eggs over which the bird sits, and the young that are in need of their mother, are generally unfit for food, and when the mother is sent away she does not see the taking of her young ones, and does not feel any pain. In most cases, however, this commandment will cause man to leave the whole nest untouched, because [the young or the eggs], which he is allowed to take, are, as a rule, unfit for food. If the Law provides that such grief should not be caused to cattle or birds, how much more careful must we be that we should not cause grief to our fellow-men. When in the Talmud (Ber. p. 33*b*) those are blamed who use in their prayer the phrase, "Thy mercy extendeth to young birds," it is the expression of the one of the two opinions mentioned by us, namely, that the precepts of the Law have no other reason but the Divine will. We follow the other opinion.

The reason why we cover the blood when we kill animals, and why we do it only when we kill clean beasts and clean birds, has already been explained by us (*supra*, chap. xlvi., p. 362).

In addition to the things prohibited by the Law, we are also commanded to observe the prohibitions enjoined by our own vows (Num. xxx.). If we say, This bread or this meat is forbidden for us, we are not allowed to partake of that food. The object of that precept is to train us in temperance, that we should be able to control our appetites for eating and drinking. Our Sages say accordingly, "Vows are a fence for abstinence." As women are easily provoked to anger, owing to their greater excitability and the weakness of their mind, their oaths, if entirely under their own control, would cause great grief, quarrel, and disorder in the family; one kind of food would be allowed for the husband, and forbidden for the wife; another kind forbidden for the daughter, and allowed for the mother. Therefore the Law gives the father of the family control over the vows of those dependent on him. A woman that is independent, and not under the authority of a chief of the family, is, as regards vows, subject to the same laws as men; I mean a woman that has no husband, or that has no father, or that is of age, i.e., twelve years and six months.

The object of Nazaritism (Num. vi.) is obvious. It keeps away from wine that has ruined people in ancient and modern times. "Many strong men have been slain by it" (Prov. xxvii. 26). "But they also have erred through wine, . . . the priest and the prophet" (Isa. xxviii. 7). In the law about the Nazarite we notice even the prohibition, "he shall eat nothing that is made of the vine tree" (Num. vi. 4), as an additional precaution, implying the lesson that man must take wine only as much as is absolutely necessary. For he who abstains from drinking it is called "holy"; his sanctity is made equal to that of the high-priest, in not being allowed to defile himself even to his father, to his mother, and the like. This honour is given him because he abstains from wine.

CHAPTER XLIX

THE precepts of the fourteenth class are those which we enumerated in the Section on Women, the Laws concerning forbidden sexual intercourse, and cross-breeding of cattle (*Sefer nashim, Hilkot issure biah ve-kaleë behemah*). The law concerning circumcision belongs also to this class. The general purpose of these precepts has already been described by us. We will now proceed to explain them singly.

It is well known that man requires friends all his lifetime. Aristotle explains this in the ninth book of his Nikomachean Ethics. When man is in good health and prosperous, he enjoys the company of his friends; in time of trouble he is in need of them; in old age, when his body is weak, he is assisted by them. This love is more frequent and more intense between parents and children, and among [other] relations. Perfect love, brotherhood, and mutual assistance is only found among those near to each other by relationship. The members of a family united by common descent from the same grandfather, or even from some more distant ancestor, have towards each other a certain feeling of love, help each other, and sympathize with each other. To effect this is one of the chief purposes of the Law. Professional harlots were therefore not tolerated in Israel (Deut. xxiii. 18), because their existence would disturb the above relationship between man and man. Their children are strangers to everybody; no one knows to what family they belong; nor does any person recognize them as relatives. And this is the greatest misfortune that can befall any child or father. Another important object in prohibiting prostitution is to restrain excessive and continual lust; for lust increases with the variety of its objects. The sight of that to which a person has been accustomed for a long time does not produce such an ardent desire for its enjoyment as is produced by objects new in form and character. Another effect of this prohibition is the removal of a cause for strife; for if the prohibition did not exist, several persons might by chance come to one woman, and would naturally quarrel with each other; they would in many cases kill one another, or they would kill the woman. This is known to have occurred in days of old, " And they assembled themselves by troops in a harlot's house " (Jer. v. 7). In order to prevent these great evils, and to effect the great boon that all men should know their relationship to each other, prostitutes (Deut. xxiii. 17) were not tolerated, and sexual intercourse was only permitted when man has chosen a certain female, and married her openly; for if it sufficed merely to choose her, many a person would bring a prostitute into his house at a certain time agreed upon between them, and say that she was his wife. Therefore it is commanded to perform the act of engagement by which he declares that he has chosen her to take her for his wife, and then to go through the public ceremony of marriage. Comp. " And Boaz took ten men," etc. (Ruth iv. 2). It may happen that husband and wife do not agree, live without love and peace, and do not enjoy the benefit of a home; in that case he is permitted to send her away. If he had been allowed to divorce her by a mere word, or by turning her out of his house, the wife would wait for some negligence [on the part of the husband], and then come out and say that she was divorced; or having committed adultery, she and the adulterer would contend that she had then been divorced. Therefore the law is that divorce can only take place by means of a document which can serve as evidence, " He shall write her a bill of divorcement " (Deut. xxiv. 1). There are frequently occasions for suspicion of adultery and doubts concerning the conduct of the wife. Laws concerning a wife suspected of adultery (*sotah*) are therefore prescribed (Num. v.) ; the effect of which is that the wife, out of fear of the "bitter waters," is most careful to prevent any ill-feeling on the part of her husband against her. Even of those that felt quite innocent and safe most were rather willing to lose all their property than to submit to the prescribed treatment ; even death was preferred to the public disgrace of uncovering the head, undoing the hair, rending the garments and exposing the heart, and being led round through the Sanctuary in the presence of all, of women and men, and also in the presence of the members of the Synhedrion. The fear of this trial keeps away great diseases that ruin the home comfort.

As every maiden expects to be married, her seducer therefore is only ordered to marry her ; for he is undoubtedly the fittest husband for her. He will better heal her wound and redeem her character than any other husband. If, however, he is rejected by her or her father, he must give the dowry (Exod. xxii. 15). If he uses violence he has to submit to the additional punishment, " he may not put her away all his days " (Deut. xxii. 29).

The reason of the law concerning marrying the deceased brother's wife is stated in the Bible (Deut. xxv. 5). It was a custom in force before the Law was given, and the Law perpetuated it. The ceremony of *ḥaliẓah* (*ibid.* 6, *seq.*), " taking off the shoe," has been introduced, because in those days it was considered disgraceful to go through that ceremony, and in order to avoid the disgrace, a person might perhaps be induced to marry his deceased brother's wife. This is evident from the words of the Law : " So shall it be done unto that man that will not build up his brother's house. And his name shall be called in Israel, The house of him that hath his shoe loosed " (Deut. xxv. 9). In the action of Judah we may perhaps notice an example of a noble conduct, and uprightness in judgment. He said : " Let her take it to her, lest we be shamed ; behold, I sent this kid, and thou hast not found her " (Gen. xxxviii. 23). For before the Lawgiving, the intercourse with a harlot was as lawful as cohabitation of husband and wife since the Lawgiving ; it was perfectly permitted, nobody considered it wrong. The hire which was in those days paid to the harlot in accordance with a previous agreement, corresponds to the *ketubah* which in our days the husband pays to his wife when he divorces her. It is a just claim on the part of the wife, and the husband is bound to pay it. The words of Judah, " Let her take it to her, lest we be shamed," etc., show that conversation about sexual intercourse, even of that which is permitted, brings shame upon us ; it is proper to be silent about it, to keep it secret, even if the silence would lead to loss of money. In this sense Judah said : It is better for us to lose property, and to let her keep what she has, than to make our affair public by inquiring after her, and bring still more shame upon us. This is the lesson, as regards conduct, to be derived from this incident. As to the uprightness to be learned therefrom, it is contained in the words of Judah when he wanted to show that he had not robbed her, that he has not in the least departed from his agreement with her. For he said, " Behold, I sent this kid, and thou hast not found her." The kid was probably very good, therefore he points to it, saying, " this kid." This is the uprightness which he had inherited from Abraham, Isaac, and Jacob : that man must not depart from his given word, nor deviate from what he agreed upon ; but he must give to others all that is due to them. It makes no difference whether he holds a portion of his neighbour's property as a loan or a trust, or whether he is in any other way his neighbour's debtor, owing him wages or the like.

The sum which the husband settles upon his wife (*ketubah*) is to be treated in the same way as the wages of a hired servant. There is no difference whether a master withholds the wages of a hired servant, or deprives his wife of that which is due to her; whether a master wrongs a hired servant, and brings charges against him with the intention to send him away without payment, or a husband treats his wife in a manner that would enable him to send her away without the payment of the promised sum.

The equity of the statutes and judgments of the Law in this regard may be noticed in the treatment of a person accused of spreading an evil report about his wife (Deut. xxii. 13, *seq.*). There is no doubt that the man that did this is bad, does not love his wife, and is not pleased with her. If he desired to divorce her in a regular manner, there is nothing to prevent him, but he would be bound to give her what is due unto her ; but instead of this, " he gives occasion of speech against her " (*ibid.* xxii. 14), in order to get rid of his wife without paying anything ; he slanders her, and utters falsehood in order to keep in his possession the fifty shekels of silver, the dowry fixed in the Law for maidens, which he is obliged to pay unto her. He is therefore sentenced to pay one hundred shekels of silver, in accordance with the principle, " Whom the judges shall condemn, he shall pay double unto his neighbour " (Exod. xxii. 9). The Law is also analogous to that about false witnesses, which we have explained above (chap. xli. p. 195). For he intended to cheat her of her fifty shekels of silver, he must therefore [add fifty, and] pay her a hundred shekels. This is his punishment for withholding from her her due, and endeavouring to keep it. But in so far as he degraded her, and spread the rumour that she was guilty of misconduct, he was also degraded, and received stripes, as is implied in the words, " and they shall chastise him " (Deut. xxii. 18). But he sinned besides in clinging to lust, and seeking only that which gave pleasure to him ; he was therefore punished by being compelled to keep his wife always, " he may not put her away all his days " (*ibid.* 19) ; for he has been brought to all this only because he may have found her ugly. Thus are these bad habits cured when they are treated according to the divine Law ; the ways of equity are never lost sight of ; they are obvious and discernible in every precept of the Law by those who consider it well. See how, according to the Law, the slanderer of his wife, who only intended to withhold from her what he is bound to give her, is treated in the same manner as a thief who has stolen the property of his neighbour ; and the false witness (Deut. xix. 16, *seq.*) who schemes to injure, although the injury was in reality not inflicted, is punished like those who have actually caused injury and wrong, viz., like the thief and the slanderer. The three kinds of sinners are tried and judged by one and the same law. See how wonderful are the divine laws, and admire His wonderful deeds. Scripture says : " The Rock, His work is perfect ; for all His ways are judgment " (Deut. xxxii. 4), i.e., as His works are most perfect, so are His laws most equitable ; but our mind is too limited to comprehend the perfection of all His works, or the equity of all His laws ; and as we are able to comprehend some of His wonderful works in the organs of living beings and the motions of the spheres, so we understand also the equity of some of His laws; that which is unknown to us of both of them is far more than that which is known to us. I will now return to the theme of the present chapter.

The law about forbidden sexual intercourse seeks in all its parts to inculcate the lesson that we ought to limit sexual intercourse altogether, hold it in contempt, and only desire it very rarely. The prohibition of pederasty (Lev. xviii. 22) and carnal intercourse with beasts (ibid. 23) is very clear. If in the natural way the act is too base to be performed except when needed, how much more base is it if performed in an unnatural manner, and only for the sake of pleasure.

The female relatives whom a man may not marry are alike in this respect—that as a rule they are constantly together with him in his house; they would easily listen to him, and do what he desires; they are near at hand, and he would have no difficulty in procuring them. No judge could blame him if found in their company. If to these relatives the same law applied as to all other unmarried women, if we were allowed to marry any of them, and were only precluded from sexual intercourse with them without marriage, most people would constantly have become guilty of misconduct with them. But as they are entirely forbidden to us, and sexual intercourse with them is most emphatically denounced unto us as a capital crime, or a sin punishable with extinction (*karet*), and as there is no means of ever legalizing such intercourse, there is reason to expect that people will not seek it, and will not think of it. That the persons included in that prohibition are, as we have stated, at hand and easily accessible, is evident. For as a rule, the mother of the wife, the grandmother, the daughter, the granddaughter, and the sister-in-law, are mostly with her; the husband meets them always when he goes out, when he comes in, and when he is at his work. The wife stays also frequently in the house of her husband's brother, father, or son. It is also well known that we are often in the company of our sisters, our aunts, and the wife of our uncle, and are frequently brought up together with them. These are all the relatives which we must not marry. This is one of the reasons why intermarriage with a near relative is forbidden. But according to my opinion the prohibition serves another object, namely, to inculcate chastity into our hearts. Licence between the root and the branch, between a man and his mother, or his daughter, is outrageous. The intercourse between root and branch is forbidden, and it makes no difference whether the male element is the root or the branch, or both root and branch combine in the intercourse with a third person, so that the same individual cohabits with the root and with the branch. On this account it is prohibited to marry a woman and her mother, the wife of the father or of the son; for in all these cases there is the intercourse between one and the same person on the one side and root and branch on the other.

The law concerning brothers is like the law concerning root and branch. The sister is forbidden, and so is also the sister of the wife and the wife of the brother; because in the latter cases two persons who are considered like root and branch, cohabit with the same person. But in these prohibitions brothers and sisters are partly considered as root and branch and partly as one body; the sister of the mother is therefore like the mother, and the sister of the father like the father, and both are prohibited; and since the daughter of the parent's brother or sister is not included in the number of prohibited relatives, so may we also marry the daughter of the brother or the sister. The apparent anomaly, that the brother of the father may marry a woman that has been the wife of his brother's son, whilst the nephew must not marry a woman that has been the wife of his father's brother, can be explained according to the above-mentioned first reason. For the nephew is frequently in the house of his uncle, and his conduct towards the wife of his uncle is the same as that towards his brother's wife. The uncle, however, is not so frequent in the house of his nephew, and he is consequently less intimate with the wife of his nephew; whilst in the case of father and son, the familiarity of the father with his daughter-in-law is the same as that of the son with the wife of his father, and therefore the law and punishment is the same for both [father and son]. The reason why it is prohibited to cohabit with a menstruous woman (Lev. xviii. 19) or with another man's wife (*ibid.* 20), is obvious, and requires no further explanation.

It is well known that we must not indulge in any sensual enjoyment whatever with the persons included in the above prohibitions; we must not even look at them if we intend to derive pleasure therefrom. We have explained this in "the laws about forbidden sexual intercourse" (*Hilkot issure biah,* xxi. 1–2), and shown that according to the Law we must not even engage our thoughts with the act of cohabitation (*ibid.* 19) or irritate the organ of generation; and when we find ourselves unintentionally in a state of irritation, we must turn our mind to other thoughts, and reflect on some other thing till we are relieved. Our Sages (B.T. Kidd 30*b*), in their moral lessons, which give perfection to the virtuous, say as follows: "My son, if that monster meets you, drag it to the house of study. It will melt if it is of iron; it will break in pieces if it is of stone: as is said in Scripture, 'Is not my word like a fire? saith the Lord, and like a hammer that breaketh the rock in pieces?'" (Jer. xxiii. 29). The author of this saying thus exhorts his son to go to the house of study when he finds his organ of generation in an irritated state. By reading, disputing, asking, and listening to questions, the irritation will certainly cease. See how properly the term monster is employed, for that irritation is indeed like a monster. Not only religion teaches this lesson, the philosophers teach the same. I have already quoted verbatim the words of Aristotle. He says: "The sense of touch which is a disgrace to us, leads us to indulge in eating and sensuality," etc. He calls people degraded who seek carnal pleasures and devote themselves to gastronomy; he denounces *in extenso* their low and objectionable conduct, and ridicules them. This passage occurs in his Ethics and in his Rhetoric.

In accordance with this excellent principle, which we ought strictly to follow, our Sages teach us that we ought not to look at beasts or birds in the moment of their copulation. According to my opinion, this is the reason why the cross-breeding of cattle is prohibited (Lev. xix. 19). It is a fact that animals of different species do not copulate together, unless by force. It is well known that the low class of breeders of mules are regularly engaged in this work. Our Law objected to it that any Israelite should degrade himself by doing these things, which require so much vulgarity and indecency, and doing that which religion forbids us even to mention, how much more to witness or to practise, except   when necessary.   Cross-breeding, however, is not necessary.   I think that the prohibition to bring together two species in any kind of work, as included in the words, "Thou shalt not plow with an ox and an ass together " (Deut. xxii. 10), is only a preventive against the intercourse of two species.   For if it were allowed to join such together in any work, we might sometimes also cause their inter-course.   That this is the reason of the commandment is proved by the fact that it applies to other animals besides ox and ass ; it is prohibited to plow not only with ox and ass together, but with any two kinds.   But Scripture mentions as an instance that which is of regular occurrence.

As regards circumcision, I think that one of its objects is to limit sexual intercourse, and to weaken the organ of generation as far as possible, and thus cause man to be moderate.   Some people believe that circumcision is to remove a defect in man's formation ; but every one can easily reply : How can products of nature be deficient so as to require external completion, especially as the use of the fore-skin to that organ is evident. This command-ment has not been enjoined as a complement to a deficient physical creation, but as a means for perfecting man's moral shortcomings.   The bodily injury caused to that organ is exactly that which is desired ; it does not interrupt any vital function, nor does it destroy the power of generation.   Circum-cision simply counteracts excessive lust; for there is no doubt that circumcision weakens the power of sexual excitement, and sometimes lessens the natural en-joyment ;   the organ necessarily becomes weak when it loses blood and is de-prived of its covering from the beginning. Our Sages (Beresh. Rabba, c. 80) say distinctly :   It is hard for a woman, with whom an uncircumcised had sexual intercourse, to separate from him. This is, as I believe, the best reason for the commandment concerning circumcision.   And who was the first to perform this commandment ?   Abraham, our father ! of whom it is well known how he feared sin ; it is described by our Sages in reference to the words, " Be-hold, now I know that thou art a fair woman to look upon " (Gen. xii. 11).

There is, however, another important object in this commandment.   It gives to all members of the same faith, i.e., to all believers in the Unity of God, a common bodily sign, so that it is impossible for any one that is a stranger, to say that he belongs to them. For sometimes people say so for the purpose of obtaining some advantage, or in order to make some attack upon the Jews.   No one, however, should circumcise himself or his son for any other reason but pure faith ; for circumcision is not like an incision on the leg, or a burning in the arm, but a very difficult operation.   It is also a fact that there is much mutual love and assistance among people that are united by the same sign when they consider it as [the symbol of] a covenant. Circumcision is likewise the [symbol of the] covenant which Abraham made in connexion with the belief in God's Unity.   So also every one that is circumcised enters the covenant of Abraham to believe in the unity of God, in accordance with the words of the Law, " To be a God unto thee, and to thy seed after thee " (Gen. xvii. 7). This purpose of the circumcision is as important as the first, and perhaps more important.

This law can only be kept and perpetuated in its perfection, if circum-cision is performed when the child is very young, and this for three good reasons.   First, if the operation were postponed till the boy had grown up, he would perhaps not submit to it. Secondly, the young child has not much pain, because the skin is tender, and the imagination weak; for grown-up persons are in dread and fear of things which they imagine as coming, some time before these actually occur. Thirdly, when a child is very young, the parents do not think much of him; because the image of the child, that leads the parents to love him, has not yet taken a firm root in their minds. That image becomes stronger by the continual sight; it grows with the development of the child, and later on the image begins again to decrease and to vanish. The parents' love for a new-born child is not so great as it is when the child is one year old; and when one year old, it is less loved by them than when six years old. The feeling and love of the father for the child would have led him to neglect the law if he were allowed to wait two or three years, whilst shortly after birth the image is very weak in the mind of the parent, especially of the father who is responsible for the execution of this commandment. The circumcision must take place on the eighth day (Lev. xii. 3), because all living beings are after birth, within the first seven days, very weak and exceedingly tender, as if they were still in the womb of their mother; not until the eighth day can they be counted among those that enjoy the light of the world. That this is also the case with beasts may be inferred from the words of Scripture: " Seven days shall it be under the dam " (Lev. xxii. 27), as if it had no vitality before the end of that period. In the same manner man is circumcised after the completion of seven days. The period has been fixed, and has not been left to everybody's judgment.

The precepts of this class include also the lesson that we must not injure in any way the organs of generation in living beings (*ibid.* xxii. 24). The lesson is based on the principle of " righteous statutes and judgments " (Deut. iv. 8); we must keep in everything the golden mean; we must not be excessive in love, but must not suppress it entirely; for the Law commands, " Be fruitful, and multiply " (Gen. i. 22). The organ is weakened by circumcision, but not destroyed by the operation. The natural faculty is left in full force, but is guarded against excess. It is prohibited for an Israelite " that is wounded in the stones, or hath his privy member cut off " (Deut. xxiii. 2), to marry an Israelitish woman; because the sexual intercourse is of no use and of no purpose; and that marriage would be a source of ruin to her, and to him who would claim her. This is very clear.

In order to create a horror of illicit marriages, a bastard was not allowed to marry an Israelitish woman (*ibid.* xxiii. 3); the adulterer and the adulteress were thus taught that by their act they bring upon their seed irreparable injury. In every language and in every nation the issue of licentious conduct has a bad name; the Law therefore raises the name of the Israelites by keeping them free from the admixture of bastards. The priests, who have a higher sanctity, are not allowed to marry a harlot, or a woman that is divorced from her husband, or that is profane (Lev. xxi 7); the high-priest, the noblest of the priests, must not marry even a widow, or a woman that has had sexual intercourse of any kind (*ibid.* xxi. 14). Of all these laws the reason is obvious. If bastards were prohibited to marry any member of the congregation of the Lord, how much more rigidly had slaves and handmaids to be excluded. The reason of the prohibition of intermarriage with other nations is stated in the Law: "And thou take of their daughters unto thy sons, and their daughters go a whoring after their gods, and make thy sons go a whoring after their gods" (Exod. xxxiv. 16).

Most of the " statutes " (*ḥukkim*), the reason of which is unknown to us serve as a fence against idolatry. That I cannot explain some details of the above laws or show their use is owing to the fact that what we hear from others is not so clear as that which we see with our own eyes. Thus my knowledge of the Sabean doctrines, which I derived from books, is not as complete as the knowledge of those who have witnessed the public practice of those idolatrous customs, especially as they have been out of practice and entirely extinct since two thousand years. If we knew all the particulars of the Sabean worship, and were informed of all the details of those doctrines, we would clearly see the reason and wisdom of every detail in the sacrificial service, in the laws concerning things that are unclean, and in other laws, the object of which I am unable to state. I have no doubt that all these laws served to blot out wrong principles from man's heart, and to exterminate the practices which are useless, and merely a waste of time in vain and purposeless things. Those principles have turned the mind of the people away from intellectual research and useful actions. Our prophets therefore describe the ways of the idolaters as follows: " (They go) after vain things which cannot profit nor deliver; for they are vain " (1 Sam. xii. 21); " Surely our fathers have inherited lies, vanity and things wherein there is no profit " (Jer. xvi. 19). Consider how great the evil consequences of idolatry are, and say whether we ought with all our power to oppose it or not! Most of the precepts serve, as has been stated by us, as a mere fence against those doctrines [of idolatry], and relieve man from the great and heavy burdens, from the pains and inflictions which formed part of the worship of idols. Every positive or negative precept, the reason of which is unknown to thee, take as a remedy against some of those diseases with which we are unacquainted at present, thank God. This should be the belief of educated men who know the true meaning of the following divine dictum: " I said not unto the seed of Jacob, Seek me in vain " (Isa. xlv. 19).

I have now mentioned all the commandments of these fourteen classses one by one, and pointed out the reason of each of them, with the exception of a few for which I was unable to give the reason, and of some details of less importance; but implicitly we have given the reason even of these, and every intelligent reader will easily find it.

The reasons of the Precepts are now complete.

CHAPTER L

THERE are in the Law portions which include deep wisdom, but have been misunderstood by many persons.; they require, therefore, an explanation. I mean the narratives contained in the Law which many consider as being of no use whatever; e.g., the list of the various families descended from Noah, with their names and their territories (Gen. x.); the sons of Seir the Horite (*ibid.* xxxvi. 20–30); the kings that reigned in Edom (*ibid.* 31, *seq.*); and the like. There is a saying of our Sages (B.T. Sanh. 99*b*) that the wicked king Manasse frequently held disgraceful meetings for the sole purpose of criticising such passages of the Law. " He held meetings and made blasphemous observations on Scripture, saying, Had Moses nothing else to write than, And the sister of Lotan was Timna " (Gen. xxxvi. 22) ? With reference to such passages, I will first give a general principle, and then discuss them *seriatim*, as I have done in the exposition of the reasons of the precepts.

Every narrative in the Law serves a certain purpose in connexion with religious teaching. It either helps to establish a principle of faith, or to regulate our actions, and to prevent wrong and injustice among men ; and I will show this in each case.

It is one of the fundamental principles of the Law that the Universe has been created *ex nihilo*, and that of the human race, one individual being, Adam, was created. As the time which elapsed from Adam to Moses was not more than about two thousand five hundred years, people would have doubted the truth of that statement if no other information had been added, seeing that the human race was spread over all parts of the earth in different families and with different languages, very unlike the one to the other. In order to remove this doubt the Law gives the genealogy of the nations (Gen. v. and x.), and the manner how they branched off from a common root. It names those of them who were well known, and tells who their fathers were, how long and where they lived. It describes also the cause that led to the dispersion of men over all parts of the earth, and to the formation of their different languages, after they had lived for a long time in one place, and spoken one language (*ibid.* xi.), as would be natural for descendants of one person. The accounts of the flood (*ibid.* vi.–viii.) and of the destruction of Sodom and Gomorrah (*ibid.* xix.), serve as an illustration of the doctrine that " Verily there is a reward for the righteous ; verily He is a God that judgeth in the earth " (Ps. lviii. 12).

The narration of the war among the nine kings (*ibid.* xiv.) shows how, by means of a miracle, Abraham, with a few undisciplined men, defeated four mighty kings. It illustrates at the same time how Abraham sympathized with his relative, who had been brought up in the same faith, and how he exposed himself to the dangers of warfare in order to save him. We further learn from this narrative how contented and satisfied Abraham was, thinking little of property, and very much of good deeds ; he said, " I will not take from a thread even to a shoe-latchet " (Gen. xiv. 23).

The list of the families of Seir and their genealogy is given in the Law (*ibid.* xxxvi. 20–30), because of one particular commandment. For God distinctly commanded the Israelites concerning Amalek to blot out his name (Deut. xxv. 17–19). Amalek was the son of Eliphas and Timna, the sister of Lotan (*ibid.* xxxvi. 12). The other sons of Esau were not included in this commandment. But Esau was by marriage connected with the Seïrites, as is distinctly stated in Scripture ; and Seïrites were therefore his children ; he reigned over them ; his seed was mixed with the seed of Seir, and ultimately all the countries and families of Seir were called after the sons of Esau who were the predominant family, and they assumed more particularly the name Amalekites, because these were the strongest in that family. If the genealogy of these families of Seir had not been described in full they would all have been killed, contrary to the plain words of the commandment. For this reason the Seïrite families are fully described, as if to say, the people that live in Seir and in the kingdom of Amalek are not all Amalekites ; they are the descendants of some other man, and are called Amalekites because the mother of Amalek was of their tribe.   The justice of God thus prevented the destruction of an [innocent] people that lived in the midst of another people [doomed to extirpation]; for the decree was only pronounced against the seed of Amalek.   The reason of this decree has already been stated by us (p. 205).

The kings that have reigned in the land of Edom are enumerated (Gen xxxvi. 31, *seq*.) on account of the law, " Thou mayst not set a stranger over thee, which is not thy brother " (Deut. xvii. 15).   For of these kings none was an Edomite; wherefore each king is described by his native land; one king from this place, another king from that place.   Now I think that it was then well known how these kings that reigned in Edom conducted themselves, what they did, and how they humiliated and oppressed the sons of Esau.   Thus God reminded the Israelites of the fate of the Edomites, as if saying unto them, Look unto your brothers, the sons of Esau, whose kings were so and so, and whose deeds are well known.   [Learn therefrom] that no nation ever chose a foreigner as king without inflicting thereby some great or small injury upon the country.   In short, what I remarked in reference to our ignorance of the Sabean worship, applies also to the history of those days.   If the religious rules of the Sabeans and the events of those days were known to us, we should be able to see plainly the reason for most of the things mentioned in the Pentateuch.

It is also necessary to note the following observations.   The view we take of things described by others is different from the view we take of things seen by us as eye-witnesses.   For that which we see contains many details which are essential, and must be fully described.   The reader of the description believes that it contains superfluous matter, or useless repetition, but if he had witnessed the event of which he reads, he would see the necessity of every part of the description.   When we therefore notice narratives in the Torah, which are in no connexion with any of the commandments, we are inclined to think that they are entirely superfluous, or too lengthy, or contain repetitions; but this is only because we do not see the particular incidents which make those narratives noteworthy.   Of this kind is the enumeration of the stations [of the Israelites in the wilderness] (Num. xxxiii.).   At first sight it appears to be entirely useless; but in order to obviate such a notion Scripture says, " And Moses wrote their goings out according to their journeys by the commandment of the Lord " (*ibid*. ver. 2).   It was indeed most necessary that these should be written.   For miracles are only convincing to those who witnessed them; whilst coming generations, who know them only from the account given by others, may consider them as untrue.   But miracles cannot continue and last for all generations; it is even inconceivable [that they should be permanent].   Now the greatest of the miracles described in the Law is the stay of the Israelites in the wilderness for forty years, with a daily supply of manna.   This wilderness, as described in Scripture, consisted of places " wherein were fiery serpents and scorpions, and drought, where there was no water " (Deut. viii. 15); places very remote from cultivated land, and naturally not adapted for the habitation of man, " It is no place of seed, or of figs, or of vines, or of pomegranates, neither is there any water to drink " (Num. xx. 5); " A land that no man passed through, and where no man dwelt " (Jer. ii. 6).   [In reference to the stay of the Israelites in the wilderness], Scripture relates, " Ye have not eaten bread, neither have ye drunk wine or strong drink " (Deut. xix. 5). All these miracles were wonderful, public, and witnessed by the people. But God knew that in future people might doubt the correctness of the account of these miracles, in the same manner as they doubt the accuracy of other narratives ; they might think that the Israelites stayed in the wilderness in a place not far from inhabited land, where it was possible for man to live [in the ordinary way] ; that it was like those deserts in which Arabs live at present ; or that they dwelt in such places in which they could plow, sow, and reap, or live on some vegetable that was growing there ; or that manna came always down in those places as an ordinary natural product ; or that there were wells of water in those places. In order to remove all these doubts and to firmly establish the accuracy of the account of these miracles, Scripture enumerates all the stations, so that coming generations may see them, and learn the greatness of the miracle which enabled human beings to live in those places forty years.

For this very reason Joshua cursed him who would ever build up Jericho (Josh. vi. 26) ; the effect of the miracle was to remain for ever, so that any one who would see the wall sunk in the ground would understand that it was not in the condition of a building pulled down by human hands, but sunk through a miracle. In a similar manner the words, " At the commandment of the Lord the children of Israel journeyed, and at the commandment of the Lord they pitched " (Num. ix. 18), would suffice as a simple statement of facts ; and the reader might at first sight consider as unnecessary additions all the details which follow, viz., " And when the cloud tarried long. . . . And so it was when the cloud was a few days. . . . Or whether it were two days," etc. (*ibid.* ix. 19–22). But I will show you the reason why all these details are added. For they serve to confirm the account, and to contradict the opinion of the nations, both of ancient and modern times, that the Israelites lost their way, and did not know where to go ; that " they were entangled in the land " (Exod. xiv. 3) ; wherefore the Arabs unto this day call that desert *Al-tih*, " the desert of going astray," imagining that the Israelites erred about, and did not know the way. Scripture, therefore, clearly states and emphatically declares that it was by God's command that the journeyings were irregular, that the Israelites returned to the same places several times, and that the duration of the stay was different in each station ; whilst the stay in one place continued for eighteen years, in another place it lasted one day, and in another one night. There was no going astray, but the journey was regulated by " the rising of the pillar of cloud " (Num. ix. 17). Therefore all these details are given. Scripture clearly states that the way was near, known, and in good condition ; I mean the way from Horeb, whither they came intentionally, according to the command of God, " Ye shall serve God upon this mountain " (Exod. ii. 12), to Kadesh-barnea, the beginning of inhabited land, as Scripture says, " Behold, we are now in Kadesh, a city in the uttermost of thy border " (Num. xx. 16). That way was a journey of eleven days ; comp. " Eleven days' journey from Horeb, by the way of mount Seir, unto Kadesh-barnea " (Deut. i. 3). In such a journey it is impossible to err about for forty years ; but Scripture states the cause of the delay.

In like manner there is a good reason for every passage the object of which we cannot see. We must always apply the words of our Sages : " It is not a vain thing for you " (Deut. xxxii. 47), and if it seems vain, it seems your fault.

CHAPTER LI

THE present chapter does not contain any additional matter that has not been treated in the [previous] chapters of this treatise. It is a kind of conclusion, and at the same time it will explain in what manner those worship God who have obtained a true knowledge concerning God ; it will direct them how to come to that worship, which is the highest aim man can attain, and show how God protects them in this world till they are removed to eternal life.

I will begin the subject of this chapter with a simile. A king is in his palace, and all his subjects are partly in the country, and partly abroad. Of the former, some have their backs turned towards the king's palace, and their faces in another direction ; and some are desirous and zealous to go to the palace, seeking " to inquire in his temple," and to minister before him, but have not yet seen even the face of the wall of the house. Of those that desire to go to the palace, some reach it, and go round about in search of the entrance gate ; others have passed through the gate, and walk about in the ante-chamber ; and others have succeeded in entering into the inner part of the palace, and being in the same room with the king in the royal palace. But even the latter do not immediately on entering the palace see the king, or speak to him ; for, after having entered the inner part of the palace, another effort is required before they can stand before the king—at a distance, or close by—hear his words, or speak to him. I will now explain the simile which I have made. The people who are abroad are all those that have no religion, neither one based on speculation nor one received by tradition. Such are the extreme Turks that wander about in the north, the Kushites who live in the south, and those in our country who are like these. I consider these as irrational beings, and not as human beings ; they are below mankind, but above monkeys, since they have the form and shape of man, and a mental faculty above that of the monkey.

Those who are in the country, but have their backs turned towards the king's palace, are those who possess religion, belief, and thought, but happen to hold false doctrines, which they either adopted in consequence of great mistakes made in their own speculations, or received from others who misled them. Because of these doctrines they recede more and more from the royal palace the more they seem to proceed. These are worse than the first class, and under certain circumstances it may become necessary to slay them, and to extirpate their doctrines, in order that others should not be misled.

Those who desire to arrive at the palace, and to enter it, but have never yet seen it, are the mass of religious people ; the multitude that observe the divine commandments, but are ignorant. Those who arrive at the palace, but go round about it, are those who devote themselves exclusively to the study of the practical law ; they believe traditionally in true principles of faith, and learn the practical worship of God, but are not trained in philosophical treatment of the principles of the Law, and do not endeavour to establish the truth of their faith by proof. Those who undertake to investigate the principles of religion, have come into the ante-chamber; and there is no doubt that these can also be divided into different grades. But those who have succeeded in finding a proof for everything that can be proved, who have a true knowledge of God, so far as a true knowledge can be attained, and are near the truth, wherever an approach to the truth is possible, they have reached the goal, and are in the palace in which the king lives.

My son, so long as you are engaged in studying the Mathematical Sciences and Logic, you belong to those who go round about the palace in search of the gate. Thus our Sages figuratively use the phrase: " Ben-zoma is still outside." When you understand Physics, you have entered the hall; and when, after completing the study of Natural Philosophy, you master Metaphysics, you have entered the innermost court, and are with the king in the same palace. You have attained the degree of the wise men, who include men of different grades of perfection. There are some who direct all their mind toward the attainment of perfection in Metaphysics, devote themselves entirely to God, exclude from their thought every other thing, and employ all their intellectual faculties in the study of the Universe, in order to derive therefrom a proof for the existence of God, and to learn in every possible way how God rules all things; they form the class of those who have entered the palace, namely, the class of prophets. One of these has attained so much knowledge, and has concentrated his thoughts to such an extent in the idea of God, that it could be said of him, " And he was with the Lord forty days," etc. (Exod. xxxiv. 28); during that holy communion he could ask Him, answer Him, speak to Him, and be addressed by Him, enjoying beatitude in that which he had obtained to such a degree that " he did neither eat bread nor drink water " (*ibid.*); his intellectual energy was so predominant that all coarser functions of the body, especially those connected with the sense of touch, were in abeyance. Some prophets are only able to see, and of these some approach near and see, whilst others see from a distance: comp. " The Lord hath appeared from far unto me " (Jer. xxxi. 3). We have already spoken of the various degrees of prophets; we will therefore return to the subject of this chapter, and exhort those who have attained a knowledge of God, to concentrate all their thoughts in God. This is the worship peculiar to those who have acquired a knowledge of the highest truths; and the more they reflect on Him, and think of Him, the more are they engaged in His worship. Those, however, who think of God, and frequently mention His name, without any correct notion of Him, but merely following some imagination, or some theory received from another person, are, in my opinion, like those who remain outside the palace and distant from it. They do not mention the name of God in truth, nor do they reflect on it. That which they imagine and mention does not correspond to any being in existence; it is a thing invented by their imagination, as has been shown by us in our discussion on the Divine Attributes (Part I. chap. l.). The true worship of God is only possible when correct notions of Him have previously been conceived. When you have arrived by way of intellectual research at a knowledge of God and His works, then commence to devote yourselves to Him, try to approach Him and strengthen the intellect, which is the link that joins you to Him. Thus Scripture says, " Unto thee it was

showed, that thou mightest know that the Lord He is God " (Deut. iv. 35);
" Know therefore this day, and consider it in thine heart, that the Lord He
is God " (*ibid.* 36) ; " Know ye that the Lord is God " (Ps. c. 3). Thus
the Law distinctly states that the highest kind of worship to which we refer
in this chapter, is only possible after the acquisition of the knowledge of God.
For it is said, " To love the Lord your God, and to serve Him with all your
heart and with all your soul " (Deut. xi. 13), and, as we have shown several
times, man's love of God is identical with His knowledge of Him. The
Divine service enjoined in these words must, accordingly, be preceded by
the love of God. Our Sages have pointed out to us that it is a service in the
heart, which explanation I understand to mean this : man concentrates all
his thoughts on the First Intellect, and is absorbed in these thoughts as much
as possible. David therefore commands his son Solomon these two things,
and exhorts him earnestly to do them : to acquire a true knowledge of God,
and to be earnest in His service after that knowledge has been acquired.
For he says, " And thou, Solomon my son, know thou the God of thy father,
and serve him with a perfect heart . . . if thou seek him, he will be found
of thee ; but if thou forsake him, he will cast thee off for ever " (1 Chron.
xxviii. 9). The exhortation refers to. the intellectual conceptions, not to
the imaginations ; for the latter are not called " knowledge," but " that
which cometh into your mind " (Ezek. xx. 32). It has thus been shown that
it must be man's aim, after having acquired the knowledge of God, to deliver himself up to Him, and to have his heart constantly filled with longing
after Him. He accomplishes this generally by seclusion and retirement.
Every pious man should therefore seek retirement and seclusion, and should
only in case of necessity associate with others.

Note.—I have shown you that the intellect which emanates from God
unto us is the link that joins us to God. You have it in your power to
strengthen that bond, if you choose to do so, or to weaken it gradually till
it breaks, if you prefer this. It will only become strong when you employ
it in the love of God, and seek that love ; it will be weakened when you direct
your thoughts to other things. You must know that even if you were the
wisest man in respect to the true knowledge of God, you break the bond
between you and God whenever you turn entirely your thoughts to the
necessary food or any necessary business ; you are then not with God, and
He is not with you ; for that relation between you and Him is actually
interrupted in those moments. The pious were therefore particular to
restrict the time in which they could not meditate upon the name of God,
and cautioned others about it, saying, " Let not your minds be vacant from
reflections upon God." In the same sense did David say, " I have set the
Lord always before me ; because he is at my right hand, I shall not be
moved " (Ps. xvi. 8) ; i.e., I do not turn my thoughts away from God ; He
is like my right hand, which I do not forget even for a moment on account
of the ease of its motions, and therefore I shall not be moved, I shall not fall.

We must bear in mind that all such religious acts as reading the Law,
praying, and the performance of other precepts, serve exclusively as the
means of causing us to occupy and fill our mind with the precepts of God,
and free it from worldly business ; for we are thus, as it were, in communication with God, and undisturbed by any other thing. If we, however,

pray with the motion of our lips, and our face toward the wall, but at the same time think of our business; if we read the Law with our tongue, whilst our heart is occupied with the building of our house, and we do not think of what we are reading; if we perform the commandments only with our limbs, we are like those who are engaged in digging in the ground, or hewing wood in the forest, without reflecting on the nature of those acts, or by whom they are commanded, or what is their object. We must not imagine that [in this way] we attain the highest perfection; on the contrary, we are then like those in reference to whom Scripture says, "Thou art near in their mouth, and far from their reins" (Jer. xii. 2).

I will now commence to show you the way how to educate and train yourselves in order to attain that great perfection.

The first thing you must do is this: Turn your thoughts away from everything while you read *Shema·* or during the *Tefillah*, and do not content yourself with being devout when you read the first verse of Shema, or the first paragraph of the prayer. When you have successfully practised this for many years, try in reading the Law or listening to it, to have all your heart and all your thought occupied with understanding what you read or hear. After some time when you have mastered this, accustom yourself to have your mind free from all other thoughts when you read any portion of the other books of the prophets, or when you say any blessing; and to have your attention directed exclusively to the perception and the understanding of what you utter. When you have succeeded in properly performing these acts of divine service, and you have your thought, during their performance, entirely abstracted from worldly affairs, take then care that your thought be not disturbed by thinking of your wants or of superfluous things. In short, think of worldly matters when you eat, drink, bathe, talk with your wife and little children, or when you converse with other people. These times, which are frequent and long, I think, must suffice to you for reflecting on everything that is necessary as regards business, household, and health. But when you are engaged in the performance of religious duties, have your mind exclusively directed to what you are doing.

When you are alone by yourself, when you are awake on your couch, be careful to meditate in such precious moments on nothing but the intellectual worship of God, viz., to approach Him and to minister before Him in the true manner which I have described to you—not in hollow emotions. This I consider as the highest perfection wise men can attain by the above training.

When we have acquired a true knowledge of God, and rejoice in that knowledge in such a manner, that whilst speaking with others, or attending to our bodily wants, our mind is all that time with God; when we are with our heart constantly near God, even whilst our body is in the society of men; when we are in that state which the Song on the relation between God and man poetically describes in the following words: "I sleep, but my heart waketh; it is the voice of my beloved that knocketh" (Song v. 2):—then we have attained not only the height of ordinary prophets, but of Moses, our Teacher, of whom Scripture relates: "And Moses alone shall come near before the Lord" (*ibid.* xxxiv. 28); "But as for thee, stand thou here by me" (Deut. v. 28). The meaning of these verses has been explained by us.

The Patriarchs likewise attained this degree of perfection; they approached God in such a manner that with them the name of God became known in the world. Thus we read in Scripture : " The God of Abraham, the God of Isaac, and the God of Jacob. . . . This is My name for ever " (Exod. iii. 15). Their mind was so identified with the knowledge of God, that He made a lasting covenant with each of them : " Then will I remember my covenant with Jacob," etc. (Lev. xxvi. 42). For it is known from statements made in Scripture that these four, viz., the Patriarchs and Moses, had their minds exclusively filled with the name of God, that is, with His knowledge and love; and that in the same measure was Divine Providence attached to them and their descendants. When we therefore find them also, engaged in ruling others, in increasing their property, and endeavouring to obtain possession of wealth and honour, we see in this fact a proof that when they were occupied in these things, only their bodily limbs were at work, whilst their heart and mind never moved away from the name of God. I think these four reached that high degree of perfection in their relation to God, and enjoyed the continual presence of Divine Providence, even in their endeavours to increase their property, feeding the flock, toiling in the field, or managing the house, only because in all these things their end and aim was to approach God as much as possible. It was the chief aim of their whole life to create a people that should know and worship God. Comp. " For I know him, that he will command his children and his household after him " (Gen. xviii. 19). The object of all their labours was to publish the Unity of God in the world, and to induce people to love Him ; and it was on this account that they succeeded in reaching that high degree ; for even those [worldly] affairs were for them a perfect worship of God. But a person like myself must not imagine that he is able to lead men up to this degree of perfection   It is only the next degree to it that can be attained by means of the above-mentioned training. And let us pray to God and beseech Him that He clear and remove from our way everything that forms an obstruction and a partition between us and Him, although most of these obstacles are our own creation, as has several times been shown in this treatise. Comp. " Your iniquities have separated between you and your God " (Isa. lix. 2).

An excellent idea presents itself here to me, which may serve to remove many doubts, and may help to solve many difficult problems in metaphysics. We have already stated in the chapters which treat of Divine Providence, that Providence watches over every rational being according to the amount of intellect which that being possesses. Those who are perfect in their perception of God, whose mind is never separated from Him, enjoy always the influence of Providence. But those who, perfect in their knowledge of God, turn their mind sometimes away from God, enjoy the presence of Divine Providence only when they meditate on God ; when their thoughts are engaged in other matters, divine Providence departs from them. The absence of Providence in this case is not like its absence in the case of those who do not reflect on God at all ; it is in this case less intense, because when a person perfect in his knowledge [of God] is busy with worldly matters, he has not knowledge in actuality, but only knowledge in potentiality [though ready to become actual]. This person is then like a trained scribe when he is not writing. Those who have no knowledge of God are like those who are in constant darkness and have never seen light. We have explained in this sense the words : " The wicked shall be silent in darkness " (1 Sam. ii. 9), whilst those who possess the knowledge of God, and have their thoughts entirely directed to that knowledge, are, as it were, always in bright sunshine ; and those who have the knowledge, but are at times engaged in other themes, have then as it were a cloudy day : the sun does not shine for them on account of the cloud that intervenes between them and God.

Hence it appears to me that it is only in times of such neglect that some of the ordinary evils befall a prophet or a perfect and pious man ; and the intensity of the evil is proportional to the duration of those moments, or to the character of the things that thus occupy their mind. Such being the case, the great difficulty is removed that led philosophers to assert that Providence does not extend to every individual, and that man is like any other living being in this respect, viz., the argument based on the fact that good and pious men are afflicted with great evils. We have thus explained this difficult question even in accordance with the philosophers' own principles. Divine Providence is constantly watching over those who have obtained that blessing which is prepared for those who endeavour to obtain it. If man frees his thoughts from worldly matters, obtains a knowledge of God in the right way, and rejoices in that knowledge, it is impossible that any kind of evil should befall him while he is with God, and God with him. When he does not meditate on God, when he is separated from God, then God is also separated from him ; then he is exposed to any evil that might befall him ; for it is only that intellectual link with God that secures the presence of Providence and protection from evil accidents. Hence it may occur that the perfect man is at times not happy, whilst no evil befalls those who are imperfect ; in these cases what happens to them is due to chance. This principle I find also expressed in the Law. Comp. " And I will hide my face from them, and they shall be devoured, and many evils and troubles shall befall them ; so that they will say in that day, Are not these evils come upon us, because our God is not among us ? " (Deut. xxxi. 17). It is clear that we ourselves are the cause of this hiding of the face, and that the screen that separates us from God is of our own creation. This is the meaning of the words : " And I will surely hide my face in that day, for all the evils which they shall have wrought " (*ibid.* ver. 18). There is undoubtedly no difference in this regard between one single person and a whole community. It is now clearly established that the cause of our being exposed to chance, and abandoned to destruction like cattle, is to be found in our separation from God. Those who have their God dwelling in their hearts, are not touched by any evil whatever. For God says : " Fear thou not, for I am with thee ; be not dismayed, for I am thy ʼGod " (Isa. xli. 10). " When thou passest through the waters, I will be with thee ; and through the rivers, they shall not overflow thee " (*ibid.* xliii. 2). For if we prepare ourselves, and attain the influence of the Divine Intellect, Providence is joined to us, and we are guarded against all evils. Comp. " The Lord is on my side ; I will not fear ; what can man do unto me ? " (Ps. cxviii. 6). " Acquaint now thyself with him, and be at peace " (Job xxii. 21) ; i.e., turn unto Him, and you will be safe from all evil.

Consider the Psalm on mishaps, and see how the author describes that great Providence, the protection and defence from all mishaps that concern the body, both from those that are common to all people, and those that concern only one certain individual; from those that are due to the laws of Nature, and those that are caused by our fellow-men. The Psalmist says: " Surely he will deliver thee from the snare of the fowler, and from the noisome pestilence. He shall cover thee with his feathers, and under his wings shalt thou trust: His truth shall be thy shield and buckler. Thou shalt not be afraid for the terror by night; nor for the arrow that flieth by day " (Ps. xci. 3–5). The author then relates how God protects us from the troubles caused by men, saying, If you happen to meet on your way with an army fighting with drawn swords, killing thousands at your left hand and myriads at your right hand, you will not suffer any harm; you will behold and see how God judges and punishes the wicked that are being slain, whilst you remain unhurt. " A thousand shall fall at thy side, and ten thousand at thy right hand; but it shall not come nigh thee. Only with thine eyes shalt thou behold and see the reward of the wicked " (ibid. vers. 7, 8). The author then continues his description of the divine defence and shelter, and shows the cause of this great protection, saying that such a man is well guarded " Because he hath set his love upon me, therefore will I deliver him: I will set him on high, because he hath known my name " (ibid. ver. 14). We have shown in previous chapters that by the " knowledge of God's name," the knowledge of God is meant. The above passage may therefore be paraphrased as follows: " This man is well guarded, because he hath known me, and then (bi chashak) loved me." You know the difference between the two Hebrew terms that signify " to love," ahab and ḥashak. When a man's love is so intense that his thought is exclusively engaged with the object of his love, it is expressed in Hebrew by the term ḥashak.

The philosophers have already explained how the bodily forces of man in his youth prevent the development of moral principles. In a greater measure this is the case as regards the purity of thought which man attains through the perfection of those ideas that lead him to an intense love of God. Man can by no means attain this so long as his bodily humours are hot. The more the forces of his body are weakened, and the fire of passion quenched, in the same measure does man's intellect increase in strength and light; his knowledge becomes purer, and he is happy with his knowledge. When this perfect man is stricken in age and is near death, his knowledge mightily increases, his joy in that knowledge grows greater, and his love for the object of his knowledge more intense, and it is in this great delight that the soul separates from the body. To this state our Sages referred, when in reference to the death of Moses, Aaron, and Miriam, they said that death was in these three cases nothing but a kiss. They say thus: We learn from the words, " And Moses the servant of the Lord died there in the land of Moab by the mouth of the Lord " (Deut. xxxiv. 5), that his death was a kiss. The same expression is used of Aaron: " And Aaron the priest went up into Mount Hor . . . by the mouth of the Lord, and died there " (Num. xxxiii. 38). Our Sages said that the same was the case with Miriam; but the phrase " by the mouth of the Lord " is not employed, because it was not considered appropriate to use these words in the description of her death as she was a female. The meaning of this saying is that these three died in the midst of the pleasure derived from the knowledge of God and their great love for Him. When our Sages figuratively call the knowledge of God united with intense love for Him a kiss, they follow the well-known poetical diction, " Let him kiss me with the kisses of his mouth " (Song i. 2). This kind of death, which in truth is deliverance from death, has been ascribed by our Sages to none but to Moses, Aaron, and Miriam. The other prophets and pious men are beneath that degree ; but their knowledge of God is strengthened when death approaches. Of them Scripture says, " Thy righteousness shall go before thee ; the glory of the Lord shall be thy rereward " (Isa. lviii. 8). The intellect of these men remains then constantly in the same condition, since the obstacle is removed that at times has intervened between the intellect and the object of its action ; it continues for ever in that great delight, which is not like bodily pleasure. We have explained this in our work, and others have explained it before us.

Try to understand this chapter, endeavour with all your might to spend more and more time in communion with God, or in the attempt to approach Him ; and to reduce the hours which you spend in other occupations, and during which you are not striving to come nearer unto Him. This instruction suffices for the object of this treatise.

CHAPTER LII

WE do not sit, move, and occupy ourselves when we are alone and at home, in the same manner as we do in the presence of a great king ; we speak and open our mouth as we please when we are with the people of our own household and with our relatives, but not so when we are in a royal assembly. If we therefore desire to attain human perfection, and to be truly men of God, we must awake from our sleep, and bear in mind that the great king that is over us, and is always joined to us, is greater than any earthly king, greater than David and Solomon. The king that cleaves to us and embraces us is the Intellect that influences us, and forms the link between us and God. We perceive God by means of that light that He sends down unto us, wherefore the Psalmist says, " In Thy light shall we see light " (Ps. xxxvi. 9) : so God looks down upon us through that same light, and is always with us beholding and watching us on account of this light. " Can any hide himself in secret places that I shall not see him ? " (Jer. xxiii. 24). Note this particularly.

When the perfect bear this in mind, they will be filled with fear of God, humility, and piety, with true, not apparent, reverence and respect of God, in such a manner that their conduct, even when alone with their wives or in the bath, will be as modest as they are in public intercourse with other people. Thus it is related of our renowned Sages that even in their sexual intercourse with their wives they behaved with great modesty. They also said, " Who is modest ? He whose conduct in the dark night is the same as in the day." You know also how much they warned us not to walk proudly, since " the fulness of the whole earth is His glory " (Isa. vi. 3). They thought that by these rules the above-mentioned idea will be firmly established in the hearts of men, viz., that we are always before God, and it is in the presence of His glory that we go to and fro. The great men among our Sages would not uncover their heads because they believed that God's glory was round them

and over them ; for the same reason they spoke little. In our Commentary
on the Sayings of the Fathers (chap. i. 17) we have fully explained how we
have to restrict our speech. Comp. " For God is in heaven and thou upon
earth, therefore let thy words be few " (Eccles. v. 1).

What I have here pointed out to you is the object of all our religious acts.
For by [carrying out] all the details of the prescribed practices, and repeating
them continually, some few pious men may attain human perfection. They
will be filled with respect and reverence towards God ; and bearing in mind
who is with them, they will perform their duty. God declares in plain
words that it is the object of all religious acts to produce in man fear of God
and obedience to His word—the state of mind which we have demonstrated
in this chapter for those who desire to know the truth, as being our duty to
seek. Comp. " If thou wilt not observe to do all the words of this law that
are written in this book, that thou mayest fear this glorious and fearful name,
the Lord thy God " (Deut. xxviii. 58). Consider how clearly it is stated
here that the only object and aim of " all the words of this law " is to [make
man] fear " the glorious and fearful name." That this end is attained by
certain acts we learn likewise from the phrase employed in this verse : " If
thou wilt not observe *to do* . . . that thou mayest fear." For this phrase
clearly shows that fear of God is inculcated [into our hearts] when we act in
accordance with the positive and the negative precepts. But the truths
which the Law teaches us—the knowledge of God's Existence and Unity—
create in us love of God, as we have shown repeatedly. You know how frequently the Law exhorts us to love God. Comp. " And thou shalt love the
Lord thy God with all thine heart, and with all thy soul, and with all thy
might " (Deut. vi. 5). The two objects, love and fear of God, are acquired
by two different means. The love is the result of the truths taught in the
Law, including the true knowledge of the Existence of God ; whilst fear of
God is produced by the practices prescribed in the Law. Note this explanation.

CHAPTER LIII

THIS chapter treats of the meaning of three terms which we find necessary
to explain, viz., *ḥesed* (" loving - kindness "), *mishpat* (" judgment "), and
ẓedakah (" righteousness ").

In our Commentary on the Sayings of the Fathers (chap. v. 7) we have
explained the expression *ḥesed* as denoting an excess [in some moral quality].
It is especially used of extraordinary kindness. Loving-kindness is practised
in two ways : first, we show kindness to those who have no claim whatever
upon us ; secondly, we are kind to those to whom it is due, in a greater
measure than is due to them. In the inspired writings the term *ḥesed* occurs
mostly in the sense of showing kindness to those who have no claim to it
whatever. For this reason the term *ḥesed* is employed to express the good
bestowed upon us by God : " I will mention the loving-kindness of the Lord "
(Isa. lxiii. 7). On this account, the very act of the creation is an act of God's
loving-kindness. " I have said, The Universe is built up in loving-kindness "
(Ps. lxxxix. 3) ; i.e., the building up of the Universe is an act of loving-kindness. Also, in the enumeration of God's attributes, Scripture says : " And
abundant in loving-kindness " (Exod. xxxiv. 6).

The term *ẓedakah* is derived from *ẓedek*, "righteousness"; it denotes the act of giving every one his due, and of showing kindness to every being according as it deserves. In Scripture, however, the expression *ẓedakah* is not used in the first sense, and does not apply to the payment of what we owe to others. When we therefore give the hired labourer his wages, or pay a debt, we do not perform an act of *ẓedakah*. But we do perform an act of *ẓedakah* when we fulfil those duties towards our fellow-men which our moral conscience imposes upon us; e.g., when we heal the wound of the sufferer. Thus Scripture says, in reference to the returning of the pledge [to the poor debtor]: "And it shall be *ẓedakah* (righteousness) unto thee" (Deut. xxiv. 11). When we walk in the way of virtue we act righteously towards our intellectual faculty, and pay what is due unto it; and because every virtue is thus *ẓedakah*, Scripture applies the term to the virtue of faith in God. Comp. "And he believed in the Lord, and he accounted it to him as righteousness" (Gen. xv. 6); "And it shall be our righteousness" (Deut. vi. 25).

The noun *mishpat*, "judgment," denotes the act of deciding upon a certain action in accordance with justice which may demand either mercy or punishment.

We have thus shown that *ḥesed* denotes pure charity; *ẓedakah* kindness, prompted by a certain moral conscience in man, and being a means of attaining perfection for his soul, whilst *mishpat* may in some cases find expression in revenge, in other cases in mercy.

In discussing the impropriety of admitting attributes of God (Part I., chap. liii., *seq.*), we stated that the divine attributes which occur in Scripture are attributes of His actions; thus He is called *ḥasid*, "kind," because He created the Universe; *ẓaddik*, "righteous," on account of His mercy with the weak, in providing for every living being according to its powers; and *shofet*, "judge," on account of the relative good and the great relative evils that are decreed by God's justice as directed by His wisdom. These three names occur in the Pentateuch: "Shall not the Judge (*shofet*) of all the earth," etc. (Gen. xviii. 25); "Righteous (*ẓaddik*) and upright is he" (Deut. xxxii. 4); "Abundant in loving-kindness" (*ḥesed*, Exod. xxxiv. 6).

We intended in explaining these three terms to prepare the reader for the next chapter.

CHAPTER LIV

THE term *ḥokmah* ("wisdom") in Hebrew is used of four different things: (1) It denotes the knowledge of those truths which lead to the knowledge of God. Comp. "But where shall wisdom be found?" (Job xxviii. 12); "If thou seekest her like silver" (Prov. ii. 4). The word occurs frequently in this sense. (2) The expression *ḥokmah* denotes also knowledge of any workmanship. Comp. "And every wise-hearted among you shall come and make all that the Lord hath commanded" (Exod. xxxv. 10); "And all the women that were wise-hearted did spin" (*ibid.* ver. 25). (3) It is also used of the acquisition of moral principles. Comp. "And teach his senators wisdom" (Ps. cv. 22); "With the ancient is wisdom" (Job xii. 12); for it is chiefly the disposition for acquiring moral principles that is developed by old age alone. (4) It implies, lastly, the notion of cunning and subtlety; comp. "Come on, let us deal wisely with them" (Exod. i. 10). In the same sense the term is used in the following passages : " And fetched thence a wise woman " (2 Sam. xiv. 2) ; " They are wise to do evil " (Jer. iv. 22). It is possible that the Hebrew *ḥokmah* (" wisdom ") expresses the idea of cunning and planning, which may serve in one case as a means of acquiring intellectual perfection, or good moral principles ; but may in another case produce skill in workmanship, or even be employed in establishing bad opinions and principles. The attribute *ḥakam* (" wise ") is therefore given to a person that possesses great intellectual faculties, or good moral principles, or skill in art ; but also to persons cunning in evil deeds and principles.

According to this explanation, a person that has a true knowledge of the whole Law is called wise in a double sense ; he is wise because the Law instructs him in the highest truths, and secondly, because it teaches him good morals. But as the truths contained in the Law are taught by way of tradition, not by a philosophical method, the knowledge of the Law, and the acquisition of true wisdom, are treated in the books of the Prophets and in the words of our Sages as two different things ; real wisdom demonstrates by proof those truths which Scripture teaches us by way of tradition. It is to this kind of wisdom, which proves the truth of the Law, that Scripture refers when it extols wisdom, and speaks of the high value of this perfection, and of the consequent paucity of men capable of acquiring it, in sayings like these : " Not many are wise " (Job xxxii. 9) ; " But where shall wisdom be found " (*ibid.* xxviii. 12) ? In the writings of our Sages we notice likewise many passages in which distinction is made between knowledge of the Law and wisdom. They say of Moses, our Teacher, that he was Father in the knowledge of the Law, in wisdom and in prophecy. When Scripture says of Solomon, " And he was wiser than all men " (1 Kings v. 11), our Sages add, " but not greater than Moses " ; and the phrase, " than all men," is explained to mean, " than all men of his generation " ; for this reason [only] " Heman, Chalcol, and Darda, the sons of Mahol," the renowned wise men of that time, are named. Our Sages further say, that man has first to render account concerning his knowledge of the Law, then concerning the acquisition of wisdom, and at last concerning the lessons derived by logical conclusions from the Law, i.e., the lessons concerning his actions. This is also the right order : we must first learn the truths by tradition, after this we must be taught how to prove them, and then investigate the actions that help to improve man's ways. The idea that man will have to render account concerning these three things in the order described, is expressed by our Sages in the following passage : " When man comes to the trial, he is first asked, ' Hast thou fixed certain seasons for the study of the Law ? Hast thou been engaged in the acquisition of wisdom ? Hast thou derived from one thing another thing ? ' " This proves that our Sages distinguished between the knowledge of the Law on the one hand, and wisdom on the other, as the means of proving the lessons taught in the Law by correct reasoning.

Hear now what I have to say after having given the above explanation. The ancient and the modern philosophers have shown that man can acquire four kinds of perfection. The first kind, the lowest, in the acquisition of which people spend their days, is perfection as regards property ; the possession of money, garments, furniture, servants, land, and the like ; the possession of the title of a great king belongs to this class. There is no close connexion between this possession and its possessor; it is a perfectly imaginary relation when on account of the great advantage a person derives from these possessions, he says, This is my house, this is my servant, this is my money, and these are my hosts and armies. For when he examines himself he will find that all these things are external, and their qualities are entirely independent of the possessor. When, therefore, that relation ceases, he that has been a great king may one morning find that there is no difference between him and the lowest person, and yet no change has taken place in the things which were ascribed to him. The philosophers have shown that he whose sole aim in all his exertions and endeavours is the possession of this kind of perfection, only seeks perfectly imaginary and transient things; and even if these remain his property all his lifetime, they do not give him any perfection.

The second kind is more closely related to man's body than the first. It includes the perfection of the shape, constitution, and form of man's body; the utmost evenness of temperaments, and the proper order and strength of his limbs. This kind of perfection must likewise be excluded from forming our chief aim; because it is a perfection of the body, and man does not possess it as man, but as a living being; he has this property besides in common with the lowest animal; and even if a person possesses the greatest possible strength, he could not be as strong as a mule, much less can he be as strong as a lion or an elephant; he, therefore, can at the utmost have strength that might enable him to carry a heavy burden, or break a thick substance, or do similar things, in which there is no great profit for the body. The soul derives no profit whatever from this kind of perfection.

The third kind of perfection is more closely connected with man himself than the second perfection. It includes moral perfection, the highest degree of excellency in man's character. Most of the precepts aim at producing this perfection; but even this kind is only a preparation for another perfection, and is not sought for its own sake. For all moral principles concern the relation of man to his neighbour; the perfection of man's moral principles is, as it were, given to man for the benefit of mankind. Imagine a person being alone, and having no connexion whatever with any other person, all his good moral principles are at rest, they are not required, and give man no perfection whatever. These principles are only necessary and useful when man comes in contact with others.

The fourth kind of perfection is the true perfection of man; the possession of the highest intellectual faculties; the possession of such notions which lead to true metaphysical opinions as regards God. With this perfection man has obtained his final object; it gives him true human perfection; it remains to him alone; it gives him immortality, and on its account he is called man. Examine the first three kinds of perfection, you will find that, if you possess them, they are not your property, but the property of others; according to the ordinary view, however, they belong to you and to others. But the last kind of perfection is exclusively yours; no one else owns any part of it, " They shall be only thine own, and not strangers' with thee " (Prov. v. 17). Your aim must therefore be to attain this [fourth] perfection that is exclusively yours, and you ought not to continue to work and weary yourself for that which belongs to others, whilst neglecting your soul till it has lost entirely its original purity through the dominion of the bodily powers over it.   The same idea is expressed in the beginning of those poems, which allegorically represent the state of our soul.   " My mother's children were angry with me ; they made me the keeper of the vineyards ; but mine own vineyard have I not kept " (Song i. 6).   Also the following passage refers to the same subject, " Lest thou give thine honour unto others, and thy years unto the cruel " (Prov. v. 9).

The prophets have likewise explained unto us these things, and have expressed the same opinion on them as the philosophers.   They say distinctly that perfection in property, in health, or in character, is not a perfection worthy to be sought as a cause of pride and glory for us ; that the knowledge of God, i.e., true wisdom, is the only perfection which we should seek, and in which we should glorify ourselves.   Jeremiah, referring to these four kinds of perfection, says :   " Thus saith the Lord, Let not the wise man glory in his wisdom, neither let the mighty man glory in his might, let not the rich man glory in his riches ; but let him that glorieth glory in this, that he understandeth and knoweth me " (Jer. ix. 22, 23).   See how the prophet arranged them according to their estimation in the eyes of the multitude. The rich man occupies the first rank ; next is the mighty man ; and then the wise man ; that is, the man of good moral principles : for in the eyes of the multitude, who are addressed in these words, he is likewise a great man. This is the reason why the three classes are enumerated in this order.

Our Sages have likewise derived from this passage the above-mentioned lessons, and stated the same theory that has been explained in this chapter, viz., that the simple term *ḥokmah*, as a rule, denotes the highest aim of man, the knowledge of God ; that those properties which man acquires, makes his peculiar treasure, and considers as his perfection, in reality do not include any perfection ; and that the religious acts prescribed in the Law, viz., the various kinds of worship and the moral principles which benefit all people in their social intercourse with each other, do not constitute the ultimate aim of man, nor can they be compared to it, for they are but preparations leading to it.   Hear the opinion of our Sages on this subject in their own words.   The passage occurs in *Bereshit Rabba*, and runs thus, " In one place Scripture says, ' And all things that are desirable (*ḥafaẓim*) are not to be compared to her ' (Prov. viii. 11) ; and in another place, ' And all things that thou desirest (*ḥafaẓeḥa*) are not to be compared unto her ' " (*ibid.* iii. 15).   By " things that are desirable " the performance of Divine precepts and good deeds is to be understood, whilst " things that thou desirest " refer to precious stones and pearls. Both—things that are desirable, and things that thou desirest—cannot be compared to wisdom, but " in this let him that glorieth glory, that he understandeth and knoweth me."   Consider how concise this saying is, and how perfect its author ;   how nothing is here omitted of all that we have put forth after lengthy explanations and preliminary remarks.

Having stated the sublime ideas contained in that Scriptural passage, and quoted the explanation of our Sages, we will now complete what the remainder of that passage teaches us.   The prophet does not content himself with explaining that the knowledge of God is the highest kind of perfection ;

for if this only had been his intention, he would have said, " But in this let him who glorieth glory, that he understandeth and knoweth me," and would have stopped there ; or he would have said, " that he understandeth and knoweth me that I am One," or, " that I have not any likeness," or, " that there is none like me," or a similar phrase. He says, however, that man can only glory in the knowledge of God and in the knowledge of His ways and attributes, which are His actions, as we have shown (Part I. liv.) in expounding the passage, " Show me now thy ways " (Exod. xxxviii. 13). We are thus told in this passage that the Divine acts which ought to be known, and ought to serve as a guide for our actions, are, *ḥesed*, " loving-kindness," *mishpat*, " judgment," and *ẓedakah*, " righteousness." Another very important lesson is taught by the additional phrase, " in the earth." It implies a fundamental principle of the Law ; it rejects the theory of those who boldly assert that God's providence does not extend below the sphere of the moon, and that the earth with its contents is abandoned, that " the Lord hath forsaken the earth " (Ez. viii. 12). It teaches, as has been taught by the greatest of all wise men in the words, " The earth is the Lord's " (Exod. ix. 29), that His providence extends to the earth in accordance with its nature, in the same manner as it controls the heavens in accordance with their nature. This is expressed in the words, " That I am the Lord which exercise loving-kindness, judgment, and righteousness in the earth." The prophet thus, in conclusion, says, " For in these things I delight, saith the Lord," i.e., My object [in saying this] is that you shall practise loving-kindness, judgment, and righteousness in the earth. In a similar manner we have shown (Part I. liv.) that the object of the enumeration of God's thirteen attributes is the lesson that we should acquire similar attributes and act accordingly. The object of the above passage is therefore to declare, that the perfection, in which man can truly glory, is attained by him when he has acquired—as far as this is possible for man—the knowledge of God, the knowledge of His Providence, and of the manner in which it influences His creatures in their production and continued existence. Having acquired this knowledge he will then be determined always to seek loving-kindness, judgment, and righteousness, and thus to imitate the ways of God. We have explained this many times in this treatise.

This is all that I thought proper to discuss in this treatise, and which I considered useful for men like you. I hope that, by the help of God, you will, after due reflection, comprehend all the things which I have treated here. May He grant us and all Israel with us to attain what He promised us, " Then the eyes of the blind shall be opened, and the ears of the deaf shall be unstopped " (Isa. xxxv. 5) ; " The people that walked in darkness have seen a great light ; they that dwell in the shadow of death upon them hath the light shined " (*ibid*. ix. 1).

God is near to all who call Him, if they call Him in truth, and turn to Him. He is found by every one who seeks Him, if he always goes towards Him, and never goes astray. AMEN.

INDEX

INDEX OF SCRIPTURAL PASSAGES.

INDEX OF QUOTATIONS FROM THE TARGUMIM.

INDEX OF QUOTATIONS FROM THE MIDRASHIM.

INDEX

INDEX OF QUOTATIONS FROM THE TALMUD.

COSIMO is a specialty publisher of books and publications that inspire, inform and engage readers. Our mission is to offer unique books to niche audiences around the world.

COSIMO CLASSICS offers a collection of distinctive titles by the great authors and thinkers throughout the ages. At COSIMO CLASSICS timeless classics find a new life as affordable books, covering a variety of subjects including: *Biographies, Business, History, Mythology, Personal Development, Philosophy, Religion and Spirituality,* and much more!

COSIMO-on-DEMAND publishes books and publications for innovative authors, non-profit organizations and businesses. COSIMO-on-DEMAND specializes in bringing books back into print, publishing new books quickly and effectively, and making these publications available to readers around the world.

COSIMO REPORTS publishes public reports that affect your world: from global trends to the economy, and from health to geo-politics.